Rick Steves'®

FLORENCE
& TUSCANY

Rick Steves & Gene Openshaw

2013

CONTENTS

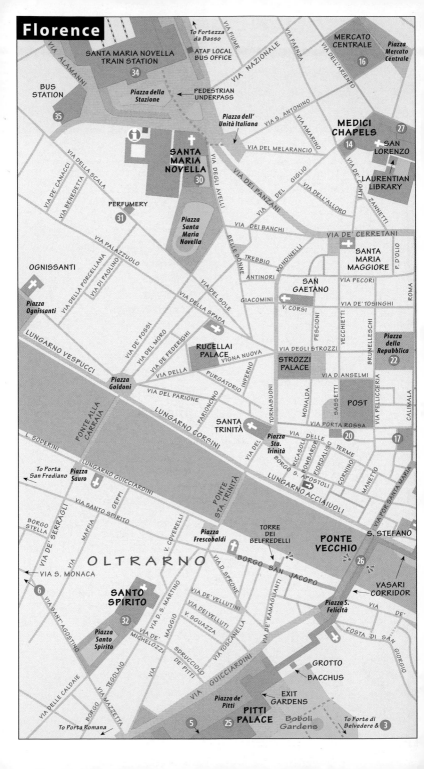

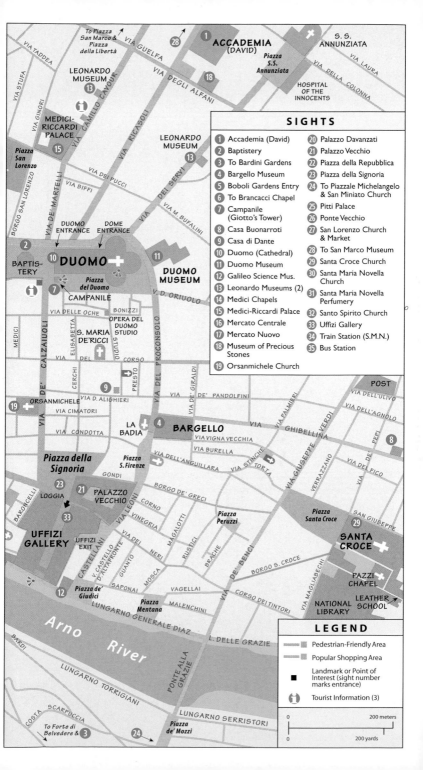

SIGHTS

1 Accademia (David)
2 Baptistery
3 To Bardini Gardens
4 Bargello Museum
5 Boboli Gardens Entry
6 To Brancacci Chapel
7 Campanile (Giotto's Tower)
8 Casa Buonarroti
9 Casa di Dante
10 Duomo (Cathedral)
11 Duomo Museum
12 Galileo Science Mus.
13 Leonardo Museums (2)
14 Medici Chapels
15 Medici-Riccardi Palace
16 Mercato Centrale
17 Mercato Nuovo
18 Museum of Precious Stones
19 Orsanmichele Church

20 Palazzo Davanzati
21 Palazzo Vecchio
22 Piazza della Repubblica
23 Piazza della Signoria
24 To Piazzale Michelangelo & San Miniato Church
25 Pitti Palace
26 Ponte Vecchio
27 San Lorenzo Church & Market
28 To San Marco Museum
29 Santa Croce Church
30 Santa Maria Novella Church
31 Santa Maria Novella Perfumery
32 Santo Spirito Church
33 Uffizi Gallery
34 Train Station (S.M.N.)
35 Bus Station

LEGEND

— Pedestrian-Friendly Area
— Popular Shopping Area
■ Landmark or Point of Interest (sight number marks entrance)
✛ Tourist Information (3)

0 — 200 meters
0 — 200 yards

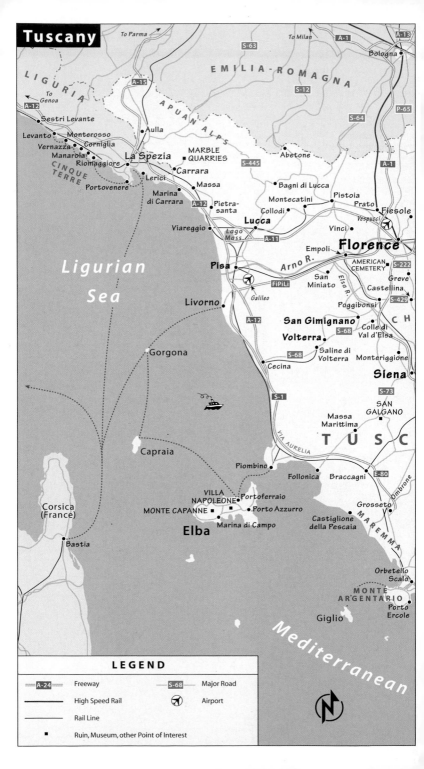

Tuscany

To Parma · To Milan · A-1 · A-13 · S-63 · Bologna

EMILIA-ROMAGNA

LIGURIA · S-12 · S-64 · P-65

To Genoa · A-15 · S-12 · A-1

A-12 · Sestri Levante · Aulla · APUAN ALPS

Levanto · Monterosso · Corniglia · Abetone

Vernazza · Manarola · La Spezia · MARBLE QUARRIES · S-445

Riomaggiore · CINQUE TERRE · Carrara · Bagni di Lucca · Pistoia

Lerici · Massa · Montecatini · Prato · Fiesole

Portovenere · Marina di Carrara · A-12 · Pietra-santa · Collodi · Vespucci ✈

Marina · Lucca · Vinci · Florence

Viareggio · Lago Mass. · A-11 · Empoli

Ligurian Sea · Pisa · Arno R. · AMERICAN CEMETERY · S-222

Galileo ✈ · FIPiLi · San Miniato · Greve · Castellina

Livorno · Elsa R. · Poggibonsi · S-429

A-12 · San Gimignano · Colle di Val d'Elsa · CH

Gorgona · Volterra · S-68 · Monteriggione

S-68 · Saline di Volterra · Siena

Cecina · S-73

S-1 · SAN GALGANO

VIA AURELIA · Massa Marittima · TUSC

Capraia · Piombino · Follonica · Braccagni · E-80

Corsica (France) · Portoferraio · VILLA NAPOLEONE · Ombrone

MONTE CAPANNE · Porto Azzurro · Grosseto · MAREMMA

Elba · Marina di Campo · Castiglione della Pescaia

Bastia · Orbetello Scalo

MONTE ARGENTARIO · Porto Ercole

Giglio · Mediterranean

LEGEND

A-24	Freeway	S-68	Major Road
	High Speed Rail	✈	Airport
	Rail Line		
■	Ruin, Museum, other Point of Interest		

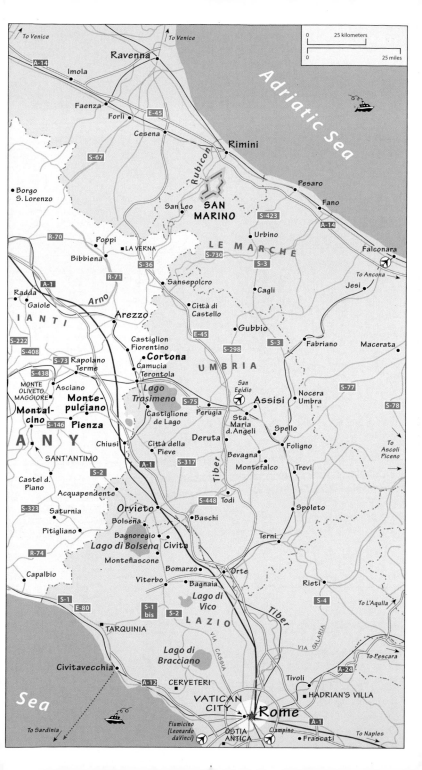

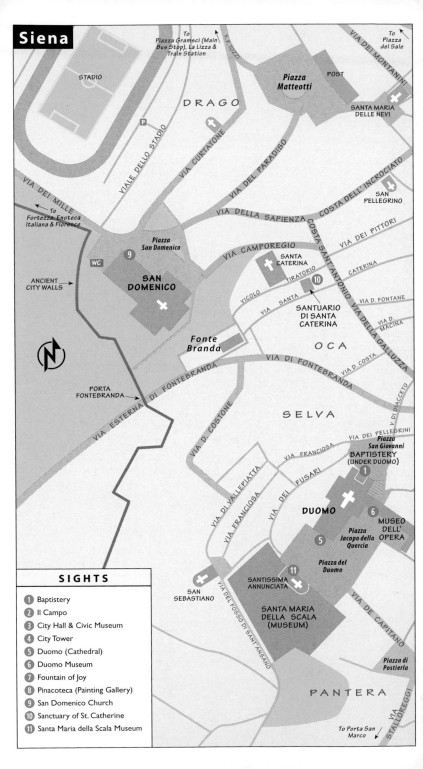

Siena

DRAGO

To Piazza Gramsci (Main Bus Stop), La Lizza & Train Station

To Piazza del Sale

To Piazza dei Montanini

STADIO

Piazza Matteotti

POST

SANTA MARIA DELLE NEVI

VIA CURTATONE

VIALE DELLO STADIO

VIA T. TOZZI

VIA DEL PARADISO

VIA DEI MILLE

To Fortezza, Enoteca Italiana & Florence

VIA DELLA SAPIENZA

COSTA DELL' INCROCIATO

SAN PELLEGRINO

P

Piazza San Domenico

VIA CAMPOREGIO

COSTA SANTANTONIO

VIA DEI PITTORI

WC

SANTA CATERINA

CATERINA

SAN DOMENICO

9

VICOLO

TIRATORIO

10

VIA D. FONTANE

ANCIENT CITY WALLS →

VIA SANTA

SANTUARIO DI SANTA CATERINA

VIA D. MACINA

VIA DELLA GALLUZZA

N

Fonte Branda

OCA

VIA DI FONTEBRANDA

VIA D. COSTA

PORTA FONTEBRANDA →

VIA ESTERNA DI FONTEBRANDA

SELVA

V. DI DIACCETO

VIA D. COSTONE

VIA DEI PELLEGRINI

VIA FRANCIOSA

Piazza San Giovanni

BAPTISTERY (UNDER DUOMO)

VIA DI VALLEPIATTA

VIA DEI FUSARI

1

VIA FRANCIOSA

DUOMO

6

MUSEO DELL' OPERA

5

Piazza Jacopo della Quercia

SAN SEBASTIANO

VIA DEL FOSSO DI SANT'ANSANO

SANTISSIMA ANNUNCIATA

11

Piazza del Duomo

VIA DE' CAPITANO

SANTA MARIA DELLA SCALA (MUSEUM)

Piazza di Postierla

PANTERA

VIA STALLOREGGI

To Porta San Marco

SIGHTS

1. Baptistery
2. Il Campo
3. City Hall & Civic Museum
4. City Tower
5. Duomo (Cathedral)
6. Duomo Museum
7. Fountain of Joy
8. Pinacoteca (Painting Gallery)
9. San Domenico Church
10. Sanctuary of St. Catherine
11. Santa Maria della Scala Museum

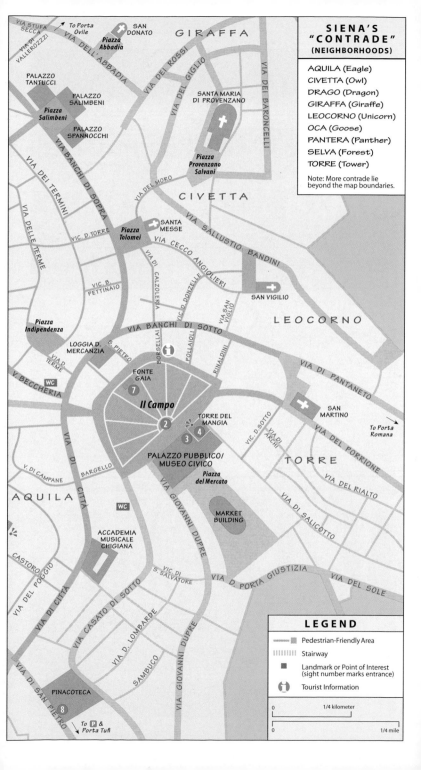

SIENA'S "CONTRADE" (NEIGHBORHOODS)

AQUILA (Eagle)
CIVETTA (Owl)
DRAGO (Dragon)
GIRAFFA (Giraffe)
LEOCORNO (Unicorn)
OCA (Goose)
PANTERA (Panther)
SELVA (Forest)
TORRE (Tower)

Note: More contrade lie beyond the map boundaries.

LEGEND

Pedestrian-Friendly Area

Stairway

Landmark or Point of Interest (sight number marks entrance)

Tourist Information

0   1/4 kilometer

0   1/4 mile

Pisa's Field of Miracles

Tuscan Farmhouse

Michelangelo's David—Accademia

Tuscan Hill Town Poppies

Brunelleschi's Dome of the Duomo, Florence

Rick Steves'®

FLORENCE & TUSCANY

2013

SANTA MARIA NOVELLA

SAN MARCO

MEDICI CHAPELS

DAVID

BAPTISTERY

CAMPANILE

DUOMO

PALAZZO VECCHIO

PONTE VECCHIO

UFFIZI

BARGELLO

BRANCACCI CHAPEL

Arno

PITTI PALACE & GARDENS

AVALON
TRAVEL

INTRODUCTION

Florence is Europe's cultural capital. As the home of the Renaissance and the birthplace of the modern world, Florence practiced the art of civilized living back when the rest of Europe was rural and crude. Democracy, science, and literature, as well as painting, sculpture, and architecture, were all championed by the proud and energetic Florentines of the 1400s.

When the Florentine poet Dante first saw the teenaged Beatrice, her beauty so inspired him that he spent the rest of his life writing poems to her. In the same way, the Renaissance opened people's eyes to the physical beauty of the world around them, inspiring them to write, paint, sculpt, and build.

Today, Florence is geographically small but culturally rich, with more artistic masterpieces per square mile than anyplace else. In a single day, you can look Michelangelo's *David* in the eyes, fall under the seductive sway of Botticelli's *Birth of Venus*, and climb the modern world's first dome, which still dominates the skyline.

Of course, there's a reality here, too. As the historic center becomes increasingly filled with visitors, rents are rising and locals are fleeing to the suburbs, threatening to make Florence a kind of Renaissance theme park. Sure, Florence is touristy. But where else can you stroll the same pedestrian streets walked by Michelangelo, Leonardo, and Botticelli while savoring the world's best gelato?

To round out your visit, see Florence and then escape to the Tuscan countryside. With its manicured fields, rustic farms, and towns clinging to nearly every hill, Tuscany is our romantic image of village Italy. Venture beyond the fringes of Florence and you'll find a series of sun- and wine-soaked villages, each with its own appeal. Stretching from the Umbrian border to the Ligurian Sea, the landscape changes from pastoral (Crete Senese) to rocky (Chianti) to mountainous (the Montagnola) to flat and brushed

Map Legend

⅃ Viewpoint	✈ Airport	) (Tunnel
↟ Entrance	Ⓣ Taxi Stand	Pedestrian Zone
ⓘ Tourist Info	Ⓣ Tram Stop	------- Railway
WC Restroom	Ⓑ Bus Stop	.... Ferry/Boat Route
Castle	Ⓜ Metro Stop	⊢—⊣ Tram
Church	Ⓟ Parking	⧙⧙⧙ Stairs
Statue/Point of Interest	) (Mtn. Pass	- - - - - Walk/Tour Route
	Park	------- Trail

Use this legend to help you navigate the maps in this book.

with sea breezes (Pisa).

During your visit, you'll discover that peaceful Tuscan villages and bustling Florence—with its rough-stone beauty, art-packed museums, children chasing pigeons, students riding Vespas, artisans sipping Chianti, and supermodels wearing Gucci fashions—offer many of the very things you came to Italy to see.

About This Book

Rick Steves' Florence & Tuscany 2013 is a personal tour guide in your pocket. Better yet, it's actually two tour guides in your pocket: The co-author of this book is Gene Openshaw. Since our first "Europe through the gutter" trip together as high school buddies in the 1970s, Gene and I have been exploring the wonders of the Old World. An inquisitive historian and lover of European culture, Gene wrote most of this book's self-guided museum tours and neighborhood walks. Together, Gene and I keep this book up-to-date and accurate (though for simplicity, from this point we've shed our respective egos to become "I").

In this book, you'll find the following chapters:

Orientation includes specifics on public transportation, helpful hints, local tour options, easy-to-read maps, and tourist information. The "Planning Your Time" section suggests a schedule for how to best use your limited time.

Sights in Florence describes the top attractions and includes their cost and hours.

The **Self-Guided Walks and Tours** take you through the core of Renaissance Florence, starting with Michelangelo's *David* and cutting through the heart of the city to Ponte Vecchio on the Arno River. You'll tour Tuscany's most fascinating museums and sights, including Florence's Accademia (home to Michelangelo's *David*), Uffizi Gallery, Bargello, Museum of San Marco, Duomo

Key to This Book

Updates

This book is updated every year—but as soon as you pin down Italy, it wiggles. For the latest, visit www.ricksteves.com /update. For a valuable list of reports and experiences—good and bad—from fellow travelers, check www.ricksteves.com /feedback.

Abbreviations and Times

I use the following symbols and abbreviations in this book:

Sights are rated:

▲▲▲	**Don't miss**
▲▲	**Try hard to see**
▲	**Worthwhile if you can make it**
No rating	**Worth knowing about**

Tourist information offices are abbreviated as **TI,** and bathrooms are **WCs.** To categorize accommodations, I use a **Sleep Code** (described on page 21).

Like Europe, this book uses the **24-hour clock.** It's the same through 12:00 noon, then keep going: 13:00, 14:00, and so on. For anything over 12, subtract 12 and add p.m. (14:00 is 2:00 p.m.).

When giving **opening times,** I include both peak season and off-season hours if they differ. So, if a museum is listed as "May-Oct daily 9:00-16:00," it should be open from 9 a.m. until 4 p.m. from the first day of May until the last day of October (but expect exceptions).

When you see a ◐ in a sight listing, it means that the sight is covered in much more detail elsewhere—either with its own self-guided tour, or as part of a self-guided walk.

For **transit** or **tour departures,** I first list the frequency, then the duration. So, a train connection listed as "2/hour, 1.5 hours" departs twice each hour and the journey lasts an hour and a half.

Museum, Palazzo Vecchio, Medici Chapels, Medici-Riccardi Palace, Church of Santa Maria Novella, Santa Croce Church, the Oltrarno (rustic Florentine district south of the Arno), Brancacci Chapel, Pitti Palace, and the Galileo Science Museum, as well as Siena's Duomo, Duomo Museum, and Civic Museum, and, in Pisa, the Leaning Tower, Duomo, and Field of Miracles.

Sleeping in Florence describes my favorite hotels, from good-value deals to cushy splurges.

Eating in Florence serves up a range of options, from inexpensive cafés to fancy restaurants.

Florence with Children includes my top recommendations for keeping your kids (and you) happy in Florence.

Shopping in Florence gives you tips for shopping painlessly

INTRODUCTION

and enjoyably, without letting it overwhelm your vacation or ruin your budget.

Nightlife in Florence is your guide to after-dark fun, including concerts, theaters, pubs, and clubs.

Florence Connections lays the groundwork for your smooth arrival and departure, covering transportation by train, bus, car, cruise ship, and by plane (with information on Florence's Amerigo Vespucci Airport).

Siena covers the highlights in this captivating Gothic city, from the stay-awhile central piazza to the 13th-century cathedral.

Pisa takes you beyond the Leaning Tower.

Lucca introduces you to the charms of this little-touristed, well-preserved city.

And **Tuscan Hill Towns** brings you the best of village Italy, featuring San Gimignano, Volterra, Montalcino, Pienza, Montepulciano, and Cortona.

The **Florentine History** chapter takes you on a whirlwind tour through the ages, covering two millennia, from ancient Tuscany to the present.

The **appendix** is a traveler's tool kit, with telephone tips, useful phone numbers, the basics on transportation in Italy, recommended books and films, a festival list, a climate chart, a handy packing checklist, a hotel reservation form, and Italian survival phrases.

Browse through this book, choose your favorite destinations, and link them up. Then have a *buono* trip! Traveling like a temporary local, you'll get the absolute most out of every mile, minute, and dollar. As you visit places I know and love, I'm happy you'll be meeting my favorite Florentines.

Planning

This section will help you get started planning your trip—with advice on trip costs, when to go, and what you should know before you take off.

Travel Smart

Many people travel through Italy and think it's a chaotic mess. They feel that any attempt at efficient travel is futile. This is dead wrong—and expensive. Italy, which seems as orderly as spilled spaghetti, actually functions quite well. Only those who understand this and travel smart can enjoy Italy on a budget.

This book can save you lots of time and money. But to have an "A" trip, you need to be an "A" student. Read it all before your trip, noting holidays, specifics on sights, and days when sights are closed. You can wait in line for two hours to get into the Uffizi—or,

Tuscany at a Glance

▲▲▲**Florence** Art-packed, bustling city—starring Michelangelo's *David,* Renaissance paintings, and Brunelleschi's dome—with the Ponte Vecchio spanning the flood-prone Arno River.

▲▲▲**Siena** Red-brick hilltop city known for its pageantry, Palio horse race, and a stunning traffic-free main square—great anytime but best after dark.

▲▲**Pisa** A city more famous for its iconic Leaning Tower than for its other equally impressive monuments on the gleaming white Field of Miracles.

▲▲**Lucca** Charming city with a lively (and flat) town center, ringed by intact old walls wide enough for biking and strolling.

▲▲**Volterra** A town off-the-beaten-path, surrounded by thick walls and hilly scenery, with a long Etruscan history.

▲▲**Montepulciano** Rugged town crowning a ridge, with dreamy vistas of the countryside and wine-tasting in inviting cantinas.

▲**San Gimignano** Epitome of a hill town, spiked with medieval towers offering superb views, popular with tourists who crowd the narrow alleys by day.

▲**Montalcino** Wine-lovers' paradise boasting a dramatic 14th-century castle, encircled by olive groves and famous vineyards.

Pienza Tiny Renaissance-planned architectural gem of a town nestled in a scenic hilly landscape.

Cortona Hillside town under the Tuscan sun, with historic churches and museums featuring Etruscan and Renaissance artifacts and art.

by planning ahead (making reservations or buying the Firenze Card), you can walk right in. Saving Michelangelo's *David* for your trip finale is risky, and on Monday, impossible. (Florence's major sights, along with some minor ones, are closed on Mondays.) If you cut your Siena day trip short, you'll miss the city's medieval magic at twilight. A smart trip is a puzzle—a fun, doable, and worthwhile challenge.

Be sure to mix intense and relaxed periods in your itinerary. To maximize rootedness in Tuscany, minimize one-night stands. It's worth a drive after dinner to be settled into a town for two nights. Every trip—and every traveler—needs slack time (laundry, picnics, people-watching, and so on). Pace yourself. Assume you will return.

Reread this book as you travel, and visit local TIs. Upon arrival in a new town, lay the groundwork for a smooth departure; write down (or print out from an online source) the schedule for the train or bus that you'll take when you depart. Drivers can study the best route to their next destination.

Get online at Internet cafés or your hotel (nearly all of which have Wi-Fi), and buy a phone card or carry a mobile phone: You can get tourist information, learn the latest on sights (special events, English tour schedules, etc.), book tickets and tours, make reservations, reconfirm hotels, research transportation connections, and keep in touch with your loved ones.

Enjoy the friendliness of your Tuscan hosts. Connect with the culture. Set up your own quest for the best gelato, piazza, *enoteca* (wine bar), or Renaissance painting or sculpture. Slow down and be open to unexpected experiences. Ask questions—most locals are eager to point you in their idea of the right direction. Keep a notepad in your pocket for confirming prices, noting directions, and organizing your thoughts. Wear your money belt, learn the currency, and figure out how to estimate prices in dollars. Those who expect to travel smart, do.

Trip Costs

Six components make up your total trip cost: airfare, surface transportation, room and board, sightseeing and entertainment, shopping and miscellany, and gelato.

Airfare: A basic, round-trip flight from the US to Florence can cost on average, about $1,000-1,800 total, depending on where you fly from and when (cheaper in winter or sometimes if flying into Milan or Rome). If your trip covers a wide area, consider saving time and money in Europe by flying into one city and out of another (for instance, into Florence and out of Paris).

Surface Transportation: Most of Florence's sights, clustered in the downtown core, are within easy walking distance of each other. If you'd rather use taxis than walk, allow $80-100 over the course of a one-week visit (taxis can be shared by up to four people). The cost of round-trip, second-class train transportation to the recommended nearby destinations is affordable (about $11 for a train ticket to Pisa or Siena, and slightly less for a bus ticket to San Gimignano). For a one-way trip between Florence's airport and the city center, allow $7 by bus or $35 by taxi (can be shared). The other cities and villages covered in this book are made for walking. For more on public transportation and car rental, see "Transportation" in the appendix.

Room and Board: You can thrive in Tuscany in 2013 on $120 a day per person for room and board. This allows $15 for lunch, $30 for dinner, and $75 for lodging (based on two people splitting the cost of a $150 double room that includes breakfast). Students and tightwads can enjoy Tuscany for as little as $60 a day ($30 for a bed, $30 for meals and snacks).

Sightseeing and Entertainment: Figure about $15 for major sights (Michelangelo's *David*, Uffizi Gallery), $5-10 for minor ones (museums, climbing church towers), and $25 for splurge experiences (e.g., walking tours and concerts). An overall average of $35 a day works for most people. Don't skimp here. After all, this category is the driving force behind your trip—you came to sightsee, enjoy, and experience Florence.

Shopping and Miscellany: Figure $3 per postcard, coffee, soft drink, or gelato. Shopping can vary in cost from nearly nothing to a small fortune. Good budget travelers find that this category has little to do with assembling a trip full of lifelong, wonderful memories.

When to Go

Tuscany's best travel months (also its busiest and most expensive) are April, May, June, September, and October. These months combine the convenience of peak season with pleasant weather.

The most grueling thing about travel in Tuscany is the summer heat in July and August, when temperatures hit the high 80s and 90s. Most mid-range hotels come with air-conditioning—a worthwhile splurge in the summer—but it's usually available only from June through September.

In April and October, you'll generally need a sweater or light jacket in the evening. In winter the temperatures can drop to the 40s or 50s (for more specifics, see the climate chart in the appendix). Off-season has none of the sweat and stress of the tourist season, but sights may have shorter hours, lunchtime breaks, and fewer activities. Confirm your sightseeing plans locally, especially when traveling off-season.

Know Before You Go

Your trip is more likely to go smoothly if you plan ahead. Check this list of things to arrange while you're still at home.

You need a **passport**—but no visa or shots—to travel in Italy. You may be denied entry into certain European countries if your passport is due to expire within three to six months of your ticketed date of return. Get it renewed if you'll be cutting it close. It

Florence Almanac

Population: Approximately 420,000 people

Currency: Euro

City Layout: Florence is the capital of Tuscany and lies on the Arno River. It's divided into five administrative wards: the Historic Center, Campo di Marte, Gavinana, Isolotto, and Rifredi.

Best Viewpoints: Piazzale Michelangelo (and San Miniato Church, above it) overlooks the city and the Duomo from across the river. For other panoramic views of Florence, climb the Campanile or the Duomo's dome (next to each other) or the tower at Palazzo Vecchio.

Sweetest Festival: In late May, the city hosts an annual gelato festival. Started in 2010, the festival features tastings and demonstrations by gelato-makers from all over Italy.

Tourist Tracks: From April to October, tourists outnumber Florence's local population. Each year, about 1.6 million tourists flock to the Uffizi Gallery to gaze at Botticelli's *Birth of Venus*.

Culture Count: A little over 90 percent of Florence's population is indigenously Italian and Roman Catholic. Immigrant groups are mostly European (3.5 percent) and East Asian (2 percent), with small percentages of North and South Americans and Northern Africans.

Famous Florentines: Florence, birthplace of the Renaissance, bred many great minds, including Michelangelo, Leonardo, Donatello, Brunelleschi, Machiavelli, Dante, and...Florence Nightingale, whose English parents named her after the city in which she was born.

Average Florentine: The average Florentine is 49 years old (7 years older than the average Italian) and will live until the age of 80. He/she is much more likely to have a leather jacket at home than a child (since less than 14 percent of the population is under 18).

can take up to six weeks to get or renew a passport (for more on passports, see www.travel.state.gov). Pack a photocopy of your passport in your luggage in case the original is lost or stolen.

Book rooms well in advance if you'll be traveling during peak season (spring and fall) and any major holidays (see page 581).

Make reservations before your trip or buy a Firenze Card in Florence to avoid standing in long lines for the Uffizi (Renaissance paintings) and Accademia (Michelangelo's *David*). The Uffizi is often booked up a month or more in advance, while the Accademia is usually full at least a few days out. Reservations are explained on page 59, and the **Firenze Card** on page 57. While reservations are mandatory (and free) for the Brancacci Chapel, you can often get them on the spot.

Call your **debit- and credit-card companies** to let them know the countries you'll be visiting, to ask about fees, request your PIN (it will be mailed to you), and more. See page 13 for details.

If you plan to hire a **local guide,** reserve ahead by email. Popular guides can get booked up.

Do your homework if you want to buy **travel insurance.** Compare the cost of the insurance to the likelihood of your using it and your potential loss if something goes wrong. Also, check whether your existing insurance (health, homeowners, or renters) covers you and your possessions overseas. For more information, see www.ricksteves.com/insurance.

Check the **Rick Steves guidebook updates** page for the latest news about Florence and Tuscany (www.ricksteves.com/update).

If you're bringing a mobile device, download any apps you might want to use on the road, such as translators, maps, and transit schedules. Be sure to check out **Rick Steves Audio Europe,** featuring audio tours of major sights, hours of travel interviews on Florence and Tuscany, and more (via www.ricksteves.com/audio europe, iTunes, Google Play, or the Rick Steves Audio Europe smartphone app; for details, see page 578).

If you're planning on **renting a car** in Italy, you'll need your driver's license. You're also technically required to have an International Driving Permit (see page 570). Driving is prohibited in some city centers; if you drive in restricted areas monitored by cameras, you can be fined without a cop ever stopping you (see page 573).

If you're taking an **overnight train** and need a couchette *(cuccetta)* or sleeper—and you must leave on a certain day—consider booking it in advance through a US agent (such as www.rail europe.com), even though it may cost more than buying it in Italy. Other Italian trains, like the high-speed ES trains, require a seat reservation, but for these it's usually possible to make arrangements in Italy just a few days ahead. (For more on train travel, see the appendix).

Because **airline carry-on restrictions** are always changing, visit the Transportation Security Administration's website (www .tsa.gov/travelers) for an up-to-date list of what you can bring on the plane with you...and what you have to check.

Practicalities

Emergency and Medical Help: In Italy, dial 113 for English-speaking police help. To summon an ambulance, call 118. If you get sick, do as the locals do and go to a pharmacist for advice. Or ask at your hotel for help; they'll know the nearest medical and emergency services.

Theft or Loss: To replace a passport, you'll need to go in person to a US embassy or consulate (see page 558). If your credit and debit cards disappear, cancel and replace them (see "Damage Control for Lost Cards" on page 15). File a police report, either on the spot or within a day or two; it's required if you submit an insurance claim for lost or stolen railpasses or travel gear, and can help with replacing your passport or credit and debit cards. For more information, see www.ricksteves.com/help. Precautionary measures can minimize the effects of loss—back up your photos and other files frequently.

Time Zones: Italy, like most of continental Europe, is generally six/nine hours ahead of the East/West Coasts of the US. The exceptions are the beginning and end of Daylight Saving Time: Europe "springs forward" the last Sunday in March (two weeks after most of North America), and "falls back" the last Sunday in October (one week before North America). For a handy online converter, try www.timeanddate.com/worldclock.

Business Hours: Traditionally, Italy uses the siesta plan, though many businesses have adopted the government's recommended 8:00 to 14:00 workday. In tourist areas, shops are open longer. People usually work from about 9:00 to 13:00 and from 15:30 to 19:30. Stores are usually closed on Sunday, and often on Monday. Many Florence shops close for a couple of weeks around August 15. Banking hours are generally Monday through Friday from 8:30 to 13:30 and 15:30 to 16:30, but can vary wildly.

Saturdays are virtually weekdays, with earlier closing hours. Sundays have the same pros and cons as they do for travelers in the US: Sightseeing attractions are generally open, while shops and banks are closed. Rowdy evenings are rare on Sundays.

Watt's Up? Europe's electrical system is 220 volts, instead of North America's 110 volts. Most newer electronics (such as laptops, battery chargers, and hair dryers) convert automatically, so you won't need a converter plug, but you will need an adapter plug with two round prongs, sold inexpensively at travel stores in the US. Avoid bringing older appliances that don't automatically convert voltage; instead, buy a cheap replacement in Europe.

Discounts: Discounts are not listed in this book. However, many sights offer discounts for youths (up to age 18), students (with proper identification cards, www.isic.org), families, seniors (loosely defined as retirees or those willing to call themselves a senior), and groups of 10 or more. Always ask. Some discounts are available only for EU citizens.

Money

This section offers advice on how to pay for purchases on your trip (including getting cash from ATMs and paying with plastic), dealing with lost or stolen cards, VAT (sales tax) refunds, and tipping.

What to Bring

Bring both a credit card and a debit card. You'll use the debit card at cash machines (ATMs) to withdraw local cash for most purchases, and the credit card to pay for larger items. Some travelers carry a third card as a backup, in case one gets demagnetized or eaten by a temperamental machine.

As an emergency backup, bring several hundred dollars in hard cash in easy-to-exchange $20 bills. Avoid using currency exchange booths (lousy rates and/or outrageous fees); if you have foreign currency to exchange, take it to a bank. Don't use traveler's checks—they're not worth the fees or long waits at slow banks.

Cash

Cash is just as desirable in Europe as it is at home. Small businesses (hotels, restaurants, shops, etc.) prefer that you pay your bills with cash. Some vendors will charge you extra for using a credit card, and some won't take credit cards at all. Cash is the best—and sometimes only—way to pay for bus fare, taxis, sights, and local guides.

Throughout Europe, ATMs (which locals call a *bancomat*) are the standard way for travelers to get cash. Most ATMs in Italy are located outside of a bank. Try to use the ATM when the branch is open; if your card is munched by a machine, you can immediately go inside for help. Stay away from "independent" ATMs such as Travelex, Euronet, or Forex, which charge huge commissions and have terrible exchange rates.

Exchange Rate

1 euro (€) = about $1.40

To convert prices in euros to dollars, add about 40 percent: €20 = about $28; €50 = about $70. (Check www.oanda.com for the latest exchange rates.) Just like the dollar, one euro is broken down into 100 cents. You'll find coins ranging from €0.01 to €2, and bills ranging from €5 to €500.

Look carefully at any €2 coin you get in change. Some unscrupulous merchants give out similar-looking, gold-rimmed old 500-lire coins (worth $0) instead of €2 coins (worth $2.80). You are now warned!

INTRODUCTION

Affordable Tuscany

Here are some ideas to help stretch your travel dollars.

Sightseeing

- Many of Florence's sights and activities are free. There is no charge for entry to the Duomo, Orsanmichele Church, Santo Spirito Church, and San Miniato Church. It's free to visit the leather school at Santa Croce Church and the perfumery near the Church of Santa Maria Novella. The three markets (Centrale for produce, Nuovo and San Lorenzo for goods) are fun to browse through.

   Free public spaces include the Uffizi and Palazzo Vecchio courtyards; the art-filled loggia on Piazza della Signoria; and Piazzale Michelangelo, with glorious views over Florence. A walk across the picturesque Ponte Vecchio costs nothing at all—unless you succumb to temptation at one of the many shops along the way. A stroll anywhere in Florence with a gelato in hand is an inexpensive treat. (This book contains information on all of these options.)

- Remember you can download lots of free information from Rick Steves Audio Europe; see page 578.

Hotels

- Choose hotels that offer a Rick Steves discount.
- Offer to pay cash to get the lowest rate.

Dining

- Don't order too much at restaurants. Servings are often big—and splittable. While restaurants frown on a cou-ple splitting just one dish, if you and your travel partner order a few small dishes and enjoy them family-style, you can sample a few different things, save some euros, and still have room for gelato. Sharing a €8 pizza makes for a cheap meal.
- Order take-out from delicatessens. Many shops have ready-to-eat entrées and side dishes, and will heat them up and send you on your way with plastic cutlery and napkins. Find a scenic picnic spot and enjoy your feast, having paid just a fraction of what you'd pay to eat in a restaurant.

To withdraw money from an ATM, you'll need a debit card (ideally with a Visa or MasterCard logo for maximum usability), plus a PIN code. Know your PIN code in numbers; there are only numbers—no letters—on European keypads. For security, it's best to shield the keypad when entering your PIN at an ATM. Although you can use a credit card for ATM transactions, it's generally more expensive (and only makes sense in an emergency), because it's considered a cash advance rather than a withdrawal.

When using an ATM, try to withdraw large sums of money to reduce the number of per-transaction bank fees you'll pay. If the machine refuses your request, try again and select a smaller amount (some cash machines limit the amount you can withdraw—don't take it personally). If that doesn't work, try a different machine. Be aware that some ATMS will tell you to take your cash within 30 seconds, and if you aren't fast enough, your cash may be sucked back into the machine...and you'll have a hassle trying to get it from the bank.

It's easier to pay for purchases with smaller bills; if the ATM gives you big bills, try to break them at a major museum or larger store.

To keep your cash safe, wear a money belt—a pouch with a strap that you buckle around your waist like a belt, and tuck under your clothes. Keep your cash, credit cards, and passport secure in your money belt, and carry only a day's spending money in your front pocket. Pickpockets target tourists. A money belt provides peace of mind, allowing you to carry lots of cash safely. Don't waste time every few days tracking down a cash machine—withdraw a week's worth of money, stuff it in your money belt, and travel!

Credit and Debit Cards

For purchases, Visa and MasterCard are more commonly accepted than American Express. Just like at home, credit or debit cards work easily at larger hotels, restaurants, and shops. I typically use my debit card to withdraw cash to pay for most purchases. I use my credit card only in a few specific situations: to book hotel reservations by phone, to cover major expenses (such as car rentals, plane tickets, and long hotel stays), and to pay for things near the end of my trip (to avoid another visit to the ATM). While you could use a debit card to make most large purchases, using a credit card offers a greater degree of fraud protection (because debit cards draw funds directly from your account).

Ask Your Credit- or Debit-Card Company: Before your trip, contact the company that issued your debit or credit cards.

• Confirm your card will work overseas, and alert them that

you'll be using it in Europe; otherwise, they may deny transactions if they perceive unusual spending patterns.

• Ask for the specifics on transaction **fees.** When you use your credit or debit card—either for purchases or ATM withdrawals—you'll often be charged additional "international transaction" fees of up to 3 percent (1 percent is normal) plus $5 per transaction. If your card's fees are too high, consider getting a card just for your trip: Capital One (www.capitalone.com) and most credit unions have low-to-no international fees.

• If you plan to withdraw cash from ATMs, confirm your daily **withdrawal limit** (€300 is usually the maximum), and if necessary, ask your bank to adjust it. Some travelers prefer a high limit that allows them to take out more cash at each ATM stop, while others prefer to set a lower limit in case their card is stolen. Note that foreign banks and ATMs also set maximum withdrawal amounts.

• Get your bank's emergency phone number in the US (but not its 800 number) to call collect if you have a problem.

• Ask for your credit card's **PIN** in case you encounter Europe's "chip and PIN" system; since the bank won't tell you your PIN over the phone, allow time for it to be mailed to you.

Chip and PIN: If your card is declined for a purchase in Europe, it may be because Europeans increasingly use chip-and-PIN cards, which are embedded with an electronic chip rather than the magnetic stripe used on our American-style cards. Most of the world, including Europe, is adopting this system, and even US banks should be issuing cards with chips by the end of 2015. You're most likely to encounter chip-and-PIN problems at automated payment machines, such as those at train and subway stations, toll roads, parking garages, luggage lockers, bike-rental kiosks, and self-serve gas pumps.

But don't panic. Most travelers who're only carrying magnetic-stripe cards never encounter any problems. Still, it pays to carry plenty of cash (you can always use an ATM with your magnetic-strip debit card), and to memorize the PIN number of your magnetic-stripe credit card (if you don't know it, ask your bank to mail it to you before you leave home). This lets you use it at many chip-and-PIN machines—just enter your PIN when prompted. If a machine won't take your card, find a cashier who can make your card work (they can print a receipt for you to sign), or find a machine that takes cash. I wouldn't bother with asking your bank for your own chip-and-PIN card just for your trip—it's not worth the cost or hassle.

Dynamic Currency Conversion: If merchants offer to convert your purchase price into dollars (called dynamic currency conversion, or DCC), refuse this "service." You'll pay even more in fees for the expensive convenience of seeing your charge in dollars.

Damage Control for Lost Cards

If you lose your credit, debit, or ATM card, you can stop people from using your card by reporting the loss immediately to the respective global customer-assistance centers. Call these 24-hour US numbers collect: Visa (tel. 303/967-1096), MasterCard (tel. 636/722-7111), and American Express (tel. 623/492-8427). European toll-free numbers (listed by country) can also be found at the websites for Visa and MasterCard.

At a minimum, you'll need to know the name of the financial institution that issued you the card, along with the type of card (classic, platinum, or whatever). Providing the following information allows for a quicker cancellation of your missing card: full card number, whether you are the primary or secondary cardholder, the cardholder's name exactly as printed on the card, billing address, home phone number, circumstances of the loss or theft, and identification verification (your birth date, your mother's maiden name, or your Social Security number—memorize this, don't carry a copy). If you are the secondary cardholder, you'll also need to provide the primary cardholder's identification-verification details. You can generally receive a temporary card within two or three business days in Europe (see www.ricksteves.com/help for more).

If you report your loss within two days, you typically won't be responsible for any unauthorized transactions on your account, although many banks charge a liability fee of $50.

Tipping

Tipping in Italy isn't as automatic and generous as it is in the US, but for special service, tips are appreciated, if not expected. As in the US, the proper amount depends on your resources, tipping philosophy, and the circumstances, but some general guidelines apply.

Restaurants: In Italy, the service charge *(servizio)* is usually built into your bill's grand total in one of two ways. If the menu states *servizio incluso* (or nothing at all), the listed prices already include service. If the menu states *servizio non incluso*, or *servizio* with a specific percentage, a fixed percentage (usually 10-15 percent of the total) will be added as a line item to the bottom of the bill. In either case, the total you pay already includes a basic tip. Some Italians don't tip beyond this, but if you're pleased with the service, you can round up the bill by a euro or two per person. If you pay your bill with a credit card, it's best to tip in cash—leave it on the table or hand it directly to your server. If you order your food at a counter, don't tip. For more tips on tipping, see page 27.

Taxis: To tip the cabbie, round up. For a typical ride, round up to the next euro on the fare (to pay a €4.50 fare, give €5). If the cabbie hauls your bags and zips you to the airport to help you catch your flight, you might want to toss in a little more. But if you feel like you're being driven in circles or otherwise ripped off, skip the tip.

Special Services: Tour guides at sights sometimes hold out their hands for tips after they give their spiel. If I've already paid for the tour, I don't tip extra unless they've really impressed me. At hotels, if you let the porter carry your luggage, it's polite to give them a euro for each bag (another reason to pack light). If you like to tip maids, leave a euro per overnight at the end of your stay.

In general, if someone in the service industry does a super job for you, a small tip (the equivalent of a euro or two) is appropriate...but not required.

When in doubt, ask. If you're not sure whether (or how much) to tip for a service, ask your hotelier or the TI; they'll fill you in on how it's done on their turf.

Getting a VAT Refund

Wrapped into the purchase price of your Italian souvenirs is a Value-Added Tax (VAT) of about 21 percent (rises to 23 percent in July 2013). You're entitled to get most of that tax back if you purchase more than €155 (about $220) worth of goods at a store that participates in the VAT-refund scheme. Typically, you must ring up the minimum at a single retailer—you can't add up your purchases from various shops to reach the required amount.

Getting your refund is usually straightforward and, if you buy a substantial amount of souvenirs, well worth the hassle. If you're lucky, the merchant will subtract the tax when you make your purchase. (This is more likely to occur if the store ships the goods to your home.) Otherwise, you'll need to:

Get the paperwork. Have the merchant completely fill out the necessary refund document, called a "cheque." You'll have to present your passport. Get the paperwork done before you leave the store to ensure you'll have everything you need (including your original sales receipt).

Get your stamp at the border or airport. Process your VAT document at your last stop in the EU (for instance, at the airport) with the customs agent who deals with VAT refunds. Before checking in for your flight, find the local customs office, and be prepared to stand in line. It's best to keep your purchases in your carry-on for viewing, but if they're too large or dangerous (such as knives), have your purchases easily accessible in the bag you're about to check, ready to show the customs agent. You're not supposed to use your purchased goods before you leave. If you show up at customs wearing your new leather shoes, officials might look the other way—or deny you a refund.

Collect your refund. You'll need to return your stamped

document to the retailer or its representative. Many merchants work with a service, such as Global Blue (www.global-blue.com) or Premier Tax Free (www.premiertaxfree.com), which have offices at major airports, ports, and border crossings (either before or after check-in and security, probably strategically located near a duty-free shop). These services, which extract a 4 percent fee, can refund your money immediately in cash or credit your card (within two billing cycles). If the retailer handles VAT refunds directly, it's up to you to contact the merchant for your refund. You can mail the documents from home, or more quickly, from your point of departure (using a stamped, self-addressed envelope or one that's been provided by the merchant). You'll then have to wait—it can take months.

Customs for American Shoppers

You are allowed to take home $800 worth of items per person duty-free, once every 30 days. You can also bring in duty-free a liter of alcohol. As for food, you can take home many processed and packaged foods: vacuum-packed cheeses, dried herbs, jams, baked goods, candy, chocolate, oil, vinegar, mustard, and honey. However, fresh fruits and vegetables and most meats are not allowed. Any liquid-containing foods must be packed in checked luggage, a potential recipe for disaster. To check customs rules and duty rates, visit www.cbp.gov.

Sightseeing

Sightseeing can be hard work. Use these tips to make your visits to Florence and Tuscany's finest sights meaningful, fun, efficient, and painless.

Plan Ahead

Set up an itinerary that allows you to fit in all your must-see sights. For a one-stop look at opening hours in Florence, see "Florence at a Glance" on page 60 (also see "Daily Reminder" on page 48). You'll find "Siena at a Glance" on page 346. Most sights keep stable hours, but you can easily confirm the latest by checking with the TI or visiting museums' websites.

For Florence, make reservations for the Uffizi and Accademia (see page 59) or plan to get a Firenze Card (see page 57). You can usually get reservations for the Brancacci Chapel when you're at the chapel, but if you don't want to take that chance, you can call to reserve a day in advance (no reservation fee; see page 243).

Don't put off visiting a must-see sight—you never know when a place will close unexpectedly for a holiday, strike, or restoration. On holidays (see list on page 581), expect reduced hours or closures—find out if a particular sight will be open by phoning ahead or checking its website. In summer, some sights may stay open late, allowing easy viewing without crowds. Many museums have shorter hours off-season.

When possible, visit the major sights in the morning (when your energy is best) and save other activities for the afternoon. Hit the highlights first, then go back to other things if you have the stamina and time.

Going at the right time helps avoid crowds. This book offers tips on specific sights. Try visiting the sight very early, at lunch, or very late. Evening visits are usually peaceful with fewer crowds.

Study up. To get the most out of the self-guided tours and sight descriptions in this book, read them before you visit.

At Sights

Here's what you can typically expect:

Many important sights have metal detectors or conduct bag searches that will slow your entry, while others require you to check daypacks and coats. They'll be kept safely. If you have something you can't bear to part with, stash it in a pocket or purse. To avoid checking a small backpack, carry it under your arm like a purse as you enter. From a guard's point of view, a backpack is generally a problem while a purse is not.

Flash photography is often banned, but taking photos without a flash is usually allowed. Look for signs or ask. Flashes damage oil paintings and distract others in the room. Even without a flash, a handheld camera will take a decent picture (or buy postcards or posters at the museum bookstore).

You may have to pay cash for the admission fee; some sights (such as the Pitti Palace and Galileo Science Museum) don't take credit cards. Museums often have special exhibits in addition to their permanent collection. Some exhibits are included in the entry price, while others come at an extra cost (which you may have to pay even if you don't want to see the exhibit).

Expect changes—artwork can be on tour, on loan, out sick, or shifted at the whim of the curator. To adapt, pick up any available free floor plans as you enter, and ask the museum staff if you can't find a particular item. Say the title or artist's name, or point to the photograph in this book and ask, *"Dov'è?"* (doh-VEH, meaning "Where is?").

Many sights rent audioguides, which generally offer excellent recorded descriptions of the art in English (about $7). If you bring along your own earbuds and a Y-jack, you can sometimes share one audioguide with your travel partner and save money. I've produced free downloadable audio tours of Florence's major sights; see page 41.

Guided tours in English are most likely to be available during peak season (usually about $10 and widely ranging in quality). Some sights also run short films featuring their highlights and history. These are generally well worth your time. I make it standard operating procedure to ask when I arrive at a sight if there is a film in English.

It helps to know the terms. Art historians and Italians refer to the great Florentine centuries by dropping a thousand years. The Trecento (300s), Quattrocento (400s), and Cinquecento (500s) were the 1300s, 1400s, and 1500s. Also, in Italian museums, art is dated with *sec* for *secolo* (century, often indicated with Roman numerals), A.C. (for *Avanti Cristo*, or B.C.), and D.C. (for *Dopo Cristo*, or A.D.). O.K.?

Important sights may have an on-site café or cafeteria (usually a good place to rejuvenate during a long visit). The WCs at many sights are free and generally clean; it's smart to carry tissues in case a WC runs out of TP.

Many places sell postcards and guidebooks that highlight their attractions. Before you leave, scan the postcards and thumb through the biggest guidebook (or skim its index) to be sure you haven't overlooked something that you'd like to see.

Most sights stop admitting people 30-60 minutes before closing time, and some rooms close early (often about 45 minutes before the actual closing time). Guards usher people out, so don't save the best for last.

Every sight or museum offers more than what is covered in this book. Use the information in this book as an introduction—not the final word.

Find Religion

Churches offer some amazing art (usually free), a cool respite from heat, and a welcome seat.

A modest dress code (no bare shoulders or shorts for anyone, even kids) is enforced at larger churches, but is often overlooked elsewhere. If you're caught by surprise, you can improvise, using maps to cover your shoulders and a jacket for your knees. A few major churches let you borrow or buy disposable ponchos to cover up in a pinch. (I wear a super-lightweight pair of long pants rather than shorts for my hot and muggy big-city Italian sightseeing.)

Some churches have coin-operated audioboxes that describe the art and history; just set the dial on English, put in your coins, and listen. Coin boxes near a piece of art illuminate the art (and present a better photo opportunity). I pop in a coin whenever I can. It improves my experience, is a favor to other visitors trying to appreciate a great piece of art in the dark, and is a little contribution to that church and its work. Whenever possible, let there be light.

Sleeping

For hassle-free efficiency, I favor hotels and restaurants that are handy to your sightseeing activities. Nearly all of my recommended accommodations are located in city or town centers, within minutes of the great sights. (To stay in the countryside, try *agriturismo* farmhouses; for more information on these rural B&Bs, see page 453.)

The hotel accommodations scene varies wildly with the season. Spring and fall are very tight and expensive, while mid-July through August is wide open and discounted. November through February is also generally empty. I've listed prices for peak season: April, May, June, September, and October.

A major feature of this book is its extensive listing of good-value accommodations. I like places that are clean, central, relatively quiet at night, reasonably priced, friendly, small enough to have a hands-on owner and stable staff, run with a respect for Italian traditions, and not listed in other guidebooks. (In Florence and Tuscany, satisfying six out of these eight criteria means it's a keeper.) I'm more impressed by a handy location and a fun-loving philosophy than flat-screen TVs and shoeshine machines.

Book your accommodations well in advance if you'll be traveling during busy times. See page 581 for a list of major holidays and festivals in Tuscany; for tips on making reservations, see page 24.

Rates and Deals

I've described my recommended accommodations using a Sleep Code (see the sidebar). Prices listed are for one-night stays in peak season, and assume you're booking directly (not through a TI or online hotel-booking engine). Using an online booking service costs the hotel about 20 percent and logically closes the door on special deals. Book direct.

While most taxes are included in the price, a tax of about €1/person per night is often added to hotel bills (and is generally not included in the prices in this book).

These days, many hotels change prices from day to day according to demand. Given the economic downturn, hoteliers are often willing and eager to make a deal. I'd suggest emailing several hotels to ask for their best price. Comparison-shop and make your choice.

As you look over the listings, you'll notice that some accommodations promise special prices to my readers who book direct (without using a room-finding service or hotel-booking website, which take a commission). To get these rates, you must mention this book when you reserve, and then show the book upon arrival. Rick Steves discounts apply to readers with ebooks as

Sleep Code

(€1 = about $1.40, country code: 39)

Price Rankings

To help you easily sort through these listings, I've divided the accommodations into three categories based on the price for a double room with bath during high season:

   $$$ Higher Priced
    $$ Moderately Priced
     $ Lower Priced

 I always rate hostels as $, whether or not they have double rooms, because they have the cheapest beds in town. Prices can change without notice; verify the hotel's current rates online or by email.

Abbreviations

To pack maximum information into a minimum of space, I use the following code to describe the recommended accommodations. Prices listed are per room, not per person. When a price range is given for a type of room (such as double rooms listing for €100-150), it means the price fluctuates with the season, size of room, or length of stay; expect to pay the upper end for peak-season stays.

 S = Single room (or price for one person in a double).
 D = Double or Twin room. "Double beds" are often two twins sheeted together and are usually big enough for nonromantic couples.
 T = Triple (generally a double bed with a single).
 Q = Quad (usually two double beds; adding an extra child's bed to a T is usually cheaper).
 b = Private bathroom with toilet and shower or tub.
 s = Private shower or tub only (the toilet is down the hall).

 According to this code, a couple staying at a "Db-€140" hotel would pay a total of €140 (about $195) for a double room with a private bathroom. Unless otherwise noted, breakfast is included, hotel staff speak basic English, and credit cards are accepted.

 If I mention "Internet access," there's a public terminal in the lobby for guests. If I specify "Wi-Fi," you can generally access it in public areas and often (though not always) in your room.

well as printed books.

In general, prices can soften up if you do any of the following: offer to pay cash, stay at least three nights, or mention this book. You can also try asking for a cheaper room or a discount, or offer to skip breakfast.

Types of Accommodations
Hotels

In Florence, you can snare a stark, clean, and comfortable double with breakfast and a private bath for about €100 (less in smaller towns). You get elegance in peak season for €160.

Solo travelers find that the cost of a *camera singola* is often only 25 percent less than a *camera doppia*. Three or four people can save money by requesting one big room. (If a Db is €110, a Qb would be about €150.) Most listed hotels have rooms for any size party from one to five people. If there's room for an extra cot, they'll cram it in for you (charging you around €25).

You'll save €30 if you request a room without a shower and just use the shower down the hall. Generally rooms with a bath or shower also have a toilet and a bidet (which Italians use for quick sponge baths). The cord that dangles over the tub or shower is not a clothesline. You pull it when you've fallen and can't get up.

Double beds are called *matrimoniale,* even though hotels aren't interested in your marital status. Twins are *due letti singoli.* Convents offer cheap accommodation but only *letti singoli.*

When you check in, the receptionist will normally ask for your passport and keep it for a couple of hours. Hotels are legally required to register each guest with the police. Relax. Americans are notorious for making this chore more difficult than it needs to be.

Assume that breakfast is included in the prices I've listed, unless otherwise noted. If breakfast is included but optional, you may want to skip it. While convenient, it's usually expensive—€5-8 per person for a simple continental buffet with ham, cheese, yogurt, and unlimited *caffè latte.* A picnic in your room followed by a coffee at the corner café can be cheaper.

More pillows and blankets are usually in the closet or available on request. In Italy, towels and linen aren't always replaced every day. Hang your towel up to dry. Some hotels use lightweight "waffle," or very thin, tablecloth-type towels; these take less water and electricity to launder and are preferred by many Italians.

Most hotel rooms have a TV, telephone, and Wi-Fi; sometimes there's an Internet terminal in the lobby. Simpler places rarely have a room phone, but often have Wi-Fi. Pricier hotels usually come with elevators, air-conditioning, and a small stocked fridge called a *frigo bar* (FREE-goh bar; pay for what you use).

Because Europeans are generally careful with energy use, you'll find government-enforced limits on heating and air-conditioning. (There's a one-month period each spring and fall when neither is allowed.) Air-conditioning sometimes costs an extra per-day charge, is worth seeking out in summer (though it may be available only at certain times of the day), and is rarely available from fall through spring. Most hotel rooms with air-conditioners come with a control stick (like a TV remote) that generally has the same symbols and features: fan icon (click to toggle), louver icon (choose steady airflow or waves), snowflake/sunshine icons (cold air or heat, depending on season), clock ("O" setting: run x hours before turning off; "I" setting: wait x hours to start), and the temperature control (21 degrees Celsius is comfortable).

If you're arriving on an early flight or an overnight train, your room probably won't be ready first thing in the morning. You should be able to safely check your bag at the hotel and dive right into sightseeing.

Hoteliers can be a great help and source of advice. Most know their cities well, and can assist you with everything from public transit and airport connections to finding a good restaurant, the nearest launderette, or an Internet café. But even at the best places, mechanical breakdowns occur: Air-conditioning malfunctions, sinks leak, hot water turns cold, and toilets gurgle and smell. Report your concerns clearly and calmly at the front desk. For more complicated problems, don't expect instant results.

If you suspect night noise will be a problem (if, for instance, your room is over a nightclub), ask for a quiet room in the back or on an upper floor. To guard against theft in your room, keep valuables out of sight. Some rooms come with a safe, and other hotels have safes at the front desk. Use them if you're concerned.

Checkout can pose problems if surprise charges pop up on your bill. If you settle up your bill the afternoon before you leave, you'll have time to discuss and address any points of contention (before 19:00, when the night shift usually arrives).

Above all, keep a positive attitude. Remember, you're on vacation. If your hotel is a disappointment, spend more time out enjoying the city you came to see.

Hostels

You'll pay about €20 per bed to stay at a hostel. Travelers of any age are welcome if they don't mind dorm-style accommodations and meeting other travelers. Most hostels offer kitchen facilities, Internet access, Wi-Fi, and a self-service laundry.

Independent hostels tend to be easygoing, colorful, and informal (no membership required); see www.hostelz.com, www .hostelseurope.com, www.hostels.com, and www.hostelworld.com.

Making Hotel Reservations

Given the good value of the accommodations I've found for this book, reserve your rooms several weeks in advance—or as soon as you've pinned down your travel dates—particularly if you'll be traveling during peak season. Note that some national holidays jam things up and merit your making reservations far in advance (see "Holidays and Festivals" on page 581).

Requesting a Reservation: It's usually easiest to book your room through the hotel's website; many have a reservation-request form built right in. Just type in your preferred dates and the website will automatically display a list of available rooms and price. Simpler websites will generate an email to the hotelier with your request. If there's no reservation form, or for complicated requests, send an email. Other options include calling (see "Phoning" below, and be mindful of time zones) or faxing. Most recommended hotels are accustomed to guests who speak only English.

The hotelier wants to know these key pieces of information about your stay (also included in the sample request form in the appendix):

- number and type of rooms
- number of nights
- date of arrival
- date of departure
- any special needs (e.g., bathroom in the room or down the hall, twin beds vs. double bed, air-conditioning, quiet, view, ground floor, etc.)

When you request a room, use the European style for writing dates: day/month/year. For example, for a two-night stay in July of 2013, I would request "1 double room for 2 nights, arrive 16/07/13, depart 18/07/13." Consider carefully how long you'll stay; don't just assume you can tack on extra days once you arrive. Make sure you mention any discounts—for Rick Steves readers or otherwise—when you make the reservation.

If you don't get a response to your email, it usually means the hotel is already fully booked—but try sending the message again or call to follow up.

Confirming a Reservation: Most places will request your credit-card number to hold the room. To confirm a room using a hotel's secure online reservation form, enter your contact information and credit-card number; the hotel will email a confirmation. For the best rates, be sure to use the hotel's official site and not a booking agency's site.

If you sent an email to request a reservation, the hotel will reply with its room availability and rates. This is not a confirmation. You must email back to say that you want the room at the given rate. While you can email your credit-card information (I do), it's safer to share that confidential info via phone call, fax, two emails (splitting your number between them), or the hotel's secure online reservation form.

Canceling a Reservation: If you must cancel your reservation, it's courteous to do so with as much advance notice as possible—at least three days. Simply make a quick phone call or send an email. Family-run places lose money if they turn away customers while holding a room for someone who doesn't show up. Understandably, many hotels bill no-shows for one night.

Cancellation policies can be strict: For example, you might lose a deposit if you cancel within two weeks of your reserved stay, or you might be billed for the entire visit if you leave early. Internet deals may require prepayment, with no refunds for cancellations. Ask about cancellation policies before you book.

If canceling via email, request confirmation that your cancellation was received to avoid being accidentally billed.

Reconfirming Your Reservation: Always call to reconfirm your room reservation a few days in advance. Smaller hotels and B&Bs appreciate knowing your estimated time of arrival. If you'll be arriving late (after 17:00), let them know. On the small chance that a hotel loses track of your reservation, bring along a hard copy of their confirmation.

Reserving Rooms as You Travel: You can make reservations as you travel, calling hotels a few days to a week before your arrival. If everything's full, don't despair. Call a day or two in advance and fill in a cancellation. If you'd rather travel without any reservations at all, you'll have greater success snaring rooms if you arrive at your destination early in the day. When you anticipate crowds (weekends are worst), call hotels at about 9:00 or 10:00 on the day you plan to arrive, when the hotel clerk knows who'll be checking out and just which rooms will be available. If you encounter a language barrier, ask the fluent receptionist at your current hotel to call for you.

Phoning: To call Italy from the US or Canada, dial 011-39 and then the local number. (The 011 is our international access code, and 39 is Italy's country code.) If you're calling Italy from another European country, dial 00-39-local number. (The 00 is Europe's international access code.) To call a Florence hotel from anywhere in Italy (including Florence), simply dial the local number. Land lines start with 0; mobile lines start with 3. For more tips on calling, see the appendix.

Official hostels are part of Hostelling International and share an online booking site (www.hihostels.com); they require that you either have a membership card or pay extra per night.

Agriturismo

For information on staying at a rural B&B *(agriturismo)* in Tuscany, see page 453.

Eating

The Italians are masters of the art of fine living. That means eating...long and well. Lengthy, multicourse lunches and dinners and endless hours sitting in outdoor cafés are the norm. Americans eat on their way to an evening event and complain if the check is slow in coming. For Italians, the meal is an end in itself, and only rude waiters rush you. When you want the bill, mime-scribble on your raised palm or ask for it: *"Il conto?"* You may have to ask for it more than once. To save time, you could ask for the check when you receive the last item you order.

Even those of us who liked dorm food will find that the cafés, cuisine, and wines become a highlight of our Italian adventure. Trust me: This is sightseeing for your palate, and even if the rest of you is sleeping in cheap hotels, your taste buds will relish an occasional first-class splurge. You can eat well without going broke. But be careful: You're just as likely to blow a small fortune on a disappointing meal as you are to dine wonderfully for €25.

Your euros will go much farther, and will net you far better food, in smaller Tuscan towns than in Florence.

Restaurants

When restaurant-hunting, choose places filled with locals, not places with big neon signs boasting "We Speak English and Accept Credit Cards." Restaurants parked on famous squares generally serve bad food at high prices to tourists. Venturing even a block or two off the main drag leads to higher-quality food for less than half the price of the tourist-oriented places. Locals eat better at lower-rent locales. Family-run places operate without hired help and can offer cheaper meals.

Good restaurants don't open for dinner before 19:00. Restaurants in Florence seem touristy in the early evening because tourists generally eat early (19:00-21:00), and Florentines often eat late (21:00 on). Also, a traffic law keeps locals with cars out of the city at night, prompting many Florentines to drive to outlying restaurants rather than walk across town to dine.

Before you sit down, look at a menu to see what extra charges a restaurant tacks on. As elsewhere in Italy, many (but not all)

Eating with the Seasons

Italian cooks love to serve you fresh produce and seafood at its tastiest. If you must have porcini mushrooms outside of October and November, they'll be frozen. To get the freshest veggies at a fine restaurant, request *'Il piatto di verdure della stagione, per favore"* ("A plate of seasonal vegetables, please").

Here are a few examples of what's fresh when:

April-May:	Squid, green beans, asparagus, artichokes, and zucchini flowers
April-May and Sept-Oct:	Black truffles
May-June:	Asparagus, zucchini, cantaloupe, and strawberries
May-Aug:	Eggplant
Oct-Nov:	Mushrooms and white truffles
Fresh year-round:	Clams, meats, and cheeses

restaurants in Florence and Tuscany add a cover charge *(coperto)* of €1.50-2.50 per person to your bill. Sometimes this is phrased as "bread and cover" *(pane e coperto)*. It's not negotiable, even if you don't eat the bread. Think of it as covering the cost of using the table for as long as you like. (Italians like to linger, and most restaurants don't depend on turning the table over multiple times in an evening.) Restaurants that tack on a separate service charge (usually 10-15 percent) are in the minority. Places with both a cover *and* a service charge are best avoided—that's a clue that a restaurant is counting on a nonlocal clientele who can't gauge a value. The same goes for the opposite: Places that advertise "no cover, no service charge" to attract tourists are likely raising their prices to compensate. Tipping isn't necessary, but it's nice to do to reward good service. To tip, round up the bill about €1 per person (or €2/person for classy places). Ideally, hand the tip to the server in cash, even if you pay with a credit card.

You can save a lot by getting fixed-priced meals, which are frequently exempt from cover and service charges. However, the cheapest ones tend to be bland and heavy, pairing a very basic pasta with reheated schnitzel and roast meats (usually around €15-20, often called *menù turistico*, or sometimes, usually falsely, *menù del giorno*—menu of the day). It's worth paying more for an inventive fixed-price meal that shows off the chef's creativity. While fixed-price meals can be easy and convenient, galloping gourmets order à la carte with the help of a menu translator. (The *Rick Steves' Italian Phrase Book & Dictionary* has a menu decoder with enough phrases for intermediate eaters.)

A full meal consists of an appetizer (antipasto, €3-6), a first course (*primo piatto,* pasta or soup, €5-12), and a second course (*secondo piatto,* expensive meat and fish dishes, €8-18). Vegetables *(contorni, verdure)* may come with the *secondo* or cost extra (€3-5) as a side dish.

The euros can add up in a hurry. Light and budget eaters get a *primo piatto* each and share an antipasto. (Italians admit the *secondo* is the least interesting part of their cuisine—though a steak can be a nice, if pricey, treat.) Another good option is sharing an array of *antipasti;* you can order several specific dishes, or at restaurants that have self-serve *antipasti* buffets, you can choose from a variety of cooked appetizers spread out like a salad bar. You pay per plate, not by weight; a typical serving costs about €8 (generally Italians don't treat buffets as all-you-can-eat, but take a one-time moderate serving; watch others and imitate).

To maximize the experience and flavors, small groups can mix *antipasti* and *primi piatti* family-style (skipping *secondi*). If you do this right (e.g., under-ordering because courses are often bigger than necessary), you can eat well in better places for less than the cost of a tourist *menù* in a cheap place.

When going to an especially good restaurant with an approachable staff, I like to find out what they're eager to serve, or I'll simply say, "Make me happy" (in this case, it's just fine to set a price limit).

Some special dishes come in large quantities meant for two people; the shorthand way of showing this on a menu is "X2" (meaning "for two people"). The price listed generally indicates the cost per person.

Note that steak and seafood are often sold by weight (priced by the kilo—1,000 grams, or just more than 2 pounds; or by the *etto*—100 grams). The letters "s.q." means according to quantity. Fish is usually served whole with the head and tail; you can't just get half a fish or a filet unless it already comes prepared as just a filet (*filetto,* sometimes *trancio*—slice, as in tuna or swordfish). However, you can ask your waiter to select a smaller fish for you. Sometimes, especially for steak, restaurants require a minimum order of four or five *etti.* Beware, or be shell-shocked by €50 entrées. Make sure you're really clear on the price before ordering.

Wine Bars *(Enoteche)*

An *enoteca* is a popular, fast option for lunch. Surrounded by the office crowd, you can get a fancy salad, a plate of meats and cheeses, and a glass of fine wine (see blackboards for the day's selection and price per glass—and go for the top end). A good *enoteca* aims to impress visitors with its wine, and will generally choose excellent-quality ingredients for the simple dishes it offers with the wine (though the prices add up—this is rarely a budget choice).

Bars/Cafés

Italian "bars" are not taverns but inexpensive cafés. These neighborhood hangouts serve coffee, mini-pizzas, sandwiches, and drinks from the cooler. Many dish up plates of fried cheese and vegetables from under the glass counter, ready to reheat. This budget choice is the Italian equivalent of English pub grub.

For quick meals, bars usually have trays of cheap, ready-made sandwiches (*panini* or *tramezzini*)—some kinds are delightful grilled. To save time for sightseeing and room for dinner, stop by a bar for a light lunch, such as a ham-and-cheese *panino* (called *toast;* have it grilled twice if you want it really hot). To get food "to go," say, *"Da portar via"* (for the road). All bars have a WC *(toilette, bagno)* in the back, and customers—and the discreet public—can use it.

Bars serve great drinks: hot, cold, sweet, or alcoholic. Chilled bottled water, still *(naturale)* or carbonated *(frizzante),* is sold cheap to go.

Coffee: If you ask for *"un caffè,"* you'll get espresso. Cappuccino is served to locals before noon and to tourists any time of day. (To an Italian, cappuccino is a breakfast drink and a travesty after eating anything with tomatoes.) Italians like their coffee only warm—to get it hot, request *"molto caldo"* (very hot) or *"più caldo, per favore"* ("hotter, please"; pew KAHL-doh, pehr fah-VOH-ray).

Experiment with a few of the options:
- Cappuccino: espresso with foamed milk on top
- *Caffè latte:* tall glass with espresso and hot milk mixed (ordering just a "latte" gets you only milk)
- *Caffè freddo:* iced sweet espresso
- Cappuccino *freddo:* iced cappuccino
- *Caffè hag:* instant decaf (any coffee drink is available decaffeinated; ask for it *decaffeinato:* day-kah-fay-een-AH-toh)
- *Caffè macchiato:* with only a little milk
- *Caffè americano:* espresso diluted with hot water
- *Caffè corretto:* espresso with a shot of liqueur (normally grappa, amaro, or Sambuca)

More Hot Drinks: *Cioccolato* is hot chocolate. *Tè* is hot tea. *Tè freddo* (iced tea) is usually from a can—sweetened and flavored with lemon or peach.

Juice: *Spremuta* means freshly squeezed, as far as *succa* (fruit juice) is concerned. (Note: *Spumante* means sparkling wine.)

Beer: Beer on tap is *alla spina*. Get it *piccola* (33 cl, 11 oz), *media* (50 cl, 17 oz), or *grande* (a liter).

Wine: To order a glass (*bicchiere*; bee-kee-AY-ray) of red (*rosso*) or white (*bianco*) wine, say, "*Un bicchiere di vino rosso/bianco*." *Corposo* means full-bodied. House wine (*vino della casa*) often comes in a quarter-liter carafe (8.5 oz, *un quarto*), half-liter pitcher (17 oz, *un mezzo*), or one-liter pitcher (34 oz, *un litro*).

Prices: You'll notice a two-tiered price system. Drinking a cup of coffee while standing at the bar is cheaper than drinking it at a table. If you're on a budget, don't sit without first checking out the financial consequences. Ask, "Same price if I sit or stand?" by saying, "*Costa uguale al tavolo o al banco?*" (KOH-stah oo-GWAH-lay ahl TAH-voh-loh oh ahl BAHN-koh?). A cup of coffee at any bar generally costs only a euro. While coffee may cost €5 at a table, you can stand at the fanciest place in town and sip your coffee at the bar for the same price as at a simple café.

Other Inexpensive Alternatives to Restaurants

Italy offers many budget options for hungry travelers. Self-service cafeterias (called "free flow" in Italian) offer the basics without add-on charges.

Döner kebab places are popping up all over Florence, selling meat, or falafel and salad fixings wrapped in pita bread. They're understandably popular for a break from Italian food (see sidebar on page 305).

Pizza is cheap and everywhere. Stop by a pizza shop for stand-up or take-out pizza. *Pizza a taglio* ("by the slice") is usually round, Naples-style pizza. *Pizza rustica* is thick, rustic, baked in a square pan, and sold by weight (clearly explain how much you want—100 grams, or *un etto*, is a hot and cheap snack; 200 grams, or *due etti*, makes a light meal). Key pizza vocabulary: *capricciosa* (generally ham, mushrooms, olives, and artichokes), *funghi* (mushrooms), *marinara* (tomato sauce, oregano, garlic, no cheese), *quattro formaggi* (four different cheeses), and *quattro stagioni* (different toppings on each of the four quarters, for those who can't choose just one menu item). If you ask for *peperoni* on your pizza, you'll get green or red peppers, not sausage. Kids like the bland *margherita* (cheese with tomato sauce) or *diavola* (the closest thing in Italy to American pepperoni). If you see a sign for a *pizzicheria*, it's not a pizzeria, but an old-timey grocery/deli.

Stop by a *rosticceria* for great cooked deli food; this makes a fast, cheap, and healthy lunch. Look for one with a buffet spread of meat and vegetables, and ask for a mixed plate of vegetables with a hunk of mozzarella (*piatto misto di verdure con mozzarella*). Don't be limited by what's displayed. If you'd like a salad with a slice of

Ordering Food at a *Rosticceria*

plate of mixed veggies	*piatto misto di verdure*	pee-AH-toh MEES-toh dee vehr-DOO-ray
"Heated, please."	*"Scaldare, per favore."*	skahl-DAH-ray, pehr fah-VOH-ray
"A taste, please."	*"Un assaggio, per favore."*	oon ah-SAH-joh, pehr fah-VOH-ray
artichoke	*carciofi*	kar-CHOH-fee
asparagus	*asparagi*	ah-SPAH-rah-jee
beans	*fagioli*	fah-JOH-lee
breadsticks	*grissini*	gree-SEE-nee
broccoli	*broccoli*	BROH-koh-lee
cantaloupe	*melone*	may-LOH-nay
carrots	*carote*	kah-ROT-ay
green beans	*fagiolini*	fah-joh-LEE-nee
ham	*prosciutto*	proh-SHOO-toh
mushrooms	*funghi*	FOONG-ghee
potatoes	*patate*	pah-TAH-tay
rice	*riso*	REE-zoh
spinach	*spinaci*	speen-AH-chee
tomatoes	*pomodori*	poh-moh-DOH-ree
zucchini	*zucchine*	zoo-KEE-nay

(Excerpted from *Rick Steves' Italian Phrase Book & Dictionary*)

cantaloupe and a hunk of cheese, they'll whip that up for you in a snap. Belly up to the bar and, with a pointing finger and key words from the chart in this chapter, you can get a fine plate of mixed vegetables. If something's a mystery, ask for *un assaggio* (oon ah-SAH-joh) to get a little taste.

Beware of cheap eateries that sport big color photos of pizza and piles of different pastas. They have no kitchens and simply microwave disgusting prepackaged food. Unless you like lasagna with ice in the center, avoid these.

Picnics

Throughout Tuscany, picnicking saves lots of euros and is a great way to sample regional specialties. In the process of assembling your meal, you get to deal with the Italians in the market scene. For a colorful experience, gather your ingredients in the morning at the produce market (Florence's is the Mercato Centrale, near the Church of San Lorenzo); you'll probably visit several market stalls to put together a complete meal (note that many close around noon). While it's fun to visit the small specialty shops, an *alimentari* is your one-stop corner grocery store; most will slice and stuff your sandwich for you if you buy the ingredients there. The rare *supermercato* (look for the Metà, Conad, Despar, and Co-op chains) gives you more efficiency with less color for less cost. At busier supermarkets, you'll need to take a number for deli service.

Juice-lovers can get a liter of O.J. for the price of a Coke or coffee. Look for "100% *succo*" (juice) on the label. Hang onto the half-liter mineral-water bottles (sold everywhere for about €1). Buy juice in cheap liter boxes, drink some, and store the extra in your water bottle. (Like locals, I refill my water bottle with tap water—*acqua del rubinetto*.)

Picnics can be an adventure in high cuisine. Be daring. Try the fresh mozzarella, *presto* pesto, shriveled olives, and any UFOs the locals are excited about. Shopkeepers are happy to sell small quantities of produce. They seem to enjoy giving you a taste *(un assaggio)*. It is customary to let the merchant choose the produce for you. Say *"Per oggi"* (pehr OH-jee), or "For today," and he or she will grab you something ready to eat, weigh it, and make the sale. A typical picnic for two might be fresh rolls, 100 grams of cheese, 100 grams of meat (*un etto* = 100 grams = about a quarter pound), two tomatoes, three carrots, two apples, yogurt, and a liter box of juice. Total cost: about €10.

Florentine Cuisine

While many restaurants in Florence and Tuscany serve your basic Italian fare—pasta and pizza, veal cutlets, and mixed salad—there are a few specialties you'll find without looking too hard. In general, Florentine cuisine is hearty, simple farmers' food: grilled meats, high-quality seasonal vegetables, fresh herbs, prized olive oil, and rustic bread. Tuscans are frugal, not wasting a single breadcrumb. They are also known as *mangiafagioli* (bean-eaters)—and upon sorting through the many beans on Florentine menus, you'll learn why. Florence is not a great pizza town.

Here are some typical foods you'll encounter throughout Tuscany:

Appetizers *(Antipasti)*

Tuscan bread: Rustic-style breads (not baguettes) with a thick crust and chewy interior. It's a type of sourdough bread, unsalted and nearly flavorless, used almost like a utensil to sop up the heartier-flavored cuisine. Slathered with olive oil and salt, it is a popular afternoon snack. Locals describe the action of dipping their crust repeatedly into the treasured olive oil as "making the *scarpetta* (little shoe)."

Bruschetta: Toasted bread brushed with olive oil and rubbed with garlic, topped with chopped tomato, mushrooms, or whatever else sounds good.

Crostini: Small toasted bread rounds topped with meat or vegetable pastes. *Alla Toscana* or "black Tuscan" generally means with chicken liver paste. *Lardo* (pork lard) is also a favorite traditional spread.

Finocchiona sbriciolona: A soft salami flavored with fennel seed.

Panzanella: A simple Tuscan salad, served only in the summer, that's made of chunks of day-old bread and chopped tomatoes, onion, and basil, tossed in a light vinaigrette.

Pecorino cheese: Fresh *(fresco)* or aged *(stagionato)*, from ewe's milk.

Porcini mushrooms: Harvested in the fall and used in pasta and soups.

Salume: Cured meat, usually pork. Two popular kinds are *prosciutto* and *pancetta*.

Tagliere: A big wooden platter with a sampling of meats and cheeses.

First Course *(Primo Piatto)*

Ribollita: "Reboiled" soup traditionally made with leftovers, including white beans *(fagioli)*, seasonal vegetables, and olive oil, with layers of day-old Tuscan bread slices.

Pappardelle sulla lepre: This broad noodle is served with a rich sauce made from wild hare.

Pici al ragù: A fat, spaghetti-like pasta served most often with a meat-tomato sauce.

Main Course *(Secondo Piatto)*

Bistecca alla fiorentina: A thick T-bone steak, generally grilled very rare and lightly seasoned. (The best is from the white Chianina breed of cattle you'll see grazing throughout Tuscany.) This dish is often sold by weight (per etto, or 100 grams), not per portion; ask what the minimum amount costs.

Cinghiale: Boar, served grilled or in soups, stews, and pasta. It is also made into many varieties of sausage and salami.

Arrosto misto: Mixed roast meats, or meats on a skewer *(spiedino)*.

Various game birds: Squab, pheasant, and guinea hen.

Trippa alla fiorentina: Tripe (intestines) and vegetables sautéed in a tomato sauce, sometimes baked with parmesan cheese.

...alla fiorentina: Anything cooked "in the Florentine style." The phrase can mean almost anything, but often means it's cooked with vegetables, especially spinach.

INTRODUCTION

Wine Labels and Lingo

The region of Tuscany produces some of the most famous and

tastiest wines in Italy. The characteristics of the soil, temperature, and exposure make each wine unique to its area. Even if you don't often drink wine, try some in Tuscany.

Choosing a wine can be intimidating, but the Italian government tries to help you choose something decent, even if you're clueless. In general, wines are designated by one of four categories:

Vino da Tavola (table wine) is the lowest grade. While inexpensive, Italy's wines are so good that, for many people, a basic vino da tavola is just fine with a meal. Many restaurants, even modest ones, take pride in their house wine (vino della casa), bottling their own or working with wineries.

Denominazione di Origine Controllata (DOC), a cut above table wine, is usually cheap, but can be surprisingly good. Hundreds of wines have earned the DOC designation, and you'll see plenty of them in Tuscany, since many DOC wines come from the Chianti region, located between Florence and Siena.

Denominazione di Origine Controllata e Guarantita (DOCG) is the highest grade, and can be identified by the pink or green label on the neck and the scary price tag on the shelf. Only a limited number of wines in Italy can be called DOCG. They're generally a good bet if you want a quality wine, but you don't know anything else about the winemaker. (Riserva is a DOC or DOCG wine matured for a longer, more specific time.)

Dessert *(Dolci)*

Panforte: Dense, dark, clove-and-cinnamon-spiced cake from Siena. Panforte makes a good, enduring gift.

Gelato: The Florentines claim they invented Italian-style ice cream. Many think they serve some of the world's best. Consider skipping dessert at the restaurant and stretching your legs before finding a good gelateria.

Cantucci and *Vin Santo:* Florentines love this simple way to end a meal, by dipping the crunchy almond biscotti in *vin santo* (literally "holy wine"), a sweet, golden dessert wine.

Indicazione Geographica Tipica (IGT) is a broad group of wines that range from basic to some of Italy's best. It includes the "Super Tuscans"—wines that don't follow the strict "recipe" required for DOC or DOCG status, but that give local vintners more opportunity to be creative. Super Tuscans are made from a mix of international grapes (such as Cabernet Sauvignon) grown in Tuscany and aged in small oak barrels for only two years. The result is a lively full-bodied wine that dances all over your head... and is worth the steep price for aficionados.

Visit a Tuscan enoteca (wine bar) and sample some of these wines side-by-side to figure out what you like—and what suits your pocketbook.

Words to Live by, or...How to Describe Wine in Italian
As you can see from many of the words listed below, adding a vowel to the English word often gets you close to the Italian one. Have some fun, gesture like a local, and you'll have no problems speaking the language of the *enoteca. Salute!*

dry	*secco*	SAY-koh
sweet	*dolce*	DOHL-chay
earthy	*terroso*	tay-ROH-zoh
tannic	*tannico*	TAH-nee-koh
young	*giovane*	JOH-vah-nay
mature	*maturo*	mah-TOO-roh
sparkling	*spumante*	spoo-MAHN-tay
fruity	*fruttoso*	froo-TOH-zoh
full-bodied	*corposo*	kor-POH-zoh
elegant	*elegante*	ay-lay-GAHN-tay

Top Local Wines

Brunello di Montalcino: One of Italy's greatest red wines, made from Sangiovese *grosso* grapes, this comes from the slopes of Montalcino, south of Siena. This full-bodied wine is aged at least four years in wooden casks, resulting in a bold, smooth character. Called "the brunette," it's dark brownish-red and has a rich, robust, complex aroma that is suitable to pair with hearty, meaty food. Really savor this one; bottles typically start at €25.

Rosso di Montalcino: This lower-priced, younger version of Brunello—a.k.a. "baby Brunello"—is also made in Montalcino from Sangiovese grapes. It lacks Brunello's depth of flavor and complexity, but it's still a great wine at a bargain price, usually €8-15.

Chianti: This hearty red from the Chianti region (20 miles south of Florence), made mostly from the Sangiovese grape, is world-famous. "Chianti Classico," with a black rooster symbol on the bottle's neck, is usually the best. Cheap, €2 Chiantis  are acidic, while better ones, starting at €8, can be flavorful, sometimes earthy or fruity.

Vino Nobile di Montepulciano: This high-quality, ruby red, dry wine—also made of Sangiovese grapes—goes well with meat dishes, especially chicken. Don't confuse this one with the inferior (but drinkable) Montepulciano wine available in most US grocery stores.

Super Tuscans: This newer breed of Italian wine is a creative mix of locally grown non-Italian grapes (usually from French grapes like Cabernet and Merlot), so the Italian regulating body does not rate them. Ask for help in choosing one of these at an enoteca. There are many choices, and because many are pricey, you don't want to be disappointed. Reliable brands are Sassicaia and Tignanello.

Vernaccia di San Gimignano: In Tuscany, this is the only choice for white-wine lovers, but even finicky red-wine fans will be able to down a glass of this medium-dry white, which pairs well with pasta and salad.

Traveling as a Temporary Local

We travel all the way to Italy to enjoy differences—to become temporary locals. You'll experience frustrations. Certain truths that we find "God-given" or "self-evident," such as cold beer, ice in drinks, bottomless cups of coffee, hot showers, and bigger being better, are suddenly not so true. One of the benefits of travel is the eye-opening realization that there are logical, civil, and even better alternatives. A willingness to go local ensures that you'll enjoy a full dose of Italian hospitality.

Europeans generally like Americans. But if there is a negative aspect to Italians' image of Americans, it's that we are big, loud, wasteful, ethnocentric, too informal (which can seem disrespectful), and a bit naive. Think about the rationale behind "crazy" Italian decisions. For instance, many hoteliers turn off the heat in spring and can't turn on air-conditioning until summer. The point is to conserve energy, and it's mandated by the Italian government. You could complain about being cold or hot...or bring a

How Was Your Trip?

Were your travels fun, smooth, and meaningful? If you'd like to share your tips, concerns, and discoveries, please fill out the survey at www.ricksteves.com/feedback. I value your feedback. Thanks in advance—it helps a lot.

sweater in winter, and in summer, be prepared to sweat a little like everyone else.

While Italians, flabbergasted by our Yankee excesses, say in disbelief, *"Mi sono cadute le braccia!"* ("I throw my arms down!"), they nearly always afford us individual travelers all the warmth we deserve. Judging from all the happy feedback I receive from travelers who have used this book, it's safe to assume you'll enjoy a great, affordable vacation—with the finesse of an independent, experienced traveler.

Thanks, and *buon viaggio!*

Back Door Travel Philosophy
From *Rick Steves' Europe Through the Back Door*

Travel is intensified living—maximum thrills per minute and one of the last great sources of legal adventure. Travel is freedom. It's recess, and we need it.

Experiencing the real Europe requires catching it by surprise, going casual..."Through the Back Door."

Affording travel is a matter of priorities. (Make do with the old car.) You can eat and sleep—simply, safely, and enjoyably—anywhere in Europe for $120 a day plus transportation costs. In many ways, spending more money only builds a thicker wall between you and what you traveled so far to see. Europe is a cultural carnival, and time after time, you'll find that its best acts are free and the best seats are the cheap ones.

A tight budget forces you to travel close to the ground, meeting and communicating with the people. Never sacrifice sleep, nutrition, safety, or cleanliness to save money. Simply enjoy the local-style alternatives to expensive hotels and restaurants.

Connecting with people carbonates your experience. Extroverts have more fun. If your trip is low on magic moments, kick yourself and make things happen. If you don't enjoy a place, maybe you don't know enough about it. Seek the truth. Recognize tourist traps. Give a culture the benefit of your open mind. See things as different, but not better or worse. Any culture has plenty to share.

Of course, travel, like the world, is a series of hills and valleys. Be fanatically positive and militantly optimistic. If something's not to your liking, change your liking.

Travel can make you a happier American, as well as a citizen of the world. Our Earth is home to seven billion equally precious people. It's humbling to travel and find that other people don't have the "American Dream"—they have their own dreams. Europeans like us, but with all due respect, they wouldn't trade passports.

Thoughtful travel engages us with the world. In tough economic times, it reminds us what is truly important. By broadening perspectives, travel teaches new ways to measure quality of life.

Globetrotting destroys ethnocentricity, helping us understand and appreciate other cultures. Rather than fear the diversity on this planet, celebrate it. Among your most prized souvenirs will be the strands of different cultures you choose to knit into your own character. The world is a cultural yarn shop, and Back Door travelers are weaving the ultimate tapestry. Join in!

FLORENCE
Firenze

ORIENTATION

The best of Florence lies on the north bank of the Arno River. The main historical sights cluster around the red-brick dome of the cathedral (Duomo). Everything is within a 20-minute walk of the train station, cathedral, or Ponte Vecchio (Old Bridge). The less famous but more characteristic Oltrarno area (south bank) is just over the bridge. Though small, Florence is intense. Prepare for scorching summer heat, slick pickpockets, few WCs, steep prices, and long lines. Easy tourist money has corrupted some locals, making them greedy and dishonest (check your bill carefully). The big news for visitors to Florence is the energetic young mayor's passion for traffic-free zones. Once brutal for pedestrians, the city is now a delight on foot.

Planning Your Time

Plan your sightseeing carefully; follow the tips and tricks in this chapter to save time and avoid lines. This is particularly important if you'll be in town for only a day or two during the crowded summer months.

The Uffizi Gallery and Accademia (starring Michelangelo's *David*) nearly always have long ticket-buying lines, especially in peak season (April-Oct) and on holiday weekends. Crowds thin out weekdays in the off-season. Whatever time of year you visit, you can easily avoid the wait by making reservations (see page 59) or buying a Firenze Card (see page 57). Note that both of these major sights are closed on Monday.

Some sights close early; see the early-closing warning in the "Daily Reminder," later in this chapter. Other museums close early only on certain days (e.g., the first Sunday of the month, second and fourth Monday, etc.). In general, Sundays and Mondays are bad, with many museums either closed or with shorter hours.

Rick Steves Audio Europe

If you're bringing a mobile device, be sure to check out **Rick Steves Audio Europe,** where you can download free audio tours and hours of travel interviews (via the Rick Steves Audio Europe smartphone app, www.ricksteves.com/audioeurope, iTunes, or Google Play).

My self-guided **audio tours** are user-friendly, easy to follow, fun, and informative, covering the major sights and neighborhoods in Florence: my Renaissance Walk, the Accademia, and the Uffizi Gallery. Compared to live tours, my audio tours are hard to beat: Nobody will stand you up, the quality is reliable, you can take the tour exactly when you like, and they're free.

Rick Steves Audio Europe also offers a far-reaching library of intriguing **travel interviews** with experts from around the globe.

Set up a good itinerary in advance. Do my recommended Renaissance Walk in the morning or late afternoon to avoid heat and crowds. Stop often for gelato.

Florence in One Brutal Day

8:30   Accademia *(David)*—reserve in advance or get a Firenze Card.

10:00   Take Renaissance Walk through town center and climb the Campanile.

12:00   Bargello (best statues).

13:30   Grab a quick lunch in or near the Mercato Centrale.

14:00   Shopping around San Lorenzo.

16:30   Uffizi Gallery (finest paintings)—reserve well in advance or get a Firenze Card.

19:30   Take the Oltrarno Walk (best local color) and have dinner across the river at 21:00.

Florence in Two Days
Day 1

8:30   Accademia *(David)*—reserve in advance or get a Firenze Card.

10:00   Museum of San Marco (art by Fra Angelico).

12:00   Explore the Mercato Centrale and have lunch there.

14:00   Medici Chapels (Michelangelo sculptures, closes early in winter).

16:30   Baptistery (closes at 14:00 on Sun).

17:00   Climb the Campanile.

18:00   Renaissance Walk through heart of old town (Duomo

ORIENTATION

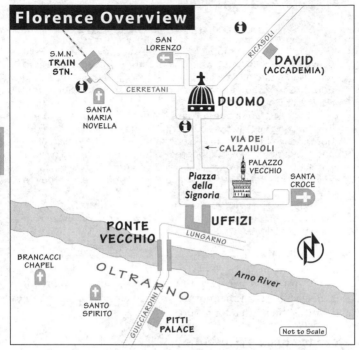

Florence Overview

SAN LORENZO

S.M.N. TRAIN STN.

RICASOLI

DAVID (ACCADEMIA)

CERRETANI

SANTA MARIA NOVELLA

DUOMO

VIA DE' CALZAIUOLI

PALAZZO VECCHIO

SANTA CROCE

Piazza della Signoria

PONTE VECCHIO

UFFIZI

LUNGARNO

BRANCACCI CHAPEL

OLTRARNO

Arno River

N

SANTO SPIRITO

GUICCIARDINI

PITTI PALACE

Not to Scale

and Orsanmichele Church interiors closed in evening, but skippable).

20:00   Dinner in the old center.

Day 2

9:00   Bargello (great statues).

11:00   Duomo Museum (intriguing statues by Donatello and Michelangelo) or Galileo Science Museum.

13:00   Lunch, free to wander and shop.

15:00   Take a bike or walking tour.

17:00   Uffizi Gallery (best paintings)—reserve well in advance or get a Firenze Card.

19:00   Oltrarno Walk.

21:00   Dinner in Oltrarno.

Florence in Three (or More) Days
Day 1

8:30   Accademia *(David)*—reserve in advance or get a Firenze Card.

10:00   Museum of San Marco (Fra Angelico).

12:00   Markets, shop, wander.

13:00   Lunch.

ORIENTATION

14:00   Medici Chapels (Michelangelo).
15:00   Take a bike or walking tour.
16:30   Baptistery (closes at 14:00 on Sun).
17:00   Climb the Campanile.
18:00   Renaissance Walk through heart of old town.
21:00   Dinner in the old center.

Day 2
9:00   Bargello (top statues).
11:00   Galileo Science Museum.
13:00   Lunch, free to wander and shop.
16:30   Uffizi Gallery (unforgettable paintings)—reserve well
         in advance or get a Firenze Card.
19:00   Take the Oltrarno Walk and have dinner in Oltrarno.

Day 3
9:00   Duomo Museum.
11:00   Santa Croce Church (opens at 14:00 on Sun).
13:00   Lunch.
16:00   San Miniato Church (Gregorian chants at 18:30
         in summer, 17:00 or 17:30 in winter), Piazzale
         Michelangelo (city views), walk back into town.

Day 4
Side-trip to Siena (sights open daily; 1.25 hours away by bus), or
consider an overnight stay to enjoy the town at twilight.

Day 5 (or More)
Visit your pick of Pisa, Lucca, and Tuscan hill towns—or take a
cooking class.

Arrival in Florence

For a rundown on Florence's train station, the bus station (next to
the train station), and nearby airports—as well as tips for arriving
by car or cruise ship—see the Florence Connections chapter.

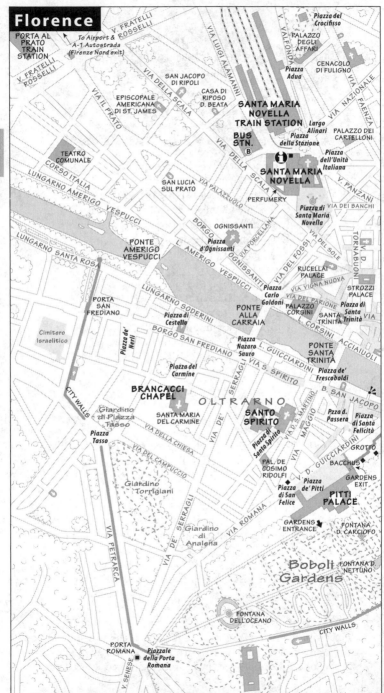

Florence

To Airport & A-1 Autostrada (Firenze Nord exit)

PORTA AL PRATO TRAIN STATION

V. FRATELLI ROSSELLI

V. FRATELLI ROSSELLI

VIA LUIGI ALAMANNI

VIA VALFONDA

Piazza del Crocifisso

PALAZZO DEGLI AFFARI

CENACOLO DI FULIGNO

SAN JACOPO DI RIPOLI

CASA DI RIPOSO D. BEATA

Piazza Adua

VIA NAZIONALE

VIA FAENZA

EPISCOPALE AMERICANA DI ST. JAMES

VIA DELLA SCALA

SANTA MARIA NOVELLA TRAIN STATION

Largo Alinari

PALAZZO DEI CARTELLONI

IL PRATO

VIA IL PRATO

BUS STN. B

Piazza della Stazione

Piazza dell'Unità Italiana

TEATRO COMUNALE

CORSO ITALIA

SAN LUCIA SUL PRATO

VIA DELLA SCALA

VIA PALAZZUOLO

SANTA MARIA NOVELLA

V. PANZANI

LUNGARNO AMERIGO VESPUCCI

PERFUMERY

Piazza di Santa Maria Novella

VIA DEI BANCHI

LUNGARNO SANTA ROSA

OGNISSANTI

Piazza d'Ognissanti

VIA PORCELLANA

VIA DEL SOLE

VIA DEL FOSSI

V. D. TORNABUONI

PONTE AMERIGO VESPUCCI

L. AMERIGO VESPUCCI

RUCELLAI PALACE

VIA VIGNA NUOVA

STROZZI PALACE

PORTA SAN FREDIANO

LUNGARNO SODERINI

Piazza Carlo Goldoni

VIA DEL PARIONE

PALAZZO CORSINI

Piazza di Santa Trinità

Cimitero Israelitico

Piazza di Cestella

PONTE ALLA CARRAIA

L. CORSINI

SANTA TRINITA

VIA

Piazza de' Nerli

BORGO SAN FREDIANO

Piazza Nazaro Sauro

L. GUICCIARDINI

PONTE SANTA TRINITA

ACCIAIUOLI

CITY WALLS

Piazza del Carmine

VIA DE' SERRAGLI

VIA S. SPIRITO

Piazza de' Frescobaldi

B. SAN JACOPO

BRANCACCI CHAPEL

OLTRARNO

VIA DE'

SANTO SPIRITO

VIA S. MARTINO

Pzza d. Passera

Piazza di Santa Felicità

Giardino di Piazza Tasso

SANTA MARIA DEL CARMINE

Piazza di Santa Spirito

VIA S. MAGGIO

GROTTO

Piazza Tasso

VIA DELLA CHIESA

BACCHUS

VIA DEL CAMPUCCIO

PAL. DE COSIMO RIDOLFI

V. D. GUICCIARDINI

GARDENS EXIT

Giardino Torrigiani

Piazza de' Pitti

Piazza di San Felice

PITTI PALACE

VIA ROMANA

Giardino di Analena

GARDENS ENTRANCE

FONTANA D. CARCIOFO

VIA DE' SERRAGLI

Boboli Gardens

FONTANA D. NETTUNO

VIA PETRARCA

FONTANA DELL'OCEANO

CITY WALLS

PORTA ROMANA

Piazzale della Porta Romana

V. SENESE

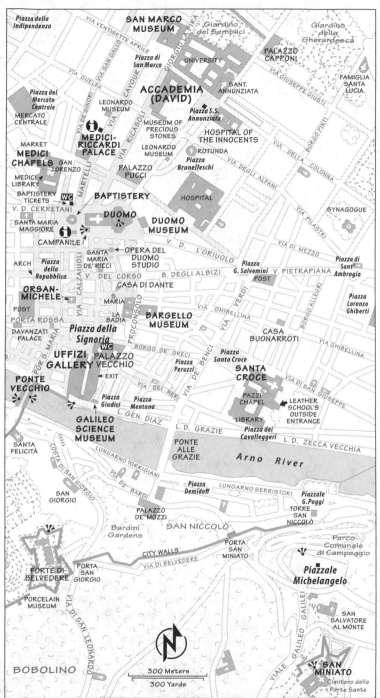

Piazza della Indipendenza

VIA VENTISETTE APRILE

SAN MARCO MUSEUM

GIORGIO LA PIRA

Giardino dei Semplici

Giardino della Gherardesca

PALAZZO CAPPONI

VIA GUELFA

VIA SAN GALLO

VIA DE GHIORI

VIA CAVOUR

Piazza di San Marco

UNIVERSITY

SANT. ANNUNZIATA

VIA GIUSEPPE GIUSTI

FAMIGLIA SANTA LUCIA

Piazza del Mercato Centrale

MERCATO CENTRALE

LEONARDO MUSEUM

ACCADEMIA (DAVID)

Piazza S.S. Annunziata

VIA RICASOLI

BORGO PINTI

MARKET

MUSEUM OF PRECIOUS STONES

HOSPITAL OF THE INNOCENTS

VIA DELLA COLONNA

MEDICI CHAPELS

MEDICI-RICCARDI PALACE

SAN LORENZO

LEONARDO MUSEUM

ROTUNDA

MEDICI LIBRARY

PALAZZO PUCCI

Piazza Brunelleschi

VIA DEGLI ALFANI

MARTELLI

BAPTISTERY TICKETS

WC

BAPTISTERY

VIA PILASTRI

V. D. CERRETANI

SANTA MARIA MAGGIORE

DUOMO

DUOMO MUSEUM

HOSPITAL

SYNAGOGUE

CAMPANILE

SANTA MARIA DE' RICCI

OPERA DEL DUOMO STUDIO

V. D. L'ORIUOLO

VIA DI MEZZO

ARCH

Piazza della Repubblica

V. CALZAIUOLI

V. DEL CORSO

B. DEGLI ALBIZI

Piazza G. Salvemini

V. PIETRAPIANA

Piazza di Sant' Ambrogio

CASA DI DANTE

POST

ORSAN-MICHELE

S. MARIA

VIA DEI PROCONSOLO

BARGELLO MUSEUM

VIA GHIBELLINA

VIA VERDI

Piazza Lorenzo Ghiberti

POST

LA BADIA

CASA BUONARROTI

VIA GHIBELLINA

PORTA ROSSA

DAVANZATI PALACE

Piazza della Signoria

WC

BORGO DE' GRECI

Piazza Santa Croce

VIA DI SAN GIUSEPPE

FOR S. MARIA

UFFIZI GALLERY

PALAZZO VECCHIO

EXIT

Piazza Peruzzi

VIA DE' BENCI

SANTA CROCE

PONTE VECCHIO

VIA DEI NERI

Piazza Giudici

Piazza Mentana

PAZZI CHAPEL

LEATHER SCHOOL'S OUTSIDE ENTRANCE

GALILEO SCIENCE MUSEUM

L. GEN. DIAZ

LIBRARY

Piazza del Cavalleggeri

L. D. ZECCA VECCHIA

SANTA FELICITA

L. D. GRAZIE

LUNGARNO TORRIGIANI

PONTE ALLE GRAZIE

Arno River

COSTA DI SAN GIORGIO

VIA DE' BARDI

Piazza Demidoff

LUNGARNO SERRISTORI

Piazzale G. Poggi

SAN GIORGIO

PALAZZO DE' MOZZI

SAN NICCOLÒ

TORRE SAN NICCOLÒ

Bardini Gardens

Parco Comunale di Campeggio

CITY WALLS

PORTA SAN MINIATO

Piazzale Michelangelo

FORTE DI BELVEDERE

PORTA SAN GIORGIO

VIA DI BELVEDERE

SAN SALVATORE AL MONTE

PORCELAIN MUSEUM

VIA DI SAN LEONARDO

VIALE GALILEO GALILEI

BOBOLINO

N

300 Meters

300 Yards

SAN MINIATO

Cimitero delle Porte Sante

Tourist Information

Florence has two separate TI organizations, which are equally helpful.

One TI has two different branches, both with a focus on the city. The main branch is across the square from the **train station** and very crowded (Mon-Sat 8:30-19:00, Sun 8:30-14:00; with your back to tracks, exit the station—it's 100 yards away, across the square in wall near corner of church at Piazza Stazione 4; if you see a "tourist information" desk inside the train station, it's a hotel-booking service in disguise; tel. 055-212-245, www.firenze turismo.it). The other branch is very centrally located at **Piazza del Duomo,** at the west corner of Via Calzaiuoli (it's inside the Bigallo Museum/Loggia; Mon-Sat 9:00-19:00, Sun 9:00-14:00).

The other TI organization covers both the city and the greater province of Florence. Its main branch is a couple of blocks **north of the Duomo** (Mon-Sat 8:30-18:30, closed Sun, just past Medici-Riccardi Palace at Via Cavour 1 red, tel. 055-290-832, international bookstore across street); a second branch is at the **airport** (daily 8:30-20:30).

At any TI, peruse these free, handy resources in English (though, since they overlap quite a bit, you probably don't need them all):

- city map (also ask for the transit map, which has bus routes of interest to tourists on the back; your hotel likely has freebie maps, too)
- current museum-hours listing (very important, since no guidebook—including this one—has ever been able to accurately predict the hours of Florence's sights for the coming year; you can also download this list at www.firenzeturismo .it)
- a list of current exhibitions
- a printout of what's happening that day
- the compact *Firenze Info* booklet, loaded with useful practical details
- the *Firenze: The Places of Interest* fold-out, with brief descriptions of sightseeing options
- information on entertainment, including the TI's monthly *Florence & Tuscany News* (good for events and entertainment listings)
- the glossy monthly *Florence Concierge Information* magazine (stuffed with ads for shopping and restaurants, but also includes some practical information)
- *The Florentine* newspaper (published every other Thu in English, for expats and tourists, with great articles giving cultural insights; download latest issue at www.theflorentine .net)

The Florence magazine and newspaper just mentioned are often available at hotels throughout town.

The TIs across from the train station and on Via Cavour sell the €50 **Firenze Card,** an expensive but handy sightseeing pass that allows you to skip the lines at top museums (see page 57).

Helpful Hints

Theft Alert: Florence has particularly hardworking thief gangs who hang out where you do: near the train station, the station's underpass (especially where the tunnel surfaces), and at major sights. American tourists—especially older ones—are considered easy targets. Some thieves even dress like tourists to fool you. Be on guard at two squares frequented by drug pushers (Santa Maria Novella and Santo Spirito). Bus #7 (to the nearby town of Fiesole, with great Florence views) is a favorite with tourists and, therefore, with thieves.

Medical Help: There's no shortage of English-speaking medical help in Florence. To reach a doctor who speaks English, call **Medical Service Firenze** at 055-475-411; the phone is answered 24/7. Rates are reasonable. For a doctor to come to your hotel within an hour of your call, you'd pay €100-200 (higher rates apply on Sun, holidays, or for late visits). You pay only €50 if you go to the clinic when the doctor's in (Mon-Fri 11:00-12:00 & 17:00-18:00, Sat 11:00-12:00, closed Sun, no appointment necessary, Via L. Magnifico 59, near Piazza della Libertà). A second clinic is available at Via Porta Rossa 1 (Mon-Sat 13:00-15:00, closed Sun).

Dr. Stephen Kerr is an English doctor specializing in helping sick tourists (drop-in clinic open Mon-Fri 15:00-17:00, other times by appointment, €50/visit, Piazza Mercato Nuovo 1, between Piazza della Repubblica and Ponte Vecchio, tel. 055-288-055, mobile 335-836-1682, www.dr-kerr.com). The TI has a list of other English-speaking doctors.

There are 24-hour **pharmacies** at the train station and on Borgo San Lorenzo (near the Baptistery).

Museum Strategies: If you want to see a lot of museums, the pricey Firenze Card—which saves you from having to wait in line or make reservations for the Uffizi and Accademia—can be a good value (see page 57).

Churches: Some churches operate like museums, charging an admission fee to see their art treasures. Modest dress for men, women, and even children is required in some churches (including the Duomo, Santa Maria Novella, Santa Croce, Santa Maria del Carmine—with the Brancacci Chapel, and the Medici Chapels), and recommended for all of them—no bare shoulders, short shorts, or short skirts. At many churches,

ORIENTATION

Daily Reminder

Sunday: The Duomo's dome, Museum of Precious Stones, and Mercato Centrale are closed.

These sights close early: Duomo Museum (at 13:40) and the Baptistery's interior (at 14:00).

A few sights are open only in the afternoon: Duomo (13:30-16:45), Santa Croce Church (14:00-17:30), Church of San Lorenzo (13:30-17:30 except closed Nov-Jan), Brancacci Chapel and Church of Santa Maria Novella (both 13:00-17:00), and Santo Spirito Church (16:00-17:30).

The Museum of San Marco and the Bargello are closed on the first, third, and fifth Sundays of the month. Palazzo Davanzati and the Medici Chapels close on the second and fourth Sundays. Need a calendar? Look in the appendix.

Monday: The biggies are closed, including the Accademia (David) and the Uffizi Gallery, as well as the Pitti Palace's Palatine Gallery, Royal Apartments, and Gallery of Modern Art.

The Museum of San Marco and the Bargello close on the second and fourth Mondays. At the Pitti Palace, the Argenti/Silverworks Museum and the Boboli and Bardini gardens close on the first and last Mondays. Palazzo Davanzati is closed on the first, third, and fifth Mondays. The San Lorenzo Market is closed Mondays in winter.

Target these sights on Mondays: the Duomo and its dome, Duomo Museum, Campanile, Baptistery, Medici-Riccardi Palace, Brancacci Chapel, Mercato Nuovo, Mercato Centrale, Casa Buonarroti, Galileo Science Museum, Palazzo Vecchio, and churches (including Santa Croce and Santa Maria Novella). Or take a walking tour.

Tuesday: Casa Buonarroti, Brancacci Chapel, and the Museum of Santa Maria Novella are closed. The Galileo Science Museum closes early (13:00).

you can borrow or buy a cheap, disposable poncho for instant respectability. Be respectful of worshippers and the paintings; don't use a flash. Churches usually close from 12:00 or 12:30 to 15:00 or 16:00.

Addresses: For reasons beyond human understanding, Florence has a ridiculously confusing system for street addresses, with separate numbering for businesses (red) and residences (black). In print, this designation is sometimes indicated by a letter following the number: "r" = red; no indication or "n" = black, for *nero*. While usually black, B&Bs can be either. The red and black numbers each appear in roughly consecutive order on streets but bear no apparent connection with each other. While the numbers are sometimes color-coded on street

Wednesday: All sights are open, except for the Medici-Riccardi Palace, Santo Spirito Church, and the Museum of Santa Maria Novella.

Thursday: All sights are open, except for the Museum of Santa Maria Novella. These sights close early: the Palazzo Vecchio (14:00) and off-season, the Duomo (16:00 Oct-May).

Friday: All sights are open.

Saturday: All sights are open, but the Duomo's dome closes earlier than usual, at 17:40.

Early-Closing Warning: Some of Florence's sights close surprisingly early most days. Palazzo Davanzati closes at 13:50 and the Museum of San Marco closes at 13:50 on weekdays (open later on Sat and when open on Sun). Off-season, the Medici Chapels and Bargello close at 13:50. The Museum of Precious Stones closes at 14:00, as does the Mercato Centrale (except in winter, when it stays open until 17:00 on Sat).

Late-Hours Relief: The Accademia and the Pitti Palace's Palatine Gallery and Royal Apartments are open until 18:50 (and the Uffizi until 18:35) daily except Monday.

Many sights are open until 19:00 on a particular day or days: San Lorenzo Market (daily, but closed Mon in winter), the Duomo's dome (Mon-Fri), and the Baptistery (Mon-Sat, except first Sat of month until 14:00).

These sights are open until 19:30: Campanile (daily), Duomo Museum (Mon-Sat), and the Boboli and Bardini gardens at the Pitti Palace (daily except some Mon, June-Aug only). The Mercato Nuovo is open daily until 20:00, as is the San Miniato Church (but closes at 19:00 in winter),

In summer (April-Sept), the best late-hours sightseeing is at the Palazzo Vecchio, which stays open until 24:00 (except on Thu, when it closes at 14:00); off-season, it's still open relatively late (Wed-Mon until 19:00).

signs, in many cases they appear in neither red nor black, but in blue! I'm lazy and don't concern myself with the distinction (if one number's wrong, I look nearby for the other) and can easily find my way around.

Chill Out: Schedule several breaks into your sightseeing when you can sit, pause, cool off, and refresh yourself with a sandwich, gelato, or coffee. Carry a water bottle to refill at Florence's twist-the-handle public fountains. Try the *fontanello* (dispenser of free cold water) on Piazza della Signoria, behind the statue of Neptune (to the left of the Palazzo Vecchio).

Internet Access: Bustling, tourist-filled Florence has many small Internet cafés. **VIP Internet** has cheap rates, numerous terminals, and long hours (€1.50/hour, daily 9:00-24:00, near recommended hotel Katti House at Via Faenza 49 red, tel. 055-264-5552). **Internet Train,** the dominant chain, is pricier, with bright and cheery rooms, speedy computers, and decent hours (€4.30/hour, cheaper for students, reusable card good for any other Internet Train location, open daily roughly 9:00-20:00, www.internettrain.it). Find branches near Piazza della Repubblica (Via Porta Rossa 38 red), behind the Duomo (Via dell'Oriolo 40), and on Piazza Santa Croce (Via de'Benci 36 red). Internet Train also offers Wi-Fi, phone cards, and other services.

Most hotels have Wi-Fi. If you have a smartphone with an Italian mobile number, you can access free Wi-Fi for an hour at various hotspots around town (the TI can give you a list of hotspots and instructions).

Bookstores: Local guidebooks (sold at kiosks) are cheap, and give you a map and a decent commentary on the sights. For brand-name guidebooks in English (including mine), try **Feltrinelli International** (Mon-Sat 9:00-19:30, closed Sun, a few blocks north of the Duomo and across the street from TI and Medici-Riccardi Palace at Via Cavour 12 red, tel. 055-219-524); **Edison Bookstore** (also has CDs, plus novels on the Renaissance and much more on its four floors; Mon-Sat 9:00-24:00, Sun 10:00-24:00, facing Piazza della Repubblica, tel. 055-213-110); **Paperback Exchange** (cheaper, all books in English, bring in your used book for a discount on a new one, Mon-Fri 9:00-19:30, Sat 10:30-19:30, closed Sun, just south of the Duomo on Via delle Oche 4 red, tel. 055-293-460); or **BM Bookshop** (with perhaps the city's largest collection of English books and guidebooks—including mine; Mon-Sat 9:30-19:30, closed Sun, near Ponte alla Carraia at Borgognissanti 4 red, tel. 055-294-575).

Services: WCs are scarce. Use them when you can, in any café or museum you patronize.

Laundry: The **Wash & Dry Lavarapido** chain offers long hours and efficient, self-service launderettes at several locations (about €7 for wash and dry, bring plenty of coins, daily 8:00-22:00, tel. 055-580-480). These are close to recommended hotels: Via dei Servi 102 red (near *David*), Via del Sole 29 red and Via della Scala 52 red (between train station and river), Via Ghibellina 143 red (Palazzo Vecchio), and Via dei Serragli 87 red (across the river in Oltrarno neighborhood). For more options, the TI has a complete list of launderettes.

Bike Rental: The **city of Florence** rents bikes cheaply at several locations: the train station, Piazza Santa Croce, and Piazza Ghiberti (€2/1 hour, €5/5 hours, €10/day, tel. 055-650-5295; information at any TI). **Florence by Bike** rents two-wheelers of all sizes (€3.50/hour, €9/5 hours, includes bike lock and helmet, child seat-€3 extra; April-Oct daily 9:00-19:30; Nov-March Mon-Sat 9:00-13:00 & 15:30-19:30, closed Sun; Via San Zanobi 120 red, tel. 055-488-992, www.florencebybike.it, info@florencebybike.it).

Travel Agency: While it's easy to buy train tickets to destinations within Italy at handy machines at the station, travel agencies can be more convenient and helpful for getting international tickets, reservations, and supplements. The cost may be the same, or there may be a minimal charge. Ask your hotelier for the nearest travel agency.

Updates to this Book: Check www.ricksteves.com/update for any significant changes that have occurred since this book was printed.

Getting Around Florence

I organize my sightseeing geographically and do it all on foot. I think of Florence as a Renaissance treadmill—it requires a lot of walking. You likely won't need public transit, except maybe to head up to Piazzale Michelangelo and San Miniato Church for the view, or to Fiesole.

Buses: The city's full-size buses don't cover the old center well (the whole area around the Duomo is off-limits to motorized traffic). The TI hands out a map of transit routes. Of the many bus lines, I find these to be of most value for seeing outlying sights:

Buses **#12** and **#13** go from the train station to Porta Romana, up to San Miniato Church and Piazzale Michelangelo, and on to Santa Croce.

Bus **#7** goes from Piazza San Marco (near the Accademia and Museum of San Marco) to Fiesole, a small town with big views of Florence.

The train station and Piazza San Marco are two major hubs near the city center; to get between these two, either walk (about 15 minutes) or take bus #1, #6, #14, or #23.

Fun little **minibuses** (many of them electric, *elettrico*) wind through the tangled old center of town and up and down the river—just €1.20 gets you a 90-minute joyride. These buses, which run every 10 minutes, are popular with sore-footed sightseers and eccentric local seniors.

Bus **#C1** stops behind the Palazzo Vecchio and Piazza Santa Croce, then heads north up to Piazza Libertà.

Bus **#C2** twists through the congested old center from the train station to Piazza Beccaria.

Bus **#C3** goes up and down the Arno River, with stops near Ponte Vecchio, the Carraia bridge to Oltrarno, and beyond.

Bus **#D** goes from the train station to Ponte Vecchio, cruises through Oltrarno, and finishes at Ponte San Niccolò.

The minibuses connect many major parking lots with the historical center (tickets sold at machines at lots).

Buy bus tickets at tobacco shops *(tabacchi)*, newsstands, or the ATAF bus office just east of the train station, on Piazza della Stazione (€1.20/90 minutes, €4.70/4 tickets, €5/24 hours, €12/3 days, 1-day and 3-day passes aren't always available in tobacco shops, validate in machine on the bus, tel. 800-424-500, www .ataf.net). You can buy tickets on board, but you'll pay more (€2) and you'll need exact change. City buses are free with the Firenze Card (see page 57). Follow general bus etiquette: Board at front or rear doors, exit out the center.

Taxi: The minimum cost for a taxi ride is €5, or €6 after 22:00 and on Sundays (rides in the center of town should be charged as tariff #1). A taxi ride from the train station to the Duomo costs about €8. Taxi fares and supplements (e.g., €2 extra if you call a cab rather than hail one) are clearly explained on signs in each taxi. It can be hard to find a cab on the street; to call one, dial 055-4390 or 055-4242.

Tours in Florence

Tour companies big and small offer plenty of tours that go out to smaller towns in the Tuscan countryside (the most popular day trips: Siena, San Gimignano, Pisa, and into Chianti country for wine-tasting). They also do Florence city tours, but for most people, the city is really best on foot (and the book you're holding provides as much information as you'll get with a generic bus tour). To sightsee on your own, download my series of free audio tours that illuminate some of Florence's top sights and neighborhoods (see sidebar on page 41 for details).

For extra insight with a personal touch, consider the tour companies and individual Florentine guides listed here. Hardworking and creative, they offer a worthwhile array of organized sightseeing activities. Study their websites for details. If you're taking a city tour, remember that individuals save money with a scheduled public tour (such as those offered daily by Florencetown or ArtViva). If you're traveling as a family or small group, however, you're likely to save money by booking a private guide (since rates are based on roughly €55/hour for any size of group).

Walking (and Biking) Tours

ArtViva Walking Tours—This company offers a variety of tours (up to 12/day year-round) featuring downtown Florence, museum highlights, and Tuscany and Cinque Terre day trips. Their guides are native English-speakers. The three-hour "Original Florence" walk hits the main sights but gets offbeat to weave a picture of Florentine life in medieval and Renaissance times. Tours go rain or shine with as few as four participants (€25, daily at 9:15). Museum tours include the Uffizi Gallery (€39, includes admission, 2 hours), Accademia (called "Original *David*" tour, €35, includes admission, 1 hour), and "Original Florence in One Day" (€94, includes admission to Uffizi and Accademia plus 3-hour town walk, 6 hours). Their brochure and website list more activities, including biking and hiking tours, wine tours, and cooking classes (Mon-Sat 8:00-18:00, Sun 8:30-13:30, near Piazza della Repubblica at Via de' Sassetti 1, second floor, above Odeon Cinema, tel. 055-264-5033 during day or mobile 329-613-2730 from 18:00-20:00, www.artviva.com).

Florencetown Tours on Foot or by Bike—This well-organized company runs a variety of English-language tours. The boss, Luca Perfetto, offers student rates (10 percent discount) to anyone with this book, with an additional 10 percent off for second tours (if booking on their website, enter the code "RICK2013" when prompted). Three tours—their basic town walk, bike tour, and cooking class—are worth considering: The "Walk and Talk Florence" tour, which takes 2.5 hours, hits all the basic spots, including the Oltrarno neighborhood (€19, daily at 10:00). The "I Bike Florence" tour gives you 2.5 hours on a vintage one-speed bike following a fast-talking guide on a blitz of the town's top sights (€25, daily at 10:00 and 15:00, helmets optional, 15 stops on both sides of the river; in bad weather, the bike tours go as a €19 walking tour). The cooking class costs €79 and includes a market tour; see the listing later. Their office is two blocks from the Palazzo Vecchio at Via de Lamberti 1 (find steps off Via de' Calzaiuoli on the river side of Orsanmichele Church); they also have an "info point" kiosk on Piazza della Repubblica, at the corner with Via Pellicceria (tel. 055-012-3994, www.florencetown.com).

Walks Inside Florence—Three art historians—Paola Barubiani and her partners Emma Molignoni and Marzia Valbonesi—provide quality guiding. Their company offers a daily 2.5-hour introductory tour (€50/person, 6 people maximum; outside except for a visit inside to see *David,* Accademia entry fee not included) and three-hour private tours (€180, €60/hour for more time, price is for groups of up to 4 people). They also offer an artisans-and-shopping tour, a guided evening walk, cooking classes with a market visit, private cruise excursions from the port of Livorno, and more—see their website for details (ask about Rick Steves discount for any tour, Paola's mobile 335-526-6496, www.walksinsideflorence.com, paola@walksinsideflorence.it).

Florentia—Top-notch private walking tours—geared for thoughtful, well-heeled travelers with longer-than-average attention spans—are led by Florentine scholars. The tours range from introductory city walks and museum visits to in-depth thematic walks, such as the Oltrarno neighborhood, Jewish Florence, and family-oriented tours (tours start at €250, includes personal assistance by email as you plan your trip, reserve in advance, www.florentia.org, info@florentia.org).

Context Florence—This scholarly group of graduate students and professors leads "walking seminars," such as a 3.5-hour study of Michelangelo's work and influence (€75/person, plus museum admission) and a two-hour evening orientation stroll (€40/person). I enjoyed the fascinating three-hour fresco workshop (€75/person plus materials, you take home a fresco you make yourself). See their website for other innovative offerings: Medici walk, lecture series, food walks, kids' tours, and programs in Venice, Rome, Naples, London, and Paris (tel. 06-967-27371, US tel. 215/609-4888 or 800-691-6036, www.contexttravel.com, info@contexttravel.com).

Cooking Classes and Market Tours

For something special, consider this five-hour experience offered by **Florencetown.** You'll start with a trip to the Mercato Centrale for shopping and tasting, then settle into their kitchen for a cooking lesson that finishes with a big feast eating everything you cooked. You'll meet butchers and bakers, and make bruschetta, pasta, a main course, and dessert (likely tiramisu). Groups are intimate and small (from 1-25 people, €79/person, 10 percent Rick Steves discount, Mon-Sat 10:00-15:00, runs rain or shine, chef Giovanni, Via de Lamberti 1, tel. 055-012-3994, www.florence town.com).

Local Guides for Private Tours

Alessandra Marchetti, a Florentine who has lived in the US, gives private walking tours of Florence and driving tours of Tuscany (€60-75/hour, mobile 347-386-9839, aleoberm@tin.it).

Paola Migliorini and her partners offer museum tours, city walking tours, private cooking classes, wine tours, and Tuscan excursions by van—you can tailor tours as you like (€60/hour without car, €70/hour in an 8-seat van, tel. 055-472-448, mobile 347-657-2611, www.florencetour.com, info@florencetour.com); they also do private tours from the cruise-ship port of Livorno.

Karin Kibby, an Oregonian living in Livorno who leads Rick Steves tours, also offers day trips throughout Tuscany, including private excursions for cruise-ship passengers docking at Livorno. She'll work with you to find the best solution for your budget and interests (2-10 people, mobile 333-108-6348, karinkintuscany @yahoo.it).

Roberto Bechi, a great guide based in Siena, can come pick you up in Florence for off-the-beaten-path tours of the Tuscan countryside (see contact information on page 345).

Hop-on, Hop-off Bus Tours

Around town, you'll see big double-decker sightseeing buses double-parking near major sights. Tourists on the top deck can listen to brief recorded descriptions of the sights, snap photos, and enjoy a drive-by look at major landmarks (€16/1 calendar day, €22/48 hours, pay as you board, www.firenze.city-sightseeing.it). As the name implies, you can hop off when you want and catch the next bus (usually every 30 minutes). But since the most important sights are buried in the old center where big buses can't go, Florence doesn't really lend itself to this kind of tour bus. Look at the route map before committing.

Driving Tours

500 Touring Club offers a unique look at Florence: from behind the wheel of one of the most iconic Italian cars, a vintage, restored Fiat 500. After a lesson in *la doppietta* (double-clutching), you'll head off in a guided convoy, following a lead car with live commentary via the radio and photo stops at the best viewpoints. Tours depart from a 15th-century villa on the edge of town; the Fiats are restored models from the 1960s and 1970s. Itineraries vary from basic sightseeing to countryside excursions with wine-making and lunch; see their website for options (2-hour tour-€60/person, US tel. 347/535-0030, Italian mobile 346-826-2324, Via Gherardo Silvani 149a, www.500touringclub.com, info@500touringclub .com, Andrea).

SIGHTS IN FLORENCE

In this chapter, Florence's most important museums have the shortest listings and are marked with a ☉. These sights are covered in much more detail in one of the self-guided tours included in this book. The Renaissance Walk chapter connects a number of Florence's major sights, from the Duomo to Ponte Vecchio over the Arno River.

Remember to check www.ricksteves.com/update for any significant changes that have occurred since this book was printed.

Opening Hours: Check opening hours carefully and plan your time well. Many museums have erratic hours (e.g., closed on alternating Sundays and Mondays), and Florence—more than most cities—has a tendency to change these hours from season to season, so it's wise to get the most up-to-date info possible at the TIs or online. The city TI has a convenient printout listing current hours for each sight; you can download the same thing at www.firenzeturismo.it (click "Art & Museums," then select "Download museums' opening times" at the bottom).

Price Hike Alert: Many of Florence's top museums have found a clever way to squeeze more money out of visitors. They host a special exhibit that few tourists really care to see, and require you to pay extra for your ticket, even if all you want to see is the permanent collection. This means already steep admission fees jump by about €3-4. For example: The Uffizi Gallery is technically only €6.50. But for most of the year, temporary exhibits raise the price to a mandatory €11. Expect this practice at the Accademia, Bargello, Pitti Palace, and others...and consider yourself lucky if you happen to visit when it's the normal price.

Sightseeing Strategies

Florence offers an array of options to help you byp̲ ̲ ̲ ̲ ̲ ̲ ̲ ̲ ̲ ̲
ticket-buying lines that can plague its most popular sights in peak
season. You can spend less time in line and more time seeing the
sights if you make use of Florence's official sightseeing pass (the
Firenze Card), advance reservations, and/or combo-tickets. Think
ahead about what you want to see,
study the options described below, and
take advantage of the option(s) that fit
your sightseeing plans and budget.

For Florence's top two sights, the
Accademia and Uffizi Gallery, you
have two good options: Either buy a
Firenze Card (expensive but handy,
especially if you plan to visit other
covered sights) or make advance **reservations** (€4 reservation fee per sight,
comes with entry time).

To beat the lines at the Duomo
and related sights (Baptistery and Campanile), you can buy a
combo-ticket at the Duomo Museum (where there are generally
no lines). And if you plan to climb the dome, you can skip the line
with the "Terraces of the Cathedral and Dome" **tour.** Note that
the Baptistery, Campanile, Duomo Museum, and dome climb are
also covered by the Firenze Card, which allows you to skip ticket-
buying lines at those sights.

Your options are described in more detail below.

Firenze Card

The Firenze Card (€50) is pricey but convenient. This three-day
sightseeing pass gives you admission to many of Florence's sights,
including the Uffizi Gallery and Accademia. Just as important, it
lets you skip the ticket-buying lines without making reservations.
For busy sightseers, the card can save some money. And for anyone, it can certainly save time.

With the card, you simply go to the entrance at a covered sight
(if there's a "with reservations" door, use it), show the card, and they
let you in (though there may be delays at popular sights if they have
reached maximum capacity). For people seeing five or six major
sights in a short time, the card is well worth it. (But if you only want
to see the Uffizi and Accademia, you'll save at least €20 by making
individual reservations instead; see "Advance Reservations," later.)

The Firenze Card is valid for 72 hours from when you validate
it at your first museum (e.g., Tue at 15:00 until Fri at 15:00). It
includes regular admission price as well as any temporary exhibits

which are commonly tacked on at major sights such as the Uffizi). The card is good for one visit per sight. It also gives you free use of Florence city buses. The card is not shareable, and there are no family or senior discounts for Americans or Canadians.

To figure out if the Firenze Card is a good deal for you, tally up the entry fees of what you want to see. For example, here's a list of popular sights and their admission fees:

- Uffizi Gallery (€6.50 base price, usually €11 with temporary exhibits, as much as €15 with €4 reservation fee)
- Accademia (same fees as Uffizi, above)
- Palazzo Vecchio (€6.50)
- Bargello (€4 base, €7 with exhibits)
- Medici Chapels (€6 base, €9 with exhibits)
- Museum of San Marco (€4)
- Medici-Riccardi Palace (€7)

SIGHTS

If you saw these sights without the card—which a busy sight-seer might reasonably expect to do in three days—you'd pay about €60, including the exhibit and reservation fees.

Other covered sights featured in this book include the various Duomo-related sights (dome climb, Campanile, Duomo Museum, and Baptistery), Pitti Palace (both Palatine Gallery and Boboli Gardens), Brancacci Chapel, Church of Santa Maria Novella, Museum of Santa Maria Novella, Santa Croce Church, Casa Buonarroti, Casa di Dante, Museum of Precious Stones, Palazzo Davanzati, and Galileo Science Museum. The card is great for popping into lesser sights you otherwise wouldn't pay for. For a complete list of included sights, see www.firenzecard.it.

The two Leonardo museums are not covered by the Firenze Card. Note that the Baptistery, Campanile, and Duomo Museum are also covered by a combo-ticket, and the dome climb by a tour option—both described later.

Getting the card makes the most sense in the peak season, from April through October, when crowds are worst. Off-season travelers could do without it.

You can buy the card at many outlets around town, including the TIs at the train station and at Via Cavour 1 red (a couple of blocks north of the Duomo) and at some sights: the Uffizi Gallery's door #2 (enter to the left of the ticket-buying line), Museum of Santa Maria Novella (near the train station), Bargello, Palazzo Vecchio, and Brancacci Chapel. You'll find the shortest (or no) lines at the Via Cavour TI and the Museum of Santa Maria Novella (around the corner from the often-crowded train-station TI); if you're doing the Uffizi first, door #2 is relatively quick. You can also buy the card online (www.firenzecard.it), obtain a voucher, and then pick up the card at any of the above locations.

Validate your card only when you're ready to tackle the cov-

Summary of Sightseeing Strategies

To spend more time sightseeing and less time waiting in ticket-buying lines, consider these options, all of which are explained in more detail in the "Sightseeing Strategies" section.

If you plan to see the...

Uffizi and Accademia only: Make reservations in advance for these two sights (it's cheaper than getting the Firenze Card); it's usually easiest to ask your hotelier to book reservations for you when you book your room.

Uffizi and Accademia, plus other covered sights (such as the Bargello, Museum of San Marco, Medici Chapels, Medici-Riccardi Palace, Palazzo Vecchio, Pitti Palace, and others): Get the Firenze Card. It's sold at some TIs and some sights; the TI on Via Cavour TI and the Museum of Santa Maria Novella have the shortest lines, or try door #2 at the Uffizi.

Duomo plus related sights (Baptistery, Campanile, and Duomo Museum): The free-to-enter Duomo is sometimes plagued with long lines. If you want to visit the Duomo and related, covered sights, get the combo-ticket at the uncrowded Duomo Museum; it allows you to enter the Duomo through its exit door, avoiding the entry line.

Duomo plus dome climb: The "Terraces of the Cathedral and Dome" tour gets you into the interior and includes the dome climb (sold at the Duomo Museum; does not include the Baptistery, Campanile, or Duomo Museum).

---

ered sights on three consecutive days. Make sure the sights you want to visit will be open (many sights are closed Sun or Mon). For details, see the "Daily Reminder" on page 48.

Advance Reservations

Florence has an optional reservation system for its state-run sights—including the Accademia, Uffizi Gallery, Bargello, Medici Chapels, and the Pitti Palace. Of these, I'd recommend reservations only for the Accademia (Michelangelo's *David*) and the Uffizi (Renaissance paintings).

If you are planning to see several other covered sights, it may make more sense to skip the reservations process altogether by getting a Firenze Card (described earlier).

The Uffizi and Accademia

If you decide not to get a Firenze Card, your best strategy is to get reservations for these two top sights as soon as you know when you'll be in town. Although you can generally get an entry time for the Accademia within a few days, reserve for the Uffizi well in advance.

Florence at a Glance

▲▲▲**Accademia** Michelangelo's *David* and powerful (unfinished) *Prisoners*. Reserve ahead or get a Firenze Card. **Hours:** Tue-Sun 8:15-18:50, closed Mon. See page 63.

▲▲▲**Duomo Museum** Underrated cathedral museum with sculptures. **Hours:** Mon-Sat 9:00-19:30, Sun 9:00-13:40. See page 75.

▲▲▲**Bargello** Underappreciated sculpture museum (Michelangelo, Donatello, Medici treasures). **Hours:** Tue-Sat 8:15-13:50, until 16:50 during special exhibits (typically April-Oct); also open first, third, and fifth Mon and second and fourth Sun of each month. See page 76.

▲▲▲**Uffizi Gallery** Greatest collection of Italian paintings anywhere. Reserve well in advance or get a Firenze Card. **Hours:** Tue-Sun 8:15-18:35, closed Mon. See page 80.

▲▲**Museum of San Marco** Best collection anywhere of artwork by the early Renaissance master Fra Angelico. **Hours:** Tue-Fri 8:15-13:50, Sat 8:15-16:50; also open 8:15-13:50 on first, third, and fifth Mon and 8:15-16:50 on second and fourth Sun of each month. See page 64.

▲▲**Medici Chapels** Tombs of Florence's great ruling family, designed and carved by Michelangelo. **Hours:** Tue-Sat April-Oct 8:15-16:50, Nov-March 8:15-13:50; also open second and fourth Mon and first, third, and fifth Sun of each month. See page 68.

▲▲**Duomo** Gothic cathedral with colorful facade and the first dome built since ancient Roman times. **Hours:** Mon-Fri 10:00-17:00, Thu until 16:00 Oct-May, Sat 10:00-16:45, Sun 13:30-16:45. See page 70.

▲▲**Palazzo Vecchio** Fortified palace, once the home of the Medici family, wallpapered with history. **Hours:** Fri-Wed 9:00-19:00, until 24:00 April-Sept; Thu 9:00-14:00 year-round. See page 81.

▲▲**Galileo Science Museum** Fascinating old clocks, telescopes, maps, and Galileo's finger. **Hours:** Wed-Mon 9:30-18:00, Tue 9:30-13:00. See page 82.

▲▲**Santa Croce Church** Precious art, tombs of famous Florentines, and Brunelleschi's Pazzi Chapel in 14th-century church. **Hours:** Mon-Sat 9:30-17:30, Sun 14:00-17:30. See page 83.

▲▲**Church of Santa Maria Novella** Thirteenth-century Dominican church with Masaccio's famous 3-D painting. **Hours:**

Church—Mon-Thu 9:00-17:30, Fri 11:00-17:30, Sat 9:00-17:00, Sun 13:00-17:00; museum—Fri-Mon 9:00-16:00, closed Tue-Thu. See page 84.

▲▲**Pitti Palace** Several museums in lavish palace plus sprawling Boboli and Bardini gardens. **Hours:** Palatine Gallery, Royal Apartments, and Gallery of Modern Art: Tue-Sun 8:15-18:50, closed Mon; Boboli and Bardini gardens, Costume Gallery, Argenti/Silverworks Museum, and Porcelain Museum: Daily 8:15-18:30 except closed first and last Mon of each month, until 19:30 June-Aug, closed first and last Mon of each month. See page 85.

▲▲**Brancacci Chapel** Works of Masaccio, early Renaissance master who reinvented perspective. **Hours:** Mon and Wed-Sat 10:00-17:00, Sun 13:00-17:00, closed Tue. Reservations required, though often available on the spot. See page 87.

▲▲**San Miniato Church** Sumptuous Renaissance chapel and sacristy showing scenes of St. Benedict. **Hours:** Daily Easter-mid-Oct 8:00-20:00 or possibly later, in winter 8:30-13:00 & 15:30-19:00. See page 89.

▲**Medici-Riccardi Palace** Lorenzo the Magnificent's home, with fine art, frescoed ceilings, and Gozzoli's lovely Chapel of the Magi. **Hours:** Thu-Tue 9:00-18:00, closed Wed. See page 69.

▲**Climbing the Duomo's Dome** Grand view into the cathedral, close-up of dome architecture, and, after 463 steps, a glorious city vista. **Hours:** Mon-Fri 8:30-19:00, Sat 8:30-17:40, closed Sun. Long slow lines—go early or take "Terraces" tour. See page 74.

▲**Campanile** Bell tower with views similar to Duomo's, 50 fewer steps, and fewer lines. **Hours:** Daily 8:30-19:30. See page 74.

▲**Baptistery** Bronze doors fit to be the gates of paradise. **Hours:** Doors always viewable; interior open Mon-Sat 12:15-19:00 except first Sat of each month 8:30-14:00, Sun 8:30-14:00. See page 74.

▲**Ponte Vecchio** Famous bridge lined with gold and silver shops. **Hours:** Bridge always open (shops closed at night). See page 81.

▲**Casa Buonarroti** Early, lesser-known works by Michelangelo. **Hours:** Wed-Mon 10:00-17:00, closed Tue. See page 83.

▲**Piazzale Michelangelo** Hilltop square with stunning view of Duomo and Florence, with San Miniato Church just uphill. **Hours:** Always open. See page 88.

SIGHTS

There are several ways to make a reservation:

• **Through Your Hotel:** When you make your hotel reservation, ask if they can book your museum reservations for you (some hoteliers will do this for free; others charge a €3-5 fee; they'll probably give you a confirmation number that you'll take to the museum, where you'll pay cash for your ticket—see "By Phone," next). This is your easiest reservation option.

• **By Phone:** Reserve by phone before you leave the States (from the US, dial 011-39-055-294-883, or within Italy call 055-294-883; €4/ticket reservation fee; booking office open Mon-Fri 8:30-18:30, Sat 8:30-12:30, closed Sun). The reservation line is often busy. Be persistent. When you get through, an English-speaking operator walks you through the process—a few minutes later you say grazie, having secured an entry time and a confirmation number. You'll need to present your confirmation number at the museum and pay cash for your ticket. The advantage to phoning versus booking online is that you pay nothing upfront when you phone.

• **Online:** Using a credit card, you can reserve your visit online. Pricey middleman sites—such as www.uffizi.com and www.tickitaly.com—are reliable, but their booking fees are exorbitant, running about €10 per ticket. Or you could take your chances with the city's troublesome official site (www.firenzemusei.it; click on gray "B-ticket" strip at the bottom). It's the cheapest place to make reservations online (€4/ticket reservation fee), but it's glitchy, runs slowly, and often reverts to Italian-only ("*Annulia operazione*" means "cancel"; if using Google Chrome browser, it can translate the form to broken English with one click). Also, you can't book a time before noon, and some readers report not receiving vouchers they've paid for. Once you've paid and booked online, you'll bring your voucher to the ticket desk to swap for an actual ticket.

• **Private Tour:** Take a tour that includes your museum admission. For example, ArtViva Walking Tours offers tours of the Uffizi (€39/person, 2 hours), Accademia (€35/person, 1 hour), and both museums (€94/person, 6 hours including 3-hour town walk; see listing on page 52).

• **Reserve in Florence:** If you arrive without a reservation, here are your choices: call the reservation number (see "By Phone" above); ask your hotelier for help; or head to a booking window, either at Orsanmichele Church (€4 reservation fee, daily 10:00-17:00, along Via de' Calzaiuoli—see location on map on page 66) or at the My Accademia Libreria bookstore across from the Accademia's exit (€4 reservation fee, Tue-Sun 8:15-17:30, closed Mon, Via Ricasoli 105 red—see map on page 116). It's also possible to go to the Uffizi's official ticket office (use door #2 and skirt to the left of the long ticket-buying line), ask if they have any short-notice reservations available, and pay cash (Tue-Sun 8:15-18:35).

Off-Season: If you're in Florence off-season (Nov-March), you can probably get into the Uffizi or Accademia without a reservation in the late afternoon (after 16:00). But why not make a reservation? After seeing hundreds of bored tourists waiting in lines, it's hard not to be amazed at their cluelessness.

Brancacci Chapel

Although Brancacci Chapel is the only sight in Florence that technically requires reservations, individuals can usually get one at the door and just walk in any time before about 15:30. Or you can reserve in advance by phone (usually the day before will do it); for details, see the Brancacci Chapel Tour chapter.

Combo-Tickets: The Duomo and Related Sights

In peak season, long lines can slow your entry to the Duomo (free), as well as its Campanile, Baptistery, and dome climb.

To waltz past the lines, consider the €15 **combo-ticket** that covers the Campanile and Baptistery, plus two sights with shorter lines: the Duomo Museum and crypt (but *not* the dome); with this ticket, you can head straight to the front of the line at each of these sights. (The crypt part of the ticket allows you to access the Duomo interior through its exit door, potentially saving a long wait at the church's main entrance.) Although the ticket is a time-saver, the cost savings are small (€2-4 if you visit everything). You can buy the ticket at any of the covered sights, but it's smartest to get it at the one that usually has no lines: the Duomo Museum, tucked behind the church. A €23 version adds the dome climb, but it's only sold at the dome entrance, so it won't help you skip that line. Either ticket is valid for four days.

A better option for dome-climbers is to take the €15 **"Terraces of the Cathedral and Dome" tour,** which allows you to skip both the long lines to enter the cathedral and the lines to climb the dome. This is the only way to skip the line for the dome, but note that it does *not* include the Baptistery, Campanile, or Duomo Museum (for more details, see page 71).

Note that the Campanile, Baptistery, Duomo Museum, and dome climb are covered by the Firenze Card.

North of the Arno River

North of the Duomo (Cathedral)

▲▲▲**Accademia (Galleria dell'Accademia)**—This museum houses Michelangelo's *David,* the consummate Renaissance statue of the buff, biblical shepherd boy ready to take on the giant. Nearby are some of the master's other works, including his powerful

(unfinished) *Prisoners*, *St. Matthew*, and a *Pietà* (possibly by one of his disciples). Florentine Michelangelo Buonarroti, who would work tirelessly through the night, believed that the sculptor was a tool of God, responsible only for chipping away at the stone until the intended sculpture emerged. Beyond the magic marble are some mildly interesting pre-Renaissance and Renaissance paintings, including a couple of lighter-than-air Botticellis, the plaster model of Giambologna's *Rape of the Sabine Women*, and a musical instrument collection with an early piano.

Cost and Hours: €6.50, up to €11 with mandatory exhibits, plus €4 reservation fee; Tue-Sun 8:15-18:50, closed Mon, last entry 30 minutes before closing; audioguide-€6, Via Ricasoli 60, reservation tel. 055-294-883, www.polomuseale.firenze.it. To avoid long lines in peak season, get the Firenze Card (described earlier) or make reservations (see page 59).

○ See the Accademia Tour chapter.

Nearby: Piazza S.S. Annunziata, behind the Accademia, displays lovely Renaissance harmony. Facing the square are two fine

buildings: the 15th-century Santissima Annunziata church (worth a peek) and Filippo Brunelleschi's Hospital of the Innocents (Spedale degli Innocenti, not worth going inside), with terra-cotta medallions by Luca della Robbia. Built in the 1420s, the hospital is considered the first Renaissance building. I love sleeping on this square (at the recommended Hotel Loggiato dei Serviti) and picnicking here during the day (with the riffraff, who remind me of the persistent gap—today as in Medici times—between those who appreciate fine art and those just looking for some cheap wine).

▲▲Museum of San Marco (Museo di San Marco)—Located one block north of the Accademia, this 15th-century monastery houses the greatest collection anywhere of frescoes and paintings by the early Renaissance master Fra Angelico. The ground floor features the monk's paintings, along with some works by Fra Bartolomeo. Upstairs are 43 cells decorated by Fra Angelico and his assistants. While the monk/painter was trained in the medieval religious style, he also learned and adopted Renaissance techniques and sensibilities, producing works that blended Christian symbols and Renaissance realism. Don't miss the cell of Savonarola, the charismatic monk who rode in from the Christian right, threw out the Medici, turned Florence into a theocracy, sponsored "bonfires of the vanities" (burning books, paintings, and so on), and was finally burned himself when Florence decided to change channels.

Cost and Hours: €4, covered by Firenze Card, Tue-Fri 8:15-13:50, Sat 8:15-16:50; also open 8:15-13:50 on first, third, and fifth Mon and 8:15-16:50 on second and fourth Sun of each month; last entry 30 minutes before closing, reservations possible but unnecessary, on Piazza San Marco, tel. 055-238-8608, www.polomuseale.firenze.it.

○ See the Museum of San Marco Tour chapter.

Museum of Precious Stones (Museo dell'Opificio delle Pietre Dure)—This unusual gem of a museum features room after room of exquisite mosaics of inlaid marble and other stones. The Medici loved colorful stone tabletops and floors; you'll even find landscapes and portraits (find Cosimo I in Room I). Upstairs, you'll see wooden work benches from the Medici workshop (1588), complete with foot-powered power tools. Rockhounds can browse 500 different stones (lapis lazuli, quartz, agate, marble, and so on) and the tools used to cut and inlay them. Borrow the English descriptions in each room.

Cost and Hours: €4, covered by Firenze Card, Mon-Sat 8:15-14:00, closed Sun, last entry 30 minutes before closing, around corner from Accademia at Via degli Alfani 78, tel. 055-265-1357.

Church of San Lorenzo—This red-brick dome—which looks like the Duomo's little sister—is the Medici church and the burial place of the family's founder, Giovanni di Bicci de' Medici (1360-1429).

Cost and Hours: €3.50, buy ticket just inside cloister next door, €6 combo-ticket covers Laurentian Library; March-Oct Mon-Sat 10:00-17:30, Sun 13:30-17:30; Nov-Jan Mon-Sat 10:00-17:30, closed Sun; last entry 30 minutes before closing.

Visiting the Church: The facade is big, ugly, and unfinished, because Pope Leo X (also a Medici) pulled the plug on the project due to dwindling funds—after Michelangelo had labored on it for four years

SIGHTS

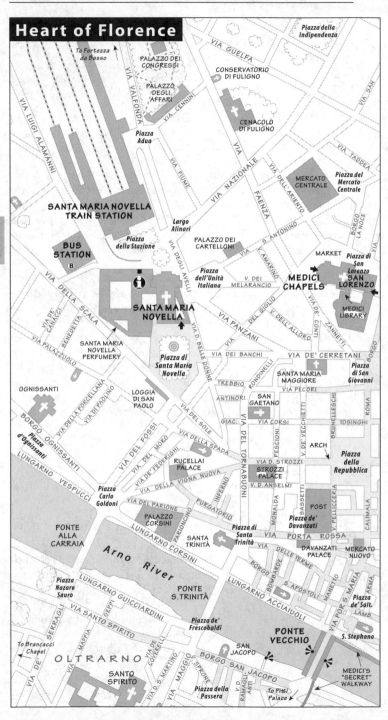

Heart of Florence

To Fortezza da Basso

Piazza della Indipendenza

VIA GUELFA

PALAZZO DEI CONGRESSI

CONSERVATORIO DI FULIGNO

PALAZZO DEGLI AFFARI

CENACOLO DI FULIGNO

VIA VALFONDA

VIA CENNINI

VIA NAZIONALE

Piazza Adua

VIA FIUME

MERCATO CENTRALE

Piazza del Mercato Centrale

VIA TADDEA

VIA DELL'ARIENTO

BORGO LA NOCE

SANTA MARIA NOVELLA TRAIN STATION

Largo Alinari

PALAZZO DEI CARTELLONI

S. ANTONINO

V. AMORINO

MARKET

Piazza di San Lorenzo

SAN LORENZO

Piazza della Stazione

VIA DEGLI AVELLI

Piazza dell'Unità Italiana

V. DEI MELARANCIO

MEDICI CHAPELS

BUS STATION

B

Piazza della Stazione

MEDICI LIBRARY

VIA DELLA SCALA

VIA DE' CANACCI

SANTA MARIA NOVELLA

VIA BENEDETTA

SANTA MARIA NOVELLA PERFUMERY

VIA PALAZZUOLO

VIA D. BELLE DONNE

DEL GIGLIO

V. DELL'ALLORO

VIA DE' CONTI

ZANNETTI

VIA PANZANI

BORGO

VIA DEI BANCHI

VIA DE' CERRETANI

Piazza di San Giovanni

TREBBIO

RONDINELLI

SANTA MARIA MAGGIORE

VIA PECORI

ROMA

OGNISSANTI

LOGGIA DI SAN PAOLO

ANTINORI

SAN GAETANO

BRUNELLESCHI

VIA DELLA PORCELLANA

VIA DI PAOLINO

VIA DEL SOLE

GIAC.

VIA CORSI

V. DE' VECCHIETTI

TOSINGHI

Piazza d'Ognissanti

VIA DEL FOSSI

VIA DEL MORO

VIA DELLA SPADA

PESCIONI

ARCH

Piazza della Repubblica

BORGO OGNISSANTI

VIA DEL TORNABUONI

VIA D. STROZZI

STROZZI PALACE

BRIGA

LUNGARNO VESPUCCI

RUCELLAI PALACE

VIA DE' FEDERIGHI

V. D. ANSELMI

VIA DELLA VIGNA NUOVA

MONALDA

SASSETTI

VIA DEL PARIONE

INFERNO

PURGATORIO

PALAZZO CORSINI

PARLASCIO

PARIONCINO

Piazza Carlo Goldoni

POST

Piazza de' Davanzati

VIA PELLICCERIA

CALIMALA

PONTE ALLA CARRAIA

LUNGARNO CORSINI

SANTA TRINITÀ

Piazza di Santa Trinità

VIA PORTA ROSSA

DAVANZATI PALACE

MERCATO NUOVO

Arno River

DELLE TERME

BOMBARDE

S. APOSTOLI

VIA POR S. MARIA

ARMA

MANETTO

Piazza Nazaro Sauro

LUNGARNO GUICCIARDINI

PONTE S. TRINITÀ

LUNGARNO ACCIAIUOLI

Piazza de' Salt.

LAMB.

VIA SERRAGLI

VIA SANTO SPIRITO

Piazza de' Frescobaldi

S. Stephano

To Brancacci Chapel

VIA DE'

VIA DI COVERELLI

VIA MAFFIA

VIA GEPPI

PONTE VECCHIO

OLTRARNO

VIA MAGGIO

VIA D. S. MARTINO

SPRONE

SAN JACOPO

BORGO SAN JACOPO

V. D. RAMAGLI ANTI

MEDICI'S "SECRET" WALKWAY

SANTO SPIRITO

Piazza della Passera

To Pitti Palace

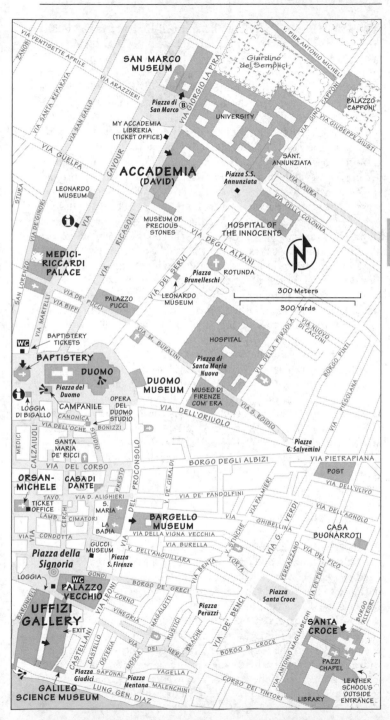

(1516-1520). Inside, though, is the spirit of Florence in the 1420s, with gray-and-white columns and arches in perfect Renaissance symmetry and simplicity. The Brunelleschi-designed church is lit by an even, diffused light. The Medici coat of arms (with the round pills of these "medics") decorates the ceiling, and everywhere are images of St. Lawrence, the Medici patron saint who was martyred on a grill.

Highlights of the church include two finely sculpted Donatello pulpits (in the nave). In the Martelli Chapel (left wall of the left transept), Filippo Lippi's *Annunciation* features a smiling angel greeting Mary in a sharply 3-D courtyard. Light shines through the vase in the foreground, like the Holy Spirit entering Mary's womb. The Old Sacristy (far left corner), designed by Brunelleschi, was the burial chapel for the Medici. Bronze doors by Donatello flank the sacristy's small altar. Overhead, the dome above the altar shows the exact arrangement of the heavens on July 4, 1442, leaving scholars to hypothesize about why that particular date was used. Back in the nave, the round inlaid marble in the floor before the main altar marks where Cosimo the Elder—Lorenzo the Magnificent's grandfather—is buried. Assistants in the church provide information on request, and the information brochure is free and in English.

Nearby: Outside the church, just to the left of the main door, is a **cloister** with peek-a-boo Duomo views and the **San Lorenzo Museum.** This collection of fancy reliquaries is included in your church admission, but is hardly worth the walk, except to see Donatello's grave. Also in the cloister is the **Laurentian Library** (€3, €6 combo-ticket with church, includes special exhibits, generally Mon and Fri-Sat 9:30-13:30, Tue-Thu 9:30-17:15, closed Sun). The library, largely designed by Michelangelo, stars his impressive staircase, which widens imperceptibly as it descends. Michelangelo also did the walls in the vestibule (entrance) that feature empty niches, scrolls, and oddly tapering pilasters. Climb the stairs and enter the Reading Room—a long, rectangular hall with a coffered-wood ceiling—designed by Michelangelo to host scholars enjoying the Medici's collection of manuscripts.

A **street market** bustles outside the church (listed after the Medici Chapels, next). Around the back end of the church is the entrance to the Medici Chapels and the New Sacristy, designed by Michelangelo for a later generation of dead Medici.

▲▲**Medici Chapels (Cappelle Medicee)**—The burial site of the ruling Medici family in the Church of San Lorenzo includes the dusky Crypt; the big, domed Chapel of Princes; and the magnificent New Sacristy, featuring architecture, tombs, and statues almost entirely by Michelangelo. The Medici made their money in textiles and banking, and patronized a dream team of Renaissance

artists that put Florence on the cultural map. Michelangelo, who spent his teen years living with the Medici, was commissioned for the family's final tribute.

Cost and Hours: €6, €9 with mandatory exhibits, covered by Firenze Card; Tue-Sat April-Oct 8:15-16:50, Nov-March 8:15-13:50; also open second and fourth Mon and first, third, and fifth Sun of each month; last entry 30 minutes before closing; reservations possible but unnecessary, audioguide-€6, modest dress required, tel. 055-238-8602, www.polomuseale.firenze.it.

○ See the Medici Chapels Tour chapter.

▲**San Lorenzo Market**—Florence's vast open-air market sprawls around the Church of San Lorenzo. Most of the leather stalls are run by Iranians selling South American leather that was tailored in Italy. Prices are soft (daily 9:00-19:00, closed Mon in winter, between the Duomo and train station).

▲**Mercato Centrale (Central Market)**—Florence's giant iron-and-glass-covered central market, a wonderland of picturesque produce, is fun to explore. While the nearby San Lorenzo Market—with its garment stalls in the streets—feels like a step up from a haphazard flea market, the Mercato Centrale retains a Florentine elegance. Wander around. You'll see parts of the cow you'd never dream of eating (no, that's not a turkey neck), enjoy generous free samples, watch pasta being made, and have your pick of plenty of fun eateries sloshing out cheap and tasty pasta to locals (Mon-Sat 7:00-14:00, in winter open Sat until 17:00, closed Sun year-round). For eating ideas in and around the market, see page 301.

▲**Medici-Riccardi Palace (Palazzo Medici-Riccardi)**—Lorenzo the Magnificent's home is worth a look for its art. The tiny Chapel of the Magi contains colorful Renaissance gems such as the *Procession of the Magi* frescoes by Benozzo Gozzoli. The former library has a Baroque ceiling fresco by Luca Giordano, a prolific artist from Naples known as "Fast Luke" *(Luca fa presto)* for his speedy workmanship. While the Medici originally occupied this 1444 house, in the 1700s it became home to the Riccardi family, who added the Baroque flourishes.

Cost and Hours: €7, covered by Firenze Card, Thu-Tue 9:00-18:00, closed Wed, last entry 30 minutes before closing, ticket entrance is north of the main gated entrance, audio/videoguide-€4, Via Cavour 3, tel. 055-276-0340, www.palazzo-medici.it.

✪ See the Medici-Riccardi Palace Tour chapter.

Leonardo Museums—Two different-but-similar entrepreneurial establishments several blocks apart show off reproductions of Leonardo's ingenious inventions.
Either one is fun for anyone who wants to crank the shaft and spin the ball bearings of Leonardo's fertile imagination. While there are no actual historic artifacts, each museum shows several dozen of Leonardo's inventions and experiments made into work-ing models. You might see a full-size armored tank, walk into a chamber of mirrors, operate a rotating crane, or watch experiments in flying. The exhibits are described in English, and what makes these places special is that you're encouraged to touch and play with the models—it's great for kids. The museum on Via dei Servi is a bit larger.

Cost and Hours: Admission to each museum is €7. Museo Leonardo da Vinci—daily 10:00-19:00, Nov-March until 18:00, Via dei Servi 66 red, tel. 055-282-966, www.mostredileonardo.com. Le Macchine di Leonardo da Vinci—April-Oct daily 9:30-19:30; Nov-March Mon-Fri 11:00-17:00, Sat-Sun 9:30-19:30; for €1 extra they'll throw in a slice of pizza and a Coke, in Galleria Michelangelo at Via Cavour 21, tel. 055-295-264, www.macchine dileonardo.com.

Duomo and Nearby

▲▲**Duomo (Cattedrale di Santa Maria del Fiore)**—Florence's Gothic cathedral has the third-longest nave in Christendom. The church's noisy neo-Gothic facade from the 1870s is covered with pink, green, and white Tuscan marble. The cathedral's claim to artistic fame is Brunelleschi's magnificent dome—the first Renaissance dome and the model for domes to follow. Massive crowds line up to see the huge church: Although it's a major sight, it's not worth a long wait. To avoid the lines, either go late (crowds subside by late afternoon), buy a combo-ticket, or take the "Terraces" tour (ticket and tour options explained below).

Cost and Hours: Free entry, Mon-Fri 10:00-17:00, Thu until

16:00 Oct-May, Sat 10:00-16:45, Sun
13:30-16:45, modest dress code enforced,
tel. 055-230-2885, www.operaduomo
.firenze.it.

Crowd-Beating Tips: There are two
ways to avoid lines at the Duomo, both
of which involve paying for related sights
(and let you skip the lines there, too). Each
one costs €15; the combo-ticket covers
more (including the highly recommended
Duomo Museum), while the "Terraces"
tour features the church interior, outdoor
view terrace, and dome climb.

The **combo-ticket** covers most of the sights associated
with the Duomo: the crypt, Duomo Museum, Baptistery, and
Campanile (sold at all of these sights, but generally no lines to buy
at the museum). A €23 version of the combo-ticket includes all the
same sights and adds the dome; however, it must be purchased at
the dome entrance, negating your time savings. Any combo-ticket
is valid for one entrance to each sight, for four days. Once you've
purchased the ticket, just show up at the exit door of the Duomo—
it's around the right side as you face the main entrance, near the
Campanile—show your ticket to the guard and he'll let you inside
(allowing you to avoid the line at the entrance).

Alternatively, taking the **"Terraces of the Cathedral and
Dome" tour** allows you to skip the long lines to enter the cathedral
and to climb the dome. After a short guided tour of the interior,
you'll climb up onto the exterior terrace, where great views reward
the hike up the stairs (see "Climbing the Duomo's Dome," later).
When the tour is finished, you can continue on your own up to the
top of the dome (€15, 45 minutes; offered Mon-Fri at 10:30, 12:00,
and 15:00 except no 15:00 tour Nov-March; Sat at 10:30 and 12:00,
no tours on Sun; buy tickets at nearby Duomo Museum and they'll
tell you where to meet your guide, tickets sold same-day only but
there's generally no problem getting a spot). If you're planning to
climb the dome anyway (€8), the tour is a fine value. Note that
the dome climb, Duomo Museum, Baptistery, and Campanile are
covered by the Firenze Card.

➔ Self-Guided Tour: Enter the Duomo (from Latin *domus*,
as it's the "house" of God). ❶ Survey the huge nave—it's 500 feet
long and 300 feet wide. The structural elements are unabash-
edly highlighted by the gray stone and cream-colored filling. In
medieval times, engineers weren't accustomed to spanning such
distances, so they used iron support bars between the columns
to ensure stability. A church has been on this spot since the fall
of Rome in c. 500 A.D. In the crypt, you can see the floor of the

SIGHTS

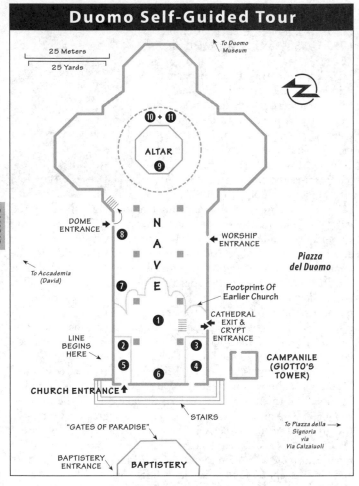

Duomo Self-Guided Tour

25 Meters
25 Yards

To Duomo
Museum

⑩ + ⑪

ALTAR
⑨

N
A
V
E

DOME
ENTRANCE

❽

WORSHIP
ENTRANCE

Piazza
del Duomo

To Accademia
(David)

❼

Footprint Of
Earlier Church

❶

CATHEDRAL
EXIT &
CRYPT
ENTRANCE

LINE
BEGINS
HERE

❷   ❸

❺   ❹

❻

CHURCH ENTRANCE ↑

CAMPANILE
(GIOTTO'S
TOWER)

STAIRS

"GATES OF PARADISE"

To Piazza della
Signoria
via
Via Calzaiuoli

BAPTISTERY
ENTRANCE

BAPTISTERY

earlier church, along with Brunelleschi's tomb—but as there's little to see and it's sparsely explained, it's not worth a visit (€3, or covered by combo-ticket; down the staircase in the nave near the exit; Brunelleschi's tomb is visible for free from the crypt's bookstore).

In 1296, the present church was begun under the architect ❷ Arnolfo di Cambio (see his bust on the left wall, inside a round medallion, second medallion from the entrance). Arnolfo, shown here holding the Duomo's blueprint, also built the Palazzo Vecchio and Santa Croce Church. Construction continued under ❸ Giotto (his bust is on the right wall, opposite Arnolfo), who started the church's Campanile and also invented modern painting.

By 1420, the nave was done, except for a 140-foot-wide hole in the roof over the altar. ❹ Filippo Brunelleschi (first medallion on the right wall) covered that with the famous dome that helped

define the Renaissance. Finally, in the 19th century, the church was completed with a multicolored facade by ❺ Emilio de Fabris (mustachioed bust in the first medallion on the left wall).

Above the main entrance is a ❻ huge clock, painted by Paolo Uccello (1443). It still works. It's a 24-hour clock, starting with sunset as the first hour, and turning counterclockwise.

As you stroll down the nave, notice the equestrian portraits on your left. The church, originally financed by the city of Florence, honors great (secular) men, such as ❼ General John Hawkwood (on horseback; 1436, it's the second horse picture, colored green). Paolo Uccello wowed Florence by creating this 3-D illusion of an equestrian statue on the flat wall. Farther up the left (north) wall is a painting of Florence's great poet ❽ Dante. He holds his *Divine Comedy*, points toward Hell (Inferno), puts his back to Mount Purgatory, and turns toward Paradise—its skyline none other than that of Florence itself.

The ❾ altar area is octagonal, echoing the shape of the Baptistery. At the base of the crucifix is a high-backed wooden

chair—the *cathedra* of Florence's bishop, which makes the Duomo a "cathedral." Standing beneath the dome, notice how it stretches halfway into the transepts— that was one big hole Brunelleschi had to cover. Look up 300 feet, into the dome, to see the expansive (if artistically uninteresting) ❿ *Last Judgment* by Giorgio Vasari and Federico Zuccari. From their graves, the dead rise into a multilevel heaven to be judged by a radiant Christ. Beneath Christ, Mary intercedes. Below them is the pagan god Kronos with the hourglass and a skeleton—symbolizing that mankind's time is up, and they (we) are entering eternity.

Just below that, on the base that supports the dome, is a ⓫ round stained-glass window by Donatello, showing *The Coronation of the Virgin*—demonstrating that human beings can eventually be exalted through the Christian faith.

▲**Climbing the Duomo's Dome**—For a grand view into the cathedral from the base of the dome, a peek at some of the tools

used in the dome's construction, a chance to see Brunelleschi's "dome-within-a-dome" construction, a glorious Florence view from the top, and the equivalent of 463 plunges on a Renaissance StairMaster, climb the dome.

Cost and Hours: €8, cash only, covered by Firenze Card, Mon-Fri 8:30-19:00, Sat 8:30-17:40, closed Sun, last entry 40 minutes before closing, enter from outside church on north side, tel. 055-230-2885. To avoid the slow-moving line, arrive by 8:30, drop by very late,

or take the "Terraces" tour of the Duomo (described earlier). For more on the dome, see page 98 of the Renaissance Walk chapter.

▲**Campanile (Giotto's Tower)**—The 270-foot bell tower has 50 fewer steps than the Duomo's dome (but that's still 413 steps— no elevator); offers a faster, relatively less-crowded climb; and has a view of that magnificent dome to boot. On the way up, there are several intermediate levels where you can catch your breath and enjoy ever-higher views. The stairs narrow as you go up, creating a mosh-pit bottleneck near the very top—but the views are worth the hassle. While the various viewpoints are enclosed by cage-like bars, the gaps are big enough to let you snap great photos.

Cost and Hours: €6, covered by Firenze Card and Duomo combo-ticket, daily 8:30-19:30, last entry 40 minutes before closing.

❂ See page 100 of the Renaissance Walk chapter.

▲**Baptistery**—Michelangelo said its bronze doors were fit to be the gates of paradise. Check out the gleaming copies of Lorenzo Ghiberti's bronze doors facing the Duomo (the original panels are in the Duomo Museum). Making a breakthrough in perspective, Ghiberti used mathematical laws to create the illusion of receding distance on a basically flat surface.

The doors on the north side of the building were designed by Ghiberti when he was young; he'd won the honor and opportunity by beating Brunelleschi in a competition (the rivals' original entries are in the Bargello).

Inside, sit and savor the medieval mosaic ceiling, where it's always Judgment Day and Jesus is giving the ultimate thumbs-up and thumbs-down.

Cost and Hours: €5, €7 with mandatory exhibits, covered by Firenze Card and Duomo combo-ticket, interior open Mon-Sat 12:15-19:00 except first Sat of month 8:30-14:00, Sun 8:30-14:00, last entry 30 minutes before closing, audioguide-€2, tel. 055-230-2885. First buy your tickets at the office just across the piazza, then enter on the north side. The bronze doors are on the outside, so they are always "open" and viewable.

✪ See page 101 of the Renaissance Walk. For more on the famous doors, see page 156 of the Bargello Tour chapter and page 178 of the Duomo Museum Tour chapter.

▲▲▲**Duomo Museum (Museo dell'Opera del Duomo)**—The underrated cathedral museum, behind the church (at Via

del Proconsolo 9), is great if you like sculpture. On the ground floor, look for a late Michelangelo *Pietà* and statues from the original Baptistery facade. Upstairs, you'll find Brunelleschi's models for his dome, as well as Donatello's anorexic *Mary Magdalene* and playful choir loft. The museum features Ghiberti's original bronze "Gates of Paradise" panels (the ones on the Baptistery's doors today are copies).

Cost and Hours: €6, covered by Firenze Card and Duomo combo-ticket; Mon-Sat 9:00-19:30, Sun 9:00-13:40, last entry 40 minutes before closing, one of the few museums in Florence always open on Mon, audioguide-€5, Via del Proconsolo 9, tel. 055-282-226, www.operaduomo.firenze.it. This museum is a good place to buy the Duomo combo-ticket (which allows you to bypass lines at the Duomo and related sights) and also sells tickets for the "Terraces of the Cathedral and Dome" tour (which allows you to skip the long cathedral-entry and dome-climbing lines). For more on these two options, see "Crowd-Beating Tips" on page 71.

✪ See the Duomo Museum Tour chapter.

SIGHTS

Between the Duomo and Piazza della Signoria

▲▲▲**Bargello (Museo Nazionale)**—This underappreciated sculpture museum is in a former police station-turned-prison that

looks like a mini-Palazzo Vecchio. It has Donatello's very influential, painfully beautiful *David* (the first male nude to be sculpted in a thousand years), works by Michelangelo, and rooms of Medici treasures. Moody Donatello, who embraced realism with his lifelike statues, set the personal and artistic style for many Renaissance artists to follow. The best pieces are in the ground-floor room at the foot of the outdoor staircase (with fine works by Michelangelo, Cellini, and Giambologna) and in the "Donatello room" directly above (with plenty by Donatello, including two different *David*s, plus Ghiberti and Brunelleschi's revolutionary dueling door panels and yet another *David* by Verrocchio).

Cost and Hours: €4, €7 with mandatory exhibits, covered by Firenze Card, Tue-Sat 8:15-13:50, until 16:50 during special exhibits (generally April-Oct); also open first, third, and fifth Mon and the second and fourth Sun of each month; last entry 30 minutes before closing, reservations possible but unnecessary, audioguide-€6, Via del Proconsolo 4, reservation tel. 055-238-8606, www.polomuseale.firenze.it.

○ See the Bargello Tour chapter.

Casa di Dante (Dante's House)—Dante Alighieri (1265-1321), the poet who gave us *The Divine Comedy*, is the Shakespeare of

Italy, the father of the modern Italian language, and the face on the country's €2 coin. However, most Americans know little of him, and this museum is not the ideal place to start. Even though it has English information, this small museum (in a building near where he likely lived) assumes visitors have prior knowledge of the poet. It's not a medieval-flavored house with period furniture—it's just a small, low-tech museum about Dante. Still, Dante lovers can trace his interesting life and works through pictures, models, and artifacts. And because the exhibits are as much about medieval Florence as they are about the man, novices can learn a little about Dante and the city he lived in.

Cost and Hours: €4, covered by Firenze Card; April-Sept

daily 10:00-18:00; Oct-March Tue-Sun 10:00-17:00, closed Mon; last entry 30 minutes before closing, near the Bargello at Via Santa Margherita 1, tel. 055-219-416, www.museocasadidante.it.

➜ **Self-Guided Tour:** Here's some background on what you'll find here—if you're new to the poet, this may help the museum seem less Dante-ing:

First Floor: In the first room, you'll see a sketch of Florence's Baptistery. Born in 1265, Dante was baptized there, and later trained as a doctor (glass cases of herbs).

Dante's life changed dramatically when he set eyes on Beatrice (look for her starry-sky picture in the first room), and fell in love with her. They ended up marrying other people, but Beatrice remained Dante's muse, inspiring him to write lofty poetry. Dante entered civic life, serving as the ambassador to Pope Boniface VIII. A model of Dante's Florence (in the second room) shows it as a walled city of many towers, housing feuding clans. Dante served in Florence's army at the decisive Battle of Campaldino, which established the city's dominance (and is explained in this floor's final room).

Second Floor: Exhibits explain the confusing politics that divided Florence between the victorious Black Guelphs and the defeated Whites, which included Dante. Politically incorrect Dante was exiled (in glass case, see the *Book of the Nail*—"*Libro del Chiodo*"—that condemns him), and never again returned to his beloved Florence. Dante probably would have liked the flattering modern portrait of him (hanging high above the book). Opposite the book is a reconstruction of a medieval bedroom—peer through the glass to see a more realistic painting of him, in red, forlorn, having received the news of his exile, with his distinctive ear-flap cap, hooked nose, and jutting chin.

Dante roamed Italy and was received by nobles. He worked on his magnum opus, *The Divine Comedy*, before he died and was buried in Ravenna in 1321. In the next room, see photos of the tomb and of his memorial in Florence's Santa Croce Church (described in the Santa Croce Tour chapter). Copies of paintings by famous artists and a video of scenes from *The Divine Comedy* in the far room demonstrate just how much Dante inspired the imagination of later artists. Some call him the father of the Renaissance.

Top Floor: Dante's most enduring legacy is the poem *The Divine Comedy*. The entire poem is displayed on the wall alongside pictures of Dante's cosmos: Hell (a spiral-shaped hole through the earth), Purgatory (a spiral-shaped mountain), and Paradise (the concentric orbits of satellites that surround earth). In the same room, you'll see bronze sculptures inspired by Dante's works. In the last room, a couple of typical costumes from Dante's era are on display.

▲**Orsanmichele Church**—In the ninth century, this loggia (covered courtyard) was a market used for selling grain (stored upstairs). Later, it was enclosed to make a church.

Outside are dynamic, statue-filled niches, some with accompanying symbols from the guilds that sponsored the art. Donatello's *St. Mark* and *St. George* (on the northeast and northwest corners) step out boldly in the new Renaissance style.

The interior has a glorious Gothic tabernacle (1359), which houses the painted wooden panel that depicts *Madonna delle Grazie* (1346). The iron bars spanning the vaults were the Italian Gothic answer to the French Gothic external buttresses. Look for the rectangular holes in the piers—these were once wheat chutes that connected to the upper floors. The museum upstairs (limited hours) displays most of the originals from the niches outside the building, by Ghiberti, Donatello, Brunelleschi, and others.

Cost and Hours: Free, daily 10:00-17:00, museum also free but open only Mon, niche sculptures always viewable from the outside. You can give the *Madonna della Grazie* a special thanks if you're in town when an evening concert is held inside the Orsanmichele (tickets sold on day of concert from door facing Via de' Calzaiuoli; also books Uffizi and Accademia tickets, ticket window open daily 10:00-17:00).

✪ See page 104 of the Renaissance Walk chapter.

A block away, you'll find the...

▲**Mercato Nuovo (a.k.a. the Straw Market)**—This market loggia is how Orsanmichele looked before it became a church. Originally a silk and straw market, Mercato Nuovo still functions as a rustic yet touristy market (at the intersection of Via Calimala and Via Porta Rossa). Prices are soft, but the San Lorenzo Market (listed earlier) is much better for haggling. Notice the circled X in the center, marking the spot where people hit after being hoisted up to the top and dropped as punishment for bankruptcy. You'll also find *Porcellino* (a statue of a wild boar nicknamed "little pig"), which people rub and give coins to in order to ensure their return to Florence. This new copy, while only a few years old, already has a polished snout. At the back corner, a wagon sells tripe (cow innards) sandwiches—a local favorite (daily 9:00-20:00).

▲**Piazza della Repubblica and Nearby**—This large square sits on the site of the original Roman Forum. Florence was a riverside garrison town set below the older town of Fiesole—essentially a rectangular fort with the square marking the intersection of the two main roads (Via Corso and Via Roma). The square's lone column—nicknamed "the belly button of Florence"—once marked the intersection (the Roman streets were about nine feet below the present street level). All that survives of Roman Florence is this column and the city's street plan. Look at any map of Florence

today, and you'll see the ghost of Rome in its streets: a grid-plan city center surrounded by what was the Roman wall. The Braille model of the city makes the design clear.

The square used to be the site of the Jewish quarter in the 1500s; in 1571, Cosimo I had it walled in and made into a ghetto.

Today's piazza, framed by a triumphal arch, is a nationalistic statement celebrating the unification of Italy. (Because it's so new, the square is not a favorite of locals.) Florence, the capital of the newly united nation of Italy (1865-1870) until Rome was "liberated" (from the Vatican), lacked a square worthy of this grand new country. So in the 1860s, the city was spiffed up for its stint as the capital—the Jewish ghetto was razed, and the city walls were taken down to make grand European-style boulevards and open up an imposing, modern forum surrounded by stately circa-1890 buildings. Notice the proud statement atop the triumphal arch, which proclaims "The squalor of the city is given a new life." Atop the lone column stands a copy of a Donatello statue of a pagan goddess of abundance, overseeing the market with her cornucopia full of produce.

Between here and the river, you'll find characteristic parts of the medieval city that give a sense of what this neighborhood felt like before it was bulldozed. Back in the Middle Ages, writers described Florence as so densely built up that when it rained, pedestrians didn't get wet. Torches were used to light the lanes in midday. The city was prickly with noble families' towers (like San Gimignano) and had *Romeo and Juliet*-type family feuds. But with the rise of city power (c. 1300), no noble family was allowed to have an architectural ego trip taller than the Town Hall, and nearly all other towers were taken down.

Venerable cafés and stores line the square. During the 19th century, intellectuals met in cafés here. The La Rinascente department store, facing Piazza della Repubblica, is one of the city's mainstays (WC on fourth floor, continue up the stairs from there to the bar with a rooftop terrace with great Duomo and city views).

▲**Palazzo Davanzati**—This five-story, late-medieval tower house offers a rare look at a noble dwelling built in the 14th century. Currently only the ground, first, and second floors are open to visitors, though the remaining floors can be visited with an escort (usually at 10:00, 11:00, and 12:00; ask when you arrive or call ahead to be sure there's space). Like other buildings of the age, the exterior is festooned with 14th-century horse-tethering rings made

out of iron, torch holders, and poles upon which to hang laundry and fly flags. Inside, though the furnishings are pretty sparse, you'll see richly painted walls, a long chute that functioned as a well, plenty of fireplaces, a lace display, and even an indoor "outhouse." While there's little posted information, you can borrow English descriptions in each room.

Cost and Hours: €2, covered by Firenze Card, Tue-Sat 8:15-13:50; also open first, third, and fifth Sun and second and fourth Mon of each month; Via Porta Rossa 13, tel. 055-238-8610.

On and near Piazza della Signoria

▲▲▲**Uffizi Gallery**—This greatest collection of Italian paintings anywhere features works by Giotto, Leonardo, Raphael, Caravaggio, Titian, and Michelangelo, and a roomful of

Botticellis, including the *Birth of Venus*. Northern Renaissance masters (Dürer, Rembrandt, and Rubens) are also well represented. Start with Giotto's early stabs at Renaissance-style realism, then move on through the 3-D experimentation of the early 1400s to the real thing rendered by the likes of Botticelli and Leonardo. Finish off with the High Renaissance—Michelangelo, Rubens, and Titian. Because only 600 visitors are allowed inside the building at any one time, there's generally a very long wait. The good news: no Louvre-style mob scenes inside. The museum is nowhere near as big as it is great. Few tourists spend more than two hours inside. The paintings are displayed on one comfortable, U-shaped floor in chronological order from the 13th through 17th centuries. The left wing, starring the Florentine Middle Ages to the Renaissance, is the best. The connecting corridor contains sculpture, and the right wing focuses on the High Renaissance and Baroque.

Cost and Hours: €6.50, €11 with mandatory exhibits, extra €4 for recommended reservation, cash required to pick up tickets reserved by phone; Tue-Sun 8:15-18:35, closed Mon, last entry 30 minutes before closing, museum info tel. 055-238-8651, reservation tel. 055-294-883, www.uffizi.firenze.it. To avoid the long ticket lines, get a Firenze Card (see page 57) or make reservations (see page 59).

✪ See the Uffizi Gallery Tour chapter.

In the Uffizi's Courtyard: Enjoy the courtyard (free), full of artists and souvenir stalls. (Swing by after dinner when it's completely empty.) The surrounding statues honor earthshaking Florentines: artists (Michelangelo), philosophers (Niccolò Machiavelli), scientists (Galileo), writers (Dante), cartographers (Amerigo Vespucci), and the great patron of so much Renaissance thinking, Lorenzo "the Magnificent" de' Medici.

✪ See page 110 of the Renaissance Walk chapter.

Nearby: The Loggia dei Lanzi, across from the Palazzo Vecchio and facing the square, is where Renaissance Florentines once debated the issues of the day; a collection of Medici-approved sculptures now stand (or writhe) under its canopy, including Cellini's bronze *Perseus*.

✪ See page 109 of the Renaissance Walk chapter.

▲▲**Palazzo Vecchio**—This castle-like fortress with the 300-foot spire dominates Florence's main square. In Renaissance times, it

was the Town Hall, where citizens pioneered the once-radical notion of self-rule. Its official name—the Palazzo della Signoria—refers to the elected members of the city council. In 1540, the tyrant Cosimo I de' Medici made the building his personal palace, redecorating the interior in lavish style. Today the building functions once again as the Town Hall.

Entry to the ground-floor courtyard is free, so even if you don't go upstairs to the museum, you can step inside and feel the essence of the Medici. Paying customers can see Cosimo's (fairly) lavish royal apartments, decorated with (fairly) top-notch paintings and statues by Michelangelo and Donatello. The highlight is the Grand Hall (Salone dei Cinquecento), a 13,000-square-foot hall lined with huge frescoes and interesting statues.

Cost and Hours: Courtyard—free to enter; museum—€6.50, €8 combo-ticket with Brancacci Chapel, covered by Firenze Card; tower only-€6.50 (418 steps), museum plus tower-€10; Fri-Wed 9:00-19:00, until 24:00 April-Sept; Thu 9:00-14:00 year-round; ticket office closes one hour earlier, Piazza della Signoria, tel. 055-276-8224, www.museicivicifiorentini.it.

✪ See the Palazzo Vecchio Tour chapter.

▲**Ponte Vecchio**—Florence's most famous bridge has long been lined with shops. Originally these were butcher shops that used the river as a handy disposal system. Then, when the powerful and princely Medici built the Vasari Corridor (described next) over the

bridge, the stinky meat market was replaced by the more
elegant gold and silver shops
that remain there to this day.
A statue of Benvenuto Cellini,
the master goldsmith of the
Renaissance, stands in the
center, ignored by the flood of
tacky tourism.

For more about the bridge, see page 111 of the Renaissance
Walk chapter and page 235 of the Oltrarno Walk chapter.

Vasari Corridor—This elevated and enclosed passageway, constructed in 1565, gave the Medici a safe, private commute over
Ponte Vecchio from their Pitti Palace home to their Palazzo
Vecchio offices. It's open only by special appointment, and while
enticing to lovers of Florence, the actual tour experience isn't
much. Entering from inside the Uffizi Gallery, you walk along a
modern-feeling hall (wide enough to carry a Medici on a sedan
chair) across Ponte Vecchio, and end in the Pitti Palace. Half the
corridor is lined with Europe's best collection of self-portraits,
along with other paintings (mostly 17th- and 18th-century) that
seem like they didn't make the cut to be hung on the walls of the
Uffizi. The best way to get inside the corridor is to go with a tour
company such as Florencetown (€89, daily at 15:30, tel. 055-012-
3994, www.florencetown.com) or ArtViva (€84, Tue and Sat at
13:30, tel. 055-264-5033, www.artviva.com). The three-hour tours,
which include a tour of the Uffizi, are expensive because of steep
city entrance fees and the requirement that groups be accompanied
by attendants and a guide.

**▲▲Galileo Science Museum (Museo Galilei e Istituto
di Storia della Scienza)**—When we think of the Florentine

Renaissance, we think of visual
arts: painting, mosaics, architecture, and sculpture. But when the
visual arts declined in the 1600s
(abused and co-opted by political
powers), music and science flour-
ished in Florence. The first opera
was written here. And Florence
hosted many scientific breakthroughs, as you'll see in this fasci-
nating collection of Renaissance and later clocks, telescopes, maps,
and ingenious gadgets. Trace the technical innovations as modern
science emerges from 1000 to 1900. One of the most talked-about
bottles in Florence is the one here that contains Galileo's finger.
Exhibits include various tools for gauging the world, from a com-

pass and thermometer to Galileo's telescopes. Other displays delve into clocks, pumps, medicine, and chemistry. It's friendly, comfortably cool, never crowded, and just a block east of the Uffizi on the Arno River.

Cost and Hours: €9, €22 family ticket, cash only, covered by Firenze Card, Wed-Mon 9:30-18:00, Tue 9:30-13:00, last entry 30 minutes before closing, audioguide-€5, Piazza dei Giudici 1, tel. 055-265-311, www.museogalileo.it.

○ See the Galileo Science Museum Tour chapter.

East of Piazza della Signoria

▲▲**Santa Croce Church**—This 14th-century Franciscan church, decorated with centuries of precious art, holds the tombs of great Florentines. The loud 19th-century

SIGHTS

Victorian Gothic facade faces a huge square ringed with tempting shops and littered with tired tourists. Escape into the church and admire its sheer height and spaciousness. Your ticket also includes the Pazzi Chapel and a small museum.

Cost and Hours: €6, €8.50 combo-ticket with Casa Buonarroti, covered by Firenze Card, Mon-Sat 9:30-17:30, Sun 14:00-17:30, last entry 30 minutes before closing, audioguide-€5, modest dress required, 10-minute walk east of Palazzo Vecchio along Borgo de' Greci, tel. 055-246-6105, www.santacroceopera.it. The **leather school** is free and sells church tickets. If the church has a long line, come here to avoid it (daily 10:00-18:00, has entry behind church plus entry within church, www.leatherschool.com).

○ See the Santa Croce Tour chapter.

▲**Casa Buonarroti (Michelangelo's House)**—Fans enjoy a house standing on property once owned by Michelangelo. The house was built after Michelangelo's death by the artist's grand-nephew, who turned it into a little museum honoring his famous relative. You'll see some of Michelangelo's early, less-than-monumental statues and a few sketches. Be warned: Michelangelo's descendants attributed everything they could to their famous relative, but very little here (beyond two marble relief panels and a couple of sketches) is actually by Michelangelo.

Cost and Hours: €6.50, €8.50 combo-ticket with Santa Croce Church, covered by Firenze Card, Wed-Mon 10:00-17:00, closed Tue, English descriptions, Via Ghibellina 70, tel. 055-241-752.

Visiting the Museum: Climb the stairs to the first-floor landing, where you come face-to-face with portraits (by his contemporaries) of 60-year-old Michelangelo, the Buonarroti family walking sticks, and some leather shoes thought to be Michelangelo's.

The room to the left of the landing displays two relief panels, Michelangelo's earliest known sculptures. Teenage Michelangelo carved every inch of the *Battle of the Centaurs* (1490-1492). This squirming tangle of battling nudes shows his fascination with anatomy. He kept this in his personal collection all his life. *The Madonna of the Stairs* (c. 1490) is as contemplative as *Centaurs* is dramatic. Throughout his long career, bipolar Michelangelo veered between these two styles—moving or still, emotional or thought-ful, pagan or Christian.

In an adjoining room is the big wooden model of a project Michelangelo took on but never completed: the facade of the Church of San Lorenzo (which remains bare brick to this day). The reclining river god was a model for one of the statues in the Medici Chapels.

The small room adjoining the landing is for the museum's vast collection of Michelangelo's sketches. Unfortunately, only a

handful of works are displayed at a time. Vasari claimed that Michelangelo wanted to burn his preliminary sketches, lest anyone think him less than perfect.

The room to the right of the landing displays small clay and wax models—some by Michelangelo, some by pupils—that the artist used to sketch out ideas for his statues.

And finally, true Michelangelomaniacs can complete their visit by exiting outside to gaze at Via Ghibellina 67 (next door to a *farmacia*). This humble doorway, lined with gray-green stone, was once the entrance to Michelangelo's actual residence, circa 1520.

Santa Maria Novella Sights near the Train Station

▲▲**Church of Santa Maria Novella**—This 13th-century Dominican church is rich in art. Along with crucifixes by Giotto and Brunelleschi, it contains every textbook's example of the early Renaissance mastery of perspective: *The Holy Trinity* by Masaccio. The exquisite chapels trace art in Florence from medieval times to early Baroque. The outside of the

church features a dash of Romanesque (horizontal stripes), Gothic (pointed arches), Renaissance (geometric shapes), and Baroque (scrolls). Step in and look down the 330-foot nave for a 14th-century optical illusion. Next to the church are the cloisters and the museum, located in the old Dominican convent of Santa Maria Novella. The museum's highlight is the breathtaking Spanish Chapel, with walls covered by a series of frescos by Andrea di Bonaiuto.

Cost and Hours: Church—€3.50, covered by Firenze Card, Mon-Thu 9:00-17:30, Fri 11:00-17:30, Sat 9:00-17:00, Sun 13:00-17:00, last entry 30 minutes before closing, audioguide-€5, modest dress required, tel. 055-219-257, www.museicivicifiorentini.it; museum—€2.70, covered by Firenze Card, Fri-Mon 9:00-16:00, closed Tue-Thu, tel. 055-282-187.

○ See the Santa Maria Novella Tour chapter.

Farmacia di Santa Maria Novella—This palatial perfumery has long been run by the Dominicans of Santa Maria Novella. Thick with the lingering aroma of centuries of spritzes, it started as the herb garden of the Santa Maria Novella monks. Well-known even today for its top-quality products, it is extremely Florentine. Pick up the history sheet at the desk, and wander deep into the shop. The first room features perfumes, the middle (green) room offers items for the home, and the third room, which sells herbal products and dates from 1612, is the most historic. From here, you can peek at one of Santa Maria Novella's cloisters with its dreamy frescoes and imagine a time before Vespas and tourists.

Cost and Hours: Free but shopping encouraged, inconsistent hours but likely daily 9:30-19:30, a block from Piazza Santa Maria Novella, 100 yards down Via della Scala at #16—located on map on page 66, tel. 055-216-276, www.smnovella.com.

South of the Arno River

The Oltrarno Walk chapter connects several of these sights, including the Pitti Palace, Brancacci Chapel, and Santo Spirito Church.

▲▲**Pitti Palace**—The imposing Pitti Palace, several blocks

southwest of Ponte Vecchio, has many separate museums and two gardens. The main reason to visit is to see the Palatine Gallery, but you can't buy a ticket for the gallery alone; to see it you'll need to buy ticket #1, which includes the Palatine Gallery, Royal Apartments, and Gallery of Modern Art. Ticket #2 covers

SIGHTS

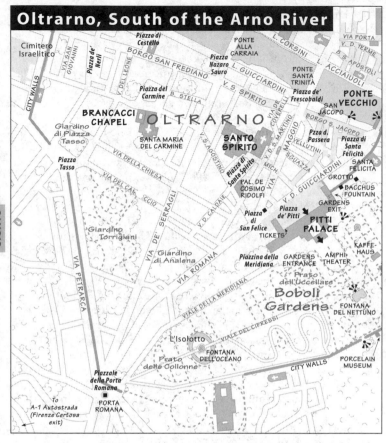

the Boboli and Bardini gardens, Costume Gallery, Argenti/
Silverworks Museum (the Medici treasures), and Porcelain
Museum. Behind door #3 is a combo-ticket covering the whole
shebang.

Cost and Hours: Ticket #1—€8.50, Tue-Sun 8:15-18:50,
closed Mon. Ticket #2—€7, daily 8:15-18:30 except closed first
and last Mon of each month, until 19:30 June-Aug, gardens close
as early as 16:30 in winter, last entry 30-60 minutes before closing. An €11.50 combo-ticket (valid 3 days) covers the entire palace complex. All tickets are cash only and increase in price with
mandatory special exhibits. Reservations are possible but unnecessary, and everything is covered by the Firenze Card. The €6 audioguide explains the sprawling palace. Tel. 055-238-8614, www.polo
museale.firenze.it.

❂ See the Pitti Palace Tour chapter.

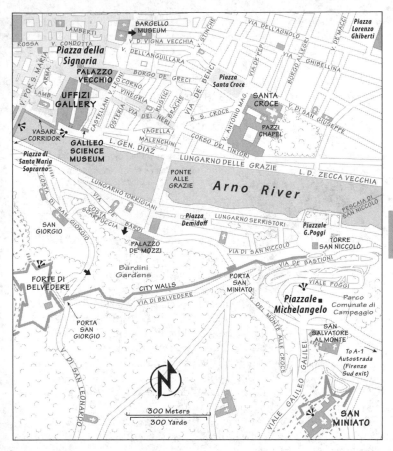

▲▲**Brancacci Chapel**—For the best look at works by Masaccio (one of the early Renaissance pioneers of perspective in paint-

ing), see his restored frescoes here. Instead of medieval religious symbols, Masaccio's paintings feature simple, strong human figures with facial expressions that reflect their emotions. The accompanying works of Masolino and Filippino Lippi provide illuminating contrasts.

Cost and Hours: €4, covered by Firenze Card, free and easy reservations required but it's usually possible to just show up and get an entry time if you arrive before 15:30, €8 combo-ticket with Palazzo Vecchio, includes worthwhile 40-minute film in English—reserve viewing time when you book entry, Mon and Wed-Sat 10:00-17:00, Sun 13:00-17:00, closed Tue, last entry 30 minutes before closing, in Church of Santa Maria del Carmine, reservations tel. 055-276-8224 or 055-276-8558, ticket desk tel. 055-284-361, www.museicivicifiorentini.it.

✪ See the Brancacci Chapel Tour chapter.

Nearby: The neighborhoods around the church are considered the last surviving bits of old Florence.

Santo Spirito Church—This church has a classic Brunelleschi interior—enjoy its pure Renaissance lines (and ignore the later

Baroque altar that replaced the original). Notice Brunelleschi's "dice"—the stone cubes added above the column capitals that contribute to the nave's playful lightness. The church's art treasure is a painted, carved wooden crucifix attributed to 17-year-old Michelangelo. The sculptor donated this early work to the monastery in appreciation for allowing him to dissect and learn about bodies. The Michelangelo *Crocifisso* is displayed in the sacristy, through a door midway down the left side of the nave (if it's closed, ask someone to let you in). Copies of Michelangelo's *Pietà* and *Risen Christ* flank the nave (near the main door). Beer-drinking, guitar-playing rowdies decorate the church steps.

Cost and Hours: Free, Mon-Tue and Thu-Sat 9:30-12:30 & 16:00-17:30, Sun 16:00-17:30 only, closed Wed, Piazza di Santo Spirito, tel. 055-210-030.

▲Piazzale Michelangelo—Overlooking the city from across the river (look for the huge statue of *David*), this square has a superb view of Florence and the stunning dome of the Duomo (see photo, right).

It's worth the 30-minute hike, drive (free parking), or bus ride (either #12 or #13 from the train station—takes 20-30 minutes, or even more in bad traffic). It makes sense to take a taxi or ride the bus up, and then enjoy the easy downhill walk back into town. An inviting café with great views is just below the overlook. The best photos are taken from the street immediately below the overlook (go around to the right and down a few steps). Off the west side of the piazza is a somewhat hidden terrace, an excellent place to retreat from the mobs. After dark, the square is packed with schoolkids licking ice cream and each other. About 200 yards beyond all the tour groups and teenagers is the stark, beautiful, crowd-free, Romanesque San Miniato Church (next listing).

The hike down is quick and enjoyable. Take the steps between the two bars on the San Miniato Church side of the parking lot (Via San Salvatore al Monte), and in a couple of minutes you walk through the old wall (Porta San Miniato) and emerge in the delightful little Oltrarno neighborhood of San Niccolò.

▲▲**San Miniato Church**—According to legend, the martyred St. Minias—this church's namesake—was beheaded on the banks

of the Arno in A.D. 250. He picked up his head and walked here (this was before the #12 bus), where he died and was buried in what became the first Christian cemetery in Florence. In the 11th century, this church was built to house Minias' remains. Imagine this fine church all alone—without any nearby buildings or fancy stairs—a peace-

ful refuge where white-robed Benedictine monks could pray and work (their motto: *ora et labora*). The evening Mass with the monks chanting in Latin offers a meditative worship experience—a peaceful way to end your visit.

Cost and Hours: Free, daily Easter-mid-Oct 8:00-20:00 or possibly later, in winter 8:30-13:00 & 15:30-19:00, tel. 055-234-2731, www.sanminiatoalmonte.it.

Getting There: It's about 200 yards above Piazzale Michelangelo. From the station, bus #12 takes you right to the San Miniato al Monte stop (hop off and hike up the grand staircase); bus #13 from the station takes you to Piazzale Michelangelo, from which you'll hike up the rest of the way.

Gregorian Chants: To experience this mystical medieval space at its full potential, time your visit to coincide with a Mass of Gregorian chants. In general, these are held each evening in summer (Easter-mid-Oct) at 18:30, and in winter at 17:00 or 17:30—but as the schedule is subject to change, double-check with any TI, check the church's website, or call ahead.

❍ Self-Guided Tour: For a thousand years, San Miniato Church—still part of a functioning monastery—has blessed the city that lies at the foot of its hill. Carved into the marble of its threshold is the Genesis verse *"Haec est Porta Coeli"* ("This is the Gate of Heaven").

Facade: The church's green-and-white marble facade (12th century) is classic Florentine Romanesque, one of the oldest in town. The perfect symmetry is a reminder of the perfection of God. The central mosaic shows Christ flanked by Mary and St. Minias. Minias, who was King of Armenia before his conversion, offers his secular crown to the heavenly king. The eagle on top, with bags of wool in his talons, reminds all who approach the church who paid for it—the wool guild.

Nave: Stepping inside, you enter the closest thing to a holy space that medieval Florentines could create. The "carpet of marble" dates from 1207. The wood ceiling is painted as it was originally. The glittering 13th-century golden mosaic that dominates the dome at the front of the nave repeats the scene on the church's facade: St. Minias offering his paltry secular crown to the king in heaven.

The Renaissance tabernacle front and center was built by the Medici. It's a résumé of early Renaissance humanism, with experiments in 3-D paintings (including St. Minias, in red) and a plush canopy of glazed terra-cotta panels by Luca della Robbia.

On the left side of the nave is an exquisite chapel dedicated to Cardinal Jacopo of Portugal. When 26-year-old Jacopo died in Florence (1459), his wealthy family mourned him by adding a chapel to the church (by cutting a hole in the church wall) and hiring the best artists of the day to decorate it. The family could enter their private chapel, take a seat on the throne (on the left), and meditate on the tomb of Jacopo (on the right).

Crypt: The church is designed like a split-level rambler, with staircases on either side of the altar, leading upstairs and down. Downstairs in the crypt, an alabaster window helps create a quiet and mysterious atmosphere. The forest of columns and capitals are all recycled...each from ancient Rome and each different. The floor is paved with the tombstones of long-forgotten big shots. Look through the window in the marble altar to see St. Minias' name, carved on the box that holds his mortal remains.

Upstairs to the Sacristy: At the staircase to the right of the main altar, notice the sinopia on the wall. A sinopia is a pattern that guides the fresco artist, and that allows the patron to have a peek at what the artist intends to create before it's set in hard plaster. There's a sinopia behind every surviving fresco in Florence.

Step upstairs and enter the sacristy (the room on the right), which is beautifully frescoed with scenes from the life of St. Benedict (circa 1350, by a follower of Giotto). Drop €2 into the electronic panel in the corner to light the room for five minutes. The elegantly bearded patron saint of Europe was the founder of the vast network of monasteries that gave the Continent some cohesiveness in the cultural darkness that followed the collapse of Rome. Benedict is shown as an active force for good, with his arm always outstretched: busy blessing, being kissed, preaching, helping, chasing the devil, bringing a man (crushed by a fallen tower) back to life, reaching out even on his death bed. Notice Benedict on the ramp, scooting up to heaven to be welcomed by an angel. And, overseeing everything, in the starry skies of the ceiling, are the four evangelists—each with his book, pen, and symbolic sidekicks.

Outside the Church: Before leaving, stroll through the cemetery behind the church to marvel at the showy crypts and headstones of Florentine hotshots from the last two centuries. And savor the views of Florence.

Near Florence: Fiesole

Perched on a hill overlooking the Arno valley, Fiesole (fee-AY-zoh-lay) gives weary travelers a break in the action and—during

the heat of summer—a breezy location from which to admire the city below. It's a small town with a main square, a few restaurants and shops, a few minor sights, and a great view. The ancient Etruscans knew a good spot when they saw one, and chose to settle here, establishing Fiesole about 400 years before the Romans founded Florence. Wealthy Renaissance families in pre-air-conditioning days also chose Fiesole as a preferred vacation spot, building villas in the surrounding hillsides. Later, 19th-century Romantics spent part of the Grand Tour admiring the vistas, much like the hordes of tourists do today. Most come here for the view—the actual sights pale in comparison to those in Florence. Shutterbugs visit in the morning for the best light.

Getting to Fiesole: From Florence's Piazza San Marco, take bus #7—enjoying a peek at gardens, vineyards, orchards, and villas—to the last stop, Piazza Mino (4/hour, fewer after 20:00, 30 minutes, €1.20, €2 if bought on bus; departs Florence from Piazza San Marco; wear your money belt—thieves frequent this bus). Taxis from Florence cost about €25-35 (ride to highest point you want to visit—La Reggia Ristorante for view terrace or Church of San Francesco—then explore downhill).

Tourist Information: The TI, immediately to the right of the Roman Archaeological Park, is a two-minute walk from the bus stop—head behind the church (daily 10:30-17:00, Via Portigiani 3, tel. 055-596-1311, www.fiesoleforyou.it).

Market Day: A modest selection of food and household items fills Via Portigiani, just off Piazza Mino, on Saturday mornings until 13:00.

Sights in Fiesole

Fiesole's main sights are either free or covered by one €10 combo-ticket, available at the Roman Theater.

▲▲Terrace and Garden with a View—Catch the sunset (and your breath) from the view terrace just below La Reggia Ristorante. It's a steep seven-minute hike from the Fiesole bus stop: Face the bell tower and take Via San Francesco, on the left. (For similar views and a peek at residential Fiesole, climb up the opposite side of the square, along the road hugging the ridgeline.)

Church of San Francesco—For even more hill-climbing, continue up from the view terrace to this charming little church. The small scale and several colorful altar paintings make this church more enjoyable than Fiesole's Duomo.

Cost and Hours: Free, Mon-Sat 8:00-12:00 & 15:00-19:00, Sun 7:00-11:00 & 15:00-19:00, Via San Francesco 13, tel. 055-59175.

Franciscan Ethnographic Missionary Museum (Museo Missionario Etnografico Francescano)—This eclectic little collection, hidden beneath the church of San Francesco, includes an Egyptian mummy, ancient coins, Chinese Buddhas, and the in situ ruins of a third-century Etruscan wall.

Cost and Hours: Free but donation suggested, Tue-Fri 10:00-12:00 & 15:00-19:00, Sat-Sun 15:00-19:00, closed Mon, unmarked door inside church leads to cloisters and museum, tel. 055-59175.

Duomo—While this church has a drab, 19th-century exterior, the interior is worth a look, if only for the blue-and-white glazed Giovanni della Robbia statue of St. Romulus over the entry door.

Cost and Hours: Free, daily 10:00-17:00, across Piazza Mino from the bus stop.

Roman Theater and Archaeological Park—Occasionally used today for plays, this well-preserved theater held up to 2,000 people. The site's other ruins are, well, ruined, and lacking in explanation. But the valley view and peaceful setting are lovely.

Cost and Hours: €8, ticket also covers Civic Archaeological Museum—described next, €10 combo-ticket adds Bandini Museum; April-Sept daily 10:00-19:00; March and Oct daily 10:00-18:00; Nov-Feb Wed-Mon 10:00-14:00, closed Tue; from the bus stop cross Piazza Mino, heading toward the back of the Duomo; www.museidifiesole.it.

Civic Archaeological Museum—Located within the Archaeological Park, the museum imparts insight into Fiesole's Etruscan and Roman roots with well-displayed artifacts and with a few sheets of English description in the corners.

Cost and Hours: €8 ticket also includes Roman theater and park, also covered by €10 combo-ticket with Bandini Museum, same hours as Roman Theater, listed earlier.

Bandini Museum—This petite museum displays the wooden panels of lesser-known Gothic and Renaissance painters as well as the glazed terra-cotta figures of Andrea della Robbia.

Cost and Hours: €5, also covered by €10 combo-ticket with archaeological museum, Roman theater, and park, daily 10:00-18:00, shorter hours off-season, behind Duomo at Via Dupre 1.

Eating in Fiesole

These two restaurants are on Piazza Mino, where the bus from Florence stops.

Ristorante Perseus, a local favorite, lacks views but serves authentic Tuscan dishes at a fair price in a rambling interior, at a few sidewalk tables, or on a shady garden terrace in fair weather (daily 12:30-14:30 & 19:30-23:30, tel. 055-59-143, Leonardo).

Ristorante Aurora is an upscale alternative with a view terrace overlooking the city of Florence (daily 12:00-14:30 & 19:00-22:30, tel. 055-59-363).

Picnics: Fiesole is made-to-order for a scenic and breezy picnic. Grab a pastry at Fiesole's best *pasticceria,* **Alcedo** (head up the main drag from the bus stop to Via Gramsci 27). Round out your goodies at the **Co-op** supermarket on Via Gramsci before walking up to the panoramic terrace. Or, for more convenience and less view, picnic at the shaded park on the way to the view terrace (walk up Via San Francesco about halfway to the terrace, and climb the stairs to the right).

RENAISSANCE WALK

*From the Duomo
to the Arno River*

After centuries of labor, Florence gave birth to the Renaissance. We'll start with the soaring church dome that stands as the proud symbol of the Renaissance spirit. Just opposite, you'll find the Baptistery doors that opened the Renaissance. Finally, we'll reach Florence's political center, dotted with monuments of that proud time. As great and rich as this city is, it's easily covered on foot. This walk through the top sights is less than a mile long, running from the Duomo to the Arno River.

Orientation

Crowd-Beating Tips: You can take this walk without entering any sights, but if you do plan to enter the Duomo and several related sights (Campanile, Baptistery, and Duomo Museum), you're probably best off getting the €15 **combo-ticket** that lets you skip the lines at all of these; buy it at the Duomo Museum (shortest lines) before you start the walk, then dip into the sights as you reach them. Dome-climbers should instead consider taking the €15 "Terraces of the Cathedral and Dome" **tour,** which let you skip the lines to enter the cathedral and dome. See page 71 for more on both options.

Duomo (Cathedral): Free, Mon-Fri 10:00-17:00, Thu until 16:00 Oct-May, Sat 10:00-16:45, Sun 13:30-16:45. A modest dress code is enforced.

Climbing the Dome: €8, cash only, Mon-Fri 8:30-19:00, Sat 8:30-17:40, closed Sun, last entry 40 minutes before closing, 463 steps.

Campanile (Giotto's Tower): €6, daily 8:30-19:30, last entry 40 minutes before closing, 413 steps.

Baptistery: €5, €7 with mandatory temporary exhibits, enter north door but first buy tickets from office across piazza, 30 paces north of entrance (see map), interior open Mon-Sat 12:15-19:00 except first Sat of month 8:30-14:00, Sun 8:30-14:00, last entry 30 minutes before closing, audioguide-€2, photos allowed inside. Facsimiles of the famous bronze doors are on the outside, so they're always viewable (and free to see; the original panels are in the Duomo Museum).

Medici-Riccardi Palace: €7, Thu-Tue 9:00-18:00, closed Wed, last entry 30 minutes before closing, Via Cavour 3.

Orsanmichele Church: Free, daily 10:00-17:00, upstairs museum open only Mon 10:00-17:00. The niche sculptures are always viewable from the outside. The church hosts evening concerts; tickets are sold on the day of the concert from the door facing Via de' Calzaiuoli. At the same ticket window, you can book tickets for the Uffizi and Accademia.

Palazzo Vecchio: €6.50, €8 combo-ticket with Brancacci Chapel, Fri-Wed 9:00-19:00, until 24:00 in April-Sept, closes at 14:00 on Thu year-round, ticket office closes one hour earlier.

Information: There's a TI right on Piazza del Duomo (just south of Baptistery, at the corner of Via de' Calzaiuoli), and another one on Via Cavour 1, a couple of blocks north of the Duomo (immediately beyond the Medici-Riccardi Palace). At either TI, ask for an updated list of museum hours.

Audio Tour: You can download this chapter as a free Rick Steves audio tour (see page 41).

Length of This Tour: Allow two hours for the walk, including interior visits of the Baptistery and Orsanmichele Church (but not the other sights mentioned).

With Limited Time: You can trim this walk by skipping the Medici-Riccardi Palace detour, and just viewing the Baptistery and Orsanmichele Church from the outside.

Services: Many cafés along the walk have WCs, and public pay toilets (€1) are at the Baptistery ticket office. You can refill your water bottle at public twist-the-handle fountains at the Duomo (left side, by the dome entrance), the Palazzo Vecchio (behind the Neptune fountain), and on Ponte Vecchio.

Photography: In churches and other sights along this walk, photos without a flash are generally OK.

Eating: You'll find plenty of cafés, self-service cafeterias, bars, and gelato shops along the route. Many good eateries along this walk are described in the Eating in Florence chapter, including Self-Service Ristorante Leonardo (near the Duomo) and the popular L'Antico Trippaio tripe-selling sandwich cart (also has non-tripe fare, a block east of Orsanmichele on Via Dante Alighieri; other cheap options are nearby). For an inexpensive drink and sandwich a half-block north of the Duomo, sneak up to the quiet upstairs café at the Libreria Martelli bookstore (26 Via de' Martelli).

Starring: Brunelleschi's dome, Ghiberti's doors, the Medici palaces, and the city of Florence—old and new.

The Tour Begins

Overview

The Duomo, the cathedral with the distinctive red dome, is the center of Florence and the orientation point for this walk. If you ever get lost, home's the dome. We'll start here, see several sights in the area, and then stroll down the city's pedestrian-only main street to the Palazzo Vecchio and the Arno River. Consider prefacing this walk with a visit to the ultimate Renaissance man: Michelangelo's *David* (✪ see the Accademia Tour chapter).

• *Stand in front of the Duomo as you get your historical bearings.*

The Florentine Renaissance (1400-1550)

In the 13th and 14th centuries, Florence was a powerful center of banking, trading, and textile manufacturing. The resulting wealth fertilized the cultural soil. Then came the Black Death in 1348. Nearly half the population died, but the infrastructure remained strong, and the city rebuilt better than ever. Led by Florence's chief family—the art-crazy Medici—and propelled by the naturally aggressive and creative spirit of the Florentines, it's no wonder that the long-awaited Renaissance finally took root here.

The Renaissance—the "rebirth" of Greek and Roman culture that swept across Europe—started around 1400 and lasted about 150 years. In politics, the Renaissance meant democracy; in science, a renewed interest in exploring nature. The general mood was optimistic and "humanistic," with a confidence in the power of the individual.

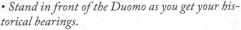

In medieval times, poverty and ignorance had made life "nasty, brutish, and short" (for lack of a better cliché). The church was the people's opiate, and their lives were only a preparation for a happier time in heaven after leaving this miserable vale of tears.

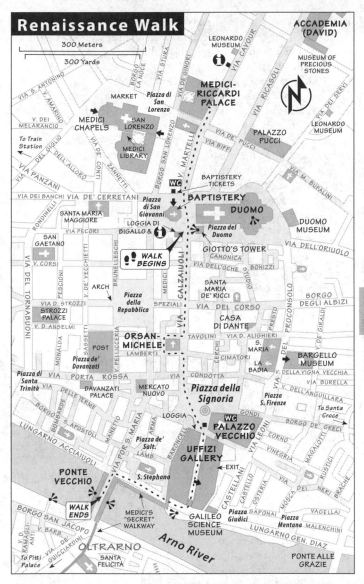

Renaissance Walk

300 Meters

300 Yards

ACCADEMIA (DAVID)

LEONARDO MUSEUM

MUSEUM OF PRECIOUS STONES

MEDICI-RICCARDI PALACE

MARKET

Piazza di San Lorenzo

MEDICI CHAPELS

SAN LORENZO

MEDICI LIBRARY

To Train Station

PALAZZO PUCCI

LEONARDO MUSEUM

BAPTISTERY TICKETS

WC

SANTA MARIA MAGGIORE

Piazza di San Giovanni

BAPTISTERY

DUOMO

DUOMO MUSEUM

SAN GAETANO

LOGGIA DI BIGALLO &

WALK BEGINS

Piazza del Duomo

GIOTTO'S TOWER

CANONICA

ARCH

Piazza della Repubblica

SANTA MARIA DE' RICCI

STROZZI PALACE

CASA DI DANTE

ORSAN-MICHELE

POST

Piazza de' Davanzati

S. MARIA LA BADIA

BARGELLO MUSEUM

Piazza di Santa Trinità

DAVANZATI PALACE

MERCATO NUOVO

Piazza della Signoria

Piazza S. Firenze

To Santa Croce

PONTE VECCHIO

Piazza de' Salt.

LOGGIA

WC

PALAZZO VECCHIO

UFFIZI GALLERY

EXIT

WALK ENDS

MEDICI'S "SECRET" WALKWAY

S. Stephano

GALILEO SCIENCE MUSEUM

Piazza Giudici

Piazza Mentana

To Pitti Palace

OLTRARNO

SANTA FELICITÀ

Arno River

PONTE ALLE GRAZIE

RENAISSANCE WALK

Medieval art was the church's servant. The noblest art form was architecture—churches themselves—and other arts were considered most worthwhile if they embellished the house of God. Painting and sculpture were narrative and symbolic, designed to tell Bible stories to the devout and illiterate masses.

As prosperity rose in Florence, so did people's confidence in life and themselves. Middle-class craftsmen, merchants, and bankers felt they could control their own destinies, rather than be at the whim of nature. They found much in common with the ancient Greeks and Romans, who valued logic and reason above superstition and blind faith.

Renaissance art was a return to the realism and balance of Greek and Roman sculpture and architecture. Domes and round arches replaced Gothic spires and pointed arches. In painting and sculpture, Renaissance artists strove for realism. Merging art and science, they used mathematics, the laws of perspective, and direct observation of nature to paint the world on a flat surface.

This was not an anti-Christian movement, though it was a logical and scientific age. Artists saw themselves as an extension of God's creative powers. At times, the church even supported the Renaissance and commissioned many of its greatest works—for instance, Raphael frescoed images of Plato and Aristotle on the walls of the Vatican. But for the first time in Europe since Roman times, there were rich laymen who wanted art simply for art's sake.

After 1,000 years of waiting, the smoldering fires of Europe's classical heritage burst into flames in Florence.

• *The dome of the Duomo is best viewed just to the right of the facade, from the corner of the pedestrian-only street.*

The Duomo—Florence's Cathedral

The dome of Florence's cathedral—visible from all over the city—inspired Florentines to do great things. (Most recently, it inspired the city to make the area around the cathedral delightfully traffic-free.) The big church itself (called the Duomo) is Gothic, built in the Middle Ages by architects who left it unfinished.

Think of the confidence of the age: The Duomo was built with a big hole in its roof, just waiting for a grand dome to cover it—but the technology needed to create such a dome had yet to be invented. *No problema.* The Florentines knew that someone would soon be able to handle the challenge. In the 1400s, the architect Filippo Brunelleschi was called on to finish the job. Brunelleschi capped the church Roman-style—with a tall, self-supporting dome as grand as the ancient Pantheon's (which he had studied).

He used a dome within a dome. First, he built the grand white skeletal ribs, which you can see, then filled them in with interlocking bricks in a herringbone pattern. The dome grew upward like an igloo, supporting itself as it proceeded from the base. When

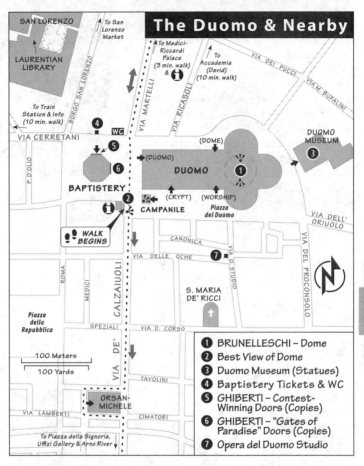

The Duomo & Nearby

❶ BRUNELLESCHI – Dome
❷ Best View of Dome
❸ Duomo Museum (Statues)
❹ Baptistery Tickets & WC
❺ GHIBERTI – Contest-Winning Doors (Copies)
❻ GHIBERTI – "Gates of Paradise" Doors (Copies)
❼ Opera del Duomo Studio

the ribs reached the top, Brunelleschi arched them in and fixed them in place with the cupola at the top. His dome, built in only 14 years, was the largest since Rome's Pantheon.

Brunelleschi's dome was the wonder of the age, the model for many domes to follow, from St. Peter's to the US Capitol. People gave it the ultimate compliment, saying, "Not even the ancients could have done it." Michelangelo, setting out to construct the dome of St. Peter's, drew inspiration from the dome of Florence. He said, "I'll make its sister...bigger, but not more beautiful."

The church's facade looks old, but is actually Neo-Gothic—only from 1870. The facade was rushed to completion (about 600 years after the building began) to celebrate Italian unity, here in the city that for a few years served as the young country's capital. Its "retro" look captures the feel of the original medieval facade, with green, white, and pink marble sheets that cover the brick

construction; Gothic (pointed) arches; and three horizontal stories decorated with mosaics and statues. Still, the facade is generally ridiculed. (While one of this book's authors thinks it's the most beautiful church facade this side of heaven, the other one naively agrees with those who call it "the cathedral in pajamas.")

The interior feels bare after being cleaned out during the Neoclassical age and by the terrible flood of 1966 (free entry, but not worth a long wait; for my brief self-guided tour of the interior, see page 71). To climb the dome, enter from outside the church on the north side (see page 74).

Campanile (Giotto's Tower)

The bell tower (to the right of the cathedral's front) offers an easier, less crowded, and faster climb than the Duomo's dome,

though the unobstructed views from the Duomo are better. Giotto, like any good pre-Renaissance genius, wore several artistic hats. Not only is he considered the father of modern painting, he's also the one who designed this 270-foot-tall bell tower for the Duomo two centuries before the age of Michelangelo. In his day, Giotto was called the ugliest man to ever walk the streets of Florence, but he designed for the city what many in our day call the most beautiful bell tower in all of Europe.

The bell tower served as a sculpture gallery for Renaissance artists—notice Donatello's four prophets on the side that faces the piazza (west). These are copies—the originals are at the wonderful Duomo Museum, just behind the church. (❂ See the Duomo Museum Tour chapter.) In the museum, you'll also get a close-up look at Brunelleschi's wooden model of his dome, Ghiberti's doors (described next), and a late *Pietà* by Michelangelo. A couple of blocks south of the Duomo, at the Opera del Duomo Studio, workers sculpt and restore statues for the cathedral (Via dello Studio 23a—see location on map on the previous page; you can peek through the doorway).

• *The Baptistery is the small octagonal building in front of the church. If you decide to go inside, enter through the north door (after getting a ticket at the office across the piazza; that's also where you can pick up*

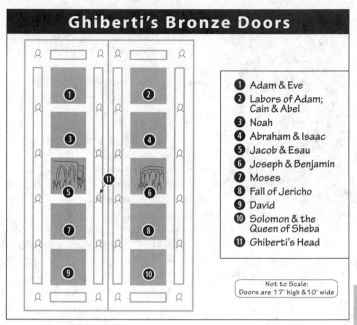

Ghiberti's Bronze Doors

1. Adam & Eve
2. Labors of Adam; Cain & Abel
3. Noah
4. Abraham & Isaac
5. Jacob & Esau
6. Joseph & Benjamin
7. Moses
8. Fall of Jericho
9. David
10. Solomon & the Queen of Sheba
11. Ghiberti's Head

Not to Scale:
Doors are 17' high & 10' wide

an audioguide). If you just want to look at the exterior doors, there's no charge, of course.

Baptistery and Ghiberti's Bronze Doors

Florence's Baptistery is dear to the soul of the city. In medieval and Renaissance times, the locals—eager to link themselves to the classical past—believed (wrongly) that this was a Roman building. It is, however, Florence's oldest building (11th century). Most festivals and parades either started or ended here.

Doors: The Baptistery's bronze doors bring us out of the Middle Ages and into the Renaissance. Some say the Renaissance began precisely in the year 1401, when Florence staged a competition to find the best artist to create the Baptistery's **north doors** (around the right side as you face the Baptistery with the Duomo at your back). Florence had strong civic spirit, with different guilds (powerful trade associations) and merchant groups embellishing their city with superb art. All the greats entered the contest, but 25-year-old Lorenzo Ghiberti won easily, beating out heavyweights such as Brunelleschi (who, having lost the Baptistery gig, was free to go to Rome, study the Pantheon, and later design the Duomo's dome). The original entries of Brunelleschi and Ghiberti are in the Bargello, where you can judge them for yourself.

Later, in 1425, Ghiberti was given another commission, for the **east doors** (facing the church). This time there was literally no

contest. The bronze panels of these doors (the ones with the crowd of tourists looking on) added a whole new dimension to art—depth. Michelangelo said these doors were fit to be the "Gates of Paradise." (These panels are copies; the originals are in the nearby Duomo Museum. For more detailed descriptions of the panels, see page 178.) Here we see how the Renaissance masters merged art and science. Realism was in, and Renaissance artists used math, illusion, and dissection to create it.

In the Jacob and Esau panel (just above eye level on the left), receding arches, floor tiles, and banisters create a background for a realistic scene. The figures in the foreground stand and move like real people, telling the Bible story with human details. Amazingly, this spacious, 3-D scene is made from bronze only a few inches deep.

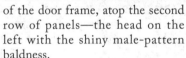

Ghiberti spent 27 years (1425-1452) working on these panels. That's him in the center of the door frame, atop the second row of panels—the head on the left with the shiny male-pattern baldness.

Interior: You'll see a fine example of pre-Renaissance mosaic art (1200s-1300s) in the Byzantine style. Workers from St. Mark's in Venice came here to make the remarkable ceiling mosaics (of Venetian glass) in the late 1200s.

The Last Judgment on the ceiling gives us a glimpse of the medieval worldview. Life was a preparation for the afterlife, when you would be judged and saved, or damned, with no in-between. Christ, peaceful and reassuring, would bless those at his right hand with heaven (thumbs up) and send those on his left to hell (the ultimate thumbs-down), to

RENAISSANCE WALK

be tortured by demons and gnashed between the teeth of monsters. This hellish scene looks like something right out of the *Inferno* by Dante, who was dipped into the baptismal waters right here.

The rest of the ceiling mosaics tell the history of the world, from Adam and Eve (over the north/entrance doors, top row) to Noah and the Flood (over south doors, top row), to the life of Christ (second row) to the beheading of John the Baptist (bottom row), all bathed in the golden glow of pre-Renaissance heaven.

• *Before we head south to the river, consider detouring a block north up Via de' Martelli (which becomes Via Cavour—the one that goes straight up from between the Duomo and Baptistery). At the intersection with Via dei Pucci is the imposing...*

Medici-Riccardi Palace

Renaissance Florence was ruled by the Medici, the rich bank-ing family who lived in this building (for more on this family, see

page 537). Studying this grand Florentine palace, you'll notice fortified lower walls and elegance limited to the fancy upper sto-ries. The Medici may have been the local Rockefellers, but hav-ing self-made wealth rather than actual noble blood, they were always a bit defensive. The Greek motifs along the eaves high-light the palace's Renaissance roots. Back then, rather than hav-ing parking spots, grand buildings came with iron rings to which you'd tether your horse.

You can step into the doorway at Via Cavour 1 and view the courtyard through an iron gate (though the entrance is farther up the street). If you pay admission, you get access to a quintessential Florentine palazzo with a courtyard and a couple of impressive rooms, most notably the sumptuous little Chapel of the Magi.

♦ See the Medici-Riccardi Palace Tour chapter.

• *Though we won't visit them on this walk, one block west of here are the Church of San Lorenzo (page 65), San Lorenzo street market (page 69), and Medici Chapels (♦ see the Medici Chapels Tour chapter). For now, return to the Duomo and continue south, entering the pedestrian-only street that runs from here toward the Arno River.*

Via de' Calzaiuoli

The pedestrian-only Via de' Calzaiuoli (kahlts-ay-WOH-lee) is lined with high-fashion shops, as Florence is a trendsetting city in trendsetting Italy. This street has always been the main axis of the city, and it was part of the ancient Roman grid plan that became Florence. In medieval times, this street connected the religious center (where we are now) with the political center (where we're heading), a five-minute walk away. In the 20th century, this historic core was a noisy snarl of car traffic. But traffic jams have been replaced by

potted plants, and now this is a pleasant place to stroll, people-watch, window-shop, lick the drips on your gelato cone, and wonder why American cities can't become more pedestrian-friendly.

And speaking of gelato...the recommended **Grom,** which keeps its *gelati* in covered metal bins, the old-fashioned way, is just a half-block detour away (daily 10:30-24:00, take your first left, to Via delle Oche 24 red). Or you could drop by any of the several nearby gelato shops. *Perché no?* (Why not?)

Continue down Via de' Calzaiuoli. Two blocks down from the Baptistery, look right on Via degli Speziali to see a triumphal arch that marks **Piazza della Repubblica.** The arch celebrates the unification of Italy in 1870 and stands as a reminder that, in ancient Roman times, this piazza was the city center. For more on this square, see page 78.

• *A block farther, at the intersection with Via Orsanmichele, is the...*

Orsanmichele Church— Florence's Medieval Roots

The Orsanmichele Church provides an interesting look at Florentine values. It's a combo church/granary. Originally, this was an open loggia (covered porch) with a huge grain warehouse upstairs. The arches of the loggia were artfully filled in (14th century), and the building gained a new purpose—as a church. This was prime real estate on what had become the main drag between the church and palace.

The niches in the walls stood empty for decades before sponsors filled them in with statues. That role fell to the rising middle class of merchants and their guilds.

Florence in 1400 was a republic, a government working for the interests not of a king, but of these guilds (much as modern America caters to corporate interests). Over time, various guilds commissioned statues as PR gestures, hiring the finest artists of the generation. As a result, the statues that ring the church (generally copies of originals stored safely in nearby museums) function as a textbook of the evolution of Florentine art.

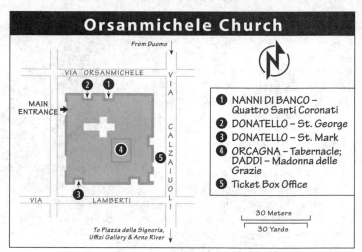

Orsanmichele Church

From Duomo

VIA ORSANMICHELE

MAIN ENTRANCE →

VIA CALZAIUOLI

VIA LAMBERTI

To Piazza della Signoria, Uffizi Gallery & Arno River ↓

1. NANNI DI BANCO – Quattro Santi Coronati
2. DONATELLO – St. George
3. DONATELLO – St. Mark
4. ORCAGNA – Tabernacle; DADDI – Madonna delle Grazie
5. Ticket Box Office

30 Meters
30 Yards

Orsanmichele Exterior

In earlier Gothic times, statues were set deep into church niches, simply embellishing the house of God. Here at the Orsanmichele Church, we see statues—as restless as man on the verge of the Renaissance—stepping out from the protection of the Church.

• *Head up Via Orsanmichele and circle the church exterior counterclockwise, looking out for these statues. Be careful not to stand right in the middle of the road—or at least keep an eye out for minibuses and horses.*

Nanni di Banco's *Quattro Santi Coronati* (c. 1415-1417)

These four early Christians were sculptors martyred by the Roman emperor Diocletian because they refused to sculpt pagan gods. They seem to be contemplating the consequences of the fatal decision they're about to make. Beneath some of the niches, you'll find the symbol of the guilds that paid for the art. Art historians differ here. Some think the work was commissioned by the carpenters' and masons' guild. Others contend it was by the guys who did discount circumcisions.

Donatello's *St. George* (c. 1417)

George is alert, perched on the edge of his niche, scanning the horizon for dragons and announcing the new age with its new outlook. His knitted brow shows there's a drama unfolding. Sure, he's anxious, but he's also self-assured. Comparing this Renaissance-style *St. George* to *Quattro Santi Coronati*, you can psychoanalyze the heady changes underway. This is humanism.

This *St. George* is a copy of the original (located in the Bargello, and described in the Bargello Tour chapter).

• *Continue around the corner of the church (bypassing the entrance for now), all the way to the opposite side.*

Donatello's *St. Mark* (1411-1413)

The evangelist cradles his gospel in his strong, veined hand and gazes out, resting his weight on the right leg while bending the left. Though subtle,

St. Mark's *contrapposto* pose (weight on one foot) was the first seen since antiquity. Commissioned by the linen-sellers' guild, the statue has elaborately detailed robes that drape around the natural contours of his weighty body. When the guild first saw the statue, they thought the oversized head and torso made it top-heavy. Only after it was lifted into its raised niche did Donatello's cleverly designed proportions look right— and the guild accepted it. Eighty years after young Donatello carved this statue, a teenage Michelangelo Buonarroti stood here and marveled at it.

• *Backtrack to the entrance and go inside.*

Orsanmichele Interior

Here's a chance to step into Florence, circa 1350. The church has

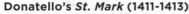

a double nave because it was adapted from a granary. Look for the pillars (on the left) with rectangular holes in them about three feet off the ground. These were once used as chutes for delivering grain from the storage rooms upstairs. Look up to see the rings hanging from the ceiling, likely used to make pulleys for lifting grain, and the iron bars spanning the vaults for support.

The fine **tabernacle** is by Andrea Orcagna. Notice how it was designed exactly for this space: Like the biggest Christmas tree possible, it's capped by an angel whose head touches the ceiling. Take in the Gothic tabernacle's medieval elegance. What it lacks in depth and realism it makes up for in color, with an intricate assemblage of marble, glass, gold, and expensive lapis lazuli. Florence had just survived the terrible bubonic plague of 1348, which killed half the population. The elaborate tabernacle was built to display Bernardo Daddi's *Madonna delle Grazie*, which received plague survivors' grateful prayers. While it's great to see art in museums, it's even better to enjoy it in its original setting—"in situ"—where the artist intended it to be seen. When you view similar altarpieces out of context in the Uffizi, think back on the candlelit medieval atmosphere that surrounds this altarpiece.

Upstairs is a free museum (open only one day a week: Mon 10:00-17:00) displaying most of the originals of the statues you just saw outside. Each one is identified by the subject, year, and sculptor, representing virtually every big name in pre-Michelangelo Florentine sculpture: Donatello, Ghiberti, Brunelleschi, Giambologna, and more.

Consider returning for one of the church's evening concerts; tickets are sold on the day of the concert from the door facing Via de' Calzaiuoli (see Orsanmichele Church map). You can also book tickets here for the Uffizi and Accademia.

• *The Bargello, with Florence's best collection of sculpture, is a few blocks east, down Via dei Tavolini. (❂ See the Bargello Tour chapter.) But let's continue down the mall 50 more yards, to the huge and historic square, Piazza della Signoria.*

Palazzo Vecchio—Florence's Political Center

The main civic center of Florence is dominated by the Palazzo Vecchio, the Uffizi Gallery, and the marble greatness of old Florence littering the cobbles. Piazza della Signoria still vibrates with the echoes of Florence's past—executions, riots, and great celebrations. There's even Roman history: Look for the **chart** showing the ancient city (on a waist-high, freestanding display to your right as you enter the square). Today, it's a tourist's world with pigeons, postcards, horse buggies, and tired hubbies. If it would make your weary companion happy, stop in at the recommended but expensive **Rivoire** café to enjoy its fine desserts, pudding-thick hot chocolate, and the best view seats in town. It's expensive—but if you linger, it can be a great value.

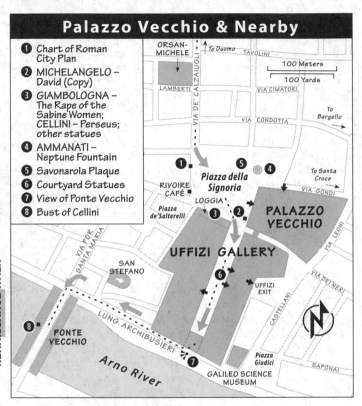

Palazzo Vecchio & Nearby

1 Chart of Roman City Plan

2 MICHELANGELO – David (Copy)

3 GIAMBOLOGNA – The Rape of the Sabine Women; CELLINI – Perseus; other statues

4 AMMANATI – Neptune Fountain

5 Savonarola Plaque

6 Courtyard Statues

7 View of Ponte Vecchio

8 Bust of Cellini

RENAISSANCE WALK

Before you towers the Palazzo Vecchio, the palatial Town Hall of the Medici—a fortress designed to contain riches and survive the many riots that went with local politics. The windows are just beyond the reach of angry stones, and the tower was a handy lookout post. Justice was doled out sternly on this square. Until 1873, Michelangelo's *David* stood where you see the replica today. The original was damaged in a 1527 riot (when a bench thrown from a palace window knocked its left arm off), but remained here for several centuries, vulnerable to erosion and pollution until it was moved indoors for its own protection.

Step past the replica *David* through the front door into the Palazzo Vecchio's courtyard (free). This palace was Florence's symbol of civic power. You're surrounded by art for art's sake—a cherub frivolously marks the courtyard's center, and ornate stuccoes and frescoes decorate the walls and columns. Such luxury represented a big change 500 years ago. For a self-guided tour of the palace, including more on this courtyard, ✪ see the Palazzo Vecchio Tour chapter.

• *Back outside, check out the statue-filled...*

Loggia dei Lanzi (a.k.a. Loggia della Signoria)

The loggia, once a forum for public debate, was perfect for a city that prided itself on its democratic traditions. But later, when the Medici figured that good art was more desirable than free speech, it was turned into an outdoor sculpture gallery. Notice the squirm-

ing Florentine themes—conquest, domination, rape, and decapitation. The statues lining the back are Roman originals brought back to Florence by a Medici when he moved home after living in Rome. Two statues in the front deserve a closer look.

The Rape of the Sabine Women, with its pulse-quickening rhythm of muscles, is from the restless Mannerist period, which followed the stately and confident Renaissance (c. 1583). The sculptor, Giambologna, proved his mastery of the medium by sculpting three entangled

bodies from one piece of marble. The composition is best viewed from below and in front. The relief panel below shows a wider view of the terrible scene. Note what looks like an IV tube on the arm of the horrified husband. It's an electrified wire that effectively keeps the pigeons away. (In the Accademia, you can see the plaster model of this statue that was used to guide Giambologna's

workers in helping him create it.)

Benvenuto **Cellini's** *Perseus* (1545-1553), the loggia's most noteworthy piece, shows the Greek hero who decapitated the snake-headed Medusa. They say Medusa was so ugly she turned humans who looked at her to stone—though one of this book's authors thinks she's kinda cute.

• *Cross the square to the big* **fountain of Neptune** *by Bartolomeo Ammanati that Florentines (including Michelangelo) consider a huge waste of marble—though one of this book's authors...*

The guy on the horse, to the left, is Cosimo I, one of the post-Renaissance Medici. Find the round bronze plaque on the ground 10 steps in front of the fountain.

Savonarola Plaque

The Medici family was briefly thrown from power by an austere monk named Savonarola, who made Florence a constitutional republic. He organized huge rallies lit by roaring bonfires here on the square where he preached. While children sang hymns, the devout brought their rich "vanities" (such as paintings, musical instruments, and playing cards) and threw them into the flames.

But not everyone wanted a return to the medieval past. Encouraged by the pope, the Florentines fought back and arrested Savonarola. For two days, they tortured him, trying unsuccessfully to persuade him to see their side of things. Finally, on the very spot where Savonarola's followers had built bonfires of vanities, the monk was burned. The bronze plaque, engraved in Italian *("Qui dove...")*, reads, "Here, Girolamo Savonarola and his Dominican brothers were hanged and burned" in the year "MCCCCXCVIII" (1498). For help in deciphering Roman numerals, see page 583.

• *Stay cool, we have 200 yards to go. Follow the gaze of the fake* David *into the courtyard of the two-tone horseshoe-shaped building...*

Uffizi Courtyard— The Renaissance Hall of Fame

The top floor of this building, known as the *uffizi* (offices) during Medici days, is filled with the greatest collection of Florentine painting anywhere. It's one of Europe's top four or five art galleries (❂ see the Uffizi Gallery Tour chapter).

The Uffizi courtyard, filled with merchants and hustling young artists, is watched over by 19th-century statues of the great figures of the Renaissance. Tourists zero in on the visual accomplishments of the era—not realizing that it was many-faceted. Let's pay tribute to the non-visual Renaissance as well, as we wander through Florence's Hall of Fame.

• *Stroll down the left side of the courtyard from the Palazzo Vecchio to the river, noticing the following greats.*

1. Lorenzo de' Medici (the Magnificent)—

LORENZO IL MAGNIFICO

RENAISSANCE WALK

whose statue is tucked under the arcade, by an Uffizi door-way—was a great art patron and cunning power broker. Excelling in everything except modesty, he set the tone for the Renaissance.

2. **Giotto,** holding the plan to the city's bell tower—named for him—was the great pre-Renaissance artist whose paintings foretold the future of Italian art.

3. **Donatello,** the sculptor who served as a role model for Michelangelo, holds a hammer and chisel.

4. **Alberti** wrote a famous book, *On Painting,* which taught early Renaissance artists the mathematics of perspective.

5. **Leonardo da Vinci** was a scientist, sculptor, musician, engineer...and not a bad painter either.

6. **Michelangelo** ponders the universe and/or stifles a belch.

7. **Dante,** with the laurel-leaf crown and lyre of a poet, says, "I am the father of the Italian language." He was the first Italian to write a popular work *(The Divine Comedy)* in non-Latin, using the Florentine dialect, which soon became "Italian" throughout the country.

8. The poet **Petrarch** wears laurel leaves from Greece, a robe from Rome, and a belt from Wal-Mart.

9. **Boccaccio** wrote *The Decameron,* stories told to pass the time during the 1348 Black Death.

10. The devious-looking **Machiavelli** is hatching a plot—his book *The Prince* taught that the end justifies the means, paving the way for the slick-and-cunning "Machiavellian" politics of today.

11. **Vespucci** (in the corner) was an explorer who gave his first name, Amerigo, to a fledgling New World.

12. **Galileo** (in the other corner) holds the humble telescope he used to spot the moons of Jupiter.

NICCOLÒ MACCHIAVELLI

• *Pause at the Arno River, overlooking Ponte Vecchio.*

Ponte Vecchio

Before you is Ponte Vecchio (Old Bridge). A bridge has spanned this narrowest part of the Arno since Roman times. While Rome "fell," Florence never really did, remaining a bustling trade center along the river. To get into the exclusive little park below (on the north bank), you'll need to join the Florence rowing club.

• *Finish your walk by hiking to the center of the bridge.*

A fine bust of the great goldsmith Cellini graces the central point of the bridge. This statue is a reminder that, in the 1500s, the Medici booted out the bridge's butchers and tanners and installed the gold- and silversmiths who still tempt visitors to this day. This is a very romantic spot late at night (when lovers gather, and a top-notch street musician performs). For more on this bridge, ❂ see the start of the Oltrarno Walk.

Look up to notice the protected and elevated passageway that led the Medici from the Palazzo Vecchio through the Uffizi, across Ponte Vecchio, and up to the immense Pitti Palace, four blocks beyond the bridge. During World War II, the Nazi occupiers were ordered to blow up Ponte Vecchio. An art-loving German consul intervened and saved the bridge. The buildings at either end were destroyed, leaving the bridge impassable but intact. *Grazie.*

ACCADEMIA TOUR: MICHELANGELO'S *DAVID*

Galleria dell'Accademia

One of Europe's great thrills is actually seeing Michelangelo's *David* in the flesh. Seventeen feet high, gleaming white, and exalted by a halo-like dome over his head, *David* rarely disappoints, even for those with high expectations. And the Accademia doesn't stop there. With a handful of other Michelangelo statues and a few other interesting sights, it makes for an uplifting visit that isn't overwhelming. *David* is a must-see on any visit to Florence, so plan for it.

Orientation

Cost: €6.50, temporary exhibits raise price to €11, additional €4 fee for recommended reservation; covered by Firenze Card.

Hours: Tue-Sun 8:15-18:50, closed Mon, last entry 30 minutes before closing.

Avoiding Lines: In peak season (April-Oct), it's smart to buy a Firenze Card or reserve ahead (see page 57 for info on both options). Those with reservations or the Firenze Card line up at the entrance labeled *With Reservations*. If you show up without a reservation or Firenze Card, and there's a long line, try dropping by the My Accademia Libreria reservation office, just across the street from the exit, to see if they have any reservations available later that day (€4 reservation charge). On off-season weekdays (Nov-March) before 8:30 or after 16:00, you can sometimes get in with no reservation and no lines.

When to Go: In peak season, the museum is most crowded on Sun, Tue, and between about 11:00 and 13:00.

Getting There: It's at Via Ricasoli 60, a 15-minute walk from the train station or a 10-minute walk northeast of the Duomo. Taxis are reasonable.

Information: Exhibits are explained in English, and a small book-store sells guidebooks near the ticket booths at the entrance. Another bookstore (inside and near the exit) and several shops outside sell postcards, books, and posters. Reservation tel. 055-294-883, www.polomuseale.firenze.it.

Audioguides: The museum rents a €6 audioguide (€10/2 people; rent from souvenir counter in ticket lobby). You can also download this chapter as a free Rick Steves audio tour (see page 41).

Length of This Tour: While *David* and the *Prisoners* can be seen in 30 minutes, allow an hour if you wish to linger and explore other parts of the museum.

Baggage Check: The museum has no bag-check service, and large backpacks are not allowed.

Services: The WCs are downstairs near the entrance/exit.

Photography: Photos and videos are prohibited.

Cuisine Art: Gelateria Carabè, popular for its sumptuous *granite* (fresh-fruit Italian ices) is a block toward the Duomo, at Via Ricasoli 60 red. Picnickers can stock up at Il Centro Supermercati, a half-block north (open daily, also has curb-side sandwich bar, Via Ricasoli 109). At Piazza San Marco, you can get pizza by the slice from Pugi (#10) and refill your water bottle (in the traffic circle park). See page 306 for eateries and picnic options.

Starring: Michelangelo's *David* and *Prisoners*.

The Tour Begins

• *From the entrance lobby, show your ticket, turn left, and look right down the long hall with* David *at the far end, under a halo-like dome. Yes, you're really here. With* David *presiding at the "altar," the* Prisoners *lining the "nave," and hordes of "pilgrims" crowding in to look, you've arrived at Florence's "cathedral of humanism."*

Start with the ultimate...

David (1501-1504)

When you look into the eyes of Michelangelo's *David*, you're looking into the eyes of Renaissance Man. This 17-foot-tall symbol of divine victory over evil represents a new century and a whole new Renaissance outlook. This is the age of Columbus and classicism, Galileo and Gutenberg, Luther and Leonardo—of Florence and the Renaissance.

In 1501, Michelangelo Buonarroti, a 26-year-old Florentine, was commissioned to carve a large-scale work for the Duomo. He was given a block of marble that other sculptors had rejected as too tall, shallow, and flawed to be of any value. But Michelangelo

picked up his hammer and chisel, knocked a knot off what became *David*'s heart, and started to work.

The figure comes from a Bible story. The Israelites, God's chosen people, are surrounded by barbarian warriors led by a brutish giant named Goliath. The giant challenges the Israelites to send out someone to fight him. Everyone is afraid except for one young shepherd boy—David. Armed only with a sling, which he's thrown over his shoulder, David gathers five smooth stones from the stream and faces Goliath.

The statue captures David as he's sizing up his enemy. He stands relaxed but alert, leaning on one leg in a classical pose known as *contrapposto*. In his powerful right hand, he fondles the handle of the sling, ready to fling a stone at the giant. His gaze is steady—searching with intense concentration, but also with extreme confidence. Michelangelo has caught the precise moment when David is saying to himself, "I can take this guy."

Note that while the label on *David* indicates that he's already slain the giant, the current director of the Accademia believes, as I do, that Michelangelo has portrayed David facing the giant. Unlike most depictions of David after the kill, this sculpture does not show the giant's severed head. There's also a question of exactly how David's sling would work. Is he holding the stone in his right or left hand? Does the right hand hold the sling's pouch or the retention handle of a sling? Scholars debate Sling Theory endlessly.

David is a symbol of Renaissance optimism. He's no brute. He's a civilized, thinking individual who can grapple with and overcome problems. He needs no armor, only his God-given body and wits. Look at his right hand, with the raised veins and strong, relaxed fingers—many complained that it was too big and overdeveloped. But this is the hand of a man with the strength of God. No mere boy could slay the giant. But David, powered by God, could... and did.

Originally, the statue was commissioned to stand along the southern roofline of the Duomo. But during the three years it took to sculpt, they decided instead to place it guarding the

ACCADEMIA

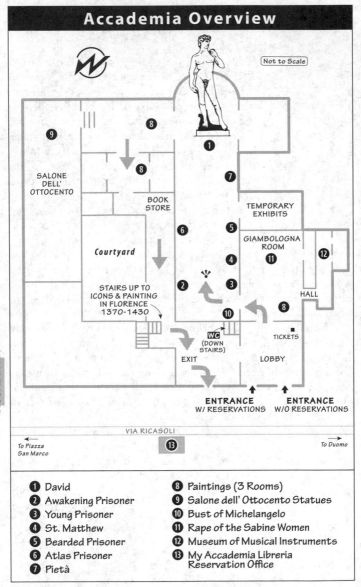

Accademia Overview

Not to Scale

SALONE DELL' OTTOCENTO

BOOK STORE

Courtyard

TEMPORARY EXHIBITS

GIAMBOLOGNA ROOM

HALL

STAIRS UP TO ICONS & PAINTING IN FLORENCE 1370-1430

WC (DOWN STAIRS)

TICKETS

EXIT

LOBBY

ENTRANCE W/ RESERVATIONS

ENTRANCE W/O RESERVATIONS

VIA RICASOLI

To Piazza San Marco

To Duomo

1. David
2. Awakening Prisoner
3. Young Prisoner
4. St. Matthew
5. Bearded Prisoner
6. Atlas Prisoner
7. Pietà
8. Paintings (3 Rooms)
9. Salone dell' Ottocento Statues
10. Bust of Michelangelo
11. Rape of the Sabine Women
12. Museum of Musical Instruments
13. My Accademia Libreria Reservation Office

entrance of Town Hall—the Palazzo Vecchio. (If the relationship between *David*'s head and body seems a bit out of proportion, it's because Michelangelo designed it to be seen "correctly" from far below the rooftop of the church.)

The colossus was placed standing up in a cart and dragged across rollers from Michelangelo's workshop (behind the Duomo) to the Palazzo Vecchio, where it replaced a work by Donatello. There *David* stood—naked and outdoors—for 350 years. In the right light, you can see signs of weathering on his shoulders. Also, note the crack in *David*'s left arm where it was broken off during a 1527 riot near the Palazzo Vecchio. In 1873, to conserve the masterpiece, the statue was finally replaced with a copy (see photo on bottom of page 115) and moved here. The real *David* now stands under a wonderful Renaissance-style dome designed just for him.

Circle *David* and view him from various angles. From the front, he's confident, but a little less so when you gaze directly into his eyes. Around back, see his sling strap, buns of steel, and Renaissance mullet. Up close, you can see the blue-veined Carrara marble and a few cracks and stains. From the sides, Michelangelo's challenge becomes clear: to sculpt a figure from a block of marble other sculptors said was too tall and narrow to accommodate a human figure.

Renaissance Florentines could identify with *David*. Like him, they considered themselves God-blessed underdogs fighting their city-state rivals. In a deeper sense, they were civilized Renaissance people slaying the ugly giant of medieval superstition, pessimism, and oppression.

• *Hang around a while. Eavesdrop on tour guides. The Plexiglas shields at the base of the statue went up after an attack by a frustrated artist, who smashed the statue's feet in 1991.*

Lining the hall leading up to David *are other statues by Michelangelo*—his Prisoners, St. Matthew, *and* Pietà. *Start with the* Awakening Prisoner, *the statue at the end of the nave (farthest from* David*). He's on your left as you face* David.

The Prisoners
(*Prigioni,* c. 1516-1534)

These unfinished figures seem to be fighting to free themselves from the stone. Michelangelo believed the sculptor was a tool of God, not creating but simply revealing the powerful and beautiful figures that God had encased in the marble. Michelangelo's job was to chip away the excess, to reveal. He needed to be in tune with God's will, and whenever the spirit came upon him, Michelangelo worked in a frenzy,

David, David, David, and *David*

Several Italian masters produced iconic sculptures of David—all of them different. Compare and contrast the artists' styles. How many ways can you slay a giant?

Donatello's *David*
(1430, Bargello, Florence)

Donatello's *David* is young and graceful, casually gloating over the head of Goliath, almost Gothic in its elegance and smooth lines. While he has a similar weight-on-one-leg *(contrapposto)* stance as Michelangelo's later version, Donatello's *David* seems feminine rather than masculine. (For further description, see page 153 of the Bargello Tour chapter.)

Andrea del Verrocchio's *David*
(c. 1470, Bargello, Florence)

Wearing a military skirt and armed with a small sword, Verrocchio's *David* is just a boy. The statue is only four feet tall—dwarfed by Michelangelo's monumental version. (For more, see page 153 of the Bargello Tour chapter.)

Michelangelo's *David*
(1501-1504, Accademia, Florence)

Michelangelo's *David* is pure Renaissance: massive, heroic in

without sleep, often for days on end.

The *Prisoners* give us a glimpse of this fitful process, showing the restless energy of someone possessed, struggling against the rock that binds him. Michelangelo himself fought to create the image he saw in his mind's eye. You can still see the grooves from the chisel, and you can picture Michelangelo hacking away in a cloud of dust. Unlike most sculptors, who built a model and then marked up their block of marble to know where to chip, Michelangelo always worked freehand, starting from the front and working back. These figures emerge from the stone (as his colleague Vasari put it) "as though surfacing from a pool of water."

The so-called *Awakening Prisoner* (the names are given by scholars, not Michelangelo) seems to be stretching after a long nap, still tangled in the "bedsheets" of uncarved rock. He's more block than statue.

On the right, the *Young Prisoner* is more finished. He buries his face in his forearm, while his other arm is chained behind him.

size, and superhuman in strength and power. The tensed right hand, which grips a stone in readiness to hurl at Goliath, is more powerful than any human hand. It's symbolic of divine strength. A model of perfection, Michelangelo's *David* is far larger and grander than we mere mortals. We know he'll win. Renaissance Man has arrived.

Gian Lorenzo Bernini's *David* (1623, Borghese Museum, Rome)

Flash forward more than a century. In this self-portrait, 25-year-old Bernini is ready to take on the world, slay the pretty-boy *David*s of the Renaissance, and invent Baroque. Unlike Michelangelo's rational, cool, restrained *David,* Bernini's is a doer: passionate, engaged, dramatic. While Renaissance *David* is simple and unadorned—carrying only a sling—Baroque Dave is "cluttered" with a braided sling, a hairy pouch, flowing cloth, and discarded armor. Bernini's *David,* with his tousled hair and set mouth, is one of us; the contest is less certain than with the other three *David*s.

To sum up: Donatello's *David* represents the first inkling of the Renaissance; Verrocchio's is early Renaissance in miniature; Michelangelo's is textbook Renaissance; and Bernini's is the epitome of Baroque.

The *Prisoners* were designed for the never-completed tomb of Pope Julius II (who also commissioned the Sistine Chapel ceiling). Michelangelo may have abandoned them simply because the project itself petered out, or he may have deliberately left them unfinished. Having perhaps satisfied himself that he'd accomplished what he set out to do, and seeing no point in polishing them into their shiny, finished state, he went on to a new project.

Walking up the nave toward *David,* you'll pass by Michelangelo's **St. Matthew** (1503), on the right. Though not one of the *Prisoners* series, he is also unfinished, perfectly illustrating Vasari's "surfacing" description.

The next statue (also on the right), the **Bearded Prisoner,** is the most finished of the four, with all four limbs, a bushy face, and even a hint of daylight between his arm and body.

Across the nave on the left, the **Atlas Prisoner** carries the unfinished marble on his stooped shoulders, his head still encased in the block.

More Michelangelo

If you're a fan of earth's greatest sculptor, you won't leave Florence until there's a check next to each of these:

- **Bargello:** Several Michelangelo sculptures, including the *Bacchus* (pictured here; see the Bargello Tour chapter).
- **Duomo Museum:** Another moving *pietà* (see page 181 of the Duomo Museum Tour chapter).
- **Medici Chapels:** The *Night* and *Day* statues, plus others done for the Medici tomb, located at the Church of San Lorenzo (see the Medici Chapels Tour chapter).
- **Laurentian Library:** Michelangelo designed the entrance staircase and more, located at the Church of San Lorenzo (see page 68).
- **Palazzo Vecchio:** His *Victory* statue (see page 195 of the Palazzo Vecchio Tour chapter).
- **Uffizi Gallery:** A rare Michelangelo painting (see page 142 of the Uffizi Gallery Tour chapter).
- **Casa Buonarroti:** Built on property Michelangelo once owned, at Via Ghibellina 70, containing some early works (see page 83).
- **Santa Croce Church:** Michelangelo's tomb (see page 83).
- **Santo Spirito Church:** Wooden crucifix thought to be by Michelangelo (see page 88).

As you study the *Prisoners*, notice Michelangelo's love and understanding of the human body. His greatest days were spent sketching the muscular, tanned, and sweating bodies of the workers in the Carrara marble quarries. The prisoners' heads and faces are the least-developed part—they "speak" with their poses. Comparing the restless, claustrophobic *Prisoners* with the serene and confident *David* gives an idea of the sheer emotional range in Michelangelo's work.

Pietà

In the unfinished *Pietà* (the threesome closest to *David*), the figures struggle to hold up the sagging body of Christ. Michelangelo (or, more likely, one of his followers) emphasizes the heaviness of Jesus' dead body, driving home the point that this divine being suffered a very human death. Christ's massive arm is almost the size of his bent and broken legs. By stretching his body—if he stood up, he'd be more than seven feet tall—the weight is exaggerated.

• *After getting your fill of Michelangelo, consider taking a spin around the rest of the Accademia. Michelangelo's statues are far and away the highlight here, but the rest of this small museum—housed in a former convent/ hospice—has a few bonuses.*

Paintings

Browse the pleasant-but-underwhelming collection of paintings in the hall near *David* and the adjoining corridor; you'll be hard-pressed to find even one by a painter whose name you recognize. (You'll find better art in the Giambologna Room near the exit; described below.)

Salone dell'Ottocento Statues

At the end of the hall to the left of *David* is a long room crammed with plaster statues and busts. These were the Academy art students' "final exams"—preparatory models for statues, many of which were later executed in marble. The black dots on the statues are sculptors' "points," guiding them on how deep to chisel. The Academy art school has been attached to the museum for centuries, and you may see the next Michelangelo wandering the streets nearby.

Bust of Michelangelo by Daniele da Volterra

At the end of the nave (farthest from *David*), a bronze bust depicts a craggy, wrinkled Michelangelo, age 89, by Daniele da Volterra. (Daniele, one of Michelangelo's colleagues and friends, is best known as the one who painted loincloths on the private parts of Michelangelo's nudes in the Sistine Chapel.) As a teenager, Michelangelo got his nose broken in a fight with a rival artist. Though Michelangelo went on to create great beauty, he was never classically handsome.

• *Enter the room near the museum entrance dominated by a large, squirming statue.*

Giambologna Room— *Rape of the Sabine Women* (1582)

This full-size plaster model guided Giambologna's assistants in completing the marble version in the Loggia dei Lanzi (on Piazza della Signoria, next to the Palazzo Vecchio, described on

ACCADEMIA

page 109). A Roman warrior tramples a fighter from the Sabine tribe and carries off the man's wife. Husband and wife exchange one final, anguished glance. Circle the statue and watch it spiral around its axis. Giambologna was clearly influenced (as a plaque with photo points out) by Michelangelo's groundbreaking *Victory* in the Palazzo Vecchio (1533-1534, described on page 195). Michelangelo's statue of a man triumphing over a fallen enemy introduced both the theme and the spiral-shaped pose that many artists imitated.

The room also contains minor **paintings** by artists you'll encounter elsewhere in Florence. There are works by Botticelli, whose *Birth of Venus* hangs in the Uffizi (see page 134). Filippino Lippi is known for his frescoes in the Brancacci Chapel and Church of Santa Maria Novella. Domenico Ghirlandaio's paintings of Renaissance Florence are behind the altar of the Church of Santa Maria Novella (see page 219). Fra Bartolomeo's dreamy portraits hang in the Museum of San Marco (see page 166). Benozzo Gozzoli decorated the personal chapel of the Medici in the Medici-Riccardi Palace (see page 211). And Francesco Granacci, a childhood friend of Michelangelo, assisted him on the Sistine Ceiling.

• *From the Giambologna Room, head down a short hallway leading to a few rooms containing the...*

Museum of Musical Instruments

Between 1400 and 1700, Florence was one of Europe's most sophisticated cities, and the Medici rulers were trendsetters. Musicians like Scarlatti and Handel flocked to the court of Prince Ferdinando (1663-1713). You'll see late-Renaissance cellos, dulcimers, violins, woodwinds, and harpsichords. (Listen to some on the computer terminals.)

As you enter, look for the two group paintings that include the prince (he's second from the right in both paintings, with the yellow bowtie) hanging out with his musician friends. The gay prince played a mean harpsichord, and he helped pioneer new variations. In the adjoining room, you'll see several experimental keyboards, including some by Florence's keyboard pioneer, Bartolomeo Cristofori. The tall piano on display (from 1739) is considered by some to be the world's first upright piano.

• *Head one more time back up the nave to say goodbye to Dave, then turn left, and left again, to go through the bookstore toward the exit. Before you leave—after the bookshop, but before the exit lobby—you'll see stairs up to one more exhibit. The stairwell is lined with a fine collection of Russian icons. At the top is...*

ACCADEMIA

Painting in Florence (Pittura a Firenze) 1370-1430

Here you'll find mostly altarpieces depicting saints and Madonnas, painted during the last gasp of the Middle Ages—the period after the Great Plague wracked Florence, but before Renaissance fever hit in full force. Gaze upon Lorenzo Monaco's *Arma Christi* (in the central hall, 1404), and mentally contrast this somber scene with the confident optimism of Michelangelo's *David*, done a century later, in the full bloom of the Florentine Renaissance.

• *The tour is finished. From here, it's a 10-minute walk to the Duomo.*

UFFIZI GALLERY TOUR

Galleria degli Uffizi

In the Renaissance, Florentine artists rediscovered the beauty of the natural world. Medieval art had been symbolic, telling Bible stories. Realism didn't matter. But Renaissance people saw the beauty of God in nature and the human body. They used math and science to capture the natural world on canvas as realistically as possible.

The Uffizi Gallery (oo-FEED-zee) has the greatest overall collection anywhere of Italian painting. We'll trace the rise of realism and savor the optimistic spirit that marked the Renaissance.

My eyes love things that are fair,
and my soul for salvation cries.
But neither will to Heaven rise
unless the sight of Beauty lifts them there.
　　—Michelangelo Buonarroti, sculptor, painter, poet

Orientation

Cost: €6.50, temporary exhibits raise price to €11, additional €4 fee for recommended reservation (if you've reserved tickets by phone, bring cash to pick them up); covered by Firenze Card.

Hours: Tue-Sun 8:15-18:35, closed Mon, last entry 30 minutes before closing.

Reservations: To avoid the notoriously long ticket-buying lines, either get a Firenze Card or book ahead (for details on both, see page 57). During summer and on weekends, the Uffizi can be booked up a month or more in advance. Sometimes, by the end of the day (an hour before closing), you can just walk right in, but generally you'll encounter lines even off-season (and waits up to three hours in peak season, April-Oct). The busiest days are Tuesday, Saturday, and Sunday.

Getting There: It's on the Arno River between the Palazzo Vecchio and Ponte Vecchio, a 15-minute walk from the train station.

Getting In: There are several entrances (see map on next page). Which one you use depends on whether you have a Firenze Card, a reservation, or neither.

Firenze Card-holders enter at door #1 (labeled *Reservation Entrance*), close to the Palazzo Vecchio. Read the signs carefully, as there are two lines at this entrance; get in the line for individuals, not groups.

People **buying a ticket on the spot** line up with everyone else at door #2. (The wait can be up to two hours.)

To **buy a Firenze Card,** or to see if there are any same-day reservations available (€4 extra, but could save you time in the ticket line), enter door #2 to the left of the ticket-buying line (marked *Booking Service and Today*).

If you've **already made a reservation** and need to pick up your ticket, go to door #3 (labeled *Reservation Ticket Office,* across the courtyard from doors #1 and #2). Tickets are available for pick-up 10 minutes before your appointed time. If you booked online, you've already prepaid with your credit card and just need to exchange your voucher for a ticket. If you (or your hotelier) booked by phone, you need to give them your confirmation number and pay for the ticket (cash only). Once you have your ticket, walk briskly past the 200-yard-long ticket-buying line—pondering the IQ of this gang—to door #1. Show your ticket and walk in.

Renovation: The Uffizi is undergoing a massive, years-long renovation that may affect your visit. Some of the items described in this chapter may be displayed in different rooms, on loan to other museums, or out for restoration—pick up a floor plan as you enter, and if you need help finding a particular piece of art, ask the guards in each room. (Rooms that are closed are posted at the entry.) On the plus side, new exhibition space is opening up all the time.

Information: There's little English (or Italian) information in the museum's rooms. For most travelers, my self-guided tour is enough, but if you want more information, you can buy Uffizi guidebooks at the ground-floor bookstore immediately upon entering, or from street vendors (€10 for basic book, €16 for more extensive version, both make good souvenirs).

UFFIZI GALLERY

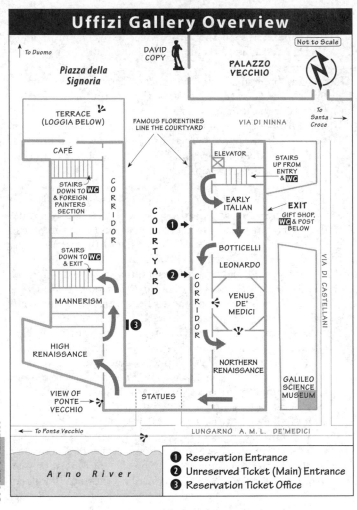

Uffizi Gallery Overview

Not to Scale

To Duomo

DAVID COPY

Piazza della Signoria

PALAZZO VECCHIO

TERRACE (LOGGIA BELOW)

To Santa Croce

FAMOUS FLORENTINES LINE THE COURTYARD

VIA DI NINNA

CAFÉ

ELEVATOR

STAIRS UP FROM ENTRY & WC

STAIRS DOWN TO WC & FOREIGN PAINTERS SECTION

CORRIDOR

EARLY ITALIAN

EXIT

GIFT SHOP, WC & POST BELOW

COURTYARD

❶

STAIRS DOWN TO WC & EXIT

BOTTICELLI

LEONARDO

❷

CORRIDOR

VENUS DE' MEDICI

MANNERISM

❸

VIA DI CASTELLANI

NORTHERN RENAISSANCE

HIGH RENAISSANCE

GALILEO SCIENCE MUSEUM

VIEW OF PONTE VECCHIO

STATUES

To Ponte Vecchio

LUNGARNO A. M. L. DE'MEDICI

Arno River

❶ Reservation Entrance
❷ Unreserved Ticket (Main) Entrance
❸ Reservation Ticket Office

Museum info tel. 055-238-8651, reservation tel. 055-294-883, www.uffizi.firenze.it.

Audioguides: A 1.5-hour audioguide costs €6 (€10/2 people; must leave ID). You can also download this chapter as a free Rick Steves audio tour (see page 41).

Length of This Tour: Allow two hours.

With Limited Time: See the Florentine Renaissance rooms (Botticelli and Leonardo) and the High Renaissance section (Michelangelo, Raphael, and Titian).

Cloakroom: Baggage check is available in the entrance lobby. No bottled liquids are allowed inside the museum.

Services: A post office and a book/gift shop are in the entrance/

exit hall on the ground floor (you'll walk right through the post office as you exit the museum). A large bank of WCs is in the basement below this hall—find stairs down near cloak-room (men use a unique marble wall/waterfall that's a urinal... or is it?). Once in the gallery, facilities are scarce—there are no WCs on the top floor (the focus of this tour), but there are some in the modern wing just downstairs from the café.

Photography: No photos are allowed.

Cuisine Art: The simple café at the end of the gallery has an out-door terrace with stunning views of the Palazzo Vecchio and the Duomo's dome. They serve €4-5 sandwiches, salads, des-serts, and fruit cups (cash only). You'll pay more to sit on the view terrace, but a €5 cappuccino outside, with that view, is one of Europe's great treats. You must finish all drinks before re-entering the museum.

Plenty of handy eateries are nearby and described in the Eating in Florence chapter.

Starring: Botticelli, Venus, Raphael, Giotto, Titian, Leonardo, and Michelangelo.

The Tour Begins

The Ascent

• *Walk up the four long flights of the monumental staircase to the top floor (those with limited mobility can take the elevator). Your brain should be fully aerated from the hike up. Past the ticket-taker, look out the window.*

The Uffizi is U-shaped, running around the courtyard. Except for a little Baroque spillover, the entire collection is on this one floor, displayed chronologically. This left wing contains Florentine paintings from medieval to Renaissance times. The right wing (which you can see across the courtyard) has art from the Roman and Venetian High Renaissance, works from the Baroque period that followed, and a café terrace facing the Duomo. A short hall-way with sculpture connects the two wings. We'll concentrate on the Uffizi's forte, the Florentine section, then get a taste of the art it inspired.

• *Head up the long hallway, enter the first door on the left, and face Giotto's giant* Madonna and Child *(straight ahead).*

Medieval—When Art Was as Flat as the World (1200-1400)

Giotto (c. 1266-1337)—*Madonna and Child with Angels (Madonna col Bambino in Trone e Angeli)*

Mary and Baby Jesus sit on a throne in a golden never-never land symbolizing heaven. It's as if medieval Christians couldn't

UFFIZI GALLERY

imagine holy people inhabiting our dreary material world. It took Renaissance painters to bring Mary down to earth and give her human realism. For the Florentines, "realism" meant "three-dimensional." In this room, pre-Renaissance paintings show the slow process of learning to paint a 3-D world on a 2-D surface.

Before concentrating on the Giotto, look at some others in the room. The **crucifixion** (on your right as you face the Giotto) was medieval 3-D: paint a crude two-dimensional work, then physically tilt the head forward. Nice try.

The three similar-looking Madonna-and-Bambinos in this room—all painted within a few decades of each other in about the year 1300—show baby steps in the march to realism. **Duccio**'s piece (on the left as you face Giotto) is the most medieval and two-dimensional. There's no background. The angels are just stacked one on top of the other, floating in the golden atmosphere. Mary's throne is crudely drawn—the left side is at a three-quarter angle while the right is practically straight on. Mary herself is a wispy cardboard-cutout figure seemingly floating just above the throne.

On the opposite wall, the work of **Cimabue**—mixing the iconic Byzantine style with budding Italian realism—is an improvement. The large throne creates an illusion of depth. Mary's foot actually sticks out over the lip of the throne. Still, the angels are stacked totem-pole-style, serving as heavenly bookends.

Giotto (JOT-oh) employs realism to make his theological points. He creates a space and fills it. Like a set designer, he builds a three-dimensional "stage"—the canopied throne—then peoples it with real beings. The throne has angels in front, prophets behind, and a canopy over the top, clearly defining its three dimensions. The steps up to the throne lead from our space to Mary's, making the scene an extension of our world. But the real triumph here is Mary herself—big and monumental, like a Roman statue. Beneath her robe, she has a real live body, with knees and breasts that stick out at us. This three-dimensionality was revolution-

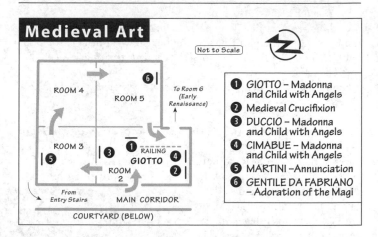

Medieval Art

Not to Scale

ROOM 4

ROOM 5

ROOM 3

ROOM 2

RAILING

GIOTTO

To Room 6
(Early
Renaissance)

From
Entry Stairs

MAIN CORRIDOR

COURTYARD (BELOW)

❶ GIOTTO – Madonna
and Child with Angels

❷ Medieval Crucifixion

❸ DUCCIO – Madonna
and Child with Angels

❹ CIMABUE – Madonna
and Child with Angels

❺ MARTINI –Annunciation

❻ GENTILE DA FABRIANO
– Adoration of the Magi

ary in its day, a taste of the Renaissance a century before it began.

Giotto was one of the first "famous" artists. In the Middle Ages, artists were mostly unglamorous craftsmen, like carpenters or cable-TV repairmen. They cranked out generic art and could have signed their work with a bar code. But Giotto was recognized as a genius, a unique individual. He died in a plague that devastated Florence. If there had been no plague, would the Renaissance have started 100 years earlier?

• *Enter room 3, to the left of Giotto.*

Simone Martini (c. 1284-1344)—*Annunciation (Annunciazione con i Santi Ansano e Massima)*

Simone Martini boils things down to the basic figures needed to get the message across: (1) The angel appears to sternly tell (2) Mary

that she'll be the mother of Jesus. In the center is (3) a vase of lilies, a symbol of purity. Above is (4) the Holy Spirit as a dove about to descend on her. If the symbols aren't enough to get the message across, Simone Martini has spelled it right out for us in Latin: *"Ave Gratia Plena..."* or, "Hail, favored one, the Lord is with you." Mary doesn't exactly look pleased as punch.

This is not a three-dimensional work. The point was not to re-create reality but to teach religion, especially to the illiterate masses. This isn't a beautiful Mary or even a real Mary. She's a generic woman without distinctive features. We know she's pure—not from her face, but only because of the halo and symbolic flowers. Before the Renaissance, artists didn't care about the beauty of individual people.

UFFIZI GALLERY

Simone Martini's *Annunciation* has medieval features you'll see in many of the paintings in the next few rooms: (1) religious subject, (2) gold background, (3) two-dimensionality, and (4) meticulous detail.

• *Pass through room 4, full of golden altarpieces, stopping at the far end of room 5.*

Gentile da Fabriano (c. 1370-1427)—*Adoration of the Magi (Adorazione dei Magi)*

Look at the incredible detail of the Three Kings' costumes, the fine horses, and the cow in the cave. The canvas is filled from top to bottom with realistic details—but it's far from realistic. While the Magi worship Jesus in the foreground, their return trip home dangles over their heads in the "background."

This is a textbook example of the International Gothic style popular with Europe's aristocrats in the early 1400s: well-dressed, elegant people in a colorful, design-oriented setting. The religious subject is just an excuse to paint secular luxuries such as jewelry and clothes made of silk brocade. And the scene's background and foreground are compressed together to create an overall design that's pleasing to the eye.

Such exquisite detail work raises the question: Was Renaissance three-dimensionality truly an improvement over Gothic, or simply a different style?

• *Exit to your right and hang a U-turn left into room 7.*

Early Renaissance (mid-1400s)

Paolo Uccello (1397-1475)—*The Battle of San Romano (La Battaglia di San Romano)*

(Consider yourself lucky if this painting, long under restoration, has returned for your visit.) In the 1400s, painters worked out the problems of painting realistically, using mathematics to create the illusion of three-dimensionality. This colorful battle scene is not so much a piece of art as an exercise in perspective. Paolo Uccello (oo-CHEL-loh) has challenged himself with every possible problem.

The broken lances at left set up a 3-D "grid" in which to place this crowded scene. The fallen horses and soldiers are experiments in "foreshortening"—diminishing the things that are farther away from us (which appear smaller) to create the illusion of distance. Some of the figures are definitely A-plus material, like the fallen gray horse in the center and the white horse at the far right walking away. But some are more like B-minus work—the kicking red

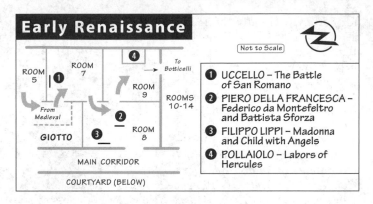

Early Renaissance

Not to Scale

ROOM 5

① ROOM 7

④ To Botticelli

ROOM 9

ROOMS 10-14

From Medieval

②

GIOTTO ③ ROOM 8

MAIN CORRIDOR

COURTYARD (BELOW)

❶ UCCELLO – The Battle of San Romano

❷ PIERO DELLA FRANCESCA – Federico da Montefeltro and Battista Sforza

❸ FILIPPO LIPPI – Madonna and Child with Angels

❹ POLLAIOLO – Labors of Hercules

horse's legs look like ham hocks at this angle, and the fallen soldier at the far right would be child-size if he stood up.

And then there's the D-minus "Are you on drugs?" work. The converging hedges in the background create a nice illusion of a distant hillside maybe 250 feet away. So what are those soldiers the size of the foreground figures doing there? And jumping the hedge, is that rabbit 40 feet tall?

UFFIZI GALLERY

Paolo Uccello almost literally went crazy trying to master the three dimensions (thank God he was born before Einstein discovered one more). Uccello got so wrapped up in it he kind of lost... perspective.

• *Enter room 8. In the center of the room stands a double portrait.*

Piero della Francesca (c. 1412-1492)—
Federico da Montefeltro and Battista Sforza
(Federico da Montefeltro e Battista Sforza)

In medieval times, only saints and angels were worthy of being painted. In the humanistic Renaissance, however, even nonreligious folk like this husband and wife had their features preserved for posterity. Usually the man would have appeared on the left, with his wife at the right. But Federico's right side was definitely not his best—he lost his right eye and part of his nose in a tournament. Renaissance artists discovered the beauty in ordinary people and painted them, literally, warts and all.

Fra Filippo Lippi (1406-1469)— *Madonna and Child with Angels (Madonna col Bambino e Angeli)*

Compare this Mary with the generic female in Simone Martini's *Annunciation*. We don't need the wispy halo over her head to tell us she's holy—she radiates sweetness and light

from her divine face. Heavenly beauty is expressed by a physically beautiful woman.

Fra (Brother) Lippi, an orphan raised as a monk, lived a less-than-monkish life. He lived with a nun who bore him two children. He spent his entire life searching for the perfect Virgin. Through his studio passed Florence's prettiest girls, many of whom decorate the walls here in this room.

Lippi painted idealized beauty, but his models were real flesh-and-blood human beings. You could look through all the thousands of paintings from the Middle Ages and not find anything so human as the mischievous face of one of Lippi's little angel boys.

• *Enter room 9, with two small works by Pollaiolo in the glass case between the windows.*

Antonio del Pollaiolo (c. 1431-1498)— *Labors of Hercules (Fatiche di Ercole)*

Hercules gets a workout in two small panels showing the human form at odd angles. The poses are the wildest imaginable, to show how each muscle twists and tightens. While Uccello worked on perspective, Pollaiolo studied anatomy. In medieval times, dissection of corpses was a sin and a crime (the two were the same then). Dissecting was a desecration of the human body, the temple of God. But Pollaiolo was willing to sell his soul to the devil for artistic knowledge. He dissected.

There's something funny about this room that I can't put my finger on...I've got it—no Madonnas. Not one. (No, that's not a Madonna; she's a Virtue.)

We've seen how Early Renaissance artists worked to conquer reality. Now let's see the fruits of their work, the flowering of Florence's Renaissance.

• *Enter the large Botticelli room and take a seat.*

Florence—The Renaissance Blossoms (1450-1500)

Florence in 1450 was in a Firenz-y of activity. There was a can-do spirit of optimism in the air, led by prosperous merchants and bankers and a strong middle class. The government was reasonably democratic, and Florentines saw themselves as citizens of a strong republic—like ancient Rome. Their civic pride showed in the public monuments and artworks they built. Man was leaving the protection of the church to stand on his own two feet.

Lorenzo de' Medici, head of the powerful Medici family, epitomized this new humanistic spirit. Strong, decisive, handsome, poetic, athletic, sensitive, charismatic, intelligent, brave, clean, and reverent, Lorenzo was a true Renaissance man, deserving of the nickname he went by—the Magnificent. He gathered Florence's best and brightest around him for evening wine and discussions of great ideas. One of this circle was the painter Botticelli (bot-i-CHEL-ee).

Sandro Botticelli (1445-1510)—
Allegory of Spring (Primavera)

It's springtime in a citrus grove. The winds of spring blow in (Mr. Blue, at right), causing the woman on the right to sprout flowers from her lips as she morphs into Flora, or Spring—who walks by, spreading flowers from her dress. At the left are Mercury and the Three Graces, dancing a delicate maypole dance. The Graces may be symbolic of the three forms of love—love of beauty, love of people, and sexual love, suggested by the raised intertwined fingers. (They forgot love of peanut butter on toast.) In the center stands Venus, the Greek goddess of love. Above her flies a blindfolded Cupid, happily shooting his arrows of love without worrying whom they'll hit.

Here is the Renaissance in its first bloom, its "springtime" of innocence. Madonna is out, Venus is in. Adam and Eve hiding their nakedness are out, glorious flesh is in. This is a return to the pre-Christian pagan world of classical Greece, where things of the

flesh are not sinful. But this is certainly no orgy—just fresh-faced innocence and playfulness.

Botticelli emphasizes pristine beauty over gritty realism. The lines of the bodies, especially of the Graces in their see-through nighties, have pleasing, S-like curves. The faces are idealized but have real human features. There's a look of thoughtfulness and even melancholy in the faces—as though everyone knows that the innocence of spring will not last forever.

• *Look at the next painting to the right.*

Botticelli—*Adoration of the Magi (Adorazione dei Magi)*

Here's the rat pack of confident young Florentines who reveled in the optimistic pagan spirit—even in a religious scene. Botticelli included himself among the adorers, at the far right, looking vain in the yellow robe. Lorenzo is the Magnificent-looking guy at the far left.

Botticelli—*Birth of Venus (Nascita di Venere)*

According to myth, Venus was born from the foam of a wave. Still only half awake, this fragile, newborn beauty floats ashore on a clam shell, blown by the winds, where her maid waits to dress her. The pose is the same S-curve of classical statues (as we'll soon see). Botticelli's pastel colors make the world itself seem fresh and newly born.

This is the purest expression of Renaissance beauty. Venus' naked body is not sensual, but innocent. Botticelli thought that

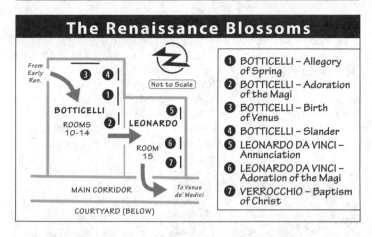

The Renaissance Blossoms

From Early Ren.

BOTTICELLI
ROOMS 10-14

LEONARDO
ROOM 15

MAIN CORRIDOR

To Venus de' Medici

COURTYARD (BELOW)

Not to Scale

1. BOTTICELLI – Allegory of Spring
2. BOTTICELLI – Adoration of the Magi
3. BOTTICELLI – Birth of Venus
4. BOTTICELLI – Slander
5. LEONARDO DA VINCI – Annunciation
6. LEONARDO DA VINCI – Adoration of the Magi
7. VERROCCHIO – Baptism of Christ

physical beauty was a way of appreciating God. Remember Michelangelo's poem: Souls will never ascend to heaven "...unless the sight of Beauty lifts them there."

Botticelli finds God in the details—Venus' windblown hair, her translucent skin, the maid's braided hair, the slight ripple of the wind god's abs, and the flowers tumbling in the slowest of slow motions, suspended like musical notes, caught at the peak of their brief life.

Mr. and Mrs. Wind intertwine—notice her hands clasped around his body. Their hair, wings, and robes mingle like the wind. But what happened to those splayed toes?

• *"Venus on the Half-Shell" (as many tourists call this) is one of the masterpieces of Western art. Take some time with it. Then find the small canvas on the wall to the right, near the* Allegory of Spring.

Botticelli—*Slander (La Calunnia)*

The spring of Florence's Renaissance had to end. Lorenzo died young. The economy faltered. Into town rode the monk Savonarola, preaching medieval hellfire and damnation for those who embraced the "pagan" Renaissance spirit. "Down, down with all gold and decoration," he roared. "Down where the body is food for the worms." He presided over huge bonfires, where the people threw in their fine clothes, jewelry, pagan books...and paintings.

Slander spells the end of the Florentine Renaissance. The architectural setting is classic Brunelleschi, but look what's tak-

ing place beneath those stately arches. These aren't proud Renaissance men and women but a ragtag, medieval-looking bunch, a Court of Thieves in an abandoned hall of justice. The accusations fly, and everyone is condemned.

The naked man pleads for mercy, but the hooded black figure, a symbol of his execution, turns away. The figure of Truth (naked Truth)—straight out of *The Birth of Venus*—looks up to heaven as if to ask, "What has happened to us?" The classical statues in their niches look on in disbelief.

Botticelli listened to Savonarola. He burned some of his own paintings and changed his tune. The last works of his life were darker, more somber, and pessimistic about humanity.

The 19th-century German poet Heinrich Heine said, "When they start by burning books, they'll end by burning people." After four short years of power, Savonarola was burned in 1498 on his own bonfire in Piazza della Signoria, but by then the city was in shambles. The first flowering of the Renaissance was over.

• *Enter the next room.*

Leonardo da Vinci (1452-1519)—*Annunciation (Annunciazione)*

A scientist, architect, engineer, musician, and painter, Leonardo was a true Renaissance man. He worked at his own pace rather than to please an employer, so he often left works unfinished. The

two paintings in this room aren't his best, but even a lesser Leonardo is enough to put a museum on the map, and they're definitely worth a look.

In the *Annunciation*,

the angel Gabriel has walked up to Mary, and now kneels on one knee like an ambassador, saluting her. See how relaxed his other hand is, draped over his knee. Mary, who's been reading, looks up with a gesture of surprise and curiosity.

Leonardo constructs a beautifully landscaped "stage" and puts his characters in it. Look at the bricks on the right wall. If you extended lines from them, the lines would all converge at the center of the painting, the distant blue mountain. Same with the edge of the sarcophagus and the railing. This subtle touch creates a subconscious feeling of balance, order, and spaciousness in the viewer.

Think back to Simone Martini's *Annunciation* to realize how much more natural, relaxed, and realistic Leonardo's version is. He's taken a miraculous event—an angel appearing out of the blue—and presented it in a very human way.

Leonardo da Vinci—*Adoration of the Magi* (*Adorazione dei Magi*)

(This piece may be under restoration during your visit.) Leonardo's human insight is even more apparent here, in this unfinished work.

The poor kings are amazed at the Christ child—even afraid of him. They scurry around like chimps around a fire. This work is as agitated as the *Annunciation* is calm, giving us an idea of Leonardo's range. Leonardo was pioneering a new era of painting, showing not just outer features but the inner personality.

The next painting to the right, **Baptism of Christ,** is by Andrea del Verrocchio, Leonardo's teacher. Leonardo painted the angel on the far left when he was only a teenager. Legend has it that when Verrocchio saw that some kid had painted an angel better than he ever would...he hung up his brush for good.

Florence saw the first blossoming of the Renaissance. But when the cultural climate turned chilly, artists flew south to warmer climes. The Renaissance shifted to Rome.

• *Exit into the main hallway. Breathe. Sit. Admire the ceiling. Look out the window. See you in five.*

Back already? Now continue down the hallway. On your left is the doorway to the recently renovated Tribuna (a.k.a. room 18). Gazing inside, you'll see the famous Venus de' Medici *statue.*

Classical Sculpture

If the Renaissance was the foundation of the modern world, the foundation of the Renaissance was classical sculpture. Sculptors,

Classical Sculpture & Northern Renaissance

ROOM 19

ROOM 20

To Sculpture Hall

ROOM 18 (TRIBUNA)

GLASS

GLASS

Not to Scale

From Leonardo

MAIN

CORRIDOR

COURTYARD (BELOW)

❶ Venus de' Medici
❷ Apollino
❸ The Wrestlers
❹ The Knife Grinder
❺ BALDUNG GRIEN – Copy of Dürer's Adam and Eve
❻ CRANACH – Adam and Eve
❼ CRANACH – Martin Luther and Katherina von Bora

painters, and poets alike turned for inspiration to these ancient Greek and Roman works as the epitome of balance, 3-D perspective, human anatomy, and beauty.

Venus de' Medici (Venere dei Medici)

Is this pose familiar? Botticelli's *Birth of Venus* has the same position of the arms, the same S-curved body, and the same lifting of

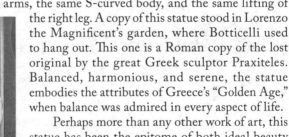

the right leg. A copy of this statue stood in Lorenzo the Magnificent's garden, where Botticelli used to hang out. This one is a Roman copy of the lost original by the great Greek sculptor Praxiteles. Balanced, harmonious, and serene, the statue embodies the attributes of Greece's "Golden Age," when balance was admired in every aspect of life.

Perhaps more than any other work of art, this statue has been the epitome of both ideal beauty and sexuality. In the 18th and 19th centuries, sex was "dirty," so the sex drive of cultured aristocrats was channeled into a love of pure beauty. Wealthy sons and daughters of Europe's aristocrats made the pilgrimage to the Uffizi to complete their classical education...where they swooned in ecstasy before the cold beauty of this goddess of love.

Louis XIV had a bronze copy made. Napoleon stole her away to Paris for himself. And in Philadelphia in the 1800s, a copy had to be kept under lock and key to prevent the innocent from catching the Venere-al disease. At first, it may be difficult for us to appreciate such passionate love of art, but if any generation knows the power of sex to sell something—be it art or underarm deodorant—it's ours.

The Other Statues

Venus de' Medici's male counterpart is on the right, facing Venus. *Apollino* (a.k.a. "Venus with a Penis") is another Greco-Roman interpretation of the master of smooth, cool lines: Praxiteles.

The other works are later Greek (Hellenistic), when quiet balance was replaced by violent motion and emotion. *The Wrestlers,* to the left of Venus, is a study in anatomy and twisted limbs—like Pollaiolo's paintings a thousand years later.

The drama of *The Knife Grinder* to the right of Venus stems from the off-stage action—he's sharpening the knife to flay a man alive.

This fine room was a showroom, or a "cabinet of wonders," back when this building still functioned as the Medici offices. Filled with family portraits, it's a holistic statement that symbolically links the Medici family with the four basic elements: air (weathervane in the lantern), water (inlaid mother of pearl in the dome), fire (red wall), and earth (inlaid stone floor).

• *Enter the next room past the Tribuna, then turn right into room 20.*

Northern Renaissance

Baldung Grien (c. 1484-1545)— Copy of Dürer's *Adam and Eve*

The warm spirit of the Renaissance blew north into Germany.

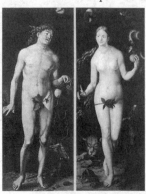

Albrecht Dürer (1471-1528), the famous German painter and engraver, traveled to Venice, where he fell in love with all things Italian. Returning home, he painted the First Couple in the Italian style—full-bodied, muscular (check out Adam's abs and Eve's knees), "carved" with strong shading, fresh-faced, and innocent in their earthly Paradise.

This copy of Dürer's original (now in the Prado) by Hans Baldung Grien was a training exercise. Like many of Europe's artists—including Michelangelo and Raphael—Baldung Grien learned technique by studying Dürer's meticulous engravings, spread by the newly invented printing press.

Lucas Cranach (1472-1553)—*Adam and Eve*

Eve sashays forward, with heavy-lidded eyes, to offer the forbidden fruit. Adam stretches to display himself and his foliage to Eve. The two panels are linked by smoldering eye contact, as Man and Woman awaken to their own nakedness. The Garden of Eden is about to be rocked by new ideas that are both liberating and troubling.

Though the German Lucas Cranach occasionally dabbled in the "Italian style," he chose to portray his Adam and Eve in the now-retro look of International Gothic.

They are slimmer than Dürer's, as well as smoother, more S-shaped, elegant, graceful, shapely, and erotic, with the dainty pinkies of the refined aristocrats who were signing Cranach's paycheck.

Though life-size, Adam and Eve are not lifelike, not monumental, not full-bodied or muscular, and are not placed in a real-world landscape with distant perspectives. Even so, Cranach was very much a man of the Renaissance, a friend of Martin Luther, and a champion of humanism.

• *Find a small, two-panel portrait featuring Martin Luther with his wife (or possibly a panel featuring Luther's colleague, Melanchthon; the museum rotates these two).*

Cranach—*Martin Luther*

Martin Luther—German monk, fiery orator, and religious whistle-blower—sparked a century of European wars by speaking out against the Catholic Church.

Luther (1483-1546) lived a turbulent life. In early adulthood, the newly ordained priest suffered a severe personal crisis of faith, before finally emerging "born again." In 1517, he openly protested

against Church corruption and was excommunicated. Defying both the pope and the emperor, he lived on the run as an outlaw, watching as his ideas sparked peasant riots. He still found time to translate the New Testament from Latin to modern German, write hymns such as "A Mighty Fortress," and spar with the humanist Erasmus and fellow-Reformer Zwingli.

In Cranach's portrait, Martin Luther (at age 46) is easing out of the fast lane. Recently married to an ex-nun, he has traded his monk's habit for street clothes, bought a house, had several kids...and has clearly been enjoying his wife's home cooking and home-brewed beer.

Cranach—*Katherina von Bora*

When "Katie" (well, Käthe) decided to leave her convent, the famous Martin Luther agreed to help find her a husband. She rejected his nominees, saying she'd marry no one...except Luther himself. In 1525, the 42-year-old ex-priest married the 26-year-old ex-nun "to please my father and annoy the pope." Martin turned his checkbook over to "my lord Katie," who also ran the family farm, raised their 6 children and 11 adopted orphans, and hosted Martin's circle of friends (including Cranach) at loud, chatty dinner parties.

• *Pass through the next couple of rooms, exiting to a great view of the Arno and Ponte Vecchio. Stroll through the...*

Sculpture Hall

A hundred years ago, no one even looked at Botticelli—they came to the Uffizi to see the sculpture collection. And today, these 2,000-year-old Roman copies of 2,500-year-old Greek originals are hardly noticed...but they should be. Only a few are displayed here now.

The most impressive is the male nude, *Doriforo* ("spear carrier"). Scholars have long suspected that this statue, a Roman marble copy of a Greek bronze original, once carried a lance in his left hand as he strolled along.

The purple statue in the center of the hall—headless and limbless—is a **female wolf** (*lupa*, c. A.D. 120) done in porphyry stone. This was the animal that raised Rome's legendary founders and became the city's symbol. Renaissance Florentines marveled at the ancient Romans' ability to create such lifelike, three-dimensional works. They learned to reproduce them in stone...and then learned to paint them on a two-dimensional surface.

• *Gaze out the windows from the hall for a...*

View of the Arno

Enjoy Florence's best view of the Arno and Ponte Vecchio. You can also see the red-tiled roof of the Vasari Corridor, the "secret" passage connecting the Palazzo Vecchio, Uffizi, Ponte Vecchio, and Pitti Palace on the other side of the river—a half-mile in all. This was a private walkway, wallpapered in great art, for the Medici family's commute from home to work.

As you appreciate the view (best at sunset), remember that it's this sort of pleasure that Renaissance painters wanted you to get from their paintings. For them, a canvas was a window you looked through to see the wide world. Their paintings re-create natural perspective: Distant objects (such as bridges) are smaller, dimmer, and higher up the "canvas," while closer objects are bigger, clearer, and lower.

We're headed down the home stretch now. If your little U-feetsies are killing you, and it feels like torture, remind yourself that it's a pleasant torture and smile...like the statue next to you.

• *In the far hallway, turn left into the first room (#25) and grab a blast of cold from the air-conditioning vent on the floor to the left.*

High Renaissance (1500-1550)— Michelangelo, Raphael, Titian

Michelangelo Buonarroti (1475-1564)—*Holy Family (Sacra Famiglia)*, a.k.a. *Doni Tondo*

This is the only completed easel painting by the greatest sculptor in history. Florentine painters were sculptors with brushes; this shows it. Instead of a painting, it's more like three clusters of statues with some clothes painted on.

The main subject is the holy family—Mary, Joseph, and Baby Jesus—and in the background are two groups of nudes looking like classical statues. The background represents the old pagan world, while Jesus in the foreground is the new age of Christianity. The figure of young John the Baptist at right is the link between the two.

This is a "peasant" Mary, with a plain face and sunburned arms. Michelangelo shows her from a very unflattering angle— we're looking up her nostrils. But Michelangelo himself was an

ugly man, and he was among the first artists to recognize the beauty in everyday people.

Michelangelo was a Florentine—in fact, he was like an adopted son of the Medici, who recognized his talent—but much of his greatest work was done in Rome as part of the pope's face-lift of the city. We can see here some of the techniques he used on the

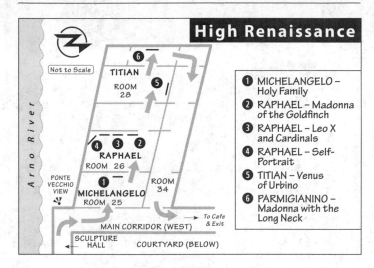

High Renaissance

Not to Scale

TITIAN
ROOM 28

RAPHAEL
ROOM 26

PONTE VECCHIO VIEW

MICHELANGELO
ROOM 25

ROOM 34

Arno River

MAIN CORRIDOR (WEST)

SCULPTURE HALL

COURTYARD (BELOW)

To Cafe & Exit

❶ MICHELANGELO – Holy Family
❷ RAPHAEL – Madonna of the Goldfinch
❸ RAPHAEL – Leo X and Cardinals
❹ RAPHAEL – Self-Portrait
❺ TITIAN – Venus of Urbino
❻ PARMIGIANINO – Madonna with the Long Neck

Sistine Chapel ceiling that revolutionized painting—monumental figures; dramatic angles (looking up Mary's nose); accentuated, rippling muscles; and bright, clashing colors (all the more apparent since both this work and the Sistine Chapel ceiling have recently been cleaned). These elements added a dramatic tension that was lacking in the graceful work of Leonardo and Botticelli.

Michelangelo painted this for his friend Agnolo Doni for 70 ducats. (Michelangelo designed, but didn't carve, the elaborate frame.) When the painting was delivered, Doni tried to talk Michelangelo down to 40. Proud Michelangelo took the painting away and would not sell it until the man finally agreed to pay double...140 ducats.

• *Enter room 26 and welcome back Raphael's* Madonna of the Goldfinch *after a laborious 10-year restoration.*

Raphael (Raffaello Sanzio, 1483-1520)—
Madonna of the Goldfinch
(La Madonna del Cardellino)

Raphael brings Mary and bambino down from heaven and into the real world of trees, water, and sky. He gives Baby Jesus (right) and John the Baptist a realistic, human playfulness. It's a tender scene painted with warm colors and a hazy background that matches the golden skin of the children.

Raphael perfected his craft in Florence, following the graceful style of Leonardo. In typical Leonardo fashion,

Six Degrees of Leo X

This sophisticated, luxury-loving pope was at the center of an international Renaissance world that spread across Europe. He crossed paths with many of the Renaissance men of his generation. Based on the theory that any two people are linked by only "six degrees of separation," let's link Leo X with the actor Kevin Bacon:

- Leo X's father was Lorenzo the Magnificent, patron of Botticelli and Leonardo.
- When Leo X was age 13, his family took in 13-year-old Michelangelo.
- Michelangelo inspired Raphael, who was later hired by Leo X.
- Raphael exchanged masterpieces with fellow genius Albrecht Dürer, who was personally converted by Martin Luther (who was friends with Lucas Cranach), who was excommunicated by...Leo X.
- Leo X was portrayed in the movie *The Agony and the Ecstasy,* which starred Charlton Heston, who was in *Planet of the Apes* with Burgess Meredith, who was in *Rocky* with Sylvester Stallone, who was in *Cop Land* with Robert De Niro, who was in *Sleepers* with...Kevin Bacon.

this group of Mary, John the Baptist, and Jesus is arranged in the shape of a pyramid, with Mary's head at the peak.

The two halves of the painting balance perfectly. Draw a line down the middle, through Mary's nose and down through her knee. John the Baptist on the left is balanced by Jesus on the right. Even the trees in the background balance each other, left and right. These things aren't immediately noticeable, but they help create the subconscious feelings of balance and order that reinforce the atmosphere of maternal security in this domestic scene—pure Renaissance.

Raphael—*Leo X and Cardinals*
(*Ritratta del Papa Leone X con i Cardinali*)

Raphael was called to Rome at the same time as Michelangelo, working next door in the Vatican apartments while Michelangelo painted the Sistine Chapel ceiling. Raphael peeked in from time to time, learning from Michelangelo's monumental, dramatic figures, and his later work is grittier and more realistic than the idealized, graceful, and "Leonardoesque" Madonna.

Pope Leo X is big, like a Michelangelo statue. And Raphael captures some of the seamier side of Vatican life in the cardinals' eyes—shrewd, suspicious, and somewhat cynical. With Raphael, the photographic realism pursued by painters since Giotto was finally achieved.

The Florentine Renaissance ended in 1520 with the death of Raphael. Raphael (see his **self-portrait** to the left of Leo X) is considered both the culmination and conclusion of the Renaissance. The realism, balance, and humanism we associate with the Renaissance are all found in Raphael's work. He

combined the grace of Leonardo with the power of Michelangelo. With his death, the Renaissance shifted again—to Venice.

• *Pass through the next room and enter Room 28.*

Titian (Tiziano Vecellio, c. 1490-1576)—*Venus of Urbino (Venere di Urbino)*

Compare this *Venus* with Botticelli's newly hatched *Venus,* and you get a good idea of the difference between the Florentine and Venetian Renaissance. Botticelli's was pure, innocent, and otherworldly. Titian's should have a staple in her belly button. This isn't a Venus, it's a centerfold—with no purpose but to please the eye and other organs. While Botticelli's allegorical *Venus* is a message, this is a massage. The bed is used.

Titian and his fellow Venetians took the pagan spirit pioneered in Florence and carried it to its logical hedonistic conclusion. Using bright, rich colors, they captured the luxurious life of happy-go-lucky Venice.

While Raphael's *Madonna of the Goldfinch* was balanced with a figure on the left and one on the right, Titian balances his paint-

ing in a different way—with color. The canvas is split down the middle by the curtain. The left half is dark, the right half lighter. The two halves are connected by a diagonal slash of luminous gold—the nude woman. The girl in the background is trying to find her some clothes.

By the way, visitors from centuries past also panted in front of this Venus. The Romantic poet Byron called it "*the* Venus." With her sensual skin, hey-sailor look, and suggestively placed hand, she must have left them blithering idiots.

• *Find the n-n-n-next painting...in Room 29.*

Parmigianino (1503-1540)—*Madonna with the Long Neck (Madonna della Collo Lungo)*

Raphael, Michelangelo, Leonardo, and Titian mastered reality. They could place any scene onto a canvas with photographic accuracy. How could future artists top that?

Mannerists such as Parmigianino tried, by going beyond realism, exaggerating it for effect. Using brighter colors and twist-

ing poses (two techniques explored by Michelangelo), they created scenes more elegant and more exciting than real life.

By stretching the neck of his Madonna, Parmigianino (like the cheese) gives her an unnatural, swanlike beauty. She has the same pose and position of hands as Botticelli's *Venus* and the *Venus de' Medici*. Her body forms an arcing S-curve—down her neck as far as her elbow, then back the other way along Jesus' body to her knee, then down to her foot. Baby Jesus seems to be blissfully gliding down this slippery slide of sheer beauty.

In the Uffizi, we've seen many images of female beauty: from ancient goddesses to medieval Madonnas to wicked Eves, from Botticelli's pristine nymphs to Michelangelo's peasant Mary, from Raphael's Madonna-and-baby to Titian's babe. Their physical beauty expresses different aspects of the human spirit.

• *As art moved into the Baroque period, artists took Renaissance realism and exaggerated it still more—more beauty, more emotion, more drama. There's lots of great stuff in the following rooms; just browse as you like.*

Pass through several rooms, returning to the main hallway. There's much more to be seen in the Uffizi. But first, head to the end of the hallway to the café for a true aesthetic experience.

Little Cappuccin Monk (Cappuccino)

This drinkable art form, born in Italy, is now enjoyed all over the world. It's called the "Little Cappuccin Monk" because the coffee's

frothy light- and dark-brown foam looks like the two-toned cowls of the Cappuccin order. Sip it on the terrace in the shadow of the towering Palazzo Vecchio, and be glad we live in an age where you don't need to be a Medici to enjoy all this fine art. *Salute.*

• *Once you're rested up, consider how much you want to tackle of...*

UFFIZI GALLERY

The Rest of the Uffizi

From the end of the gallery near the café, you'll find two stair-cases: one modern (right next to the café, with elevators), and one older (backtrack up the corridor, near room 41). The older staircase leads to an outside exit (offering a Caravaggio detour en route—described later); if you're ready to leave now, this is your quickest exit.

The modern staircase (with elevators), right next to the café, takes you down several flights to the new **Foreign Painters Section.** Loosely organized by nationality, this collection empha-sizes Flemish and Dutch painters. You'll see canvases by Steen, Van Dyck, Rubens, the Brueghel clan, and more. Room 49 dis-plays several Rembrandts, including two self-portraits. Paintings by artists from France, Spain, and other countries round out the collection. While there are few, if any, masterpieces here, this sec-tion would rank as a fine museum all on its own if it weren't over-shadowed by the Uffizi's substantial Italian collections.

If you're here after all the renovation work is finished, you may be able to exit the museum directly from the Foreign Painters Section. Until then, however, you'll likely have to climb the stairs (or take the elevator) back up to the top (café) level to find the sec-ond, older staircase.

The older staircase (near room 41), leads from the top floor down through a long series of temporary exhibition rooms. Near the end you can detour to the **Caravaggio Rooms**, which include the shocking ultra-realism of Caravaggio's *Sacrifice of Isaac*. The surrounding rooms feature many other works—by Caravaggio and his less-talented imitators—featuring his trademark *chiaroscuro* technique, which juxtaposes light and dark in high contrast.

• *As you head for the exit, you'll pass WCs (if the first one is too crowded, there's another farther along, plus the main WC in the basement under the entrance/exit hall).*

BARGELLO TOUR

The Renaissance began with sculpture. The great Florentine painters were "sculptors with brushes." You can see the birth of this revolution of 3-D in the Bargello (bar-JEL-oh), which boasts the best collection of Florentine sculpture. It's a small, uncrowded museum and a pleasant break from the intensity of the rest of Florence.

Orientation

Cost: €4, but mandatory special exhibits often raise the price to €7. Covered by Firenze Card.

Hours: Tue-Sat 8:15-13:50, until 16:50 during special exhibits (typically April-Oct); also open first, third, and fifth Mon and second and fourth Sun of each month; last entry 30 minutes before closing. You can reserve an entrance time, but it's unnecessary. Tel. 055-238-8606, www.polomuseale.firenze.it.

Getting There: It's located at Via del Proconsolo 4, a three-minute walk northeast of the Uffizi. Facing the Palazzo Vecchio, go behind the Palazzo and turn left. Look for a rustic brick building with a spire that looks like a baby Palazzo Vecchio. If lost ask, *"Dov'è Bargello?"* (doh-VEH bar-JEL-oh).

Getting In: You must pass through a metal detector to enter. No liquids are allowed in the museum.

Audioguide: You can rent one for €6 (€10/2 people).

Length of This Tour: Allow one hour.

With Limited Time: Be sure to see the Donatello room upstairs on the first floor, which has three statues of *David* side-by-side for easy comparison.

Photography: Permitted only in the courtyard.

Cuisine Art: Inexpensive bars and cafés await in the surrounding streets. See recommended eateries on page 308.

Starring: Michelangelo, Donatello, Brunelleschi, Ghiberti, and four different *David*s.

The Tour Begins

Courtyard

• *Buy your ticket and take a seat in the courtyard.*

The Bargello, built in 1255, was once Florence's original Town Hall and also served as a police station *(bargello)*, and later a prison. The

heavy fortifications tell us that keeping the peace in medieval Florence had its occupational hazards.

The Bargello, a three-story rectangular building, surrounds this cool and peaceful courtyard. The best statues are found in two rooms—one on the ground floor at the foot of the outdoor stair-

case, and another one flight up, directly above. We'll proceed from Michelangelo to Donatello to Verrocchio.

But first, meander around this courtyard and get a feel for sculpture in general and the medium of stone in particular. Sculpture is a much more robust art form than painting. Think of just the engineering problems of the sculpting process: quarrying and cutting the stone, transporting the block to the artist's studio, all the hours of chiseling away chips, then the painstaking process of sanding the final product by hand. A sculptor must be strong enough to gouge into the stone, but delicate enough to groove out the smallest details. Think of Michelangelo's approach to sculpting: He wasn't creating a figure—he was liberating it from the rock that surrounded it.

The Renaissance was centered on humanism—and sculpture is the perfect medium in which to express it. It shows the human form, standing alone, independent of church, state, or society, ready to create itself.

Finally, a viewing tip. Every sculpture has an invisible "frame" around it—the stone block it was cut from. Visualizing this frame helps you find the center of the composition.

Bargello—Ground Floor

50 Feet

To Duomo

VIA GHIBELLINA

TOWER

ENTRANCE → TICKETS

TEMPORARY EXHIBITS

COURTYARD

WELL

WC & ELEVATOR

VIA PROCONSOLO

STAIRS UP TO DONATELLO ROOM (FIRST FLOOR)

VIA DELLA VIGNA VECCHIA

To Palazzo Vecchio & Uffizi

To Santa Croce

① MICHELANGELO – Bacchus
② MICHELANGELO – Brutus
③ MICHELANGELO – David (Apollo)
④ Copies of Michelangelo's Works
⑤ DANIELE – Bust of Michelangelo
⑥ CELLINI – Models of Perseus (2)
⑦ GIAMBOLOGNA – Mercury
⑧ GIAMBOLOGNA – Florence Victorious over Pisa

Ground Floor

• *Head into the room at the foot of the courtyard's grand staircase. Enter, turn left, and watch for a party animal on the right.*

Michelangelo—*Bacchus* (*Baccho*, c. 1497)

Bacchus, the god of wine and revelry, raises another cup to his lips, while his little companion goes straight for the grapes.

Maybe Michelangelo had a sense of humor after all. Mentally compare this tipsy Greek god of wine with his sturdy, sober *David*, begun a few years later. Raucous *Bacchus* isn't nearly so muscular, so monumental...or so sure on his feet. Hope he's not driving. The pose, the smooth muscles, the beer belly, and swaying hips look more like Donatello's boyish *David*.

This was Michelangelo's first major commission. He often vacillated between showing man as strong and noble, or as weak and perverse. This isn't the nobility of the classical world, but the decadent side of orgies and indulgence.

• *Just beyond Bacchus is...*

Michelangelo—*Brutus* (*Bruto,* 1540)

Another example of the influence of Donatello is this so-ugly-he's-beautiful bust by Michelangelo. His rough intensity gives him

the look of a man who has succeeded against all odds, a dignified and heroic quality that would be missing if he were too pretty.

The subject is Brutus, the Roman who, for the love of liberty, murdered his friend and dictator, Julius Caesar *("Et tu...?").* Michelangelo could understand this man's dilemma. He himself was torn between his love of

the democratic tradition of Florence and loyalty to his friends the Medici, who had become dictators.

So he gives us two sides of a political assassin. The right profile (the front view) is heroic. But the hidden side, with the drooping mouth and squinting eye, makes him more cunning, sneering, and ominous.

• *Farther along is...*

Michelangelo—*David* (also known as *Apollo,* 1530-1532)

This restless, twisting man is either David or Apollo. (Is he reaching for a sling or a quiver?) Demure (and left unfinished), this statue is light years away from Michelangelo's famous *David* in the Accademia, which is so much larger than life in every way. We'll see three more *David*s upstairs. As you check out each one, compare and contrast the artists' styles.

In the glass cases in the corner, behind the partitions, are small-scale copies of some of Michelangelo's most famous works. Behind the adjacent pillar is a bust of Michelangelo by his fellow sculptor Daniele da Volterra, capturing his broken nose and brooding nature. (You may recognize this bust from the Accademia, which has a copy.)

• *Doubling back toward the entrance, you'll find...*

Cellini—Models of *Perseus* (*Perseo,* 1545-1554)

The life-size statue of Perseus slaying Medusa, located in the open-air loggia next to the Palazzo Vecchio, is cast bronze. Benvenuto Cellini started with these smaller models (one in wax, one in bronze) to get the difficult process down. When it came time to cast the full-size work, everything was going fine...until he realized he didn't have enough metal! He ran around the studio,

Donatello
(1386-1466)

Donatello was the first great Renaissance genius, a model for Michelangelo and others. He mastered realism, creating the first truly lifelike statues of people since ancient times. Donatello's work is highly personal. Unlike the ancient Greeks—but like the ancient Romans—he often sculpted real people, not idealized versions of pretty gods and goddesses. Some of these people are downright ugly. In the true spirit of Renaissance humanism, Donatello appreciated the beauty of flesh-and-blood human beings.

Donatello's personality was also a model for later artists. He was moody and irascible, purposely setting himself apart from others in order to concentrate on his sculpting. He developed the role of the "mad genius" that Michelangelo would later perfect.

gathering up pewterware and throwing it in, narrowly avoiding a mess-terpiece.

Giambologna—*Mercury* (c. 1564-1580)

Catch this statue while you can—he's in a hurry to deliver those flowers. Despite all the bustle and motion, *Mercury* has a solid Renaissance core: the line of balance that runs straight up the center, from toes to hip to fingertip. He's caught in mid-stride. His top half leans forward, counterbalanced by his right leg in back, while the center of gravity rests firmly at the hipbone. Down at the toes, notice the cupid practicing for the circus.

Giambologna—*Florence Victorious over Pisa (Firenze Trionfa su Pisa*, c. 1529-1608)

This sculpture shows the fierce Florentine chauvinism that was born in an era when Italy's cities struggled for economic and political

BARGELLO

dominance...and Florence won.
• *To see the roots of Florence's Renaissance, climb the courtyard staircase to the next floor up and turn right into the large Donatello room.*

First Floor
• *Entering the room, cross to the middle of the far wall, and check out the first of three Davids in this room (the one wearing the long skirt).*

Donatello—An early *David* (marble, 1408)
This is young Donatello's first take on the popular subject of *David* slaying Goliath. His dainty pose makes him a little unsteady on his feet. He's dressed like a medieval knight (fully clothed but showing some leg through the slit skirt). The generic face and blank, vacant eyes give him the look not of a real man but of an anonymous decoration on a church facade. At age 22, Donatello still had one foot in the old Gothic style. To tell the story of David, Donatello plants a huge rock right in the middle of Goliath's forehead.
• *From here, circle the room clockwise. The next statue is the same subject, by a different artist.*

Andrea del Verrocchio—*David* (c. 1470)

Verrocchio (1435-1488) is best known as the teacher of Leonardo da Vinci, but he was also the premier sculptor of the generation between Donatello and Michelangelo. Verrocchio's *David* is definitely the shepherd "boy" described in the Bible. (Some have speculated that the statue was modeled on Verrocchio's young, handsome, curly-haired apprentice, Leonardo da Vinci.) David leans on one leg, not with a firm, commanding stance but a nimble one (especially noticeable from behind). Compare the smug smile of the victor with Goliath's "Oh, have I got a headache" expression.
• *Finally, near the corner, is...*

Donatello—*David* (bronze, c. 1430)
He's naked. Donatello sees David as a teenage boy wearing only a helmet, boots, and sword (this sculpture is often cited by scholars who think the artist, who never married, was homosexual). The smooth-skinned warrior sways gracefully, poking his sword playfully at the severed head of the giant Goliath. His *contrapposto* stance is similar to Michelangelo's *David*, resting his weight on one

Bargello—First Floor

50 Feet

1 DONATELLO – David (1408)
2 VERROCCHIO – David (c. 1470)
3 DONATELLO – David (1430)
4 DONATELLO – Niccolò da Uzzano
5 DONATELLO – St. George
6 DESIDERIO (and DONATELLO) – St. John the Baptist
7 GHIBERTI and BRUNELLESCHI – Abraham Sacrificing Isaac (2 versions)
8 DELLA ROBBIA – Terra-Cotta Relief Panels

leg in the classical style, but it gives him a feminine rather than masculine look. Gazing into his coy eyes and at his bulging belly is a very different experience from confronting Michelangelo's older and sturdier Renaissance Man.

This *David* paved the way for Michelangelo's. Europe hadn't seen a freestanding male nude like this in a thousand years. In the Middle Ages, the human body was considered a dirty thing, a symbol of man's weakness, something to be covered up in shame. The church prohibited exhibitions of nudity like this one and certainly would never decorate a church with it. But in the Renaissance, a new class of rich and powerful merchants appeared, and they bought art for personal enjoyment. Reading Plato's *Symposium,* they saw the ideal of Beauty in the form of a young man. This particular statue stood in the palace of the Medici (today's Medici-Riccardi Palace)...where Michelangelo, practically an adopted son, grew up admiring it.

Now's a good time to compare the four different *David*s that we've seen. Verrocchio's saucy, impertinent *David* has more attitude than Donatello's generic warrior, and is younger and more masculine than Donatello's girlish, gloating *David*. He's more vig-

orous than Michelangelo's unfinished *David/Apollo* but he's a far cry from Michelangelo's monumental version.
• *Along the wall behind the last* David *is...*

Donatello—*Niccolò da Uzzano* (c. 1420)

Not an emperor, not a king, not a pope, saint, or prince, this is one of Florence's leading businessmen in a toga, portrayed in the style of an ancient Roman bust. In the 1400s, when Florence was inventing the Renaissance that all Europe would soon follow, there was an optimistic spirit of democracy that gloried in everyday people. Donatello has portrayed this man as he was—with wrinkles, a quizzical look, and bags under his eyes.
• *In the niche just above and to the right of* Uzzano, *you'll see...*

Donatello—*St. George* (*S. Giorgio,* 1416)

The proud warrior has both feet planted firmly on the ground and stands on the edge of his niche looking out alertly. He tenses his

powerful right hand as he prepares to attack. George, the Christian slayer of dragons, was just the sort of righteous warrior proud Renaissance Florentines could rally around in their struggles with nearby cities. Nearly a century later, Michelangelo's *David* replaced *George* as the unofficial symbol of Florence, but *David* was clearly inspired by *George*'s relaxed intensity and determination. (This is the original statue; a copy stands in its original niche at Orsanmichele Church—see page 105.)

The relief panel below shows George doing what he's been pondering. To his right, the sketchy arches and trees create the illusion of a distant landscape. Donatello, who apprenticed in Ghiberti's studio, is credited with teaching his master how to create 3-D illusions like this.
• St. John the Baptist, *begun by Donatello and finished by his student, is to the right.*

Desiderio da Settignano (and Donatello)—
St. John the Baptist (*San Giovannino,* c. 1455-1460)
John the Baptist was the wild-eyed, wildcat prophet who lived in

the desert preaching, living on bugs 'n' honey, and baptizing Saviors of the world. Donatello, the mad prophet of the coming Renaissance, might have identified with this original eccentric.

• *On the wall next to* George, *you'll find some bronze relief panels. Don't look at the labels just yet.*

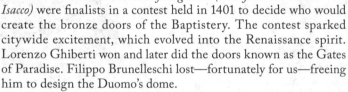

Ghiberti and Brunelleschi—Baptistery Door Competition Entries, titled *Abraham Sacrificing Isaac (Sacrificio di Isacco,* 1401)

Some would say these two different relief panels represent the first works of the Renaissance. These two versions of *Abraham Sacrificing Isaac (Sacrificio di Isacco)* were finalists in a contest held in 1401 to decide who would create the bronze doors of the Baptistery. The contest sparked citywide excitement, which evolved into the Renaissance spirit. Lorenzo Ghiberti won and later did the doors known as the Gates of Paradise. Filippo Brunelleschi lost—fortunately for us—freeing him to design the Duomo's dome.

Both artists catch the crucial moment when Abraham, obeying God's orders, prepares to slaughter and burn his only son as a sacrifice. At the last moment—after Abraham has passed this test of faith—an angel of God appears to stop the bloodshed.

Let's look at the composition of the two panels: One is integrated and cohesive (yet dynamic), while the other is a balanced knickknack shelf of segments. Human drama: One has bodies and faces that speak. The boy's body is a fine classical nude in itself, so real and vulnerable. Abraham's face is intense and ready to follow God's will. Perspective: An angel zooms in from out of nowhere to save the boy in the nick of time.

Is one panel clearly better than the other? You be the judge.

Ghiberti's, on the left, won.

Pictured at the bottom of the previous page are the two finalists for the Baptistery door competition—Ghiberti's and Brunelleschi's. Which do you like best?

It was obviously a tough call, but Ghiberti's was chosen, perhaps because his goldsmith training made him better suited for the technical end.

• *Cross all the way back to the far end of the room. Along the walls back near the entrance, you'll find several colorful terra-cotta reliefs.*

Luca della Robbia—Terra-Cotta Relief Panels

Mary and baby Jesus with accompanying angels look their most serene in these panels by the master of painted, glazed porcelain. Polished blue, white, green, and yellow, they have a gentle and feminine look that softens the rough masculine stone of this room. Luca was just one of a family of della Robbias who pioneered art in terra-cotta.

The Rest of the Bargello

You've already seen the undisputed highlights of this compact museum. With more time, you can do some exploring. Browse around the two upper floors, filled with objects that provide a look at life in Renaissance Florence. In the rooms branching off from the Donatello room are ivories, jewelry, and Renaissance dinnerware.

Also consider strolling through the easy-to-miss second floor. To reach it, exit the Donatello room through the same door you entered. Cross to the rooms on the other side of the courtyard. Take your first left, then immediately turn right and find the carpeted staircase (marked *Al 2° Piano*) that leads up to the second floor. (Note that the second floor is sometimes closed off-season.) Scattered through these rooms are medallions and terra-cotta panels of Mary with Baby Jesus, done by other members of the della Robbia clan. The most interesting room has large glass cases filled with miniature bronze models of famous statues. For example, look for small-scale, alternate versions of works by Giambologna, including his *Mercury* and *Rape of the Sabine Women*.

From swords to statues, from *Brutus* to Brunelleschi, from *David* to *David* to *David* to *David*—the Bargello's collection of civilized artifacts makes it clear why Florence dominated the Italian Renaissance.

BARGELLO

MUSEUM OF SAN MARCO TOUR

Museo di San Marco

Two of Florence's brightest lights lived in the San Marco Monastery, a reminder that the Renaissance was not just a secular phenomenon. At the Museum of San Marco, you'll find these two different expressions of 15th-century Christianity—Fra Angelico's radiant paintings, fusing medieval faith with Renaissance realism, and Savonarola's moral reforms, fusing medieval faith with modern politics.

Orientation

Cost: €4 or covered by Firenze Card.

Hours: Tue-Fri 8:15-13:50, Sat 8:15-16:50; also open 8:15-13:50 on first, third, and fifth Mon and 8:15-16:50 on second and fourth Sun of each month; last entry 30 minutes before closing. You can reserve an entrance time, but it's unnecessary.

Getting There: It's on Piazza San Marco, a block north of the Accademia, and several long blocks northeast of the Duomo (head up Via Ricasoli or Via Cavour).

Information: Consider picking up the compact, worthwhile, official guide (€9.50) at the bookstore. Tel. 055-238-8608, www .polomuseale.firenze.it.

Length of This Tour: Allow one hour.

Baggage Check: None is available, and large bags are not allowed in the museum (but if you ask nicely, the ticket-taker might watch your bag for you).

Photography: Prohibited.

Cuisine Art: See page 306 for recommended eateries nearby.

Starring: Fra Angelico's paintings and Savonarola's living quarters.

The Tour Begins

Overview

The ground floor features the world's best collection of Fra Angelico paintings. The upstairs contains the monks' cells (living quarters), decorated by Fra Angelico, and the cell of the most famous resident, Savonarola. Restoration is ongoing; expect that some paintings will be out and a room or two may be closed.

• *Buy your ticket and enter the courtyard/cloister.*

Ground Floor

The Courtyard/Cloister

Stepping into the cloister, you can feel the spirituality of this place, a respite from the hubbub of modern Florence. You'll see Renaissance arches frame Gothic cross-vaulting—an apt introduction to a monastery built during an optimistic time, when Renaissance humanism dovetailed with medieval spirituality.

In 1439, Cosimo the Elder (the founder of the Medici ruling dynasty and Lorenzo the Magnificent's grandpa) hired the architect Michelozzo to build the monastery, and invited Fra Angelico's Dominican community to move here from Fiesole. Fra Angelico (c. 1400-1455) turned down an offer to be archbishop of Florence, instead becoming prior (head monk). He quickly began decorating the monastery walls with frescoes.

• *From the entrance, walk straight ahead. On the wall at the end of the first corridor, in the corner of the cloister, is...*

Fra Angelico—*Crucifixion with St. Dominic* (*San Domenico in Adorazione del Crocifisso*)

The fresco by Fra Angelico shows Dominic, the founder of the order, hugging the bloody cross like a groupie adoring a rock star.

Monks who lived here—including Fra Angelico, Savonarola, and Fra Bartolomeo—renounced money, sex, ego, and pop music to follow a simple, regimented life, meditating on Christ's ultimate sacrifice.

Fra Angelico considered painting to be a form of prayer. He worked to bridge the gap between the infinite (Christ) and the finite (a mortal's ability to relate to God) by injecting an ethereal atmosphere into his frescoes.

• *Now head to the opposite corner of the cloister and enter the Hospice (Ospizio).*

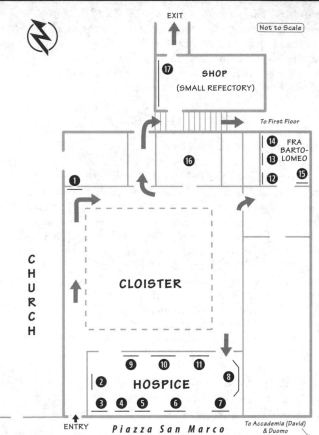

Museum of San Marco—
Ground Floor

EXIT

Not to Scale

17 SHOP
(SMALL REFECTORY)

To First Floor

14 FRA
BARTO-
13 LOMEO

16

12

15

1

C
H
U
R
C
H

CLOISTER

9   **10**   **11**

2   HOSPICE   **8**

3   **4**   **5**   **6**   **7**

ENTRY   *Piazza San Marco*   To Accademia (David)
& Duomo

1 FRA ANGELICO – Crucifixion
with St. Dominic

2 FRA ANGELICO – Deposition
from the Cross

3 FRA ANGELICO – Triptych of
St. Peter Martyr

4 FRA ANGELICO – Wedding &
Funeral of the Virgin

5 FRA ANGELICO –
Last Judgment

6 FRA ANGELICO – Door Panels
of a Silverware Storeroom

7 FRA ANGELICO – Lamentation

8 FRA ANGELICO – Altarpiece
of the Linen-Drapers

9 FRA ANGELICO –
Annalena Altarpiece

10 FRA ANGELICO –
San Marco Altarpiece

11 FRA ANGELICO – Bosco ai
Frati Altarpiece

12 FRA BARTOLOMEO –
Ecce Homo

13 FRA BARTOLOMEO –
St. Dominic

14 FRA BARTOLOMEO –
St. Thomas Aquinas

15 FRA BARTOLOMEO –
Portrait of Savonarola

16 FRA ANGELICO –
Crucifixion with Saints

17 GHIRLANDAIO –
Last Supper

The Hospice (Ospizio) and Nearby

Fra Angelico—equal parts monk and painter—fused early-Renaissance technique with medieval spirituality. His works can be admired for their beauty or contemplated as spiritual visions. Browse the room, and you'll find serene-faced Marys, Christs, and saints wearing gold halos (often painted on altarpieces), bright primary colors (red-blue-yellow/gold), evenly lit scenes, and meticulous detail—all creating a mystical world apart, glowing from within like stained-glass windows.

• *Start with the large three-peaked altarpiece—showing the* Deposition—*at the end of the room.*

Fra Angelico—*Deposition from the Cross* (*Pala di Santa Trinità*)

Christ's body is lowered from the cross, mourned by haloed women (on the left) and contemporary Florentines (right). There's a clearly

 defined foreground (the kneeling, curly-headed man and the woman with her back to us), background (the distant city and hills), and middle distance (the trees).

Though trained in medieval religious painting, Fra Angelico never closed his eyes to the innovations of the budding Renaissance, using both styles all his life. There are Gothic elements, such as the altarpiece frame, inherited from his former teacher (who painted the pinnacles on top). The holy wear halos, and the stretched-out "body of Christ" is symbolically "displayed" like the communion bread.

But it's truly a Renaissance work. The man in green, lowering Christ, bends forward at a strongly foreshortened (difficult to draw) angle. Christ's toes, kissed by Mary Magdalene, cross the triptych wall, ignoring the frame's traditional three-arch divisions. Fra Angelico was boldly "coloring outside the lines" to create a single, realistic scene.

And the holy scene has been removed from its golden heaven and placed in the first great Renaissance landscape—on a lawn, among flowers, trees, cloud masses, real people, and the hillsides of Fiesole overlooking Florence. Fra Angelico, the ascetic monk, refused to renounce one pleasure—his joy in the natural beauty of God's creation.

• *Moving counterclockwise around the room, you'll find the following works (among others).*

Fra Angelico—*Triptych of St. Peter Martyr*
(Trittico di San Pietro Martire)

In this early, more "medieval" work, Fra Angelico sets (big) Mary and Child in a gold background flanked by (small) saints standing obediently in their niches. When

he joined the Dominican community in Fiesole, the artist took the name Giovanni (as he was known in his lifetime), and he wore the same attire as these famous Dominicans (including St. Dominic, far left, and St. Thomas Aquinas, far right)—white robe, blue cape, and tonsured haircut.

Peter Martyr (next to Mary, with bloody head) exemplified the unbending Dominican spirit. Attacked by heretics (see the scene above Peter), he was hacked in the head with a dagger but died still preaching, writing with his own blood: *"Credo in Deum"* ("I believe in God").

• *Continuing counterclockwise, look at the two small panels sharing one long frame.*

Fra Angelico—Two Panels: *Wedding* and
Funeral of the Virgin (Sposalizio, Funerali della Vergine)

Fra Angelico's teenage training was as a miniaturist, so even these small predella panels (part of a larger altarpiece) are surprisingly

realistic. The folds in the clothes, the gold-brocade hemlines, and the precisely outlined people are as though etched in glass. Notice the Renaissance perspective tricks he was exploring, setting the wedding in front of receding

buildings and the funeral among candles that get shorter at the back of the scene.

• *Next up is...*

Fra Angelico—*Last Judgment*
(Giudizio Universale)

Despite the Renaissance, Florence in the 1420s was still a city in the Christian universe described by Dante. Hell (to the right) is a hierarchical barbecue where sinners are burned, boiled, and tortured by a minotaur-like Satan, who rules the

bottom of the pit. The blessed in heaven (left) play ring-around-the-rosy with angels. In the center, a row of open tombs creates a 3-D highway to hell, stretching ominously to that final Judgment Day.

• *On the other side of the pillar are several panels. Look at the one on the left.*

Fra Angelico (and Assistants)—*Door Panels of a Silverware Storeroom (Panelli dell'Armadio degli Argenti)*

The first nine scenes in this life of Christ (the big panel on the left end) are by Fra Angelico himself (the rest by assistants). Like storyboards for a movie, these natural, realistic, and straightforward panels "show" through action, they don't just "tell" through symbols. (The Latin inscription beneath each panel is redundant.) The miraculous is presented as an everyday occurrence.

1. The Wheel of Ezekiel (OK, that's medieval symbolism) prophesies Christ's coming.
2. In the Annunciation, the angel gestures to tell Mary that she'll give birth.
3. Newborn Jesus glows, amazing his parents, while timid shepherds sneak a peek.
4. Precocious Jesus splays himself and says, "Cut me."
5. One of the Magi kneels to kiss the babe's foot.
6. In the temple, the tiny baby is dwarfed by elongated priests and columns.
7. Mary and the baby ride, while Joseph carries the luggage.
8. Meanwhile, babies are slaughtered in a jumble of gore, dramatic poses, and agonized faces.
9. The commotion contrasts with the serenity of the child Jesus in the temple.

This work by 50-year-old Fra Angelico—master of many styles, famous in Italy—has the fresh, simple, and spontaneous storytelling of a children's book.

• *Near the left end of this wall is...*

Fra Angelico—*Lamentation (Compianto sul Cristo Morto)*

This painting of the executed Christ being mourned silently by loved ones was the last thing many condemned prisoners saw during their final hours. It once hung in a church where the soon-to-be executed were incarcerated.

The melancholy mood is understated, suggested by a series of horizontal layers—Christ's body, the line of mourners, the city

walls, landscape horizon, layered
clouds, and the crossbar. It's as
though Christ is being welcomed
into peaceful rest, a comforting
message from Fra Angelico to
the condemned.

"Fra Angelico" (Angelic
Brother) is a nickname that
describes the artist's reputation
for sweetness, humility, and compassion. It's said he couldn't paint
a Crucifixion without crying. In 1984, he was beatified by Pope
John Paul II and made patron of artists.

• *At the far end of the room hangs the...*

Fra Angelico—*Altarpiece of the Linen-Drapers (Tabernacolo dei Linaioli)*

Check out the impressive size and
marble frame (by Ghiberti, of baptistery-door fame), which attest to Fra
Angelico's worldly success and collaboration with the Renaissance greats.
The monumental Mary and Child,
as well as the saints on the doors, are
gold-backed and elegant, to please
conservative patrons. In the three
predella panels below, Fra Angelico
gets to display his Renaissance chops,
showing haloed saints mingling with
well-dressed Florentines amid local
cityscapes and landscapes. (Find
Ghiberti in the left panel, kneeling,
in blue.)

• *On the long wall are three similar-
looking altarpieces. Move left to right,
watching the...*

Evolution of the *Sacra Conversazione*

Fra Angelico (largely) invented what became a common
Renaissance theme: Mary and Child surrounded by saints "con-
versing" informally about holy matters. Four examples in this
room show how Fra Angelico, exploring Renaissance techniques,
developed the idea over his lifetime.

Fra Angelico—*Annalena Altarpiece (Pala d'Annalena)*

In the *Annalena Altarpiece* (c. 1435)—considered Florence's first
true *Sacra Conversazione*—the saints flank Mary in a neat line,

backed by medieval gold in the form of a curtain. Everyone is either facing out or in profile—not the natural poses of a true crowd. There's little eye contact, and certainly no "conversation."

Mary and Jesus direct our eye to Mary's brooch, the first in a series of circles radiating out from the center: brooch, halo, canopy arch, circle of saints. Set in a square frame, this painting has the circle-in-a-square composition that marks many *Sacra Conversaziones.*

Fra Angelico—*San Marco Altarpiece (Pala di San Marco)*

Cosimo the Elder commissioned this painting (c. 1440) as the centerpiece of the new church (next door). For the dedication Mass, Fra Angelico theatrically "opens the curtain," revealing a stage set with a distant backdrop of trees, kneeling saints in the foreground, and a crowd gathered around Mary and Child at center stage on a raised, canopied throne. The carpet makes a chessboard-like pattern to establish 3-D perspective. The altarpiece was like a window onto a marvelous world where the holy mill about on earth as naturally as mortals.

To show just how far we've come from Gothic, Fra Angelico gives us a painting-in-a-painting—a crude, gold-backed Crucifixion.

Fra Angelico—*Bosco ai Frati Altarpiece (Pala di Bosco ai Frati)*

This altarpiece (c. 1450) is Fra Angelico's last great work, and he uses every stylistic arrow in his quiver: detailed friezes of the miniaturist; medieval halos and gold backdrop; monumental, naturally posed figures in the style of Masaccio (especially St. Francis, on the left, with his relaxed *contrapposto*); 3-D perspective established by the floor tiles; and Renaissance love of natural beauty (the trees and sky).

Fra Angelico's bright colors are eye-catching. The gold backdrop sets off the red-pink handmaidens, which set off Jesus' pale skin. The deep blue of Mary's dress, frosted with a precious gold hem, turns out at her feet to show a swath of the green inner lining, suggesting the 3-D body within.

Despite Renaissance realism, Fra Angelico creates a world

of his own—perfectly lit, with no moody shadows, dirt, frayed clothing, or imperfection. The faces are certainly realistic, but they express no human emotion. These mortals, through sacrifice and meditation, have risen above the petty passions celebrated by humanist painters, to achieve a serenity that lights them from within.

• *From here, we'll circle the cloister counterclockwise. Exit the Hospice back into the courtyard, walk to the end of the corridor, and enter the next set of rooms (marked* Lavabo e Refettorio). *The small room on the left has paintings and fresco fragments by...*

Fra Bartolomeo

Fra Bartolomeo (1472-1517) lived and worked in this monastery a generation after the "Angelic" brother. *Ecce Homo* shows the kind of Christ that young, idealistic Dominican monks (like Fra Bartolomeo) adored in their meditations—curly-haired, creamy-faced, dreamy-eyed, bearing the torments of the secular world with humble serenity.

• *From Jesus, the third panel on the right is...*

Fra Bartolomeo—*St. Dominic (San Domenico)*

St. Dominic holds a finger to his lips—"Shh! We have strict rules in my order." Dominic (c. 1170-1221), a friend of St. Francis of Assisi, formed his rules after seeing the austere *perfetti* (perfect ones) of the heretical Cathar sect of southern France. He figured they could only be converted by someone just as extreme, following Christ's simple, possession-free lifestyle. Nearing 50, Dominic made a 3,400-mile preaching tour—on foot, carrying his luggage—from Rome to Spain to Paris and back. Dominic is often portrayed with the star of revelation over his head.

• *One more panel to the right is...*

Fra Bartolomeo—*St. Thomas Aquinas (San Tommaso d'Aquino)*

St. Thomas Aquinas (c. 1225-1274, wearing a hood)—the intellectual giant of the U. of Paris—used logic and Aristotelian models to defend and explain Christianity (building the hierarchical belief system known as Scholasticism). He's often shown with a heavy build and the sun of knowledge burning in his chest.

• *As you face the door, to the left you'll see...*

Fra Bartolomeo—*Portrait of Savonarola (Ritratto di Fra' Girolamo Savonarola)*

This is the famous portrait—in profile, hooded, with big nose and

clear eyes, gazing intently into the
darkness—of the man reviled as the
evil opponent of Renaissance goodness. Would it surprise you to learn
that it was Savonarola who inspired
Fra Bartolomeo's art? Bartolomeo was
so moved by Savonarola's sermons
that he burned his early nude paintings (and back issues of *Penthouse*),
became a monk, gave up painting for a
few years...then resurfaced to paint the
simple, sweet frescoes we see here.

• *Leaving the world of Fra Bartolomeo, return to the courtyard and continue to the next room (Capitolo), which contains the large wall fresco...*

Fra Angelico—*Crucifixion with Saints (Crocifissione dell'Angelico)*

This Crucifixion, against a bleak background, is one of more than
20 versions of Christ's torture/execution in the monastery. It was

in this room that naughty monks
were examined and judged.

Among the group of hermits,
martyrs, and religious extremists
who surround the cross, locate
Dominic (kneeling at the foot
of the cross, in Dominican white
robe, blue cape, and tonsured
hair, with star on head), Peter Martyr (kneeling in right corner,
with bloody head), and Thomas Aquinas (standing behind Peter,
with jowls and sun on chest).

The bell in the room is the original church bell, the one that
rang a warning to Savonarola the night he was arrested. (The mob
was so enraged that they exiled the bell for 10 years.)

• *Return to the courtyard, go through the next door, and head upstairs
to the first floor. At the top of the staircase, you'll come face-to-face with
Fra Angelico's* Annunciation.

First Floor

Fra Angelico—*Annunciation (Annunciazione)*

Sway back and forth and watch the angel's wings sparkle (from
glitter mixed into the fresco) as he delivers "the good news" to the
very humble and accepting Virgin. Mary is under an arcade that's
remarkably similar to the one in the monastery courtyard. Fra
Angelico brings this scene home to the monks quite literally.

Paintings such as this one made Fra Angelico so famous that

Museum of San Marco—First Floor

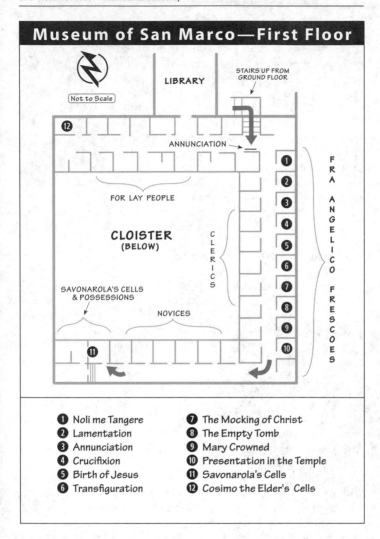

Not to Scale

LIBRARY

STAIRS UP FROM
GROUND FLOOR

ANNUNCIATION

FRA ANGELICO FRESCOES

FOR LAY PEOPLE

CLOISTER
(BELOW)

CLERICS

SAVONAROLA'S CELLS
& POSSESSIONS

NOVICES

❶ Noli me Tangere
❷ Lamentation
❸ Annunciation
❹ Crucifixion
❺ Birth of Jesus
❻ Transfiguration
❼ The Mocking of Christ
❽ The Empty Tomb
❾ Mary Crowned
❿ Presentation in the Temple
⓫ Savonarola's Cells
⓬ Cosimo the Elder's Cells

the pope called on him to paint the Vatican. Yet this work, like the other frescoes here, was meant only for the private eyes of humble monks. Monks gathered near the *Annunciation* for common prayers, contemplating Christ's life from beginning *(Annunciation)* to end *(Crucifixion with St. Dominic*, over your shoulder). The caption reads: Remember to say your Hail Marys.

The Monastery's Living Quarters

This floor is lined with the cells (bedrooms) of those who lived in the monastery: monks (in the corridor to your left), novice monks (farther down), and lay people and support staff (to your right).

We'll see Savonarola's quarters in the far corner. Each room was frescoed by Fra Angelico or his assistants.

• *From the* Annunciation, *take a few steps to the left, and look down the (east) corridor lined with monks' cells to find...*

Fra Angelico's Frescoes

After a long day of prayer, meditation, reading, frugal meals, chopping wood, hauling water, translating Greek, attending Mass, and more prayer, a monk retired to one of these small, bare, lamp-lit rooms. His "late-night TV" was programmed by the prior—Fra Angelico—in the form of a fresco to meditate on before sleep. In monastic life, everything is a form of prayer. Pondering these scenes, monks learned the various aspects of worship: humility, adoration, flagellation, reflection, and so on.

All in all, 43 cells were decorated in the early 1440s by Fra Angelico and his assistants. Many feature a crucifix and St. Dominic, but each shows Dominic in a different physical posture (kneeling, head bowed, head raised, hands folded), which the monks copied in order to attain a more spiritual state.

• *Some of Fra Angelico's best work is found in the 10 cells along the left-hand side. Begin with the first of these cells.*

Cell ❶—*Noli me Tangere:* The resurrected Jesus, appearing as a hoe-carrying gardener, says, "Don't touch me" and gingerly sidesteps Mary Magdalene's grasp. The flowers and trees represent the blossoming of new life, and they're about the last we'll see. Most scenes have stark, bare backgrounds, to concentrate the monk's focus on just the essential subject.

Cell ❷—*Lamentation:* Christ and mourners are a reverse image of the *Lamentation* downstairs. Christ levitates, not really supported by the ladies' laps. The colors are muted grays, browns, and pinks. Dominic (star on head) stands contemplating, just as the monk should do, by mentally transporting himself to the scene.

Cell ❸—*Annunciation:* The painting's arches echo the room's real arch. (And they, in turn, harmoniously "frame" the "arch" of Mary and the angel bending toward each other to talk.) Peter Martyr (bloody head) looks on.

You can't call these cells a wrap until you've found at least six crosses, three Dominics, three Peters, and a Thomas Aquinas. Ready...go.

Cell ❹—*Crucifixion:* That's one cross. And another Dominic.

Cell ❺—*Birth of Jesus:* And there's your second Peter.

Cell ❻—*Transfiguration:* Forsaking Renaissance realism, Fra Angelico emphasizes the miraculous. In an aura of blinding light, Christ spreads his arms cross-like, dazzling the three witnesses at the bottom of the "mountain." He's joined by disembodied heads of prophets, all spinning in a circle echoed by the room's arch. These rooms, which housed senior monks, have some of the most complex and intellectually demanding symbolism.

Cell ❼—*The Mocking of Christ:* From Renaissance realism to Dalí surrealism. Dominic, while reading the Passion, conjures an image of Christ—the true king, on a throne with a globe and scepter—now blindfolded, spit upon, slapped, and clubbed by...a painting of medieval symbols of torment. This must have been a puzzling riddle from the Master to a fellow monk.

Cell ❽—*The Empty Tomb:* The worried women are reassured by an angel that "he is risen." Jesus, far away in the clouds, seems annoyed that they didn't listen to him.

Cell ❾—*Mary Crowned:* ...triumphantly in heaven, while Dominic, Peter, Aquinas, Francis, and others prepare to celebrate with high-fives.

Cell ❿—*Presentation in the Temple:* Baby Jesus is swaddled like a mummy. And there's your final Peter.

• *Continue around the bend—Savonarola's three rooms are at the far end of the corridor.*

Savonarola's Cells (Celle del Savonarola)

Girolamo Savonarola (1452-1498) occupied the cluster of rooms ⓫ at the end of the hall. But before you climb the three steps to his cells, stop at the last two rooms along the hall (on the right).

First enter the next-to-last room. Home-schooled by his Scholastic grandfather, the 22-year-old Savonarola's life was changed when he heard a sermon on repentance. He traded his scholar's robes for the blue cloak of a simple Dominican monk. He quickly became known for his asceticism, devotion, and knowledge of the Bible. His followers rallied around a **banner** *(Lo Stendardo del Savonarola)* painted with a gruesome Crucifixion scene in the Fra Angelico style. They paraded through the streets reminding all that Christ paid for their worldly Renaissance sins.

In the next room (the last one before the steps), you'll find a number of his possessions, including his **blue cloak** and personal **crucifix,** scattered about.
• *Now enter the Celle del Savonarola.*

First Room
The **portrait bust** shows the hooded monk, whose personal charisma and prophetic fervor led him from humble scholar to celebrity preacher to prior of San Marco to leader of Florence to controversial martyr. The **relief** under the portrait bust shows Savonarola at his greatest moment. He stands before the Florence city council and pledges allegiance to Florence's constitution, assuming control of the city after the exile of the Medici (1494). Reviled as a fanatical, regressive tyrant and praised as a saint, reformer, and champion of democracy, Savonarola was a complex man in a position of great power during turbulent times.

Various **paintings** depict Savonarola in action, including one by Federico Andreotti, which shows the powerful monk reproaching two troublemakers in his study.
• *The next room is Savonarola's...*

Study (Studiolo)
Seated at this **desk,** in his ecclesiastical folding **chair,** Savonarola scoured his Bible for clues to solve Florence's civic strife.

In 1482 at age 30, the monk had come to San Marco as a lecturer. He was bright, humble...and boring. Then, after experiencing divine revelations, he spiced his sermons with prophecies of future events...which started coming true. His sermons on Ezekiel, Amos, Exodus, and the Apocalypse predicted doom for the Medici family. He made brazen references to the pope's embezzling and stable of mistresses, and preached hope for a glorious future after city and church were cleansed.

Packed houses heard him rail against the "prostitute church... the monster of abomination." Witnesses wrote that "the church echoed with weeping and wailing," and afterward "everyone wandered the city streets dazed and speechless." From this humble desk, he corresponded with the worldly pope, the humanist Pico della Mirandola, and fans, such as Lorenzo the Magnificent, who begrudgingly admired his courage.

Lorenzo died, the bankrupt Medici were exiled, and Florence was invaded by France...as Savonarola had prophesied. In the power vacuum, the masses saw Savonarola as a moderate voice who championed a return to Florence's traditional constitution. He was made head of a Christian commonwealth.

• Finally, step into the...

Room with Savonarola's Possessions (Le Reliquie di Savonarola)

Savonarola's personal moral authority was unquestioned, as his simple **wool clothes** and **rosary** attest.

At first, his rule was just. He cut taxes, reduced street crime, shifted power from rich Medici to citizens, and even boldly proposed banning Vespas from tourist zones.

However, Savonarola had an uncompromising and fanatical side, as his **hair-shirt girdle** suggests. His government passed strict morality laws against swearing, blasphemy, gambling, and ostentatious clothes, which were enforced by gangs of thuggish teenagers. At the height of the Christian Republic, during Lent of 1497, followers built a huge "bonfire of vanities" on Piazza della Signoria, where they burned wigs, carnival masks, dice, playing cards, musical instruments, and discredited books and paintings.

In 1498, several forces undermined Savonarola's Republic: scheming Medici, crop failure, rival cities, a pissed-off pope threatening excommunication for Savonarola and political isolation for Florence, and a public tiring of puritanism. Gangs of opponents (called Arrabbiati, "Rabid Dogs") battled Savonarola's supporters (the "Weepers"). Meanwhile, Savonarola was slowly easing out of public life, refusing to embroil the church in a lengthy trial, retiring to his routine of study, prayer, and personal austerity.

Egged on by city leaders and the pope, a bloodthirsty mob marched on San Marco to arrest Savonarola. Arrabbiati fought monks with clubs (imagine it in the **courtyard** out the window), while the church bells clanged and the monks shouted, "*Salvum fac populum tuum, Domine!*" ("Save thy people, Lord!"). The Arrabbiati stormed up the stairs to this floor, and Savonarola was handed over to the authorities. He was taken to the Palazzo Vecchio, tortured, tried, and sentenced.

On May 23, 1498 (see the **painting** *Supplizio del Savonarola in Piazza della Signoria*), before a huge crowd in front of the Palazzo Vecchio (where today a memorial plaque is embedded in the pavement of the Piazza della Signoria), Savonarola was publicly defrocked, then publicly forgiven by a papal emissary. Then he was hanged—not Old West-style, in which the neck snaps, but instead

slowly strangled, dangling from a rope, while teenage boys hooted and threw rocks.

The crowd looked upon the lifeless body of this man who had once captivated their minds, as they lit a pyre under the scaffold—see the **stick** *(palo)* from the fire. The flames rose up, engulfing the body, when suddenly...his arm shot upward!—like a final blessing or curse—and the terrified crowd stampeded, killing several. Savonarola's ashes were thrown in the Arno.

The Rest of the Museum

The corridor near Fra Angelico's *Annunciation* has the library (also designed by Michelozzo), which contains music and other manuscripts. In a cell across the hall and a bit to the right is Fra Angelico's *Kiss of Judas* fresco—a theme that proved prophetic, since it was outside that cell that Savonarola was arrested. At the end of the corridor (right side) are ⓬ the cells where Cosimo the Elder—the builder of this monastery—often retired for spiritual renewal. Inside, the painting of the Magi includes a kneeling Magus kissing the baby's little holy toes—a portrait of Cosimo.

• *To exit, return to the stairway and descend. Take a right at the bottom into a bookshop decorated with a fine Ghirlandaio Last Supper fresco (are you as tired as John is?). WCs are in the next hallway. Pass through corridors filled with a hodgepodge of architectural fragments and on to the exit. On the street, turn right, then right again, and you'll see the Duomo.*

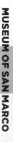

DUOMO MUSEUM TOUR

Museo dell'Opera del Duomo

Brunelleschi's dome, Ghiberti's bronze doors, and Donatello's statues—these creations define the 1400s (the Quattrocento) in Florence, when the city blossomed and classical arts were reborn. All are featured at the Duomo Museum, plus a Michelangelo *Pietà* that was intended as his sculptural epitaph. While copies now decorate the exteriors of the Duomo (cathedral), Baptistery, and Campanile (bell tower, called Giotto's Tower), the original sculptured masterpieces of the complex are now restored and displayed safely indoors, filling the Duomo Museum. This refurbished museum is a delight, though it's overlooked by most visitors to Florence. There's never a line.

Orientation

Cost: €6, covered by Firenze Card. It's also covered by the €15 combo-ticket that includes the Baptistery, Campanile, and Duomo's crypt (allowing you to enter all of those sights without a wait). A €23 version of the combo-ticket adds the dome climb, but you have to buy it at the dome entrance (which can have long lines). Either version is valid for four days.

You can also buy €15 tickets here for the "Terraces of the Cathedral and Dome" tour, allowing you to bypass the long cathedral-entry and dome-climbing lines.

For details on both options, see page 71.

Hours: Mon-Sat 9:00-19:30, Sun 9:00-13:40, last entry 40 minutes before closing. Note that this is one of the few museums in Florence that's open every Monday. It also stays open later than most.

Getting There: The museum is across the street from the Duomo on the east side, at Via del Proconsolo 9.

Information: Tel. 055-282-226, www.operaduomo.firenze.it.
Tours: The audioguide costs €5. Guided English tours are generally offered daily in summer for €3 (as they use volunteer guides, schedules vary—stop by or call to ask).
Length of This Tour: Allow 1.5 hours.
With Limited Time: Focus on Ghiberti's doors, Michelangelo's *Pietà*, Donatello's sculptures, and the pair of finely carved choir lofts *(cantorie)*.
Photography: Allowed, but no flash around paintings.
Starring: Brunelleschi, Ghiberti, Donatello, and Michelangelo.

The Tour Begins

Ghiberti's doors (if on view when you visit) are on the ground floor, while Donatello's statues are on the first floor. The *Pietà* is on a landing halfway between floors.

Ground Floor

The Medieval Cathedral

• *Browse the first few small rooms.*

Roman sarcophagi, Etruscan fragments, a chronological chart, and broken **Baptistery statues** attest to the 2,000-year history of

Florence's Duomo, Baptistery, and Campanile. The Baptistery was likely built on the site of a pagan Roman temple. It was flanked by a humble church that, by the 1200s, was not big enough to contain the exuberant spirit of a city growing rich from the wool trade and banking. In 1296, the cornerstone was laid for a huge church—today's Duomo—intended to be the biggest in Christendom.

• *The first large room (with a pope sitting at one end) is lined with statues from the original facade (1296-1587). On the long wall you'll find...*

Madonna with the Glass Eyes (Madonna in Trono col Bambino)

The architect Arnolfo di Cambio designed this statue to sit in a niche on the church's exterior. The building was dedicated to Mary—starry-eyed over the birth of baby Jesus. She sits, crowned like a chess-set queen, above the main door, framed with

DUOMO MUSEUM

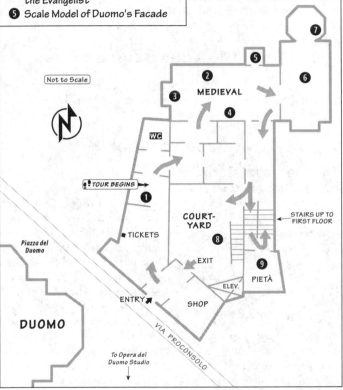

Duomo Museum—Ground Floor

1. Roman Sarcophagi, Etruscan Fragments, Chronological Chart & Baptistery Statues
2. Madonna with the Glass Eyes
3. Statue of Pope Boniface VIII
4. DONATELLO – St. John the Evangelist
5. Scale Model of Duomo's Facade
6. Room of Altarpieces & Reliquaries
7. John the Baptist's Finger
8. GHIBERTI – "Gates of Paradise" Doors
9. MICHELANGELO – Pietà

Not to Scale

MEDIEVAL

WC

TOUR BEGINS

Piazza del Duomo

TICKETS

COURT-YARD

STAIRS UP TO FIRST FLOOR

EXIT

ELEV.

PIETÀ

ENTRY

SHOP

DUOMO

VIA PROCONSOLO

To Opera del Duomo Studio

a dazzling mosaic halo. She's accompanied (to our right) by St. Zenobius, Florence's first bishop during Roman times, whose raised hand consecrates the formerly pagan ground as Christian.

Statue of Pope Boniface VIII

Despised by Dante for his meddling in politics, this pope paid 3,000 florins to get his image in a box seat on the facade. His XL shirt size made him look correct when viewed from below. Though the statue is stylized, Arnolfo realistically shows the pope's

custom-made, extra-tall hat and bony face. (Most of the room's statues are straight-backed, to hang on the facade.)
• *On the long wall opposite the Madonna, find...*

Donatello—*St. John the Evangelist* (*San Giovanni Evangelista*)

A hundred years later, Arnolfo's medieval facade became a show-case for Renaissance sculptors.

John sits gazing at a distant horizon, his tall head rising high above his massive body. This visionary foresees a new age...and the coming Renaissance. The right hand is massive—as relaxed as though it were dangling over the back of a chair, but full of powerful tension. Like the mighty right hand of Michelangelo's *David,* and the beard of Michelangelo's *Moses,* this work is a hundred years ahead of its time.

At 22 years old, Donatello (c. 1386-1466) sculpted this work just before becoming a celebrity for his inspiring statue of *St. George* (original in the Bargello, copy on the exterior of the Orsanmichele Church). Donatello, like most early Renaissance artists, was a blue-collar worker, raised as a workshop apprentice among knuckle-dragging musclemen. He proudly combined physical skill with technical know-how to create beauty (Art + Science = Renaissance Beauty). His statues are thinkers with big hands who can put theory into practice.
• *To the right of the Madonna, in an adjoining room, find a...*

Scale Model of the Duomo's Original Facade

In Renaissance times, this is what the Duomo would have looked like. (The model, by Franco Gizdulich, is 1:20.) The glassy-eyed Madonna was over the main doorway, Pope Boniface was to the left, high up, and Donatello's St. John was to the left, farther

down. You can see that only the bottom third was ever completed with marble facing—the upper part was bare brick. Had Arnolfo's design been completed, the three-story facade would have looked much like today's colorful, Neo-Gothic version, with pointed arches and white, pink, and green marble, studded with statues and gleaming with gold mosaics. In 1587, the still-incomplete facade was torn down.

• *Up a few steps at the end of the long statue room is a...*

Room of Altarpieces and Reliquaries

These medieval altarpieces, which once adorned chapels and altars inside the Duomo, show saints and angels suspended in a gold never-never land. In the adjoining room, the ornate reliquaries hold bones and objects of the saints (Peter's chains, Jerome's jawbone, and so on), many bought from a single, slick 14th-century con artist preying on medieval superstition.

In the 1400s, tastes changed, and these symbols of crude medievalism were purged from the Duomo and stacked in storage. Soon artists replaced the golden heavenly scenes with flesh-and-blood humans who inhabited the physical world of rocks, trees, and sky...the Renaissance.

• *Go into the little chapel at the far end of this room. The first glass case on the right as you enter the chapel contains...*

John the Baptist's Finger in a Reliquary
(Reliquario di un Dito Indice di San Giovanni)

The severed index finger of the beheaded prophet is the most revered relic of all the holy body parts in this museum.

• *Pass through a few more rooms into the ground-floor courtyard, where you'll find...*

The Renaissance Church—
Ghiberti's Baptistery Doors

The Renaissance began in 1401 with a citywide competition to build new doors for the Baptistery. Lorenzo Ghiberti (c. 1378-1455) won the job and built the doors (now on the Baptistery's north side), which everyone loved. He then was hired to make another set of doors—these panels—for the main entrance facing the Duomo. These bronze "Gates of Paradise" (1425-1452) revolutionized the way Renaissance people saw the world around them.

The original 10 panels from the Gates of Paradise were moved from the Baptistery to the museum to better preserve them. (Copies now adorn the Baptistery itself—see the graphic on page 101 for the original layout.) But even indoors, corrosive oxides gathered between the bronze panels and their gilding. After recent preservation efforts, the doors are now back on display. The panels are under glass to protect against natural light, and gassed with nitrogen to protect them against oxygen and humidity.

• *Here's a description of a few of the panels:*

Joseph and Benjamin (Storie di Giuseppe e Beniamino)

With just the depth of a thumb-nail, Ghiberti creates a temple in the round inhabited by workers. This round temple wowed Florence. Armed with the rules of perspective, Ghiberti rendered reality with a mathematical precision we don't normally impose on what we see, when our eyes and minds settle for ballpark estimates about relative size and distance. For Florentines, suddenly the world acquired a whole new dimension—depth.

Adam and Eve (La Creazione e Storie di Adamo ed Eva)

Ghiberti tells several stories in one panel—a common medieval technique—using different thicknesses in the relief. In the sketchy

background (very low relief), God in a bubble conducts the Creation. In the center (a little thicker), Eve springs from Adam's side. Finally, in the lower left (in high relief), an elegantly robed God pulls Adam, as naked as the day he was born, from the mud.

Ghiberti welcomed the innovations of other artists. See the angel flying through an arch (right side). This arch is in very low relief but still looks fully 3-D because it's rendered sideways, using the perspective tricks of painting. Ghiberti learned the technique from one of his employees, the young Donatello.

Jacob and Esau (Storie di Giacobbe ed Esau)

The "background" arches and the space they create are as interesting as the scenes themselves. At the center is the so-called vanishing point on the distant horizon, where all the arches and floor tiles converge. This calm center gives us an eye-level reference point for all the figures. Those closest to us, at the bottom of the panel, are big and clearly defined. Distant figures are smaller, fuzzier, and higher up.

Ghiberti has placed us about 20 feet away from the

scene, part of this casual crowd of holy people—some with their backs to us—milling around an arcade.

Labors of Adam, and Cain and Abel
(Il Lavoro dei Progenitori e Storie di Caino e Abele)

On one mountain, we see Cain and Abel offering a sacrifice at the top, Adam waving at the bottom, and the first murder in between.

In early panels such as this one (pictured at right) Ghiberti used only a sketchy landscape as a backdrop for human activities.

Ghiberti, the illegitimate son of a goldsmith, labored all his working life (more than 50 years) on the two Baptistery doors. Their execution was a major manufacturing job, requiring a large workshop of artists and artisans for each stage of the process: making the door frames that hold the panels, designing and making models of the panels (forming them in wax in order to cast them in bronze), gilding the panels (by bathing them in powdered gold dissolved in mercury, then heating until the gold and bronze blended), polishing the panels, mounting them, installing the doors...and signing paychecks for everyone along the way. Ghiberti was as much businessman as artist.

Solomon and the Queen of Sheba
(Salomone e la Regina di Saba)

The receding arches stretch into infinity, giving the airy feeling that we can see forever. All of the arches and steps converge at the center of the panel, where the two monarchs meet, uniting their respective peoples. Ghiberti's subject was likely influenced by the warm ecumenical breeze blowing through Florence in 1439, as religious leaders convened here in an attempt to reunite the eastern (Constantinople) and western (Rome) realms of Christendom.

If the Renaissance began in 1401 with Ghiberti's doors, it ended in 1555 with Michelangelo's *Pietà*.

• *In the courtyard are two staircases almost side by side. Ascend the old (not new) staircase to the first landing.*

Michelangelo—*Pietà* (1547-1555)

The aging Michelangelo (1475-1564) designed his own tomb, with this as the centerpiece. He was depressed by old age, the recent death of his soul mate, and the grim reality that by sculpting this statue he was writing his own obituary. Done on his own dime, it's fair to consider this an introspective and very personal work.

Three mourners tend the broken body of the crucified Christ. We see Mary, his mother (the shadowy figure on our right); Mary Magdalene (on the left, polished up by a pupil); and Nicodemus, the converted Pharisee, whose face is clearly that of Michelangelo himself. The polished body of Christ stands out from the unfinished background. Michelangelo (as Nicodemus), who spent a lifetime bringing statues to life by "freeing" them from the stone,

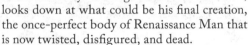

looks down at what could be his final creation, the once-perfect body of Renaissance Man that is now twisted, disfigured, and dead.

Seen face-on, the four figures form a powerful geometric shape of a circle inside a triangle, split down the middle by Christ's massive (but very dead) arm. Seen from the right side, they seem to interact with each other, their sketchy faces changing emotions from grief to melancholy to peaceful acceptance.

Fifty years earlier, a confident Michelangelo had worked here on these very premises, skillfully carving *David* from an imperfect block. But he hated this marble for the *Pietà;* it was hard and grainy, and gave off sparks when hit wrong. (The chisel grooves in the base remind us of the sheer physical effort of a senior citizen sculpting.) Worst of all, his housekeeper kept bugging him with the same question that Pope Julius II used to ask about the Sistine Chapel— "When will you finish?" Pushed to the edge, Michelangelo grabbed a hammer and attacked the flawed marble statue, hacking away and breaking off limbs, then turned to the servant and said, "There! It's finished!" (An assistant later repaired some of the damage, but cracks are still visible in Christ's left arm and only leg.)

• *Continue upstairs to the first floor, entering a large room lined with statues and two balconies. Donatello's prophets are at the far end.*

First Floor

Room of the *Cantorie*

The room displays two choir boxes *(cantorie)* and the original 16 statues (by several sculptors) from the bell tower's third story, where copies stand today.

DUOMO MUSEUM

Duomo Museum—First Floor

⑩ DONATELLO – Habakkuk & Jeremiah
⑪ DELLA ROBBIA – Cantoria
⑫ "Lamb of God" Panel
⑬ DONATELLO – Cantoria
⑭ DONATELLO – Mary Magdalene
⑮ Silver Altar
⑯ Silver Cross
⑰ Medieval Crucifix
⑱ PISANO (& Others) – The Campanile Panels
⑲ BRUNELLESCHI – Lantern Model, Scaffolding, Tools & Death Mask
⑳ Facade Models
㉑ Emilio De Fabris & Designs

Not to Scale

COURT-YARD (BELOW)

STAIRS UP FROM GROUND FLOOR

Piazza del Duomo

VIA PROCONSOLO

ELEV.   PIETÀ

DUOMO

To Opera del Duomo Studio

Donatello's Prophets

Donatello did several statues of the prophets, plus some others in collaboration. (Some of the statues may be under restoration during your visit.)

Donatello ("Little Donato") invented the Renaissance style that Michelangelo would later perfect—powerful statues that are ultra-realistic, even ugly, sculpted in an "unfinished" style by an artist known for experimentation and his prickly, brooding personality. Both men were famous but lived like peasants, married only to their work.

DUOMO MUSEUM

Donatello—*Habakkuk (Abacuc)*

Donatello's signature piece shows us the wiry man beneath the heavy mantle of a prophet. Habakkuk's rumpled cloak falls down the front, dividing the body lengthwise. From the deep furrows emerges a bare arm with well-defined tendons and that power-

ful right hand. His long, muscled neck leads to a bald head (the Italians call the statue *Lo Zuccone,* meaning "pumpkinhead").

The ugly face, with several days' growth of beard, crossed eyes, and tongue-tied mouth, looks crazed. This is no confident Charlton Heston prophet, but a man who's spent too much time alone, fasting in the wilderness, searching for his calling, and who now returns to babble his vision on a street corner.

Donatello, the eccentric prophet of a new style, identified with this statue, talking to it, swearing at it, yelling at it: "Speak!"

• *Nearby, look for...*

Donatello—*Jeremiah (Geremia)*

Watching Jerusalem burn in the distance, the ignored prophet reflects on why the Israelites wouldn't listen when he warned them that the Babylonian kings would conquer the city. He purses his lips bitterly, and his down-turned mouth is accentuated by his plunging neck muscle and sagging shoulders. The folds in the clothes are very deep, evoking the anger, sorrow, and disgust that Jeremiah feels but cannot share, as it is too late.

Movement, realism, and human drama were Donatello's great contributions to sculpture.

The *Cantorie*

The two marble balconies in this room are choir lofts. They once sat above the sacristy doors of the Duomo. Donatello's is on the right (from the entrance); Luca della Robbia's on the left. Della Robbia's is a reconstruction from casts, with the original 10 panels displayed below.

Luca della Robbia—*Cantoria* (1430-c. 1438)

After almost 150 years of construction, the cathedral was nearly done, and the Opera del Duomo, the workshop in charge, began preparing the interior for the celebration. Brunelleschi hired a little-known sculptor, 30-year-old Luca della Robbia, to make this balcony choir-box *(cantoria)* for singers in the cathedral. It sums up the exuberance of the Quattrocento. The panels are a celebration of music, song, and dance performed by toddlers, children, and teenagers.

The *cantoria* brings Psalm 150 ("Praise ye the Lord") to life like a YouTube video. Each panel depicts one verse. Latin speakers can read the text, while the rest can follow along with the pictures. Start in the upper left and read left-to-right and top-to-bottom.

The banner along the top—*"Laudate D.N.M."*—reads "Praise the Lord. Praise him in his holy place, in the firmament *(Firmamento)* for his mighty deeds *(Virtu)* and greatness *(Magnitudinem)."*

In the first panel (upper left), we see children laugh and dance to the sound of trumpets: "Praise him with the sound of trumpets *(sono Tubae)."* Next, they play guitars and autoharps: "Praise him with psalter and zither *(Psalterio et Cythara)...* Praise him with tambourines *(Timpano)...*and dancing *(Choro)."*

In the next level down, kids dance ring-around-the-rosy. Della Robbia sculpts a scene in the round on an almost-flat surface, showing front, back, and in-between poses. The children dance "...with pipes and strings *(Organo)...*and with jubilant cymbals *(Cimbalis)."*

The Psalm ends: "Everybody praise the Lord!"

Della Robbia's choir box was a triumph, a celebration of

Florence's youthful boom time. Perhaps sensing he could never top it, the young sculptor hung up his hammer and chisel and concentrated on the colorful glazed terracotta for which he's best known. (Find the **round "Lamb of God" panel** over your left shoulder, above a doorway nearby, by Luca's nephew, who took over the workshop.)

Donatello—*Cantoria* (1433-c. 1440)

If Della Robbia's balcony looks like afternoon recess, Donatello's looks like an all-night rave. Donatello's figures are sketchier, murky, and filled with frenetic activity, as the dancing kids hurl themselves around the balcony. Imagine candles lighting this as the scenes seem to come to life. If the dance feels almost pagan,

Pop. 100,000...But Still a Small Town

At the dawn of the Renaissance, Florence was bursting with creative geniuses, all of whom knew each other and worked together. For example, after Ghiberti won the bronze-door competition, Brunelleschi took teenage Donatello with him to Rome. Donatello returned to join Ghiberti's workshop. Ghiberti helped Brunelleschi with dome plans. Brunelleschi, Donatello, and Luca della Robbia collaborated on the Pazzi Chapel. And so on, and so on.

there's a reason.

Recently returned from a trip to Rome, Donatello carved in the style of classical friezes of dancing *putti* (chubby, playful toddlers). This choir box stood in a dark area of the Duomo, so Donatello chose colorful mosaics and marbles to catch the eye, while purposely leaving the dancers unfinished and shadowy, tangled figures flitting inside the columns. In the dim light, worshippers swore they saw them move.

• *Beneath Donatello's* cantoria *is a statue of...*

Donatello—*Mary Magdalene (Maddalena,* c. 1455)

Carved from white poplar, originally painted with realistic colors (like the medieval crucifix displayed in the next room), this statue is less a Renaissance work of beauty than a medieval object of intense devotion.

Mary Magdalene—the prostitute rescued from the streets by Jesus—folds her hands in humble prayer. Her once-beautiful face and body have been scarred by fasting, repentance, and the fires of her own remorse. The matted hair sticks to her face; veins and tendons line the emaciated arms and neck. The rippling hair suggests emotional turmoil within. But from her hollow, tired eyes, a new beauty shines, an enlightened soul that doesn't rely on the external beauty of human flesh.

The man who helped re-birth the classical style now shocked Florence by turning his back on it. Picking up a knife, he experimented in the difficult medium of wood carving, where subtlety can get lost when the wood splits off in larger-than-wanted slivers.

Sixty-five-year-old Donatello had just returned to Florence, after years away. His city had changed. Friends were dying (Brunelleschi died before they could reconcile after a bitter fight), favorite pubs were overrun with frat boys, and Florence was gaga over Greek gods in pretty, gleaming marble. Donatello fell into a five-year funk, completing only two statues, including this one.

The Rest of the Museum
• *Enter the adjoining room (to the right as you face* Mary Magdalene*).*

Silver Altar and Cross
The exquisite half-ton silver altarpiece and cross honoring John the Baptist, which dominate this room, once stood in the Baptistery. Each of the immaculately restored silver panels depicts an episode from John the Baptist's life: birth, baptizing Jesus, and so on. Around the right side are his execution and the presentation of his disembodied head to Herod during a feast.

Also in this room, near the door, is a wood-carved **crucifix** that's colorfully painted (as Donatello's *Mary Magdalene* was originally).
• *Pass back through the large room of the* cantorie *and into the next room. Work clockwise from the entrance.*

Andrea Pisano (and others)—*The Campanile Panels* (c. 1334-1359)
These 28 hexagonal and 28 diamond-shaped, blue-glazed panels decorated the Duomo's Campanile, seven per side (where copies stand today). The original design scheme was perhaps Giotto's, but his successor, Andrea Pisano, and assistants executed most of the panels.

The panels celebrate technology, showing workers, inventors, and thinkers. Allegorically, they depict humanity's long march to "civilization"—a blend of art and science, brain and brawn. But realistically, they're snapshots of that industrious generation that helped Florence bounce back ferociously from the Black Death of 1348.

The lower, **hexagonal panels** (reading clockwise from the entrance) show God starting the chain of creation by inventing (1) man and (2) woman, then (3) Adam and Eve continuing the work, (4) Jabal learning to domesticate sheep, (5) Jubal blowing a horn, inventing music...
• *Continuing along the next wall...*

(6) Tubalcain the blacksmith and (7) Noah inventing wine and Miller Time. (8) An astronomer sights along a quadrant to chart the heavens and the (round, tilted-on-axis, pre-Columbian) earth, (9) a master builder supervises his little apprentices building a brick wall, (10) a doctor holds a flask of urine to the light for analysis (yes, that's what it is), and so on.

• *Skip ahead to the fourth wall, the second panel.*

(20) The invention of sculpture, as a man chisels a figure to life.

The upper **diamond-shaped panels,** of marble on blue majolica (tin-glazed pottery tinged blue with copper sulfate), add religion (sacraments and virtues) to the civilization equation.

• *Enter the next, narrow room to find tools, scaffolding, and, at the end of the corridor, a wooden model of the cathedral dome's lantern.*

Model of the Lantern (Cupola di S. Maria del Fiore)

Look at this model of the dome's top portion (or look out the window—if it's open—at the real thing). Brunelleschi's dome, a feat of engineering that was both functional and beautiful, put mathematics in stone. It rises 330 feet from the ground, with eight white, pointed-arch ribs, filled in with red brick and capped with a "lantern" (cupola) to hold it all in place.

In designing the dome, Brunelleschi faced a number of challenges: The dome had to cover a gaping 140-foot hole in the roof of the church (a drag on rainy Sundays), a hole too wide to be spanned by the wooden scaffolding that traditionally supported a dome under construction. (An earlier architect suggested supporting the dome with a great mound of dirt inside the church...filled

with coins, so peasants would later cart it away for free.) In addition, the eight-sided "drum" that the dome was to rest on was too weak to support its weight, and there were no side buildings on the church on which to attach Gothic-style buttresses.

The solution was a dome within a dome, leaving a hollow space between to make the structure lighter. And the dome had to be self-supporting, both while being built and when finished, so as not to require buttresses.

Brunelleschi used wooden models such as these to demonstrate his ideas to skeptical approval committees.

Scaffolding

Although no scaffolding supported the dome itself, the stone masons needed exterior scaffolding to stand on as they worked.

Support timbers were stuck into postholes in the drum (some are visible on the church today).

The dome rose in rings. First, the workers stacked a few blocks of white marble to create part of the ribs, then connected the ribs with horizontal crosspieces before filling in the space with red brick, in a herringbone pattern. When the ring was complete and self-supporting, they'd move the scaffolding up and do another section.

Tools

The dome weighs 80 million pounds—as much as the entire population of Florence—so Brunelleschi had to design special tools and machines to lift and work all that stone. (The lantern alone—which caps the dome—is a marble building nearly as tall as the Baptistery.) You'll see sun-dried bricks, brick molds, rope, a tool belt, compasses, stone pincers, and various pulleys for lifting. Brunelleschi also designed a machine (not on display) that used horses to turn a shaft that reeled in rope, lifting heavy loads.

The dome was completed in 16 short years, capping 150 years of construction on the church. Brunelleschi enjoyed the dedication ceremonies, but he died before the lantern was completed. His legacy is a dome that stands as a proud symbol of man's ingenuity, proving that art and science can unite to make beauty.

• *Facing the lantern model, find...*

Brunelleschi's Death Mask *(Maschera Funebre)*

Filippo Brunelleschi (1377-1446) was uniquely qualified to create the dome. Trained in sculpture, he gave it up in disgust after losing the Baptistery-door gig. In Rome, he visualized placing the Pantheon on top of Florence's Duomo, and dissected the Pantheon's mathematics and engineering.

Back home, he astounded Florence with a super-realistic painting of the Baptistery, as seen from the Duomo's front steps. Florentines lined up to see the painting (now lost) displayed side by side with the real thing, marveling at the 3-D realism. (Brunelleschi's mathematics of linear perspective were later expanded and popularized by Alberti.)

In 1420 Brunelleschi was declared *capomaestro* of the dome project. He was a jack-of-all-trades and now master of all as well, overseeing every aspect of the dome, the lantern, and the machinery to build them. Despite all his planning, it's clear from documentary evidence that he was making it up as he went along,

exuding confidence to workers and city officials while privately improvising.
• *The models you'll find two rooms farther along represent the...*

Facade from the 16th to the 19th Centuries
The church wasn't done. In 1587, the medieval facade by Arnolfo was considered hopelessly outdated and torn down like so much old linoleum. But work on a replacement never got off the ground, and the front of the church sat bare for nearly 300 years while church fathers debated proposal after proposal (like the models in this room) by many famous architects. Most versions champion the Renaissance style to match Brunelleschi's dome, rather than Gothic to fit the church.
• *Two rooms later, we reach the conclusion to the Duomo's long history.*

The 19th-Century Facade
Finally, in the 1800s, as Italy was unifying and filled with a can-do spirit, there was a push to finish the facade. **Emilio De Fabris (portrait)** won a competition, and began to build a neo-Gothic facade that echoed the original work of Arnolfo. The new-old facade was dedicated in 1887. Notice that even De Fabris changed designs as he went—the spikes along the roofline in some of the designs are not there today.

Critics may charge that De Fabris' facade is too retro, but it was the style of the church beloved by Ghiberti, Donatello, Brunelleschi, and the industrious citizens of Florence's Quattrocento, who saw it as Florence's finest art gallery.

The Opera del Duomo Today
If you climb the stairs to the sparse third-floor landing, you might see lab-coated workers busy in the restoration studio. They belong

to the Opera del Duomo, the organization that does the continual work required to keep the cathedral's art in good repair (*opera* is Italian for "work").

For another behind-the-scenes peek, make one more stop after leaving the Duomo Museum: Head to the left around the back of the Duomo to find Via dello Studio (near the south transept), then walk a block toward the river to #23a (freestanding yellow house on the right; see map on page 99). You can look through the open doorway of the **Opera del Duomo art studio** and see workers sculpting new statues, restoring old ones, or making exact copies. They're carrying on an artistic tradition that dates back to the days of Brunelleschi. The "opera" continues.

PALAZZO VECCHIO TOUR

With its distinctive castle turret and rustic stonework, this fortified "Old Palace"—Florence's past and present Town Hall—is a
Florentine landmark. The highlight of the interior is the Grand
Hall: With a Michelangelo sculpture and epic paintings of great
moments in Florentine history, it was the impressive epicenter
of Medici power. The richly decorated rooms of the royal apartments—though hardly the most sumptuous royal quarters in
Europe—show off some famous art, creative decorative flourishes,
and aristocratic curiosities. It's open very late in summer, making
it a fine after-dinner sightseeing option.

Orientation

Cost and Hours: Ground-floor courtyard—free; museum—€6.50,
    covered by Firenze Card, €8 combo-ticket with Brancacci
    Chapel; tower only-€6.50 (418 steps), museum plus tower-
    €10; Fri-Wed 9:00-19:00, until 24:00 in April-Sept; Thu 9:00-
    14:00 year-round; ticket office closes one hour earlier.
Information: Tel. 055-276-8224, www.museicivicifiorentini.it.
Tours: Tours in English are offered daily, but the schedule varies
    and you must reserve (tel. 055-276-8224). The tour costs the
    same as an entry ticket (€6.50), but tour takers don't get any
    free time inside unless they pay an extra €2. A new audio/vid-
    eoguide may be available when you visit; ask for details.
Activities for Kids: The palace's "Children's Museum" program
    offers an ever-changing range of activities, usually lasting a
    little over an hour, and requiring reservations—check online,
    call, or ask at the reception by the ticket office (no activities
    after 17:00).

Nighttime Terrace Visits: In summer, you can join an escort for an unnarrated walk along the "patrol path"—the balcony that runs just below the crenellated top of the building (€2 plus regular admission ticket, every 30 minutes between 20:00 and 23:00, no tours Oct-March). Note that this tour doesn't go to the top of the tower, but just to the top of the main building.

Expect Changes: Florence's spunky young mayor is trying to make the palazzo more inviting to the public. By the time you visit, the entry procedure may have been changed and new parts of the palace may be open to the public.

Length of This Tour: One hour.

Starring: The spacious Grand Hall, lavish royal apartments, and statues by Michelangelo and Donatello.

The Tour Begins

• *Stand in Florence's main square, Piazza della Signoria, and take in the palace's grand facade.*

Exterior

Around the year 1300, the citizens of Florence broke ground on a new Town Hall, designed by Arnolfo di Cambio, who also did the Duomo. Arnolfo's design expanded on an earlier palace on the site, turning its small tower into today's 308-foot spire and increasing the building's architectural footprint, which is why the tower ended up slightly off-center.

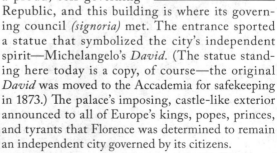

In Renaissance times, Florence was a proud, self-governing Republic, and this building is where its governing council *(signoria)* met. The entrance sported a statue that symbolized the city's independent spirit—Michelangelo's *David*. (The statue standing here today is a copy, of course—the original *David* was moved to the Accademia for safekeeping in 1873.) The palace's imposing, castle-like exterior announced to all of Europe's kings, popes, princes, and tyrants that Florence was determined to remain an independent city governed by its citizens.

• *Enter the courtyard, walking past the fake* David *and Bandinelli's* Hercules and Cacus.

Courtyard

This courtyard has long been a showcase for great Florentine art—art that made a statement to the city's populace.

Anchoring the courtyard is a copy of *Putto with Dolphin*, an innovative work of Renaissance 3-D by Verrocchio, Leonardo da Vinci's teacher. With a twisting spiral form, this statue was one of the first intended to be equally enjoyable from any angle—an improvement on medieval statues that only worked when seen from the front. It stands where the original used to, spouting water piped in from the Boboli Gardens.

Verrocchio's cherub took the place of Donatello's bronze *David* (now in the Bargello, and described on page 153), an even more groundbreaking statue. As the first male nude sculpted in a thousand years, it was a radical humanist statement: art for art's sake—created not for the glory of God, but for the enjoyment of everyday citizens. Secular art hadn't been displayed in a public place since ancient times. The statue also made a bold political statement with an inscription meant to rally Florentines: "The hero is he who defends the fatherland. Behold, a boy defeated a tyrant, so fight on, citizens!"

Stroll around. The faded maps indicate foreign-policy concerns of the Duchy of Tuscany. The squiggly wall painting was inspired by ancient Roman art, which was being excavated at the time (c. 1500). The style is called *grotteschi* (Grotesque), because the ancient villas were discovered underground, and looked like grottoes. You may also see temporary exhibits displayed in this area.

While the Palazzo Vecchio's exterior and courtyard reflect the tastes and ideas of the Florentine Republic, most of the interior decoration dates from a later era. In the 16th century, Florence came under the rule of Cosimo I de' Medici. He suspended the city council and ruled as a "Grand Duke." He transformed this building from a civic center of the people into his personal palatial residence.

• *To see the rest of the palace, you'll have to buy a ticket at the desk deeper in the complex.*

After buying your ticket, look for the small but fascinating exhibit (near the foot of the stairs) with paintings, maps, and other depictions of old-time Florence. You can see how much—or how little—the city has changed over the centuries. Head upstairs to the highlight of the palace, the 13,000-square-foot...

Palazzo Vecchio—First Floor

50 Feet

STAGE

GRAND HALL
SALONE DEI CINQUECENTO

Courtyard

MICHELANGELO'S VICTORY

Piazza della Signoria

Court-yard

LORENZO THE MAGNIFICENT ROOM

STAIRS UP FROM ENTRY COURTYARD

STATUE OF LEO X

LEO X ROOM

SHADED AREA SHOWS ROOMS OPEN TO VISIT

STAIRS UP TO 2ND FLOOR

APARTMENTS OF LEO X

PALAZZO VECCHIO

Grand Hall (Sala Grande)

This vast room—170' by 75'—is also called the Salone dei Cinquecento (Hall of Five Hundred). Originally built under

Savonarola in 1494 to house the Florentine Republic's 500 Grand Councilors, it was expanded under Cosimo I to accommodate 500 party-goers. The ceiling and huge wall paintings, all by Giorgio Vasari and his assistants, are a celebration of the power of Florence, specifically the power of the Medici. Consider this magnificent room in its proper context: In an age when there

was no mass media to use as a mouthpiece, this was how a fabulously wealthy person waged a public-relations campaign (and kept the people down).

Cosimo I is the star here, looking down from the circular medallion in the center of the ceiling. He's dressed as an emperor, with his highness-ness affirmed by the crown of the Holy Roman Emperor and

Cosimo I de' Medici
(1519-1574)

This palace is all about Cosimo I de' Medici. His presence is everywhere. In the famous statue on the square outside the palace, he sits like a Roman emperor astride a horse. Inside, in the Grand Hall, he looms high above in a ceiling painting. And his aesthetic vision is on full display in the Royal Apartments, which were personally decorated with care by Cosimo and his high-maintenance wife Eleonora.

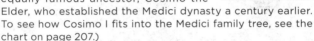

Cosimo's Medici forebears had been Florentine big shots, but Cosimo was the first to have a royal title, after the pope made him a Grand Duke in 1569. Don't confuse Grand Duke Cosimo I with his equally famous ancestor, Cosimo the Elder, who established the Medici dynasty a century earlier. To see how Cosimo I fits into the Medici family tree, see the chart on page 207.)

Before Cosimo I took charge, the loggia in front of the palace (Loggia dei Lanzi) had been used as a gathering place, where Florentines discussed the issues of the day. Cosimo changed it into an art gallery, swapping out public discourse for statues that personified the power and strength of his family. Perseus, holding the head of Medusa, sent a clear message about how the Medici dealt with their enemies.

It was Cosimo I who moved the family out of the Medici-Riccardi Palace and into these digs—officially called the Palazzo della Signoria. Cosimo left the exterior as-is, which is why it still looks like a medieval fortress. But he completely revamped the inside, updating it to match the outlook of the Renaissance. Later, when his wife Eleonora complained about needing a fancier place with a bigger yard, they moved across the river to the Pitti Palace, where she could stroll the sprawling Boboli Gardens. The Vasari Corridor was built over Ponte Vecchio to connect the two palaces. After they'd moved out, the Palazzo della Signoria began to be known as the "old" palace—the Palazzo "Vecchio."

blessed by the staff and cross of the pope. He's circled by a kaleidoscope of symbols of Florentine craft and art guilds, and the shields of his domain, all asserting his power. Notice that in place of the Roman motto of SPQR (*Senatus Populus Que Romanus*—the Senate and People of Rome), he uses "SPQF," implying that Florence is the new Rome. From the stage at the far end of the room, Cosimo sat on his throne, overseeing his fawning subjects.

In the niche in the front of the room is a statue of **Pope Leo X,** looking down from his own throne. The son of Lorenzo

the Magnificent, Leo X was the first of three Medici popes. When he became pope in 1513, the family suddenly had religious authority and some seriously good connections, helping them eventually become bankers to the Vatican.

Vasari's **wall paintings** show great Florentine victories: over Pisa in 1497 (on the left) and over Siena in 1555 (on the right). In the upper-left corner of the painting of Pisa, you can see the Field of Miracles, with its tower leaning long before it was a tourist attraction. In the Siena painting, watch the Florentines storm Siena's gate by lantern light.

While Vasari's battle scenes are impressive, they pale in comparison to what some scholars believe was first painted on these walls. Around 1500, this hall was to have been the scene of a painting contest between two towering geniuses—young Michelangelo and aging Leonardo da Vinci. Unfortunately, Michelangelo never got around to starting his proposed *Battle of Cascina* (and his paper sketch of it is lost to history). But Leonardo may have painted the *Battle of Anghiari* here. Art historians have long suspected that this famous-but-unseen Leonardo masterpiece lies hidden beneath Vasari's *Battle of Marciano* (on the Siena wall). Vasari himself may have hinted at it to later scholars, by painting an enigmatic clue: a banner (40 feet up, hard to find) that reads *Cerca trova*—"He who seeks, finds."

The **statues** lining the hall show the labors of Hercules— the half-human, half-god who earned his divinity through great deeds...thereby setting an example for the power-hungry Medici.

Underneath Siena, in the middle of the right wall, stands **Michelangelo's *Victory*** (*La Vittoria,* 1533-1534), showing a young man triumphing over an older man. It was designed to ornament the never-finished tomb of Pope Julius II in St. Peter's Basilica in Rome. *Victory* was the prototype of the hall's many spiral-shaped statues by other artists.

• *From the Grand Hall, climb the stairs, following* Museo *arrows that point the rest of the one-way route through the palace.*

Royal Apartments

In 1540, Cosimo I and his wife Eleonora of Toledo moved into the Palazzo Vecchio, turning the Town Hall into their private

Giorgio Vasari
(1511-1574)

Giorgio Vasari—painter, architect, and writer—has been dismissed by history as a Renaissance hack, a man who was equally mediocre at many things. But his influence on Renaissance history is undeniable.

During his lifetime, Vasari enjoyed respect and accumulated a considerable fortune. He was consistently employed by patrons in the Medici family in Florence and Rome. In Florence, you'll see his mark everywhere. His huge frescoes color the main hall of the Palazzo Vecchio and the dome of the Duomo (see page 73). His oil paintings hang in the Church of Santa Maria Novella (see page 222) and the Uffizi Gallery. He built the tomb for his hero Michelangelo in Santa Croce Church (page 227). As an architect, he designed the Uffizi Gallery and the Vasari Corridor over Ponte Vecchio, which connects the Uffizi with the Pitti Palace.

Vasari is most famous, though, as the first Italian art historian. His book, *The Lives of the Artists,* was an early work that chronicled the Renaissance (with a bias that favored Florentine painters, sculptors, and architects). For that classic alone, we can say *"Grazie tante!"*

residence. They set about redecorating with frescoes and coffered ceilings in the Mannerist style.

The rooms are well-described in English; many are named for the subject painted on the ceiling. Not all of the rooms are open to the public, as the building still functions as Florence's Town Hall, housing the offices of the city's mayor—a popular, young, get-things-done guy who's credited with making the center of town so pedestrian-friendly.

• *Follow signs for* Apartments of Leo X. *One of the apartments is dedicated to the greatest of the Medici.*

Lorenzo the Magnificent Room

(The room is unmarked from the outside, but look for the label posted inside.) Here you feel the passion of this avid patron of the arts. Lorenzo died in 1492, when Florence was at its pinnacle (and still a self-governing republic), when the New World was still a mystery and the center of European power hadn't yet moved west. Enjoy the fine examples of the erotic, mystical, and fanciful art of his time.

Palazzo Vecchio—Second Floor

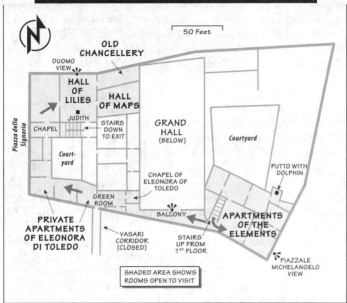

• *From here walk through the Room of Leo X and go up the staircase (built by Vasari) to the second floor, then turn left, entering the...*

Apartments of the Elements (Quartiere degli Elementi)

These five rooms were Cosimo's personal living rooms. In the first room (with paintings by Vasari and assistants), we see Cosimo I as a new god, controlling the four classical elements: air, earth, fire, and water (represented by the water-birth of Venus). Cosimo's coat of arms shows a cherub sailing a turtle. It's a bit of Medici symbol-

ism, referencing Cosimo I's motto, *festina lente* ("make haste, slowly")—that is, do urgent things properly and with care (or, perhaps, "measure twice, cut once").

Circling around this wing, find the balcony with a stunning view of Piazzale Michelangelo. One room displays Verrocchio's original *Putto with Dolphin* (1476), from the courtyard downstairs. The statue originally stood in the Medici family's rural villa before Cosimo I brought it to the Palazzo Vecchio.

• *Go back to the top of the stairs and cross over to the balcony overlooking the Grand Hall. Gaze out over the opulence and imagine it filled by a lavish Medici wedding celebration with a 500-person guest list. As you pass through the Green Room (Sala Verde), find the (locked) door, which leads onto the Vasari Corridor, Cosimo's private passageway leading to the Uffizi, across Ponte Vecchio, and into the Pitti Palace.*

Next, we enter the...

Private Apartments of Grand Duchess Eleonora di Toledo

Eleonora of Toledo (1522-1562) married Cosimo I in 1539. Their marriage united the Medici clan with royal bloodlines all over Europe. The following year, the couple moved out of the Medici-Riccardi Palace (as it's now known) and settled in here. As Florence's "first lady," Eleonora used her natural grace and beauty to mollify Florentine democrats chafing under Cosimo's absolutist rule.

This series of rooms features virtuous women of renown—the Sabine women abducted by the Romans, the Biblical Esther, Homer's Penelope—thus, of course, putting Eleonora in their company. On the whole, these rooms are relatively dull, except for the elaborately frescoed chapel done by Bronzino, Cosimo's court painter. The Penelope Room has a *Madonna and Child* by Botticelli.

• *Continue through these rooms to reach the large hall with the high, gilded ceiling.*

Hall of Lilies (Sala dei Gigli)

The coffered ceiling (from the 1460s) sports the fleur-de-lis—the three-petaled lily that's the symbol of Florence. Check out the

great view of the Duomo out the window, and compare it with a painting on the wall (by Ghirlandaio) showing a glimpse of the Duomo, circa 1482.

The room's highlight is Donatello's 11-piece bronze, *Judith and Holofernes*—cast in 1457, when the artist was in his prime. It shows a Biblical scene easily interpreted by its Renaissance audience: the victory of the weak-but-virtuous Judith over Holofernes the tyrant. The statue was commissioned by Cosimo the Elder to use as a fountain in the garden of the Medici-Riccardi Palace (note the holes in the cushion's corners). Since then, it's served as Florentine propaganda, displayed to justify the strength of whoever was in power. The Medici saw themselves as the noble Judith slaying their (drunken, sleepy) ene-mies. But when the Medici were driven out by Savonarola in the 1490s, the Florentines took the statue from the Medici-Riccardi Palace and placed it at the Palazzo Vecchio doorway (where the fake *David* now stands) as a symbol of their triumph over the corrupt family. A decade later, it was replaced by Michelangelo's *David*, the symbol of Florence victorious.

• *End your tour with a visit to two nearby rooms.*

Old Chancellery and Hall of Geographical Maps

The **Old Chancellery** (Sala delle Cancelleria) was once the office of Niccolò Machiavelli (1469-1527). Ponder the bust of the man who

faithfully served the Florentine Republic as a civil servant from 1498 to 1512, while the Medici were exiled as tyrants. When the Medici returned to power (under Pope Leo X), they tortured and exiled Machiavelli. He then wrote *The Prince,* a poly-sci treatise about how a ruler can ruthlessly gain and maintain power. Ironically, Machiavelli's cautionary advice soon came to be exploited by the man who would end the Florentine Republic for good—Grand Duke Cosimo I.

Finally, the **Hall of Geographical Maps** (Sala delle Carte Geografiche, the palace's former wardrobe) is full of maps made in a fit of post-1492 fascination with the wider world. Most date from about 1560, and show how serious cartography had become in the first 70 years after Columbus landed in the New World. They also say a great deal about what 16th-century Europeans did—and didn't—know about faraway lands. For example, Cosimo's huge *mappa mundi* globe was clearly made before the discovery of Australia. On other maps, some Texans and Southern Californians can even find their hometowns (far right corner of the hall, upper level). Florentines excelled at creating and publishing maps—which is why, even though Columbus beat the Florentine Amerigo Vespucci to the New World, our continent isn't called "North Columbia."

• *To exit, return to the Hall of Lilies; the door on the left leads to stairs that take you down to the courtyard. You're at the center of Florence—the city awaits.*

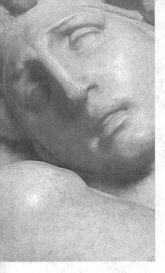

MEDICI CHAPELS TOUR

Cappelle Medicee

The Medici (MED-ee-chee) Chapels contain tombs of Florence's great ruling family, from Lorenzo the Magnificent to those less so. The highlight is a chapel designed by Michelangelo at the height of his creative powers. This is Renaissance Man's greatest "installation," a room completely under one artist's control, featuring innovative architecture, tombs, and sculpture. His statues tell of a middle-aged man's brooding meditation on mortality, the fall of the Medici Golden Age, and the relentless passage of time—from *Dawn* to *Day* to *Dusk* to *Night*.

Orientation

Cost: €6, €9 with mandatory temporary exhibits.

Hours: Tue-Sat April-Oct 8:15-16:50, Nov-March 8:15-13:50; also open second and fourth Mon and first, third, and fifth Sun of each month; last entry 30 minutes before closing. Reservations are possible but unnecessary.

Dress Code: No tank tops, short shorts, or short skirts.

Getting There: It's in the Church of San Lorenzo—the one with the smaller dome on Florence's skyline (5-minute walk northwest of Duomo). The bustling outdoor market almost obscures the chapel entrance at the back (west end) of the church. See page 68 for more about the Church of San Lorenzo.

Information: The audioguide costs €6 (€10/2 people). Tel. 055-238-8602, www.polomuseale.firenze.it.

Length of This Tour: Allow 45 minutes.

With Limited Time: Make a beeline to Michelangelo's New Sacristy.

Services: WCs are located midway up the staircase that leads from the Crypt to the Chapel of Princes. Look for the

camouflaged doorway.
Photography: Prohibited.
Starring: Michelangelo's statues *Day, Night, Dawn,* and *Dusk.*

The Tour Begins

Overview
The Medici Chapels consist of three burial places: the unimpressive Crypt; the large and gaudy Chapel of Princes; and—the highlight—Michelangelo's New Sacristy, a room completely designed by him to honor four Medici. Due to restoration work, scaffolding in the Chapel of Princes may obscure some (lesser) sights when you visit.
• *Enter the Chapel and buy tickets. Immediately after you show your ticket, you're in...*

The Crypt
This gloomy, low-ceilinged room with gravestones underfoot reminds us that these "chapels" are really tombs. You'll see a few Lorenzos buried in this room (after all, "Laurentius," or Lawrence, was the family's patron saint)...but none that is "Magnificent" (he's later). The collection of ornate silver and gold reliquaries is appropriately macabre and worth a quick look.
• *Head upstairs via the staircase on the right and into the large, domed, multicolored chapel, which is* not *by Michelangelo.*

Chapel of Princes
(La Cappella dei Principi, 1602-1743)
The impressive **dome** overhead (seen from outside, it's the big, red-brick "mini-Duomo") tops an octagonal room that echoes the

Baptistery and Duomo drum. It's lined with six tombs of Medici rulers and is decorated everywhere with the **Medici coat of arms**—a shield with six balls thought to represent the pills of doctors *(medici),* reputedly their original occupation. Along with many different-colored marbles, geologists will recognize jasper, porphyry, quartz, alabaster, coral, mother-of-pearl, and lapis lazuli.

    Sixteen shields ring the room at eye level, each representing one of the Tuscan cities ("Civitas") ruled by Florence's dukes. Find Florence, with its fleur-de-lis ("Florentiae"), and Pisa ("Pisarum"), both just left of the altar.
The bronze **statues** honor two of the "later" Medici, the cultured but oppressive dukes who ruled Florence after the city's

glorious Renaissance. In the first niche to the right (as you face the altar) stands Ferdinando I (ruled 1587-1609), dressed in an ermine cape and jewels. He started the work on this Chapel of Princes and tore down the Duomo's medieval facade. His son, Cosimo II (ruled 1609-1621, to the right), appointed Galileo "first professor" of science at Pisa U., inspiring him to label the moons of Jupiter "the Medici Stars."

The **altar** was finished in 1939 for a visit from Hitler and Mussolini. The altar itself is the only Christian symbolism in this spacious but stifling temple to power, wealth, and mediocre Medici.

(*Psst.* A room behind the altar—though it may be blocked by scaffolding—displays relics and the pastoral staff of Pope Leo X, who was Lorenzo the Magnificent's son and Michelangelo's classmate.)

• *Continue down the hall, passing statues of Roman armor with worms sprouting out, to Michelangelo's New Sacristy.*

New Sacristy (Sacrestia Nuova)—Michelangelo

The entire room—architecture, tombs, and statues—was designed by Michelangelo over a 14-year period (1520-1534) to house the bodies of four of the Medici family. Michelangelo, who spent his teen years in the Medici household and personally knew three of the four family members buried here, was emotionally attached to the project. This is the work of a middle-aged man (he started at age 45 and finished at 59) reflecting on his contemporaries dying around him, and on his own mortality.

• *There are tombs decorated with statues against three of the walls, and an altar on the fourth. Start with the tomb on the left wall (as you enter and face the altar).*

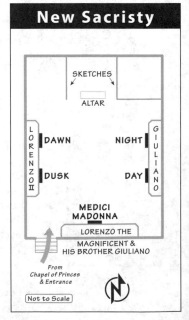

Tomb of Lorenzo II, Duke of Urbino

Lorenzo II—the grandson of Lorenzo the Magnificent—is shown as a Roman general, seated, arm resting on a Medici-bank money box, and bowing his head in contemplation. He had been the model for Machiavelli's *The Prince,* and when he died at 27 (of tuberculosis and syphilis) without a male heir, the line of great princes stretching back to Cosimo the Elder died with him.

His sarcophagus, with a curved, scrolled lid, bears the reclining statues that Michelangelo
named *Dusk* and *Dawn. Dusk*
(the man), worn out after a long
day, slumps his chin on his chest
and reflects on the day's events.
Dawn (the woman) stirs restlessly after a long night, with an
anguished face, as though waking from a bad dream. *Dusk* and
Dawn, with their counterparts

Day and *Night* (opposite wall), represented to Michelangelo the
swift passage of time, which kills everyone and causes our glorious
deeds on earth to quickly fade.

During the years he worked here, Michelangelo suffered the deaths of his father, his favorite brother, and his unofficial step-brother, Pope Leo X Medici. In addition, plagues in 1522 and 1527 killed thousands in Florence. In 1527, his adoptive city of Rome was looted by mercenaries. Michelangelo's letters reveal that, upon turning 50, he was feeling old, tired ("If I work one day, I need four to recuperate"), and depressed (he called it *mio pazzo,* "my madness"). He was also facing up to the sad fact that the master-piece of his youth—the grand tomb of Pope Julius II—was never going to be completed.

Overachievers in severe midlife crises may wish to avoid the Medici Chapels.

• *On the opposite wall is the...*

Tomb of Giuliano, Duke of Nemours

Overshadowed by his famous father (Lorenzo the Magnificent) and

big brother (Pope Leo X), **Giuliano** led a wine-women-and-song life, dying young without a male heir. His statue as a Roman general, with scepter, powerful Moses-esque pose, and alert, intelligent face, looks in the direction of the Madonna statue, as though asking forgiveness for a wasted life. The likeness is not at

MEDICI CHAPELS

all accurate. Michelangelo said, "In a thousand years, no one will know how they looked."

Giuliano's "active" pose complements the "contemplative" one of Lorenzo, showing the two elements (thought + action) that Plato and Michelangelo believed made up the soul of man.

Night (the woman) does a crossover sit-up in her sleep, toning the fleshy abs that look marvelously supple and waxlike, not like hard stone. She's highly polished, shimmering, and finished with minute details. Michelangelo's females—musclemen with coconut-shell breasts—are generally more complete and (some think) less interesting than his men.

Michelangelo was homosexual. While his private sex life (or lack thereof) remains a mystery, his public expressions of affection were clearly weighted toward men. Some say he was less interested in female bodies and felt he could easily sum them up in a statue.

Day (the man) works out a crick in his back, each limb twisting a different direction, turning away from us. He looks over his shoulder with an expression (suspicious? angry? arrogant?) forever veiled behind chisel marks suggestive of Impressionist brush strokes. In fact, none of the four reclining statues' faces expresses a clear emotion, as all are turned inward, letting body language speak.

If, as some say, Michelangelo purposely left these statues "unfinished" while liberating them from their stone prison, it certainly adds mystery and a contrast in color and texture. *Night*'s moonlit clarity and *Day*'s rough-hewn grogginess may also reflect Michelangelo's own work schedule—a notorious day-sleeper and guilt-ridden layabout ("Dear to me is sleep") who, when inspired (as a friend wrote), "works much, eats little, and sleeps less."

Among *Night*'s symbols (the crescent moon on her forehead, owl under knee, and poppies underfoot) is a grotesque **mask** with, perhaps, a self-portrait. Michelangelo, a serious poet (so much so that he almost considered sculpting his "day job"), has *Night* say in one of his poems: "As long as shame and sorrow exist / I'd rather not see or hear / So speak softly and let me sleep."

Day, Night, Dawn, and *Dusk*—brought to life in this room where Michelangelo had his workshop, and where they've been ever since—meditate eternally on Death, squirming restlessly, unable to come to terms with it.

• *On the entrance wall is the...*

Tomb of Lorenzo the Magnificent and his Brother Giuliano

As the tomb was never completed, all that really marks where The Magnificent One's body lies is a marble slab, now topped with a statue of the Madonna flanked by saints. Perhaps Michelangelo was working up to the grand finale to honor the man who not only was the greatest Medici, but who also plucked a poor 13-year-old Michelangelo from an obscure apprenticeship to dine at the Medici table with cardinals and kings.

Lorenzo's beloved younger brother, Giuliano, died in 1478 in a "hit" by a rival family, stabbed to death before the altar of the Duomo during Easter Mass. (Lorenzo, wounded, drew his sword and backpedaled to safety. Enraged supporters grabbed the assassins—including two priests planted there by the pope—and literally tore them apart.)

The **Medici Madonna,** unlike many Michelangelo women, is thin, vertical, and elegant, her sad face veiled under chisel marks. Aware of the hard life her son has ahead of him, she tolerates the squirming, two-year-old Jesus, who seems to want to breast-feed. Mary's right foot is still buried in stone, so this unfinished statue was certainly meant to be worked on more. The saints **Cosmas** and **Damian** were done by assistants.

The Unfinished Project

The Chapel project (1520-1534) was plagued by delays: design changes, late shipments of Carrara marble, the death of patrons, Michelangelo's other obligations (including the Laurentian Library next door), his own depression, and...revolution.

In 1527, Florence rose up against the Medici pope and declared itself an independent republic. Michelangelo, torn between his love of Florence and loyalty to the Medici of his youth, walked a fine line. He continued to work for the pope while simultaneously designing fortified city walls to defend Florence from the pope's troops. In 1530, the besieged city fell, republicans were rounded up and executed, and Michelangelo went into hiding (perhaps in the chapel basement, down the steps to the left of the altar). Fortunately, his status as both an artist and a staunch Florentine spared him from reprisals.

In 1534, a new pope enticed Michelangelo to come back to Rome with a challenging new project: painting the *Last Judgment*

The Medici in a Minute and a Half

The Medici family—part *Sopranos,* part Kennedys, part John-D-and-Catherine-T art patrons—dominated Florentine politics for 300 years (c. 1434-1737). Originally a hardworking, middle-class family in the cloth, silk, and banking businesses, they used their wealth, blue-collar popularity, and philanthropy to rise into Europe's nobility, producing popes and queens.

1400s: The Princes

Lorenzo the Magnificent (ruled 1469-1492), Cosimo the Elder's grandson, epitomized the Medici ruling style: publicly praising Florence's constitution while privately holding the purse strings. A true Renaissance Man, Lorenzo's personal charisma, public festivals, and support of Leonardo, Botticelli, and teenage Michelangelo made Florence Europe's most enlightened city.

1494-1532: Exile in Rome

After Lorenzo's early death, the family was exiled by the Florentines. The Medici became victims of bank failure, Savonarola's reforms, and the Florentine tradition of democracy. They built a power base in Rome under Lorenzo's son (Pope Leo X, who made forays into Florence) and nephew (Pope Clement VII, who finally invaded Florence and crushed the republic).

1537-1737: The Grand Duchy—Mediocre Medici

Backed by Europe's popes and kings, the "later" Medici—descendants of Cosimo the Elder's brother—ruled Florence and Tuscany as just another duchy. Grand Duke Cosimo I was politically repressive but a generous patron of the arts, leaving his mark on the Palazzo Vecchio, the Uffizi, and the Pitti Palace. Cosimo II supported Galileo. Famous throughout Europe, the Medici married into Europe's royal families (Catherine and Marie de' Medici were queens of France), even while Florence declined as a political and economic power.

over the altar in the Sistine Chapel. Michelangelo left, never to return to the Medici Chapels. Assistants gathered up statues and fragments from the chapel floor (and the Madonna from Michelangelo's house) and did their best to assemble the pieces according to Michelangelo's designs.

• *The apse is the area behind the altar. This has the best view of the chapel as a whole.*

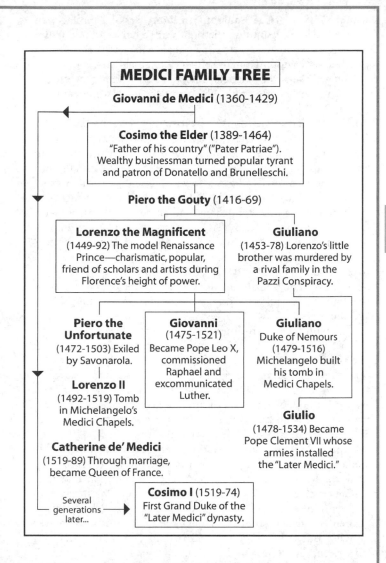

MEDICI FAMILY TREE

Giovanni de Medici (1360-1429)

Cosimo the Elder (1389-1464)
"Father of his country" ("Pater Patriae").
Wealthy businessman turned popular tyrant
and patron of Donatello and Brunelleschi.

Piero the Gouty (1416-69)

Lorenzo the Magnificent
(1449-92) The model Renaissance
Prince—charismatic, popular,
friend of scholars and artists during
Florence's height of power.

Giuliano
(1453-78) Lorenzo's little
brother was murdered by
a rival family in the
Pazzi Conspiracy.

Piero the Unfortunate
(1472-1503) Exiled
by Savonarola.

Giovanni
(1475-1521)
Became Pope Leo X,
commissioned
Raphael and
excommunicated
Luther.

Giuliano
Duke of Nemours
(1479-1516)
Michelangelo built
his tomb in
Medici Chapels.

Lorenzo II
(1492-1519) Tomb
in Michelangelo's
Medici Chapels.

Giulio
(1478-1534) Became
Pope Clement VII whose
armies installed
the "Later Medici."

Catherine de' Medici
(1519-89) Through marriage,
became Queen of France.

Several
generations →
later...

Cosimo I (1519-74)
First Grand Duke of the
"Later Medici" dynasty.

MEDICI CHAPELS

Sketches on the Walls of the Apse

Michelangelo's many design changes and improvisational style come to life in these (dimly lit and hard to see behind Plexiglas) black chalk and charcoal doodles, presumably by Michelangelo and assistants.

• *Starting on the left wall and working clockwise at about eye level...*

Look at all the marks: hash marks counting off days worked,

a window frame for the Laurentian Library, scribbles, a face, an arch, a bearded face, and (on the right wall) a horse, a nude figure crouching under an arch, a twisting female nude with her dog, and a tiny, wacky, cartoon Roman soldier with shield and spurs. You really do get a sense of Michelangelo and staff working, sweating, arguing, and just goofing off as the hammers pound and dust flies.

The Whole Ensemble—Michelangelo's Vision

The New Sacristy was the first chance for Michelangelo to use his arsenal of talents—as sculptor, architect, and Thinker of Big Ideas—on a single multimedia project. The resulting "installation" (a 20th-century term) produces a powerful overall effect that's different for everyone—"somber," "meditative," "redemptive," "ugly."

The room is a cube topped with a Pantheon-style dome, with three distinct stories—the heavy tombs at ground level, upper-level windows with simpler wall decoration, and the dome, better-lit and simpler still. The whole effect draws the eye upward, from dark and "busy" to light and airy. (It's intensified by an optical illusion—Michelangelo made the dome's coffers, the upper windows, and round lunettes all taper imperceptibly at the top so they'd look taller and higher.)

The white walls are lined in gray-brown-green stone. The half columns, arches, and triangular pediments are traditional Renaissance forms, but with no regard for the traditional "orders" of the time (matching the right capital with the right base, the correct width-to-height ratio of columns, upper story taller than lower, etc.). Michelangelo had Baroque-en the rules, baffling his contemporaries and pointing the way to a new, more ornate style that used old forms as mere decoration.

Finally, Michelangelo, a serious neo-Platonist, wanted this room to symbolize the big philosophical questions that death presents to the living. Summing up these capital-letter concepts (far, far more crudely than was ever intended), the room might say:

Time (the four reclining statues) kills Mortal Men (statues of Lorenzo and Giuliano) and mocks their Glory (Roman power symbols). But if we Focus (Lorenzo and Giuliano's gaze) on God's Grace (Madonna and Child), our Souls (both Active and Contemplative parts) can be Resurrected (the Chapel was consecrated to this) and rise from this drab Earth (the dark, heavy ground floor) up into the Light (the windows and lantern) of Heaven (the geometrically perfect dome), where God and Plato's Ideas are forever Immortal.

And that, folks, is a Mouthful.

MEDICI-RICCARDI PALACE TOUR

Palazzo Medici-Riccardi

Cosimo the Elder, the founder of the ruling Medici family dynasty, lived here with his upwardly mobile clan, including his grandson, Lorenzo the Magnificent. Besides the immediate family, the palace also hosted many famous Florentines: teenage Michelangelo, who lived almost as an adopted son; Leonardo da Vinci, who played the lute at Medici parties; and Botticelli, who studied the classical sculpture that dotted the gardens. The historical ambience is captured in a few well-preserved rooms and in a 15th-century fresco that brings the colorful Medici world to life.

Orientation

Cost: €7, covered by Firenze Card.

Hours: Thu-Tue 9:00-18:00, closed Wed, last entry 30 minutes before closing.

Crowd Alert: While the palace is rarely mobbed, you may encounter a slight bottleneck at the tiny Chapel of the Magi (Cappella di Gozzoli). Only 10 people are allowed in at a time, but the line moves quickly.

Getting There: It's one block north of the Duomo at Via Cavour 3. The ticket entrance is a bit north of what appears to be the main entrance (which is often gated shut).

Information: The €1 brochure available at the entrance is worth considering. You can also rent an audio/videoguide with 25 minutes of commentary and interactive maps (€4). Tel. 055-276-0340, www.palazzo-medici.it.

Length of This Tour: Allow an hour.

With Limited Time: Focus on the Chapel of the Magi.

Photography: Photography without a flash is OK, except in the Chapel of the Magi, where photos are not allowed.

Starring: Cosimo the Elder and Lorenzo the Magnificent as depicted in Gozzoli's colorful Magi frescoes.

The Tour Begins

Exterior

Cosimo the Elder hired the architect Michelozzo to build the pal-

ace (1444), whose three-story facade set the tone for the rest of Florence—rough stones at bottom, rising to smooth and elegant on top. Two generations later, Michelangelo added the distinctive "kneeling windows" (with scrolls), an innovation that later cropped up on palaces the world over. In the 1700s, the palace was extended northward (keeping the same style) by its next owners, the Riccardi family.

• *Buy your ticket, pass through one small courtyard, and continue into the...*

Courtyard

As with many Italian homes, the courtyard served as an open-air meeting point and "living room" for the extended family. The statue of Orpheus (who calmed wild animals with his harp) reminded visitors that the Medici family calmed wild Florence with smart and soothing politics. Find the family shield above the arches, with the six pills of these doctors *(medici)*-turned-cloth merchants-turned-international bankers. The Riccardi family later gilded this Renaissance lily with Baroque decor and adorned this courtyard with their collection of classical sculpture. Temporary exhibits (included in your ticket) often inhabit rooms adjoining the courtyard.

Garden

Pop into the fragrant garden with its greenhouse for lemon trees. This tiny oasis is a mere fraction of the once-spacious gardens that stretched for a city block to the north. In the past, the grounds were studded with many more fountains and statues, including the *Venus de' Medici* (Uffizi). Donatello's *David* (Bargello) likely stood in the courtyard. Teenage Michelangelo studied sculpture and liberal arts in the family school located in the gardens.

At the far end of the garden and down the stairs is the Museo degli Marmi, included in your ticket. At some point, you may want to visit its small collection of rare busts of ancient gods (Hercules, or *Ercole*), philosophers, emperors (Caracalla), and ordinary citizens (a *bambino* and the handsome Riccardi Athlete).

• *Enter the room to Orpheus' left.*

Lorenzo's Workshop/"Virtual Visit"

This room was once Lorenzo the Magnificent's public office. It now houses a multimedia *Star Wars*-meets-art history setup that allows you to see close-ups of Gozzoli's Magi frescoes. Stand on the lighted square and use your arm to point at marked areas of the large video screen. It zooms in, and a narrator explains the selected detail. A smaller plasma screen takes you through what Lorenzo's workshop would have been like in 1492.

• *Check out any temporary exhibits (in the room to Orpheus' right), then head upstairs. From the courtyard, a stairway leads to the...*

Chapel of the Magi
(Cappella di Benozzo Gozzoli)

This sumptuous little room was the nuclear family's private chapel, where they could kneel at the altar and pray to a *Madonna and Child* by Fra Filippo Lippi (where a copy stands now). At the time, it was rare and highly prestigious for a family to have a private chapel (this is one of only three in Florence). But Cosimo the Elder was the pope's banker—he even bankrolled one of the Crusades. He could afford it.

The three walls around the altar display *The Journey of the Magi* (the three kings—one king per wall) by Benozzo Gozzoli (1459).

Each wall has a dominant color of white, green, or red: the Medici family colors.

On the biggest wall, a curly-haired young king, dressed in white and riding a white horse, leads a parade of men through a rocky landscape. (Some scholars have suggested that the young Magus may be Lorenzo the Magnificent, but others dismiss the idea. Lorenzo is pictured elsewhere—read on.) The scene takes you not to Bethlehem, but to

15th-century Medici-populated Tuscany. Riding behind the king are Cosimo the Elder (in red hat, riding a modest brown donkey) and his son Piero (also in a red hat, on a gray-white horse), who succeeded Cosimo the Elder as ruler of Florence. In the line of young men behind them, find Piero's 10-year-old son and future ruler—Lorenzo the Magnificent (sixth in from the left, in red cap, with scoop nose, and brown bowl-cut hair; he looks to the right with an intense gaze). Little Lorenzo grew up surrounded by these beautiful frescoes that celebrate the natural world. One day, he would commission his own great art.

Above Lorenzo (and slightly to the right) is Gozzoli himself. The sour-faced man in the cap above Gozzoli is Pope Pius II, often called "the first humanist" (see "Piccolomini Library" on page 367). Lost? Ask the attendant where they are: *"Dov'è* (doh-VEH) *Benozzo Gozzoli? Dov'è Cosimo? Dov'è Lorenzo?"*

The next wall (working clockwise) sets the king and his entourage in a green, spacious, and obviously Tuscan landscape. The men wear colorful clothes that set trends throughout Europe. Every year on Epiphany (January 6), the Medici men would actually dress up like this and parade through the streets to celebrate the holiday of the three kings.

On the last wall, notice that the white-bearded king on his white donkey (far left) got cut off when the room was later remodeled. But the fresco was preserved—find the horse's ass on the other side of the doorway.

Gozzoli's crystal-clear, shadowless scenes reflect the style of his teacher, Fra Angelico. The portraits are realistic, showing the leading characters of 1459 Florence.

The room itself functioned both as a chapel and as the place where Cosimo the Elder received VIPs. By portraying his own family in this religious setting, Cosimo made a classy display of cool power and sophistication. When learned rival powers came here, they thought, "Damn, these Medici are good."

• *Exit the Gozzoli room into several...*

Palatial Rooms with Temporary Exhibitions

Though the displays change often, the rooms themselves give a small sense of the former luxury of the palace—suggested now by a few chandeliers, tapestries, and furnishings. From roughly 1400 to 1700, the city of Florence set the tone for fashion and interior decor throughout Europe. This palace was ground zero of international style.

• *Eventually you'll reach a room displaying a painting in a glass case.*

Fra Filippo Lippi—*Madonna and Child*

Lippi's cheek-to-cheek *Madonna and Child* demonstrates his specialty— humanizing the son of God and the Virgin. Baby Jesus' transparent shirt, Mary's transparent scarf, and their transparent halos make this late Lippi work especially ethereal. Mary's eyes are sad, while Jesus stares into his spiritual future. She gives him a tender hug before he's off on his mission.

• *Several rooms branching off the Lippi room are government offices.*

The Palace as Civic Center

Today, the palace is a functioning county government building. As you wander around, notice the bureaucrats at work. Occasionally, the provincial council meeting room (Sala Quattro Stagione) is open for viewing. You'll see a few dozen modern-looking seats for the council members, amid chandeliered elegance. The tapestries on the wall depict the four seasons *(quattro stagione).*

• *Complete your visit in the nearby...*

Luca Giordano Room

This Baroque, Versailles-like former reception hall was added

by the Riccardi family. The ceiling (*The Apotheosis of the Medici Family,* frescoed in 1685 by the Naples artist Luca Giordano) features Medici big shots (with starbursts over their heads) frolicking with Greek gods. Walk slowly toward the center of the room and watch as the Medici appear to rise up into heaven to be crowned by Zeus. Ringing the base of the ceiling are various Greek myths—find Poseidon with his trident (to the left) and Hades carrying off Persephone (to the right). Claiming her place among the ancients, the blue-robed woman over the entrance is Florence, who re-birthed the classical world.

• *Your tour is done. Now head back out into the modern world and take your place among the ancients—and youth—of Florence.*

SANTA MARIA NOVELLA TOUR

Chiesa di Santa Maria Novella

The Church of Santa Maria Novella, chock-full of ground-breaking paintings and statues, is a reminder that the Renaissance was not simply a secular phenomenon. Many wealthy families paid for chapels inside this church that today are appreciated for their fine art.

Masaccio's fresco *The Trinity* (1427), the first painting of modern times to portray three-dimensional space, blew a "hole in the wall" of this church. From then on, a painting wasn't just a decorated panel, but a window into the spacious 3-D world of light and color. With Masaccio's *Trinity* as the centerpiece, the church traces Florentine art from the medieval to the Quattrocento (1400s) to the onset of Baroque.

Orientation

Cost: €3.50, covered by Firenze Card.

Hours: Mon-Thu 9:00-17:30, Fri 11:00-17:30, Sat 9:00-17:00, Sun 13:00-17:00, last entry 30 minutes before closing.

Dress Code: No bare shoulders or short skirts or short shorts for adults. Your clothing must cover your knees. Free poncho-like coverings are available.

Getting There: It's on Piazza Santa Maria Novella, a block south of the train station.

Information: The audioguide costs €5 (€8/2 people). Tel. 055-219-257, www.museicivicifiorentini.it.

Length of This Tour: Allow 45 minutes.

With Limited Time: Masaccio's *Trinity* and Ghirlandaio's Mary and John the Baptist fresco cycles are a must.

Services: Pay WCs (€0.60) are to the left of the church; the free WCs in the museum are for people who have paid admission.

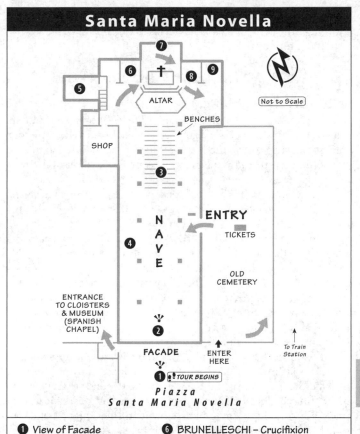

Santa Maria Novella

① View of Facade
② View down the Nave
③ GIOTTO – Crucifixion
④ MASACCIO – The Trinity
⑤ ORCAGNA BROTHERS – Hell, Purgatory & Heaven

⑥ BRUNELLESCHI – Crucifixion
⑦ GHIRLANDAIO – Fresco Cycles of Mary and John the Baptist
⑧ FILIPPINO LIPPI – St. Philip at the Temple of Mars & St. John the Evangelist Raising Drusiana
⑨ VASARI – Madonna of the Rosary

Photography: Prohibited.

Eating: For recommended restaurants in the area, see page 301.

Nearby: Ardent art lovers can seek out the adjacent cloisters and **Museum of Santa Maria Novella,** with its frescoed Spanish Chapel (€2.70, covered by Firenze Card, entry to the left of church's facade; Fri-Mon 9:00-16:00, closed Tue-Thu, tel. 055-282-187).

A block away from the church is a fancy **perfumery** (Farmacia di Santa Maria Novella). This store, which feels like a small museum, is free and fun to visit (inconsistent hours but likely daily 9:30-19:30, Via della Scala 16, tel.

055-216-276); see page 85 for details.

Starring: The early Renaissance—Masaccio, Giotto, Brunelleschi, and Ghirlandaio.

The Tour Begins

❶ Exterior—The Facade

The green-and-white marble facade (1456-1470) by Leon Battista Alberti contains elements of Florence's whole history: Romanesque (horizontal stripes, like the Baptistery), Gothic (pointed arches on the bottom level), and Renaissance (geometric squares and circles on the upper level).

The church itself is cross-shaped, with a high central nave and low-ceilinged side aisles. The scrolls on the facade help bridge the two levels.

Before stepping inside, turn around and survey Piazza Santa Maria Novella. This marked the Dominican Quarter, just outside the city walls, while the Franciscans flanked the city on the opposite side of town at Santa Croce. The monks here built a hospice (the fine arcade opposite the church), ran a pharmacy (around the corner), and for centuries provided a kind of neighborhood clinic (which still functions as an emergency room—notice the ambulances parked on the right).

The obelisks at either end of the square were commissioned by Cosimo I (a 16th-century Medici duke—don't confuse him with Cosimo the Elder). His symbol was the turtle, and turtles seem to be holding up the obelisks, which served as end posts for a race-track. Imagine high-energy horse races in this square as jockeys rode bareback, to the delight of Florentine spectators.

• *Enter the courtyard to the right of the main door, passing through the cemetery, where you'll pay to enter. Masaccio's* Trinity *is on the opposite wall from the entrance. But we'll start our tour at the central doorway in the facade, looking down the long nave to the altar.*

❷ Interior—View down the Nave from the Main Entrance

The long, 330-foot nave looks even longer, thanks to a 14th-century perspective illusion. The columns converge as you approach the altar, the space between them gets smaller, the arches get lower, and the floor gets higher, creating the illusion that the nave stretches farther into the distance than it actually does. Gothic architects were

aware of the rules of perspective, just not how to render it on a two-dimensional canvas.

• *Hanging from the ceiling in the middle of the nave is a painting by...*

❸ Giotto—*Crucifixion*

The altarpiece by Giotto (c. 1266-1337) originally stood on the main altar. Stately and understated, it avoids the gruesome excesses of many medieval crucifixes. The tragic tilt of Christ's head, the parted lips, and the stretched rib cage tell more about human suffering than an excess of spurting blood.

On either side of the crossbar, Mary and John sit in a golden iconic heaven, but they are fully human, turned at a three-quarter angle, with knowing, sympathetic expressions. Giotto, the proto-Renaissance experimenter in perspective, creates the illusion that Christ's hands are actually turned out, palms down, and not hammered flat against the cross.

• *Masaccio's* Trinity *is on the left wall, about midway along the nave (opposite the entrance). For the best perspective, stand about 20 feet from it, then take four steps to your left, standing on the shield with a crown. Masaccio positioned it to be seen by the faithful as they dipped fingers into a (missing) font and crossed themselves—"Father, Son, and Holy Ghost."*

❹ Masaccio—*The Trinity* (1425-1427)

In his short but influential five-year career, Masaccio (1401-1428) was the first painter since ancient times to portray Man in Nature—real humans with real emotions, in a spacious three-dimensional world. (Unfortunately for tourists, his best portrayal of 3-D space is here, but his best portrayal of humans is in the Brancacci Chapel across the river.)

With simple pinks and blues (now faded), Masaccio creates the illusion that we're looking into a raised, cube-shaped chapel (about nine feet tall) topped with an arched ceiling and framed at the entrance with classical columns. Inside the chapel, God the Father stands on an altar, holding up the cross of Christ. (Where's the dove of the Holy Spirit? Why is God's "white collar" crooked?) John looks up at Christ while Mary looks down at us. Two donors (husband and wife, most likely) kneel on the front step outside the chapel, their cloaks spilling out of the niche. Below this fake chapel sits a fake tomb with the skeleton of Adam; compare it with the real tomb and niche to the right.

The checkerboard-coffered ceiling creates a 3-D tunnel effect, with rows of panels that appear to converge at the back, the panels getting smaller, lower, and closer together. Earlier painters had played with tricks like this, but Masaccio went further. He gave such thought to the proper perspective that we, as viewers, know right where we stand in relation to this virtual chapel.

He knew that, in real life, the rows of coffers would, if extended, stretch to the distant horizon. Lay a mental ruler along them, and you'll find the "vanishing point"—where all the lines intersect—all the way down below the foot of the cross. Masaccio places us there, looking "up" into the chapel.

Having fixed where the distant horizon is and where the viewer is, Masaccio draws a checkerboard grid in between, then places the figures on it (actually underneath it) like chess pieces. What's truly amazing is that young Masaccio seemed to grasp this stuff intuitively—as a "natural"—eyeballing it and sketching freehand what later artists would have to work out with a pencil and paper.

What Masaccio learned intuitively, Brunelleschi analyzed mathematically, and Alberti (who did the facade) codified in his famous 1435 treatise, *On Painting*. Soon, artists everywhere were drawing Alberti checkerboards on the ground, creating spacious, perfectly lit, 3-D scenes filled with chess-piece humans.

• *The Orcagna Chapel is at the far end of the left transept. As you approach, view the chapel from a distance. This is the illusion that Masaccio tried to create—of a raised chapel set in a wall with people inside—using only paint on a flat surface. Climb the steps to see...*

❺ Orcagna Brothers—Frescoes of the Last Judgment: *Hell, Purgatory,* and *Heaven* (*Inferno, Purgatorio,* and *Paradiso,* 1340-1357)

In 1347-1348, Florence was hit with the terrible Black Death (bubonic plague) that killed half the population. Here, in the Orcagna Chapel, the fading frescoes from that grim time show hundreds of figures, and not a single smile.

It's the Day of Judgment (center wall), and God (above the stained-glass window) spreads his hands to divide the good from the evil. God has selected Dante as the interior decorator for heaven and hell. (Find Dante all in white, with his ear-flap cap, among the crowd to the left of the window, about a third of the way up.) Notice that God is bigger than the angels, who dwarf the hallowed saints, who are bigger than ordinary souls such as Dante, mirroring the feudal hierarchy of king, nobles, knights, and serfs.

In *Heaven* (left wall), Hotel Paradiso is *completo,* stacked with gold-haloed saints. *Hell* (faded right wall) is a series of layers, the descending rings of Dante's Inferno. A river of fire runs through it, dividing *Purgatory* (above) and *Hell* (below). At the bottom of the pit, where dogs and winged demons run wild, naked souls in caves beg for mercy and get none.

• *In a chapel to the left of the church's main altar, you'll find...*

❻ Filippo Brunelleschi—*Crucifixion*

Filippo Brunelleschi (1377-1446)—architect, painter, sculptor—used his skills as an analyst of nature to carve (in wood) a

perfectly realistic *Crucifixion,* neither prettified nor with the grotesque exaggeration of medieval religious objects. His Christ is buck naked, not particularly muscular or handsome, with bulging veins, armpit hair, tensed leg muscles, and bent feet. The tilt of Christ's head frees a tendril of hair that directs our eye down to the wound and the dripping blood, dropping straight from his side to his thigh to his calf—a strong vertical line that sets off the curve of Christ's body. Brunelleschi carved this to outdo a crucifix his friend Donatello had done elsewhere. He thought Donatello's Christ looked like an agonized peasant; Brunelleschi's was a dignified noble. (BTW, Donatello was impressed.)

• *In the choir area behind the main altar are Ghirlandaio's 21 frescoes, stacked seven to a wall. We'll concentrate on just the six panels on the bottom.*

❼ Domenico Ghirlandaio—Fresco Cycles of Mary and John the Baptist (1485-1490)

At the peak of Florence's power, wealth, and confidence, Domenico Ghirlandaio (1449-1494) painted portraits of his fellow Florentines

SANTA MARIA NOVELLA

in their Sunday best, inhabiting video-game landscapes of mixed classical and contemporary buildings, rubbing shoulders with saints and angels. The religious subjects get lost in the colorful scenes of everyday life—perhaps a metaphor for how Renaissance humanism was marginalizing religion.

• *Start with the left wall and work clockwise along the bottom. The first scene shows the...*

Expulsion of Joachim from the Temple

Proud, young Florentine men (the group at left) seem oblivious to

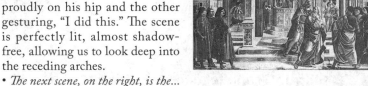

bearded, robed saints rushing from the arcade. There's Ghirlandaio himself (in the group on the right) looking out at us, with one hand proudly on his hip and the other gesturing, "I did this." The scene is perfectly lit, almost shadow-free, allowing us to look deep into the receding arches.

• *The next scene, on the right, is the...*

Birth of the Virgin

Five beautiful young women, led by the pregnant daughter of Ghirlandaio's patron, parade up to newborn Mary. The pregnant

girl's brocade dress is a microcosm of the room's decorations. Dancing babies in the room's classical frieze celebrate Mary's birth, obviously echoing Donatello's beloved *cantoria* in Florence's Duomo Museum.

True, Ghirlandaio's works are "busy"—each scene crammed with portraits, designs, fantasy architecture, and great costumes—but if you mentally frame off small sections, you discover a collection of mini-masterpieces.

• *On the lowest part of the center wall, flanking the stained-glass window, are two matching panels.*

Giovanni Tornabuoni Kneeling and
Francesca Tornabuoni (his wife) Kneeling

Giovanni Tornabuoni, who paid for these frescoes, was a successful executive in the Medici Company (and Lorenzo the Magnificent's uncle). However, by the time these frescoes were being finished, the Medici bank was slipping seriously into the red, and soon the

family had to flee Florence, creditors on their heels.
• *On the right wall...*

Mary Meets Elizabeth

In a spacious, airy landscape (with the pointed steeple of Santa Maria Novella in the distance), Mary and Elizabeth embrace,

uniting their respective entourages. The parade of ladies in contemporary dress echoes the one on the opposite wall. This panel celebrates youth, beauty, the city, trees, rocks, and life.

A generation after Brunelleschi and Alberti, all artists—including the near-genius Ghirlandaio—had mastered perspective tricks. Here, Alberti's famed checkerboard is laid on its side, making a sharply receding wall to create the illusion of great distance.

Ghirlandaio employed many assistants in his productive workshop: "Johnson, you do the ladies' dresses. Anderson, you're great at birds and trees. And Michelangelo... you do young men's butts." The three small figures leaning over the wall (above Mary and Elizabeth) were likely done by 13-year-old Michelangelo, an apprentice here before being "discovered" by Lorenzo the Magnificent. Relaxed and natural, they cast real shadows, as true to life as anyone in Ghirlandaio's perfect-posture, face-the-camera world.

Ghirlandaio was reportedly

jealous (and talented Michelangelo contemptuous), but, before they parted ways, Michelangelo learned how to lay fresco from the man who did it as well as anyone in Florence.
• *On the far right, find the...*

Appearance of an Angel to Zechariah

In a crowded temple, old Zechariah is going about his business, when an angel strolls up. "Uh, excuse me..." The event is supposedly miraculous, but there's nothing supernatural about this scene: no clouds of fire or rays of light. The crowd doesn't even notice the angel. Ghirlandaio presents the holy in a completely secular way.
• *In the chapel to the right of the altar, Filippino Lippi did the frescoes on the left and right walls. Look first at the right wall, lower level...*

❽ Filippino Lippi

St. Philip at the Temple of Mars

In an elaborate shrine, a statue of the angry god Mars waves his broken lance menacingly. The Christian Philip points back up at

him and says, "I'm not afraid of him—that's a false god." To prove it, he opens a hole in the base of the altar, letting out a little dragon, who promptly farts (believe it when you see it), causing the pagan king's son to swoon and die. The overcome spectators clutch their foreheads and noses.

If Ghirlandaio was "busy," Lippi is downright hyperactive, filling every square inch with something frilly—rumpled hair, folds in clothes, dramatic gestures, twisting friezes, windblown flags, and flatulent dragons.

• *On the left wall, lower level, is...*

St. John the Evangelist Raising Drusiana from the Dead

The miracle takes place in a spacious 3-D architectural setting, but Lippi has all his actors in a chorus line across the front of the

stage. Filippino Lippi (1457-1504, the son of the more famous Fra Filippo Lippi) was apprenticed to Botticelli and exaggerated his bright colors, shadowless lighting, and elegant curves.

The sober, dignified realism of Florence's Quattrocento was ending. Michelangelo would extend it, building on Masaccio's spacious, solemn, dimly lit scenes. But Lippi championed a style (later called Mannerism, which led to Baroque) that loved color, dramatic excitement, and the exotic.

• *In the next chapel to the right of the altar, on the central wall, find...*

❾ Giorgio Vasari—*Madonna of the Rosary*

The picture-plane is saturated with images from top to bottom. Saints and angels twist and squirm around Mary (the red patch in the center), but their body language is gibberish, just an excuse for Vasari to exhibit his technique.

Giorgio Vasari (1511-1574) was a prolific artist. As a Mannerist, he copied the "manner" of, say, a twisting Michelangelo statue, but violated the sober spirit, multiplying by 100 and cramming the canvas. I've tried to defend Vasari from the art critics who unanimously call his art superficial and garish...but doggone it, they're right.

With Vasari, who immortalized the Florentine Renaissance with his writing, the Renaissance ended.

• *After leaving the church, you can step into the medieval cloisters next door. You'll see how the flood of 1966 ruined a series of frescoes by Paolo Uccello. If you're interested in the museum, pay its separate admission fee (not included with church).*

Museum of Santa Maria Novella

Located in the old Dominican monastery, the highlight of the museum is its breathtaking Spanish Chapel. Once the former chapter house of the monastery, the sheer size of the vault put this place on the map when it was built in the 1320s (it became known as the Spanish Chapel after Cosimo I gave it to his bride Eleonora of Toledo). Covering the chapel's walls is Andrea di Bonaiuto's 14th-century fresco series, *Allegory of the Active and Triumphant Church and of the Dominican Order* (c. 1365). The fresco is a visual Sunday-school class—complete with Peter's fishing boat. Follow the long and tricky road to salvation, ending high above, where the saved are finally greeted by Peter at his gate.

On the left wall, find the 13th-century Dominican theologian Thomas Aquinas (dark robe) seated in glory amid virtues, authors of books of the Bible, and angels. The central wall tells the Passion story: Christ carries his cross (lower left), is crucified between two thieves (center), then rises triumphant (right) to trample and spook the demons of death. On the right wall, the pinkish church was inspired by designs for the Duomo, which was then under construction. Using the museum's chart, find medieval celebrities in the fresco, including Dante and Beatrice, and artists Giotto and Cimabue. Along the bottom of the fresco, dogs fight off the wolves of heresy. They're led by St. Dominic, whose fiercely loyal Dominicans (*Dominicanus* in Latin) rightly earned their medieval play-on-words nickname of "Domini canes"—God's dogs.

SANTA MARIA NOVELLA

SANTA CROCE TOUR

Chiesa di Santa Croce

Santa Croce, one of Florence's biggest and oldest churches, gives us a glimpse into the medieval roots of the Renaissance. The church was the centerpiece of a monastery for Franciscans, and was built by Arnolfo di Cambio, who also designed the Duomo, and frescoed by Giotto, the proto-Renaissance pioneer.

In the cloisters is a small chapel that some consider the finest example of early-Renaissance architecture. The church was host to many famous Florentines, including Michelangelo and Galileo, who are both buried here. Today, the church complex houses a leather school, a display on the disastrous 1966 flood, and a museum housed in the monks' former dining hall.

Orientation

Cost: €6 (or €8.50 combo-ticket with nearby Casa Buonarroti), includes the church, Pazzi Chapel, and museum. Covered by Firenze Card. The leather school is always free.

Hours: Church—Mon-Sat 9:30-17:30, Sun 14:00-17:30, last entry 30 minutes before closing. Leather school—daily 10:00-18:00.

Crowd-Beating Tips: A limited number of people are allowed to enter at one time, sometimes resulting in waits of up to 40 minutes in summer. Go early or late in the day, or use the...

Back Door Entrance: The leather school, tucked in the back of the church, is never crowded, and also sells entrance tickets to the church, letting you skip the line. To find the school, walk west along the left side of the church, and enter the doorway at Via San Giuseppe 5 red (labeled *Leather School of Florence*). Follow *Scuola del Cuoio* signs through the small garden and humble parking lot to the low-key back entrance of the school. Don't be shy—they want you to visit their store. Once inside, pass through the workshops and displays to the room with the cash register, and tell the cashier you want a church ticket. With your ticket in hand, go down the hallway that leads into the church. You'll find yourself at #12 on the Santa Croce map (see next page). Find your way to the nave to start this tour.

Dress Code: A modest dress code (no short shorts or bare shoulders) is enforced. A vending machine at the entrance dispenses disposable ponchos for €0.50.

Getting There: It's a 10-minute walk east of the Palazzo Vecchio along the street called Borgo de' Greci.

Information: The audioguide is €5 (€8/2 people). Tel. 055-246-6105, www.santacroceopera.it. The leather school has its own website (www.leatherschool.com).

Length of This Tour: Allow one hour.

With Limited Time: Focus on the tombs of VIFs (Very Important Florentines) and the Giotto frescoes.

Photography: Permitted in most areas, without flash.

Eating: Recommended eateries are nearby (see page 310).

Starring: Tombs of Michelangelo and Galileo, Giotto's frescoes, St. Francis' robe, and Brunelleschi's Pazzi Chapel.

The Tour Begins

· *Begin on the square in front of the church.*

Piazza Santa Croce

Santa Croce Church was built from 1294 to 1442. Architect Arnolfo di Cambio's design was so impressive, the city also hired

him to do the Duomo and the Palazzo Vecchio.

The church's colorful marble facade, left unfinished for centuries, was finally added in the 1850s. A statue of the medieval poet Dante adorns the church steps.

The church presides over a vast square ringed with a few old palazzos, notably the late-Renaissance building at the far end. Piazza Santa Croce has always been one of Florence's gathering spots, for Carnival, May Day, and community events. If you're here in the third week of June, the square is covered with dirt and surrounded by bleachers for the annual soccer/rugby match, which since 1530 has pitted neighborhood against neighborhood.

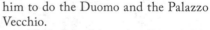

Santa Croce

FENCE

50 Feet

LEATHER
SCHOOL
OUTSIDE
ENTRANCE

**LEATHER
SCHOOL**

To Leather School
(Enter at #5 red)

SACRISTY

⑩
BOOKS
⑪
⑫
⑧

⑨

**PAZZI
CHAPEL**

ENTRANCE →

N
A
V
E

⑦

⑬

⑥

CLOISTERS

⑤

⑭

④

To Casa
Buonarotti

②

③

⑮

⑯

MUSEUM

① TOUR BEGINS

WC

STAIRS

EXIT

REFECTORY

To Arno
River

VIA SAN GIUSEPPE

SANTA CROCE

*Piazza
Santa Croce*

To Piazza
della Signoria

① View down the Nave
② Galileo's Tomb
③ Michelangelo's Tomb
④ Dante's Memorial
⑤ Machiavelli's Tomb
⑥ DONATELLO – Annunciation
⑦ Rossini's Tomb
⑧ GIOTTO – Death of St. Francis

⑨ GADDI – Frescoes in the Baroncelli Chapel
⑩ St. Francis' Tunic
⑪ Leather School
⑫ Flood Photos
⑬ Pazzi Chapel
⑭ Romantic Graves Gallery
⑮ CIMABUE – Crucifixion
⑯ GADDI – Tree of the Cross and Last Supper

If you were here on November 4, 1966, you would have found the square covered with 15 feet of water. The Arno flooded that day, submerging the church steps and rising halfway up the central doorway. (More on the flood later.)

• *Buy your ticket and enter. Start at the far end of the nave (farthest from the altar). Face the altar and gaze down the long nave.*

The Nave

The effect here is one of great spaciousness. The nave is 375 feet long, lined with columns that are tall, slender, and spaced far apart, supporting wide, airy arches. As in most Gothic churches, there's no attempt to hide the structural skeleton of columns and pointed

arches. Instead, they're the stars of this show, demonstrating the mathematical perfection of the design and the builders' technical prowess.

The Tombs

Hundreds of people are buried in the Santa Croce complex, including 276 of them under your feet, marked by plaques in the floor. More famous folk line the walls.

• *Nearby, find the tombs of two particularly well-known people.*

On the left wall (as you face the altar) is the **tomb of Galileo Galilei** (1564-1642), the Pisan who lived his last years under house arrest near Florence. His crime? Defying the Church by saying that the earth revolved around the sun. His heretical remains were only allowed in the church long after his death. (For more on Galileo, see his relics in the Galileo Science Museum.)

Directly opposite (on the right wall) is the **tomb of Michelangelo Buonarroti** (1475-1564). Santa Croce was Michelangelo's childhood church, as he grew up a block west of here at Via dei Bentaccordi 15 (where nothing but a plaque marks the spot). He took Florentine culture and spread it across Europe. In his later years, Michelangelo envisioned that his tomb would be marked with a *pietà* he carved himself. (Left unfinished, it's now in the Duomo Museum.) The garish tomb he actually got—with the allegorical figures of painting, architecture, and sculpture—was designed by Michelangelo's great admirer, the artist/biographer Giorgio Vasari. Vasari also did the series of paintings that line the left side of the nave, using the twisting poses and bulky muscles that Michelangelo pioneered.

• *Stroll up the nave, finding more tombs and monuments along the right wall.*

At the memorial to the poet **Dante Alighieri** (1265-1321), there's no body inside, since Dante was banished by his hometown because of his politics and was buried elsewhere. Exiled Dante looks weary, the Muse of Poetry mourns, and Lady Florence gestures to say, "Look what we missed out on."

Two tombs ahead, the **tomb of Niccolò Machiavelli** (1469-1527) features Lady Justice presenting a medallion with his portrait on it. Machiavelli, a champion of democratic Florence, opposed the Medici as tyrants. When they returned to power, he was arrested and tortured. He retired to his farm to write *The Prince,* a how-to manual on hardball politics.

A few steps farther along, Donatello's carved gray-and-gold **relief** (1430-1435) depicting the Annunciation shows a kneeling angel gently breaking the news to an astonished Mary. Notable for its then-unprecedented realism, the wispy Mary (on the right) is considered one of the artistic breakthroughs that marked the beginning of the long-overdue Renaissance.

Two tombs up is **Gioacchino Rossini** (1792-1868), the Italian composer of many operas and the *William Tell Overture* (a.k.a. the *Lone Ranger* theme). Rossini died in Paris, but his body was later moved here, to his homeland, during a wave of Italian nationalism in the late 19th century.

• *Head for the main altar. In the first chapel to the right of the altar are the...*

Giotto Frescoes in the Bardi Chapel (c. 1325)

The left wall has the famous *Death of St. Francis.* With simple but eloquent gestures, Francis' brothers bid him a sad farewell. One folds his hands and stares longingly at Francis' serene face. Another

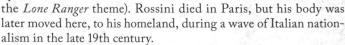

bends to kiss Francis' hand, while others raise their arms in grief. It's one of the first expressions of human emotion in modern painting. It's also one of the first to create a real three-dimensional grouping of figures. Giotto places three kneeling men (with their backs to us) in the foreground, puts some others standing behind Francis, and turns the rest to profile.

Giotto and his army of assistants were hired to plaster much of the church in colorful frescoes. But over the years, most were chiseled off, replaced by more modern works (like Vasari's). This chapel was only whitewashed over, and the groundbreaking frescoes were rediscovered in the 19th century.

• *Facing the altar, turn right, and head into the right (south) transept. At the far end, enter the chapel decorated with colorful frescoes.*

Gaddi Frescoes in the Baroncelli Chapel (c. 1328-1338)

After assisting Giotto in the Bardi Chapel, Taddeo Gaddi (1300-1366)—Giotto's beloved godson—was charged with painting this chapel. His lively frescoes cover both the wall to the left (as you enter), and the wall straight ahead (with stained-glass windows by Gaddi and an altar by Giotto).

Start with the wall to the left. The story of Mary, the mother of Jesus, unfolds from top to bottom, left to right. At the very

top (under the pointed arch), is a temple scene. Mary's future dad, Joachim (with a beard and a halo), is turned away from the temple because he's childless. Ashamed, he retreats to the wilderness (right side), where an angel promises him a daughter. Overjoyed, Joachim rushes to his wife, Anna, and they embrace (next level down, left panel). Anna soon gives birth to baby Mary (badly damaged panel, right side). Still a child, Mary climbs the steps of the temple (bottom level, left panel; most of her body is missing from peeling plaster) to the chief priest (cone-shaped hat), who would raise her. When it comes time for Mary to marry, the priest assembles all the eligible bachelors (bottom-right panel). Joseph's staff sprouts leaves and a dove (center of scene, to left of priest), signaling that he is chosen. In the foreground, a sore loser bends over and breaks his own staff.

Mary's life continues on the altar/stained-glass wall. At the top left, an angel swoops down to tell Mary that she'll give birth to Jesus. Perhaps Gaddi's most impressive scene is just below: A sleeping shepherd is awakened by an angel, who announces that Christ is born. Gaddi, an early pioneer in lighting effects, placed these windows where the natural light coming through would mix with the supernatural light from the radiant angel. (It's said that Gaddi studied solar eclipses to the point of near-blindness.) Finally, Mary's story comes to its culmination (right of window): She gives birth to the Son of God in a stable.

• *Exiting the chapel, immediately do a U-turn right, into a long hallway. Enter the first door on the left to reach the sacristy.*

St. Francis' Tunic

In a glass case along the wall, find a bit of **St. Francis' tunic** (*Parte della Tonaca*, scrunched up in a small gold frame). Francis

(c. 1182-1226), a monk from nearby Assisi, caused a stir by challenging the decadence of Church government and society in general. Adopting the poor, wandering lifestyle of Jesus Christ, he preached a message of non-materialism and love. His charismatic presence and stirring sermons attracted many followers, including the monks who founded Santa Croce. Francis' humanistic outlook and appreciation for the beauty of nature helped sow the seeds that would bloom into the Florentine Renaissance. Also displayed is a Papal Bull *(Regula Ordinis)*, which finally legitimized the once-controversial Franciscan movement.

• *The sacristy leads into the bookstore, which leads to the...*

Leather School
(Scuola del Cuoio)

After World War II, the Franciscan monks created a "Boys Town" here to give war orphans a trade: making leather products. It was the first shop of what is now a popular leather district. The Gori family of merchants helped found the school and the grandson still runs it today. Wander through the former dorms for monks, watch

SANTA CROCE

Floods in Florence

Summer visitors to Florence gaze at the lazy green creek called the Arno River and have a tough time imagining it being a destructive giant. But rare, powerful flooding is a part of life in this city. The Arno River washed away Ponte Vecchio in 1177 and 1333. And on November 4, 1966, a huge rainstorm turned the Arno into a wall of water, inundating the city with mud stacked as high as 20 feet. Nearly 14,000 families were left homeless, and tens of thousands of important frescoes, paintings, sculptures, and books were destroyed or damaged.

Almost as impressive as the flood was the huge outpouring of support, as the art-loving world came to the city's rescue. While money poured in from far and wide, volunteers, nicknamed "mud angels," mopped things up. After the flood, scientists made great gains in restoration techniques as they cleaned and repaired masterpieces from medieval and Renaissance times. Cimabue's *Crucifixion*, now displayed in Santa Croce's Refectory, is a prime example.

You'll see plaques around town showing the high-water marks from 1966 (about six feet high at the Duomo). Now that a dam has tamed the Arno, kayakers glide peacefully on the river, sightseers enjoy the great art with no thought of a flood, and locals...still get nervous after every heavy rain.

the leatherworking in action, and browse the finished products—for sale, of course. Angled mirrors let you look over the shoulders of the busy leatherworkers. At the start of the long hallway, see the photos of visiting celebrities, from Jimmy Stewart to "Miss" Barbara Bush to Robert Downey, Jr.

• *Backtrack through the bookstore, which spills out into a hallway that features a display on...*

Flood Photos

Located close to the Arno, Santa Croce was especially hard-hit by the devastating flood of November 1966. Water spilled into the church complex (including the museum/refectory we'll see later), carrying off furnishings and artwork, and leaving several feet of mud in its wake. Cimabue's famous *Crucifixion* was badly damaged, but survived (you'll see it in the refectory—described later).

• *Return to the nave and exit between the Rossini and Machiavelli tombs into the delightful cloister (open-air courtyard). Descend the stairs and turn left into the...*

SANTA CROCE

Pazzi Chapel

Begun in 1430 by Brunelleschi, this small chapel captures the Renaissance in miniature. As with his Duomo dome, Brunelleschi was inspired by Rome's ancient Pantheon. The circle-in-square design reflects the ancient Romans' (and Renaissance Florentines') belief in the unity and harmony of perfect shapes. Notice how the color scheme of white plaster and gray sandstone accentuates the architectural lines, so that only a little decoration is

needed. The creamy colors help diffuse the light from the dome's windows, making the chapel evenly lit and meditative. The four medallions showing the evangelists (at the base of the dome) may be by Donatello; the medallions of apostles (on the walls) are by Luca della Robbia. While originally used as a monk's assembly room (chapter house), this later became the Pazzi family's private chapel. Imagine how modern this chapel must have seemed after Brunelleschi capped it with a dome.

• *Exiting into the courtyard, notice the long building on the right that houses the Romantic Graves Gallery (19th-century headstones), which is also included in your church admission. On the left is the entrance to the...*

Museum (Museo) and Refectory

Stroll through several rooms of paintings, statues, medieval altarpieces, and frescoes, until you come out into the large room that was originally the monks' refectory, or dining hall, under heavy timber beams.

Cimabue's *Crucifixion* (1423) was heavily damaged in the 1966 flood, and most of Christ's face and body were washed away. Rescued and restored (as best they could), it became a symbol of the flood's destruction and the international community's efforts to rebuild the historic city.

The refectory's entire far wall is frescoed with the impressive, 1,300-square-foot *Tree of the Cross and Last Supper*, by Taddeo Gaddi. A crucifix sprouts branches blossoming with medieval symbolism, which dining monks ate up. Francis kneels at the base of the cross and makes sympathetic eye contact with Jesus. In one of the scenes that flank the cross (upper left), Francis has a vision in which he receives the stigmata—the same wounds in his hands, feet, and side that Christ suffered when he was crucified. Beneath the Tree of the Cross is the Last Supper, a scene that gave the monastery's residents the illusion that they were eating in the symbolic company of Jesus and the apostles.

OLTRARNO WALK

A Loop Trip South from Ponte Vecchio

Staying in the tourist zone leaves you with an incomplete impression of Florence. Most of its people live and work outside the touristy center. The best place to get a sense of rustic, old Florence is in the Oltrarno neighborhood, south of the Arno River. While the essence of the Oltrarno is best enjoyed by simply wandering, this walk gives you a structure in which to cover its highlights.

We'll start at Ponte Vecchio, walk to the Pitti Palace, explore some colorful (and slightly seedy) back streets, pass by the Brancacci Chapel, and return to where we started—Ponte Vecchio. This walk is a helpful way to link some of the Oltrarno sights worth seeing.

Orientation

Pitti Palace: €11.50 combo-ticket covers the entire palace complex (valid 3 days, cash only). Two cheaper combo-tickets make sense for less-thorough visits. The Palatine Gallery is open Tue-Sun 8:15-18:50, closed Mon.

Santo Spirito Church: Free, Mon-Tue and Thu-Sat 9:30-12:30 & 16:00-17:30, Sun 16:00-17:30 only, closed Wed.

Brancacci Chapel: €4, €8 combo-ticket with the Palazzo Vecchio, Mon and Wed-Sat 10:00-17:00, Sun 13:00-17:00, closed Tue; free reservations are required, but it's usually possible to just show up and get a time right away (especially if you arrive before 15:30).

When to Go: Mornings and evenings are best. Mid-afternoon is sleepy and many shops and churches are closed. Artisan shops are closed on weekends.

Getting There: Start at Ponte Vecchio, which crosses the Arno River (a 10-minute walk south of the Duomo).

Length of This Tour: Allow about an hour, not including visits to church interiors, the Brancacci Chapel, or the Pitti Palace.

With Limited Time: Finish the walk early, at Piazza Santo Spirito (explained below, in the listing for the square).

Eating: You'll pass a number of recommended restaurants, described on page 312.

Starring: Views of the Arno, Florence's medieval past, present-day artisans at work, and few tourists.

The Tour Begins

What you'll see on this walk varies with the time of day. In the morning, shops and artisans dominate the scene. In the evening, cafés, restaurants, and strolling people—both locals and tourists—leave the strongest impression.

• *Start in the middle of Ponte Vecchio.*

Ponte Vecchio

The Arno River separates the city center from the Oltrarno—the neighborhood on the "other" *(altro)* side of the river. The two sides have historically been connected by this oldest bridge—Ponte Vecchio (current version built in 1345)—lined with its character-istic shops.

Florence was born on the north bank (founded by the Romans in the first century B.C.) and, since the 1200s, the Oltrarno has been the city's poorer, working-class cousin. As the Oltrarno grew in medieval times, the wooden walls were replaced by stone, and two more bridges were added, connecting it with the city center. Looking upstream (east), you'll see the lone crenellated tower that marks the wall that once defined the medieval city. By Michelangelo's day, the Oltrarno had grown enough that this bridge was about mid-Florence.

Look above to see the Vasari Corridor (the yellow wall with the round windows), which was named for its architect, Giorgio Vasari. This was the personal passageway built for the Medici family to give them a private commute from the Uffizi (center of city government) to the Pitti Palace, their palatial home (which we'll see a bit later). The corridor, built in five months in 1565, drilled straight through people's homes. The only detour is where it curves around the tower at the end of the bridge. (The fam-ily who owned that tower must have had a lot of clout.) With Medici princes prancing back and forth in their corridor, the smells of the traditional shops

OLTRARNO WALK

Oltrarno Walk

- **1** Ponte Vecchio
- **2** Torre dei Barbadori, Torre dei Belfredelli & Photo Op
- **3** Via Toscanella
- **4** Pitti Palace
- **5** Piazza Santo Spirito
- **6** Piazza del Carmine
- **7** Piazza de' Frescobaldi
- **8** Borgo San Jacopo
- **9** Torre di Marsili

had to go. That's when Ponte Vecchio's original merchants— butchers and fish mongers—were replaced by today's gold- and silversmiths.

Ponte Vecchio has seen a lot of turmoil. The plaque above the crowds on the uphill side honors Gerhard Wolf, the German consul in Florence who is credited with saving the bridge (as well as other art treasures) from destruction during World War II. In August 1944, as Hitler's occupying troops fled the city, they were ordered to destroy all of Florence's bridges to cover their retreat. Ponte Santa Trinità was demolished (rebuilt in 1958), and Ponte Vecchio was next in line. But thankfully, Wolf understood the bridge's historic value, and instead of destroying it, he had the buildings at either end blown up to render the bridge unusable. The flood of 1966, which later inundated the city, destroyed still more bridges and dramatically thrust entire

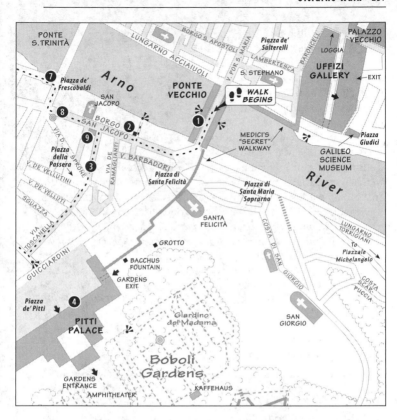

trees like spears through buildings on Ponte Vecchio.
• *Cross the bridge, turn right on Borgo San Jacopo, and walk one block. You'll pass ugly buildings from the 1950s, built after the damage from WWII-era bombs. Stop at the twin towers.*

Torre dei Barbadori, Torre dei Belfredelli, and Photo Op

The tower of the Barbadori family is typical of countless towers that created Florence's 12th-century skyline. Across the street is the ivy-covered tower of the Belfredellis, another noble family. Just as the Montagues and Capulets feuded in nearby Verona, neighbors here also needed to fortify their mansions. At the corner of the Barbadori tower, next to the "do not enter" sign, notice the high-water mark from the 1966 flood.

OLTRARNO WALK

Step out to Hotel Lungarno's little riverside viewpoint for a good look at Ponte Vecchio. Envision a city turned inward, facing its main commercial artery, the river. Barges of goods from Pisa moored here through the ages (loaded with cargo, including marble for artists such as Michelangelo). Today's strict building codes leave

the view essentially the same as you see in engravings from 1700. In a more poetic vein (see the plaque), this is a good spot to watch the rippling Arno and sail into the beyond with your thoughts.

• *Continue down Borgo San Jacopo a half-block to the intersection (on the left) with the tiny street called Via Toscanella. On the corner, look up to find a little modern statue of a woman holding her nose—a Dumpster is often left here. Turn left and enter Via Toscanella, following the lane away from the river...and deeper into the Oltrarno. Notice how Via Toscanella opens up a bit wider 20 yards down. In the 1950s, this former pedestrian-only promenade was widened to accommodate modern traffic.*

Via Toscanella

You're on a quiet and characteristic lane typical of the Oltrarno. A high stone wall hides a private garden (common in this city). The street is named for the family of Paolo Toscanelli (1397-1482), the scientist who used Brunelleschi's dome as a giant sundial and convinced Columbus to reach the East by sailing west. For a glimpse of the clothing styles of today's locals, look up at their laundry.

The little square ahead is Piazza della Passera. The recommended Trattoria 4 Leoni dominates the square, and the classic

little Caffè degli Artigiani is a reminder of the earthy pride of this once rustic district, now gaining affluence as it becomes trendier. Demographically, the Oltrarno is an interesting melting pot of traditional craftspeople, immigrants, retired people, and yuppies.

Continue down Via Toscanella. You'll pass artisan shops on this and neighboring streets. Their doors are open to welcome browsers. Be comfortable stepping in and enjoying the proud work of the artisan. It's polite to say *"Buon giorno"* and *"Ciao."* "Can I take a look?" is *"Posso guardare?"* (POH-soh gwahr-DAH-ray). Long a working-class neighborhood, the Oltrarno is where artisans still

OLTRARNO WALK

ply the traditional trades of their forebears. You'll find handmade furniture,
jewelry, leather items, shoes, pottery,
and picture frames in a centuries-old
style. Craftsmen bind books and make
marbled paper. Antique pieces are
refurbished by people who've become
curators of the dying techniques of
gilding, engraving, etching, enamel-
ing, mosaics, and repoussé metal work.
It was in artisan workshops like these
that boys like Leonardo, Michelangelo,
and little Sandy Botticelli apprenticed.

• *Continue to the end of Via Toscanella and turn left. You'll soon see the
stony facade of a huge palace.*

Pitti Palace

The massive palace, with its rusticated stonework so pleasing to
noble egos, sits conveniently in front of the quarry from where all

that stone was cut. This behemoth
shows the Renaissance aesthetics
of symmetry and mathematical
order on a giant scale. In the 15th
century, the Oltrarno became a
fashionable spot for Florentine
nobles to build palaces.

Originally built for the Pitti
family (15th century), the palace
was later bought and enlarged by
the Medici (16th century). In the 1860s, when Florence briefly
ruled Italy as the interim capital, the palace was the "White
House" for the ruling Savoy family. While stark on the outside, it
is much warmer on the inside, and its bulk hides the lush Boboli
Gardens. It's been a museum since the early 1900s (✪ see the Pitti
Palace Tour chapter).

• *Turn 180 degrees and—with your back to the Pitti Palace—double
back down the street called Sdrucciolo de' Pitti (enjoy wrapping your
tongue around that "sdr"). Continue west, crossing busy Via Maggio.
You'll come to a big church facing a square.*

Piazza Santo Spirito

Piazza Santo Spirito, with its bald-faced church, is the community
center, hosting a colorful produce market in the morning. Later in
the day, bohemians and winos move in to drink and strum guitars
on the church steps. Steer clear of any seedy characters camping
out near the fountain.

OLTRARNO WALK

Santo Spirito Church is worth a visit (see page 88) for its Brunelleschi-designed interior and crucifix by Michelangelo. As a teenager, Michelangelo was allowed to dissect bodies from the adjacent monastic mortuary in order to learn the secrets of anatomy—something he considered key to portraying bodies accurately. As thanks, he made the crucifix.

The church's blank facade prompted the neighborhood to have a contest to design a fun finish: The nearby Ricchi Caffè displays the hundred or so entries on its walls. Choose your favorite while enjoying an ice cream or drink.

• *To end the walk here: To return to the Arno River, face Santo Spirito Church and walk north, along the right side of the church, up Via del Presto di San Martino. At the end of the block, turn right and enter a busy five-way intersection, Piazza de' Frescobaldi. From here you'll see Ponte Santa Trinità arcing over the Arno, decorated with statues on the end. You can finish the walk here, in the middle of Florence, free to explore.*

To continue the walk: From the far end of Piazza Santo Spirito (opposite the church), turn right on Via Sant'Agostino. Stroll westward for 5 or 10 minutes, enjoying more people-watching and browsing the small antique and fashion shops, until you reach a big square.

Piazza del Carmine

Piazza del Carmine (the ugliest square in Florence) hosts the Church of Santa Maria del Carmine, with its famous Brancacci Chapel and Masaccio frescoes. Just a few years ago, most of Europe's main squares were parking lots just like this. Now this square is an exception.

Step into Santa Maria del Carmine. Redone after a 1714 fire, the church offers a good look at textbook Baroque art. Don't miss the impressive 3-D work on the ceiling. Just as the Renaissance originated in Florence and went from here to Rome, Baroque originated in Rome and went from there to Florence. The adjacent Brancacci Chapel is covered with frescoes by Masaccio—some of the most exquisite art in Florence (❂ see the Brancacci Chapel Tour chapter).

• *From Piazza del Carmine, head back toward the river. At Borgo San Frediano, consider detouring a couple of blocks left to see the **Porta San Frediano** city gate (see sidebar). Otherwise, turn right onto Borgo San Frediano, then take the first left to Ponte alla Carraia.*

For a drink, snack, or treat, you have a couple of options: First,

Porta San Frediano

Porta San Frediano (c. 1333) is one of the gates in Florence's medieval wall, which stretches impressively from here to

the river. This gate straddled the road to Pisa. In medieval times, a three-quarter-mile-wide strip outside the wall was cleared to deny attackers any cover. The tower, originally twice as high, was built when gravity ruled warfare. During the Renaissance, gunpowder became the weapon of choice, and the tower—now just an easy target—was lopped.

Florence's symbol, the lily (fleur-de-lis), decorates the top of the tower. The 40-foot doors weigh 16 tons each, and are studded with fat iron nails to withstand battering rams. Take a close look at the hardware. Touch it. Clang a ring.

before turning onto Ponte alla Carraia, watch for La Cité Libreria Café, a cool local hangout with a leftist vibe and a good aperitivo scene in the evening (20 red on Borgo San Frediano). Or, facing the bridge, drop into Gelateria la Carraia for an ice-cream cone.

From the Carraia bridge, turn right and walk along the river toward Ponte Vecchio to the next square...

Piazza de' Frescobaldi

At this small square, along the river, two statues flank the Trinità bridge. The elegant Palazzo Frescobaldi faces the river. A block up from the river, on the corner, look for the picturesque little Medici-era fountain that decorates a flat-iron corner.

Before moving on, just stand at the intersection, watch traffic come and go, and marvel at how the chaos all seems to work out fine.

• *Now, cross the square and turn left, down Borgo San Jacopo.*

Borgo San Jacopo— Torre di Marsili

See how quickly the rough-around-the-edges neighborhood becomes an upscale, pedestrian-friendly lane of fashion stores, antique and jewelry shops, and

nice restaurants. Stop at #17 (on the right), at **Torre di Marsili,** to admire the terra-cotta figurines above the door, especially the fine Annunciation scene.

• *A few steps past the tower are Via Toscanella and the twin towers, and—just like that—we're back at Ponte Vecchio. Ciao.*

BRANCACCI CHAPEL TOUR

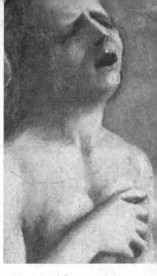

Cappella Brancacci

In the Brancacci (bran-KAH-chee) Chapel, Masaccio created a world in paint that looked like the world we inhabit. For the first time in a thousand years, Man and Nature were frozen for inspection. Masaccio's painting techniques were copied by many Renaissance artists, and his people—sturdy, intelligent, and dignified, with expressions of understated astonishment—helped shape Renaissance men and women's own self-images.

Orientation

Cost: €4, €8 combo-ticket with the Palazzo Vecchio; covered by Firenze Card.

Hours: Mon and Wed-Sat 10:00-17:00, Sun 13:00-17:00, closed Tue, last entry 30 minutes before closing.

Reservations: Reserving an entry time is required (and free), but if you come before 15:30, you can usually just show up and be assigned a time more or less right away. Officially, reservation times begin every 15 minutes, with a maximum of 30 visitors per time slot (you have 15 minutes inside the chapel). But when it's not too busy, they generally let people come and go at will, and stay as long as they like.

The most crowded time is around 16:00, just before closing time; the least crowded time tends to be 12:00-14:00. If, before you head out for the sight, you want to find out if there's a long line, you can call ahead to the ticket desk just to ask how busy it is (tel. 055-284-361).

Firenze Card users don't need a reservation at all, and can walk in whenever they like.

If it's worth the peace of mind for you to reserve in advance, call the chapel a day ahead (tel. 055-276-8224 or

055-276-8558, English spoken, call center open Mon-Sat 9:30-17:00, Sun 9:30-12:30). If the line is busy, keep trying—it's best to call around 13:00-15:00. When you call to reserve, you can also book a time to see the film (see "Film," later).

Dress Code: Shorts and bare shoulders are OK in the chapel, but modest dress is requested when visiting the rest of the church.

Getting There: The Brancacci Chapel is in the Church of Santa Maria del Carmine, on Piazza del Carmine, in the Oltrarno neighborhood south of the Arno River. It's about a 20-minute walk or short taxi ride (about €11) from downtown Florence. From Ponte Vecchio, cross to the Oltrarno side, turn right on Borgo San Jacopo, walk 10 minutes, then turn left into Piazza del Carmine. (**◑** See the previous Oltrarno Walk chapter for a nice walking route.)

Getting In: The chapel is accessible only through the paid entrance to the right of the church.

Information: Tel. 055-284-361, www.museicivicifiorentini.it.

Film: Your ticket includes a 40-minute film in English on the church, the frescoes, and Renaissance Florence (reserve a viewing time when you book your entry). The film starts promptly at the top of the hour (first shown at 10:00, last shown at 15:00). Computer animation brings the paintings to life—making them appear to move and giving them 3-D depth—while narration describes the events depicted in the panels. Yes, it's a long time commitment, and the film takes liberties with the art. But it's visually interesting and your best way to see the frescoes close up. The film works great either before or after you visit the frescoes.

Length of This Tour: Allow 30 minutes (plus 40 minutes if you see the film).

Photography: Allowed without a flash.

Starring: Masaccio, Masolino, and Filippino Lippi.

The Tour Begins

Overview

The chapel has frescoes that tell the story of Peter—half are by Masaccio and half by either Masolino or Filippino Lippi (the son of Filippo Lippi). Although Masaccio is the star, the panels by his colleagues are interesting and provide a good contrast in styles. Masaccio's works are sprinkled among the others, mostly on the left and center walls.

The panels are displayed roughly in the order they were painted, from upper left to lower right—the upper six by Masaccio and Masolino (1424-1425), the lower ones by Masaccio (1426-1427)

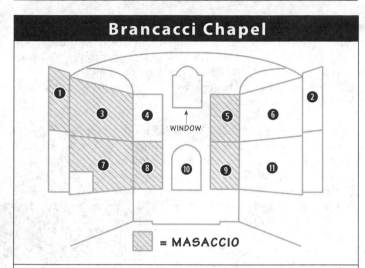

Brancacci Chapel

WINDOW

= MASACCIO

❶ MASACCIO – Adam and Eve Banished from Eden
❷ MASOLINO – Adam and Eve Tempted by the Serpent
❸ MASACCIO – Jesus, Peter & Disciples Pay the Tribute Money
❹ MASOLINO – Peter Preaches to a Crowd
❺ MASACCIO – Peter Baptizing Converts
❻ MASOLINO – Peter Heals a Cripple and Resurrects Tabitha

❼ MASACCIO – Peter Resurrects the Son of Theophilus
❽ MASACCIO – Peter Heals the Sick with his Shadow
❾ MASACCIO – Peter Shares the Wealth with the Poor
❿ ANONYMOUS – The Madonna of the People
⓫ FILIPPINO LIPPI – Peter Crucified

and Filippino Lippi (1481-1485).

It's best to read this chapter before you enter, because if it's busy, you'll have only 15 minutes in the chapel.

• *Start with the left wall, the small panel in the upper left.*

Masaccio—*Adam and Eve Banished from Eden*

Renaissance man and woman—as nude as they can be—turn their backs on the skinny, unrealistic, medieval Gate of Paradise

and take their first step as mortal humans in the real world. For the first time in a thousand years of painting, these figures cast a realistic shadow, seemingly lit by the same light we are—the natural light through the Brancacci Chapel's window.

Eve wails from deep within. (The first time I saw her, I thought

Eve's gaping mouth was way over the top, until I later saw the very same expression on someone dealing with a brother's death.) Adam buries his face in shame. These simple human gestures speak louder than the heavy-handed religious symbols of medieval art.

• *Compare Masaccio's* Adam and Eve *with the one on the opposite wall, by his colleague Masolino.*

Masolino—*Adam and Eve Tempted by the Serpent*

Masolino's elegant, innocent First Couple float in an ethereal Garden of Eden with no clear foreground or background (Eve hugs a tree or she'd float away). Their bodies are lit evenly by a pristine, all-encompassing, morning-in-springtime light that casts no shad-

ows. Satan and Eve share the same face—a motif later Renaissance artists would copy.

In 1424, Masolino da Panicale (1383-1435) was hired by the Brancacci family to decorate this chapel with the story of Peter (beginning with the Original Sin that Peter's "Good News" saves man from). Masolino, a 40-year-old contractor with too many other commitments,

invited 23-year-old Masaccio (1401-1428) to help him. The two set up scaffolding and worked side by side—the older, workmanlike master and the younger, intuitive genius—in a harmonious collaboration. They just divvied up the panels, never (or rarely) working together on the same scene.

• *Return to the left wall, upper level. From here, we'll work clockwise around the chapel. After* Adam and Eve, *the second panel is...*

Masaccio—*Jesus, Peter, and the Disciples Pay the Tribute Money*

The tax collector (in red miniskirt, with his back to us) tells Jesus that he must pay a temple tax. Jesus gestures to say, "OK, but the money's over there." Peter, his right-hand man (gray hair and beard, brown robe), says, "Yeah, over there." Peter goes over there to the lake (left side of panel), takes off his robe, stoops down at an odd angle, and miraculously pulls a coin from the mouth of a fish. He puts his robe back on (right side of panel) and pays the man.

Some consider this the first modern painting, placing real humans in a real setting, seen from a single viewpoint—ours. Earlier painters had done far more detailed landscapes than Masaccio's sketchy mountains, lake, trees, clouds, and buildings, but they never fixed where the viewer was in relation to these things.

Masaccio tells us exactly where we stand—near the crowd, farther from the trees, with the sun to our right casting late-after-noon shadows. We're no longer detached spectators, but an extension of the scene. Masaccio lets us stand in the presence of the human Jesus. While a good attempt at three-dimensionality, Masaccio's work is far from perfect. Later artists would perfect mathematically what Masaccio eyeballed intuitively.

The disciples all have strong, broad-shouldered bodies, but each face is unique. Blond, curly-haired, clean-shaven John is as handsome as the head on a Roman coin (Masaccio had just returned from Rome). Thomas (far right, with a five-o'clock shadow) is intense. Their different reactions—with faces half in shadow, half in light—tell us that they're divided over paying the tax.

Masaccio's people have one thing in common—a faraway look in the eye, as though hit with a spiritual two-by-four. They're deep in thought, reflective, and awestruck, aware they've just experienced something miraculous. But they're also dazzled, glazed over, and a bit disoriented, like tourists at the Brancacci Chapel.

• *Continuing clockwise, we move to the next panel, on the center wall.*

Masolino—*Peter Preaches to a Crowd*

Masolino and Masaccio were different in so many ways, but they were both fans of Giotto (c. 1266-1337), who told stories with simple gestures and minimal acting, adding the human drama by showing the reaction of bystanders. Here, the miraculous power

of the sermon is not evident in Peter (who just raises his hand) but in the faces of the crowd. The lady in the front row is riveted, while others close their eyes to meditate. The big nun (far right) is skeptical, but wants to hear more. The tonsured monk's mouth slips open in awe, while the gentleman to the left finds it interesting enough to come a little closer.

Masolino never mastered 3-D space like Masaccio. Peter's extreme profile is a cardboard cut-out, his left leg stands too high to plant him realistically on flat ground, the people in the back have their gazes fixed somewhere above Peter, and the "Masacciesque" mountains in the background remain just that, background.

• *Continuing clockwise to the other side of the window, come to...*

Masaccio—*Peter Baptizing Converts*

A muscular man kneels in the stream to join the cult of Jesus. On the bank (far right), another young man waits his turn, shivering in his jockstrap. Among the crowd, a just-baptized man wrestles with his robe, while the man in blue, his hair still dripping, but-

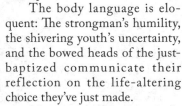

tons up.

The body language is eloquent: The strongman's humility, the shivering youth's uncertainty, and the bowed heads of the just-baptized communicate their reflection on the life-altering choice they've just made.

Masaccio builds these bodies with patches of color (an especially effective technique in fresco, where colors can bleed together). He knew that a kneeling man's body, when lit from the left (the direction of the chapel window), would look like a patchwork of bright hills (his pecs) and dark crevasses (his sternum). He assembles the pieces into a sculptural, 3-D figure, "modeled" by light and shade.

Again, Masaccio was the first artist to paint real humans—with 3-D bodies and individual faces, reflecting inner emotions—in a real-world setting.

• *Continue clockwise to the right wall.*

Masolino—*Peter Heals a Cripple* (left side)
and *Resurrects Tabitha* (right side)

Masolino takes a crack at the 3-D style of his young partner, setting two separate stories in a single Florentine square, defined by an arcade on the left and a porch on the right. Crude elements of the future Renaissance style abound: The receding buildings establish the viewer's point of reference; the rocks scattered through the square define 3-D space; there are secular details in the background (mother and child, laundry on a balcony, a monkey on a ledge); and the cripple (left) is shown at an odd angle (foreshortening). Masaccio may have helped on this panel.

But the stars of the work are the two sharply dressed gentlemen strolling across the square, who help to divide (and unite) the two stories of Peter. The patterned coat is a textbook example of the International Gothic style that was the rage in Florence—elegant, refined, graceful, with curvy lines creating a complex, pleasing pattern. The man walking is at a three-quarters angle, but Masolino

shows the coat from the front to catch the
full display. The picture is evenly lit, with
only a hint of shadow, accentuating the
colorful clothes and cheerful atmosphere.

In mid-project (1426), Masolino
took another job in Hungary, leaving
Masaccio to finish the lower half of the
chapel. Masolino never again explored
the Renaissance style, building a successful career with the eternal springtime of
International Gothic.

• *Move to the lower level. Start on the left wall
with the second panel and work clockwise.*

Masaccio—*Peter Resurrects the Son of Theophilus*

Peter (in that same brown robe...like Masaccio, who was careless
about his appearance) raises the boy from the world of bones, win-
ning his freedom from stern Theophilus (seated in a niche to the
left).

The courtyard setting is fully 3-D, Masaccio having recently
learned a bit of perspective mathematics from his (older) friends
Brunelleschi and Donatello. At the far right of the painting are
three of the Quattrocento (1400s) giants who invented painting
perspective (from right to left): Brunelleschi, who broke down

reality mathematically; Alberti,
who popularized the math with
his book, *On Painting;* and
Masaccio himself (looking out at
us), who opened everyone's eyes to
the powerful psychological possi-
bilities of perspective.

Little is known of Masaccio's
short life. "Masaccio" is a nick-
name (often translated as "Lumbering Antonio") describing his
personality—stumbling through life with careless abandon, not
worrying about money, clothes, or fame...a lovable doofus. Imagine
the absent-minded professor,
completely absorbed in his art.

Next to Masaccio's self-
portrait is a painting within a
painting of Peter on a throne.
On a flat surface with a blank
background, Masaccio has created a hovering hologram, a
human more 3-D than even a
statue made in medieval times.

"Wow," said Brother Philip, a 20-year-old Carmelite monk stationed here when Masaccio painted this. Fra Filippo ("Brother Philip") Lippi was inspired by these frescoes and went on to become a famous painter himself. At age 50, while painting in a convent, he fell in love with a young nun, and they eloped. Nine months later, "Little Philip" was born, and he too grew to be a famous painter—Filippino Lippi, who in 1481 was chosen to complete the Brancacci Chapel.

Filippino Lippi painted substantial portions of this fresco, including the group in the far left (five heads but only eight feet).

• *Moving clockwise to the center wall, you'll see...*

Masaccio—*Peter Heals the Sick with his Shadow*

Peter is a powerful Donatello statue come to life, walking toward us along a Florentine street. Next to him, in the red cap, is bearded

Donatello, Masaccio's friend and mentor.

Masaccio inspired more than painters. He gave ordinary people a new self-image of what it was to be human. Masaccio's people are individuals, not generic Greek gods, not always pretty (like the old bald guy) but still robust and handsome in their own way. They exude a seriousness that makes them very adult. Compare these street people with Masolino's two well-dressed dandies, and you see the difference between Florence's working-class, urban, "democratic" spirit (Guelphs) and the courtly grace of Europe's landed gentry (Ghibellines).

• *The next panel, on the other side of the altar, is...*

Masaccio—
Peter Shares the Wealth with the Poor

Early Christians practiced a form of communal sharing. The wealthy Ananias lies about his contribution, and he drops dead at Peter's feet. Peter takes the missing share and gives it to a poor lady who can't even afford baby pants. The shy baby, the grateful woman, and the admiring man on crutches show Masaccio's blue-collar sympathies.

The scene reflects an actual event in Florence—a tax-reform measure to make things equal for everyone. Florentines were championing a new form of government where, if we all contribute our fair share through taxes, we don't need kings and nobles.

• *The altar under the window holds a painting that is not by Masaccio, Masolino, or Lippi.*

Anonymous (possibly Coppo di Marcovaldo)— *The Madonna of the People*

This medieval altarpiece replaces the now-destroyed fresco by Masaccio that was the centerpiece of the whole design—Peter's crucifixion.

With several panels still unfinished, Masaccio traveled to Rome to meet up with Masolino. Masaccio died there (possibly poisoned) in 1428, at age 27. After his death, the political and artistic climate changed, the chapel was left unfinished (the lower right wall), and some of his frescoes were scraped off whole (his *Crucifixion of Peter*) or in part (in *Peter Resurrects the Son of Theophilus*, several exiled Brancaccis were erased from history, later to be replaced).

Finally, in 1481, new funding arrived and Filippino Lippi, the son of the monk-turned-painter, was hired to complete the blank panels and retouch some destroyed frescoes.

• *The right wall, lower section, contains two panels by Filippino Lippi. The first and biggest is...*

Filippino Lippi—*Peter Crucified*

Lippi completes the story of Peter with his upside-down crucifix-

ion. Lippi tried to match the solemn style of Masaccio, but the compositions are busier, and his figures are less statuesque, more colorful and detailed. Still, compared with Lippi's other, more hyperactive works found elsewhere, he's reined himself in admirably here to honor the great pioneer.

In fact, while Masaccio's perspective techniques were enormously influential, learned by every Tuscan artist, his sober style was not terribly popular. Another strain of Tuscan painting diverged from Masaccio. From Fra Filippo Lippi to

Botticelli, Ghirlandaio, and Filippino Lippi, artists mixed in the bright colors, line patterns, and even lighting of International Gothic. But Masaccio's legacy remained strong, emerging in the grave, statuesque, harsh-shadow creations of two Florentine giants—Leonardo da Vinci and Michelangelo.

PITTI PALACE TOUR

Palazzo Pitti, Galleria Palatina

The Pitti Palace offers many reasons for a visit: the palace itself, with its imposing exterior and lavish interior; the second-best collection of paintings in town; the statue-dotted Boboli Gardens; and a host of secondary museums. However, seeing it all is impossible, and choosing where to spend your time can be confusing. While famous, the Pitti Palace exhausts tourists. Do yourself (and your travel partner) a favor and stay focused on the highlights: Stick to the Palatine Gallery, which has the painting collection, plus the sumptuous rooms of the Royal Apartments. The paintings pick up where the Uffizi leaves off, at the High Renaissance. Lovers of Raphael's Madonnas and Titian's portraits will find some of the world's best at the Pitti Palace. For fashionistas, the Costume Museum is worth a peek. And if it's a nice day, take a stroll in the Boboli Gardens, a rare and inviting patch of extensive green space within old Florence.

Orientation

Cost: Everything is covered by the Firenze Card. Otherwise, you have three different ticket options:

Ticket #1 (the tour described in this chapter) costs €8.50. This ticket covers the recommended Palatine Gallery, Royal Apartments, and Gallery of Modern Art. You can't buy a ticket for just the Palatine Gallery.

Ticket #2 is €7, and covers the Boboli and Bardini gardens, Costume Gallery, Argenti/Silverworks Museum (the Medici treasures), and Porcelain Museum.

Ticket #3, a combo-ticket covering all of the above, costs €11.50 (valid 3 days).

All tickets are cash only. When there are special exhibits,

PITTI PALACE

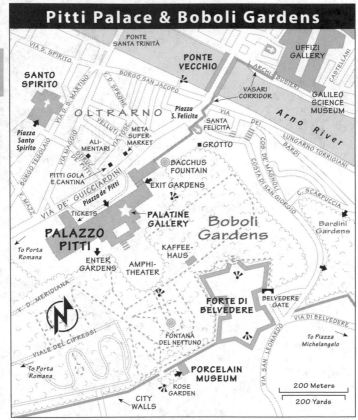

Pitti Palace & Boboli Gardens

ticket prices go up several euros and the combo-ticket may not be available.

Hours: The "ticket #1" sights (Palatine Gallery, Royal Apartments, and Gallery of Modern Art) are open the same hours year-round: Tue-Sun 8:15-18:50, closed Mon. The "ticket #2" sights (Boboli and Bardini gardens, Costume Gallery, Argenti/Silverworks Museum, and Porcelain Museum) vary depending on the season: daily 8:15-18:30 except closed first and last Mon of each month, until 19:30 June-Aug, gardens close as early as 16:30 in winter, last entry 30-60 minutes before closing.

Reservations: Not necessary. If there's a long line, you can bypass it by making a €3 "reservation" on the spot for immediate entry (just march up to the head of the line and go to the window on the right, marked *reservation desk*). You can also skip lines if you have a Firenze Card.

Getting There: The Pitti Palace is located several blocks southwest of Ponte Vecchio, in the Oltrarno neighborhood. Bus

#C3 from the Santa Croce Church stops right in front.

Getting In: The ticket office is at the far right of the massive facade. Once you have your ticket, enter through the main doorway in the center of the facade. Firenze Card-holders should go directly to the main entrance (where you may be ushered to the head of the security checkpoint); then go to the bookstore on the left side of the courtyard to have your card swiped and get your tickets.

Information: Each room has some descriptions in English, and the paintings themselves have limited English labels. An audioguide is available from the ticket office (€6, or €10/2 people); if you're interested in the sprawling palace beyond this Palatine Gallery, this can help bring meaning to your visit. Tel. 055-238-8614, www.polomuseale.firenze.it.

Length of This Tour: Allow one hour for the Palatine Gallery and Royal Apartments.

Services: WCs are in the basement corridor underneath the café and the Palatine Gallery/Royal Apartments staircase.

Photography: Photography is not allowed in the Palatine Gallery.

Eating: While there's a basic café inside the palace courtyard, it's disappointing and overpriced. A better idea is to eat nearby before or after your visit. Several recommended Oltrarno restaurants are a few blocks away (see page 312). Across the plaza is a cozy wine-by-the-glass *enoteca*, Pitti Gola e Cantina, which also serves €10 *antipasti* plates, €8-12 lunches, and €14 homemade pastas (daily, Piazza Pitti 16, tel. 055-212-704). For picnics, a tiny *alimentari* is a half-block directly away from the palace (€3-5 made-to-order sandwiches, Sdrucciolo de' Pitti 6), and a Metà supermarket is across from the palace (see page 315). A drinking fountain is in front of the palace, at the base of the square.

Starring: Raphael, Titian, and the most ornate palace you can tour in Florence.

The Tour Begins

The plain and brutal Pitti Palace facade is like other hide-your-wealth palace exteriors in Florence. The Pitti family (rivals of the Medici family) began building it in 1458 but ran out of money. It sat unfinished until the Medici bought it, expanded it, and moved in during the mid-1500s, choosing to keep the name.

It's an imposing facade—more than two football fields long, made of heavy blocks of unpolished stone, and set on a hill. For nearly two centuries (1549-1737), this palace was arguably Europe's cultural center, setting trends in the arts, sciences, and social mores.

• *Enter the palace through the central doorway, passing through the metal detector and into the courtyard. From here, all of the sights are well-marked: The Palatine Gallery entrance is to your right, the Boboli Gardens entrance is straight ahead, and the Argenti/Silverworks Museum is to the left. Climb several flights of stairs to the Palatine Gallery (Galleria Palatina), housed in the Royal Apartments.*

Palatine Gallery and Royal Apartments

• *Enter room 1 of the Palatine Gallery. (If there's a temporary exhibit, your visit may begin in the large white ballroom, which then leads into room 1.)*

The collection is all on one floor. To see the highlights, walk straight down the spine through a dozen or so rooms. (Avoid the rooms that branch off to the side.) At the far end, make a U-turn left and double back. After the Galleria Palatina, the route flows naturally into the even-more-lavish rooms of the Royal Apartments.

You'll walk through one palatial room after another, with frescoed ceilings that celebrate the Medici family and give the rooms their names (the Venus Room, Apollo Room, and so on). The walls sag with floor-to-ceiling paintings in gilded frames, stacked three and four high, different artists and time periods all jumbled together. Use the information folders in each room to help find the featured paintings. Even with their help, it's still difficult to pick out the masterpieces from the minor pieces. Focus on my recommended highlights first, then let yourself browse.

Rooms 1 and 2
• *Immediately to your right as you enter is the...*

Bronze Bust of Cosimo I
Thank Cosimo I de' Medici (1519-1574, with beard and crown) for this palace. Cosimo I (not to be confused with Cosimo the Elder, the 15th-century founder of the Medici clan) was the first Grand Duke, and the man who revived the Medici family's dominance a generation after the death of Lorenzo the Magnificent. Cosimo I's wife, Eleonora, bought the palace from the Pittis and convinced him and their 11 children to move there from their home in the Palazzo Vecchio. They used their wealth to expand the Pitti, building the gardens and amassing the rich painting collection. This would be the Medici family home for the next 200 years.

PITTI PALACE

Pitti Palace—Palatine Gallery

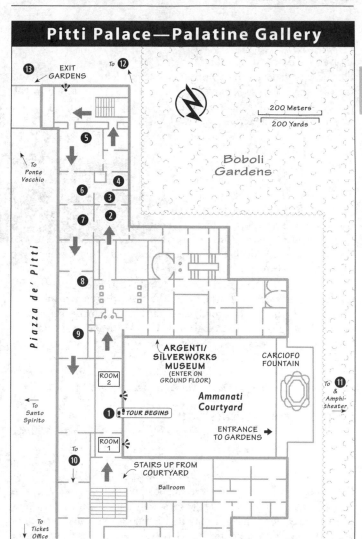

Boboli Gardens

200 Meters
200 Yards

To Ponte Vecchio

Piazza de' Pitti

To Santo Spirito

EXIT GARDENS

⑬

To ⑫

⑤

④

⑥

③

②

⑦

⑧

⑨

ROOM 2

ARGENTI/ SILVERWORKS MUSEUM (ENTER ON GROUND FLOOR)

CARCIOFO FOUNTAIN

Ammanati Courtyard

To ⑪ & Amphi- theater

① ▪ TOUR BEGINS

ENTRANCE TO GARDENS

ROOM 1

To ⑩

STAIRS UP FROM COURTYARD

Ballroom

To Ticket Office

① Bust of Cosimo I & Garden Views
② FILIPPO LIPPI – Madonna and Child
③ RAPHAEL – Holy Family
④ Napoleon's Bathroom
⑤ RAPHAEL – Portrait of a Woman
⑥ RAPHAEL – Madonna of the Grand Duke; Tommaso Inghirami; Agnolo and Maddalena Doni; Madonna with Child and St. John the Baptist
⑦ RAPHAEL – Veiled Woman
⑧ TITIAN – Mary Magdalene; Portrait of a Man
⑨ TITIAN – Portrait of a Lady; Pietro Aretino; The Concert
CANOVA – Venus Italica
⑩ To Royal Apartments
⑪ To Porcelain Museum & City Views
⑫ To Grotto of Buontalenti
⑬ Bacchus Fountain

• *Look out the windows to enjoy...*

Views of Boboli Gardens

Dotted with statues and fountains, the gardens seem to stretch forever. The courtyard below (by Ammanati) is surrounded by the palace on three sides; the fourth side opens up theatrically onto the gardens, which rise in terraces up the hillside. Cosimo I and his descendants could look out their windows at eye level onto the garden's amphitheater, ringed with seats around an obelisk that once stood in the Temple of Ramses II in Egypt. At this amphitheater

the Medici enjoyed plays and spectacles, including perhaps the first opera, *Euridice* (1600).

From the amphitheater, the central axis of the Boboli Gardens stair-steps up to the top of the hill (where there are great views of Florence and beyond). The gardens' expansive sightlines, sculpted foliage, geometric patterns, Greek statues, and bubbling fountains would serve as the model a century later for the gardens at Versailles.

• *Continue straight ahead through a handful of rooms until you reach a green-and-gold room virtually wallpapered with paintings.*

Sala di Prometeo (Room 17)

• *Inside this room, look for the fireplace topped with a round-framed painting.*

Fra Filippo Lippi—*Madonna and Child* (c. 1452)

This pure, radiant Virgin cradles a playful Jesus as he eats a pomegranate. Lippi's work combines medieval piety with new Renaissance techniques. It may be Florence's first tondo (circular artwork), an innovative format that soon became a Renaissance staple. Seed-eating Jesus adds a human touch, but the pomegranate was also a medieval symbol for new life and the Resurrection. In medieval style, the background relates episodes from different places and times, including Mary's birth to Anne (in bed, at left) and the meeting of Mary's parents (distant background, right). But these stories are set in rooms that are textbook

Renaissance 3-D, with floor tiles and ceiling coffers that create the illusion of depth. The ladies bringing gifts to celebrate Mary's birth add another element of everyday Renaissance realism.

Compare Lippi's Madonna with two by Lippi's star pupil, **Botticelli** (one on the left wall, one on the right, both hung high). Botticelli borrowed much from Lippi, including the same facial features, pale skin, precise lines, and everyday details.

• *The next room is the...*

Sala di Ulisse (Room 22)

This was the Grand Duke's bedroom. One of Cosimo I's favorite paintings hangs above the fireplace.

Raphael (Raffaello Sanzio)—*Holy Family (Sacra Famiglia, a.k.a. Madonna dell'Impannata,* 1512-1514)

This work introduces us to the range of this great artist. There's the creamy, rosy beauty of the Virgin alongside the gritty wrin-

kles of St. Anne/Elizabeth. At first glance, it seems like a stately scene, until you notice that Jesus is getting tickled. Everyone is in motion—gazes pointed in all different directions—but they're also posed in a harmonious pyramid, with Jesus' crotch at the center. Little John the Baptist sticks a foot in our face and points to Jesus as The One. Also typical of the always-busy Raphael: The work was probably completed by some of his 50-plus assistants.

• *The next small room you pass by is known as...*

Napoleon's Bathroom (Bagno di Napoleone)

The white-marble luxury and sarcophagus-shaped bathtub were intended for the great French conqueror, Napoleon Bonaparte, when he ruled Florence (1799-1814). Napoleon installed his little sister Elisa as Grand Duchess, and she spent her years here redecorating the palace, awaiting her brother's return. But Napoleon was not destined to meet this water loo. After he was toppled from power, the palace returned to its previous owners.

Over the centuries, the palace hosted several rulers: 200 years of Medici (c. 1549-1737); 100 years of Austrians (the Habsburg-Lorraines, 1737-1860); 15 years of Napoleon (1799-1814); and 60 years under the Savoys, Italy's first royal family (1860-1919), who made the Pitti their "White House" when Florence was briefly the capital of modern Italy.

• *Pass through the final rooms and exit out the far end into the stairwell*

PITTI PALACE

Raphael
(1483-1520)

Raphael (like most Renaissance greats, known by a single name) is considered the culmination of the High Renaissance. (Note that the museum uses his Italian name Raffaello, or Raffaello Sanzio.) He combined symmetry, grace, beauty, and emotion. With his debonair personality and lavish lifestyle, Raphael also epitomized the worldly spirit of the Renaissance.

Raphael lived a charmed life. Handsome and sophisticated, he quickly became a celebrity in the Medici family's high-living circle of bankers, princes, and popes. He painted masterpieces by day and partied by night. Both in his life and art, he exuded what his contemporaries called *sprezzatura*—an effortless, unpretentious elegance. In a different decade, he might have been thrown out of the Church as a great sinner, but his love affairs and devil-may-care personality were perfectly in keeping with the optimism of the times.

Raphael employed a wide range of styles and techniques, but there are some recurring elements. His paintings are bathed in an even light, with few shadows. His brushwork is smooth and blended, and colors are restrained. Works from the Florence years (1504-1508) show Leonardo's influence: Mona Lisa poses,

(with some handy benches). Ahhh. Admire the views of the Duomo, Palazzo Vecchio, and green hills of Fiesole in the distance. The Medici could commute from here to downtown Florence by way of a private, covered passageway (Vasari Corridor) that goes from the Pitti Palace and across Ponte Vecchio to the Palazzo Vecchio. If you look down into the Boboli Gardens, you can see the melted-frosting entrance to the Buontalenti Grotto.

Double back through the second half of the collection. The first room you enter is the...

Sala dell' Iliade (Room 27)

This is the first of several former state rooms, used for grand public receptions. For centuries, Europe's nobles, ladies, and statesmen passed through these rooms as they visited the Medici. They wrote home with wonder about the ceiling frescoes and masterpiece-covered walls. The ceiling frescoes depict the Greek gods cavorting with Medici princes, developing the idea of rule by divine right—themes that decades later would influence the deco-

sfumato brushwork (soft outlines), and lots of sweet Madonnas and Holy Families in a pyramid format. On the other hand, Raphael's portraits are never saccharine. The poses are natural, and individual quirks are never glossed over. He captures the personality without a hint of caricature.

In his later years, Raphael experimented with more complex compositions and stronger emotions. In group scenes, Raphael wants you to follow his subjects' gazes as they exchange glances or look off in different directions. This adds a sense of motion and psychological tension to otherwise well-balanced scenes. Raphael's compositions always have a strong geometric template. Figures are arranged into a pyramid or a circle. Human bodies are composed of oval faces, cylindrical arms, and arched shoulders. Subconsciously, this creates the feeling that God's created world is geometrically perfect. But Raphael always lets a bit of messy reality spill over the lines so his scenes don't appear static. His work comes across as simple and unforced... *sprezzatura.*

When Raphael died in 1520, he was one of Europe's most celebrated painters (along with Michelangelo and Titian). His style went out of fashion with the twisted forms of Mannerism and over-the-top drama of Baroque. The 1700s saw a revival, and today's museums are stuffed with sappy Madonnas by Raphael's many imitators. It's easy to dismiss his work and lump him in with his wannabes. Don't. This is the real deal.

ration of Versailles. Turn your attention to the painting by the entrance door.

Raphael—*Portrait of a Woman (Ritratto di Donna*, a.k.a. *La Gravida,* 1505-1506)

This rather plain-looking woman has one hand on her stomach and a serious expression on her face. She's pregnant. Though she is no Madonna, and her eyes don't sparkle, the woman has presence. Raphael's sober realism cuts through the saccharine excesses of the surrounding paintings.

As one of Raphael's earliest portraits, from his time in Florence, it shows the influence of Leonardo da Vinci. Like Mona Lisa, she's a human pyramid turned at a three-quarters angle, supporting her arm on an armrest that's almost at the level of the frame itself. It's as if she's sitting near the edge of an open window, looking out at us.

• *Enter the next room.*

Sala di Saturno (Room 28)

This room boasts the second-biggest Raphael collection in the world—the Vatican beats it by one. A half-dozen Raphael paintings ring the room at eye level, ranging from dreamy soft-focus Madonnas to down-to-earth, five-o'clock-shadow portraits.

• *Next to the door you just came through, find...*

Raphael—*Madonna of the Grand Duke* (*Madonna del Granduca*, 1505)

Raphael presents Mary in an unusually simple pose—standing, while she cradles baby Jesus under his bum. With no background,

the whole focus is on Mother, lost in thought, and Child, looking right at us. Mary's dreamy face and Jesus' golden body seem to emerge from the shadows. Try as you might, you can't quite discern the outlines of the figures, as they blend seamlessly into the dark background (Leonardo's *sfumato* technique).

The apparently simple pose is actually a skillful, geometric composition. Mary's head and flowing mantle form a triangle. The triangle's base is, first, the neckline of her dress, then her belt, then the horizontal line formed by her arm and Jesus' thighs. The geometric symmetry is livened by an off-kilter touch of reality: Mary's head tilts ever-so-slightly to the side.

This Madonna radiates tenderness and holiness, the divine embodied in human form. The iconic face, the pale colors, the simple pose, the geometric perfection—all are classic Raphael.

• *Now survey a few more paintings, moving clockwise through the room. At the right end of the same wall is...*

Raphael—*Portrait of Tommaso Inghirami* (c. 1510)

Wearing his bright red Cardinal's suit, Tommaso was the friend and librarian of the Medici pope, Leo X. Raphael captures him during an unposed moment, as he pauses to think while writing. Without glossing over anything, Raphael shows us the man just as he was, complete with cleft chin, jowls, lazy eye, and all.

• *On the next wall, look for...*

PITTI PALACE

Raphael—Two Companion Portraits (*Ritratto*) of Agnolo and Maddalena Doni (c. 1505-1506)

These portraits are as crystal clear as the *Madonna del Granduca* is hazy. They're a straightforward look at an upwardly mobile Florentine couple. He was a successful businessman in the textile trade (who commissioned Michelangelo's *Holy Family* in the Uffizi), and she was the daughter of one of the city's richest families. Raphael places them right at the edge of the picture plane, showing off his fine clothes and her jewelry.

• *Immediately to the left of the door leading to the next room is...*

Raphael—*Madonna with Child and St. John the Baptist* (*Madonna dell' Seggiola*, c. 1514-1516)

This colorful, round-framed painting (also known as the *Madonna of the Chair*) is one of Raphael's best-known and most-copied works. Mary hugs Baby Jesus, squeezing him along with little John the Baptist. This Mary is no distant Madonna; she wears a peasant's scarf and a colorful dress and looks directly out at us with a cheerful half-smile. The composition plays on the theme of circles and spheres. The whole canvas is patterned after round sculpture-relief tondi. Mary's halo is a circle, her scarf forms a half-circle, and her face is an oval. The pudgier-than-normal Bambino exaggerates the overall roundness of the scene. Mother and child fit together like interlocking half-circles. As in a cameo, the figures seem to bulge out from the surface, suggesting roundness. Bathed in a golden glow, Mary enfolds her child into the safe circle of motherly love.

• *Head into the next room.*

Sala di Giove (Room 29)

Here in the throne room, the Grand Duke once saw visitors beneath a ceiling fresco showing Jupiter receiving legendary guests.

• *To the left of the door leading into the next room is...*

Raphael—*Veiled Woman* (*La Velata*, 1514-1515)

The dark-haired beauty's dark eyes stare intently at the viewer. The elaborate folds of her shiny silk dress

contrast with her creamy complexion. It's a study in varying shades of white and brown, bathed in a diffuse golden glow. A geometric perfection underlies this woman's soft, flesh-and-blood beauty: Her ovoid face, almond eyes, arch-shaped eyebrows, and circular necklace are all framed by a triangular veil. She is the very picture of perfection...except for that single wisp of loose hair that gives her the added charm of human imperfection.

Who is she? She may be the same woman Raphael depicted topless for a painting in Rome and as a Virgin (in Dresden). The biographer Vasari claims (and scholars debate) that La Velata is Raphael's beloved girlfriend Margherita Luti, known to history as La Fornarina, or the baker's daughter. Raphael became so obsessed with her that he had to have her near him to work. Vasari says that Raphael's sudden and premature death at age 37 came after a night of wild sex with her. Whoever La Velata is, she's one of the beauties of Western art.

• *Pass through the Sala di Marte (room 30) and into the Sala di Apollo (room 31). Two paintings by Titian flank the entrance door.*

Sala di Apollo (Room 31)
Titian (Tiziano Vecellio)—*Mary Magdalene*
(La Maddalena, c. 1530-1535)
According to medieval lore (but not the Bible), Mary Magdalene was a prostitute who repented when she heard the message of Jesus.

Titian captures her right on the cusp between whore and saint. She's naked, though covered by her hair, which she pulls around her like a cloak as she gazes heavenward, lips parted. Her hair is a rainbow of red, gold, and brown, and her ample flesh radiates gold. The rippling locks (echoed by gathering clouds in the background) suggest the inner turmoil and spiritual awakening of this passionate soul.

Among the upper classes in Renaissance times, Mary Magdalene was a symbol of how sensual enjoyment (food, money, sex) could be a way of celebrating God's creation. The way this Mary Magdalene places her hand to her breast and gathers her hair around her is also the classic "Venus Pudica" pose of many ancient Greek statues. It's simultaneously a gesture of modesty and a way of drawing attention to her voluptuous nudity.

Titian—*Portrait of a Man (Ritratto Virile, c. 1545)*
This unknown subject has so mesmerized viewers that his portrait has become known by various monikers, including *The Young Englishman, The Gray-Eyed Nobleman,* and *Doctor McDreamy's Evil*

Twin. The man is dressed in dark clothes and set against a dim background, so we only really see his face and hands, set off by a ruffled collar and sleeves. He nonchalantly places his hand on his hip while holding a glove, and stares out. The man is unforgettable, with a larger-than-life torso and those piercing blue-gray eyes that gaze right at us with extreme intensity. Scholars have speculated that the man could be a well-known lawyer...eternally cross-examining the museum-goers.

• *In the next room you'll find several more Titians.*

Sala di Venere (Room 32)

• *Survey the room in a clockwise order. First up, turn around and face the door you just came through. Immediately to the right is...*

Titian—*Portrait of a Lady (Ritratto di Donna,* a.k.a. *La Bella,* c. 1536)

Titian presents a beautiful *(bella)* woman in a beautiful dress to create a beautiful ensemble of colors: the aqua-and-brown dress, the gold necklace, pearl earrings, creamy complexion, auburn hair, and dark jewel-like eyes. She embodies the sensual, sophisticated, high-society world that Titian ran around in. The woman is likely Titian's Venus of Urbino, standing up and with her clothes on (see page 145). Scholars speculate on who she really was; perhaps she's Eleonora the Duchess of Urbino, or the mistress of the previous Duke, or maybe she's just a paid model that Titian found to be...beautiful.

• *At the right end of the same wall is...*

Titian—*Portrait of Pietro Aretino* (c. 1545)

The most notorious and outrageous figure in Renaissance high society was the writer Pietro Aretino (1492-1556). In 1527, he fled Rome, having scandalized the city with a collection of erotic/pornographic sonnets known as the *Sixteen Ways* (or sex positions). He took refuge in luxury-loving Venice, where he befriended Titian, a fellow connoisseur of eroticism and the arts. Titian and Aretino were both commoners, but they moved easily in court circles:

Titian
(c. 1490-1576)

Titian the Venetian (the museum uses his Italian name Tiziano or Tiziano Vecellio) captures the lusty spirit of his hometown. Titian was one of the most prolific painters ever, cranking out a painting a month for almost 80 years. He excelled in every subject: portraits of kings, racy nudes for bedrooms, creamy-faced Madonnas for churches, and pagan scenes from Greek mythology. He was cultured and witty, a fine musician and businessman—an all-around Renaissance kind of guy. Titian was famous and adored by high society, including Cosimo I and other Medici.

Titian's style changed over his long career. In his youth, he painted alongside Giorgione, even working on the same canvases (scholars still debate who did what). When he reached middle age, he found his voice: bright colors (particularly the famed "Titian red"), large-scale canvases, exuberant motion, and complex compositions, rebelling against the strict symmetry of early Renaissance. In his sixties, his technique became more impressionistic. He applied the paint in rough, thick brushstrokes, even using his fingers. In these late works, his figures don't pop from the background; instead they blend in, creating a moody atmosphere.

Throughout his life, his bread and butter were portraits of Europe's movers and shakers—kings, popes, countesses, mistresses, artists, and thinkers. Without ever making his sitters more handsome or heroic than they were, he captured both their outer likeness and their inner essence. Their clothes and accessories tell us about their social circle, so collectively, his portraits are a chronicle of the Renaissance in all its sensual glory.

Titian the diplomat and Aretino the fiery satirist who tweaked the noses of arrogant princes. (In fact, Aretino was part of the Rat Pack of rowdy Medici that included the father of Cosimo I.)

This portrait captures the self-confidence that allowed Aretino to stand up to royalty. Titian portrays him with the bearded face of an ancient satyr (a lecherous, untamed creature in Greek mythology). His torso is huge, like a smoldering volcano of irreverence that could erupt at any moment. Rather than the seamless brushstrokes and elaborate detail of Titian's earlier works, the figure of

Aretino is composed of many rough strokes of gold and brown paint. Around age 60, Titian radically altered his style, adopting this "unfinished" look that the Impressionists would elaborate on centuries later. Aretino joked when he saw the portrait: "It breathes and moves as I do in the flesh. But perhaps [Titian] would have spent more time on my fine clothes—the robe, the silk, the gold chain—if I'd paid him more." Aretino gave the portrait to Cosimo I as a gift.

• *On the facing wall, just over the small table, find...*

Titian—*The Concert* (*Concerto*, 1510-1512)

An organ-playing man leans back toward his fellow musician (a monk), who's put down his cello to tap him on the shoulder. A young dandy in fancy clothes and a feathered cap looks on. The meaning of the work is a puzzle, perhaps intentionally so. Titian may have collaborated on this early painting with his colleague Giorgione, who specialized in enigmatic works used by cultured hosts as conversation starters.

Maybe it's just a slice-of-life snapshot of Venetian musicians briefly united in their common task. Or maybe it's a philosophical metaphor, in which a middle-aged man, blithely engaged in the gay music of his youth, is interrupted by a glimpse at his future— the bass notes and receding hairline of old age.

• *In the middle of the Sala di Venere stands...*

Canova—*Venus Italica* (*Venere*, 1810)

This pure white marble statue of Venus looks like the *Venus de' Medici* with a sheet (see page 138). Like the Medici Venus, she's nude, modestly crossing her hands in front of her (the "Venus Pudica" pose), while turning her head to the side. But Canova's Venus clutches a garment, which only highlights her naked vulnerability.

In 1796, a young French general named Napoleon Bonaparte toured the Uffizi and fell in love with the *Venus de' Medici*. A few years later, when he conquered Italy, he carried Venus off with him to Paris. To replace it, the great Venetian sculptor Canova was asked to make a copy. He refused to make an exact replica, but he agreed to do his own interpretation, combining motifs from many ancient Venuses of the Pudica (modest) and Callipigia (ample derriere) styles. Canova's *Venus Italica* stood in the Uffizi until Napoleon was conquered and *Venus de' Medici* returned.

• *From here, the rooms of the Palatine Gallery lead into the...*

Royal Apartments

These 14 rooms (of which only a few are open at any one time) are where Florence's aristocrats lived in the 18th and 19th centuries. The decor reflects both Italian and French styles. In the 16th century, the two countries cross-pollinated when Catherine de' Medici (Lorenzo the Magnificent's great-granddaughter) married the king of France. Soon power shifted northward, which is why many of these rooms mimic the Versailles style, rather than vice versa. You'll see rooms of different themes and color schemes. Each room features the style of a particular time period. Ogle the velvety wallpaper, heavy curtains, white-and-gold stucco ceilings, chandeliers, and Louis XIV-style chairs, canopied beds, clocks, and candelabras. Gazing over it all are portraits of some of the people who lived in these rooms. Here, you get a real feel for the splendor of the dukes' world.

The Rest of the Pitti Palace

If you've got the energy and interest, it'd be a Pitti to miss the palace's other offerings: the Boboli and Bardini gardens, Argenti/Silverworks Museum (the Medici treasures), Costume Gallery, and Porcelain Museum (all covered by ticket #3).

Other Palatine Gallery Works

Art lovers can hunt down Titian's *Portrait of Filippo II of Spain* and *Portrait of Ippolito de' Medici;* Giorgione's *Three Ages of Man;* Caravaggio's *Sleeping Cupid;* and many more.

Modern Art Gallery

On the second floor, this gallery features Romantic, Neoclassical, and Impressionist works by 19th- and 20th-century Tuscan painters.

Costume Gallery

Also on the second floor, this fine collection displays centuries' worth of men's and women's fashions, with thoughtful explanations about the philosophical underpinnings of clothing styles. This is worth a linger for those interested in fashion, and interesting to anybody. The darkened room at the far end of the exhibit displays the clothes that Cosimo I and Eleonora of Toledo were buried in (later retrieved from their tombs and preserved—a rare chance to see original 16th-century garments).

Argenti/Silverworks Museum

This Medici treasure chest (on the ground and mezzanine floors) holds items such as jeweled crucifixes, exotic porcelain, rock-crystal goblets, and gilded ostrich eggs, made to entertain fans of the applied arts.

PITTI PALACE

Boboli and Bardini Gardens

For those eager to escape the halls upon halls of fancy apartments, two adjoining gardens are located behind the palace. Enter the Boboli Gardens directly from the Pitti Palace courtyard. The less-visited Bardini Gardens are higher up and farther out behind the Boboli, rising in terraces toward Piazzale Michelangelo. Both gardens are similar, providing a pleasant and shady refuge from the city heat, with statues, fountains, and scenic vistas down tree-lined avenues.

A few fun little sights are in the low-lying area just to the left as you enter the Boboli Gardens. First, near the end of the palace, is the much-photographed **Bacchus Fountain** (Fontana di Bacco, 1560), starring Cosimo I's fat dwarf jester straddling a turtle—a fitting metaphor for this heavyweight palace.

Just beyond Bacchus is the **Grotto of Buontalenti,** an artificial cave crusted with fake stalactites and copies of Michelangelo's *Prisoners,* which once stood here (and are now in the Accademia). Playful figures—a hunter with his dog, goats, a monster—seem to morph into existence from the cottage cheese-like walls. At the top of the hour (check posted schedules) the grotto gates are opened for five minutes of frolicking among the statues.

You can also stroll up the steep terraces directly behind the palace. From the top, you're greeted by a panoramic view of the palace and Oltrarno churches (but only peek-a-boo views of the old town center, the Palazzo Vecchio, and Duomo). On your way up, you'll pass the **amphitheater** (ringed with statues). At the top, just beyond the hillcrest, is a pleasant **rose garden** with bucolic views of the rolling Tuscan hills (punctuated by cypress trees). The small building adjoining the rose garden houses the **Porcelain Museum,** with a modest and sparsely described collection of ducal dinnerware. From here, you can follow signs around to the **Belvedere Fortress,** with even higher and better views, and the Belvedere Gate, which leads to the Bardini Gardens.

GALILEO SCIENCE MUSEUM TOUR

Museo Galilei e Istituto di Storia della Scienza

Enough art, already! Forget the Madonnas and Venuses for a while to ponder weird contraptions from the birth of modern science. The same spirit of discovery that fueled the artistic Renaissance helped free the sciences from medieval mumbo jumbo. This museum offers a historical overview of technical innovations from roughly A.D. 1000 to 1900, featuring early telescopes, clocks, experiments, and Galileo's finger in a jar.

English majors will enjoy expanding their knowledge. Art lovers can admire the sheer beauty of functional devices. Engineers will be in hog heaven among endless arrays of gadgets. Everyone will be fully amused by my feeble attempts to explain technical concepts. And admission to the museum gives you access to one of the marvels of modern science: air-conditioning.

Orientation

Cost: €9, €22 family ticket covers 2 adults and 2 kids age 18 and under, cash only, tickets good all day, covered by Firenze Card.

Hours: Wed-Mon 9:30-18:00, Tue 9:30-13:00, last entry 30 minutes before closing.

Getting There: The museum is located one block east of the Uffizi on the north bank of the Arno River at Piazza dei Giudici 1.

Information: Excellent English descriptions are posted throughout. Engaging video screens in many rooms illustrate the inventions and scientific principles (with information in English). Tel. 055-265-311, www.museogalileo.it.

Tours: The €5 **audioguide** is well-produced, and offers both a highlights tour as well as dial-up info (with video) on each exhibit. The 1.5-hour English-language **guided tour** covers the collection plus behind-the-scenes areas, and includes hands-on demonstrations of some of the devices (€50 flat fee for 2-14 people, cash only, doesn't include museum entry, book at least a week in advance, great for kids, tel. 055-234-3723, groups@museogalileo.it).

Length of this Tour: Allow one hour (or more, especially for those interested in science).

Photography: Permitted without a flash.

Starring: Galileo's telescopes, experiment models, and finger.

The Tour Begins

The collection is on the first and second floors. Take advantage of the helpful English-speaking docents. They're available to answer questions about how these scientific gadgets work. In fact, the staff is happy that you're there to see this museum, and not just lost on your way to the Uffizi.

• *Buy your ticket and head up the stairs to the first floor, room I.*

Room I: The Medici Collections

In this room, you immediately get a sense of the variety of devices to be found in the collection: everything from a big wooden quadrant and maps to optical illusions and old science books. These belonged to that trend-setting family, the Medici, who always seemed at the forefront of Europe's arts and sciences. Many of the objects we'll see measured the world around us—the height of distant mountains, the length of a man's arm, the movement of  the sun and stars across the sky. In fact, one of the bold first steps in science was to observe nature and measure it. What scientists found is that nature—seemingly ever-changing and chaotic—actually behaves in an orderly way, following rather simple mathematical formulas.

Room II: Astronomy and Time

This room has (triangle-shaped) quadrants and (round) astrolabes. In medieval times, sailors used these to help them find their way at sea. They mapped the constellations as a starting point. Next they had to figure out where they stood in relation to those stars.

Quadrants: A *quad*-rant is one-*fourth* of a 360-degree circle, or 90 degrees. You'd grab this wedge-shaped object by its curved edge, point it away from you, and sight along the top edge toward, say, a distant tower or star. Then you'd read the scale etched along

the curved edge to find how many degrees above the horizon the object was.

The quadrant *(quadrante)* measured the triangle formed by you, the horizon, and a distant object. Once you knew at least three of the triangle's six variables (three angles and three sides), you could calculate the others. (That's trigonometry.) Armed with this knowledge, you could use the quadrant to measure all kinds of things. On land, you could calculate how high or how far away a building was. At sea, you could figure your position relative to the sun and stars.

Astrolabes: Astrolabes—invented by the ancient Greeks and pioneered by medieval Arab sailors—combined a quadrant with a map of the sky (a star chart), allowing you to calculate your position against the stars without doing all of the math. You'd hang the metal disk from your thumb and sight along the central crossbeam, locate a star, then read its altitude above the horizon on the measuring scale etched around the rim.

Next, you'd enter this information by turning a little handle on the astrolabe's face. This set the wheels-within-wheels into motion, and the constellations would spin across a backdrop of coordinates. You'd keep turning until the astrolabe mirrored the current heavens. With your known coordinates dialed in, the astrolabe calculated the unknowns, and you could read out your position along the rim.

Knowing the position of the stars and sun also revealed the current time of day, which was especially useful for Arab

traders (i.e., Muslims) in their daily prayers.
• *Continue to room III, dominated by a big globe.*

Room III: The Representation of the World

The big globe is an **armillary sphere,** a model of the universe as conceived by ancient Greeks and medieval Europeans. You'd turn

a crank and watch the stars and planets orbit around the earth in the center. This earth-centered view of the universe—which matches our common-sense observations of the night sky—was codified by Ptolemy, a Greek-speaking Egyptian of the second century A.D.

Ptolemy (silent P) summed up Aristotle's knowledge of the heavens and worked out the mathematics explaining its movements. His math was complex, especially when trying to explain the planets, which occasionally lag behind the stars in their paths across the night sky. (We now know it's because fast-orbiting earth passes the outer planets in their longer, more time-consuming orbits around the sun.)

Ptolemy's system dominated Europe for 1,500 years. It worked most of the time and fit well with medieval Christianity's human-centered theology. But, finally, Nicolaus Copernicus (and Galileo) made the mental leap to a sun-centered system. This simplified the math, explained the movement of planets, and—most importantly—changed earthlings' conception of themselves forever.

Thanks to Columbus' voyages, the Europeans' world suddenly got bigger and rounder. Increasingly, maps began to portray the spherical world on a flat surface.
• *Pass through room IV (with more globes and a map where south is up) and enter...*

Room V: The Science of Navigation

This room has more quadrants and maps, plus a new navigational feature: clocks. By measuring time accurately, sailors could not only establish their latitude (north-south on the globe), but also their longitude (east-west).

In the 1600s, with overseas trade booming, there was a crying need for an accurate and durable clock to help in navigation. Sighting by the stars told you your latitude but was less certain on whether you were near Florence, Italy (latitude 44), or Portland, Maine (also latitude 44). You needed a way to time earth's 24-hour rotation, to know exactly where you were on that daily journey—that is, your longitude. Reward money was offered for a good clock that could be taken to sea, and science sprang into action.

The longitude problem was finally solved—and a £20,000 prize won—by John Harrison of England (1693-1776), who developed the "chronometer" (not in this museum), a spring-driven clock that was set in a suspension device, to keep it horizontal. It was accurate within three seconds a day, far better than any clock displayed here.

• *Room VI (The Science of Warfare), displays not weapons but surveyors' tools, crucial for plotting the trajectory of, say, a cannonball. Next up is one of the museum's highlights.*

Room VII: Galileo's New World

Galileo Galilei (1564-1642) is known as the father of modern science. His discoveries pioneered many scientific fields, and he was among the first to blend mathematics with hands-on observation of nature to find practical applications. Raised in Pisa, he achieved fame teaching at the University of Padua before working for the Grand Duke of Florence. The museum displays several of his possessions (lens, two telescopes, compass, and thermometer), models illustrating his early experiments, and his finger, preserved in a jar.

• *In the glass case at the end of the benches, look for...*

Galileo's Finger: Galileo is perhaps best known as a martyr for science. He popularized the belief (conceived by the Polish astronomer Nicolaus Copernicus in the early 1500s) that the earth orbits around the sun. At the time, the Catholic Church (and most of Europe) preached an earth-centered universe. At the age of 70, Galileo was hauled before the Inquisition in Rome and forced to kneel and publicly proclaim that the earth did not move around the sun. As he walked away, legend has it, he whispered to his followers, "But it does move!"

After his death, Galileo's students preserved this finger bone *(Dito Medio della Mano Destra di Galileo),* displayed on an alabaster pedestal, as a kind of sacred relic in this shrine to science. (This case also holds two other fingers, and a tooth, that were found a few years ago.) Galileo's beliefs eventually triumphed over the Inquisition, and, appropriately, we have his right middle finger raised upward for all those blind to science.

• *On the right side of the room, look for the case containing...*

Galileo's Telescopes: Galileo was the first earthling to see the moons of Jupiter. With a homemade telescope, he looked through the lens and saw three moons lined up next to Jupiter. This discovery also irked the Church, which insisted that all heavenly bodies orbited the earth. You could see Jupiter's moons with your own eyes if you simply looked through the telescope, but few church scholars bothered to do so, content to believe what they'd read in ancient books.

Galileo built these telescopes, based on reports he'd read from Holland. He was the first person to seriously study the heavens

with telescopes. Though these only magnified the image about 30 times ("30 power," which is less than today's binoculars), he saw Jupiter's four largest moons, Saturn's rings, the craters of the moon (which he named "seas"), and blemishes (sunspots) on the supposedly perfect sun.

• *In the same case is a...*

Pendulum Clock Model: Galileo's restless mind roamed to other subjects. It's said that during a church service in Pisa, Galileo looked up to see the cathedral's chandelier swaying slowly back and forth, like a pendulum. He noticed that a wide-but-fast arc took the same amount of time as a narrow-but-slow arc. "Hmmm. Maybe that regular pendulum motion could be used to time things..."

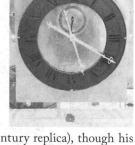

• *The last case on this wall contains a...*

Thermoscope: Galileo also invented the thermometer (or thermoscope—similar to the museum's 19th-century replica), though his glass tube filled with air would later be replaced by thermometers filled with mercury.

• *Across the room is a giant model of an...*

Inclined Plane: The large wooden ramp figures in one of the most enduring of scientific legends. Legend has it that Galileo dropped cannonballs from the Leaning Tower of Pisa to see whether heavier objects fall faster than lighter ones, as the ancient philosopher Aristotle (and most people) believed. In fact, Galileo probably didn't drop objects from the Leaning Tower, but likely rolled them down a wooden ramp like

this reconstructed one.

Rolling balls of different weights down the ramp, he timed them as they rang the bells posted along the way. (The bells are spaced increasingly far apart, but a ball—accelerating as it drops—will ring them at regular intervals.) What Galileo found is that—if you discount air resistance—all objects fall at the same rate, regardless of their weight. (It's the air resistance, not the weight, that makes a feather fall more slowly than a cannonball.)

He also found that falling objects accelerate at a regular rate (9.8 meters per second faster every second), summed up in a mathematical formula (distance is proportional to the time squared).

Galileo pioneered the art of experimentation. He built devices that could simulate nature on a small scale in a controlled laboratory setting, where natural forces could be duplicated and measured. In the following rooms, we'll see many of the experimental tools and techniques he inspired.

• *Room VIII has early glass beakers, jars, and test tubes. Continue on to...*

Room IX: After Galileo—Exploring the Physical and Biological World

This room has both telescopes (for observing objects far away) and microscopes (to see the world up close).

A **telescope** is essentially an empty tube with a lens at the

far end to gather light, and another lens at the near end to magnify the image. The farther apart the lenses, the greater the magnification, which is why telescopes have increased in size over time. The longest ever built was 160 feet, but the slightest movement would jiggle the image.

Galileo used a "refracting telescope," made with lenses that bend (refract) light. Later on, scientists started using "reflecting telescopes," which were often thick-barreled, with the eyepiece sticking out the side. These telescopes use mirrors (not lenses) to bounce light rays back and forth through several lenses, thereby increasing magnification without the long tubes and distortion of refractors.

• *Ascend to the second floor and enter room X.*

Room X: The Lorraine Collections— Medical Science

Look at the big table with all the drawers and jars in the glass case in the center of the room. Back when the same guy who cut

your hair removed your appendix, medicine was crude. In the 1700s, there were no anesthetics beyond a bottle of wine, nor was there any knowledge of antiseptics. The best they could do was resort to the healing powers of herbs and plants. Consider what was thought to be therapeutic in the 1700s: cocaine, anise, poisonous plants like belladonna, tea, and ipecac.

GALILEO SCIENCE MUSEUM

The room also displays models detailing the varieties of complications that could arise during childbirth. Not a pretty sight, but crucial to finding ways to save lives.

Room XI: The Spectacle of Science

This room is filled with odd-looking devices used by scientists to instruct and amaze. Chief among them, in the middle of the room, are the turn-the-crank machines dealing with electricity.

Electromagnetism: Lightning, magnets, and static cling mystified humans for millennia. Little did they know that these quite different phenomena are all generated by the same invisible force—electromagnetism.

In the 1700s, scientists began to study, harness, and play with electricity. As a popular party amusement, they devised big static electricity-generating machines. You turned a crank to spin a glass disk, which rubbed against silk cloth and generated static electricity. The electricity could then be stored in a glass Leyden jar (a jar coated with metal and filled with water). A metal rod sticking out of the top of the jar gave off a small charge when touched, enough to create a spark, shock a party guest, or tenderize a turkey (as Ben Franklin attempted one Thanksgiving). But such static generators could never produce enough electricity for practical use.

• *In the corner near where you entered, look for...*

Model for Demonstrating Newton's Mechanics: Isaac Newton (1642-1727) explained all of the universe's motion ("mechanics")—from spinning planets to rolling rocks—in a few simple mathematical formulas.

The museum's collision balls (the big wooden frame with hanging balls), a popular desktop toy in the 1970s, demonstrate Newton's three famous laws.

1. Inertia: The balls just sit there unless something moves them, and once they're set in motion, they'll keep moving the same way until something stops them.

2. Force = Mass × Acceleration: The harder you strike the balls, the more they accelerate (change speeds). Strike with two balls to pack twice the punch.

3. For every action, there's an equal and opposite reaction: When one ball swings in and strikes the rest, the ball at the other end swings out, then returns and strikes back.

• *Rooms XII and XIII have more demonstration and teaching devices. In room XIII is a famous model.*

Room XIII: Teaching Science— The Archimedes Screw Model

Back in third-century B.C. Greece, Archimedes—the man who gave us the phrase "Eureka!" ("I've found it!")—invented a way

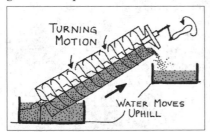

to pump water that's still occasionally used today. It's a screw in a cylinder. Simply turn the handle and the screw spins, channeling the water up in a spiral path. Dutch windmills powered big Archimedes screws to push water over dikes, reclaiming land from the sea.

Room XIV: Precision Instruments

This room shows the development of big reflecting **telescopes** and finer **microscopes.**

One day, a Dutchman picked something from his teeth, looked at it under his crude microscope, and discovered a mini-universe, crawling with thousands of "very little animalcules, very prettily a-moving" (i.e., bacteria and protozoa). Antonie van Leeuwenhoek (1632-1723) popularized the microscope, finding that fleas have fleas, semen contains sperm, and one-celled creatures are our fellow animals.

Tick, Tock, Clocks

Pop into the museum's ground-floor bookshop, where some impressive clocks are on display.

In an ever-changing universe, what is constant enough to measure the passage of time? The sun and stars passing over every 24 hours work for calendar time, but not for hours, minutes, or seconds. Since the time of the Greeks, man used sundials, or the steady flow of water or sand through an opening, but these were only approximate.

In medieval times, humans invented mechanical clocks that work similar to the classic grandfather clock. The clock is powered by suspended weights that slowly "fall," producing enough energy to turn a series of cogwheels that methodically move the clock hands around the dial. The whole thing is regulated by a pendulum rocking back and forth, once a second. A clock has three essential components:

1. Power (falling weights).
2. An "escapement" (the cogs that transform the "falling" power into turning power).
3. A regulator (swinging pendulum) that keeps the gears turning evenly.

Later clocks were powered by a metal spring that slowly uncoiled (also used in most watches). The power was regulated by a pendulum—Galileo's contribution. Unfortunately, a rocking pendulum on a rocking ship wasn't going to work.

During the so-called Age of Reason (1600s) and Age of Enlightenment (1700s), the clock was the perfect metaphor for the orderly workings of God's well-crafted universe. So, wondered the philosophers/scientists, would the universe eventually wind down like an old clock? In fact, in every energy exchange (as stated in the second law of thermodynamics), a certain amount of energy is transformed into nonrecyclable heat, meaning a perpetual motion machine is impossible. This principle of entropy (the trend toward dissipation of energy) has led philosophers to ponder the eventual cold, lifeless fate of the universe itself.

Microscopes can be either simple or compound. A simple one is just a single convex lens—what we'd call a magnifying glass. A compound microscope contains two (or more) lenses in a tube, working like a telescope: One lens magnifies the object, and the eyepiece lens magnifies the magnified image. Van Leeuwenhoek opted for a simple microscope (not in this museum), since early compound ones often blurred and colored objects around the edges. His glass bead-size lens could make a flea look 275 times bigger.

Room XV: Atmosphere and Light

Even nature's most changeable force—the weather—was analyzed by human reason, using thermometers and barometers.

Thermometers: You'll see many interesting thermometers—spiral ones, tall ones, and skinny ones on distinctive bases. All operate on the basic principle that heat expands things. So, liquid in a closed glass tube will expand and climb upward as the temperature rises.

Galileo's early thermoscope was not hermetically sealed, so it was too easily affected by changing air pressure. So scientists experimented with various liquids in a vacuum tube—first water, then alcohol. Finally, Gabriel Fahrenheit (1686-1736) tried mercury, the densest liquid, which expands evenly. He set his scale to the freezing point of a water/salt/ice mixture (zero degrees) and his own body temperature (96 degrees). With these parameters, water froze at 32 degrees and boiled at 212 degrees. Anders Celsius (1701-1744) used water as the standard, and called the freezing point 0 and the boiling point 100.

Barometers: To make a barometer, take a long, skinny glass tube (like the ones in the wood frames), fill it with liquid mercury,

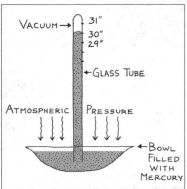

then turn it upside-down and put the open end into a bowlful of more mercury. The column of mercury does not drain out, because the air in the room "pushes back," pressing down on the surface of the mercury in the bowl.

Changing air pressure signals a shift in the weather. Hot air expands, pressing down harder on the mercury's surface, thereby causing the mercury column to rise above 30 inches; this indicates the "pushing away" of clouds and points to good, dry weather. Low pressure lets the mercury drop, warning of rain. If you have a barometer at home, it probably has a round dial with a needle (or a digital readout), but it operates on a similar principle.

• *In the next room, you'll find (among magnets, generators, and small machines), a couple of early batteries.*

Room XVI: Electricity

Alessandro Volta (1745-1827) built the first battery in Europe. (Although the museum does not have one of Volta's batteries, it

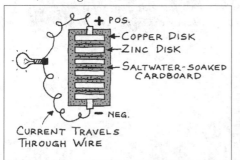

does have similar devices.) A battery generates electricity from a chemical reaction. Volta (and others) stacked metal disks of zinc and copper between disks of cardboard soaked with salt water. The zinc slowly dissolves, releasing electrons into the liquid. Hook a wire to each end

of the battery, and the current flows. When the zinc is gone, your battery is dead.

England's Michael Faraday (c. 1831) created the first true electric motor, which could generate electricity by moving a magnet through a coil of copper wire. Faraday shocked the world (and occasionally himself), and his invention soon led to the production of electricity on a large scale.

Room XVII: Making Science Useful

Chemistry: Antoine Lavoisier (1743-1794) was the Galileo of chemistry, introducing sound methodology and transforming the

mumbo jumbo of medieval alchemy into hard science. He created the precursor to our modern periodic table of the elements, and used the standardized terminology of suffixes that describe the different forms a single element can take (sulfur, sulf-ide, sulf-ate, sulf-uric, etc.).

The large object-with-lenses nearby was used, I believe, by 18th-century dukes to burn bugs.

• *In the case to the left of this primitive bug zapper, look for the metal rod in a wooden box.*

Standard Meter: Much of the purpose of science is to use constants to measure an ever-changing universe. For centuries, one of these constants was the meter-long metal rod, established in 1790 as the fundamental unit by which all distances are measured.

The rod is exactly one meter. Or 39.37 inches. Or 1/1,000th of the distance from the Galileo Science Museum to *David*. Or 1/10,000,000th of the distance from the equator to the North Pole. Or, according to the updated definition from 1960, a meter is the length of 1,650,763.73 wavelengths in a vacuum of the orange-red radiation of krypton 86.

Ain't science wonderful?

• *On the way out, you'll pass through a fun kids' zone with hands-on exhibits and touchscreens, and (just before the shop) lots of clocks from various historical periods.*

SLEEPING IN FLORENCE

Competition among hotels is stiff. When things slow down, fancy hotels drop their prices and become a much better value for travelers than the cheap, low-end places. For information and tips on pricing, getting deals, making reservations, seasonal differences (peak season versus off-season), and much more, see page 20 of the Introduction.

I like hotels that are handy to the great sights. Nearly all of my recommended accommodations are located in the center of Florence. If arriving by train, you can either walk (usually around 10 minutes) or take a taxi (roughly €8-10) to reach most of my recommended accommodations, as buses don't cover the city center very well.

Florence is notorious for its mosquitoes. If your hotel lacks air-conditioning, request a fan and don't open your windows, especially at night. Many hotels furnish a small plug-in bulb *(zanzariere)*—usually set in the ashtray—that helps keep the blood-suckers at bay. If not, you can purchase one cheaply at any pharmacy *(farmacia)*.

Museumgoers take note: If you don't plan to get a Firenze Card (see page 57), ask if your hotelier will reserve entry times for you to visit the popular Uffizi Gallery and the Accademia (Michelangelo's *David*). Request this service when you book your room; it's fast, easy, and offered free or for a small fee by most hotels—the only requirement is advance notice. Ask them to reserve your visits for any time the day after your arrival. Most likely they'll book by phone, then give you a confirmation number that you'll take to the museum, where you'll pay cash for your ticket. If your hotel does charge a fee, you could save several euros per reservation by booking it yourself (see page 59 for details), but it may not be worth the hassle.

North of the Arno River

Between the Duomo and the Train Station

$$$ Hotel Centrale is indeed central, just a short walk from the Duomo. The 31 spacious but slightly overpriced rooms—with a tasteful mix of old and new decor—are over a businesslike conference center (Db-€170, bigger superior Db-€212, Tb-€210, suites available, 10 percent discount with this book, ask for Rick Steves rate when you reserve, 20 percent discount if booked 3 months in advance, air-con, elevator, free Internet access and Wi-Fi, Via dei Conti 3, check in at big front desk on ground floor, tel. 055-215-761, fax 055-215-216, www.hotelcentralefirenze.it, info@hotel centralefirenze.it, Margherita and Roberto).

$$ Hotel Accademia, which comes with marble stairs, parquet floors, and attractive public areas, has 21 pleasant rooms and a floor plan that defies logic (Db-€145, Tb-€170, 10 percent discount with this book if you book direct and pay cash, air-con, free Internet access and Wi-Fi, Via Faenza 7, tel. 055-293-451, fax 055-219-771, www.hotelaccademiafirenze.com, info@hotelaccademia firenze.com, Tea and Paolo).

$ Hotel Lorena, just across from the Medici Chapels, has 19 rooms (six of which have shared bathrooms) and a tiny lobby. Though it's a bit like a youth hostel, it's cheap and conveniently located. Chatty Roberto speaks little English, but is eager to please (S-€35, Sb-€50, D-€60, Db-€75, Tb-€95, very flexible rates, breakfast-€5, air-con, free Wi-Fi, Via Faenza 1, tel. 055-282-785, fax 055-288-300, www.hotellorena.com, info@hotellorena.com).

$ Katti House and the nearby **Soggiorno Annamaria** are run by house-proud mama-and-daughter team Maria and Katti, who rent a total of 15 rooms on a bustling pedestrian street. While both offer comparable comfort, Soggiorno Annamaria has a more historic setting, with frescoed ceilings, unique tiles, timbered beams, and quieter rooms. Katti House serves as reception for both places, but mostly you interact with Maria; while she's a fine hostess, she speaks virtually no English so communication can be challenging (Sb-€85, D-€85, Db-€100, skimpy breakfast served in your room, air-con, free Internet access and Wi-Fi—only in Katti, Via Faenza 21, if no answer check in at Trattoria Katti next door, tel. & fax 055-213-410, www.kattihouse.com, info@kattihouse.com).

North of the Duomo

North of the Mercato Centrale

After dark, this neighborhood can feel a little deserted, but I've never heard of anyone running into harm here. It's a short walk from the train station and an easy stroll to all the sightseeing action. While workaday, it's practical, with plenty of good budget

Sleep Code

(€1 = about $1.40, country code: 39)
S = Single, **D** = Double/Twin, **T** = Triple, **Q** = Quad, **b** = bathroom,
s = shower only.

You can assume a hotel takes credit cards unless you see "cash only" in the listing. Unless otherwise noted, hotel staff speak basic English and breakfast is included.

Florence charges a hotel tax of €1 per star (according to the hotel's official star rating), per person, per night. So a couple staying at a three-star hotel would pay €3 each, or €6 total, per night. This tax is generally not included in the prices I've listed here.

To help you easily sort through these listings, I've divided the accommodations into three categories based on the price for a standard double room with bath during high season:

$$$ Higher Priced—Most rooms €160 or more.
 $$ Moderately Priced—Most rooms between €100-160.
  $ Lower Priced—Most rooms €100 or less.

Prices can change without notice; verify the hotel's current rates online or by email.

restaurants and markets nearby.

$$ Grand Tour Firenze has six charming rooms on a nondescript street between the train station and the Accademia. This cozy B&B will make you feel right at home; it's thoughtfully appointed and the owners, Cristina and Giuseppe, live there. The delightful and spacious suites come with a garden ambience on the ground floor (Db-€110, suite-€130, 10 percent discount when you book direct and pay cash, includes breakfast voucher for the corner bar—or skip it to save €10/person, air-con, free Wi-Fi, Via Santa Reparata 21, tel. 055-283-955, www.florencegrandtour.com, info @florencegrandtour.com). They run another more romantic, pricier place a couple of blocks away.

$$ Galileo Hotel, a classy business hotel with 31 rooms on a chaotic and congested street, is run with familial warmth (Sb-€100, Db-€130, Tb-€150, ask for 10 percent Rick Steves discount when you book direct and pay cash, quadruple-pane windows effectively shut out street noise, air-con, elevator, free Internet access and Wi-Fi, Via Nazionale 22a, tel. 055-496-645, fax 055-496-447, www.galileohotel.it, info@galileohotel.it).

$ Hotel Il Bargellino, run by Bostonian Carmel and her Italian husband Pino, feels like it's in a residential neighborhood. They rent 10 summery rooms decorated with funky antique furniture and Pino's modern paintings. Guests enjoy relaxing with

SLEEPING IN FLORENCE

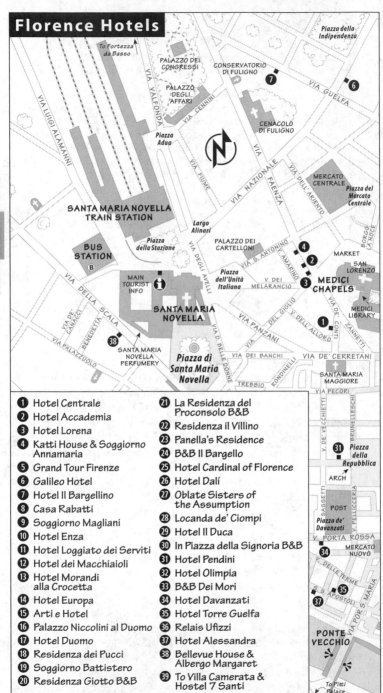

Florence Hotels

1. Hotel Centrale
2. Hotel Accademia
3. Hotel Lorena
4. Katti House & Soggiorno Annamaria
5. Grand Tour Firenze
6. Galileo Hotel
7. Hotel Il Bargellino
8. Casa Rabatti
9. Soggiorno Magliani
10. Hotel Enza
11. Hotel Loggiato dei Serviti
12. Hotel dei Macchiaioli
13. Hotel Morandi alla Crocetta
14. Hotel Europa
15. Arti e Hotel
16. Palazzo Niccolini al Duomo
17. Hotel Duomo
18. Residenza dei Pucci
19. Soggiorno Battistero
20. Residenza Giotto B&B
21. La Residenza del Proconsolo B&B
22. Residenza il Villino
23. Panella's Residence
24. B&B Il Bargello
25. Hotel Cardinal of Florence
26. Hotel Dalí
27. Oblate Sisters of the Assumption
28. Locanda de' Ciompi
29. Hotel Il Duca
30. In Piazza della Signoria B&B
31. Hotel Pendini
32. Hotel Olimpia
33. B&B Dei Mori
34. Hotel Davanzati
35. Hotel Torre Guelfa
36. Relais Uffizi
37. Hotel Alessandra
38. Bellevue House & Albergo Margaret
39. To Villa Camerata & Hostel 7 Santi

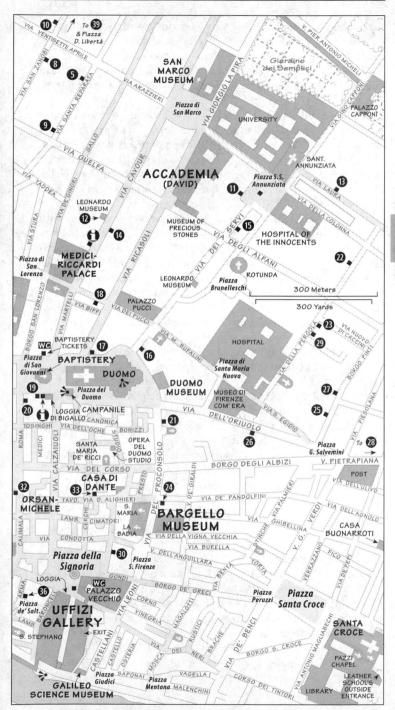

Carmel and Leopoldo the parrot on the big, breezy, momentum-slowing terrace adorned with lemon shrubs (S-€45, D-€80, Db-€90, ask for Rick Steves discount if you book direct and pay cash, extra bed-€25, no breakfast, free Wi-Fi, north of the train station at Via Guelfa 87, tel. 055-238-2658, www.ilbargellino.com, carmel@ilbargellino.com).

$ **Casa Rabatti** is the ultimate if you always wanted to have a Florentine mama. Its four simple, clean rooms are run with warmth by Marcella. This is a great place to practice your Italian, since Marcella loves to chat and speaks minimal English. Seeing nearly two decades of my family Christmas cards on their walls, I'm reminded of how long she has been keeping budget travelers happy (D-€50, Db-€60, €25 extra per bed in shared quad or quint, prices good with this book, cash only but secure reservation with credit card, no breakfast, fans available, free Wi-Fi, 5 blocks from station at Via San Zanobi 48 black, tel. 055-212-393, casarabatti @inwind.it). If Marcella's booked, she'll put you up in her daughter's place nearby, at Via Nazionale 20 (five big, airy, family-friendly rooms; €25/person, fans, no breakfast, closer to the station). While daughter Patrizia works, her mom runs the place. Getting bumped to Patrizia's gives you slightly more comfort and slightly less personality...certainly not a net negative.

$ **Soggiorno Magliani** is central and humble, with six bright, no-frills rooms (sharing two baths) that feel and smell like a great-grandmother's home. It's run by the friendly duo Vincenza and her English-speaking daughter Cristina, and the price is right (S-€36, D-€46, T-€65, cash only but secure reservation with credit card, no breakfast, near Via Guelfa at Via Santa Reparata 1, tel. 055-287-378, hotel-magliani@libero.it).

$ **Hotel Enza** rents 19 dark, musty, straightforward rooms. The prices are reasonable for predictable hotel comfort (S-€45, Sb-€55, Db-€80, these prices promised through 2013 with this book, extra bed-€20, optional breakfast-€8, air-con, free Internet access and Wi-Fi, Via San Zanobi 45 black, tel. 055-490-990, fax 055-473-672, www.hotelenza.it, info@hotelenza.it, Diana).

Near the Accademia
$$$ **Hotel Loggiato dei Serviti,** at the most prestigious address in Florence on the most Renaissance square in town, gives you Old World romance with hair dryers. Stone stairways lead you under open-beam ceilings through this 16th-century monastery's monumental public rooms—it's so artful, you'll be snapping photos everywhere. The 38 cells—with air-conditioning, TVs, mini-bars, free Wi-Fi, and telephones—would be unrecognizable to their original inhabitants. The hotel staff is both professional and warm (Sb-€140, Db-€160, superior Db-€180, family suites from

€263, ask for Rick Steves rate when you book, elevator, valet parking-€21/day, Piazza S.S. Annunziata 3, tel. 055-289-592, fax 055-289-595, www.loggiato deiservitihotel.it, info@loggiato deiservitihotel.it; Simonetta, Gianni, and two Chiaras). When full, they rent five spacious and sophisticated rooms in a 17th-century annex a block away. While it lacks the monastic mystique, the annex rooms are bigger, gorgeous, and cost the same.

SLEEPING IN FLORENCE

$$$ **Hotel dei Macchiaioli** offers 15 fresh and spacious rooms on one high-ceilinged, noble floor in a restored *palazzo* owned for generations by a well-to-do Florentine family. You'll eat breakfast under original frescoed ceilings while enjoying modern comforts (Sb-€100, Db-€180, Tb-€220, 10 percent Rick Steves discount if you book direct and pay cash, air-con, free Wi-Fi, Via Cavour 21, tel. 055-213-154, www.hoteldeimacchiaioli.com, info@hoteldei macchiaioli.com, helpful Francesca and Paolo).

$$ **Hotel Morandi alla Crocetta,** a former convent, envelops you in a 16th-century cocoon. Located on a quiet street with 12 rooms, period furnishings, parquet floors, and wood-beamed or painted ceilings, it takes you back a few centuries and up a few social classes (Sb-€105, Db-€155, Tb-€185, low-season discounts online, air-con, free Wi-Fi, a block off Piazza S.S. Annunziata at Via Laura 50, tel. 055-234-4747, fax 055-248-0954, www.hotel morandi.it, welcome@hotelmorandi.it, well-run by Maurizio, Rolando, and Ertol).

$$ **Hotel Europa,** run by cheery Miriam, Roberto, and daughters Priscilla and Isabel since 1970, has a welcoming atmosphere. The breakfast room is spacious, and some of the 20 rooms have views of the Duomo (Sb-€89, Db-€150, Tb-€180, Qb-€250, a little extra for a private balcony, €10-15 more for bigger "deluxe" room, 10 percent discount if you pay cash, mention Rick Steves to get their best available room, air-con, old-timey elevator, free Wi-Fi, Via Cavour 14, tel. 055-239-6715, fax 055-268-984, www .webhoteleuropa.com, firenze@webhoteleuropa.com).

$$ **Arti e Hotel** rents 11 large, tastefully furnished rooms well-located on a quiet street just far enough away from the tourist scene. As there's no real public space, the emphasis is on the classy rooms (Db-€135, 10 percent discount if you book direct and pay cash—ask for their Rick Steves price, third bed-€30, air-con, elevator, free Wi-Fi, Via dei Servi 38, tel. 055-267-8553, fax 055-290-140, www.artiehotel.it, info@artiehotel.it, Carlo).

Near the Duomo

All of these places are within a block of Florence's biggest church and main landmark.

$$$ Palazzo Niccolini al Duomo, one of five elite Historic Residence Hotels in Florence, is run by Niccolini da Camugliano. The lounge (where free chamomile tea is served in the evenings) is palatial, but the 12 rooms, while splendid, vary wildly in size. If you have the money and want a Florentine palace to call home, this can be a good bet (Db-€180-€450 depending on type of room, ask for 10 percent Rick Steves discount when you book, check online to choose a room and consider last-minute deals, elevator, free Internet access and Wi-Fi, Via dei Servi 2, tel. 055-282-412, fax 055-290-979, www.niccolinidomepalace.com, info@niccolini domepalace.com).

$$$ Hotel Duomo, big and venerable, rents 24 rooms four floors up. The Duomo looms like a monster outside the hotel's windows; most (but not all) rooms come with views. The rooms are modern and comfortable enough, and the location can't be beat (Sb-€90, Db-€160, Tb-€180, 10 percent discount with this book if you pay cash, air-con, elevator, free Wi-Fi, Piazza del Duomo 1, tel. 055-219-922, www.hotelduomofirenze.it, info@hotelduomo firenze.it; Alberto, Sonia, and Karen).

$$ Residenza dei Pucci rents 12 pleasant rooms (each one different) spread over three floors. The decor, a mix of soothing earth tones and aristocratic furniture, makes this place feel upscale for this price range (Sb-€135, Db-€150, Tb-€170, Qb-€238, rates can vary, 10 percent discount with cash and this book, air-con, no elevator, free slow Wi-Fi or pay for fast Wi-Fi, reception open 9:00-20:00—let them know if you'll arrive late, Via dei Pucci 9, tel. 055-281-886, fax 055-264-314, www.residenzadeipucci.com, residenzadeipucci@residenzadeipucci.com, Mirella and Marina).

$$ Soggiorno Battistero rents seven simple, airy rooms, most with great views, overlooking the Baptistery and the Duomo square. Choose a view or a quieter room in the back when you book by email. It's a pristine, fresh, and minimalist place run by Italian Luca and his American wife Kelly, who makes the hotel particularly welcoming (Sb-€83, Db-€110, Tb-€145, Qb-€155, prices good with this book, 5 percent discount if you book direct and pay cash, breakfast served in room, air-con available June-Aug, free Wi-Fi, Piazza San Giovanni 1, third floor—new elevator planned for 2013, tel. 055-295-143, fax 055-268-189, www.soggiorno battistero.it, info@soggiornobattistero.it).

$$ Residenza Giotto B&B offers you the chance to stay on Florence's upscale shopping drag, Via Roma. Occupying the top floor of a 19th-century building, this place has six bright, smallish rooms and a terrace with knockout views of the Duomo's tower.

Reception is generally open 9:00-17:00; let them know your arrival time in advance (Sb-€90, Db-€130, view rooms-€10 extra, extra bed-€25, 10 percent discount if you book direct and pay cash, air-con, elevator, free Wi-Fi, Via Roma 6, tel. 055-214-593, fax 055-264-8568, www.residenzagiotto.it, info@residenzagiotto.it, Giorgio).

$$ **La Residenza del Proconsolo B&B,** run by helpful Mariano, has five older-feeling rooms a minute from the Duomo (three rooms have Duomo views). The place lacks public spaces, but the rooms are quite large and nice—perfect for eating breakfast, which is served in your room (Sb-€90, Db-€120, Tb-€140, air-con, free Wi-Fi, Via del Proconsolo 18 black, tel. 055-264-5657, mobile 335-657-4840, www.proconsolo.com, info@proconsolo.com).

East of the Duomo

$$ **Residenza il Villino,** popular and friendly, aspires to offer a Florentine home away from home. It has 10 charmingly rustic rooms and a picturesque, peaceful little courtyard. As it's in a "little villa" (as the name implies) set back from the street, this is a quiet refuge from the bustle of Florence (small Db-€110, Db-€130, family suite that sleeps up to six—price upon request, 5 percent discount with cash and this book, air-con, free Internet access and Wi-Fi, just north of Via degli Alfani at Via della Pergola 53, tel. 055-200-1116, fax 055-200-1101, www.ilvillino.it, info@ilvillino.it; Sergio—who looks a bit like Henry Winkler, Elisabetta, and son Lorenzo).

$$ **Panella's Residence,** once a convent and today part of owner Graziella's extensive home, is a classy B&B, with six chic, romantic, and ample rooms, antique furnishings, and historic architectural touches (Db-€140, bigger superior Db-€165, even bigger deluxe Db-€180, these prices are with cash, discounts for 3 or more nights, air-con, free Wi-Fi, Via della Pergola 42, tel. & fax 055-234-7202, mobile 345-972-1541, www.panellaresidence.com, panella_residence@yahoo.it).

$ **B&B Il Bargello** is a home away from home, run by friendly and helpful Canadian expat Gabriella. Hike up three long flights (no elevator) to reach six smart, relaxing rooms. Gabriella offers a cozy communal living room, kitchen access, and an inviting roof-top terrace with close-up views of Florence's towers (Db-€100, ask for Rick Steves rate when you book direct and pay cash, air-con, free Internet access and Wi-Fi, 20 yards off Via Proconsolo at Via de' Pandolfini 33 black, tel. 055-215-330, mobile 339-175-3110, www.firenze-bedandbreakfast.it, info@firenze-bedandbreakfast.it).

$ **Hotel Cardinal of Florence** is a third-floor walk-up with 17 spartan, tidy, and sun-splashed rooms overlooking either a silent courtyard (many with views of Brunelleschi's dome) or quiet street. Relax and enjoy Florence's rooftops from the sun terrace (Sb-€60, Db-€95, these prices for Rick Steves readers, additional €5 discount if you pay cash, air-con, free Wi-Fi, Borgo Pinti 5, tel. 055-234-0780, fax 055-234-3389, www.hotelcardinalofflorence .com, info@hotelcardinalofflorence.com, Mauro and Ida).

$ **Hotel Dalí** has 10 cheap and cheery rooms with new baths and floors in a nice location for a great price. Samanta and Marco, who run this guesthouse with a charming passion and idealism, are a delight to know (S-€40, D-€70, Db-€85, extra bed-€25, no breakfast, fans but no air-con, request quiet room when you book, no elevator, free Wi-Fi, free parking, 2 blocks behind the Duomo at Via dell'Oriuolo 17 on the second floor, tel. & fax 055-234-0706, www.hoteldali.com, hoteldali@tin.it).

$ **Oblate Sisters of the Assumption** run an institutional 30-room hotel in a Renaissance building with a dreamy garden, great public spaces, appropriately simple rooms, and a quiet, prayerful ambience (€45/person in single, double, triple, or quad rooms with bathrooms, €38/person with shared bathrooms, cash only, single beds only, air-con, elevator, Wi-Fi with suggested donation, €10/day limited parking—request when you book, Borgo Pinti 15, tel. 055-248-0582, fax 055-234-6291, sroblateborgopinti@virgilio .it, sisters are likely to speak French but not English, Sister Theresa is very helpful).

$ **Locanda de' Ciompi,** overlooking the inviting Piazza dei Ciompi antiques market in a young and lively neighborhood, is just right for travelers who want to feel like a part of the town. Riccardo runs a minimalist place—just five quiet, clean, tasteful rooms along a thin hallway (Db-€100, Tb-€115, 10 percent discount with this book if you book direct and pay cash, includes breakfast at nearby bar, air-con, free Wi-Fi, 8 blocks behind the Duomo at Via Pietrapiana 28, tel. 055-263-8034, www.locandade ciompi.it, locandadeciompi@yahoo.it).

$ **Hotel Il Duca**—a big, bright place on a quiet street a few blocks behind the Duomo—seems like a basic building wearing a fancy coat. Its 13 pleasant rooms are a great value, but don't expect a warm welcome or personal service (Sb-€85, Db-€90, third bed-€25, air-con, free Wi-Fi, Via della Pergola 34, tel. 055-906-2167, www.hotelilduca.it, info@hotelilduca.it, Angela).

South of the Duomo
Between the Duomo and Piazza della Signoria
These are the most central of my accommodations recommendations (and therefore a little overpriced). While worth the extra cost for many, given Florence's walkable, essentially traffic-free core, nearly every hotel I recommend can be considered central.

$$$ In Piazza della Signoria B&B, overlooking Piazza della Signoria, is peaceful, refined, and homey at the same time. Fit for a honeymoon, the 10 rooms come with all the special touches and little extras you'd expect in a top-end American B&B. However, the rates are high, and the "partial view" rooms require craning your neck to see anything—not worth the extra euros (viewless Db-€250, partial-view Db-€280, full-view "deluxe" Db-€300, Tb-€280, partial-view Tb-€300, ask for 10 percent discount when you book direct with this book, family apartments, lavish bathrooms, air-con, tiny elevator, free Internet access and Wi-Fi, Via dei Magazzini 2, tel. 055-239-9546, mobile 348-321-0565, fax 055-267-6616, www.inpiazzadellasignoria.com, info@inpiazzadella signoria.com, Sonia and Alessandro).

$$$ Hotel Pendini, with 42 rooms and three slightly tarnished stars, fills the top floor of a grand building constructed to celebrate Italian unification in the late 19th century. It overlooks Piazza della Repubblica, and as you walk into the lobby, you feel as if you are walking back in time (Sb-€139, Db-€189, deluxe Db with square view and noise-€239, air-con, elevator, free Internet access and Wi-Fi, Via degli Strozzi 2, tel. 055-211-170, www.hotel pendini.it, info@hotelpendini.it).

$$$ Hotel Olimpia is a friendly, well-worn, established place renting 24 quite dated rooms on the fourth floor overlooking Piazza della Repubblica (some rooms have views and noise). You pay for the location (Db-€160, air-con, elevator, pay Wi-Fi, Piazza della Repubblica 2, tel. 055-219-781, fax 055-267-0383, www.hotel -olimpia.it, hotelolimpia@tin.it, Marziano).

$$ B&B Dei Mori, a peaceful haven with a convivial and welcoming living room, rents five tastefully appointed rooms ideally located on a quiet pedestrian street near Casa di Dante—within a five-minute walk of the Duomo, the Bargello, or Piazza della Signoria. Accommodating Suzanne, Daniele, and Peter pride themselves on offering personal service, including lots of tips on dining and sightseeing in Florence. But if they're full, I'd skip their offer of an apartment nearby (D-€100, Db-€120, 10 percent discount for my readers—ask when you book, air-con-€5, free Wi-Fi, reception open 8:00-19:00, Via Dante Alighieri 12, tel. 055-211-438, www.deimori.com, deimori@bnb.it).

Near Ponte Vecchio

$$$ Hotel Davanzati, bright and shiny with artistic touches, has 22 cheerful rooms with all the comforts. The place is a family affair, thoughtfully run by friendly Tommaso and father Fabrizio, who offer drinks and snacks each evening at their candlelit happy hour, plus lots of other extras (Sb-€132, Db-€199, Tb-€259, these rates good with this book though prices soft off-season, 10 percent discount if you pay cash, free loaner laptop in every room, free on-demand movies—including my Italy TV shows—on your room TV, air-con, free Wi-Fi, next to Piazza Davanzati at Via Porta Rossa 5—easy to miss so watch for low-profile sign above the door, tel. 055-286-666, fax 055-265-8252, www.hoteldavanzati.it, info @hoteldavanzati.it).

$$$ Hotel Torre Guelfa has grand (almost royal) public spaces and is topped by a fun medieval tower with a panoramic rooftop terrace. Its 31 pricey rooms vary wildly in size and layout. Room 315, with a private terrace (€245), is worth reserving several months in advance (Db-€170-190, Db junior suite-€230, ask for Rick Steves discount, family deals, check their website for promotions, air-con, elevator, free Internet access and Wi-Fi in lobby, a couple blocks northwest of Ponte Vecchio, Borgo S.S. Apostoli 8, tel. 055-239-6338, fax 055-239-8577, www.hoteltorreguelfa.com, info@hoteltorreguelfa.com, Sandro and Barbara).

$$$ Relais Uffizi is a peaceful little gem, with 15 classy rooms tucked away down a tiny alleyway off Piazza della Signoria. The lounge has a huge window overlooking the action in the square below (Sb-€120, Db-€180, Tb-€220, more for deluxe rooms, buffet breakfast, air-con, elevator, free Wi-Fi, Chiasso de Baroncelli/ Chiasso del Buco 16, tel. 055-267-6239, fax 055-265-7909, www .relaisuffizi.it, info@relaisuffizi.it, charming Alessandro and Elizabetta).

$$ Hotel Alessandra is 16th-century, tranquil, and sprawling, with 27 big, tasteful rooms and an old-school, peeling-wallpaper vibe (S-€67-€88, Sb-€110, D-€110, Db-€150, Tb-€195, Qb-€215, 5 percent cash discount, air-con, free Internet access and Wi-Fi, Borgo S.S. Apostoli 17, tel. 055-283-438, fax 055-210-619, www .hotelalessandra.com, info@hotelalessandra.com, Anna and son Andrea).

Near the Train Station

$ Bellevue House is a third-floor (no elevator) oasis of tranquility, with six spacious, old-fashioned rooms flanking a long, mellow-yellow lobby. It's a peaceful time warp thoughtfully run by Rosanna and Antonio di Grazia (Db-€70-95, family deals; 10 percent discount if you stay two nights, pay cash, and book direct; optional €3 breakfast in street-level bar, air-con, free Wi-Fi, Via della Scala 21, tel. 055-260-8932, mobile 333-612-5973, fax 055-265-5315, www.bellevuehouse.it, info@bellevuehouse.it).

$ Albergo Margaret, homey yet minimalist, doesn't have a public lounge or offer breakfast. Run by the Cristantielli family, it has seven peaceful and simple rooms (D-€40, Ds-€60, Db-€75, 10 percent discount if you book direct and pay cash, extra bed-€10, air-con, free Wi-Fi, near Santa Maria Novella at Via della Scala 25, tel. & fax 055-210-138, www.hotel-margaret.it, info@hotel -margaret.it; Francesco, Anna, and Graziano).

Hostels away from the Center

These two hostels, northeast of downtown, are a bus ride from the action. A far more central hostel is in the Oltrarno (see listing at the end of this chapter).

$ Villa Camerata, classy for an IYHF hostel, is in a pretty villa three miles northeast of the train station, on the outskirts of Florence (€18/bed with breakfast, 4- to 6-bed rooms, non-members pay €3/night more, free Wi-Fi, self-serve laundry, Via Righi 2—take bus #11 from the train station to Salviatino or bus #17 to Via Cento Stelle, tel. 055-601-451, fax 055-610-300, www .aighostels.com, firenze@aighostels.com).

$ Hostel 7 Santi calls itself a "travelers' haven." It fills a for-mer convent, but you'll feel like you're in an old school. Still, it offers some of the best cheap beds in town, is friendly to older travelers, and comes with the services you'd expect in a big, mod-ern hostel, including free Wi-Fi and self-serve laundry. It's in a more residential neighborhood near the Campo di Marte stadium, about a 10-minute bus ride from the center (200 beds in 60 rooms, mostly 4- or 6-bed dorms with a floor of doubles and triples, €16-18/dorm bed, Sb-€45, Db-€60, Tb-€75, Qb-€85, includes sheets and towels, breakfast and dinner available but cost extra, no cur-few, free Internet access and Wi-Fi; Viale dei Mille 11—from train station, take bus #10, #17, or #20, direction: Campo di Marte, to bus stop Chiesa dei Sette Santi; tel. 055-504-8452, www.7santi .com, info@7santi.com).

South of the Arno River, in the Oltrarno

Across the river in the Oltrarno area, between the Pitti Palace and Ponte Vecchio, you'll find small, traditional crafts shops, neigh-borly piazzas, and family eateries. The following places are an easy walk from Ponte Vecchio. Only the first two are real hotels—the rest are a ragtag gang of budget alternatives.

$$$ Hotel Silla is a classic three-star hotel with 36 cheery, spacious, pastel, and modern rooms. It faces the river and overlooks a park opposite Santa Croce Church (Db-€180, bigger "superior" Db-€210, ask for Rick Steves rate when you book, extra bed-€35,

SLEEPING IN FLORENCE

Oltrarno Hotels & Restaurants

Arno

To Porta San Frediano & **10**

LUNGARNO GUICCIARDINI

To Santa Maria Novella

BORGO SAN FREDIANO   **4**

Piazza Nazaro Sauro

8

VIA DI SANTO SPIRITO

VIA DELL'ONEE

5   Piazza del Carmine

BORGO STELLA

VIA DEI SERRAGLI

VIA MAFFIA

VIA DE' COVERELLI

BRANCACCI CHAPEL

VIA SANTA MONACA   **6**   O L T R A R N O

SANTA MARIA DEL CARMINE

To **12**

SANTO SPIRITO

VIA S. AGOSTINO

VIA D. S. MARTINO

3

VIA

15

SDRUCCIOLO DE PITTI

Piazza di Santo Spirito   **14**   MICH.   **13**

VIA DELLA CHIESA

VIA MAGGIO

MARSILI

VIA DEL CAMPUCCIO

VIA DEL TEGOLAIO

PAL. DE COSIMO RIDOLFI

VIA MAZZETTA

BORGO

Piazza di San Felice

Giardino Torrigiani

VIA DEI SERRAGLI

VIA DELLE CALDAIE

TICKET OFFICE

Piazzina della Meridiana

ROMANA

To Porta Romana

VIALE DELLA MERIDIANA

VIALE DEL CIPRESSI

L'Isolotto

FONTANA DELL'OCEANO

1 To Hotel Silla & Il Gelato di Filo
2 Hotel la Scaletta
3 Istituto Gould
4 Soggiorno Alessandra
5 Casa Santo Nome di Gesù
6 Ostello Santa Monaca
7 Golden View Open Bar
8 Il Santo Bevitore Ristorante & Enoteca Il Santino Gastronomia
9 Trattoria 4 Leoni
10 To Antico Ristoro Di' Cambi, Trattoria da Sergio & Trattoria Sabatino
11 Olio & Convivium Gastronomia
12 To Trattoria Al Tranvai
13 Trattoria Casalinga
14 Borgo Antico, Volume Bar & Ricchi Caffè
15 Pop Café
16 Meta Supermarket

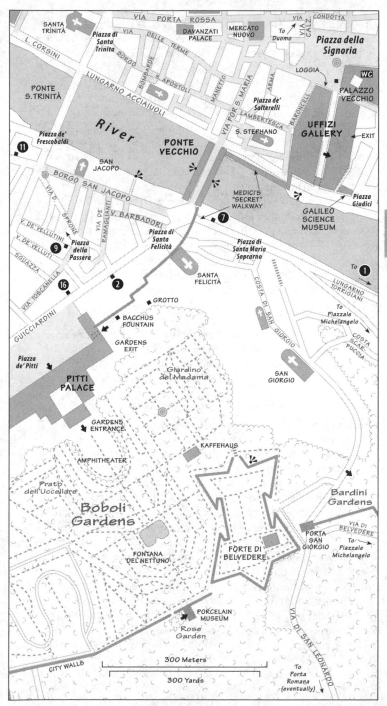

air-con, elevator, free Internet access and Wi-Fi, parking-€19/day, Via dei Renai 5, tel. 055-234-2888, fax 055-234-1437, www.hotelsilla.it, hotelsilla@hotelsilla.it; Laura, Chiara, Massimo, and Stefano).

$$ Hotel la Scaletta has 17 functional but colorful rooms hiding in a tortured floor plan, plus a fabulous rooftop terrace overlooking Boboli Gardens (Db-€130, third bed-€20, breakfast-€7, air-con, elevator, free Internet access and Wi-Fi, Via de' Guicciardini 13, tel. 055-283-028, fax 055-283-013, www.hotel lascaletta.it, info@hotellascaletta.it).

$ Istituto Gould is a Protestant Church-run place with 39 clean and spartan rooms that have twin beds and modern facilities. It's located in a 17th-century palace with a beautiful garden courtyard. The complex also houses kids from troubled homes, and proceeds raised from renting rooms help fund that important work (Sb-€55, Db-€60, €20 more for garden rooms that are quieter and have air-con, Tb-€81, Qb-€100, breakfast-€6, non-air-con rooms have fans, free Wi-Fi in lobby, Via dei Serragli 49, tel. 055-212-576, fax 055-280-274, www.istitutogould.it, foresteriafirenze@diaconia valdese.org). You must arrive when the office is open (Mon-Fri 8:45-13:00 & 15:00-19:30, Sat 9:00-13:30 & 14:30-18:00, no live check-in on Sundays but they'll email you a code).

$ Soggiorno Alessandra has five bright, comfy, and smallish rooms. Because of its double-paned windows, you'll hardly notice the traffic noise (D-€73, Db-€78, Tb-€98, Qb-€128, cheaper off-season, includes basic breakfast in room, air-con-€8, free Wi-Fi, just past the Carraia Bridge at Via Borgo San Frediano 6, tel. 055-290-424, fax 055-218-464, www.soggiornoalessandra.it, info @soggiornoalessandra.it, Alessandra).

$ Casa Santo Nome di Gesù is a grand, 29-room convent whose sisters—Franciscan Missionaries of Mary—are thankful to rent rooms to tourists. Staying in this 15th-century palace, you'll be immersed in the tranquil atmosphere created by a huge, peaceful garden, generous and prayerful public spaces, and smiling nuns. The monastic rooms have only twin beds (D-€70, Db-€85, T-€100, Tb-€120, book direct to avoid fees, no air-con but rooms have fans, memorable convent-like breakfast room, elevator, strict 23:29 curfew, Piazza del Carmine 21, tel. 055-213-856, fax 055-281-835, www.fmmfirenze.it, info@fmmfirenze.it).

Hostel: **$ Ostello Santa Monaca,** a well-run, institutional-feeling hostel a long block south of the Brancacci Chapel. As clean as its guests, its 112 beds in 15 rooms (2- to 20-bed dorms) attract a young backpacking crowd (€18-26/bed with sheets and towel, 10:00-14:00 lock-out, 2:00 in the morning curfew, free Internet access and Wi-Fi, self-serve laundry, kitchen, bike rental, Via

Santa Monaca 6, tel. 055-268-338, fax 055-280-185, www.ostello
santamonaca.com, info@ostellosantamonaca.com).

Rural *Agriturismo* South of Florence

The Tuscan countryside south of Florence is loaded with enticing rural farms offering accommodations, called *agriturismi* (for
details, see page 453). I've listed several good choices near Siena
(see page 387) and throughout the Tuscan Hill Towns chapter.
This option is a bit closer to Florence (about 45 minutes south), in
the Chianti region.

$$$ I Greppi di Silli is a lovely, family-run *agriturismo* set
among rolling hills south of Florence. Owners Anna and Giuliano
Alfani cultivate Chianti grapes and olive trees, and offer six care-
fully remodeled apartments with beds for 2-6 people, some with
panoramic views and/or terraces; a seventh apartment (sleeps 8) is
a mile away in an old country house (Db-€115-250 or €735-1,900/
week, price depends on apartment, less off-season; one-week
minimum—Sat-to-Sat—in July-Aug, fewer nights possible in
shoulder and low season—but generally still a 3-night minimum;
breakfast-€9, pool, kids' play area, table tennis, bocce ball court,
loaner bikes, weekly farm dinners-€28/person—less for kids, Via
Vallacchio 19, near San Casciano and just outside the village of
Mercatale Val di Pesa, about 45 minutes' drive to Florence or San
Gimignano and one hour from Siena, tel. 055-821-7959, www
.igreppidisilli.it, info@igreppidisilli.it).

Apartment Rentals

Cross-Pollinate is an online booking agency representing
B&Bs and apartments in a handful of European cities, includ-
ing Florence. Unlike huge aggregator websites like HomeAway or
VRBO, Cross-Pollinate handpicks its listings, selectively present-
ing each one as if recommending it to a friend. Search their website
for a listing you like, then submit your reservation online. If the
place is available, you'll be charged a small deposit and emailed the
location and check-in details. Policies vary from owner to owner,
but in most cases you'll pay the balance on arrival in cash. Florence
listings range from a B&B room for two near Santa Maria Novella
for €50 per night to a two-bedroom Ponte Vecchio apartment
sleeping six for €165 per night. Minimum stays vary from one to
three nights (US tel. 800-270-1190, Italy tel. 06-9936-9799, www
.cross-pollinate.com, info@cross-pollinate.com).

EATING IN FLORENCE

Florence is a Tuscan tour for your taste buds, but be warned: My readers fill many of the mom-and-pop eateries listed here. Still, even when packed with travelers, these personality-driven places are a fine value and offer high quality. If you want to steer away from my readers, grab another spot. If it's in the center, it'll probably have less value and just as many tourists. To really escape from the crowds, you need to get away from the town center...though I'd rather stick around. The Oltrarno, just across the river, is a good compromise: far enough away to not feel completely overrun by tourists, but close enough for an easy commute by foot.

You may have the best luck finding local ambience at lunch, since that's when many restaurants in the center cater to office workers. For dinner, those same places fill with tourists early; then, after about 21:00, the tourists are replaced by locals dining later. If you're on a budget and are planning to visit any small Tuscan towns, your splurge dollars will go much farther there than in expensive Florence...and you'll get generally better food, to boot.

For an overview of restaurants, other types of eateries, and Florentine cuisine, along with tips on tipping, see page 26 in the Introduction. Remember, restaurants like to serve what's fresh. If you're into flavor, go for the seasonal best bets—featured in the *piatti del giorno* ("special of the day") section on menus. For dessert, it's gelato (see sidebar later in this chapter).

To save money and time for sights, keep lunches fast and simple, eating in one of the countless pizzerias and self-service cafeterias. Picnicking is easy—there's no shortage of corner *supermercatos*, or you can picnic your way through the Mercato Centrale.

North of the Arno River

Near the Church of Santa Maria Novella

Trattoria al Trebbio serves traditional food, especially rabbit and steak, with simple Florentine elegance in its candlelit interior. Inside, it feels like a throwback; the room is decorated with old movie posters. Outside, tables spill out onto a romantic little square—an oasis of Roman Trastevere-like charm (€7-10 pastas, €10-14 *secondi,* daily 12:00-15:00 & 19:15-23:00, closed for lunch Tue off-season, reserve for outdoor seating, half a block off of Piazza Santa Maria Novella at Via delle Belle Donne 47, tel. 055-287-089, Antonio).

Trattoria "da Giorgio" is a family-style diner on a sketchy street serving up piping-hot, delicious home cooking to happy locals and tourists alike. Their three-course, fixed-price meal, including water and a drink, is a great value (€12 at lunch, €13 at dinner). Choose from among the daily specials or the regular menu (Mon-Sat 12:00-14:30 & 18:30-22:00, closed Sun, Via Palazzuolo 100 red, tel. 055-284-302, Silvano).

Trattoria Marione serves sincerely home cooked-style meals to a mixed group of tourists and Florentines beneath hanging ham hocks. The ambience is happy, crowded, food-loving, and steamy (€8-11 pastas, €10-12 *secondi,* daily 12:00-17:30 & 19:00-23:00, Via della Spada 27 red, tel. 055-214-756, Fabio).

Trattoria Sostanza-Troia, characteristic and well established, is famous for its beef. Hearty steaks and pastas are splittable. Whirling ceiling fans and walls strewn with old photos evoke earlier times, while the artichoke pies remind locals of Grandma's cooking. Crowded, shared tables with paper tablecloths give this place a bistro feel. They offer two dinner seatings, at 19:30 and 21:00, which require reservations (dinners for about €30 plus wine, cash only, lunch Mon-Sat 12:30-14:00, closed Sun, closed Sat off-season, Via del Porcellana 25 red, tel. 055-212-691).

Trattoria 13 Gobbi ("13 Hunchbacks") is a trendy and slightly self-important eatery, atmospherically cluttered and glowing with candles around a tiny garden. Romantic in front and more kid-friendly in back, it serves beautifully presented Tuscan food (they're enthusiastic about their steak) on big, fancy plates to a mostly tourist crowd (€10-12 pastas, €14-19 *secondi,* daily 12:30-15:00 & 19:30-23:00, Via del Porcellana 9 red, tel. 055-284-015, Enrico).

Near the Mercato Centrale

The following market-neighborhood eateries all have a distinct vibe. They're within a few blocks of each other: Scout around and choose your favorite.

EATING IN FLORENCE

EATING IN FLORENCE

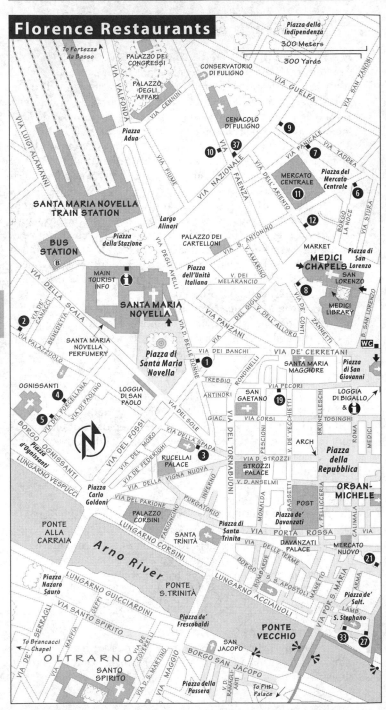

Florence Restaurants

1. Trattoria al Trebbio
2. Trattoria "da Giorgio"
3. Trattoria Marione
4. Trattoria Sostanza-Troia
5. Trattoria 13 Gobbi
6. Trattoria Zà-Zà & Trattoria Mario's
7. Trattoria la Burrasca
8. Trattoria Lo Stracotto
9. Osteria Vineria i'Brincello
10. Trattoria Nerone Pizzeria
11. Mercato Centrale & Nerbone in the Market
12. Casa del Vino
13. Pugi Pizza
14. Barbecue Döner Kebab
15. Pasticceria Robiglio
16. La Mescita Fiaschetteria
17. Il Centro Supermercati
18. To Antica Trattoria da Tito
19. Self-Service Rist. Leonardo
20. Turkuaz Döner Kebab
21. Rivoire Café
22. Frescobaldi Rist. & Wine Bar
23. Ristorante Paoli, Cantinetta dei Verrazzano & Perchè No! Gelateria
24. Osteria Vini e Vecchi Sapori
25. I Fratellini
26. L'Antico Trippaio, Pizzeria Totò & Supermarket
27. 'Ino Bottega di Alimentari e Vini
28. Ristorante del Fagioli
29. Boccadama Enoteca Rist.
30. Trattoria Anita
31. Trattoria l'cche C'è C'è
32. Gelateria Grom
33. Gelateria Carrozze
34. Gelateria Carabè
35. Vivoli's Gelateria
36. Gelateria de' Neri
37. The Bermuda Triangle

EATING IN FLORENCE

Trattoria Zà-Zà is a fun, characteristic, high-energy place facing the Mercato Centrale. It offers a family-friendly festival of standard Tuscan dishes such as *ribollita* and *bistecca alla fiorentina*, plus a variety of big, splittable €8 salads. Though it's more touristy than ever, the food is still great, and everyone's happy. Arrive early or make a reservation. Choose between the folkloric interior or the fine outdoor piazza. Understand your itemized bill, and don't mistake their outside seating with the neighboring restaurant's (€8-10 pastas, €10-16 *secondi*, daily 11:00-23:00, Piazza del Mercato Centrale 26 red, tel. 055-215-411). Their **bar/osteria,** nearby, has a similar menu (with a few differences, including more of an emphasis on seafood and *taglieri*—cheese-and-meat plates), a trendier-feeling interior, and a smaller, more open outdoor-dining zone.

Trattoria la Burrasca is Flintstone-chic. Friendly duo Elio and Simone offer a limited menu with good-value seasonal specials of Tuscan home cooking. It's small—10 tables—and often filled with my readers. If Archie Bunker were Italian, he'd eat at this trattoria for special nights out (€6 pastas, €7-15 *secondi*, no cover or service charge, Tue-Sun 12:00-15:00 & 19:00-22:30, closed Mon, Via Panicale 6, north corner of Mercato Centrale, tel. 055-215-827).

Trattoria Lo Stracotto is a truffle-colored eatery with sophisticated ambience just steps away from the Medici Chapels. It's run by cousins Francesco and Tommaso, who serve up tasty, traditional dishes such as *bistecca alla fiorentina* and *ribollita* (based on grandfather's recipe), and good chocolate soufflé. Enjoy the candlelit ambience and soft music as you sit either in the dining room or out on the terrace (€8-10 pastas, €9-15 *secondi*, daily 12:00-15:00 & 18:00-22:30, Piazza Madonna degli Aldobrandi 16/17, tel. 055-230-2062).

Osteria Vineria i'Brincello is a bright, happy, no-frills diner with tasty food, lots of spirit, friendly service, and no hint of snobbishness. It features a list of Tuscan daily specials hanging from the ceiling and great prices on good bottled wine (€7-8 pastas, €8-15 *secondi*, €5 takeout homemade pasta, daily 12:00-15:00 & 19:00-23:00, near corner of Via Nazionale and Via Chiara at Via Nazionale 110 red, tel. 055-282-645, Fredi cooks while Claudia serves).

Trattoria Nerone Pizzeria, serving up cheap, hearty Tuscan dishes and decent pizzas, is a tourist-friendly, practical standby in the hotel district. The lively, flamboyantly outfitted space (once the garden courtyard of a convent) feels like a good but kitschy Italian-American chain restaurant (€5-8 pizzas, €6-8 pastas, €8-12 *secondi*, daily 12:00-15:00 & 18:30-23:00, just north of Via Nazionale at Via Faenza 95 red, tel. 055-291-217, Tulio).

Döner Kebab—Cheap, Fast, and Not a Hint of Pasta

Because of the influx of Middle Eastern immigrants into Italy, "ethnic cuisine" has become more prevalent in recent years. Today, shops selling *döner kebab* (roasted meat, salad, and sauce wrapped in thin bread) are sprouting everywhere.

Döner kebab shops offer cheap, filling, healthy alternatives to your average slice of pizza or ham-and-cheese *panino*. The kebab itself consists of chicken or veal, which has been cut into thick slabs, piled high onto a skewer, and slow-roasted on a vertical spit. Once it's cooked, the rich, savory meat is sliced ultra-thin with a razor and stuffed into your choice of pita bread *(panino)* or a wrap *(piadina),* along with tomatoes, onions, lettuce, tangy yogurt sauce, and (optional) hot chili sauce. A vegetarian alternative is falafel (a fried garbanzo-bean patty) served with the same works. Dishes cost about €3-5, and shops are generally open from 11:00 in the morning until midnight.

Two particularly good and handy places are **Turkuaz** (two blocks from the Duomo at Via dei Servi 65) and **Barbecue: The Taste of Istanbul** (west of the Accademia at Via Cavour 41, a few doors north of the TI).

EATING IN FLORENCE

Eating Cheaply in or near the Mercato Centrale

Note that none of these eateries is open for dinner.

Mercato Centrale (Central Market) is great for an ad-lib lunch. It offers colorful piles of picnic produce, people-watching, and rustic sandwiches (Mon-Sat 7:00-14:00, Sat in winter until 17:00, closed Sun, a block north of San Lorenzo street market). Meat, fish, and cheese are sold on the ground level, with fruit and veggies mostly upstairs. The thriving ground-level eateries within the market (such as Nerbone, described next) serve some of the cheapest hot meals in town. The fancy deli, Perini, is famous for its quality products and generous free samples. Buy a picnic of fresh mozzarella cheese, olives, fruit, and crunchy bread to munch on the steps of the nearby Church of San Lorenzo, overlooking the bustling street market.

Nerbone in the Market is a venerable café and the best place for a sit-down meal within the Mercato Centrale. Join the shoppers and workers who crowd up to the bar to grab their €4-6 plates. Of the several cheap market diners, this feels the most authentic. As intestines are close to Florentines' hearts, tripe is very big here (lunch menu served Mon-Sat 12:00-14:00, sandwiches available 8:00-12:00, closed Sun, cash only, inside Mercato Centrale on the side closest to the Church of San Lorenzo, mobile 339-648-0251).

Trattoria Mario's, around the corner from Trattoria Zà-Zà (listed earlier), has been serving hearty lunches to market-goers since 1953 (Fabio and Romeo are the latest generation). Their simple formula: bustling service, old-fashioned good value, a lunch-only fixed-price meal, and shared tables. It's *cucina casalinga*—home cooking *con brio*. This place is high-energy and jam-packed. Their best dishes often sell out first, so go early. If there's a line, put your name on the list (€5-6 pastas, €8 *secondi*, cash only, Mon-Sat 12:00-15:30, closed Sun and Aug, no reservations, Via Rosina 2, tel. 055-218-550).

Casa del Vino, Florence's oldest operating wine shop, offers glasses of wine from among 25 open bottles (see the list tacked to the bar). Owner Gianni, whose family has owned the Casa for more than 70 years, is a class act. Gianni's *carta dei panini* lists delightful €3.50 sandwiches and €1 crostini; the *I Nostri Panini* (classic sandwiches) richly reward adventurous eaters. During busy times, it's a mob scene. You'll eat standing outside alongside workers on a quick lunch break (Mon-Fri 9:30-20:00 year-round, Sat 9:30-17:00 June-Sept only, closed Sun year-round and Sat off-season, hidden behind stalls of San Lorenzo Market at Via dell'Ariento 16 red, tel. 055-215-609).

Near the Accademia
Budget-Lunch Places Surrounding the Accademia

For pizza by the slice, try **Pugi,** at Piazza San Marco 10. For a break from pasta and pizza, grab a quick kebab lunch from **Barbecue: The Taste of Istanbul** (Via Cavour 41; see sidebar on page 305).

Pasticceria Robiglio, a smart little café, opens up its stately dining area and sets out a few tables on the sidewalk for lunch. They have a small menu of daily pasta and *secondi* specials, and seem determined to do things like they did in the elegant, pre-tourism days (generous €9-10 plates, a great €8 *niçoise*-like "fantasy salad," pretty pastries, smiling service, daily 12:00-15:00, longer hours as a café, a block toward the Duomo off Piazza S.S. Annunziata at Via dei Servi 112 red, tel. 055-212-784). Before you leave, be tempted by their pastries—famous among Florentines.

La Mescita Fiaschetteria is a characteristic hole-in-the-wall just around the corner from *David*—but a world away from all the tourism. It's where locals and students enjoy daily pasta specials and hearty sandwiches with good €1.50 house wine. You can trust Mirco and Alessio (as far as you can throw them)—just point to what looks good (such as their €5-6 pasta plate or €6-7 *secondi*), and you'll soon be eating well and inexpensively. The place can either be mobbed by students or in a peaceful time warp, depending on when you stop by (Mon-Sat 10:45-16:00, closed Sun, Via degli Alfani 70 red, mobile 347-795-1604 or 338-992-2640).

Picnic on the Ultimate Renaissance Square: **Il Centro Supermercati,** a handy supermarket a half-block north of the Accademia, has a curbside sandwich bar (Panineria) with an easy English menu that includes salads to go (Mon-Sat 9:00-19:30, Sun 10:00-19:00, sandwich bar may close earlier, Via Ricasoli 109). With your picnic in hand, hike around the block and join the bums on Piazza S.S. Annunziata, the first Renaissance square in Florence (don't confuse this with the less-interesting Piazza San Marco, closer to the supermarket). There's a fountain for washing fruit on the square. Grab a stony seat anywhere you like, and savor one of my favorite cheap Florence eating experiences. Or, drop by any of the places listed earlier for an easy lunch (pizza, kebab, or sandwich plus juice) to go.

Dining with Bobo away from the Center

Antica Trattoria da Tito, a 10-minute hike from the Accademia along Via San Gallo, is a long, drawn-out event of a meal. The boss, Bobo, is a fire hose of restaurateur energy who has clearly found his niche—making people happy with quality traditional food and lots of wine. His staff is as loyal as his clientele. While the food is great, there's no pretense. It's just a playground of Tuscan cuisine with "no romance allowed." As for the music he plays, Bobo says, "We are slaves of '80s." I'd come late and plan to party. To gorge on a feast of *antipasti* (meats, cheeses, fava beans, and bruschetta), consider ordering *fermami* (literally "stop me")— for €14, Bobo brings you food until you say, *"Fermami!"* A couple can get *fermami,* desserts, and a nice bottle of wine for €60 total. Ask for *vino* recommendations to experience that perfect pairing of food and wine. If you go with the flow here, you'll walk back to your hotel fat and filled with memories (€10 pastas, €12 *secondi,* €14 *gran tagliere*—big plate of cheese and meat, travelers with this book get a free after-dinner drink, Mon-Sat 12:30-15:00 & 19:00-23:00, closed Sun, reservations generally necessary, Via San Gallo 112 red, tel. 055-472-475).

Fast and Cheap near the Duomo

Self-Service Ristorante Leonardo is inexpensive, air-conditioned, quick, and handy. Eating here, you'll get the sense that they're passionate about the quality of their food. Stefano and Luciano (like Pavarotti) run the place with enthusiasm and put out free pitchers of tap water. It's just a block from the Duomo, southwest of the Baptistery (tasty €5 pastas, €6 main courses, Sun-Fri 11:45-14:45 & 18:45-21:45, closed Sat, upstairs at Via Pecori 11, tel. 055-284-446).

Döner Kebab: A good place to try this cheap Middle Eastern specialty is **Turkuaz,** a couple of blocks northeast of the Duomo (Via dei Servi 65; see sidebar on page 305).

Near Piazza della Signoria

Piazza della Signoria, the scenic square facing Palazzo Vecchio, is ringed by beautifully situated yet touristy eateries serving over-priced, bad-value, and probably microwaved food. If you're deter-mined to eat on the square, have pizza at Ristorante il Cavallino or bar food from the Irish pub next door. Piazza della Signoria's saving grace is **Rivoire** café, famous for its fancy desserts and thick hot chocolate. While obscenely expensive, it has the best view tables on the square (Tue-Sun 7:30-24:00, closed Mon, tel. 055-214-412).

Fine Dining

Frescobaldi Ristorante and Wine Bar, the showcase of Italy's aristocratic wine family, is a good choice for a formal dinner in Florence. Candlelight reflects off glasses of wine, and high-vaulted ceilings complement the sophisticated dishes. They offer the same menu in three different dining areas: cozy interior, woody wine bar, and breezy terrace. If coming for dinner, make a reservation, dress up, and hit an ATM (€11-14 appetizers and pastas, €18-24 *secondi*, lighter wine-bar menu at lunch, Tue-Sat 12:00-14:30 & 19:00-22:30, Mon 19:00-22:30, closed Sun and much of Aug, air-con, half a block north of Palazzo Vecchio at Via dei Magazzini 2-4 red, tel. 055-284-724, Francesco is the lead waiter).

Ristorante Paoli dishes up wonderful, traditional cuisine to loads of cheerful eaters being served by jolly little old men under a richly frescoed Gothic vault. It feels old-school and Old World... it's all about the setting. Because of its fame and central location, it's filled mostly with tourists, but for a sophisticated, traditional Tuscan splurge meal, this is a fine choice. Salads are dramati-cally cut and mixed from a trolley right at your table. The walls are sweaty with memories that go back to 1824, and the service is flamboyant and fun-loving (but don't get taken—confirm prices). Woodrow Wilson slurped spaghetti here—his bust looks down on you as you eat (€10-15 pastas, €12-20 *secondi*, daily 12:00-15:00 & 19:00-23:00, reserve for dinner, between Piazza della Signoria and the Duomo at Via dei Tavolini 12 red, tel. 055-216-215).

Eating Cheaply and Simply near Piazza della Signoria

Cantinetta dei Verrazzano, a long-established bakery/café/wine bar, serves delightful sandwich plates in an old-time setting. Their *selection Verrazzano* is a fine plate of four little crostini (like mini-bruschetta) proudly featuring different breads, cheeses, and meats from the Chianti region (€7.50). The *tagliere di focacce*, a sampler plate of mini-focaccia sandwiches, is also fun (€14 for big plate for two). Add a €5 glass of Chianti to either of these dishes to make a fine, light meal. Office workers pop in for a quick lunch, and it's traditional to share tables. Be warned: Prices can add up here in a hurry (Mon-Sat 8:00-21:00, Sun 10:00-17:00, no reservations taken, just off Via de' Calzaiuoli, across from Orsanmichele Church at Via dei Tavolini 18, tel. 055-268-590). They also have benches and tiny tables for eating at take-out prices. Simply step to the back and point to a hot *focacce* sandwich (€3), order a drink at the bar, and take away your food or sit with Florentines and watch the action while you munch.

Osteria Vini e Vecchi Sapori, half a block north of the Palazzo Vecchio, is a colorful 16-seat hole-in-the-wall restaurant serving Tuscan food with a fun, accessible menu of delicious €7-9 pastas and €9-10 *secondi* (Tue-Sat 12:30-15:00 & 19:30-22:00, Sun 12:30-15:00, closed Mon, reserve for dinner; facing the bronze equestrian statue in Piazza della Signoria, go behind its tail into the corner and to your left; Via dei Magazzini 3 red, tel. 055-293-045, run by Mario while wife Rosanna cooks and son Thomas serves).

I Fratellini is an informal eatery where the "little brothers" have served peasants 29 different kinds of sandwiches and cheap glasses of Chianti wine (see list on wall) since 1875. Join the local crowd to order, then sit on a nearby curb or windowsill to eat, placing your glass on the wall rack before you leave (€2.50 sandwiches, daily 9:00-20:00 or until the bread runs out, closed Sun in winter, 20 yards in front of Orsanmichele Church on Via dei Cimatori, tel. 055-239-6096). Be adventurous with the menu (easy-order by number). Consider *finocchiona* (#15, a special Tuscan salami), *lardo di Colonnata* (#22, lard aged in Carrara marble), and *cinghiale* (#19, spicy wild boar) sandwiches. Order the most expensive wine they're selling by the glass (Brunello for €5; bottles are labeled).

Cheap Takeout on Via Dante Alighieri: Three handy places line up on this street, just a couple of blocks from the Duomo. **L'Antico Trippaio,** an antique tripe stand, is a fixture in the town center. Cheap and authentic as can be, this is where locals come daily for €4-6 sandwiches *(panino),* featuring specialties like *trippa alla fiorentina* (tripe), *lampredotto* (cow's stomach), and a list of more appetizing options. Roberto and Maurizio offer a free plastic glass of rotgut Chianti with each sandwich for travelers with this book (daily 9:00-20:00, on Via Dante Alighieri, mobile 339-742-5692). If tripe isn't your cup of offal, **Pizzeria Totò,** just next to the tripe stand, has very good €2.50-3 slices (Via Dante Alighieri 28 red, tel. 055-290-406). And a few steps in the opposite direction is a **Metà supermarket**, with cheap drinks and snacks and a fine *antipasti* case inside (daily 8:30-21:30, Sun from 9:00, Via Dante Alighieri 20-24). If you pick up lunch at any of these, the best people-watching place to enjoy your sandwich is three blocks away, on Piazza della Signoria.

Gelato

Gelato is an edible art form. Italy's best ice cream is in Florence—and it's one souvenir that can't break and won't clutter your luggage. But beware of scams at touristy joints on busy streets that turn a simple request for a cone into a €10 "tourist special" rip-off. To avoid this, survey the size options and be very clear in your order (for example, "a €3 cone").

A key to gelato appreciation is sampling liberally and choosing flavors that go well together. Ask, as Italians do, for "Un assaggio, per favore?" (A taste, please?; oon ah-SAH-joh pehr fah-VOH-ray) and "Che si sposano bene?" (What marries well?; kay see spoh-ZAH-noh BEN-ay).

Artiginale, nostra produzione, and *produzione propia* mean gelato is made on the premises; also, gelato displayed in covered metal tins (rather than white plastic) is more likely to be homemade. Gelato aficionados avoid colors that don't appear in nature—for fewer chemicals and real flavor, go for mellow hues (bright colors attract children). If you see giant mounds of bright colors, skip it.

All of these places, which are a cut above, are open daily for long hours.

Near the Duomo: The recent favorite in town, **Grom** uses organic ingredients and seasonal fresh fruit, along with biodegradable spoons and tubs. This clever Italy-wide chain markets its traditional approach with a staff quick to tell customers, "This gelato reminds me of my childhood." A few purists grumble that a chain gelateria can't possibly compare with a local one-off,

Wine Bar near Ponte Vecchio

'Ino Bottega di Alimentari e Vini is a mod little shop filled with gifty edibles. Alessandro and his staff serve sandwiches and wine—you'll get your €5-8 sandwich on a napkin with an included glass of their wine of the day as you perch on a tiny stool. They can also make a fine €12 *piatto misto* of cheeses and meats with bread (daily 11:00-16:30, immediately behind Uffizi Gallery on Ponte Vecchio side, Via dei Georgofili 3 red, tel. 055-219-208).

Between Palazzo Vecchio and Santa Croce Church

Ristorante del Fagioli is an enthusiastically run eatery where you feel the heritage. The dad, Gigi, commands the kitchen while family members Antonio, Maurizio, and Simone keep the throngs of but so far Grom has maintained an impressively high quality—likely because the menu follows what's in season, changing every month (Via delle Oche 24 red).

Near Ponte Vecchio: **Gelateria Carrozze** is a longtime favorite (on riverfront 30 yards from Ponte Vecchio toward the Uffizi at Piazza del Pesce 3).

Near the Accademia: A Sicilian choice on a tourist thoroughfare, **Gelateria Carabè** is particularly famous for its luscious *granite*—Italian ices made with fresh fruit. A cremolata is a granita with a dollop of gelato—a delicious combination (from the Accademia, it's a block toward the Duomo at Via Ricasoli 60 red).

Near Orsanmichele Church: **Perchè No!** is located just off the busy main pedestrian drag, Via de' Calzaiuoli, and serves a wide array of flavors (Via dei Tavolini 19).

Near the Church of Santa Croce: The venerable favorite, **Vivoli's** still has great gelato—but it's more expensive, and stingy in its servings. Before ordering, try a free sample of their rice flavor—*riso* (closed Mon, Aug, and Jan; opposite the Church of Santa Croce, go down Via Torta a block and turn right on Via Stinche). Locals flock to **Gelateria de' Neri** (Via de' Neri 26 red), also owned by Vivoli's.

Near the Mercato Centrale: **The Bermuda Triangle** (a.k.a., I Gelati Del Bondi) is a hit both for its fresh ingredients and for the big-hearted energy of its owner, Vetulio (Via Nazionale 61 red, where it crosses Via Faenza, tel. 055-287-490).

Across the River: If you want an excuse to check out the little village-like neighborhood across the river from Santa Croce, enjoy a gelato at the tiny **Il Gelato di Filo** (named for Filippo and Lorenzo) at Via San Miniato 5 red, a few steps toward the river from Porta San Miniato. Gelato chef Edmir is proud of his fruity sorbet as well.

loyal customers returning. The cuisine: home-style bread-soups, hearty steaks, and Florentine classics. Don't worry—while *fagioli* means "beans," that's the family name, not the extent of the menu (€9 pastas, €9 *secondi*, cash only, Mon-Fri 12:30-14:30 & 19:30-24:00, closed Sat-Sun, reserve for dinner, between Santa Croce Church and the Alle Grazie bridge at Corso dei Tintori 47, tel. 055-244-285).

Boccadama Enoteca Ristorante is a stylish, shabby-chic wine bistro serving an easy-to-navigate menu of capably executed traditional Tuscan fare based on seasonal produce. Eat in the intimate dining room with candles reflecting off bottle-lined walls or at one of the few tables on the dramatic Piazza Santa Croce. As this place is popular with groups, reservations are smart (€8-9 *primi*, €12-16 *secondi*, daily 11:00-16:00 & 18:30-24:00, on south side of Piazza Santa Croce at 25-26 red, tel. 055-243-640, Marco).

Trattoria Anita, midway between the Uffizi and Santa Croce, feels old-school, with wood paneling and rows of wine bottles. Brothers Nicola, Gianni, and Maurizio offer a good lunch special: three hearty Tuscan courses for €9 on weekdays (€7-8 pastas, €7-12 *secondi,* Mon-Sat 12:00-14:30 & 19:00-22:15, closed Sun, on the corner of Via Vinegia and Via del Parlagio at #2 red, tel. 055-218-698).

Trattoria I'cche C'è C'è (EE-kay chay chay; dialect for "whatever there is, there is") is a small, family-style restaurant where fun-loving Gino and his wife Mara serve functional local food, including a €13 three-course, fixed-price meal. While filled with tourists, the place has a charming mom-and-pop warmth (€7-12 pastas, €12-18 *secondi,* Tue-Sun 12:30-14:30 & 19:30-22:30, closed Mon and two weeks in Aug, midway between Bargello and river at Via Magalotti 11 red, tel. 055-216-589).

South of the River, in the Oltrarno

In general, dining in the Oltrarno offers a more authentic experience; although it's quite close to the old center, tourists imagine that it's another world and tend to stay away. At many of these places, Florentines may even outnumber my readers. For locations, see the map on page 296.

Dining with a Ponte Vecchio View

Golden View Open Bar is a lively, trendy bistro, good for a romantic meal or just a salad, pizza, or pasta with fine wine and a fine view of Ponte Vecchio and the Arno River. Its white, minimalist interior is a stark contrast to atmospheric old Florence. Reservations for window tables are essential unless you drop in early for dinner (€10 pizzas, €11-15 pastas, big €11-14 salads, €20-30 *secondi,* daily 11:30-24:00, impressive wine bar, 50 yards east of Ponte Vecchio at Via dei Bardi 58, tel. 055-214-502, run by Antonio, Marco, and Tomaso). They have four seating areas (with the same menu and prices) for whatever mood you're in: a riverside pizza place, a classier restaurant, a jazzy lounge, and a wine bar (they also serve a buffet of appetizers free with your drink from 19:00 to 21:00). Mixing their fine wine, river views, and live jazz makes for a wonderful evening (jazz nightly at 21:00 except Tue and Thu off-season).

Dining Well in the Oltrarno

Of the many good and colorful restaurants in the Oltrarno, these are my favorites. You can survey most of them while following the route in the Oltrarno Walk chapter before making a choice.

Reservations are a good idea in the evening.

Il Santo Bevitore Ristorante, lit like a Rembrandt painting and filled with dressy tables, serves creative Tuscan cuisine. They're enthusiastic about matching quality produce from the area with the right wine. This is a good break from the big, sloppy plates of pasta you'll get at many Florence eateries (€9-12 pastas, €8-12 meat-and-cheese *taglieri*, €10-17 *secondi*, good wine list by the glass or bottle, daily 12:30-14:30 & 19:30-22:30, closed Sun for lunch, come early or make reservations, no outside seating, Via di Santo Spirito 64, tel. 055-211-264). Their smaller wine bar next door, **Enoteca Il Santino Gastronomia,** feels like the perfect after-work hangout for foodies who'd like a glass of wine and some light food. Tight, cozy, and atmospheric, one wall is occupied by the bar, where you can assemble an €8-12 *tagliere* of local cheeses and *salumi* (also available to take away). They also have a few €6-8 hot dishes. Both the food and the wine is locally sourced from small producers (daily 12:30-23:00, Via di Santo Spirito 60 red, tel. 055-230-2820).

Trattoria 4 Leoni creates the quintessential Oltrarno dinner scene. The Tuscan-style food is made with an innovative twist and an appreciation for vegetables. You'll enjoy the fun energy and characteristic seating, both outside on the colorful square, Canto ai Quattro Pagoni, and inside, where you'll dine in exposed-stone sophistication. While the wines by the glass are pricey, the house wine is very good (€10 pastas, €10-15 *secondi*, daily 12:00-24:00, dinner reservations smart; from Ponte Vecchio walk four blocks up Via de' Guicciardini, turn right on Via dello Sprone, then slightly left to Via de' Vellutini 1; tel. 055-218-562).

Antico Ristoro Di' Cambi is a meat-lover's dream—thick with Tuscan traditions, rustic touches, and T-bone steaks. The bustling scene has a memorable, beer-hall energy. As you walk in, you'll pass a glass case filled with red chunks of Chianina beef that's priced by weight (for the famous *bistecca alla fiorentina*, €40/kilo, standard serving is half a kilo per person). Before you OK your investment, they'll show you the cut and tell you the weight. While the steak comes nearly uncooked, it's air dried for 21 days so it's not really raw, just very tasty and tender—it'll make you happy you're at the top of the food chain. Sit inside the convivial woody interior or outside on a square (€8-10 pastas, €10-18 *secondi*, Mon-Sat 12:00-14:30 & 18:30-22:30, closed Sun, reserve on weekends and to sit outside, Via Sant'Onofrio 1 red, one block south of Ponte Amerigo Vespucci, tel. 055-217-134, run by Stefano and Fabio, the Cambi cousins).

Olio & Convivium Gastronomia is primarily a catering company for top-end events, and this is where they showcase their cooking. It started as an elegant deli whose refined olive-oil-tasting room morphed into a romantic, aristocratic restaurant. Their three intimate rooms are surrounded by fine *prosciutti,* cheeses, and wine shelves. It can seem intimidating and a little pretentious, but well-dressed foodies will appreciate this place for its quiet atmosphere. Their list of €14-25 *gastronomia* plates offers an array of taste treats and fine wines by the glass (€14-16 pastas, €20-22 *secondi,* stylish €18 lunches with wine, Tue-Sat 12:00-14:30 & 19:00-22:30, Mon 12:00-14:30 only, closed Sun, strong air-con, Via di Santo Spirito 4, tel. 055-265-8198, Monica).

Trattoria da Sergio is a tiny eatery about a block before Porta San Frediano, one of Florence's medieval gates. It has charm and a strong following, so reservations are a must. The food is on the gourmet side of home-cooking—mama's favorites with a modern twist—and therefore a bit more expensive (€9-10 pastas, €12-20 *secondi,* Tue-Sun 12:00-14:00 & 19:30-22:45, closed Mon, Borgo San Frediano 145 red, tel. 055-223-449, Sergio and Marco).

Trattoria Al Tranvai, with tight seating and small dark-wood tables, looks like an old-time tram filled with the neighborhood gang. A 10-minute walk from the river at the edge of the Oltrarno, it feels like a small town's favorite eatery (€9 pastas, €10-13 *secondi,* Mon 19:00-24:00, Tue-Sat 11:00-15:00 & 19:00-24:00, closed Sun, Piazza T. Tasso 14 red, tel. 055-225-197).

Eating Cheaply in the Oltrarno

Trattoria Sabatino, farthest away and least touristy of my Oltrarno listings, is a spacious, brightly lit mess hall. It's disturbingly cheap, with family character and a simple menu—a super place to watch locals munch. You'll find it just outside Porta San Frediano, a 15-minute walk from Ponte Vecchio (€4 pastas, €5 *secondi,* Mon-Fri 12:00-15:00 & 19:15-22:00, closed Sat-Sun, Via Pisana 2 red, tel. 055-225-955, little English spoken). Let eating here be your reward after following the stroll in my Oltrarno Walk chapter.

Trattoria Casalinga, an inexpensive standby, comes with aproned women bustling around the kitchen. Florentines and tourists alike pack the place and leave full and happy, with euros to spare for gelato (€7 pastas, €8-10 *secondi,* Mon-Sat 12:00-14:30 & 19:00-21:45, after 20:00 reserve or wait, closed Sun and Aug, just off Piazza di Santo Spirito, near the church at Via de' Michelozzi 9 red, tel. 055-218-624, Andrea and Paolo).

Borgo Antico is the hit of Piazza di Santo Spirito, with enticing pizzas, big deluxe plates of pasta, a delightful setting, and a trendy and boisterous young crowd (€8-10 pizza and pasta, €14-18 *secondi,* daily 12:00-23:00, best to reserve for a seat on the square, Piazza di Santo Spirito 6 red, tel. 055-210-437, Andrea and Michele—feel his forearm). **Volume,** the bar next door, is run by the same gang (see page 326 in the Nightlife in Florence chapter).

Ricchi Caffè, next to Borgo Antico, has fine gelato, home-made desserts, shaded outdoor tables, and €9 pasta dishes at lunch (daily 7:00-24:00, tel. 055-215-864). After noting the plain facade of the Brunelleschi church facing the square, step inside the café and pick your favorite picture of the many ways the church might be finished.

Supermarket: Facing the Pitti Palace, **Metà Supermarket** seems designed to rescue poor, hungry, and thirsty travelers (daily 9:00-20:30, Piazza de' Pitti 33 red). For other good options near Pitti Palace, see page 255.

FLORENCE WITH CHILDREN

Florence with kids: not ideal. But it's certainly good for them! Here are a few thoughts on family fun in the art capital of Europe.

- Book ahead to avoid lines whenever possible, especially at the Uffizi and Accademia; see page 59. (Or you can get a Firenze Card and bypass lines, but at €50 and with no price break for kids, it's an expensive alternative.) Long museum lines add insult to injury for the preteen dragged into another old building filled with more old paintings.
- Avoid the midday heat by planning on a cool break, such as an air-conditioned, kid-friendly place for lunch.
- Public WCs are hard to find: Try museums, bars, gelato shops, and fast-food restaurants.
- The smart tour guide/parent incorporates the child's interests into each day's plans. When a child is unhappy, no one has fun.
- Guidebooks can make history more accessible for kids. Try *Florence: Just Add Water* (excellent for travelers aged 10 to adult), easy to find in the US or in Florence. (See bookstores on page 50.) The pocket-size, spiral-bound *Kids Go Europe: Treasure Hunt Florence,* available in the US, encourages youngsters to journal and sketch.
- Context Florence offers a children's tour program run by scholarly guides who make the city's great art and culture accessible to kids (contact info on page 54). Local guide Alessandra Marchetti also does kid-tailored tours (see contact info on page 54).
- Give your kids a business card from your hotel, along with your contact information, just in case you get separated.
- Riding the little minibuses around the old town and up and down the river could be entertaining to some children.

Propose the challenge of covering as many routes on the #C2, #C3, and #D lines as you can in 90 minutes—the amount of time a ticket is valid.

- If you're taking the train to another city, ask if there's a family discount ("Offerta Familia") when buying tickets at a counter. Or, at a ticket machine, click "Yes" to the "Do you want ticket issue?" prompt, then click "Familia." With the discount, families of 3-5 people with at least one kid (age 12 or under) get 50 percent off the kids' tickets, and 20 percent off the adults' fare. Not all trains or routes are discounted.

Sights and Activities

After touring a bunch of hands-off museums, squirming kids will enjoy the hands-on activities at either one of the **Leonardo museums,** where all that human energy can be used to power modern re-creations of the brilliant scientist's machines (see page 70).

Climbing the dome of the cathedral is almost like climbing an urban mountain—you'll spiral up in a strange dome-within-a-dome space, see some musty old tools used in the construction, get a bird's-eye peek into the nave from way up, and then pop out to see the best city view in town (dome closed Sun). To beat the crowds, arrive by 8:30, drop by very late, or take the "Terraces of the Cathedral and Dome" tour (see page 71).

Every kid will want to see Michelangelo's *David* (closed Mon; ✪ see the Accademia Tour chapter). But the most interesting collection of statues—with many bizarre poses—is in the **Bargello** (closed some Sun and Mon; ✪ see the Bargello Tour chapter).

The **Palazzo Vecchio** has a "children's museum" (Museo dei Ragazzi) program which offers a variety of activities (for age four to teens), usually requiring reservations. As the offerings are always in flux, call, check online, or drop by to find out what your options are (included in Palazzo Vecchio entry: €6, children 3-17-€2, families-€14-16; Fri-Wed 9:00-17:00, Thu 9:00-14:00; tel. 055-276-8224, www.palazzovecchio-familymuseum.it, info.museoragazzi @comune.fi.it).

The **Galileo Science Museum** has Galileo's finger on display, plus cool old telescopes and early chemical and science lab stuff. Engaging video screens illustrate scientific principles. Be warned that some parents find the museum's displays on childbirth inappropriate for kids (✪ see the Galileo Science Museum Tour chapter).

The **Museum of Precious Stones** displays 500 different kinds of stones and demonstrates the fascinating techniques of inlay and mosaic work (closed Sun, around corner from *David;* see page 65).

The **Uffizi courtyard** is ringed by statues of all the famous

Florentines (Amerigo Vespucci, Machiavelli, Leonardo, and so on)—great for putting a face on a sweep through history (see page 110 of the Renaissance Walk chapter).

Florence's various **open-air markets** are fun for kids (❂ see the Shopping in Florence chapter). Remember to haggle.

The **Boboli Gardens** (and adjacent Bardini Gardens) are landscaped wonderlands. While designed to give adults a break from the city, they're kid-friendly, too (closed first and last Mon of the month; ❂ see the Pitti Palace Tour chapter). To get to Florence's sprawling public park, **Parco delle Cascine,** head west of the old center along the north side of the river (10-minute walk, lots of grass, playground, swimming pool open daily May-Aug, tel. 055-362-233).

The peaceful and breezy **Piazza d'Azeglio** park—complete with playground—can be a welcome refuge from touring madness (daily dawn to dusk, 15-minute walk east from Duomo or take bus #12 or #13 from train station or Piazza San Marco bus stop just north of Duomo).

Older kids may enjoy hiking up to **Piazzale Michelangelo** for the view, or taking a **bike tour.** Florencetown's I Bike Florence Tour, led by a quick-talking guide, is a 2.5-hour, 15-stop blitz of the town's top sights (€25, daily at 10:00 and 15:00, helmets optional, Via de Lamberti 1, tel. 055-012-3994, www.florencetown.com). For bike rentals, see page 50.

For kids running on their gelato buzz well into the evening hours, the vibrant **Piazza della Repubblica** has a sparkling carousel and lively street musicians.

Of all the possible side-trips from Florence, a jaunt to see the Leaning Tower in **Pisa** is probably the most interesting for kids (❂ see the Leaning Tower Tour chapter; note that kids under age eight aren't allowed to climb the tower).

Eating

Eat dinner early (at about 19:00), and you'll miss the romantic crowd. (Restaurants are less kid-friendly after 21:00.) Skip the famous places. Look instead for self-serve cafeterias, bars (children are welcome), or fast-food restaurants where kids can move around without bothering others. Picnic lunches and dinners work well. For ready-made picnics, drop by a *rosticceria* (deli) or a *pizza rustica* shop (cheap take-out pizza; *diavola* is the closest thing on the menu to kid-friendly pepperoni).

For fast and kid-approved meals in the old center, there are plenty of hamburger and pizza joints. For a good cafeteria, try Self-Service Ristorante Leonardo (a block from the Duomo). *Gelaterie* such as Perchè No! (Via dei Tavolini 19) are brash and neon, providing some of the best high-calorie memories in town. All of these are described in the Eating in Florence chapter.

SHOPPING IN FLORENCE

Florence is a great shopping town—known for its sense of style since the Medici days. Many people spend entire days shopping. Smaller stores are generally open 9:00-13:00 and 15:30-19:30, usually closed on Sunday, often closed on Monday, and sometimes closed for a couple of weeks around August 15. Many stores have promotional stalls in the market squares.

For shopping ideas, ads, and a list of markets, see *The Florentine* newspaper or *Florence Concierge Information* magazine (free from TI and many hotels). For a list of bookstores, see page 50. For information on VAT refunds and customs regulations, see page 16.

If you end up going overboard on Florentine finds, you can buy a cheap extra suitcase at the stalls outside the Church of Santa Maria Novella, opposite the train station. A big suitcase with wheels costs about €25, and should last long enough to haul your purchases home.

Markets

Busy street scenes and markets abound. Prices are soft in the markets—go ahead and bargain. Perhaps the biggest market is the one that fills the streets around the Church of San Lorenzo (see page 69), with countless stalls selling lower-end leather, clothing, T-shirts, handbags, and souvenirs (daily 9:00-19:00, closed Mon in winter, between the Duomo and train station). Beware of fake "genuine" leather and "Venetian" glass. The neighboring Mercato Centrale

(Central Market) is a giant covered food market (see "Edible Goodies," later).

Other popular shopping centers are: the Santa Croce area, known for leather (check out the leather school actually inside Santa Croce Church; enter to the right of the altar or use the outside entrance—see description on page 230); Ponte Vecchio's gold and silver shops; and the old, covered Mercato Nuovo (three blocks north of Ponte Vecchio, described on page 78).

Wander the city's "Left Bank," the Oltrarno, for antiques and artisan shops (on Via Toscanella and neighboring streets, south of the river; ✪ see the Oltrarno Walk chapter).

A **flea market** litters Piazza dei Ciompi with antiques and odds and ends daily, but is only really big on the last Sunday of each month (9:00-20:00, near Piazza Santa Croce).

Boutiques and High Fashion

The entire area between the river and the cathedral is busy with inviting boutiques that show off ritzy Italian fashions. The street Via de' Tornabuoni is best for boutique browsing.

The main **Ferragamo** store fills a classy 800-year-old building with a fine selection of shoes and bags (daily 10:00-19:30, Via de' Tornabuoni 2). They have an interesting, four-room **shoe museum** (€5, Wed-Mon 10:00-18:00, closed Tue, near the Santa Trinità bridge at Piazza Santa Trinità 5, tel. 055-336-0846).

The new **Gucci Museum,** right on Piazza della Signoria, tells the story of that famous designer with many original samples (€6, daily 10:00-20:00, tel. 055-7592-33027).

For more boutiques, meander the following streets: Via della Vigna Nuova (runs west from Via de' Tornabuoni), Via del Parione, and Via Strozzi (runs east from Via de' Tornabuoni to Piazza della Repubblica).

Department Stores

Typical chain department stores are **Coin,** the Italian equivalent of Macy's (Mon-Sat 10:00-19:30, Sun 10:30-19:30, on Via de' Calzaiuoli, near Orsanmichele Church); the similar, upscale **La Rinascente** (Mon-Sat 9:00-21:00, Sun 10:30-20:00, on Piazza della Repubblica); and **Oviesse,** a discount clothing chain, the local JCPenney (Mon-Sat 9:00-19:30, Sun 10:00-19:30, near train station at intersection of Via Panzani and Via del Giglio).

Souvenir Ideas

Shoppers in Florence can easily buy art reproductions (posters, calendars, books, prints, and so on—a breeze to find in and near the Uffizi and Accademia museums). With its history as a literary center, Florence offers traditional marbled stationery and leather-bound journals (try the Il Papiro chain stores), plus reproductions of old documents, maps, and manuscripts. Find silk ties, scarves, and Tuscan ceramics at the San Lorenzo street market, where haggling is expected. Goofy knickknacks featuring Renaissance masterpieces are fun gifts: Botticelli mouse pads, Raphael

lipstick-holders, and plaster *David*s. For soaps, skin creams, herbal remedies, and perfumes, sniff out the antique and palatial perfumery, **Farmacia di Santa Maria Novella** (Via della Scala 16; see page 85).

Edible Goodies

The **Mercato Centrale** is a prime spot for stocking up on culinary souvenirs (Mon-Sat 7:00-14:00, in winter open Sat until 17:00, closed Sun year-round, a block north of the Church of San Lorenzo). Classic purchases include olives, Parmigiano-Reggiano cheese, unusually shaped and colored pasta, and jars of pestos and sauces (such as pesto *genovese* or *tartufo*—truffle).

Upstairs, where produce and bulk products are sold, the price of dried porcini mushrooms is less than a quarter of what it is at the airport Duty Free. While many bring home a special bottle of Chianti Classico or Brunello di Montalcino, I take home only the names of my favorite wines—and buy them later at my hometown wine shop (rather than flying with hard-to-pack bottles).

NIGHTLIFE IN FLORENCE

With so many American and international college students in town, Florence by night can have a frat-party atmosphere. For me, nighttime is for eating a late meal, catching a concert, attending a lecture, strolling through the old-town pedestrian zone and piazzas with a gelato, or hitting one of the many pubs.

The latest on nightlife and concerts is listed in several publications available free at the TI (such as the biweekly *The Florentine*) or for a small price at newsstands (consider the monthly *Firenze Spettacolo,* which has an English section—www.firenzespettacolo .it). The TI prints a daily listing of musical events. Also check www.firenzeturismo.it.

Strolling After Dark

The historic center has a floodlit ambience that's ideal for strolling. The entire pedestrian zone around the Duomo and along Via de' Calzaiuoli, between the Uffizi and the Duomo, is lively with people. Piazza della Repubblica, lined with venerable 19th-century cafés, offers good people-watching. In the evening, it's a hub of activity, with opera singers, violinists, harpists, bizarre street performers, and a cover band that plays cheesy tunes for the seating area of one of the piazza's bars. Ponte Vecchio is a popular place to enjoy river views (and kiss). Some squares feel creepy after dark. Use good judgment. I'd skip the seedy area north of the Mercato Centrale.

Sightseeing

Certain sights in Florence stay open later, allowing you to extend your sightseeing into the evening. You can get a pre-dinner workout by climbing the Duomo's dome (Mon-Fri until 19:00) or Campanile (daily until 19:30). Or you can do some early-evening sightseeing at the Accademia (Tue-Sun until 18:50), Uffizi (Tue-Sun until 18:35), Duomo Museum (Mon-Sat until 19:30), and others. The Palazzo Vecchio is open until 24:00 from April through September (except on Thu). For a list of late-night sights, see page 49.

Sunsets

For the perfect end to the day, watch the sun descend over the Arno River from any of the bridges, especially Ponte Vecchio. Piazzale

Michelangelo, perched on a hilltop across the river (bus #12 or #13 from the train station), is also awesome for sunset-watching; it's packed with Romeos and Juliets on weekend evenings. The nearby San Miniato Church (200 yards uphill) is quieter and comes with the same commanding view. If you're going after dark, it's more efficient to zip up there by taxi (rather than take a one-hour round-trip hike). While side-tripping out to Fiesole for the sunset is popular (described on page 91), I'd stick with Piazzale Michelangelo.

Live Music

Frequent **live concerts** enhance Florence's beautiful setting. In the summertime, piazzas host a wide range of performers, including pop bands on temporary stages. The lovely sounds of classical music fill churches year-round for special performances. At the TI, pick up a printout of current musical events, and keep an eye open for posters as you wander around town.

Orsanmichele Church regularly holds concerts under its Gothic arches. Tickets are sold on the day of the concert from the door facing Via de' Calzaiuoli.

Orchestra della Toscana presents classical concerts from November to May in the Teatro Verdi (€11-16, box office open Mon-Sat 10:00-13:00 & 16:00-19:00, closed Sun, near Bargello at Via Ghibellina 99 red, tel. 055-212-320, www.orchestradella toscana.it or www.teatroverdionline.it).

St. Mark's English Church offers opera music several nights each week from March through October (with fewer dates in the winter). Check the website or call to see what's playing (full opera performance-€30, opera concerts-€20, Via Maggio 18, mobile 340-811-9192, www.concertoclassico.info).

Santo Stefano Church hosts concerts almost nightly at 21:15 (€12, on Piazza San Stefano, near north end of Ponte Vecchio, tel.

055-289-367, mobile 330-885-951, www.notearmoniche.com).

Dinner Theater at Teatro del Sale is a quirky place for dinner and theater. Every night (except Sun-Mon) at 19:30 they kick off a buffet with a fun array of tasty dishes for an hour and a half. Then they take away the tables, and there's an hour-long show. Sometimes the show is great for non-Italian speakers—and sometimes it's not (call or check their website). The old theater is not technically a restaurant, so you'll pay a €5 membership fee to "join" the association, plus €30 for the evening, including drinks (10 blocks behind the Duomo, northeast of Santa Croce at Via dei Macci 111, tel. 055-200-1492, www.teatrodelsale.com).

The recommended **Golden View Open Bar** complements its Arno River views with live jazz (nightly at 21:00, no jazz off-season Tue and Thu; near Ponte Vecchio—see listing on page 312).

The **Box Office** sells tickets for rock concerts and theater productions in Italian (Mon-Fri 9:30-19:00, Sat 9:00-14:00, Sun 9:30-14:00, east of Santa Croce Church at Via delle Vecchie Carceri 1, tel. 055-210-804, www.boxofficetoscana.it).

Ponte Vecchio often hosts a fine street musician late each evening in summer. He plugs in his amp, while young people get comfortable on the curb. There's generally a street concert nightly in the **Uffizi courtyard.**

Wine Bars

A wine bar *(enoteca)* is fun for sampling regional wines and enjoying munchies, especially pre-dinnertime. Throughout the old town, *enoteche* serve fine Italian wines by the glass with memorable atmospheres.

Le Volpi e l'Uva, specializing only in small wine producers, has a cozy interior and romantic seating on a quiet little piazza. They have 40 open bottles to choose from and a short menu of appropriate dishes. For maximum tasting, they are happy to arrange a set of half-glasses and make a little plate of mixed meats and cheeses (Mon-Sat 11:00-21:00, closed Sun, 65 yards south of Ponte Vecchio—walk through Piazza Santa Felicità to Piazza dei Rossi 1, tel. 055-239-8132, www.levolpieluva.com, run by wine experts Riccardo, Ciro, and Emilio).

Movies

Find first-run films in their original languages—including English—at Odeon Cinema, a half-block west of Piazza della Repubblica (Piazza Strozzi, tel. 055-214-068, www.odeon.in toscana.it; for schedule of original-language films, look under *"Original Sound"*).

Late-Night Local Scenes

American university students in Florence seem to do more drinking than studying during their semesters abroad. Despite the college party vibe, there is something for everyone in Florence after-hours.

Piazza Santa Croce: It's a hangout at night, often with concerts in front of the church. The epicenter of American student partying is around this square, where you'll find lots of bars and more foreigners than Italians. The neighboring Via de' Benci is busy with night spots. **Moyo**—a slick, gold-lit lounge popular with a hip local crowd—offers a happy-hour buffet. Order a €5-7 cocktail and you can munch what's basically a free dinner (no cover, open daily until late, buffet 19:00-22:30, dancing from 22:30, free Wi-Fi, just off Piazza Santa Croce at Via de' Benci 23 red, tel. 055-247-738, www.moyo.it). There are tables outside, if you want to hear yourself talk, and another inviting lounge next door.

Near the Duomo: La Congrega Lounge Bar, a tiny wine/champagne/coffee bar, is a handy little retreat day or night tucked into a tiny lane. It offers a chic mix of old and new (Mon-Thu 9:00-1:00 in the morning, Fri-Sun 9:00-2:30 in the morning, between the Duomo and Piazza della Repubblica at Via Tosinghi 3/4 red, mobile 338-482-3597, www.lacongregaloungebar.com, Maya).

Piazza Demidoff: To rub elbows with the locals, head across the river toward tiny Piazza Demidoff (cross the bridge east of Ponte Vecchio and turn left). These two places have outdoor seating, chichi interiors, and Florentines flaunting their latest shoe purchases: **Negroni** (Mon-Fri 8:00-3:00 in the morning, Sat-Sun 19:00-3:00 in the morning, Via dei Renai 17 red, tel. 055-243-647) and **Zoe** (Mon-Sat 8:30-2:00 in the morning, Sun 18:00-2:00 in the morning, Via dei Renai 13 red, tel. 055-243-111).

Piazza di Santo Spirito: This square—long known for its riff-raff and druggies—has become a more mainstream place to enjoy the evening. It's lined with lively bars and restaurants, including the recommended **Borgo Antico** (see page 314). The same people run **Volume,** the adjacent bar that's famous for its *aperitivo* (buy a €6-8 cocktail and make a meal out of their free munchies, daily 17:00-24:00, see map on page 296 for location, manager Neri). On the opposite side of the square, **Pop Café** offers a "free" buffet if you buy a €5-10 drink between 20:00 and 22:00. It feels trendy, but is plastic-plate simple, with students getting comfortable on the curbs and cobbles (Piazza di Santo Spirito 18, tel. 055-213-852).

FLORENCE CONNECTIONS

Florence is Tuscany's transportation hub, with fine train, bus, and plane connections to virtually anywhere in Italy. The city has several train stations, a bus station (next to the main train station), and an airport (plus Pisa's airport is nearby). Livorno, on the coast west of Florence, is a major cruise-ship port for passengers visiting Florence, Pisa, and other nearby destinations.

By Train

Florence's main train station is called **Santa Maria Novella** (*Firenze S.M.N.* on schedules and signs). Florence also has two suburban train stations: **Firenze Rifredi** and **Firenze Campo di Marte.** Note that some trains don't stop at the main station—before boarding, confirm that you're heading for S.M.N., or you may overshoot the city. (If this happens, don't panic; the other stations are a short taxi ride from the center.)

Santa Maria Novella Station

Built in Mussolini's "Rationalism" style back between the wars, in some ways the station seems to have changed little—notice the 1930s-era lettering and architecture.

To orient yourself to the station and nearby services, stand with your back to the tracks. Look left to see a 24-hour pharmacy (*Farmacia,* near McDonald's) and baggage storage halfway down track 16 (€5/5 hours, then €0.70/hour for 6-12 hours and €0.30/hour for over 12 hours, daily 6:00-23:50, passport required, maximum 40 pounds, no explosives—sorry). Directly ahead of you is the main hall (*salone biglietti,* with ticket windows). Avoid the station's fake "Tourist Information" office, funded by hotels, if it's still around. To reach the real TI, walk away from the tracks and exit the station; it's straight across the square, 100 yards away, by the stone church. (If there's construction, circle around the torn-up square to the left to reach it.)

Buying Tickets: If you need tickets to travel within Italy, there's no reason to stand in line at a window. Take advantage of the user-friendly, automated "Fast Ticket" machines that display schedules, issue tickets, and even make reservations for railpass-holders. Some take only credit cards; others take cards and cash. Using them is easy—it actually can be fun; just tap "English." Be aware there are two train companies: TrenItalia, with most connections, has green-and-white machines (toll tel. 892-021, www .trenitalia.it); the red machines are for the new Italo service, run by a private operator (tel. 06-0708, www.italotreno.it).

To get international tickets, you'll need to either go to a ticket window (in the main hall) or a travel agency. For more on train travel in Italy—including your ticket-buying options—see page 560.

Cheap Eats: The large cafeteria near McDonald's has various food stands. Better yet, the handy Margherita/Conad supermarket—with sandwiches and salads to go—is just around the corner (with your back to the tracks, leave the station to the right, go down the steps, and it's immediately on your right on Via Luigi Alamanni; Mon-Sat 8:00-20:00, closed Sun).

Getting to the Duomo and City Center

The Duomo and town center are to your left (with your back to the tracks). Out the doorway to the left, you'll find city buses and the taxi stand. **Taxis** cost about €8 to the Duomo, and the line moves fast, except on holidays. **Buses** generally don't cover the center well and probably aren't the best way to reach your hotel (walking could be faster), but if you need to take one, buy a ticket at the small ATAF ticket office outside the main entrance. Minibus #C2 (which runs through the middle of town) departs from across the square, at the corner beyond the TI and Santa Maria Novella underpass; however, by the time you walk to the stop, you're already halfway to downtown.

To **walk** into town (10-15 minutes), exit the station to the left and find the stairs/escalators down to the underground passageway/mall called Galleria S.M. Novella. Head toward the Church of Santa Maria Novella. (Warning: Pickpockets—often dressed as tourists—frequent this tunnel, especially the surface point near the church.) You come out on the other side of the square; head down Via dei Panzani, which leads directly to the Duomo.

Train Connections

From Florence by Train to: Pisa (2-3/hour, 45-75 minutes, €7.10),

Lucca (2/hour, 1.5 hours, €6.40), **Siena** (direct trains hourly, 1.5-2 hours, €7.70; bus is better because Siena's train station is far from the center), **Camucia-Cortona** (hourly, 1.5 hours, €8.90), **Livorno**—cruise ship port described later (hourly, 1.5 hours, some change in Pisa, €8.20), **La Spezia** (for the Cinque Terre, 5/day direct, 2.5 hours, otherwise nearly hourly with change in Pisa, €11.30), **Milan** (hourly, 1.75 hours, €53), **Milan's Malpensa Airport** (2/day direct, 2.75 hours, €58), **Venice** (hourly, 2-3 hours, may transfer in Bologna; often crowded—reserve ahead, €43), **Assisi** (8/day direct, 2-3 hours, €12), **Orvieto** (hourly, 2 hours, some with change in Campo di Marte or Rifredi station, €19), **Rome** (at least hourly, 1.5 hours, most connections require seat reservations, €45), **Naples** (hourly, 3 hours, €72), **Brindisi** (8/day, 8 hours with change in Bologna or Rome, €75), **Interlaken** (5/day, 5.5-6 hours, 2-3 changes), **Frankfurt** (1/day, 12 hours, 1-3 changes), **Paris** (3/day, 10-15 hours, 1-2 changes, important to reserve over-night train ahead), **Vienna** (1 direct overnight train, or 5/day with 1-3 changes, 10-16 hours). Note that these are all TrenItalia connections; the new Italo company may offer additional options (check www.italotreno.it).

By Bus

SITA Bus Station

The SITA bus station (100 yards west of the Florence train station on Via Santa Caterina da Siena) is traveler-friendly—a big, old-school lot with numbered stalls and all the services you'd expect. Schedules for regional trips are posted everywhere, and TV monitors show imminent departures. Bus service drops dramatically on Sunday.

Getting to the Train Station and City Center: Exit the station through the main door, and turn left along the busy street toward the brick dome. The train station is on your left, while downtown Florence is straight ahead and a bit to the right.

From Florence by Bus to: San Gimignano (hourly, less on Sun, 1.5-2 hours, change in Poggibonsi, €6.80), **Siena** (about 2/hour, 1.25-hour *rapida/via superstrada* buses are faster than the train, avoid the 2-hour *ordinaria* buses, €7.20), **Volterra** (4/day Mon-Sat, 1/day Sun, 2 hours, change in Colle Val d'Elsa where you catch a convenient CPT bus, €8.35), **Montepulciano** (2/day with a change in Bettole, 2 hours, €8.70), Florence's **Amerigo Vespucci Airport** (2/hour, 30 minutes, €5, pay driver and immediately validate ticket, always from platform 1). Generally buy bus tickets in the station, as you'll pay 30 percent more if you buy tickets on the bus. Bus info: www.sitabus.it or tel. 800-373-760 (Mon-Fri 8:30-12:30 & 15:00-18:00, closed Sat-Sun).

By Taxi

For small groups with more money than time, zipping to nearby towns by taxi can be a good value (e.g., €120 from your Florence hotel to your Siena hotel).

A more comfortable alternative is to hire a private car service. Florence-based **Transfer Chauffeur Service** has a fleet of modern vehicles with drivers who can whisk you between cities, to and from the cruise ship port at Livorno, and through the Tuscan countryside for around the same price as a cab (tel. 055-614-2182, mobile 338-862-3129, www.transfercs.com, marco.masala@transfer cs.com, Marco).

By Car

The autostrada has several exits for Florence. Get off at the *Nord, Sud,* or *Certosa* exits and follow signs toward—but not into—the *Centro.*

Don't even attempt driving into the city center. Florence has a traffic-reduction system that's complicated and confusing even to locals. Every car passing into the *Zona Traffico Limitato (ZTL)* is photographed; those who haven't jumped through bureaucratic hoops to get a permit can expect to receive a €100 ticket in the mail. If you get lost and cross the line several times...you get several fines. The no-go zone (defined basically by the old medieval wall, now a boulevard circling the historic center of town—watch for *Zona Traffico Limitato* signs) is roughly the area between the river, main train station, Piazza della Libertà, Piazza Donatello, and Piazza Beccaria.

Parking: The city center is ringed with big, efficient parking lots (signposted with the standard big *P*), each with taxi and bus service into the center. Check www.firenzeparcheggi.it for details on parking lots, availability, and prices. From the freeway, follow the signs to *Centro,* then *Stadio,* then *P.* I usually head for "Parcheggio del Parterre," just beyond Piazza della Libertà (€2/hour, €20/day, €65/week, open 24 hours daily, tel. 055-500-1994, 600 spots, automated, pay with cash or credit card, never fills up completely). To get into town, find the taxi stand at the elevator exit, or ride one of the minibuses that connect all of the major parking lots with the city center (see www.ataf.net for routes).

You can park for free along any suburban curb near a bus stop that feels safe and take the bus into the city center from there. Check for signs that indicate parking restrictions—for example, a circle with a slash through it and "*dispari giovedi,* 0,00-06,00" means "don't park on Thursdays between midnight and six in the morning."

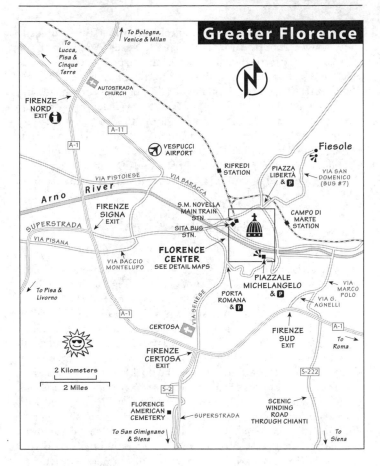

Free parking is easy up at Piazzale Michelangelo (see page 88), but don't park where the buses drop off passengers; park on the side of the piazza farthest from the view. To get from Piazzale Michelangelo to the center of town, take bus #12 or #13.

Car Rental: If you're picking up a rental car upon departure, don't struggle with driving into the center. Taxi with your luggage to the car-rental office, and head out from there. For more information on car rental and driving in Italy, see page 570. For tips on driving in Tuscany, see page 452.

By Plane

Amerigo Vespucci Airport

Also called Peretola Airport, Florence's airport is about five miles northwest of the city (open 5:10-24:00, no overnighting allowed, TI, cash machines, car-rental agencies, airport code: FLR, airport info tel. 055-306-1630, flight info tel. 055-306-1700—domestic only, www.aeroporto.firenze.it). Shuttle buses (far right of airport as you exit arrivals hall) connect the airport with Florence's SITA bus station, 100 yards west of the train station on Via Santa Caterina da Siena (2/hour, 30 minutes, €5, buy ticket on board and validate immediately, daily 6:00-23:30, first bus leaves for airport from Florence at 5:30). If you're changing to a different intercity bus in Florence (for instance, one bound for Siena), stay on the bus through the first stop (at the train station); it will continue on to the bus station nearby. Allow about €25 and 30 minutes for a taxi.

For information on Pisa's **Galileo Galilei Airport,** see page 430.

By Cruise Ship

Livorno

If you're arriving in Tuscany by cruise ship, you'll disembark in the coastal town of Livorno (sometimes called "Leghorn" in English), located about 60 miles west of Florence. Around 900,000 travelers pass through Livorno's cruise ship ports each year.

Of the excursion options, **Florence** is the most time-consuming to reach (roughly two hours each way by public transit). You have three good options for getting into Florence: take the train; share a minibus taxi (arrange this at the dock); or take a cruise-line excursion (either fully guided or transportation-only). **Pisa** is closer (about an hour each way), and—since Pisa is well-connected with **Lucca**—it's possible to combine those two cities into one long day. (If doing this, save Pisa until after lunch to avoid the cruise crowds that flock there in the morning, and be aware that most shops and restaurants in Lucca are closed Sun-Mon.) No matter where you go, if you're taking the train, keep in mind that it takes 30 minutes just to get from Livorno's cruise port to the train station across town. Plan your day conservatively, as trains can be delayed.

Arrival at the Port: Livorno's port (at the western edge of town) is vast and sprawling, but most cruise ships dock in one of two places: Molo 75, at the Porto Mediceo; or the adjacent Molo Capitaneria. At either pier, you'll find cruise-line excursion buses, a tiny TI desk, drivers hustling to fill their minibus taxis for trips into Florence, and a shuttle bus leaving every few minutes for Piazza del Municipio in the center of Livorno.

Tourist Information: Livorno's TI kiosk is on Piazza del Municipio, a 10-20 minute walk or quick shuttle ride from the port. The kiosk is right next to the stop for the shuttle bus (kiosk open May-Oct daily 8:00-18:00; Nov-April Mon-Sat 9:00-17:00, closed Sun; tel. 0586-204-611). Public **WCs** are in City Hall, across the street from the TI on Piazza del Municipio.

Connecting Livorno and Florence, Pisa, or Lucca

With a little patience, budget-minded travelers can use public transportation to go from Livorno to Florence, Pisa, or Lucca, and back again before the ship departs. Taxis to these places are very expensive, though if splitting the cost with a group, this can be a decent way to go.

By Public Transportation

To visit Florence, Pisa, or Lucca by public transit, follow this basic plan: Walk or ride the cruise line's shuttle bus from the port to downtown Livorno; then ride a public bus to Livorno's train station; then take the train to wherever you're going.

Getting Between the Port and Downtown Livorno: Most cruise lines offer a **shuttle bus** to the center of Livorno, dropping you off at a bus stop near the TI kiosk in Piazza del Municipio (sometimes free, otherwise about €5-8 round-trip).

If the line for the shuttle bus is too long—or if you're in the mood for a stroll—you can **walk** from most areas of the port to downtown Livorno in about 10-20 minutes. If you arrive at Molo 75/Porto Mediceo, walk around the little sailboat harbor, then bear right over the wide bridge and up Via Grande. From Molo Capitaneria, walk through the port area, cross the wide bridge, and continue straight up Via Grande. Via Grande—an elegant-feeling, arcaded street lined with shops and fashion boutiques—takes you straight to Piazza Grande in the heart of town.

Getting to Livorno Centrale Train Station: Livorno's city center clusters around two nearby squares: Piazza Grande (stop for bus #1 to train station) and Piazza del Municipio (TI, public WCs, stop for shuttle bus to the port). The squares are connected by a long, covered pedestrian mall (with the main TI inside).

Shuttle buses from the port drop off cruise passengers at Piazza del Municipio. You'll find plenty of transportation and tour deals being hawked here by a gaggle of small-time guides and tour operators eager to win your business. There's also a very helpful TI kiosk catering to your needs (and trying to entice you to simply stay put and have fun in Livorno).

Livorno's public **bus** #1 departs from the middle of Piazza Grande (in front of the church; from the shuttle-bus stop on Piazza del Municipio, just turn right out of the bus and walk two short blocks on Via Cogorano to Piazza Grande). From here, the bus heads to Livorno Centrale train station, the end of the line (€1, 8/hour Mon-Sat, 4-6/hour Sun, 10 minutes). Before boarding, buy your bus ticket at a tobacco shop or newsstand; at the same place, you can also buy train tickets to Pisa, Lucca, or Florence (doing this now will help you save time and avoid lines at the train station).

The 35-minute **walk** from Piazza Grande to the train station is long and boring; don't do it—the bus is simple.

Getting to Florence, Pisa, and Lucca: From Livorno Centrale Station, trains zip to Florence, Pisa, Lucca, and other points in Italy. Note that all train lines go first to Pisa, then split: north to Lucca or east to Florence.

To Florence: Hourly, usually departs at :10 after the hour, arrive in Florence at :32 past the following hour—1 hour and 22 minutes total, €8.20 on a regional train. (There are also a few departures that are a few minutes shorter, but require you to change trains at Pisa Centrale.)

To Pisa: 2-3/hour, 20 minutes, €1.90 on a regional train.

To Lucca: About hourly, 1-1.25 hours, transfer at Pisa Centrale, €3.70 on a regional train.

To Lucca and Pisa: If you want to visit Lucca and Pisa in one day, take the train to Lucca first. A handy bus connects Lucca's Piazzale Giuseppe Verdi to Pisa's Field of Miracles (hourly Mon-Sat, fewer on Sun, 30 minutes, €3).

Pisa Bus Alternative: If you want to go straight from downtown Livorno to Pisa, consider taking bus #101 (1/hour, no buses Sat-Sun, 55 minutes, €2.30, schedule posted at stop). In Livorno, catch bus #101 at the Largo Duomo stop behind the cathedral (which faces Piazza Grande). The bus first goes to Pisa's airport and then leaves you about a block from Pisa's train station, across town from the Field of Miracles and Leaning Tower (see "Arrival in Pisa," page 399). Notice that the bus runs less frequently than the train, and not at all on weekends. It also takes more than twice as long as the train (which takes only 20 minutes)—but it saves you the trip from downtown Livorno to the train station.

By Taxi and Shared Minibus

Taxis wait at the dock to hustle up business as travelers disembark. Private taxis are costly, but you'll also find enterprising drivers with eight-seat minibuses gathering groups to split their €400 fee. At €50/person, this is actually a great deal—you'll be driven one hour into Florence, dropped off near the center for four or five hours of free time, and then taken back to the port. Some groups cram in a stop at Pisa on the way back, which, while rushing a tour of Florence, is doable. If you have friends on board, this is a wonderful option worth considering and talking up before you arrive in Livorno.

Here are some ballpark round-trip fares for a four-seat car: **Pisa**—€120, **Pisa and Lucca**—€220, **Florence**—€320. In general, drivers at the port prefer to take passengers who will pay them for the whole day, so it can be difficult to get someone to take you just one-way (especially the long haul into Florence). You might have better luck for shorter trips if you take the shuttle bus into downtown Livorno and then catch a taxi there (maximum prices one-way: Livorno-Pisa-€60, Livorno-Lucca-€80, Livorno-Florence-€250, Pisa-Lucca-€50).

Taxis both at the port and in the city offer the same rates. Clarify the fare beforehand, even though by law the driver must have the meter on (the quoted price will usually be less than the meter). And don't pay for a round-trip excursion until your cabbie has returned you back to your ship...safe, sound, and on time.

TUSCANY
Toscana

Tuscany

To Milan
To Venice
To Venice

Bologna

Ravenna

Adriatic Sea

EMILIA-ROMAGNA

Imola

To Milan

Apuan Alps

LIG.

La Spezia

Carrara

Faenza

Cesena

SAN MARINO

CINQUE TERRE

Montecatini Terme

Pistoia

VESPUCCI

Fiesole

LE MARCHE

To Urbino

Lucca

A-11

Viareggio

Vinci

Arno R.

Florence

Arno R.

Ligurian Sea

Pisa

GALILEO

Empoli

U.S. CEM.

S-222

Sansepolcro

Livorno

Poggibonsi

CHIANTI

Arezzo

UMBRIA

San Gimignano

Volterra

Colle Val d'Elsa

Castellina

Cortona

Lisciano

S-68

Saline

Siena

Monteriggione

S-326

Camucia

Ter.

Perugia

20 Kilometers

20 Miles

Ancaiano

TUSCANY

SAN GALGANO

Ascano

S-438

S-146

Pienza

Lake Trasimeno

Chiusi

Assisi

Montalcino

Monte-pulciano

SANT' ANTIMO

S-2

A-1

Todi

Piombino

Portoferraio

Elba

Grosseto

Orvieto

MAREMMA

Lake Bolsena

Bagnoregio

Civita

Autostrada
Other Roads
Rail
Border of Tuscany
Border of Province

Monte Argentario

Viterbo

To Rome

LAZIO

SIENA

Siena was medieval Florence's archrival. And while Florence ultimately won the battle for political and economic superiority, Siena still competes for the tourists. Sure, Florence has the heavyweight sights. But Siena seems to be every Italy connoisseur's favorite town. In my office, whenever Siena is mentioned, someone moans, "Siena? I looove Siena!"

Once upon a time (about 1260-1348), Siena was a major banking and trade center, and a military power in a class with Florence, Venice, and Genoa. With a population of 60,000, it was even bigger than Paris. Situated on the north-south road to Rome (Via Francigena), Siena traded with all of Europe. Then, in 1348, the Black Death (bubonic plague) swept through Europe, hitting Siena and cutting the population by more than a third. Siena never recovered. In the 1550s, Florence, with the help of Philip II's Spanish army, conquered the flailing city-state, forever rendering Siena a non-threatening backwater. Siena's loss became our sight-seeing gain, as its political and economic irrelevance pickled the city in a purely medieval brine. Today, Siena's population is still 60,000, compared with Florence's 370,000.

Siena, situated atop three hills, qualifies as Italy's ultimate "hill town" (though it's much larger than its cousins covered in the Tuscan Hill Towns chapter). Its thriving historic center, with red-brick lanes cascading every which way, offers Italy's best medieval city experience. Most people do Siena, just 35 miles south of Florence, as a day trip, but it's best experienced at twilight. While Florence has the blockbuster museums, Siena has an easy-to-enjoy soul: Courtyards sport flower-decked wells, alleys dead-end at rooftop views, and the sky is a rich blue dome.

For those who dream of a Fiat-free Italy, Siena is a haven. Pedestrians rule in the old center of town. Sit at a café on the main square. Wander narrow streets lined with colorful flags and studded with iron rings to tether horses. Take time to savor the first European city to eliminate automobile traffic from its main square (1966) and then, just to be silly, wonder what would happen if they did it in your hometown.

Planning Your Time

On a quick trip, consider spending two nights in Siena (or three nights with a whole-day side-trip into Florence). Whatever you do, be sure to enjoy a sleepy medieval evening in Siena. The next morning, you can see the city's major sights in half a day. Or consider using Siena as your jet-lag pillow. With its lazy small-town ambience, impressive but user-friendly sights, and easy connection by bus to Florence's airport (simply change at downtown Florence's bus station), this is a fine way to settle into Italian life.

Orientation to Siena

Siena lounges atop a hill, stretching its three legs out from Il Campo. This main square, the historic meeting point of Siena's neighborhoods, is pedestrian-only—and most of those pedestrians are students from the university.

Just about everything mentioned in this chapter is within a 15-minute walk of the square. Navigate by three major landmarks (Il Campo, Duomo, and Church of San Domenico), following the excellent system of street-corner signs. The typical visitor sticks to the Il Campo-San Domenico axis. Make a point to stray from this main artery. Sienese streets go in anything but a straight line, so it's easy to get lost—but equally easy to get found. Don't be afraid to explore.

Siena itself is one big sight. Its individual sights come in two little clusters: the square (Civic Museum and City Tower) and the cathedral (Baptistery and Duomo Museum, with its surprise viewpoint). Check these sights off, and then you're free to wander.

Tourist Information

The TI on Il Campo can be an exasperating place. Think about the importance of tourism in this town—and yet this office charges €0.50 for a map and lets tour commissions color its advice (Mon-Sat 10:00-18:30, Sun 10:00-17:00, on Il Campo at #56, tel. 0577-280-551, www.terresiena.it). They hand out a few pretty booklets (including *Siena* and the regional *Terre di Siena* guide), sell maps and books, and may be able to answer a few questions. The TI

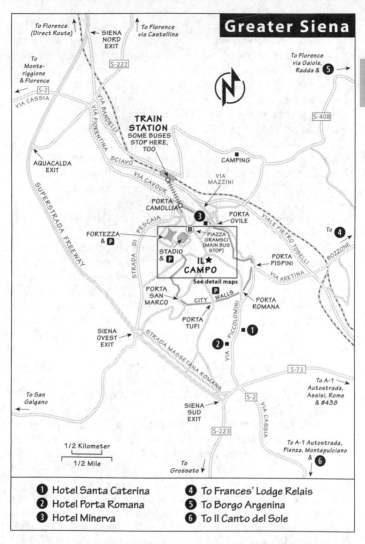

Greater Siena

To Florence (Direct Route)
To Florence via Castellina
SIENA NORD EXIT
To Monte-riggione & Florence
VIA CASSIA
S-2
S-222
VIA BANDELLI
VIA FIORENTINA
To Florence via Gaiole, Radda & **5**
S-408
TRAIN STATION SOME BUSES STOP HERE, TOO
SCIAVO
VIA CAVOUR
CAMPING
VIA MAZZINI
AQUACALDA EXIT
SUPERSTRADA FREEWAY
STRADA DI PESCAIA
PORTA CAMOLLIA
FORTEZZA & P
3
B
PIAZZA GRAMSCI (MAIN BUS STOP)
PORTA OVILE
VIALE PIETRO TOSELLI
To **4**
BOZZONE
STADIO & P
IL CAMPO ★
See detail maps
PORTA PISPINI
VIA ARETINA
PORTA SAN MARCO
P
CITY WALLS
PORTA TUFI
PORTA ROMANA
VIA PICCOLOMINI
1
SIENA OVEST EXIT
STRADA MASSETANA ROMANA
2
S-73
To San Galgano
SIENA SUD EXIT
S-2
VIA CASSIA
To A-1 Autostrada, Assisi, Rome & #438
S-223
To A-1 Autostrada, Pienza, Montepulciano & **6**
1/2 Kilometer
1/2 Mile
To Grosseto

1 Hotel Santa Caterina
2 Hotel Porta Romana
3 Hotel Minerva
4 To Frances' Lodge Relais
5 To Borgo Argenina
6 To Il Canto del Sole

SIENA

organizes walking tours of the old town (€20, daily April-Oct at 11:00, 2 hours, no interiors, guide usually explains in both English and Italian). Ignore the second "TI" across from the Church of San Domenico, which is a useless private agency run by the local hotel association.

Arrival in Siena

By Train

The small train station, located at the base of the hill on the edge of town, has a bar, a bus office (Mon-Fri 7:15-19:30, Sat 7:15-17:45,

Sun 8:30-12:30 & 14:30-18:30), and a newsstand (which sells local bus tickets—buy one now if you're taking the city bus into town), but no baggage check or lockers (stow bags at Piazza Gramsci— see "By Intercity Bus," later). A shopping mall with a supermarket (handy for picnic supplies) is across the plaza right in front of the station.

Getting from the Train Station to the City Center: To reach central Siena, you can hop aboard the city bus, ride a long series of escalators (which involves a bit of walking), or take a taxi. To reach either the bus or the escalators, head for the shopping mall across the plaza. From the tracks, go down the stairs into the tunnel that connects the platforms; this leads (with escalators) right up into the mall. Alternatively, you can exit the station out the front door, cross over to the plaza, turn left and walk to the far end of the plaza, then turn right to enter the mall's glass doors.

To ride the **city bus,** go through the shopping mall's right-hand door and use the elevator to go down to the subterranean bus stop. If you didn't buy bus tickets in the train station, you can get them from the blue machine (press "F" to toggle to English, then select "A" for type of ticket). Buses leave frequently (6/hour, fewer on Sun and after 22:00, €1.10, about a 10-minute ride into town depending on route). Smaller shuttle buses go up to Piazza del Sale, while bigger city buses head to nearby Piazza Gramsci (both are at the north end of town, walkable to most of my recommended hotels). Before boarding, double-check the destination with the driver by asking *"Centro?"* Punch your ticket in the machine onboard to validate it.

Riding the **escalator** into town takes a few minutes longer and requires more walking than the bus. From the station, follow the instructions above and enter the mall at the far-left end. Once inside, go straight ahead and ride the escalators up two floors to the food court. Continue directly through the glass doors to another escalator (marked *Porta Camollia/Centro*) that takes you gradually, up, up, up into town (free). Exiting the escalator, turn left down the big street, bear left at the fork, then continue straight through the town gate. From here, landmarks are well-signed (go up Via Camollia).

The **taxi stand** is to your right as you exit the train station, but as the city is chronically short on cabs, getting one here can take a while (about €9 to Il Campo, taxi tel. 0577-49222).

Getting to the Train Station from the City Center: If you're leaving Siena by train, you can ride a smaller shuttle bus from Piazza del Sale (which goes straight to the station), or catch an orange or red-and-silver city bus from Piazza Gramsci (which may take a more roundabout route). Multiple bus routes make this trip—look for *Ferrovia* or *Stazione* on schedules and marked on the bus. City buses drop off right in front of the station. Confirm with the driver that the bus is going to the *stazione* (stat-zee-OH-nay); remember to purchase your ticket in advance from a tobacco shop or the blue machine, then validate it on board.

By Intercity Bus

Most buses arrive in Siena at Piazza Gramsci, a few blocks north of the city center. (Some buses only go to the train station; others go first to the train station, then continue to Piazza Gramsci—to find out, ask your driver, "pee-aht-sah GRAM-chee?") The main bus companies are Sena and Tiemme/Siena Mobilità (formerly called Tra-In). Day-trippers can store baggage in the passageway underneath Piazza Gramsci called Sottopassaggio la Lizza (€5.50/day, open daily 7:00-19:00, carry-on-sized luggage no more than 33 pounds, no overnight storage). From Piazza Gramsci, it's an easy walk into the town center—just head in the opposite direction of the tree-filled park. For more on buses, see page 394.

By Car

Siena is not a good place to drive. Plan on parking in a big lot or garage and walking into town.

Drivers coming from the autostrada take the *Siena Ovest* exit and follow signs for *Centro,* then *Stadio* (stadium). The soccer-ball signs take you to the stadium lot (Parcheggio Stadio, €1.70/hour, pay when you leave) near Piazza Gramsci and the huge, bare-brick Church of San Domenico. The nearby Fortezza lot charges the same amount. Another good option is the underground Santa Caterina garage (you'll see signs on the way to the stadium lot, same price). From the garage, hike 150 yards uphill through a gate to an escalator on the right, which carries you up into the city. If you're staying in the south end of town, try the Il Campo lot, near Porta Tufi.

On parking spots, blue stripes mean pay and display; white stripes mean free parking. You can park for free in the lot west of the Fortezza; in white-striped spots behind the Hotel Villa Liberty (south of the Fortezza); and overnight in most city lots from 20:00 to 8:00. Watch for signs showing a street cleaner and a day of the week—that's when the street is closed to cars for cleaning.

Driving within Siena's city center is restricted to local cars and policed by automatic cameras. If you drive or park anywhere marked *Zona Traffico Limitato (ZTL),* you'll likely have a hefty ticket waiting for you in the mail back home.

Technically, hotel customers are allowed to drop off bags at their hotel before finding a place to park overnight, but getting permission to do so isn't worth the trouble.

Helpful Hints

Combo-Tickets: Siena always seems to be experimenting with different combo-tickets, but in general, only two are worth considering: the €10 Opa Si combo-ticket that includes the Duomo, Duomo Museum, Crypt, and Baptistery (a savings of €8 if you plan on seeing all those sights; sold only at the ticket office just right of the Duomo, near the Duomo Museum entrance), and the €13 combo-ticket covering the Civic Museum and City Tower (a €3 savings; must purchase at City Tower).

Wednesday Morning Market: The weekly market (clothes, knick-knacks, and food) sprawls between the Fortezza and Piazza Gramsci along Viale Cesare Maccari and the adjacent Viale XXV Aprile. The fact that this is more local than touristy makes it, for some, even more interesting.

Internet Access: In this university town, there are lots of places to get plugged in. **Cheap Phone Center** is hidden in a small shopping mall near Il Campo (€2/hour to use terminals, €1/hour for Wi-Fi, daily 10:00-22:00, Sun from 12:00; coming from Il Campo, go uphill past recommended Albergo Tre Donzelle, turn left at Via Cecco Angiolieri, after 20 yards look for #16). **Internet Point** is located upstairs at Via di Città 80, with the entrance around the corner on Via delle Campane (€3/hour, daily 9:00-21:00).

Post Office: It's on Piazza Matteotti (Mon-Fri 8:15-19:00, Sat 8:15-13:30, closed Sun).

Books: Libreria Senese sells books (including my guidebooks), newspapers, and magazines in English, with an emphasis on Italian-related topics (daily 9:00-20:00, Via di Città 62, tel. 0577-280-845). The **Feltrinelli** bookstore at Banchi di Sopra 52 also sells books and magazines in English (Mon-Sat 9:00-19:30, closed Sun, tel. 0577-271-104; the bigger Feltrinelli branch farther down the street at #64 has no English books).

Laundry: Onda Blu is a modern, self-service launderette just 50 yards from Il Campo (about €6 wash and dry, daily 8:00-22:00, last load at 21:00, Via del Casato di Sotto 17

Travel Agency: Palio Viaggi, on Piazza Gramsci, sells plane tickets upstairs. Their downstairs office (go down the ramp to the door below the arch) sells train tickets, railpass reservations, and some bus tickets (only for the longer-distance Sena buses, not the regional Tiemme/Siena Mobilità buses). They charge a €1 fee per bus or train ticket, but this saves you a trip to the train station (Mon-Fri 9:00-12:45 & 15:00-18:30, Sat 9:00-12:30, closed Sun, opposite the columns of NH Excelsior Hotel at La Lizza 12, tel. 0577-280-828, info@palioviaggi.it).

Wine Classes: The **Tuscan Wine School** gives two-hour classes in English on Italian wine and food. Morning classes (11:00) cover rotating topics: wines from all over Italy, olive-oil tasting, or a "Savor Siena" food tour that visits several vendors around town (check website for specific schedule). Afternoon classes (16:00) focus on Tuscan wines, including samples of five vintages. They also offer a one-hour "crash course" at 14:00. Rebecca and her fellow sommeliers keep things entertaining and offer classes for as few as two people (€40/person, 20 percent student discount to anyone with this book, €25 for one-hour course, classes offered Mon-Sat, closed Sun, reservations recommended—especially in peak season, Via di Stalloreggi 26, 30 yards from recommended Hotel Duomo, tel. 0577-221-704, mobile 333-722-9716, www.tuscanwineschool.com, info @tuscanwineschool.com). Their outlet store sells wine from local producers at cost (Mon-Sat 11:00-18:00, closed Sun).

Updates to this Book: For news about changes to this book's coverage since it was published, see www.ricksteves.com/update.

Tours in Siena

Roberto's Tuscany Tours—**Roberto Bechi,** a hardworking Sienese guide, specializes in off-the-beaten-path minibus tours of the surrounding countryside (up to eight passengers, convenient pickup at hotel). Married to an American (Patti) and having run restaurants in Siena and the US, Roberto communicates well with Americans. His passions are Sienese culture, Tuscan history, and local cuisine. It's ideal to book well in advance, but you might be able to schedule a tour if you call the day before (seven different tours—explained on his website, €90/person for full-day tours, €60/person for off-season four-hour tours, entry fees extra, assistant Anna can schedule city tours as well as other guides if Roberto is booked, Anna's mobile 320-147-6590, Roberto's mobile 328-425-5648, www.toursbyroberto.com, toursbyroberto@gmail .com). Roberto also does multiday tours. If you book any tour with Roberto, he can advise you on other aspects of your trip.

Other Local Guides—**Federica Olla,** who leads walking tours of Siena, is a smart, youthful guide with a knack for creative teaching (€55/hour, mobile 338-133-9525, info@ollaeventi.com).

GSO Guides Co-op is a group of 10 young professional guides who offer good tours covering all of Tuscany and Umbria (€130/half-day, €260/full day, 10 percent discount for Rick Steves readers, mobile 338-611-0127, www.guidesienaeoltre.com). Among them, charming Stefania Fabrizi specializes in Siena (mobile 338-640-7796).

Bus Tours—Somehow a company called My Tour has a lock on all hotel tour-promotion space. Every hotel has a rack of their

Siena at a Glance

▲▲▲**Il Campo** Best square in Italy. **Hours:** Always open. See page 347.

▲▲▲**Duomo** Art-packed cathedral with mosaic floors and statues by Michelangelo and Bernini. **Hours:** March-Oct Mon-Sat 10:30-19:00, Sun 13:30-18:00; Nov-Feb Mon-Sat 10:30-17:30, Sun 13:30-17:30. See page 355.

▲▲**Civic Museum** City museum in City Hall with Sienese frescoes, the *Effects of Good and Bad Government.* **Hours:** Daily mid-March-Oct 10:00-19:00, Nov-mid-March 10:00-18:00. See page 351.

▲▲**Duomo Museum** Siena's best museum, displaying cathedral art (including Duccio's *Maestá*) and offering sweeping Tuscan views. **Hours:** Daily March-Oct 10:30-19:00, Nov-Feb 10:30-17:30. See page 355.

▲**City Tower** 330-foot tower climb. **Hours:** Daily March-mid-Oct 10:00-19:00, mid-Oct-Feb 10:00-16:00. See page 351.

▲**Pinacoteca** Fine Sienese paintings. **Hours:** Tue-Sat 8:15-19:15, Sun-Mon 9:00-13:00. See page 352.

▲**Baptistery** Cave-like building with baptismal font decorated by Ghiberti and Donatello. **Hours:** Daily March-Oct 10:30-19:00, Nov-Feb 10:30-17:30. See page 356.

▲**Santa Maria della Scala** Museum with vibrant ceiling and wall frescoes depicting day-to-day life in a medieval hospital, much of the original *Fountain of Joy,* and an Etruscan artifact exhibit. **Hours:** Daily March-Oct 10:30-18:00, Nov-Feb 10:30-16:00. See page 356.

Crypt Site of 12th-century church, housing some of Siena's oldest frescoes. **Hours:** Daily March-Oct 10:30-19:00, Nov-Feb 10:30-17:30. See page 356.

Church of San Domenico Huge brick church with St. Catherine's head and thumb. **Hours:** Daily 7:00-18:30. See page 357.

Sanctuary of St. Catherine Home of St. Catherine. **Hours:** Daily 9:00-18:00, church closed 12:30-15:00. See page 359.

brochures, which advertise a variety of five-hour big-bus tours into the countryside (€38, depart from Piazza Gramsci).

Sights in Siena

On Il Campo, the Main Square

▲▲▲**Il Campo**—This square is the heart, both geographically and metaphorically, of Siena. It fans out from City Hall (Palazzo Pubblico) to create an amphitheater.

It's the only town square I've ever seen where people stretch out as if at the beach. Il Campo's shining moment is the famous Palio horse races, which take place in summer (see sidebar on page 352).

Originally, this area was just a field *(campo)* located outside the former city walls. Bits of those original walls, which circled the Duomo (and curved against today's square), can be seen above the pharmacy (the black-and-white stones,

to the right as you face City Hall). In the 1200s, with the advent of the Sienese Republic, the city expanded—once a small medieval town circling its cathedral, it became a larger, humanistic city gathered around its towering City Hall. In this newer and relatively secular age, the focus of power shifted from the bishop to the city council.

As the city expanded, Il Campo eventually became the historic junction of Siena's various competing *contrade* (neighborhood districts) and the old marketplace. The brick surface is divided into nine sections, representing the council of nine merchants and city bigwigs who ruled medieval Siena. The square and its buildings are the color of the soil upon which they stand—a color known to artists and Crayola users as "Burnt Sienna."

City Hall: This secular building, with its 330-foot tower, dominates the square. In medieval Siena, this was the center of

the city, and the whole focus of Il Campo still flows down to it.

The building's facade features the various symbols of the city. The **sun** hearkens back to St. Bernardino of Siena. Born on the day that St. Catherine of Siena died, he grew up here and went on to travel throughout Italy, giving spirited and humorous sermons

SIENA

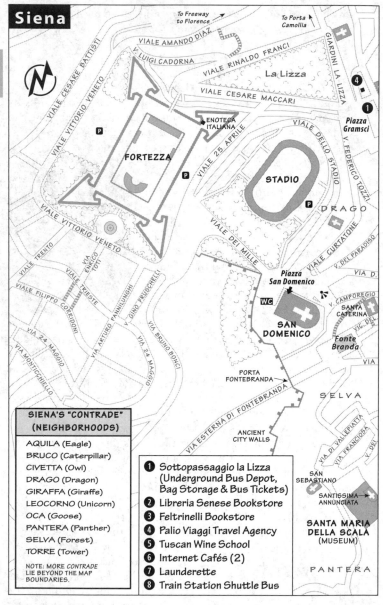

Siena

To Freeway to Florence
To Porta Camollia

VIALE AMANDO DIAZ
V. LUIGI CADORNA
VIALE RINALDO FRANCI
La Lizza
GIARDINI LA LIZZA
VIALE CESARE MACCARI
VIALE CESARE BATTISTI
VIALE VITTORIO VENETO
ENOTECA ITALIANA
VIALE 25 APRILE
VIALE DELLO STADIO
Piazza Gramsci
V. FEDERICO TOZZI
FORTEZZA
STADIO
VIALE VITTORIO VENETO
VIALE DEI MILLE
DRAGO
VIALE CURTATONE
V. DEL PARADISO
VIA D.
VIALE TRENTO
VIA ENRICO TOTI
VIALE TRIESTE
VIALE FILIPPO CORRIDONI
VIA GINO FRUSCHELLI
VIA ARTURO PANNILUNGHI
Piazza San Domenico
V. CAMPOREGIO
VIA
SANTA CATERINA
VIG. DEL
WC
SAN DOMENICO
Fonte Branda
VIA 24 MAGGIO
VIA BRUNO BONCI
VIA
VIA 24 MAGGIO
VIA MONTICCHIELLO
PORTA FONTEBRANDA
SELVA
VIA ESTERNA DI FONTEBRANDA
VIA DI VALLEPIATTA
VIA FRANCIOSA
V. DEL
ANCIENT CITY WALLS
SAN SEBASTIANO
SANTISSIMA ANNUNCIATA
SANTA MARIA DELLA SCALA (MUSEUM)
PANTERA

SIENA'S "CONTRADE" (NEIGHBORHOODS)

AQUILA (Eagle)
BRUCO (Caterpillar)
CIVETTA (Owl)
DRAGO (Dragon)
GIRAFFA (Giraffe)
LEOCORNO (Unicorn)
OCA (Goose)
PANTERA (Panther)
SELVA (Forest)
TORRE (Tower)

NOTE: MORE *CONTRADE* LIE BEYOND THE MAP BOUNDARIES.

1 Sottopassaggio la Lizza (Underground Bus Depot, Bag Storage & Bus Tickets)
2 Libreria Senese Bookstore
3 Feltrinelli Bookstore
4 Palio Viaggi Travel Agency
5 Tuscan Wine School
6 Internet Cafés (2)
7 Launderette
8 Train Station Shuttle Bus

SIENA

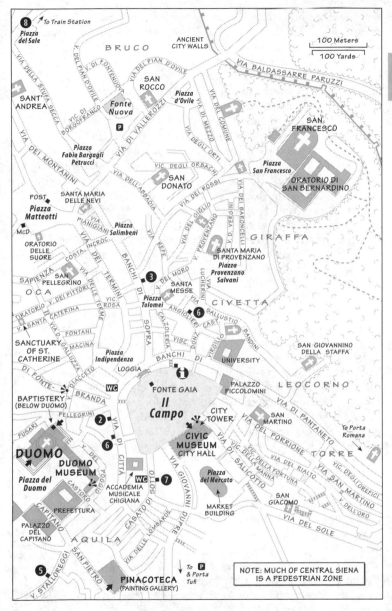

To Train Station
8 Piazza del Sale

BRUCO

ANCIENT CITY WALLS

VIA BALDASSARRE PARUZZI

100 Meters
100 Yards

SANT' ANDREA

VIA DELLA STUFA SECCA

V. DEL PIAN D'OVILE
VIA DI FONTENUTI
VIA DEL PIAN D'OVILE

SAN ROCCO

Piazza d'Ovile

Fonte Nuova
P

VIA DI VALLEROZZI

VIA DEL COMUNE

VIA DEL MEZZO

SAN FRANCESCO

VIC. DI BORGOFRANCO

Piazza Fabio Bargagli Petrucci

VIA DEI MONTANINI

VIA DELL'ABBADIA

VIC. DEGLI ORBACHI

SAN DONATO

VIA DEGLI ORTI

VIA DEI ROSSI

Piazza San Francesca

ORATORIO DI SAN BERNARDINO

POST
Piazza Matteotti

SANTA MARIA DELLE NEVI

VIA PIANIGIANI

Piazza Salimbeni

VIA DEL GIGLIO

VIA DEL BARONCELLI

GIRAFFA

McD

ORATORIO DELLE SUORE

VIA INCROC

BANCHI DI SOPRA

VIA DELLE TERME

SANTA MARIA DI PROVENZANO

Piazza Provenzano Salvani

VIA PROVENZANO

SAPIENZA

OCA

SAN PELLEGRINO

COSTA DI

V. DEI PITTORI

3
Piazza Tolomei

DEL MORO

SANTA MESSE

CIVETTA

TIRATOIO

V. SANTA CATERINA

VIA GALLUZZA

FONTANI

VIC. ROSA

CALZOLERIA

ANGIOLIERI

6
VIA SALLUSTIO BANDINI

VIRGILIO

SAN GIOVANNINO DELLA STAFFA

SANCTUARY OF ST. CATHERINE

MACINA

Piazza Indipendenza

BANCHI DI

VISC.

UNIVERSITY

LEOCORNO

DI FONTE

LOGGIA

FONTE GAIA

i

PALAZZO PICCOLOMINI

VIA DI PANTANETO

BRANDA

WC

Il Campo

CITY TOWER

SAN MARTINO

To Porta Romana

BAPTISTERY (BELOW DUOMO)

PELLEGRINI

2
VIA DI CITTÀ

6

CIVIC MUSEUM CITY HALL

VIC. DEL PORRIONE

TORRE

FUSARI

V. DEL POGGIO

VIC. DELLA FORTUNA

VIA DEL RIALTO

VIC. DEGLI OREFICI

DUOMO

DUOMO MUSEUM

CASTORO

WC
7

Piazza del Mercato

VIC. DI SALICOTTO

SAN MARTINO

Piazza del Duomo

ACCADEMIA MUSICALE CHIGIANA

CASATO DI SOTTO

VIA GIOVANNI DUPRÈ

SAN GIACOMO

V. DELL'ORO

PREFETTURA

MARKET BUILDING

VIA DEL SOLE

PALAZZO DEL CAPITANO

CAPITANO

SAN PIETRO

AQUILA

VIA DELLE LOMBARDE

5

V. STALLOREGGI

PINACOTECA (PAINTING GALLERY)

To P & Porta Tufi

NOTE: MUCH OF CENTRAL SIENA IS A PEDESTRIAN ZONE

that preached peace between warring political factions. His sermons often ended with reconciling parties exchanging a *bacio di pace* (kiss of peace). In Siena he would stand in front of the Palazzo and preach to crowds discreetly segregated by gender with a curtain down the middle. Bernardino personally designed the sun logo to attract crowds, and later he became the patron saint of advertising (and of Siena).

To either side of the sun logo, **she-wolf gargoyles** lean out and snarl, "Don't mess with Siena, Mister Pope!" This Ghibelline city prided itself on its political independence from the papacy; it embraced as a city symbol the pagan she-wolf who suckled Romulus and Remus (Remus' son was Siena's legendary founder). The black-and-white **shields** over the windows are another city symbol. Near ground level, the metal rings are for tying your horse, while the fixtures above once held flags.

The **City Tower** (Torre del Mangia) is Italy's tallest secular tower. It was named after a hedonistic watchman who consumed his earnings like a glutton consumes food. His chewed-up statue is in the courtyard, to the left as you enter. (For details on climbing the tower, see "City Tower" listing, later.)

The open **chapel** located at the base of the tower was built in 1348 as thanks to God for ending the Black Death (after it killed more than a third of the population). It should also be used to thank God that the top-heavy tower—just plunked onto the building with no extra foundation and no iron reinforcement—still stands. These days, the chapel is used solely to bless the Palio contestants, and the tower's bell only rings for the race.

Fountain of Joy (Fonte Gaia): This 15th-century work by Jacopo della Quercia marks the square's high point. The joy is all about how the Sienese Republic blessed its people with water. Notice Lady Justice with her scales (also holding a sword, right of center), overseeing the free distribution of water to all. Imagine residents gathering here in the 1400s to fill their jugs. The Fountain of Joy still reminds locals that life in Siena is good. Notice the pigeons politely waiting their turn to tightrope gingerly down slippery spouts to slurp a drink from wolves' snouts. The relief panel on

the left shows God creating Adam by helping him to his feet. It's said that this reclining Adam influenced Michelangelo when he painted his Sistine Chapel ceiling. This fountain is a copy—you can see most of the original fountain in an interesting exhibit at Siena's Santa Maria della Scala (described later).

To say that Siena and Florence have always been competitive is an understatement. In medieval times, a statue of Venus stood on Il Campo. After the plague hit Siena, the monks blamed the pagan statue. The people cut it to pieces and buried it along the walls of Florence.

▲▲Civic Museum (Museo Civico)—At the base of the tower is Siena's City Hall, the spot where secular government got its start in early Renaissance Europe. There you'll find city government still at work, along with a sampling of local art, including Siena's first fresco (with a groundbreaking down-to-earth depiction of the Madonna). While pricey, it's worth strolling through the dramatic halls to see fascinating frescoes and portraits extolling Siena's greats, saints, and the city-as-utopia.

Cost and Hours: €8, €13 combo-ticket with tower (must be purchased at the tower), daily mid-March-Oct 10:00-19:00, Nov-mid March 10:00-18:00, last entry 45 minutes before closing, tel. 0577-292-615, www.comune.siena.it.

✪ See the Civic Museum Tour chapter.

▲City Tower (Torre del Mangia)—Siena gathers around its City Hall more than its church. Medieval Siena was a proud republic, and this tall tower is the exclamation point of its "declaration of independence." Its 300 steps get pretty skinny at the top, but the reward is one of Italy's best views.

Cost and Hours: €8, €13 combo-ticket with Civic Museum, daily March-mid-Oct 10:00-19:00, mid-Oct-Feb 10:00-16:00, last entry 45 minutes before closing, closed in rain, free and mandatory bag check. Wait at the bottom of the stairs for the green *Avanti* light. Admission is limited to 50 people at a time, so be prepared for long lines or for tickets to be sold out. Try to avoid midday crowds (up to an hour wait at peak times).

Near Il Campo

Via Banchi di Sopra and Via Banchi di Sotto—These main drags in town are named "upper row of banks" and "lower row of banks." They were once lined with market tables *(banchi)*, and rents were paid to the city for a table's position along the street. If the owner of a *banco* neglected to pay the rent for his space, thugs came along and literally broke *(rotto)* his table. It is from this practice—*banco rotto*, broken table—that we get the English word "bankrupt."

In medieval times, these two streets were part of the Via

Siena's Palio

In the Palio, the feisty spirit of Siena's 17 neighborhoods lives on. Each neighborhood, or *contrada,* has a parish church, well or fountain, and sometimes even a historical museum. Each is represented by a mascot (porcupine, unicorn, wolf, etc.) and unique colors worn proudly by residents.

Contrada pride is evident year-round in Siena's parades and colorful banners, lamps, and wall plaques. (If you hear the thunder of distant drumming, run to it for some medieval action—there's a good chance it'll feature flag-throwers.) You are welcome to participate in these lively neighborhood festivals. Buy a scarf in *contrada* colors, grab a glass of Chianti, munch on some panforte, and join in the merriment.

Contrada passion is most visible twice a year—on July 2 and August 16—when the city erupts during its world-famous horse race, the Palio di Siena. Ten of the 17 neighborhoods compete (chosen by rotation and lot), hurling themselves with medieval abandon into several days of trial races and traditional revelry. Jockeys—usually from out of town—are considered hired guns, no better than paid mercenaries. Bets are placed on which *contrada* will win...and lose. Despite the shady behind-the-scenes dealing, on the big day the horses are taken into their *contrada's* church to be blessed. ("Go and return victorious," says the priest.) It's considered a sign of luck if a horse leaves droppings in the church.

On the evening of the race, Il Campo is stuffed to the brim with locals and tourists. Dirt is brought in and packed down over the gray pavement of the perimeter to create the track's surface, while mattresses pad the walls of surrounding buildings. The most treacherous spots are the sharp corners, where many a rider has bitten the dust.

Francigena, the main thoroughfare between Rome, London, and Santiago de Compostela in Spain. The medieval Sienese traded wool with passing travelers, requiring money-changers, which led to banks. As Siena was a secular town, local Christians were allowed to loan money and work as bankers. Today, strollers out each evening for their *passeggiata* fill Via Banchi di Sopra.

▲**Pinacoteca**—If you're into medieval art, you'll likely find this quiet, uncrowded, colorful museum delightful. The museum walks you through Siena's art chronologically, from the 12th through the 16th centuries, when a revolution in realism was percolating in Tuscany.

Cost and Hours: €4, Tue-Sat 8:15-19:15, Sun-Mon 9:00-

Picture the scene: Ten snorting horses and their nervous riders line up near the pharmacy (on the west side of the square) to await the starting signal. Then they race like crazy while spectators wave the scarves of their neighborhoods. Every possible vantage point and perch is packed with people straining to see the action. One lap around the course is about a third of a mile (350 meters); three laps make a full circuit. In this literally no-holds-barred race—which lasts just over a minute—a horse can win even without its rider (jockeys perch precariously without saddles on the sweaty horses' backs, and often fall off).

When the winner crosses the line, 1/17th of Siena—the prevailing neighborhood—goes berserk. Winners receive a *palio* (banner), typically painted by a local artist and always featuring the Virgin Mary. But the true prize is proving that your *contrada* is *numero uno,* and mocking your losing rivals.

All over town, sketches and posters depict the Palio. This is not some folkloric event—it's a real medieval moment. If you're packed onto the square with 60,000 people, all hungry for victory, you won't see much, but you'll feel it. Bleacher and balcony seats are expensive, but it's free to join the masses in the square. Be sure to go with an empty bladder as there are no WCs, and be prepared to surrender any sense of personal space.

While the actual Palio packs the city, you could side-trip in from Florence to see the horse-race trials—called *prove* (proh-vay)—on any of the three days before the main event (usually at 9:00 and after 19:00, free seats in bleachers). For more information, visit www.ilpalio.org.

13:00, last entry 30 minutes before closing, free and mandatory bag check; from Il Campo, walk out Via di Città and go left on Via San Pietro to #29; tel. 0577-281-161 or 0577-286-143, www.pinacotecanazionale.siena.it.

❍ **Self-Guided Tour:** In general, the collection lets you follow the evolution of painting styles from Byzantine to Gothic, then to International Gothic, and finally to Renaissance.

• *The core of the collection is on the second floor, in Rooms 1-19. To reach them, ascend two floors and go up a little landing to your right.*

Long after Florentine art went realistic, the Sienese embraced a timeless, otherworldly style glittering with lots of gold. But Sienese art features more than just paintings. In this city of proud craftsmen, the gilding and carpentry of the frames almost compete with the actual paintings. The exquisite attention to detail gives a glimpse into the wealth of the 14th and 15th centuries, Siena's Golden Age. As you walk through the museum, take time to trace the delicate features with your eyes. The woven silk and gold clothing you'll see was worn by the very people who once walked these halls, when this was a private mansion (appreciate the colonnaded courtyard).

Room 1 mostly features the pre-Duccio art world. (Duccio created the *Maestà* in the Duomo Museum, the Duomo's big stained-glass window, and a fresco in the Civic Museum.) Altarpieces emphasize the heavenly and otherworldly, rather than the human realism that Duccio helped to pioneer. (You may see a Duccio in here, as well.)

Rooms 2-4 contain a number of works by Duccio (and assistants), whose groundbreaking innovations are subtle to the layman's eyes: less gold-leaf background, fewer gold creases in robes, transparent garments, inlaid-marble thrones, and a more human Mary and Jesus. Notice that the Madonna-and-Bambino pose is eerily identical in each version.

In **Room 5** are works by Duccio's one-time assistant, Simone Martini, including his *St. Augustine of Siena*. The saint's life is set in pretty realistic Sienese streets, buildings, and landscapes. In each panel, the saint pops out at the oddest (difficult to draw) angles to save the day. (Simone Martini also did the *Maestà* and possibly the Guidoriccio frescoes in the Civic Museum.)

Room 7 includes religious works by the hometown Lorenzetti brothers (Ambrogio is best known for the secular masterpiece, the *Effects of Good and Bad Government,* in the Civic Museum). The rest of the rooms on this floor are a menagerie of gold-backed saints and Madonnas.

In **Room 12** are two famous small wooden panels: *Città sul Mare (City by the Sea)* and *Castello in Riva al Lago (Castle on the Lakeshore).* These pieces, done by an early 14th-century Sienese painter (some scholars think it could be Ambrogio Lorenzetti), feature the strange, medieval landscape Cubism seen in the work of the contemporaneous *Guidoriccio da Fogliano* (in the Civic Museum). Notice the weird, melancholy light that captures the sense of the Dark Ages. These images are replicated on postcards found throughout the city.

• *Loop through the rest of this level, then descend one floor to view a minor collection of later art.*

In **Room 20,** suddenly the gold is gone—Madonna is set on earth. See works by the painter/biographer Giorgio Vasari **(Room 22),** a stunning view out the window **(Room 26),** and several colorful rooms **(27-30)** dedicated to Domenico Beccafumi (1486-1551).

Beccafumi designed many of the Duomo's inlaid pavement panels (including *Slaughter of the Innocents*), and his original cartoons are displayed in **Room 30.** With strong bodies, twisting poses, and dramatic gestures, Beccafumi's works epitomize the Mannerist style.

Room 31 has the sympathetic *Christ on the Column* by Sodoma (Giovanni Bazzi), and the long **Room 32** displays large-scale works by Sodoma, Beccafumi, and others. And finally, Bernardino Mei **(Room 33)** gives a Sienese take on the wrinkled saints and dark shadows of Caravaggio.

Cathedral Area

Each of the first four sights (Duomo, Duomo Museum, Crypt, and Baptistery) is covered by a separate ticket, or by the €10 Opa Si combo-ticket. If you're planning to visit only the Duomo and Duomo Museum, this is a bad deal; but if you're curious about the Crypt and Baptistery, the combo-ticket lets you peek into those sights for just €1 more. Individual tickets for any of these sights and the Opa Si combo-ticket are sold only at the ticket office near the entrance to the Duomo Museum—to the right as you face the cathedral facade (no tickets sold at sight entrances).

▲▲▲**Duomo**—This 13th-century Gothic cathedral, with its six-story striped bell tower—Siena's ultimate tribute to the Virgin

Mary—is heaped with statues, plastered with frescoes, and paved with art. Soak up the richly ornamented facade before venturing inside, where 1,000 years of popes keep watch from on high. The interior is a Renaissance riot of striped columns, remarkably intricate inlaid-marble floors, a Michelangelo statue, and evocative Bernini sculptures. The Piccolomini Library features a series of 15th-century frescoes chronicling the adventures of Siena's philanderer-turned-pope, Aeneas Piccolomini.

Cost and Hours: €3 includes cathedral and Piccolomini Library, also covered by Opa Si combo-ticket, buy tickets near Duomo Museum entry; March-Oct Mon-Sat 10:30-19:00, Sun 13:30-18:00; Nov-Feb Mon-Sat 10:30-17:30, Sun 13:30-17:30; last entry 30 minutes before closing; modest dress is required to enter, but paper ponchos are provided; tel. 0577-286-300, www.operaduomo.siena.it.

✪ See the Siena Duomo Tour chapter.

▲▲**Duomo Museum (Museo dell'Opera e Panorama)**—Located in a corner of the Duomo's grand but unfinished extension

SIENA

(to the right as you face the main facade), Siena's most enjoyable museum was built to house the cathedral's art. The ground floor features the original Duccio stained-glass window that once hung over the high altar, along with an army of statues from the facade. Upstairs is Duccio's *Maestà* (*Enthroned Virgin*, 1311), one of the great pieces of medieval art. The flip side of the *Maestà* (displayed on the opposite wall) has 26 panels—the medieval equivalent of pages—showing scenes from the Passion of Christ. Finally, climb up to the Panorama dal Facciatone. From the first landing, take the skinny second spiral for Siena's surprise view.

Cost and Hours: €6, also covered by Opa Si combo-ticket, buy tickets near Duomo Museum entry, daily March-Oct 10:30-19:00, Nov-Feb 10:30-17:30, last entry 30 minutes before closing, tel. 0577-286-300, www.operaduomo.siena.it.

✪ See the Siena Duomo Museum Tour chapter.

▲**Baptistery**—Siena is so hilly that there wasn't enough flat ground on which to build a big church. What to do? Build a big church anyway and prop up the overhanging edge with the Baptistery. This dark and quietly tucked-away cave of art is worth a look for its cool, tranquil bronze panels and angels by Ghiberti, Donatello, and others that adorn the pedestal of the baptismal font.

Cost and Hours: €3, also covered by Opa Si combo-ticket, buy tickets near Duomo Museum entry, daily March-Oct 10:30-19:00, Nov-Feb 10:30-17:30, last entry 30 minutes before closing.

Crypt—The cathedral "crypt" is archaeologically important. The site of a small 12th-century Romanesque church, it was filled in with dirt a century after its creation to provide a foundation for the huge church that sits atop it today. Recently excavated, the several rediscovered frescoed rooms show off what are likely the oldest frescoes in town.

Cost and Hours: €6, also covered by Opa Si combo-ticket, buy tickets near Duomo Museum entry, daily March-Oct 10:30-19:00, Nov-Feb 10:30-17:30, last entry 30 minutes before closing, entrance is halfway up the stairs between the Baptistery and Duomo Museum.

▲**Santa Maria della Scala**—This museum (opposite the Duomo entrance) was used as a hospital until the 1980s. Its labyrinthine 12th-century cellars—carved out of volcanic tuff and finished with brick—go down several floors and during medieval times were used to store supplies for the hospital upstairs. Today, the hospital and its cellars are filled with exhibits (well-described in English) and can be a welcome refuge from the hot streets. Stop in for a cool and quiet break in the air-conditioned lobby, which offers a fine bookshop and big, comfy couches, all under great 15th-century timbers.

Cost and Hours: €6, daily March-Oct 10:30-18:00, Nov-Feb 10:30-16:00, last entry 30 minutes before closing, bookstore, tel. 0577-534-511, www.santamariadellascala.com.

Visiting the Museum: It's easy to get lost in this gigantic complex, so stay focused on the main attractions—the fancily frescoed Pellegrinaio Hall (ground floor), most of the original *Fountain of Joy* (first basement), and the Etruscan collection in the Archaeological Museum (second basement). Just inside the complex (enter from the square) is the Church of the Santissima Annunziata.

• *From the entrance, walk down the lengthy hall to the long room with the colorful frescoes.*

The sumptuously frescoed walls of **Pellegrinaio Hall** show medieval Siena's innovative health care and social welfare system in action (c. 1442, wonderfully described in English). Starting in the 11th century, the hospital nursed the sick and cared for abandoned children, as is vividly portrayed in these frescoes. The good works paid off, as bequests and donations poured in, creating the wealth that's evident throughout this building.

• *Head down the stairs, then continue straight into the darkened rooms with pieces of Siena's landmark fountain—follow signs to* Fonte Gaia.

An engaging exhibit explains Jacopo della Quercia's early 15th-century *Fountain of Joy (Fonte Gaia)*—and displays the disassembled pieces of the original fountain itself. In the 19th century, after serious deterioration, the ornate fountain was dismantled and plaster casts were made. (From these casts, they formed the replica that graces Il Campo today.) Here you'll see the eroded original panels paired with their restored casts, along with the actual statues that once stood on the edges of the fountain.

• *Descend into the cavernous second basement.*

Under the groin vaults of the **Archaeological Museum,** you're alone with piles of ancient Etruscan stuff excavated from tombs dating centuries before Christ (displayed in a labyrinthine exhibit). Remember, the Etruscans dominated this part of Italy before the Roman Empire swept through—some historians think even Rome originated as an Etruscan town.

San Domenico Area

Church of San Domenico—
This huge brick church is worth a quick look. The spacious, plain interior (except for the colorful flags of the city's 17 *contrade*, or neighborhoods) fits the austere philosophy of the Dominicans and invites meditation on the

St. Catherine of Siena
(1347-1380)

The youngest of 25 children born to a Sienese cloth dyer, Catherine began experiencing heavenly visions as a child. At

16 she became a Dominican nun, locking herself away for three years in a room in her family's house. She lived the life of an ascetic, which culminated in a vision wherein she married Christ. Catherine emerged from solitude to join her Dominican sisters, sharing her experiences, caring for the sick, and gathering both disciples and enemies. At age 23, she lapsed into a spiritual coma, waking with the heavenly command to spread her message to the world. She wrote essays and letters to kings, dukes, bishops, and popes, imploring them to find peace for a war-ravaged Italy. While visiting Pisa during Lent of 1375, she had a vision in which she received the stigmata, the wounds of Christ.

Still in her twenties, Catherine was invited to Avignon, France, where the pope had taken up residence. With her charm, sincerity, and reputation for holiness, she helped convince Pope Gregory XI to return the papacy to the city of Rome. Catherine also went to Rome, where she died young. She was canonized in the next generation (by a Sienese pope), and her relics were distributed to churches around Italy.

Because of her intervention in the papal schism, today Catherine is revered (along with St. Benedict) as the patron saint of Europe, and remembered as a rare outspoken medieval woman still appreciated for her universal message: that this world is not a gift from our fathers, but a loan from our children.

thoughts and deeds of St. Catherine. Walk up the steps in the rear to see paintings from her life. Halfway up the church on the right, find a metal bust of St. Catherine, a small case housing her thumb (on the left), and a glass box on the lowest shelf containing the chain she used to scourge herself. In the chapel (15 feet to the left) surrounded with candles, you'll see Catherine's actual head atop the altar. Through the door just beyond are the sacristy and the bookstore.

Cost and Hours: Free, daily 7:00-18:30, gift shop tel. 0577-286-848, www.basilicacateriniana.com. A WC (€0.50) is at the far end of the parking lot, to the right as you face the church entrance.

Sanctuary of St. Catherine (Santuario di Santa Caterina)—
Step into the cool and peaceful site of Catherine's home. Siena
remembers its favorite hometown gal, a simple, unschooled, but
mystically devout soul who, in the mid-1300s, helped convince the
pope to return from France to Rome. Pilgrims have visited this
place since 1464, and architects and artists have greatly embellished what was probably once a humble home (her family worked
as wool dyers). You'll see paintings throughout showing scenes
from her life.

Enter through the courtyard, and walk down the stairs at the
far end. The church on your right contains the wooden crucifix
upon which Catherine was meditating when she received the stigmata. Take a pew, gaze at it, and try to imagine the scene. Back
outside, the oratory across the courtyard stands where the kitchen
once was. Go down the stairs (left of the gift shop) to reach the
saint's room. Catherine's bare cell is behind wrought-iron doors.

Cost and Hours: Free, daily 9:00-18:00, church closed
12:30-15:00, a few downhill blocks toward the center from San
Domenico—follow signs to *Santuario di Santa Caterina*—at Costa
di Sant'Antonio 6, tel. 0577-288-175.

Shopping in Siena

The main drag, Via Banchi di Sopra, is a cancan of fancy shops.
Here are some things to look for:

Flags: For easy-to-pack souvenirs, get some of the large, colorful scarves/flags that depict the symbols of Siena's 17 different
neighborhoods (such as the wolf, the turtle, or the snail). They're

good for gifts or to decorate your
home (sold in varying sizes at souvenir
stands).

Sweets: All over town, Prodotti
Tipici shops sell Sienese specialties.
Siena's claim to caloric fame is its
panforte, a rich, chewy concoction of
nuts, honey, and candied fruits that
impresses even fruitcake-haters. There
are a few varieties: *Margherita,* dusted
in powdered sugar, is more fruity,
while *panpepato* has a spicy, peppery crust. Locals prefer a chewy,
white macaroon-and-almond cookie called *ricciarelli.*

SIENA DUOMO TOUR

The Duomo sits atop Siena's highest point, with one of the most extravagant facades in all of Europe. And this ornate but surprisingly secular shrine to the Virgin Mary is stacked with colorful art inside and out, from the inlaid-marble floors to the stained-glass windows. Along with sculptures by Bernini and Michelangelo, the church features the Piccolomini Library, where a series of captivating frescoes by the Umbrian painter Pinturicchio tells the story of Aeneas Piccolomini, Siena's consummate Renaissance Man, who became Pope Pius II.

Orientation

Cost: €3 includes cathedral and Piccolomini Library, buy ticket at Duomo Museum entrance (facing the cathedral entry, the museum is 100 yards to the right, near the south transept). To add the Duomo Museum, Crypt, and Baptistery, consider the €10 Opa Si combo-ticket. Check the line to get into the Duomo before buying tickets—if there's a long wait, you can pay an extra €1 for a (misnamed) "reservation" that lets you skip the line (not possible to book in advance—just buy it on the spot).

Hours: March-Oct Mon-Sat 10:30-19:00, Sun 13:30-18:00; Nov-Feb Mon-Sat 10:30-17:30, Sun 13:30-17:30; last entry 30 minutes before closing; tel. 0577-286-300, www.operaduomo .siena.it.

Dress Code: Modest dress is required, but stylish paper ponchos are provided for the inappropriately clothed.

Getting There: Just look up and head for the black-and-white-striped tower.

Audioguides: Inside the Duomo are €2 video terminals that give a history of the cathedral floor. In the nave, you can rent a small tablet computer (like a mini-iPad) with audio commentary, colorful photographs, and an extremely dry but informative tour of the cathedral and related sights (for Duomo only: €6, €10/2 people; for Duomo plus Duomo Museum, Crypt, and Baptistery: €8, €14/2 people). Considering the expense and hassle (you have to return the audioguide to the nave), it's probably not worth it for most visitors, who should find the commentary in this chapter and the next one to be plenty.

Length of This Tour: Allow one hour.

Photography: No flash permitted.

The Tour Begins

Exterior

Grab a spot on a stone bench opposite the entry to take in this architectural festival of green, white, pink, and gold. Like a medi-

eval altarpiece, the facade is divided into sections, each frame filled with patriarchs and prophets, studded with roaring gargoyles, and topped with prickly pinnacles. Imagine pilgrims arriving at this church, its facade trumpeting the coming of Christ and the true path to salvation.

The current structure dates back to 1215, with the major decoration done during Siena's heyday (1250-1350). The lower story, by Giovanni Pisano (who worked from 1284 to 1297), features remnants of the fading Romanesque style (round arches over the doors), topped with the pointed arches of the new Gothic style that was seeping in from France. The upper half, in full-blown Gothic, was designed and built a century later.

The six-story bell tower (c. 1315) looks even taller, thanks to an optical illusion: The white marble stripes get narrower toward the top, making the upper part seem farther away.

On columns flanking the entrance are statues of the Roman she-wolf suckling Romulus and Remus, the mythical founders of Rome. Legend has it that Remus' son Senio ("Siena") rode north on a black horse to found the city of Siena.

• *Step inside, putting yourself in the mindset of a pilgrim as you take in this trove of religious art. (With a maximum capacity of 700 visitors, you may have to wait—the current number is indicated on a computer screen at the turnstile. Remember, if the line is dreadfully long, you can pay €1 for a "reservation" at the ticket desk to skip the line.)*

SIENA DUOMO

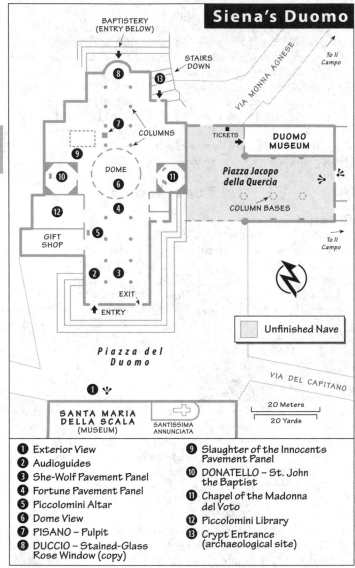

Siena's Duomo

BAPTISTERY
(ENTRY BELOW)

STAIRS
DOWN

VIA MONNA AGNESE

To Il Campo

❽

⓭

❼
COLUMNS

TICKETS

DUOMO MUSEUM

❾

❿

DOME
❻

Piazza Jacopo della Quercia

⓫

COLUMN BASES

❹

⓬

GIFT SHOP

❺

To Il Campo

❷   ❸

EXIT

↑ ENTRY

Unfinished Nave

Piazza del Duomo

VIA DEL CAPITANO

❶ ⚲

SANTA MARIA
DELLA SCALA
(MUSEUM)

SANTISSIMA
ANNUNCIATA

20 Meters

20 Yards

❶ Exterior View
❷ Audioguides
❸ She-Wolf Pavement Panel
❹ Fortune Pavement Panel
❺ Piccolomini Altar
❻ Dome View
❼ PISANO – Pulpit
❽ DUCCIO – Stained-Glass Rose Window (copy)

❾ Slaughter of the Innocents Pavement Panel
❿ DONATELLO – St. John the Baptist
⓫ Chapel of the Madonna del Voto
⓬ Piccolomini Library
⓭ Crypt Entrance (archaeological site)

Nave

The heads of 172 popes—who reigned from Peter to the 12th century—peer down from above, looking over the fine inlaid art on the floor. With a forest of striped columns, a coffered dome, a large stained-glass window at the far end (it's a copy—the original is viewable up close in the nearby Duomo Museum), and an art gallery's worth of early Renaissance art, this is one busy inte-

Siena's Big Plans and Slow Fade

After rival republic Florence began its grand cathedral (1296), proud Siena planned to build one even bigger, the biggest church in all Christendom. Construction began in the 1330s on an extension off the right side of the existing Duomo (today's cathedral would have been used as a transept). The vision was grand, but it underestimated the complexity of constructing such a building without enough land for it to sit upon. That, coupled with the devastating effects of a plague, killed the city's ability and will to finish the project. Many Sienese saw the plague as a sign from God, punishing them for their pride. They canceled their plans and humbly faded into the background of Tuscan history.

rior. If you look closely at the popes, you'll see the same four faces repeated over and over.

For almost two centuries (1373-1547), 40 artists paved the marble floor with scenes from the Old Testament, allegories, and intricate patterns.

The series starts near the entrance with historical allegories; the larger, more elaborate scenes surrounding the altar are mostly stories from the Old Testament. Many of the floor panels are roped off—and occasionally even covered—to prevent further wear and tear.

• *On the floor, find the second pavement panel from the entrance.*

She-Wolf Pavement Panel

Depicted as a she-wolf, the proud city of Siena is the center of the Italian universe, orbited by such lesser lights as Roma, Florentia (Florence), and Pisa. This is pretty secular stuff for such prime church real estate. Five yards to the left and right are panels with pre-Christian imagery—the ancient Greek prophetesses known as the sibyls. This church's mix of pre-Christian wisdom, secular humanism, and Christian piety gives an insight into the Sienese approach to religion.

• *The fifth pavement panel from the entrance is the...*

Fortune Panel

Lady Luck (lower right) parachutes down to earth, where she teeters back and forth on a ball and a tipsy boat. The lesson? Fortune is an unstable foundation for life. Truth-seekers wind their way up the precarious path to the top, where Socrates accompanies Lady Wisdom. Having attained wisdom, the world's richest man ("Crates," upper right) realizes that money doesn't buy happiness, and he dumps his jewels out. They fall to earth, and the cycle of

Fortune begins again.

On the right wall hangs a dim **painting of St. Catherine** (fourth from entrance). Siena's homegrown saint (see page 358) had a vision in which she mystically married Christ. Here's the wedding ceremony in heaven. Jesus places the ring on Catherine's finger as her future mother-in-law, Mary, looks on.

• *On the opposite wall is a marble altarpiece decorated with statues.*

Piccolomini Altar

The Piccolomini Altar was designed for the tomb of the Sienese-born Pope Pius III. It was commissioned when he was the cardinal of Siena, but because he later became a pope (see the fresco of his coronation with Pius wearing the golden robe—above and to the right of the Michelangelo statue), he was buried in the Vatican and this fancy tomb was never used. It's most interesting for its statues: one by Michelangelo and three by his students. Michelangelo was originally contracted to do 15 statues, but another sculp-

tor had started the marble blocks, and Michelangelo's heart was never in the project. He personally finished only the figure of St. Paul (lower right, clearly more interesting than the bland, bored popes above him).

Paul has the look of Michelangelo's *Moses,* the broken-nosed self-portrait of the sculptor himself, and the relaxed hand of his *David.* It was the chance to sculpt *David* in Florence that convinced Michelangelo to abandon the Siena project.

• *Now grab a seat to study the...*

Dome (and Surrounding Area)

The dome sits on a 12-sided base, but its "coffered" ceiling is actually a painted illusion.

Get oriented to the array of sights by thinking of the church floor as a big 12-hour clock. You're the middle, and the altar is high noon: You'll find the *Slaughter of the Innocents* roped off on the floor at 10 o'clock, Pisano's pulpit between two pillars at 11 o'clock, a copy of Duccio's round stained-glass window at high noon, Bernini's chapel at 3 o'clock, the Piccolomini Altar with the Michelangelo statue (next to doorway leading to a shop, snacks, and WC) at 7 o'clock, the Piccolomini Library at 8 o'clock, and a Donatello statue at 9 o'clock.

Attached to columns (easy to miss, at 7 o'clock and 5 o'clock) are two 65-foot wooden poles that are dear to any Sienese heart.

These were the **flagpoles,** bearing the Florentine flag, captured during the pivotal Battle of Montaperti (1260, fought near Siena), when 20,000 Sienese squared off against 35,000 soldiers from their archrival city, Florence. The two armies battled back and forth all day, until one of the Florentine soldiers—actually, a Sienese spy under cover—attacked the Florentine standard-bearer from behind. Florence's flag fell to the ground, the army lost its bearings and confidence, and Siena seized the moment to counterattack and win. It was the city's finest hour, ushering in its 80-year Golden Age.

The church was intended to be much larger. Look into the right transept and mentally blow a hole in the wall. You'd be looking down the nave of the massive extension of the church—that is, if the original grandiose plan had been completed (see sidebar, previous page).

Pisano's Pulpit

The octagonal Carrara marble pulpit (1268) rests on the backs of lions, symbols of Christianity triumphant. Like the lions, the Church eats its catch (devouring paganism) and nurses its cubs. The seven relief panels tell the life of Christ in rich detail. The pulpit is the work of Nicola Pisano (c. 1220-1278), the "Giotto of sculpture," whose revival of classical forms (columns, sarcophagus-like relief panels) signaled the coming Renaissance. His son Giovanni (c. 1240-1319) carved many of the panels, mixing his dad's classicism and realism with the decorative detail and curvy lines of French Gothic—a style that would influence Donatello and the other Florentines.

The Crucifixion panel (facing the nave under the eagle) is proto-Renaissance. Christ's anatomy is realistic. Mary (bottom left) swoons into the arms of the other women, a very human outburst of emotion. And a Roman soldier (to the right, by Giovanni) turns to look back with an easy motion that breaks the stiff, frontal Gothic mold.

Look at the two panels facing the altar. It's Judgment Day, and Christ is flanked by the saved (on his right, almost hypnotized by the presence of their savior) and, on his left, the desperate damned.

If you visit Pisa, you'll see two similar Pisano pulpits there. (See pages 414 and 421 for more on the Pisanos and their pulpits.)

Duccio's Stained-Glass Rose Window

This is a copy of the original window, which was moved to the Duomo Museum a couple of years ago. The famous rose window was created in 1288 and dedicated to the Virgin Mary (read the complete description on page 371).

• *As you face the window, in the floor to the left (in the transept) is the...*

Slaughter of the Innocents Pavement Panel

Herod (left), sitting enthroned amid Renaissance arches, orders the massacre of all babies to prevent the coming of the promised Messiah. It's a chaotic scene of angry soldiers, grieving mothers, and dead babies, reminding locals that a republic ruled by a tyrant will always experience misery.

The work was designed by the Sienese Matteo di Giovanni (late 1400s) and inlaid with a colorful array of marble, including yellow marble, a Sienese specialty quarried nearby.

• *Step into the chapel just beyond the pavement panel (next to the Piccolomini Library) to see...*

Donatello's St. John the Baptist

The rugged saint in his famous rags stands in a quiet chapel. Donatello, the aging Florentine sculptor, whose style was now considered passé in Florence, came here to build bronze doors for the church (similar to Ghiberti's in Florence). He didn't complete the door project, but he did finish this bronze statue (1457). Notice the cherubs high above it, playfully dangling their feet.

• *Cross beneath the dome to find the Chigi Chapel, also known as the...*

Chapel of the Madonna del Voto

To understand why Bernini is considered the greatest Baroque sculptor, step into this sumptuous chapel (designed in the early 1660s for Fabio Chigi, a.k.a. Pope Alexander VII). Move up to the altar and look back at the **two Bernini statues:** Mary Magdalene in a state of spiritual ecstasy and St. Jerome playing the crucifix like a violinist lost in beautiful music. It's enough to make even a Lutheran light a candle.

The chapel is classic Baroque, combining colored marble, statues, stained glass, a dome, and golden angels holding an icon-like framed painting, creating a multimedia extravaganza that offers a glimpse of heaven.

That painting over the altar is the *Madonna del Voto,* a Madonna and Child adorned with a real crown of gold and jewels (painted by an unknown Italian master in the mid-13th century). In typical medieval fashion, the scene is set in the golden light of heaven. Mary has the almond eyes, long fingers, and golden folds in her robe that are found in orthodox icons of the time. Still, this Mary tilts her head and looks out sympathetically, ready to listen to the prayers of the faithful. This is the Mary to whom the Palio is dedicated, dear to the hearts of the Sienese.

For untold generations, the Sienese have prayed to the *Madonna del Voto* for help. In thanks, they give **offerings** of silver hearts and medallions, many of which hang now on the wall just to the left as you exit the chapel. On the other side of the chapel door is a glass display case that looks like a jewelry store's front window—with rings, necklaces, and other precious items given by thankful worshippers. Want to leave an offering yourself? Light a candle for a €0.50 donation.

• *Cross back to the other side of the church and head toward the main door. On the right, just before the big Piccolomini Altar we saw earlier, look for the door to the...*

Piccolomini Library

If crowds slow your way into this library, spend your waiting time by reading ahead. Brilliantly frescoed, the library captures the exuberant, optimistic spirit of the 1400s, when humanism and the Renaissance were born. The never-restored frescoes look nearly as vivid now as the day they were finished 550 years ago. (With the bright window light, candles were unnecessary in this room—and didn't sully the art with soot.) The painter Pinturicchio (c. 1454-1513) was hired to celebrate the life of one of Siena's hometown boys—a man many call "the first humanist," Aeneas Piccolomini (1405-1464), who became Pope Pius II. Each of the 10 scenes is framed with an arch, as if Pinturicchio were opening a window onto the spacious 3-D world we inhabit. Begin with the episode to the right of the window, and let your eyes follow the frescoes clockwise to trace their progression:

1. Leaving for Basel: Twenty-seven-year-old Aeneas, riding a white horse and decked out in an outrageous hat, pauses to take

one last look back as he leaves Siena to charge off on the first of many adventures in his some-times sunny, sometimes stormy life. Born poor but noble, he got all A's in his classics classes in Siena. Now, having soaked up all the secular knowledge available, he leaves home to crash a church council in Switzerland, where he would take sides against the pope.

2. Meeting James II of Scotland: Aeneas (with long brown hair) charmed King James and the well-dressed, educated, worldly crowd of Europe's courts. Among his many travels, he visited London (writing home about Westminster Abbey and St. Paul's), barely survived a storm at sea, negotiated peace between England and France, and fathered (at least) two illegitimate children.

3. Crowned Poet by Frederick III: Next we find Aeneas in Vienna, working as secretary to the German king. Aeneas kneels to ceremonially receive the laurel crown of a poet. Aeneas wrote love poetry, bawdy stories, and a play, and is best known for his candid autobiography. Everyone was talking about Aeneas—a writer, speaker, diplomat, and lover of the arts and pretty women, who was the very essence of the *uomo universale*, a.k.a. Renaissance Man.

4. Submitting to Pope Eugene IV: At age 40, after a serious illness, Aeneas changes his life. He journeys to Rome and kisses the pope's foot, apologizing for his heretical opposition. He repents for his wild youth and becomes a priest. (In his autobiography, he says it was time to change anyway, as women no longer aroused him...and he no longer attracted them.)

5. Introducing Frederick III and Eleanora: Quickly named Bishop of Siena, Aeneas (in white pointed bishop's hat) makes his hometown a romantic getaway for his friend Frederick and his fiancée. Notice the Duomo's bell tower in the distance and the city walls (upper left). Aeneas always seemed to be present at Europe's most important political, religious, and social events.

6. Made Cardinal: Kneeling before the pope, with shaved head and praying hands, Aeneas receives the flat red hat of a cardinal. In many of these panels, the artist Pinturicchio uses all the latest 3-D effects—floor tiles and carpets, distant landscapes, receding lines—to suck you into the scene. He tears down palace walls and lets us peek inside into the day's centers of power.

7. Made Pope: In 1458, at age 53, Aeneas is elected to be Pope Pius II. Carried in triumph, he blesses the crowd. One of his first acts as pope is to declare as heresy the anti-pope doctrines he championed in his youth. (Pius II fans can visit his birthplace in Pienza, described in the Tuscan Hill Towns chapter.)

8. Proclaims a Crusade: He calls on all of Europe to liberate the Christian city of Constantinople, which had recently fallen (in 1453) to the Ottoman Turks. Europe is reluctant to follow his call, but Aeneas pushes the measure through.

9. Canonizes St. Catherine: From his papal throne, Aeneas looks down on the mortal remains of Catherine (clutching her symbol, the lily) and proclaims his fellow Sienese a saint. The well-dressed candle-holders in the foreground pose proudly.

10. Arrival in Ancona: Old and sick, the pope has to be carried everywhere on a litter because of rheumatic feet. He travels to Ancona, ready to board a ship to go fight the Turks. But only a handful of Venetian galleys arrive at the appointed time, the crusade peters out, and Aeneas, disheartened, dies. He wrote: "I do not deny my past. I have been a great wanderer, wandering away from the right path. But at least I know it, and hope the knowledge has not come too late."

Circle around a second time to appreciate the library's intricately decorated, illuminated music scores and a statue (a Roman

copy of a Greek original) of the Three Graces, who almost seem to dance to the beat. The oddly huge sheepskin sheets of music are from the days before individual hymnals—they had to be big so that many singers could read the music at the same time from a distance. If the musical notation looks off, that's because 15th-century Italians used a sliding C clef, not the fixed C and G clefs musicians know today. This clef marked middle C, and the melodies could be chanted in relation to it. Appreciate the fine painted decorations on the music—the gold-leaf highlights, the blue tones from newly discovered (and quite expensive) cobalt, and the miniature figures. All of this exquisite detail was lovingly crafted by Benedictine monks for the glory of God. Find your favorite—I like the blue, totally wild god of wind with the big hair (in the fourth case).

• *Exit the Duomo and make a U-turn to the left, walking alongside the church to Piazza Jacopo della Quercia.*

The Unfinished Church

The nave of the Duomo was supposed to be where the piazza is today. Worshippers would have entered the church from the far end

of the piazza through the unfinished wall. (Look way up at the highest part of the wall. That's the viewpoint accessible from inside the Duomo Museum.) Some of the nave's green-and-white-striped columns were built, but are now filled in with a brick wall. White stones in the pavement mark where a row of pillars would have been. Look through the unfinished entrance facade, note blue sky where the stained-glass windows would have been, and ponder the struggles, triumphs, and failures of the human spirit.

SIENA DUOMO MUSEUM TOUR

Museo dell'Opera del Duomo

Siena's most enjoyable museum was built to house the cathedral's art. Stand eye-to-eye with the saints and angels who once languished unknown in the church's upper reaches (where copies are found today). The museum's centerpiece—an altarpiece by Duccio—once stood in the center of the church. And the museum's high point is one of the loftiest in town, offering expansive views of the church and the city.

Orientation

Cost: €6, also covered by Opa Si combo-ticket, buy tickets near Duomo Museum entry.

Hours: Daily March-Oct 10:30-19:00, Nov-Feb 10:30-17:30, last entry 30 minutes before closing; tel. 0577-286-300, www .operaduomo.siena.it.

Getting There: It's next to the Duomo, in the skeleton of the unfinished part of the church on the Il Campo side; look for the white banner.

Audioguides: You can rent an audio/videoguide on a tablet computer for €4 (€6/2 people). You can pay more for one that also covers the Duomo and other sights, but you have to pick it up and drop it off inside the cathedral (for details, see page 361).

Photography: Not allowed except from the viewpoint.

Length of This Tour: Allow one hour.

Starring: Duccio, the Virgin Mary, and the Tuscan view.

The Tour Begins

Ground Floor

The ground floor houses the church's original statues, mainly from the facade and exterior. After descending a few steps, turn your back on the hall of statues and wrought-iron gate.

• *You're now face-to-face with...*

Donatello's *Madonna and Child*

In this round, carved relief, a slender and tender Mary gazes down at her chubby-cheeked baby. The thick folds of her headdress stream down around her smooth face. Her sad eyes say that she knows the eventual fate of her son. Donatello creates the illusion of Mary's three-dimensional "lap" using only a few inches of depth cut into the creamy-rose stone. Move to the far right and look at Mary's face from an angle (try not to notice impish Jesus); think of the challenge involved in carving the illusion of such depth.

• *On the opposite side of the room is...*

Duccio's Stained-Glass Window

Until recently, this splendid original window was located above and behind the Duomo's altar. Now the church has a copy, and art lovers can enjoy a close-up look at this masterpiece. The rose window—20 feet across, made in 1288—is dedicated (like the church and the city itself) to the Virgin Mary. In the window's bottom panel, Mary (in blue) lies stretched across a red coffin while a crowd of mourners looks on. Miraculously, Mary was spared the pain of death (the Assumption, central panel); winged angels carry her up in a holy bubble to heaven (top panel), where Christ sets her on a throne beside him and crowns her.

The work was designed by Siena's most famous artist, Duccio di Buoninsegna (c. 1255-1319). Duccio combined elements from rigid Byzantine icons (Mary's almond-shaped bubble, called a *mandorla,* and the full-frontal saints that flank her) with a budding sense of 3-D realism (the throne turned at a three-quarter angle to simulate depth, with angels behind). Also notice how the angels in the central panel spread their wings out beyond the border of the window frame.

The Sienese army defeated Florence in the bloody battle of Montaperti, thanks, many believed, to the divine intervention of the Virgin. For the next 80 years of prosperity, Sienese artists cranked out countless Madonnas as a way of saying *grazie.* Bear in mind that the Duomo's main altar was originally dominated by Duccio's *Maestà,* a huge golden altarpiece of the Virgin in Majesty (which you'll see upstairs) that was bathed in the golden-blue light from this window.

• Lining this main room are...

Pisano's Statues

Giovanni Pisano spent a decade (c. 1285-1296) carving and orchestrating the decoration of the cathedral—saints, prophets, sibyls, animals, and the original she-wolf with Romulus and Remus. These life-size, robed saints stand in a relaxed *contrapposto*, with open mouths and expressive gestures. Their heads jut out—Pisano's way of making them more visible from below. Some turn and seem to converse with their neighbors, especially evident with Moses *(Mosè)* and the sister who raised him like a mother, Miriam (*Maria di Mosè*, on the left side of the room). The copies of these two stand on the right side of the church, where they appear to interact.

Down a few steps in Rooms 11 and 12 are the two lions that once looked down from the church's main entrance, and Pisano's 12 apostles who originally lined the nave. (See old photos on the wall.) Tastes changed over the centuries, and the apostles were later moved up to the roof, where they eroded. Pisano's relaxed realism and expressive gestures were a major influence on later Florentine sculptors such as Donatello.

• Retrace your steps and go up to the...

First Floor

• Head to the left, through a glass door into the darkened Room 6, for a private audience with Duccio's Madonna.

Duccio—*Maestà* and Passion Panels, 1311

The panels in this room were once part of the Duomo's main altarpiece. Grab a seat and study one of the great pieces of medieval art. Although the former altarpiece was disassembled (and the frame was lost), most of the pieces are displayed here, with the front side (*Maestà*, with Mary and saints; pronounced my-STAH) at one end of the room and the back side (26 Passion panels) at the other.

Imagine these separate panels pieced together, set into their original gold, prickly, 15-by-15-foot wood frame and placed on the main altar in the Duomo. For two centuries it gave the congregation something to look at while the priests turned their backs at Communion time. The Christ Child stared back.

Maestà (Enthroned Virgin)

At the center of the front side sit the Virgin and Child, surrounded by angels and saints. Mary is a melancholy queen on an inlaid-marble throne. Young angels lean their elbows on the back of the throne and sigh. We see the throne head-on, unnaturally splayed open (a Byzantine style popular at the time in Siena). Mary is massive, twice the size of the saints around her, and she clearly stands

SIENA DUOMO MUSEUM

out from the golden background. Unlike traditional full-frontal Byzantine icons, she turns slightly sideways to touch her baby, who does not bless us.

The city of Siena is dedicated to this Lady, who backed the Sienese against Florence in the bloody battle of Montaperti in 1260. Here, she's triumphant, visited by Siena's four patron saints (kneeling in front), John the Baptist and other saints (the first choir row), more angels in a row (soprano section), and, chiming in from up in the balcony, James the Great and the 12 apostles.

The painting was revolutionary for the time in its sheer size and opulence, and in Duccio's budding realism, which broke standard conventions. Duccio, at the height of his powers, used every innovative arrow in his quiver. He replaced the standard gold-leaf background (symbolizing heaven) with a gold, intricately patterned curtain draped over the throne. Mary's blue robe opens to reveal her body, and the curve of her knee suggests real anatomy beneath the robe. Baby Jesus wears a delicately transparent garment. Their faces are modeled with light—a patchwork of bright flesh and shadowy valleys, as if lit from the left (a technique he likely learned from his contemporary Giotto during a visit to Florence).

Along the base of Mary's throne is an inscription (*"Mater sancta dei..."* or "Holy Mother of God...") asking Mary to bring peace to Siena *(Senis)* and long life to Duccio *(Ducio)*—quite a tribute in a time when painters were usually treated as anonymous craftsmen.

• *Look on the opposite wall to find scenes from...*

The Passion of Christ

The flip side of the altarpiece featured 26 smaller panels—the medieval equivalent of book pages—showing colorful scenes from the Passion of Christ.

The panels showcase the budding Tuscan style that united realism and storytelling. It doesn't take a Bible scholar to "read" these panels, left to right. Christ on a donkey (lower left) makes his triumphal entry into the city gate of Jerusalem (or is it Siena?). Next, he washes his disciples' feet in a realistic, three-dimensional room. But Duccio hasn't fully mastered perspective—in the Last Supper, we see Christ eye-to-eye, but view the table from above. Christ is arrested in Gethsemane, and so on, until the climactic Crucifixion. The Crucifixion is given the standard gold background, but the cross is set in a real-world location: on a terraced hillside, amid the crowd. Jesus' followers express human emotion rarely seen in earlier art.

The crowd scenes in the Passion panels aren't arranged in neat choir rows, but in more natural-looking groups. Duccio sets figures in motion, with individual faces expressing sorrow, anger, and agitation. Duccio's human realism would be taken to the next level by his Florentine counterpart Giotto, often called the proto-Renaissance painter.

Duccio and assistants (possibly including Simone Martini) spent three years on this massive altarpiece. It was a triumph, and at its dedication the satisfied Sienese marched it around the Campo and into the church in a public procession.

But by 1506, at the height of the Renaissance, Duccio's medieval altarpiece looked musty and old-fashioned, and was moved to a side altar. In 1771 it was disassembled and stored in the church offices (now the Duomo Museum). Today, scholars debate how to reassemble it accurately, and hail it as a quantum leap in the evolution of art.

Room 9, to the left and behind the *Maestà*, contains wooden models of the Duomo's inlaid-marble floor and close-ups of the individual floor panels for easier inspection.

• *Return to the stairs and continue up. Take a right at the first landing. At the landing just before the top floor, turn right and walk past the rooms, going through the small doorway to the stairwell. Climb down the steps and then up about 60 claustrophobic spiral stairs to the first viewpoint. You can continue up another similar spiral staircase to reach the very top.*

Panorama dal Facciatone

Standing on the wall from this high point in the city, you're rewarded with a stunning view of Siena...and an interesting perspective.

Look toward the Duomo and remember this: To outdo Florence, Siena had planned to enlarge this cathedral by turning it into a transept and constructing an enormous nave (see sidebar on page 363). You're standing on top of what would have been the new entrance facade (see map on page 362). Columns would have stood where you see the rows of white stones in the pavement below. Had the church been completed, you'd be looking straight down the nave toward the altar.

CIVIC MUSEUM TOUR

Museo Civico

Siena's City Hall (Palazzo Pubblico), still the seat of city government, symbolizes a republic independent from the pope and the Holy Roman Emperor. It also represents a rising secular society, one that appeared first in Tuscany and then spread throughout Europe in the Renaissance. City Hall also has a fine and manageable museum that displays a good sampling of Sienese art. Stroll through this civic center and let its fine day-in-the-life frescoes take you back to a time when this proud town understandably considered itself the vanguard of Western civilization.

Orientation

Cost: €8, €13 combo-ticket with tower (must be purchased at the tower).

Hours: Daily mid-March-Oct 10:00-19:00, Nov-mid-March 10:00-18:00, last entry 45 minutes before closing, tel. 0577-292-615, www.comune.siena.it.

Getting There: As the focus of the main square, it's hard to miss.

Length of This Tour: Allow one hour.

Photography: Not allowed.

Starring: Frescoes by Martini and Lorenzetti's *Effects of Good and Bad Government.*

The Tour Begins

• *Climb two flights of stairs (elevator on request—ask at ticket desk), pass through the gift shop, and enter the...*

CIVIC MUSEUM

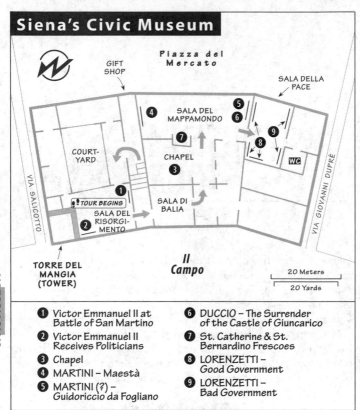

Siena's Civic Museum

GIFT SHOP

Piazza del Mercato

SALA DELLA PACE

4 SALA DEL MAPPAMONDO

5
6

COURT-YARD

7

8 **9**

CHAPEL

3

WC

VIA GIOVANNI DUPRÈ

VIA SALICOTTO

1 TOUR BEGINS

SALA DEL RISORGI-MENTO **2**

SALA DI BALIA

TORRE DEL MANGIA (TOWER)

Il Campo

20 Meters
20 Yards

1 Victor Emmanuel II at Battle of San Martino	**6** DUCCIO – The Surrender of the Castle of Giuncarico
2 Victor Emmanuel II Receives Politicians	**7** St. Catherine & St. Bernardino Frescoes
3 Chapel	**8** LORENZETTI – Good Government
4 MARTINI – Maestà	**9** LORENZETTI – Bad Government
5 MARTINI (?) – Guidoriccio da Fogliano	

Sala del Risorgimento (Hall of Italian Unification)

This hall has dramatic scenes of the 19th-century unification of Italy (surrounded by statues that don't seem to care). In the paintings, see Victor Emmanuel II (left wall as you enter, with beard and pointy moustache), king of a small northern Italian province. His status as the only Italian-blooded provincial king made him a natural to become the first king of a united Italy. Here we see him on horseback at the Battle of San Martino (1859) while leading a united Italian nation against its Austrian oppressors. Beneath that, you'll see the coat he's wearing in the painting. Next (clockwise above the windows), the king's red-shirted troops cheer as he shakes hands with the dashing general Giuseppe Garibaldi. There was a concern that Garibaldi, the charismatic revolutionary who had won the south, might not submit to the king. In this scene, even as the king's white horse seems to honor Garibaldi, the revolutionary famously says, "I obey." Victorious, the king receives politicians (next painting), who bow and present the election results that made Italy united and democratic, with Victor Emmanuel II as a symbolic head. When he died in 1878 (see his funeral procession passing through Rome's Pantheon portico, filled with real portraits, on the far wall), Italy was well on the way to modern nationhood. The mythological grandeur on the ceiling seems designed to legitimize the Italian Republic, a latecomer to the European family of nations.

• *Pass through the hallway to the left, and walk through the Sala di Balia. In the next room, turn left to find the chapel where the city's governors and bureaucrats prayed. Continue into the large...*

Sala del Mappamondo (Hall of the World Map)

This room, where the Grand Council met, pumped up governors and citizens alike with its images of military victories and the blessings of Mary. On opposite ends of the room, you'll find two large frescoes. The beautiful *Maestà* (*Enthroned Virgin*, 1315), by Siena's great Simone Martini (c. 1280-1344), was the secular counterpart to Duccio's *Maestà* (then in the Duomo, now in the Duomo Museum). Mary sits on a throne under a red silk canopy, a model to Siena's city council of what a just ruler should be. Siena's black-and-white coat of arms is woven into both the canopy and the picture frame. Mary is surrounded by saints and angels, clearly echoing the *Maestà* of Simone's teacher, Duccio.

But this is a groundbreaking work. It's Siena's first fresco showing a Madonna not in a faraway, gold-leaf heaven, but under the blue sky of the real world that we inhabit. As Mary delicately holds Baby Jesus, her expressive face anticipates the sacrifice of her son. A scraggly John the Baptist connects viewers with the scene.

The canopy creates a 3-D stage, with saints in front of, behind, and underneath it. Some saints' faces are actually blocked by the support poles. These saints are not a generic conga-line of Byzantine icons, but a milling crowd of 30 individuals with expressive faces. Some look straight out, some are in profile, and some turn at that difficult-to-draw three-quarter angle, grabbing onto the canopy poles. And the Virgin's brooch is painted so well that it almost looks...uh, real.

With unbeatable Florence to its north, Siena expanded south. Facing the *Maestà* is the famous *Equestrian Portrait of Guidoriccio da Fogliano* (1330; long attributed to Simone Martini, but more recently art historians have debated its authorship). The year is MCCCXXVIII (1328), and Siena's renowned mercenary commander Guidoriccio da Fogliano rides across a barren landscape and surveys the imposing castle that his armies have just conquered. He has just successfully finished a six-month-long siege—see his camp on the right. This is one of Europe's first secular portraits. (Guido and his horse have the same tailor.)

On the same wall, just below the horse and rider, *The Surrender of the Castle of Giuncarico*, by Duccio (1314), shows a man in green about to hand over his sword to a representative of the Sienese republic (not pictured—the scene was obliterated when it was covered by a later fresco). In the background is the man's castle and village on a rocky outcrop. Duccio's *Surrender* apparently inspired the 3-D landscape of *Guidoriccio da Fogliano*.

Also in the room (among those painted between the arches) are frescoes of two saints with local connections, St. Catherine (see page 358) and St. Bernardino (1380-1444). Bernardino's charismatic sermons in Siena could hold a Campo crowd for several days. At sunset, he'd announce that he would begin speaking again at sunrise...and people would come back. He brought together sworn enemies to share a *bacio di pace*—kiss of peace.

• *Continue into the next room.*

Sala della Pace, a.k.a. Sala dei Nove (Hall of Peace/Hall of the Nine)

The Council of Nine, who ruled Siena from 1287 to 1355, met in this room. Looking down on the oligarchy during their meetings was a fascinating fresco series showing the *Effects of Good and Bad Government*, by Ambrogio Lorenzetti (1337-1340).

The short wall opposite the window features the *Allegory of Good Government*, which celebrates the Sienese social system: "Siena," the stately, bearded man on the throne, is flanked by the six virtues. The central virtue, Peace (Pax), lounges on a pile of discarded armor. Justice (in red on the left) is punishing and forgiving under the figure of wisdom. Justice holds a scale, with angels on either side, to execute her judgments. Wrongdoers (lower right) are rounded up by the authorities. At the foot of the stage, prominent Sienese citizens file by. Concordia (below the figure of Justice) makes society just and equal with the wooden plane on her lap. And the symbolic foundation of it all is the she-wolf with Romulus and Remus, recalling a myth meant to connect Siena's

origins to the glory of ancient Rome (explained on page 350).

The allegory continues on the long wall with a well-preserved fresco depicting the effects of good government in town and country. Notice the whistle-while-you-work happiness of the utopian community ruled by the utopian government. The city and the countryside are exactly the same width (20 feet), an indication that they work together and need each other. Amid Siena's skyline (Duomo at upper left), young people dance to the beat of a tambourine, workers repair roofs, a professor teaches, and the conversation flows. The blessings of a good government extend even to the countryside, which feels safe and prosperous. Bringing stability and safety to the land outside the city walls was a big accomplishment in the 14th century. The fields are tilled, the Via Francigena is busy, and angels fly overhead.

Study this intimate and rare look at medieval commerce, and take in the details of the 14th-century cityscape. Notice, for instance, how today's exposed brick work, so "typical" of Siena, had then been stuccoed over and brightly painted. Notice also the pointy skyline, showing the city's proud towers before they were lopped off by the Florentines. The toppled towers ended up providing building material for the huge Fortezza—a repurposing that wasn't just practical but psychological, serving as a reminder of the Florentine Medici's success in keeping the Sienese down.

On the opposite long wall, in the *Allegory of Bad Government*

(badly damaged), a horned, fanged, wine-drinking devil sets the vices loose ("Avarice," "Vainglory"). Rather than dancing in the streets, people are being arrested. Arsonists torch homes and fields, soldiers rape and pillage, crime is rampant, fields are barren, and frescoes get damaged. The only person still working is making weapons. Justice slumps at the devil's feet, bound, too depressed to look up. The countryside is dark and devastated, and no one leaves the city unarmed. The message: Without justice, there can be no prosperity.

• *An enlightened city government also provides convenient toilets for the public—which you'll find just off this room. On your way out, just before the Sala del Risorgimento, find the lo-o-o-o-ong stairs and head up for...*

A Grand View

Cap your visit by climbing up to the loggia for a sweeping view of the city and its surroundings. (For a less impressive version of this view, you could skip the stairs and simply peek behind the curtains in the Sala della Pace.)

SIENA SLEEPING, EATING & CONNECTIONS

Sleeping in Siena

Finding a room in Siena is tough during Easter (March 31 in 2013) or the Palio (July 2 and Aug 16). Many hotels won't take reservations until the end of May for the Palio, and even then they might require a four-night stay. While day-tripping tour groups turn the town into a Gothic amusement park in midsummer, Siena is basically yours in the evenings and off-season.

Part of Siena's charm is its lively, festive character—this means that all hotels can be plagued with noise, even (and sometimes especially) the hotels in the pedestrian-only zone. If tranquility is important for your sanity, ask for a room that's off the street, or consider staying at one of the recommended places outside the center.

Fancy Sleeps, Southwest of Il Campo

These well-run places are a 10-minute walk from Il Campo.

$$$ Pensione Palazzo Ravizza is elegant and friendly, with 38 rooms and an aristocratic feel—fitting, as it was once the luxurious residence of a noble. Guests enjoy a peaceful garden set on a dramatic bluff, along with a Steinway in the upper lounge (Sb-€170, small loft Db-€130, standard Db-€170, superior Db-€200, Tb-€230, family suites-€300, rates can vary, see website for room differences, rooms in back overlook countryside, air-con, elevator, free Wi-Fi, Via Piano dei Mantellini 34, tel. 0577-280-462, fax 0577-221-597, www.palazzoravizza.com, bureau@palazzoravizza .it, Ariol). As parking is free and the hotel is easily walkable from the center, this is a particularly good value for drivers.

$$$ Hotel Duomo has 20 spacious but slightly dated rooms, a picnic-friendly roof terrace, and a bizarre floor plan (Sb-€105,

Sleep Code

(€1 = about $1.40, country code: 39)
S = Single, **D** = Double/Twin, **T** = Triple, **Q** = Quad, **b** = bathroom,
s = shower only.

Breakfast is included unless otherwise noted. If your hotel doesn't provide breakfast, eat at a bar on Il Campo or near your hotel. Credit cards are generally accepted, but I note in the listings if they aren't. (If not, there are ATMs all over town.) Hotel staff generally speak English unless noted otherwise. Siena levies a hotel tax of €2 per person, per night, which must be paid in cash (not included in the rates I've quoted).

To help you easily sort through these listings, I've divided the accommodations into three categories based on the price for a standard double room with bath during high season:

  $$$ Higher Priced—Most rooms €130 or more.
   $$ Moderately Priced—Most rooms between €90-130.
    $ Lower Priced—Most rooms €90 or less.

Prices can change without notice; verify the hotel's current rates online or by email.

Db-€130, Db suite-€180, Tb-€180, Qb-€230, elevator with some stairs, air-con, free Wi-Fi, discounted parking-€20/day; follow Via di Città, which becomes Via di Stalloreggi, to #38; tel. 0577-289-088, fax 0577-43-043, www.hotelduomo.it, booking@hotelduomo.it, Alessandro). If you're arriving by train, take a taxi (€10) or ride bus #3 to the Porta Tufi stop, just a few minutes' walk from the hotel; you can also arrange to have Alessandro take you to/from the train station or airport (with this book: train station-€10, Florence's Vespucci Airport-€105, Pisa's Galilei Airport-€165; he'll also take you to nearby hill towns, e.g. Florence-€105 and Pisa-€165). If you're driving, go to Porta San Marco, turn right, and follow signs to the hotel—drop your bags, then park in the nearby Il Campo lot near Porta Tufi.

Simple Places near Il Campo

Most of these listings are forgettable but inexpensive, and just a horse wreck away from one of Italy's most wonderful civic spaces.

$$ Piccolo Hotel Etruria, with 20 straightforward rooms, is overpriced for what it is—though well-located and restful (S-€50, Sb-€60, Db-€90-110, Tb-€120-138, Qb-€145-166, higher rates are for peak-of-peak times, optional breakfast-€6, air-con June-Oct only, next to recommended Albergo Tre Donzelle at Via delle Donzelle 1-3, tel. 0577-288-088, fax 0577-288-461,

SIENA SLEEPING

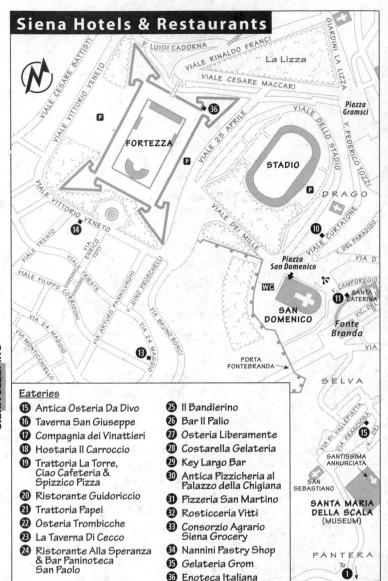

Siena Hotels & Restaurants

FORTEZZA

La Lizza

STADIO

Piazza Gramsci

DRAGO

Piazza San Domenico

WC

SAN DOMENICO

Fonte Branda

PORTA FONTEBRANDA

SELVA

SANTISSIMA ANNUNCIATA

SAN SEBASTIANO

SANTA MARIA DELLA SCALA (MUSEUM)

PANTERA

Eateries
15 Antica Osteria Da Divo
16 Taverna San Giuseppe
17 Compagnia dei Vinattieri
18 Hostaria Il Carroccio
19 Trattoria La Torre, Ciao Cafeteria & Spizzico Pizza
20 Ristorante Guidoriccio
21 Trattoria Papei
22 Osteria Trombicche
23 La Taverna Di Cecco
24 Ristorante Alla Speranza & Bar Paninoteca San Paolo
25 Il Bandierino
26 Bar Il Palio
27 Osteria Liberamente
28 Costarella Gelateria
29 Key Largo Bar
30 Antica Pizzicheria al Palazzo della Chigiana
31 Pizzeria San Martino
32 Rosticceria Vitti
33 Consorzio Agrario Siena Grocery
34 Nannini Pastry Shop
35 Gelateria Grom
36 Enoteca Italiana

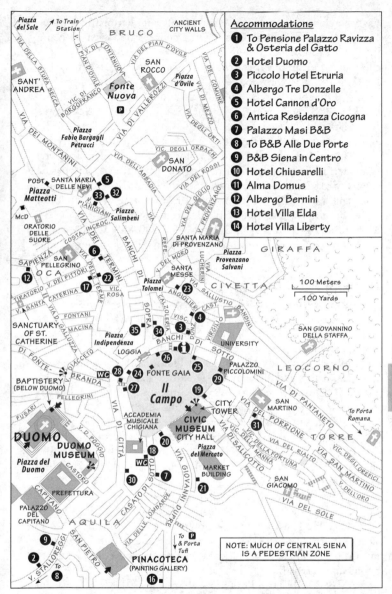

Accommodations

1. To Pensione Palazzo Ravizza & Osteria del Gatto
2. Hotel Duomo
3. Piccolo Hotel Etruria
4. Albergo Tre Donzelle
5. Hotel Cannon d'Oro
6. Antica Residenza Cicogna
7. Palazzo Masi B&B
8. To B&B Alle Due Porte
9. B&B Siena in Centro
10. Hotel Chiusarelli
11. Alma Domus
12. Albergo Bernini
13. Hotel Villa Elda
14. Hotel Villa Liberty

100 Meters

100 Yards

NOTE: MUCH OF CENTRAL SIENA IS A PEDESTRIAN ZONE

SIENA SLEEPING

www.hoteletruria.com, info@hoteletruria.com, Fattorini family).

$ Albergo Tre Donzelle is a fine budget value with 20 plain, well-worn rooms. Although the showers have seen better days, these may be the cheapest rooms in the center. Don't hang out here...think of Il Campo, a block away, as your terrace (S-€38, D-€49, Db-€60, T-€70, Tb-€85, no rooms available for Palio, breakfast-€5, free Wi-Fi; with your back to the tower, head away from Il Campo toward 2 o'clock to Via delle Donzelle 5; tel. 0577-280-358, www.tredonzelle.com, info@tredonzelle.com, Maurizio).

$ Hotel Cannon d'Oro, a few blocks up Via Banchi di Sopra, is a labyrinthine slumbermill renting 30 institutional, overpriced rooms (Sb-€71, Db-€90, Tb-€115, Qb-€136, these discounted prices good with this book through 2013, fans, free Wi-Fi in lobby and some rooms, a couple of blocks from the bus hub at Via dei Montanini 28, tel. 0577-44-321, fax 0577-280-868, www.cannon doro.com, info@cannondoro.com; Maurizio, Tommaso, and Rodrigo).

B&Bs in the Old Center

$$ Antica Residenza Cicogna is a seven-room guesthouse with a homey elegance and an ideal location. It's warmly run by the young and charming Elisa and her dad Fabio, who set out biscotti, *vin santo*, and tea all day for their guests. With artfully frescoed walls and ceilings, this is remarkably genteel for the price (Db-€95, suite Db-€120, third bed-€15, air-con, free Internet access and Wi-Fi, Via dei Termini 76, tel. 0577-285-613, mobile 347-007-2888, www .anticaresidenzacicogna.it, info@anticaresidenzacicogna.it).

$$ Palazzo Masi B&B, run by Alizzardo and Daniela, is just below Il Campo. They rent six pleasant, spacious, antique-furnished rooms with shared common areas on the second and third floors of an old building. While a bit pricey, the fine location and warm welcome are appreciated (D-€80, Db-€120 if you book direct, discounts for 4 or more nights, cash only, breakfast-€8, free Wi-Fi, discounted parking at nearby Il Campo lot-€25/24 hours; from City Hall, walk 50 yards down Via del Casato di Sotto to #29; mobile 349-600-9155, www.palazzomasi.com, info@palazzo masi.it). The place is sometimes unstaffed, so it's important to phone upon arrival.

$ B&B Alle Due Porte is a charming little establishment renting four big rooms with sweet furniture under big medieval beams. The shared breakfast room is delightful. The manager, Egisto, is a phone call and five-minute scooter ride away (Db-€85, windowless Db with small bed-€65, Tb-€110, free Wi-Fi, Via di Stalloreggi 51, tel. 0577-287-670, mobile 368-352-3530, www.siena tur.it, soldatini@interfree.it).

$ B&B Siena in Centro is a clearinghouse managing five good and centrally located private apartments. Their handy office functions as a reception renting out a total of about 20 rooms; stop by here to pick up your key and be escorted to your apartment. The rooms are generally spacious, quiet, and comfortable, but with no air-conditioning or Wi-Fi. Their website lets you visualize your options (Sb-€45-60, Db-€70-90, Tb-€90-120, reception open 9:00-13:30 & 15:00-19:00, later in high season, other times by phone request, OK to leave bags at reception, Via di Stalloreggi 14, tel. 0577-43041, mobile 331-281-4137 or 347-465-9753, www.bbsienaincentro.com, info@bbsienaincentro.com; Patrizia, Paolo, Gioia, and Michela).

Near San Domenico Church

These hotels are within a 10-minute walk northwest of Il Campo. Note that Albergo Bernini and Alma Domus offer fine panoramas of the old town for reasonable prices.

$$$ Hotel Chiusarelli, with 48 classy rooms in a beautiful Neoclassical villa, has a handy location but is on a very busy street. Expect traffic noise at night—ask for a quieter room in the back (can be guaranteed with reservation). The bells of San Domenico are your 7:00 wake-up call (Sb-€108, Db-€155, Tb-€190, ask for Rick Steves discount when you book, air-con, free Wi-Fi with this book, across from San Domenico at Viale Curtatone 15, tel. 0577-280-562, fax 0577-271-177, www.chiusarelli.com, info@chiusarelli.com).

$ Alma Domus is a church-run hotel renting 43 spartan rooms with quaint balconies, some fantastic views (ask for a room *con vista*), stately public rooms, and a pleasant atmosphere. While the setting is tranquil, thin doors, echoey halls, and nearby church bells will make you glad you brought earplugs. The 10:00 checkout time is strict, but they will store your luggage in their secure courtyard (Sb-€48, Db-€80, Tb-€105, €5 extra for best views on fourth floor, central air-con, elevator, pay Internet access and Wi-Fi; from San Domenico, walk downhill toward the view with the church on your right, turn left down Via Camporegio, make a U-turn down the brick steps to Via Camporegio 37; tel. 0577-44-177, fax 0577-47-601, www.hotelalmadomus.it, info@hotelalmadomus.it, Louis).

$ Albergo Bernini makes you part of a Sienese family in a modest, clean home with 10 traditional rooms. Giovanni, charming wife Daniela, and their three daughters welcome you to their spectacular view terrace for breakfast and picnic lunches and dinners (S-€55, D-€65, Sb or small Db with view-€78, Db-€85, less in winter, optional breakfast-€3.50/small or €7.50/big, cash only, free Wi-Fi, on the main Il Campo-San Domenico drag at Via della

Sapienza 15, tel. & fax 0577-289-047, www.albergobernini.com, hbernin@tin.it).

Farther from the Center

These options, a 10- to 20-minute walk from the center, are great for drivers.

Near Porta Romana City Gate

These two fine spots are about 200 yards outside the Porta Romana (see locations on the map on page 341). To get to downtown Siena from here, catch minibus line A uphill to Piazza al Mercato, just behind Il Campo (€1.10). To reach the bus and train stations, take bus #2 (which becomes #17 at Piazza del Sale; when arriving, catch #17 from the station). If driving, from the freeway, take the Siena Sud exit, continue in direction Romana, then at the first light turn left, following *Pta Romana/Centro* signs for about half a mile until you see the big city gate.

$$$ Hotel Santa Caterina is a three-star, 18th-century place renting 22 comfy rooms. It's professionally run with real attention to quality. While it's on a big city street, it has a delightful garden terrace with views over the countryside (Sb-€125, four small Db-€125, Db-€165, split-level Tb or Qb-€215, prices promised with this book through 2013, can be cheaper in low season, garden side is quieter, air-con, fridge in room, elevator, free Wi-Fi, parking-€15/day—request when you reserve, Via E.S. Piccolomini 7, tel. 0577-221-105, fax 0577-271-087, www.hscsiena.it, info@hscsiena.it, Lorenza and her crew).

$$ Hotel Porta Romana is at the edge of town, off a busy road. Some of its 15 rooms face the open countryside (request one of these), and breakfast is served in the garden (Sb-€90, Db-€110, extra person-€20, 10 percent Rick Steves discount if you book direct and pay cash, air-con in some rooms, free Internet access, free Wi-Fi with this book, free parking, inviting sun terrace, Via E.S. Piccolomini 35, tel. 0577-42299, fax 0577-232-905, www.hotelportaromana.com, info@hotelportaromana.com; Marco and Evelia).

In the Posh Neighborhood South of the Fortress

These two places are in a villa-studded residential neighborhood across a gully from San Domenico Church. They're about 5-10 minutes farther than the listings under "Near San Domenico Church," earlier, but the extra walking gets you to a swankier address.

$$$ Hotel Villa Elda rents 11 bright and light rooms in a recently renovated villa. It's classy, stately, pricey, and run with a feminine charm (Db-€140-170, about €20 more for view, extra person-€30, air-con, free Wi-Fi, garden and view terrace, Viale

SIENA SLEEPING

Ventiquattro Maggio 10, tel. 0577-247-927, www.villaeldasiena.it, info@villaeldasiena.it).

$$$ Hotel Villa Liberty, across a busy street from the fortress, is a former private mansion. It has 17 big, bright, comfortable rooms and some road noise (Sb-€80, Db-€150, Tb-€180, €10 more for superior room, air-con, elevator, free Wi-Fi, bar, courtyard, free and easy street parking, facing fortress at Viale Vittorio Veneto 11, tel. 0577-44-966, fax 0577-44-770, www.villaliberty.it, info@villaliberty.it).

Just Inside Porta Ovile, at the North End of Town

$$ Hotel Minerva is your big, professional, plain, efficient option. It's the most impersonal of my listings, with zero personality but predictable comfort. While its 56 rooms are boring, they don't hide any unpleasant surprises. It works best for those with cars—parking is reasonable (€12/day), and it's only a 10-minute walk from the action (Sb-€76, Db-€122, Tb-€168, bigger suites available for more, air-con, elevator, free Internet access, pay Wi-Fi, Via Garibaldi 72, see map on page 341 for location, tel. 0577-284-474, fax 0577-43343, www.albergominerva.it, info@albergominerva.it).

Outside Siena

The following accommodations are set in the lush, peaceful countryside surrounding Siena, and are best for those traveling by car (see locations on the map on page 454).

$$$ Frances' Lodge Relais is a tranquil and delightfully managed farmhouse B&B a mile out of Siena. Each of its six rooms is bursting with character (all well-described on their website). Franca and Franco run this rustic-yet-elegant old place, which features a 19th-century orangery that's been made into a "better homes and palaces" living room, as well as a peaceful garden, eight acres of olive trees and vineyards, and great views of Siena and its countryside—even from the swimming pool (small Db-€170, Db-€190, Db suite-€220, Tb-€210-220, Tb suite-€280, Qb suite-€340, these prices promised to Rick Steves readers through 2013, possibly cheaper for longer stays, air-con-€10, free Internet access and Wi-Fi, free parking, Strada di Valdipugna 2, tel. & fax 0577-42379, mobile 337-671-608, www.franceslodge.it). To the center, it's a five-minute bus ride (€1.10, they'll call to arrange) plus a five-minute walk, or €10 by taxi. Consider having an al fresco dinner in the gazebo, complete with view (make your own picnic, or have your hosts assemble a very fancy one for €20/person).

$$$ Borgo Argenina has seven rooms in a well-maintained, pricey splurge of a B&B. Run by helpful Elena Nappa, it's 20 minutes north of Siena by car in the Chianti region (Db-€170, beautiful gardens, free Wi-Fi, tel. 0577-747-117, www.borgoargenina.it, info@borgoargenina.it).

$$ Il Canto del Sole is a restored 18th-century farmhouse turned family-friendly B&B located about six miles outside the Porta Romana city gate. Run by Laura, Luciano, and their son Marco, it features 10 bright and airy rooms and two apartments with original antique furnishings, a saltwater swimming pool, a game room, and bike rentals (Db-€120, Tb-€140, extra bed-€30, apartment-€180-220, air-con, free Wi-Fi, free parking, dinner cooked on request, Val di Villa Canina 1292, 53014 Loc. Cuna, tel. 0577-375-127, fax 0577-373-378, www.ilcantodelsole.com, info @ilcantodelsole.com).

Eating in Siena

Sienese restaurants are reasonable by Florentine and Venetian standards. You can enjoy ordering high on the menu here without going broke. For me, the best €5 you can spend in Siena is on a cocktail at Bar Il Palio, overlooking Il Campo. For pasta, a good option is *pici* (PEE-chee), a thick Sienese spaghetti that seems to be at the top of every menu.

Fine Dining in the Old Town

For only a few euros more, these four places deliver a more upscale ambience and generally better food than my later recommendations.

Antica Osteria Da Divo is *the* place for a dressy and atmospheric €45 meal. The kitchen is creative, the ambience is flowery and candlelit, some of the seating fills old Etruscan tombs, and the food is fresh, delicate, and top-notch. While the cuisine is flamboyant and almost over-the-top, Chef Pino and his wife Susanna serve up my favorite splurge dinner in town. Pino is a fanatic for fresh ingredients, enjoys giving traditional dishes his creative spin, and is understandably proud of his desserts. The wine is good, too—you can order it by the glass (€4-7) if you ask (€10-12 pastas, €20-26 *secondi*, €3 cover, Wed-Mon 12:00-14:30 & 19:00-22:30, closed Tue, reservations smart; facing Baptistery door, take the far right street and walk one long curving block to Via Franciosa 29; tel. 0577-284-381). Those dining here with this book can finish with a complimentary biscotti and *vin santo* or coffee (upon request).

Taverna San Giuseppe, a local favorite, offers modern Tuscan cuisine in a chic grotto atmosphere. While the vibe is high energy and casual, the food compares favorably with the slightly more upscale places listed here. The wine-and-cheese cellar in back is cut from an Etruscan tomb. Check the posters tacked around the entry for daily specials. Reserve or arrive early to get a table (€8-10 pastas, €15-20 *secondi,* Mon-Sat 12:00-14:30 & 19:00-22:00, closed Sun, air-con, 7-minute climb up street to the right of City Hall at Via Giovanni Dupre 132, tel. 0577-42-286, Matteo).

Compagnia dei Vinattieri serves modern Tuscan dishes with a creative twist. In this elegantly unpretentious space, you can enjoy a quiet and romantic meal under graceful brick arches. The menu is small and accessible, and the young staff will help you match your meal with the right wine. Marco, the owner, is happy to take you down to their marvelous wine cellar (€9-12 pastas, €16-18 *secondi,* leave this book on the table for a complimentary *aperitivo* or dessert drink, daily 12:30-15:00 & 19:30-23:00, near Via dei Pittori at Via delle Terme 79, tel. 0577-236-568).

Hostaria Il Carroccio, artsy and convivial, seats guests in a tight, sea-foam green dining room and serves elegantly presented, traditional "slow food" recipes with innovative flair at affordable prices (€8 pastas, €14-18 *secondi,* €30 tasting *menu*—minimum two people, cash only, reservations wise, Thu-Tue 12:30-15:00 & 19:30-22:00, closed Wed, Via del Casato di Sotto 32, tel. 0577-41-165, sweet Renata and Mauro).

Traditional and Rustic Places in the Old Town

Trattoria La Torre is a thriving, unfussy *casalinga* (home-cooking) eatery, popular for its homemade pasta, plates of which entice customers as they enter. The sound of its busy open kitchen adds to the conviviality. Ten tables are packed under one medieval brick arch. Service is brisk and casual, and despite its priceless position below the namesake tower, it feels more like a local hangout than a tourist trap. Study the menu in the window before entering; otherwise, the owner likes to just recite his long list of dishes (€7-8 pastas, €8-10 *secondi,* €2 cover, Fri-Wed 12:00-15:00 & 19:00-22:00, closed Thu, just steps below Il Campo at Via Salicotto 7, tel. 0577-287-548, Alberto Boccini).

Osteria del Gatto is a classic little hole-in-the-wall, thriving with townspeople and powered by a passion for serving good Sienese cuisine. Marco Coradeschi and his engaged staff cook and serve daily specials with attitude. As it's so small and popular, it can get loud (€8-9 pastas, €8-10 *secondi,* Mon-Fri 12:30-15:00 & 19:30-22:00, Sat 19:30-22:00 only, closed Sun, 5-minute walk away from the center at Via di San Marco 8, tel. 0577-287-133).

Ristorante Guidoriccio, just a few steps below Il Campo, feels warm and welcoming. You'll get smiling service from Ercole and Elisabetta. While mostly filled with tourists, the place has a charm—especially if you let gentle Ercole explore the menu with you and follow his suggestions (€9 pastas, €13-14 *secondi,* Mon-Sat 12:30-14:30 & 19:00-22:30, closed Sun, air-con, Via Giovanni Dupre 2, tel. 0577-44-350).

Trattoria Papei is a Sienese favorite, featuring a casual, rollicking family atmosphere and friendly servers dishing out generous portions of rib-stickin' Tuscan specialties and grilled meats. This big, sprawling place under tents in a parking lot is in all the guidebooks and often jammed—so call to reserve (€7 pastas, €8-12 *secondi*, daily 12:00-15:00 & 19:00-22:30, closed Mon June-Sept, on the market square directly behind City Hall at Piazza del Mercato 6, tel. 0577-280-894; for 50 years Signora Giuliana has ruled her kitchen, Amadeo and Eduardo speak English).

Osteria Trombicche takes you back to another age—cheap and small, with tight indoor seating and two tiny outdoor tables from which to watch the street scene. Bobby (who speaks English) and monolingual Davide serve fast, hearty food to a local crowd (€6.50 *ribollita*—bean-and-vegetable soup—in winter, €5 *panzanella*—bread salad with tomato and basil—in summer, €8-10 mixed-vegetable antipasto plates, hand-cut prosciutto, Mon-Sat 11:00-15:00 & 17:30-22:00, closed Sun, Via delle Terme 66, tel. 0577-288-089).

La Taverna Di Cecco is a simple, comfortable little eatery on an uncrowded back lane where earnest Luca and Gianni serve tasty salads and Sienese specialties made from fresh ingredients for a fair price (€8-12 pastas, €10-15 *secondi*, daily 12:00-16:00 & 19:00-24:00, Via Cecco Angiolieri 19, tel. 0577-288-518).

Places on Il Campo

If you choose to eat on perhaps the finest town square in Italy, you'll pay a premium, meet waiters who don't need to hustle, and get mediocre food. And yet I recommend it. The clamshell-shaped square is lined with venerable cafés, bars, restaurants, and pizzerias.

To experience Il Campo without paying for a full meal, consider having drinks or breakfast on the square. Some bars serve food. And if your hotel doesn't include breakfast or if you'd like something more memorable, Il Campo has plenty of options. A cappuccino and a *cornetto* (croissant) run about €5-6.

Dining and Drinks on the Square

Ristorante Alla Speranza has perhaps the best view in all of Italy. If you're looking to eat reasonably on Il Campo, this is your place (€8-10 pastas and pizzas, €13-15 *secondi*, €2 cover charge, daily 9:00-late, tel. 0577-280-190). It's smart to reserve the view table of your choice by phone—or simply stop by earlier in the day while you're sightseeing in the square.

Il Bandierino is another decent option with an angled view of City Hall (€8-12 salads, €11-12 pizzas, €13-15 pastas; no cover but a 20 percent service fee, daily 11:00-23:00, tel. 0577-282-217).

Nightlife in Siena

Evenings are a wonderful time to be out and about in Siena, after the tour groups have left for the day.

Join the evening *passeggiata* (peak strolling time is 19:00) along Via Banchi di Sopra with gelato in hand. I like **Gelateria Grom,** which serves "Gelato like it used to be." Its seasonal flavors and all-natural ingredients make it a popular stop for any Sienese in need of something cool and sweet to lick while strolling (a little pricier than the competition, daily 11:00-24:00, Banchi di Sopra 13).

A fun trend in Siena is the *aperitivo.* All over town, you'll find bars attracting an early evening crowd by serving a free buffet of food with the purchase of a drink. For many, this can be a light dinner for the cost of a drink. Or consider starting or ending a meal with a drink or dessert on Il Campo. For suggestions, see "Places on Il Campo."

Enoteca Italiana is a good wine bar in a cellar in the Fortezza, funded in part by the government to promote Italian wine production. They have 30 different bottles open on any given day, and they offer tastings at three different prices: €3, €4, and €6.50. To get there, enter the Fortezza via the bridge, cross the running track, and—after passing a tree—go left down a ramp (Mon-Sat 12:00-24:00, closed Sun, snacks served when the bar's pricey restaurant is between mealtimes, outside terrace, tel. 0577-228-832).

SIENA EATING

Bar Il Palio is the best bar on Il Campo for a pre- or post-dinner drink: It has straightforward prices, no cover, decent waiters, and a fantastic perspective out over the square.

Dynamic little **Osteria Liberamente** (on the square, not above it) has a trendy vibe and is popular with young people (fine wine by the glass, €7 cocktails with good tapas, Wed-Mon 8:00 until late, closed Tue, Pino).

Drinks or Snacks from Balconies Overlooking Il Campo

Three places have skinny balconies with benches overlooking the main square for their customers. Sipping a coffee or nibbling a pastry here while marveling at the Il Campo scene is one of my favorite things to do in Europe. And it's very cheap. Survey these three places from Il Campo (with your back to the tower, they are at 10 o'clock, high noon, and 3 o'clock, respectively).

The little **Costarella Gelateria,** on the corner of Via di Città and Costa dei Barbieri, has good drinks and light snacks, such as cute little €3.50 sandwiches, though the gelato tastes artificial (daily 8:00-late, Via di Città 33). While the restaurant is for regular service, you're welcome to take anything from the bar out to the simple benches (just walk through the "table service only" section upstairs) and eat with a grand view overlooking Il Campo.

Bar Paninoteca San Paolo has a youthful pub ambience and a row of stools lining a skinny balcony overlooking the square. It serves big €7 salads and 50 kinds of €4 sandwiches, hot and cold—not authentic Italian, but quick and filling (order and pay at the counter, food served daily 12:00-2:00 in the morning, on Vicolo di San Paolo, tel. 0577-226-622).

Key Largo Bar has two long, second-story benches in the corner offering a wonderful secret perch. Buy your drink or snack at the bar (no cover and no extra charge to sit on balcony), climb upstairs, and slide the ancient bar to open the door. Enjoy stretching out, and try to imagine how, during the Palio, three layers of spectators cram into this space—note the iron railing used to plaster the top row of sardines up against the wall. Suddenly you're picturing Palio ponies zipping wildly around the corner (€4 cocktails, daily 7:00-24:00, on the corner of Via Rinaldini). If you can't get a seat on the outdoor benches, skip the otherwise nondescript, youthful interior.

Eating Cheaply in the Center

Antica Pizzicheria al Palazzo della Chigiana (look for the sign reading *Pizzicheria de Miccoli*) may be the official name, but I bet locals just call it Antonio's. For most of his life, frenzied Antonio has carved salami and cheese for the neighborhood. Most of the day, a hungry line spills onto the street as people wait for their sandwiches—meat and cheese sold by weight—with a good €10 bottle of Chianti (Italian law dictates that he must sell you a bottle of wine—cheap and good—and lend you the glasses). Antonio and his boys offer a big cheese-and-meat plate (about €18 gets you 30 minutes of eating) and pull out a tiny tabletop in the corner so you can munch or sip while standing and watching the ham-hock-y scene. Or just grab a €4-5 sandwich. Even if you don't eat here, pop in to inhale the commotion or peruse Antonio's gifty traditional edibles (daily 8:00-20:00, Via di Città 95, tel. 0577-289-164).

Ciao Cafeteria, at the bottom of Il Campo, offers good-value, self-service lunches, but no ambience or views (hearty €5-7 meals, daily 12:00-15:00). The crowded **Spizzico,** a pizza counter in the front half of Ciao, serves huge €4-5 quarter-pizzas. For both places, the food and ambience recall a cut-rate truck stop—but on sunny days, people take the pizza out on Il Campo for a memorable picnic (daily 11:00-21:00, to left of City Tower as you face it).

Pizza: Spizzico (listed above) is worth considering only if you're standing on Il Campo, desperate for pizza, and unashamedly lazy. Budget eaters look for *pizza al taglio* shops, scattered throughout Siena, selling better pizza by the slice. One good bet, **San Martino,** a couple of blocks behind Il Campo, is a local-feeling spot with €2-3 slices and sandwiches (Mon-Sat 8:00-14:30 & 16:30-21:00, closed Sun, Via del Porrione 64).

Rosticcerie: For cheap take-out food, look for a *rosticceria* (explained on page 31). One affordable, central option that feels at least partly untouristed is **Rosticceria Vitti,** near Piazza Gramsci's bus terminus (point to what you want in the glass case, figure €5 for a light meal, Sun-Fri 9:00-21:30, closed Sat, Via Montanini 14/16, tel. 0577-289-291).

Supermarket: You won't find many cheap grocery shops in the touristy center of Siena. But one handy (if fancy) option is **Consorzio Agrario Siena.** Ask them to make you up a *panino.* As this place specializes in artisanal Tuscan foods, both the quality and prices are high (Mon-Sat 8:00-19:30, sometimes open Sun, a block off Piazza Matteotti, toward Il Campo at Via Pianigiani 5).

Desserts and Treats

For a special dessert or a sweet treat any time of day, stop by **Nannini**—considered the top-end pastry shop and *the* place to go for quality local specialties (Mon-Sat 7:30-21:00, Sun 8:00-21:00, Banchi di Sopra 24). Across the street is the wonderful **Gelateria Grom** (see "Nightlife in Siena" sidebar)—but you have my permission to sample every gelateria in town to pick your own favorite.

Siena Connections

Siena has sparse train connections but is a great hub for buses to the hill towns, though frequency drops on Sundays and holidays. For most, Florence is the gateway to Siena. Even if you are a railpass-user, connect these two cities by bus—it's faster than the train, and Siena's bus station is more convenient and central than its train station. (Note: Many travelers mistake old signs for a former bus company, Tra-In, as signs for trains or the train station. Those buses have nothing to do with the railway.)

By Train

Siena's train station is at the edge of town. For details on getting between the town center and the station, see page 342.

From Siena by Train to: Florence (direct trains hourly, 1.5-2 hours, €7.70; bus is better), **Pisa** (2/hour, 1.75 hours, change at Empoli, €8.90), **Assisi** (8/day, 4-5 hours, most involve 2 changes, €11.05, bus is faster), **Rome** (1-2/hour, 3-3.5 hours, change in Florence or Chiusi, €24-53), **Orvieto** (12/day, 2-2.5 hours, change in Chiusi, €14.10). For more information, visit www.trenitalia .com.

By Bus

The main bus companies are **Tiemme** (part of a larger company called Siena Mobilità and formerly called Tra-In; mostly handles buses to regional destinations, tel. 0577-204-246, www.siena mobilita.it) and **Sena** (for long-distance connections, tel. 0577-208-282, www.sena.it). On schedules, the fastest buses are marked *rapida*. I'd stick with these. Most buses depart Siena from Piazza Gramsci; others leave from the train station (confirm when you buy your ticket).

Tiemme/Siena Mobilità Buses go to: Florence (about 2/hour, 1.25-hour *rapida/via superstrada* buses are faster than the train, avoid the 2-hour *ordinaria* buses unless you have time to enjoy the beautiful scenery en route, €7.20; to avoid line at bus-ticket office, tickets also available at tobacco shops/*tabacchi*; generally leaves from Piazza Gramsci as well as train station), **San Gimignano** (Mon-Fri 10/day, Sat 7/day, none direct on Sun, 1.25 hours, €6, leaves from Piazza Gramsci), **Volterra** (4/day Mon-Sat, no buses on Sun, 2 hours, change in Colle Val d'Elsa, €5.75, leaves from Piazza Gramsci), **Montepulciano** (8/day, none on Sun, 1.25 hours, €5.45, leaves from train station), **Pienza** (6/day, none on Sun, 1.5 hours, €4.40, leaves from train station), **Montalcino** (6/day Mon-Sat, 4/day Sun, 1.25 hours, €3.85, leaves from train station or Piazza del Sale), and **Pisa's Galileo Galilei Airport** (3/day, 1.75 hours, €14, one direct, two via Poggibonsi).

Sena Buses go to: Rome (9-10/day, 3 hours, €22, from Piazza Gramsci, arrives at Rome's Tiburtina station on Metro line B with easy connections to the central Termini train station), **Naples** (1/day overnight bus, 6.5 hours, bus departs at 23:59, €30), and **Milan** (4/day, 4 hours, €36, departs from Piazza Gramsci, arrives at Milan's Cadorna Station with Metro access and direct trains to Malpensa Airport).

To reach the town center of **Pisa,** the train is better (described earlier).

Tickets and Information: You can buy tickets in the underground passageway (called Sottopassaggio la Lizza) beneath Piazza Gramsci—look for stairwells in front of NH Excelsior Hotel. Once down there, be sure to find the correct office: The larger one (marked *Siena Mobilità*) handles Tiemme/Siena Mobilità buses (Mon-Fri 6:30-19:30, Sat-Sun 7:00-19:30). The smaller one is for Sena buses (Mon-Sat 8:30-19:45 only; on Sun, when the Sena bus ticket office is closed, buy tickets next door at Tiemme/Siena Mobilità office). Both offices accept credit cards. You can also get tickets for both Tiemme/Siena Mobilità buses and Sena buses at the train station (look for bus-ticket kiosk just inside main door—see page 341 for hours). If necessary, you can buy tickets from the driver, but it costs €3 extra.

Services: Sottopassaggio la Lizza also has luggage storage (at the Tiemme/Siena Mobilità office, see page 343 for details), posted bus schedules, TV monitors listing imminent departures for several bus companies, and WCs (€0.50).

PISA

In A.D. 1200, Pisa's power peaked. For nearly three centuries (1000-1300), Pisa rivaled Venice and Genoa as a sea-trading power, exchanging European goods for luxury items in Muslim lands. As a port near the mouth of the Arno River (six miles from the coast), the city enjoyed easy access to the Mediterranean, plus the protection of sitting a bit upstream. The Romans had made it a naval base, and by medieval times the city was a major player.

Pisa's 150-foot galleys cruised the Mediterranean, gaining control of the sea, establishing outposts on the islands of Corsica, Sardinia, and Sicily, and trading with other Europeans, Muslims, and Byzantine Christians as far south as North Africa and as far east as Syria. European Crusaders hired Pisan boats to carry them and their supplies as they headed off to conquer the Muslim-held Holy Land. The Pisan "Republic" prided itself on its independence from both popes and emperors. The city used its sea-trading wealth to build the grand monuments of the Field of Miracles, including the now-famous Leaning Tower.

But the Pisan fleet was routed in battle by Genoa (1284, at Meloria, off Livorno), and their overseas outposts were taken away. Then the port silted up, and Pisa was left high and dry, with only its Field of Miracles and its university keeping it on the map.

Pisa's three important sights—the Duomo, Baptistery, and the Tower—float regally on the best lawn in Italy. The style throughout is Pisa's very own "Pisan Romanesque." Even as the church was being built, Piazza del Duomo was nicknamed the "Campo dei Miracoli," or Field of Miracles, for the grandness of the undertaking.

The Tower recently underwent a decade of restoration and topple-prevention. To ascend, you'll have to get your ticket and book a time at least a few hours in advance (for details, see page 407).

Planning Your Time

For most visitors, Pisa is a touristy quickie—seeing the Tower, visiting the square, and wandering through the church are 90 percent of their Pisan thrills. But it's a shame to skip the rest of the city. Considering the city's historic importance and the wonderful ambience created by its rich architectural heritage and vibrant student population, the city deserves a half-day visit. For many, the lack of tourists outside the Field of Miracles is both a surprise and a relief.

If you want to climb the Tower, go straight to the ticket office upon arrival in the city to snag an appointment—usually for a couple of hours later (for directions to the Field of Miracles, see "Arrival in Pisa," later). For an extra €2, you can book a time in advance online (at least 15 days beforehand) at www.opapisa.it. If you'll be seeing both the town and the Field of Miracles, plan on a six-hour stop. If just blitzing the Field of Miracles, three hours is the minimum. Spending the night lets you savor a great Italian city scene.

If you're day-tripping to Pisa from Lucca, or doing a Lucca/Pisa day trip from Florence, note that a handy bus runs hourly (less frequent on Sun) between the Field of Miracles and Lucca, saving time and hassle (see page 430).

Orientation to Pisa

PISA

The city of Pisa is framed on the north by the Field of Miracles (Leaning Tower) and on the south by the Pisa Centrale train station.

The Arno River flows east to west, bisecting the city. Walking from Pisa Centrale directly to the Tower takes about 30 minutes (but allow up to an hour if you take my self-guided walk). The two main streets for tourists and shoppers are Via Santa Maria (running south from the Tower) and Corso Italia/Borgo Stretto (running north from the station).

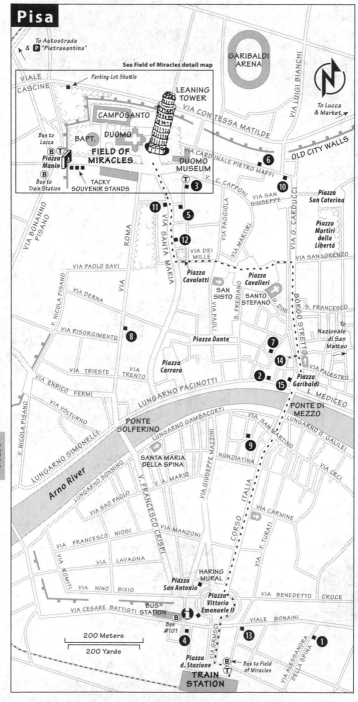

Pisa

To Autostrada & P "Pietrasantina"

See Field of Miracles detail map

Parking-Lot Shuttle

VIALE CASCINE

LEANING TOWER

CAMPOSANTO

GARIBALDI ARENA

VIA CONTESSA MATILDE

To Lucca & Market

VIA LUIGI BIANCHI

Bus to Lucca

Piazza Manin

Bus to Train Station

BAPT. DUOMO

FIELD OF MIRACLES

DUOMO MUSEUM

TACKY SOUVENIR STANDS

VIA CARDINALE PIETRO MAFFI

V. C. CAPPONI

6

OLD CITY WALLS

3

10

VIA SAN GIUSEPPE

VIA G. CARDUCCI

Piazza San Caterina

Piazza Martiri della Libertà

VIA BONANNO PISANO

ROMA

VIA SANTA MARIA

11

5

12

VIA FAGGIOLA

VIA MARTIRI

VIA DEI MILLE

VIA SAN LORENZO

VIA PAOLO SAVI

VIA DERNA

VIA

Piazza Cavalotti

SAN SISTO

VIA S. FREDIANO

Piazza Cavalieri

SANTO STEFANO

U. DINI

BORGO STRETTO

S. FRANCESCO

To Nazionale di San Matteo

V. NICOLA PISANO

VIA RISORGIMENTO

8

VIA PAOLI

Piazza Dante

7

14

VIA PALESTRO

VIA TRIESTE

VIA TRENTO

Piazza Carrara

2

15

Piazza Garibaldi

L. MEDICEO

VIA ENRICO FERMI

LUNGARNO PACINOTTI

PONTE DI MEZZO

V. NICOLA PISANO

VIA VOLTURNO

PONTE SOLFERINO

LUNGARNO GAMBACORTI

9

VIA SAN MARTINO

LUNGARNO G. GALILEI

VIA CECI

LUNGARNO SIMONELLI

SANTA MARIA DELLA SPINA

LUNGARNO SONNINO

V. A. MARIO

NUNZIATINA

Arno River

VIA SAO PAOLO

V. FRANCESCO CRISPI

VIA GIUSEPPE MAZZINI

CORSO ITALIA

VIA CARMINE

VIA F. TURATI

VIA FRANCESCO NIOSI

VIA MANZONI

VIA LAVAGNA

V. COMITI

VIA NINO BIXIO

HARING MURAL

Piazza San Antonio

VIA BENEDETTO CROCE

VIA CESARE BATTISTI

BUS STATION

Bus #101

4

Piazza Vittorio Emanuele II

VIA GRAMSCI

13

VIALE BONAINI

1

VIA ALESSANDRA DELLA SPINA

200 Meters

200 Yards

Piazza d. Stazione

Bus to Field of Miracles

TRAIN STATION

PISA

Pisa Key

① Hotel Alessandro della Spina
② Hotel Royal Victoria & Caffè dell'Ussero
③ Hotel Villa Kinzica
④ Hotel Milano
⑤ Pensione Helvetia
⑥ Two Steps from the Tower B&B
⑦ Antica Trattoria il Campano
⑧ Ristorante Masala
⑨ Ristorante Bagus
⑩ Pizzeria al Bagno di Nerone
⑪ Paninoteca il Canguro
⑫ Panetteria Antiche Tradizioni
⑬ La Lupa Ghiotta Tavola Calda
⑭ Via delle Colonne Produce Market & Restaurants
⑮ La Bottega del Gelato

Tourist Information

The TI is about 200 yards from Pisa Centrale train station—exit and walk straight up the left side of the street to the big, circular Piazza Vittorio Emanuele II. The TI is on the left, around the corner from #16 (daily 9:00-19:00, closes Sun at 16:00 off-season, tel. 050-42291). There's also a TI at the airport (daily 8:30-23:30).

Arrival in Pisa

By Train

Most trains (and visitors) arrive at Pisa Centrale Station, about a mile south of the Tower and Field of Miracles. A few trains, particularly those from Lucca, also stop at the smaller Pisa San Rossore Station, which is just four blocks from the Tower (not all trains stop here, but if yours does, hop off).

Pisa Centrale: This station has a baggage-check desk—look for *deposito bagagli* (€3/bag for 12 hours, daily 6:00-21:00, they photocopy your passport to check ID). As you get off the train, it's to the right at the far end of platform 1, just after the police station.

To get from this station to the Field of Miracles, you can **walk** (get free map from TI, 30 minutes direct, one hour if you follow my self-guided walk), take a **taxi** (€7-10, tel. 050-541-600, taxi stand at station), or go by **bus.** Take bus LAM Rossa (4-6/hour, after 20:00 3/hour, 15 minutes), which stops across the street from the train station, in front of the NH Cavalieri Hotel. Buy a €1.10 bus ticket from the tobacco/magazine kiosk in the train station's main hall or at any tobacco shop (€1.50 if you buy it on board, smart to have exact change, good for 70 minutes, round-trip permitted). Before getting on the bus, confirm that it is indeed going to "Campo dei Miracoli" (ask driver, a local, or TI) or risk taking a long tour of Pisa's suburbs. The correct buses let you off at Piazza Manin, in front of the gate to the Field of Miracles; drivers make sure tourists don't miss the stop.

To return to the train station from the Tower, catch the bus

PISA

in front of the BNL bank, across the street from where you got off (again, confirm the destination—"Stazione Centrale," staht-see-OHN-ay chen-TRAHL-ay). You'll also find a taxi stand 30 yards from the Tower (at Bar Duomo).

Pisa San Rossore: From this station to the Field of Miracles, it's just a four-block walk. Follow Viale delle Cascine east, continuing as it turns into Via Contessa Matilde, and follow signs to *La Torre*—or just head toward the dome of the Baptistery.

By Car

It's best to leave your car at the big Pietrasantina parking lot, designed for tour buses (which pay €110 to park) and tourists with cars (who park for free). From there, a regular city bus shuttles you to the Field of Miracles (driving in the city center will likely net you a steep fine—cameras catch you and the city sends you a ticket by mail).

To reach the parking lot, exit the autostrada at *Pisa Nord* and follow signs to *Pisa* (on the left). Pass the second traffic light and turn left toward the city center. Go straight, following the *Bus Parking* signs, until you see the gas station. The parking lot is on the left. Here you'll find a cafeteria, WC, lots of big buses, and a bus stop for the Line C shuttle that goes back and forth between the lot and the Largo Cocco Griffi bus stop, just behind the walls of the Field of Miracles (6/hour, daily 8:30-19:20, €1.50, buy round-trip ticket on board). Or, if you have more time and want to follow my self-guided walk through Pisa to the Field of Miracles, take bus LAM Rossa to Pisa Centrale train station (4-6/hour, after 20:00 3/hour, €1.10 if you buy ticket at parking-lot cafeteria, €1.50 if purchased on board, also stops near the Tower en route).

By Plane

For details on Pisa's Galileo Galilei Airport, see page 430.

Helpful Hints

Markets: An open-air produce market attracts picnickers to Piazza della Vettovaglie, one block north of the Arno River near Ponte di Mezzo, and nearby Piazza Sant'Uomobuono (Mon-Sat 7:00-18:00, main section closes at 13:00, closed Sun). A street market—with more practical goods than food—bustles on Wednesday and Saturday mornings between Via del Brennero and Via Paparrelli (8:00-13:00, just outside of wall, about 6 blocks east of the Tower).

Festivals: The first half of June has many events, culminating in a celebration for Pisa's patron saint (June 16-17).

Local Guide: Dottore Vincenzo Riolo is a great guide for Pisa and the surrounding area (€130/3 hours, mobile 338-211-2939, www.pisatour.it, info@pisatour.it).

Tours: The TI coordinates with local guides to offer walking tours most days. The theme and schedule change every day; check with the TI for the latest information.

Updates to this Book: For news about changes to this book's coverage since it was published, see www.ricksteves.com/update.

Self-Guided Walk

Welcome to Pisa: From Pisa Centrale Train Station to the Tower

A leisurely one-hour stroll from the station to the Tower is a great way to get acquainted with the more subtle virtues of this Renaissance city. Because the hordes who descend daily on the Tower rarely bother with the rest of the town, you'll find most of Pisa to be delightfully untouristy—a student-filled, classy, Old World town with an Arno-scape much like its upstream rival, Florence. Pisa is pretty small, with just 100,000 people. But its 45,000 students keep it lively, especially at night.

• *From Pisa Centrale train station, walk north up Viale Antonio Gramsci to the circular square called...*

Piazza Vittorio Emanuele II

The Allies considered Pisa to be strategically important in World War II, and both the train station and its main bridge were targeted for bombing. Forty percent of this district was destroyed. The piazza has been recently rebuilt, and now this generous public space with grass and benches is actually a lid for an under-

ground parking lot. The TI is on this piazza, in the arcade. The entire wall of a building just to the left of the piazza was painted by American artist Keith Haring in 1989 to create *Tuttomondo (Whole Wide World)*. Haring (who died of AIDS in 1990) brought New York City graffiti into the mainstream. This painting is a celebration of diversity, chaos, and the liveliness of our world, vibrating with energy.

• *Walk up Corso Italia to the river.*

Corso Italia

Cutting through the center of town, this is Pisa's main drag. As you leave Piazza Vittorio Emanuele II, look to the right to see the circa-1960 wall map of Pisa with a steam train (on the wall of the bar on the corner). You'll also see plenty of youthful fashions, as kids are out making the scene here. Be on guard for pickpockets—too young to arrest, they can only be kicked out of town. Pushed out of their former happy hunting grounds, the Field of Miracles, they now work the crowds here, often dressed as tourists.

• *Follow the pedestrianized Corso Italia straight north to the Arno River and Ponte di Mezzo. Stop in the center of the bridge.*

Ponte di Mezzo

This modern bridge, constructed on the same site where the Romans built one, marks the center of Pisa. In the Middle Ages, this bridge (like Florence's Ponte Vecchio) was lined with shops. It's been destroyed several times by floods and in 1943 by British and American bombers. Enjoy the view from the center of the bridge of the elegant mansions that line the riverbank, recalling Pisa's days of trading glory—the cityscape feels a bit like Venice's Grand Canal. Pisa sits on shifting delta sand, making construction tricky. The entire town leans. With innovative arches above ground and below, architects didn't stop the leaning—but they have made buildings that wobble without being threatened.

• *Cross the bridge to...*

Piazza Garibaldi

This square is named for the charismatic leader of the Risorgimento, the unification movement that led to Italian independence in 1870. Knowing Pisa was strongly nationalist, Garibaldi came here when wounded to be nursed back to health; many Pisans died in the national struggle. **La Bottega del Gelato,** Pisa's favorite gelato place, is on Piazza Garibaldi (daily 11:30-24:00). You can side-trip about 100 yards downstream to **Caffè dell'Ussero** (famous for its fine 14th-century red terra-cotta original facade, at #28, Sun-Fri 7:00-21:00, closed Sat) and browse its time-warp interior, lined with portraits and documents from the struggle for Italian independence.

• *Continue north up the elegantly arcaded...*

Borgo Stretto

Welcome to Pisa's main shopping street. On the right, the Church of St. Michael, with its fine Pisan Romanesque facade, still sports some 16th-century graffiti. I'll bet you can see some modern graffiti across the street. Students have been pushing their causes here—or simply defacing things—for five centuries.

From here, look farther up the street and notice how it undulates like a flowing river. In the sixth century B.C., Pisa was born when two parallel rivers were connected by canals. This street echoes the flow of one of those canals. An 11th-century landslide rerouted the second river, destroying ancient Pisa, and the entire city had to regenerate.

• *After a few steps, detour left onto Via delle Colonne, and walk one block down to...*

Piazza delle Vettovaglie

Pisa's historic market square, Piazza delle Vettovaglie, is lively day and night. Its Renaissance loggia has hosted the fish and vegetable market for generations. The stalls are set up in this piazza during the morning (Mon-Sat 7:00-13:00, closed Sun) and stay open later in the neighboring piazza to the west (Piazza Sant'Uomobuono, Mon-Sat 7:00-18:00, closed Sun). You could cobble together a picnic from the sandwich shops and fruit-and-veggie stalls ringing these squares.

• *Continue north on Borgo Stretto another 100 yards, passing an ugly bomb site on the right, with its horrible 1960s reconstruction. Take the second left on nondescript Via Ulisse Dini (it's not obvious—turn left immediately at the arcade's end, just before the pharmacy). This leads to Pisa's historic core, Piazza dei Cavalieri.*

Piazza dei Cavalieri

With its old clock and colorfully decorated palace, this piazza was once the seat of the independent Republic of Pisa's government. In

around 1500, Florence conquered Pisa and made this square the training place for the knights of its navy. The statue of Cosimo I de' Medici shows the Florentine who ruled Pisa in the 16th century. With a foot on a dolphin, he reminded all who passed that the Florentine navy controlled the sea—at least a little of it. The frescoes on the exterior of the square's buildings, though damaged by salty sea air and years of neglect, reflect Pisa's fading glory under the Medici.

With Napoleon, this complex of grand buildings became part of the University of Pisa. The university is one of Europe's oldest, with roots in a law school that dates back as far as the 11th century. In the mid-16th century, the city was a hotbed of controversy, as spacey professors like Galileo Galilei studied the solar system—with results that challenged the church's powerful doctrine. More recently, the blind tenor Andrea Bocelli attended law school in Pisa before embarking on his well-known musical career.

From here, take Via Corsica (to the left of the clock). The humble **Church of San Sisto,** ahead on the left (side entrance on Via Corsica), is worth a quick look. With simple bricks, assorted reused columns, heavy walls, and few windows, this was the

Field of Miracles Tickets

Pisa has a combo-ticket scheme designed to get you into its neglected secondary sights: the Baptistery, Camposanto Cemetery, Duomo Museum, and Museum of the Sinopias (fresco pattern museum). For €5, you get your choice of one of these sights; for two of these sights or one plus the Duomo, the cost is €6; and for the works, you'll pay €10 (credit cards accepted). By comparison, the Duomo alone is a bargain (€2).

You can buy any of these tickets either behind the Leaning Tower or at the Museum of the Sinopias (near Baptistery, almost suffocated by souvenir stands). Both ticket offices have big, yellow, triangle-shaped signs. .

No matter which ticket you get, you'll have to pay an additional €15 if you want to climb the Tower. Tickets for the Tower are sold at the ticket offices or online at least 15 days in advance at www.opapisa.it (€2 fee).

typical Romanesque style that predated the more lavish Pisan Romanesque style of the Field of Miracles structures.

Follow Via Corsica as it turns into Via dei Mille, then turn right on Via Santa Maria, which leads north (and grab a quick bite at the recommended **Panetteria Antiche Tradizioni**). You'll pass through increasingly touristy claptrap, directly to the Field of Miracles and the Tower.

Sights in Pisa

▲▲▲**Leaning Tower**—A 15-foot lean from the vertical makes the Tower one of Europe's most recognizable images. You can see it for free; it's always viewable, or you can pay to climb its 294 stairs to the top.

Cost and Hours: €15, kids under eight not allowed, daily April-Sept 8:00-20:00, Oct 9:00-19:00, Nov-Feb 10:00-17:00, March 9:00-18:00, ticket office opens 30 minutes early, last entry 30 minutes before closing, timed entry, reservations recommended, www.opapisa.it.

❂ See the Leaning Tower Tour chapter.

▲▲**Duomo (Cathedral)**—The gargantuan Pisan Romanesque church has a Pisano pulpit, modest dress code, and no baggage check.

Cost and Hours: €2, daily April-Sept 10:00-20:00, Oct 10:00-19:00, Nov-Feb 10:00-13:00 & 14:00-17:00, March 10:00-18:00, last entry 30 minutes before closing.

☼ See the Pisa Duomo Tour chapter.

▲▲▲**Field of Miracles (Campo dei Miracoli)**—Scattered across a golf-course-green lawn are five grand buildings: the cathedral (or Duomo), its bell tower (the Leaning Tower), the Baptistery, the hospital (today's Museum of the Sinopias), and

the Camposanto Cemetery. The buildings are constructed from similar materials—bright white marble—and have comparable decoration. Each has a simple ground floor and rows of delicate columns and arches that form open-air arcades, giving the Campo a pleasant visual unity.

The style is called Pisan Romanesque. Unlike traditional Romanesque, with its heavy fortress-like feel—thick walls, barrel arches, few windows—Pisan Romanesque is light and elegant. At ground level, most of the structures have simple half-columns and arches. On the upper levels, you'll see a little of everything—tight rows of thin columns; pointed Gothic gables and prickly spires; Byzantine mosaics and horseshoe arches; and geometric designs (such as diamonds) and striped, colored marbles inspired by mosques in Muslim lands.

Architecturally, the Campo is unique and exotic. Theologically, the Campo's buildings mark the main events of every Pisan's life: christened in the Baptistery, married in the Duomo, honored in ceremonies at the Tower, healed in the hospital, and buried in the Camposanto Cemetery.

Lining this field of artistic pearls is a gauntlet of Europe's tackiest souvenir stands, as well as dozens of amateur mimes "propping up" the Leaning Tower while tourists take photos.

The next four sights—the Baptistery, Camposanto Cemetery, Museum of the Sinopias, and Duomo Museum—share the same pricing and schedule. All are covered in more detail within the ☼ Field of Miracles Tour chapter.

▲**Baptistery**—The round Baptistery, located in front of the Duomo, has superb acoustics and another fine Pisano pulpit.

Cost and Hours: €5, but most visitors buy one of the vari-

PISA

ous combo-tickets to save money (see sidebar on page 404), daily
April-Sept 8:00-20:00, Oct 9:00-19:00, Nov-Feb 10:00-17:00,
March 9:00-18:00, last entry 30 minutes before closing.

Camposanto Cemetery—Lined with faint frescoes, this centuries-old cemetery on the north side of the Campo is famous for its
"Holy Land" dirt, reputedly brought here from the Middle East
in the 12th century and said to reduce a body to a skeleton within
a day. Artillery fire during World War II set the lead roof ablaze,
greatly damaging the building and its frescoes (same cost and
hours as Baptistery).

Museum of the Sinopias (Museo delle Sinopie)—Across from
the Baptistery, housed in a 13th-century hospital (with its entrance
nearly obscured by souvenir stands), this museum displays some of
the original preliminary sketches (sinopias) that lay beneath the
frescoed walls of the Camposanto Cemetery—the drawings were
recovered after a WWII fire severely damaged the frescoes themselves. This museum comes with two free, short, introductory videos that you can watch even without a ticket. Good students might
want to come here first for this orientation (same cost and hours as
Baptistery).

Duomo Museum (Museo dell'Opera del Duomo)—Located
behind the Leaning Tower, the Duomo Museum is big on Pisan
art, displaying treasures of the cathedral, paintings, silverware,
and sculptures (from the 12th to 14th centuries, particularly
by the Pisano dynasty), as well as ancient Egyptian, Etruscan,
and Roman artifacts (same cost and hours as Baptistery, Piazza
Arcivescovado 18).

Museo Nazionale di San Matteo—On the river and in a former
convent, this art museum displays 12th- to 15th-century sculptures, illuminated manuscripts, and paintings on wood by pre- and
early Renaissance masters Martini, Masaccio, and others. It's a
fine collection—especially its painted wood crucifixes—and gives
you a chance to see Pisan innovation in 11th- to 13th-century art,
before Florence took the lead.

   Cost and Hours: €5, Tue-Sat 9:00-19:00, Sun 9:00-13:00,
closed Mon, near Piazza San Paolo at Lungarno Mediceo, a
5-minute walk upriver from the main bridge, tel. 050-541-865.

LEANING TOWER TOUR

You've seen it in TV ads, in movies, and on posters, key chains, and souvenir dishes—now it's time to see it in the flesh. And, the funny thing is, it's one iconic image that really looks like its famous reproductions.

The off-kilter Tower parallels Pisa's history. It was started in the late 12th century, when Pisa was at its peak: one of the world's richest, most powerful, and most sophisticated cities. They'd built their huge cathedral to reflect Pisa's superpower status, and the cathedral's bell tower—the Leaning Tower—was the perfect complement. But as Pisa's power declined, the Tower reclined, and ever since, both have required a great deal of effort to prop. However, after a 10-year renovation, the Tower's been stabilized. You can admire it in all its cockeyed glory and even climb to the top for a commanding view.

Orientation

Cost: Free to look, €15 to go inside and climb to the top (restrictions apply to youth; see "Reservations to Climb the Tower," below).

Hours: Always viewable from the outside. It's open to climb daily April-Sept 8:00-20:00, Oct 9:00-19:00, Nov-Feb 10:00-17:00, March 9:00-18:00, ticket office opens 30 minutes early, last entry 30 minutes before closing.

Reservations to Climb the Tower: Entry to the tower is by a timed ticket good for a 30-minute visit. Every 20 minutes, 45 people can clamber up the 294 tilting stairs to the top. Children under age eight are not allowed to go up. Children ages 8-12 must be accompanied by—and hold hands at all times with—

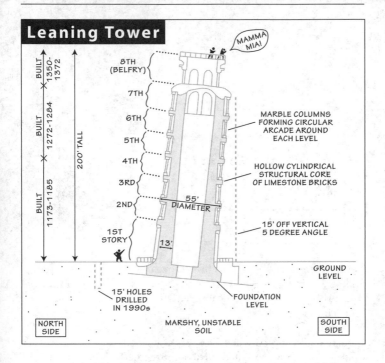

Leaning Tower

8TH (BELFRY)
7TH
6TH
5TH
4TH
3RD
2ND
1ST STORY

BUILT 1350-1372
BUILT 1272-1284
BUILT 1173-1185
200' TALL

MARBLE COLUMNS FORMING CIRCULAR ARCADE AROUND EACH LEVEL

HOLLOW CYLINDRICAL STRUCTURAL CORE OF LIMESTONE BRICKS

55' DIAMETER

15' OFF VERTICAL 5 DEGREE ANGLE

13'

GROUND LEVEL

15' HOLES DRILLED IN 1990s

FOUNDATION LEVEL

MARSHY, UNSTABLE SOIL

NORTH SIDE

SOUTH SIDE

MAMMA MIA!

an adult. Teenagers (up to and including 18-year-olds) must also be accompanied by an adult.

Reserve your timed entry in person at the ticket office (see below), or for an extra €2, book a time online at www .opapisa.it.

Online bookings are accepted no more than 45 days—and no fewer than 15 days—in advance. You must pick up your ticket(s) at least 30 minutes before your entry time. Show up 10 minutes before your appointment at the meeting point outside the ticket office.

To reserve in person, go to the **ticket office** behind the Tower, on the left in the yellow building, or to the Museum of the Sinopias ticket office hidden behind the souvenir stalls. In summer, for same-day entry, it will likely be a couple of hours before you're able to go up (see the rest of the monuments and grab lunch while waiting). The wait is usually much shorter at the beginning or end of the day.

Getting There: From Pisa Centrale train station, you can walk (30 minutes), take a taxi (€7-10), or catch bus LAM Rossa (4-6/ hour, after 20:00 3/hour, 15 minutes; see page 399 for details).

Remember, if your train stops at the smaller Pisa San Rossore Station, get off there and you're only about four blocks from the Tower (head for the Baptistery's dome).

PISA TOWER

If you're traveling by car, see "Arrival in Pisa: By Car," on page 400.

The Climb: You wind your way up the outside of the Tower along a spiraling ramp. For your 30-minute time slot, figure about 10 minutes to climb and 10 to descend, leaving about 10 minutes for vertigo at the top. Even though it's technically a "guided" visit, that only means you're accompanied by a museum guard who makes sure you don't stay up past your scheduled appointment time.

Baggage Check: You can't take any bags up the Tower, but day-bag-size lockers are available at the ticket office—show your Tower ticket to check your bag. You may check your bag 10 minutes before your reservation time and must pick it up immediately after your Tower visit.

Caution: The railings are skinny, the steps are slanted, and rain makes the marble slippery. Anyone with balance issues of any sort should think twice before ascending.

Starring: The Tower's frilly Pisan Romanesque look and its famous lean.

The Tour Begins

Yep, There It Is

Rising up alongside the cathedral, the Tower is nearly 200 feet tall and 55 feet wide, weighing 14,000 tons and currently leaning at a five-degree angle (15 feet off the vertical axis). It started to lean almost immediately after construction began (it would take two centuries to finish the structure). Count the eight stories—a simple base, six stories of columns (forming arcades), and a belfry on top. The inner structural core is a hollow cylinder built of limestone bricks, faced with white marble brought here by barge from San Giuliano, northeast of the city. The thin columns of the open-air arcades make the heavy Tower seem light and graceful.

The Building of the Tower

The Tower was built over two centuries by at least three differ-

ent architects. You can see how each successive architect tried to correct the leaning problem—once halfway up (after the fourth story), once at the belfry on the top.

The first stones were laid in 1173, probably under the direction of the architect Bonanno Pisano (who also designed the Duomo's bronze back door). Five years later, just as

PISA TOWER

Galileo's Experiments

The Leaning Tower figures prominently in scientific lore. Legend has it that the scientific pioneer Galileo Galilei dropped objects off the Tower in attempts to understand gravity. Galileo (1564-1642) was born in Pisa, grew up here on Via Giuseppe Giusti (where the family home still stands, adorned with a humble plaque), and taught math at the university. Galileo is said to have climbed the Tower and dropped two balls: one heavy and metal, the other a lighter wooden ball. Which object hit the ground first? The heavier object, of course—but through further reasoning and experimentation, Galileo figured out that the lighter object fell more slowly only because of air resistance. In doing so, he shattered the conventional wisdom, established by Aristotle, that heavier objects accelerate faster. We don't know whether Galileo actually dropped those orbs from this Tower, but we do know he tested this theory of gravity by rolling balls of different weights down ramps, which would have been easier to time (see page 275). These experiments led to Isaac Newton's formulation of the laws of gravity. Moreover, by forging theories through rigorous testing, rather than through reasoning alone (as Aristotle had), Galileo helped re-envision science itself.

they'd finished the base and the first arcade, someone said, "Is it just me, or does that look crooked?" The heavy Tower—resting on a very shallow 13-foot foundation—was obviously sinking on the south side into the marshy, multilayered, unstable soil. (Actually, all the Campo's buildings tilt somewhat.) The builders carried on anyway, until they'd finished four stories (the base, plus three arcade floors). Then, construction suddenly halted—no one knows why—and for a century the Tower sat half-finished and visibly leaning.

Around 1272, the next architect continued, trying to correct the problem by angling the next three stories backward, in the opposite direction of the lean. The project then again sat mysteriously idle for nearly another century. Finally, Tommaso Pisano put the belfry on the top (c. 1350-1372), also kinking it backward.

Man Versus Gravity

After the Tower's completion, several attempts were made to stop its slow-motion fall. The architect/artist/writer Giorgio Vasari reinforced the base in 1550, and it actually worked. But in 1838, well-intentioned engineers pumped out groundwater, destabilizing the Tower and causing it to increase its lean at a rate of a millimeter per year.

It got so bad that in 1990 the Tower was closed for repairs, and $30 million was spent trying to stabilize it. Engineers dried the soil with steam pipes, anchored the Tower to the ground with steel cables, and buried 600 tons of lead on the north side as a counterweight (not visible)—all with little success. The breakthrough came when they drilled 15-foot-long holes in the ground on the north side and sucked out 60 tons of soil, allowing the Tower to sink on the north side and straighten out its lean by about six inches.

As well as gravity, erosion threatens the Tower. Since its construction, 135 of the Tower's 180 marble columns have had to be replaced. Stone decay, deposits of lime and calcium phosphate, accumulations of dirt and moss, cracking from the stress of the lean—all of these are factors in its decline.

Thanks to the Tower's lean, there are special trouble spots. The lower south side (which is protected from cleansing rain and wind) is a magnet for dirty airborne particles, while the stone on the upper areas has more decay (from eroding rain and wind).

The Tower, now stabilized, has been cleaned as well. Cracks have been filled, and accumulations removed with carefully formulated atomized water sprays and poultices of various solvents.

All the work to shore up, straighten, and clean the Tower has probably turned the clock back a few centuries. In fact, art historians figure it leans today as much as it did when Galileo reputedly conducted his gravity experiment here 400 years ago.

PISA DUOMO TOUR

The huge Pisan Romanesque cathedral, with its carved pulpit by Giovanni Pisano, is artistically more important than its more famous bell tower.

Orientation

Cost: €2, covered by various combo-tickets (see sidebar on page 404).

Hours: Daily April-Sept 10:00-20:00, Oct 10:00-19:00, Nov-Feb 10:00-13:00 & 14:00-17:00, March 10:00-18:00, last entry 30 minutes before closing.

Dress Code: Shorts are OK as long as they're not too short, and shoulders should be covered (although it's not really enforced).

Audioguides: Don't let the sparkle of the new coin-operated "phone guides" tempt you. These €2 machines still use narration from a bygone era.

Length of This Tour: Allow one hour.

Baggage: Big backpacks are not allowed, nor is storage provided. If you have a day bag, carry it.

Starring: Pisano's pulpit, Galileo's lamp, and the remains of a saint.

The Tour Begins

❶ Exterior

The Duomo is the centerpiece of the Field of Miracles' complex of religious buildings. Begun in 1063, it was financed by a galley-load of booty ransacked that year from the Muslim-held capital of Palermo, Sicily. The architect Buschetto created the style of Pisan

Pisa Duomo

To
Leaning Tower

③ APSE

⑨

⑧

⑥ DOME ⑦

④

⑤

N
A
V
E

❶ Exterior View
❷ Nave
❸ Apse Mosaic
❹ Dome
❺ Giovanni's Pulpit
❻ Galileo's Lamp
❼ St. Ranieri's Body
❽ Emperor Henry VII's Tomb
❾ Bronze Doors of St. Ranieri

❷

EXIT

ENTRANCE

❶

FIELD OF MIRACLES

To
Tacky Souvenir
Stands

To Baptistery

Romanesque that set the tone for the Baptistery and Tower. Five decades later (1118), the architect Rainaldo added the impressive main-entrance facade (which also leans out about a foot).

The lower half of the church is simple Romanesque, with blind arches. The upper half has four rows of columns that form arcades. Stripes of black-and-white marble, mosaics, stone inlay, and even recycled Roman tombstones complete the decoration.

• *Enter the church at the facade, opposite the Baptistery.*

❷ Nave

The 320-foot nave was the longest in Christendom when it was built. It's modeled on a traditional Roman basilica, with 68 Corinthian columns of granite (most shipped from Sardinia in

1063) dividing the space into five aisles. But the striped marble and arches-on-columns give the nave an exotic, almost mosque-like feel. Dim light filters in from the small upper windows of the galleries, where the women worshipped. At the center of the gilded coffered ceiling is the shield of Florence's Medici family; the round symbols around its edges are thought to represent medicinal pills—an allusion to the literal meaning of their name (Medici = "doctors"). This powerful merchant and banking family took over Pisa after its glory days had passed.

• *In the apse (behind the altar) is the...*

❸ Apse Mosaic

The mosaic (c. 1300, partly done by the great artist Cimabue) shows Christ as the Ruler of All (Pantocrator) between Mary and St. John the Evangelist. The Pantocrator image of Christ is standard fare among Eastern Orthodox Christians—that is, the "Byzantine" people who were Pisa's partners in trade.

As King of the Universe, Christ sits on a throne, facing directly out, with penetrating eyes. Only Christ can wear this style of halo, divided with a cross. In his left hand is a Bible open to the verse *"Ego Lux Sum Mundi"*—"I am the light of the world." While his feet crush the devil in serpent form, Christ blesses us with his right hand. His fingers form the Greek letters *chi* and *rho,* the first two letters of "Christos." The thumb (almost) touches the fingers, symbolizing how Christ unites both his divinity and his humanity.

❹ Dome

Looking up into the dome, the heavens open, and rings of saints and angels spiral up to a hazy God. Beneath the dome is an inlaid-marble, Cosmati-style mosaic floor. The modern (and therefore controversial) marble altar and pulpit were carved by a Florentine artist in 2002.

• *Near the center of the church you'll find...*

❺ Giovanni's Pulpit (1301-1311)

The 15-foot-tall, octagonal pulpit by Giovanni Pisano (c. 1240-1319) is the last, biggest, and most complex of the four pulpits by the Pisano father-and-son team. Giovanni's father, Nicola, started the family tradition four decades earlier, carving the pulpit in the Baptistery. Giovanni grew up working side-by-side with his dad on numerous projects. Now on his own, he crams everything he's learned into his crowning achievement.

Giovanni left no stone uncarved in his pursuit of beauty. Four hundred intricately sculpted figures smother the pulpit, blurring the architectural outlines. In addition, the relief panels are actually curved, making it look less like an octagon than a circle. The creamy-white Carrara marble has the look and feel of carved French ivories, which the Pisanos loved. Originally, this and the other pulpits were frosted with paint, gilding, and colored pastes.

At the base, lions roar and crouch over their prey, symbolizing how Christ (the lion) triumphs over Satan (the horse, as in the Four Horsemen of the Apocalypse).

Four of the pulpit's support "columns" are statues. The central "column" features three graceful ladies representing Faith, Hope, and Charity, the three pillars of Christianity. They in turn stand on the sturdy base of knowledge, representing the liberal arts taught at the U. of Pisa. Another column is Hercules, standing *contrapposto*, nude, holding his club and lion skin. Nearby, Lady Church suckles the babies of the Old and New Testaments, while at her feet are the Four Virtues, including Justice (with her scales), Moderation (modestly covering her nakedness), Courage (holding a lion), and Wisdom (with a horn of plenty).

Around the top of the pulpit, Christ's life unfolds in a series of panels saturated with carvings. The panels tilt out from the top, so the viewer below has a better look, and they're bordered on top with a heavy cornice as a backdrop. Since the panels are curved and unframed, you "read" Christ's life less like a nine-frame comic strip and more like a continuous scroll.

The story unfolds from left to right, beginning at the back near the stairs:

1. Story of Elizabeth and Zechariah: John the Baptist's parents.

2. Nativity: Mary lounges across a bed, unfazed by labor and delivery. Her pose is clearly inspired by carved Roman sarcophagi (which you can see in the Camposanto Cemetery), showing the dearly departed relaxing for eternity atop their coffins. Mary and the babe are surrounded by angels (above) and shepherds (right).

3. Adoration of the Magi: The Wise Men ride in with horses and camels.

4. Presentation in the Temple (left side): Joseph and Mary hold Baby Jesus between them. On the right side of the panel, Giovanni adds the next scene in the story, when the nuclear family gets on a donkey and escapes into Egypt.

5. Massacre of the Innocents: Herod (at the top) turns and gestures dramatically, ordering the slaughter of all babies. A mother (bottom left corner) grabs her head in despair. Giovanni uses thick lips and big noses to let the faces speak the full range of human emotions. The soldiers in the tangled chaos are almost freestanding.

6. Kiss of Judas: Jesus is betrayed by a kiss (left side).

7. Crucifixion: An emaciated Christ is mourned by his followers, who turn every which way. A Roman horseman (bottom right corner) rides directly away from us—an example of Renaissance "foreshortening" a century before its time.

8. and **9. Last Judgment:** Christ sits in the center, the dead rise from their graves, and he sends the good to heaven (left) and the bad to hell (right).

Giovanni was a better pure sculptor than his father. Armed with more sophisticated chisels, he could cut even deeper into the marble, freeing heads from the stone backdrop, creating almost freestanding, 3-D figures. Where Nicola shows figures either facing forward or in profile, Giovanni mastered the difficult three-quarters angle.

If the pulpit seems a bit cluttered and asymmetrical, blame Mussolini. Originally, Giovanni built the pulpit standing on the right side of the altar (the traditional location). But after a massive fire in 1595 (when the roof burned), the pulpit was disassembled and stored away for three centuries. In 1926, they pulled it out of storage, reassembled it on this spot...and ended up with pieces left over (now in other museums), leading scholars to debate the authenticity of the current look.

• *Hanging from the ceiling of the north transept (to the left of the altar) is...*

❻ Galileo's Lamp

The bronze incense burner is said to be the one (actually, this is a replacement for the original) that caught teenage Galileo's attention one day in church. Someone left a church door open, and a gust of wind set the lamp swinging. Galileo timed the swings and realized that the burner swung back and forth in the same amount of time regardless of how wide the arc. (This pendulum motion was a constant that allowed Galileo to measure our ever-changing universe.)

Galileo Galilei (1564-1642) was born in Pisa, grew up here on Via Giuseppe Giusti, and taught math at the university (1584-1591). Legend says he dropped things off the Tower to time their falls, fascinated by gravity (see sidebar on page 410).

• *Find the following two sights in the right (south) transept, near the back of the church. First, enter the Ranieri Chapel to take a look at...*

❼ St. Ranieri's Body

In a glass-lined casket on the altar, Pisa's patron saint lies mummi-fied, encased in silver at his head and feet, with his hair shirt cov-ering his body. The silver, mask-like face dates from 2000 and is as realistic as possible—derived from an FBI-style computer scan of Ranieri's skull.

Ranieri Scuggeri (1117-1161) was born into the city of Pisa at its peak, when the Field of Miracles was a construction zone. (Ranieri was one year old when this Duomo was consecrated in thanks for Pisa's lucrative victory over the Muslim Saracens.) The son of a rich sea-trader, Ranieri chose the life of a hard-partying, popular, touring musician. Backstage one night, he met a mysteri-ous stranger who changed his life. Ranieri was inspired to take his musical instrument and set it on fire, while opening his arms to the heavens (à la Jimi Hendrix). He returned to his father's ship-ping business and amassed a fortune. Then, one day, he smelled something funky—his own money. He gave it all away, joined a monastery, and put on a hair shirt.

The former wandering troubadour, traveling salesman, and pilgrimaging monk finally settled down in his hometown of Pisa. He devoured the Bible, then used his showmanship to wow audi-ences here—in the Duomo—when he took the stage atop the pul-pit to deliver spirited sermons.

Ranieri, honored in grand style on June 16 and 17, is cause for Pisa's biggest local event—the Luminara—celebrated along the Arno with tens of thousands of candles lining the buildings and floating on the river. The next day, rowing teams play a game of capture-the-flag, racing to a boat in the Arno and shimmying up a long rope to claim the prize.

• *To the left of the chapel, look on the wall to find...*

❽ Emperor Henry VII's Tomb

Pause at the tomb of Holy Roman Emperor Henry VII, whose untimely death plunged Pisa into its centuries-long decline. Henry lies sleeping, arms folded, his head turned to the side, resting on a soft pillow.

This German king (c. 1275-1313) invaded Italy and was wel-comed by Pisans as a nonpartisan leader who could bring peace to Italy's warring Guelphs and Ghibellines. In 1312, he was crowned emperor by the pope in Rome. He returned to his base in Pisa and was preparing to polish off the last opposition when he caught a fever (or was poisoned by a priest) and died. Ghibelline Pisa was suddenly at the mercy of Guelph rivals such as rising Florence, and Pisa never recovered.

• *Exit the church and walk around to its back end (facing the Tower), where you'll find the...*

PISA DUOMO

❾ Bronze Doors of St. Ranieri (Porta San Ranieri)

Designed by Bonanno Pisano (c. 1186)—who is thought by some historians to have been the Tower's first architect—the doors have 24 different panels that show Christ's story using the same simple, skinny figures found in Byzantine icons. (The doors are actually copies; the originals are housed—but not always on display—in the Duomo Museum.)

The story begins in the lower right panel ("Magis"), as the three Wise Men ride up a hill, heading toward...the panel to the left, where tiny Baby Jesus lies in a manger while angels and shepherds look down from above. Above the manger scene, King Herod ("Erodi") sits under a canopy (in Pisan Romanesque style) and orders a soldier to raise his sword to kill all potential Messiahs. The terrified mother pulls her hair out. In the panel to the right, John the Baptist stands under a swaying palm and baptizes the adult Jesus, who wears the rippling River Jordan like a blanket.

Cast using the lost-wax technique, these doors were an inspiration for Lorenzo Ghiberti's bronze doors in Florence.

FIELD OF MIRACLES TOUR

Campo dei Miracoli

Imagine arriving in Pisa as a sailor in the 11th century when the Arno came to just outside the walls surrounding this square, the church here was the biggest in the world, and this ensemble in gleaming white marble was the most impressive space in Christendom. Calling it the Field of Miracles (Campo dei Miracoli) would not have been hyperbole.

The Leaning Tower nearly steals the show from the massive cathedral, which muscles out the other sights. But don't neglect the rest of the Field of Miracles: the Baptistery, Camposanto Cemetery, Museum of the Sinopias, and the Duomo Museum.

Orientation

Cost: €10 combo-ticket includes all the sights, plus the Duomo (credit cards accepted; see sidebar on page 404 for run-down on various combo-tickets).

Hours: All of the sights on this tour share the same schedule: daily April-Sept 8:00-20:00, Oct 9:00-19:00, Nov-Feb 10:00-17:00, March 9:00-18:00, last entry 30 minutes before closing.

Location: The Baptistery is located in front of the Duomo's facade. The Camposanto Cemetery is behind the church on the north side of the Field of Miracles. The Museum of the Sinopias is hidden behind souvenir stands, across the street from the Baptistery entrance. The Duomo Museum is housed behind the Tower.

Length of This Tour: Allow two hours.

The Tour Begins

Baptistery

Pisa's Baptistery is Italy's biggest. It's interesting for its pulpit and interior ambience, and especially great for its acoustics.

Exterior

The building is 180 feet tall—John the Baptist on top looks eye-to-eye with the tourists atop the nearly 200-foot Leaning Tower.

Notice that the Baptistery leans nearly six feet to the north (the Tower leans 15 feet to the south). The building (begun in 1153) is modeled on the circular-domed Church of the Holy Sepulchre in Jerusalem, seen by Pisan Crusaders who occupied Jerusalem in 1099.

From the outside, you see three distinct sections, which reflect the changing tastes of the years spent building it: simple Romanesque blind arches at the base (1153), ornate Gothic spires and pointed arches in the middle (1250), and a Renaissance dome (15th century). The roofing looks mismatched but was intentionally designed with red clay tiles on the seaward side and lead tiles (more prestigious but prone to corrosion) on the sheltered east side. The statues of the midsection are by Nicola Pisano (c. 1220-1278, Giovanni's father), who sculpted the pulpit inside.

Interior

Inside, it's simple, spacious, and baptized with light. Tall arches atop thin columns once again echo the Campo's architectural theme of arches above blank spaces. The columns encircle just a few pieces of religious furniture.

In the center sits the beautiful marble **octagonal font** (1246). A statue of the first Baptist, John the Baptist, stretches out his

hand and says, "Welcome to my Baptistery." The font contains plenty of space for baptizing adults by immersion (the medieval custom), plus four wells for dunking babies.

Baptismal fonts—where sinners symbolically die and are reborn—are traditionally octagons. The shape suggests a cross (symbolizing Christ's death), and the eight sides

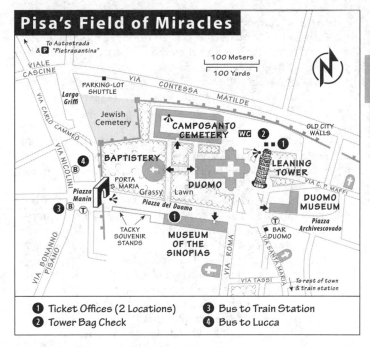

Pisa's Field of Miracles

To Autostrada
& **P** "Pietrasantina"

VIALE CASCINE

100 Meters
100 Yards

VIA CONTESSA MATILDE

PARKING-LOT SHUTTLE

Largo Griffi

VIA CARLO CAMMEO

Jewish Cemetery

CAMPOSANTO CEMETERY **WC** **2** **1**

OLD CITY WALLS

VIA NICOLINI

4 **B**

BAPTISTERY

PORTA S. MARIA

Piazza Manin

LEANING TOWER

VIA C. P. MAFFI

3 **B** **T**

Grassy Lawn

DUOMO

Piazza del Duomo

1

DUOMO MUSEUM

Piazza Archivescovado

TACKY SOUVENIR STANDS

MUSEUM OF THE SINOPIAS

VIA ROMA

T BAR DUOMO

VIA SANTA MARIA

VIA BONANNO PISANO

VIA TASSI

To rest of town
& train station

- **1** Ticket Offices (2 Locations)
- **2** Tower Bag Check
- **3** Bus to Train Station
- **4** Bus to Lucca

represent the eighth day of Christ's ordeal, when he was resurrected. The font's sides, carved with inlaid multicolored marble, feature circle-in-a-square patterns, indicating the interlocking of heaven and earth. The circles are studded with interesting faces, both human and animal. Behind the font, the altar features similar inlaid-marble work.

Nicola Pisano's Pulpit

Is this the world's first Renaissance sculpture? It's the first authenticated (signed) work by the "Giotto of sculpture," working in what came to be called the Renaissance style. The freestanding sculpture has classical columns, realistic people and animals, and 3-D effects in the carved panels.

The 15-foot-tall, hexagonal pulpit is by Nicola Pisano, and the earliest (1260) and simplest of the four pulpits by the Pisano father-and-son team. Nicola, born in southern Italy, settled in Pisa, where he found steady work. Ten-year-old Giovanni learned the art of pulpit-making here at the feet of his father.

The speaker's platform stands on columns that rest on the backs of animals, representing

Christianity's triumph over paganism. The white Carrara-marble panels are framed by dark rose-colored marble, making a pleasant contrast. Originally, this and the other pulpits were touched up with paint, gilding, and colored pastes.

The relief panels, with scenes from the life of Christ, are more readable than the Duomo pulpit. They show bigger, simpler figures in dark marble "frames." Read left to right, starting from the back:

1. Nativity: Mary reclines across a bed like a Roman matron, a pose inspired by Roman sarcophagi, which had been found around Pisa in Nicola's day (on display in the Camposanto Cemetery, described later).

2. Adoration of the Magi: The Three Kings kneel before Baby Jesus in simple profile; but notice the strong 3-D of the horses' heads coming straight out of the panel. Just below this relief, note the small statue of Hercules. Many art historians consider this the first Renaissance carving. Sculpted in 1260—200 years before Michelangelo—it's a nude depiction of a pagan character, with a realistic body standing in a believable *contrapposto* pose. This was clearly inspired by carvings found on ancient sarcophagi.

3. Presentation in the Temple: It lacks the star of the scene, the Christ Child, who got broken off, but on the panel's right side, a powerful, bearded man in a voluminous robe epitomizes Nicola's solemn classical style.

4. Crucifixion: Everyone faces either straight out or in profile; the Roman in front actually has to look back over his shoulder to razz Jesus.

5. Last Judgment: Christ reigns over crowded, barely controlled chaos. The pulpit's lectern is an eagle clutching its prey, echoing the "triumph of Christianity" theme of the base.

Acoustics

Make a sound in here and it echoes for a good 10 seconds. A priest standing at the baptismal font (or a security guard today) can sing three tones within those 10 seconds—"Ave Maria"—and make a chord, singing haunting harmonies with himself. This medieval form of digital delay is due to the 250-foot-wide dome. Recent computer analysis suggests that the 15th-century architects who built the dome intended this building to function not just as a Baptistery, but also as a musical instrument. A security guard sings every half-hour, starting when the doors open in the morning.

Climb 75 steps to the interior gallery (midway up) for an impressive view back down on the baptismal font.

Camposanto Cemetery

The cemetery is enclosed within the long white building (1278-1465) that borders the Field of Miracles on the north. This site has been a cemetery since at least the 12th century. Highlights are the building's cloistered interior courtyard, some ancient  sarcophagi, and the large 14th-century fresco, *The Triumph of Death.*

Courtyard

The delightful open-air courtyard is surrounded by an arcade with intricately carved tracery in the arches. The courtyard's grass grows on special dirt (said to turn a body into bones in a single day) shipped here by returning Crusaders from Jerusalem's Mount Calvary, where Christ was crucified.

The arcade floor is paved with the **coats of arms** of some 600 dearly departed Pisans. In death all are equal—the most humble peasant (or tourist) can walk upon these VIP tombstones. Today much of the marble flooring is scarred, the result of lead melting from the roof during WWII bombing.

Displayed in the arcade are dozens of ancient Roman **sarcophagi.** These coffins, which originally held dead Romans, were reused by medieval big shots. In anticipation of death, a wealthy Pisan would shop around, choose a good sarcophagus, and chip his message into it. When he died, his marble box was placed with the others around the exterior of the cathedral. Great sculptors such as Nicola and Giovanni Pisano passed them daily, gaining inspiration.

Circle the courtyard clockwise, noticing **traces of fresco** on the bare-brick walls. (We'll see some reconstructed frescoes later.) The huge **chains** on the west wall once stretched across the mouth of Pisa's harbor as a defense. Then Genoa attacked, broke the chains, carried them off as a war trophy, and gave them to Pisa's archrival Florence. After unification, they were returned to Pisa as a token of friendship.

Straight ahead is the cemetery's oldest object, an ochre-colored Greek tombstone. This **stele,** dating from the time of Alexander the Great (fourth century B.C.), shows a woman (seated) who's just given birth. A maid (standing) shows the baby while the mother gazes on adoringly.

In the floor 10 yards away, by the corner of the courtyard, is a **pavement slab** dedicated to an American artist, Deane Keller.

After serving in Italy during World War II, he helped rebuild the Camposanto Cemetery and restore its frescoes.

On the wall in the corner, what looks like a big, faded **bull's-eye** is the politically correct 14th-century view of the universe—everything held by Christ, with the earth clearly in the center.

World War II Photos

At the back of the courtyard (opposite where you entered), step through the door to see photos of the bombed-out Camposanto. By the summer of 1944, Allied troops had secured much of southern Italy and pushed Nazi forces to the north bank of the Arno. German Field Marshal Kesselring dug in at Pisa, surrounded by the US Army's 91st Infantry. Germans and Americans lobbed artillery shells at each other. (The Americans even considered blowing up the Leaning Tower—the "Tiltin' Hilton" was suspected to be the German lookout point.) Most of the Field of Miracles was miraculously unscathed, but the Camposanto took a direct hit from a Yankee incendiary grenade. It melted the lead-covered arcade roof and peeled historic frescoes from the walls—one of the many tragic art losses of World War II. The Americans liberated the city on September 2 and rebuilt the Camposanto.

Some of the much-damaged frescoes are displayed in the adjoining room. (After careful restoration, these are now slowly and steadily being returned to their original spots on the walls of the Camposanto.)

The Triumph of Death

This 1,000-square-foot fresco (on the left wall, c. 1340, by an unknown 14th-century master) captures late-medieval Europe's concern with death—predating but still accurately depicting Pisa's mood in the wake of the bubonic plague (1348), which killed one in three Pisans. Well-dressed ladies and gents (left half of the painting) are riding gaily through the countryside when they come across three coffins with corpses (bottom left). Confronted with death, they each react differently—a woman puts her hand thoughtfully to her chin, a man holds his nose against the stench, while a horse leans in for a better whiff. Above them, a monk scours the Bible for the meaning of death. Mr. Death, a winged demon with a scythe, stands to the right of center and eyes his future victims.

In the right half of the painting, young people gather in a garden (bottom right) to play music (symbolizing earthly pleasure), oblivious to the death around them. Winged demons swoop down from above to pluck souls from a pile of corpses, while winged angels fight them for the souls. The action continues in the next fresco (the room's far wall), where Jesus and Mary judge the dead at the Last Judgment. The wicked are led away to hell (the right wall of the room) to be tortured by a horned Satan. Grim stuff, but appropriate for the Camposanto's permanent residents—and to anyone alive who needed a reminder of the fleeting and corruptive nature of wealth and worldly pleasures.

As you leave the fresco room, look left to see a third-century A.D. **Roman sarcophagus** carved with mythological scenes. Near the corner, another sarcophagus features a couple—the deceased—relaxing atop their coffin.

Back Outside

Stepping back into the piazza, consider how this richly artistic but utilitarian square fit into the big picture of life. The ensemble around you includes the Baptistery, the cathedral, the bell tower, the hospital (present-day Museum of the Sinopias), and the Christian cemetery you just visited. The Jewish cemetery is adjacent but just outside the walls. Pisa, a pragmatic port town, needed the money and business connections of the Jews and treated them relatively well for the age. Unlike in Rome or Venice, there was no Jewish ghetto here in the Middle Ages.

Museum of the Sinopias (Museo delle Sinopie)

Housed in a 13th-century hospital, this museum features the preparatory sketches (sinopias) for the Camposanto's WWII-damaged frescoes. If you loved *The Triumph of Death* and others in the Camposanto, or if you're interested in fresco technique, this museum is worthwhile. If not, you'll wonder why you're here.

Whether or not you pay to go in, you can watch two free videos in the entry lobby that serve to orient you to the square: a 10-minute, 3-D computer tour of the complex and a 15-minute story of the Tower, its tilt, and its fix.

Just past the ticket-taker, you'll see the multiringed, earth-centric, Ptolemaic universe of the *Theological Cosmography*. Continue to your right to find a faint *Crucifixion* and scenes from the Old Testament. At the end of the long hall, climb the stairs to the next floor to find (midway along the right wall) the red-tinted sinopias for *The Triumph of Death* and the *Last Judgment and Hell*.

Sinopias are sketches made in red paint directly on the wall, designed to guide the making of the final colored fresco. The master always did the sinopia himself. It was a way for him (and for those who paid for the work) to see exactly how the scene would look in its designated spot. If it wasn't quite right, the master changed a detail here and there. Next, assistants made a "cartoon" by tracing the sinopia onto large sheets of paper *(cartone)*. Then the sinopia was plastered over. To put the drawing back on the wall, assistants perforated the drawing on the cartoon, hung the cartoon over the wall, and dabbed it with a powdered bag of charcoal. This process printed dotted lines onto the newly plastered wall, re-creating the cartoon. While the plaster was still wet, the master and his team quickly filled in the color and details, producing the final frescoes (now on display at the Camposanto). These sinopias—never meant to be seen—were uncovered by the bombing and restoration of the Camposanto and brought here.

Duomo Museum
(Museo dell'Opera del Duomo)

Near the Tower is the entrance to the Duomo Museum, which houses many of the original statues and much of the artwork that once adorned the Campo's buildings (where copies stand today), notably the statues by Nicola and Giovanni Pisano. You can stand face-to-face with the Pisanos' very human busts, which once ringed the outside of the Baptistery. Giovanni Pisano's stone *Madonna del Colloquio* solemnly exchanges gazes with baby Jesus in her arms. The most charming piece is Giovanni's carved ivory *Madonna and Child*. Mary leans back gracefully to admire baby Jesus, her pose matching the original shape of what she's carved from—an elephant's tusk. Here, too, are the Duomo's original 12th-century bronze doors of St. Ranieri, with scenes from the life of Jesus, done by Bonanno Pisano.

You'll see a mythical sculpted hippogriff (a medieval jack-alope) and other oddities brought back from the Holy Land by Pisan Crusaders. The museum also has several large-scale wooden models of the Duomo, Baptistery, and Tower. The church treasury is here, with vestments, chalices, and bishops' staves.

On the next floor up are the illuminated manuscripts, along with fine inlaid woodwork that once graced the choir stalls of the sacristy. The collection of antiquities includes Etruscan funerary urns with reclining people—the inspiration for the Roman sarcophagi that inspired the Pisanos. Beyond the ancient sculptures are beautiful small-scale copies of the Camposanto frescoes, painted in the 1830s. There's also a scene that shows the building's appearance before it was bombed.

The museum's grassy interior courtyard has a two-story, tourist-free view of the Tower, Duomo, and Baptistery.

PISA SLEEPING, EATING & CONNECTIONS

Sleeping in Pisa

To locate these hotels, see the map on page 398.

$$$ Hotel Alessandro della Spina, in a nondescript neighborhood near Pisa Centrale train station, has 16 elegant and colorful rooms, each named after a flower (Sb-€120, Db-€140, discounts off-season and online, air-con, Internet access, free Wi-Fi, parking-€10/day; head straight out of train station, turn right on Viale F. Bonaini, and take the third right on Via Alessandro della Spina to find the hotel on your left at #5; tel. 050-502-777, fax 050-20583, www.hoteldellaspina.it, info@hoteldellaspina.it).

$$ Hotel Royal Victoria, a classy place on the Arno River, has been run by the Piegaja family since 1837. With 48 creaky, historic rooms filled with antiques, it's ideal for romantics who missed out on the Grand Tour. The location, dead-center between the Tower and Pisa Centrale train station, is the most atmospheric of my listings (D-€80, standard Db-€110, better Db-€130, suite-€190, family room-€228, 10 percent discount with this book if you pay cash and book direct, check website for special deals, air-con on request, Wi-Fi, parking garage-€20/day, lush communal terrace, Lungarno Pacinotti 12, tel. 050-940-111, fax 050-940-180, www.royalvictoria.it, mail@royalvictoria.it).

$$ Hotel Villa Kinzica has 30 tired, worn rooms with high ceilings, indifferent management, and a prime location just steps away from the Field of Miracles—ask for a room with a view of the Tower (Sb-€70, Db-€95, Tb-€109, Qb-€119, air-con, elevator, Piazza Arcivescovado 2, tel. 050-560-419, fax 050-551-204, www.hotelvillakinzica.it, info@hotelvillakinzica.it).

$ Hotel Milano, near Pisa Centrale train station, offers 10 simple, clean rooms (D-€55, Db-€78, 10 percent discount for Rick

PISA EATING

Sleep Code

(€1 = about $1.40, country code: 39)
S = Single, **D** = Double/Twin, **T** = Triple, **Q** = Quad, **b** = bathroom, **s** = shower only. Unless otherwise noted, credit cards are accepted, breakfast is included, and English is generally spoken. Many towns in Italy levy a hotel tax of about €2 per person, per night, which is generally not included in the rates I've quoted.

To help you sort easily through these listings, I've divided the accommodations into three categories based on the price for a standard double room with bath:

$$$ Higher Priced—Most rooms €120 or more.
$$ Moderately Priced—Most rooms between €80-120.
$ Lower Priced—Most rooms €80 or less.

Prices can change without notice; verify the hotel's current rates online or by email.

Steves readers if you pay cash and book direct, breakfast extra, air-con, Via Mascagni 14, tel. 050-23-162, fax 050-44-237, www .hotelmilano.pisa.it, info@hotelmilano.pisa.it).

$ Pensione Helvetia is a no-frills, homey, clean, and quiet inn just 100 yards from the Tower. Its 29 economical rooms are spread over four floors (no elevator); the lower your room number, the lower your altitude (S-€54, Sb-€60, D-€70, Db-€79, lower prices off-season, no breakfast but small lounge with vending machines, ceiling fans, free Wi-Fi, Via Don G. Boschi 31, reception around the corner at Hotel Francesco on Via Santa Maria, tel. 050-553-084, www.pensionehelvetiapisa.com, helvetiapisatravel @gmail.com).

$ Two Steps from the Tower B&B, in the historic center just a few blocks east of the Field of Miracles, offers three Ikea-style rooms (Sb-€35-40, Db-€60-65, extra bed-€15, weekly rates available, free Wi-Fi, kitchen use-€10/day, Via Cardinale Pietro Maffi 6, tel. 347-394-6559, www.2stepsfromtower.com, info@2stepsfromtower.com).

Eating in Pisa

Antica Trattoria il Campano, just off the market square, has a typically Tuscan menu and a candlelit, stay-awhile atmosphere. Their €30-€35 tasting menus include wine and generous portions of local specialties (Thu-Tue 12:30-15:00 & 19:30-22:45, closed Wed, reservations smart, Via Cavalca 19, tel. 050-580-585).

Ristorante Masala serves tasty, authentic Indian cuisine just a few blocks from the Tower. As there is a large Indian community in Pisa, this is a great place to take a break from pizza and pasta (€4-9 curries, vegetarian options, Tue-Sun 19:00-23:00, lunch Fri-Sun 12:00-14:30, closed Mon, Via Roma 52, tel. 050-48513).

At **Ristorante Bagus** the specialties are an extra-rare burger made with the famous Chianina beef and trendy twists on typical Tuscan fare (€25 fixed-price meal, Mon-Fri 12:30-14:30 & 19:30-22:00, Sat 19:30-22:00 only, closed Sun; heading south on Corso Italia, turn right on Via Nunziata and take your first right after Piazza Griletti to Piazza dei Facchini 13; tel. 050-26196).

Pizzeria al Bagno di Nerone is a local favorite and particularly popular with students. Belly up to the bar and grab a slice to go, or sit in their small dining room for a whole pie. Try the *cecina*, a crepe-like garbanzo-bean cake (Wed-Mon 11:30-14:30 & 18:45-22:30, closed Tue, a 5-minute walk from the Tower at Largo Carlo Fedeli 26, tel. 050-551-085).

At **Paninoteca il Canguro,** Mario makes warm, hearty sandwiches to order. Check the chalkboard for seasonal specials, such as *porchetta* (daily 10:00-24:00, Via Santa Maria 151, tel. 050-561-942).

Panetteria Antiche Tradizioni—not to be confused with another panetteria across the street—is a sandwich/bread shop with complete fixings for a picnic on the lawn at the Field of Miracles. Build your own sandwich with homemade bread or focaccia, then choose fruit from the counter, fresh pastries from the window, and cold drinks or wine to round out your meal (daily 8:00-20:00, Via Santa Maria 66, mobile 327-570-5210).

Drop by cheery **La Lupa Ghiotta Tavola Calda** for a cheap, fast, and tasty meal a few steps from Pisa Centrale train station. It's got everything you'd want from a *ristorante* at half the price and with faster service (build your own salad—five ingredients for €4.50; Mon and Wed-Sat 12:15-15:00 & 19:15-23:30, Tue 12:15-15:00 only, closed Sun, Viale F. Bonaini 113, tel. 050-21018).

The street that houses the daily market, **Via delle Colonne** (a block north of the Arno, west of Borgo Stretto), has a few atmospheric, mid-priced restaurants and several fun, greasy take-out options.

Pisa Connections

Pisa is well-connected by trains, buses (particularly with Lucca), and highways, with a busy airport nearby.

From Pisa Centrale Station by Train to: Florence (2-3/hour, 45-75 minutes, €7.10), **Livorno** (2-3/hour, 20 minutes, €1.90), **Rome** (2/hour, many change in Florence, 3-4 hours), **La Spezia,**

gateway to Cinque Terre (about hourly, 1-1.5 hours), **Siena** (2/hour, 1.75 hours, change at Empoli, €8.90), **Lucca** (1-2/hour, 30 minutes, bus is better except on Sun—see below, €3). Even the fastest trains stop in Pisa, so you might change trains here whether you plan to stop or not.

By Bus to Lucca: A handy bus connects the Field of Miracles with Lucca's Piazzale Giuseppe Verdi in 30 minutes (Mon-Sat hourly, fewer on Sun; in Pisa, wait at the Vai Bus signpost, immediately outside the wall behind the Baptistery on the right; buy €3 ticket on bus, toll-free tel. 800-602-947). This makes a half-day side-trip to Pisa from Lucca particularly easy.

By Car: The drive between Pisa and Florence is that rare case where the non-autostrada highway (free, more direct, and at least as fast) is a better deal than the autostrada.

By Plane: Pisa's **Galileo Galilei Airport** handles more and more international and domestic flights (TI open daily 8:30-23:30, cash machine, car-rental agencies, baggage storage from 8:00-20:00 only, €7/bag; self-service cafeteria, airport code: PSA, tel. 050-849-300, www.pisa-airport.com).

To get into **Pisa,** you can take bus LAM Rossa (4-6/hour, after 20:00 3/hour, 15 minutes, €1.10, departs from in front of the arrivals hall); a train (departs from the far left of the arrivals hall as you face the exits); or a taxi (€10-12).

You can connect to **Florence** easily by train (2-3/hour, 1.25 hours, €5.80, most transfer at Pisa Centrale) or by Terravision bus (about hourly, 1.25 hours, €10 one-way, ticket kiosk is at the right end of the arrivals hall as you're facing the exits, catch bus outside and to the far right of the bus parking lot, www.terravision.eu).

LUCCA

Surrounded by well-preserved ramparts, layered with history, alternately quaint and urbane, Lucca charms its visitors. The city is a paradox. Though it hasn't been involved in a war since 1430, it is Italy's most impressive fortress city, encircled by a perfectly intact wall. Most cities tear down their wall to make way for modern traffic, but Lucca's effectively keeps out both traffic and, it seems, the stress of the modern world. Locals are very protective of their wall, which they enjoy like a community roof garden.

Lucca, known for being Europe's leading producer of toilet paper and tissue (with a monopoly on the special machinery that makes it), is nothing to sneeze at. However, the town has no single monumental sight to attract tourists—it's simply a uniquely human and undamaged, never-bombed city. Romanesque churches seem to be around every corner, as do fun-loving and shady piazzas filled with soccer-playing children.

Locals say Lucca is like a cake with a cherry filling in the middle... every slice is equally good. Despite Lucca's charm, few tourists seem to put it on their maps, and it remains a city for the Lucchesi (loo-KAY-zee).

Planning Your Time

Low-impact Lucca has no must-see sights, but its pleasant ambience, ample churches, and pristine piazzas reward any time you've got. With the better part of a day, stroll through the town center, dipping into the sights that interest you. Once you've had your fill, rent a bike and do a few spins around the ramparts (or do the loop in slow motion, by foot) before dinner.

Orientation to Lucca

Tourist Information

Lucca has two TIs. The bigger TI, on **Piazzale Giuseppe Verdi,** offers city information and a no-fee room-booking service (daily 9:00-19:00, futuristic WC-€0.60, tel. 0583-583-150, www.luccaitinera.it). It also has Internet access, baggage storage, and bike rentals (all described later, under "Helpful Hints") and guided city walks (see "Tours in Lucca," later).

The other TI is in a kiosk near the train station. As you exit the piazza in front of the station, look for it to the right on **Piazza Curtatone** (daily May-Sept 9:00-19:00, Oct-April 9:00-13:00 & 14:00-18:00, no-fee room booking, baggage storage—see "Helpful Hints," later, tel. 0583-496-639).

Arrival in Lucca

By Train: There is no baggage check at the train station, but you can leave your luggage at either TI described above, or in a pinch, at the recommended Hotel Rex, near the train station (see "Helpful Hints," later).

To reach the city center from the train station, walk toward the walls and head left, to the entry at Porta San Pietro. Taxis are sparse, but try calling 025-353 (ignore any recorded message— just wait for a live operator); a ride from the station to Piazza dell'Anfiteatro costs about €6.

By Bus: Buses from Pisa, Viareggio, and from nearby villages arrive inside the walls at Piazzale Giuseppe Verdi, where the main TI is located.

By Car: The key for drivers—don't try to drive within the walls. The old town is ringed by parking lots (with two just inside the walls, both usually full).

An easy option is to park near the tour bus lot, not far from the southwest wall. As you leave the autostrada, follow signs for *Bus Turistico Checkpoint*, which will lead you to parking lots on Via Luporini—one is for buses but the other has free and paid parking for cars. White lines denote free parking, and blue lines are paid parking (daily 8:00-20:00, €1-1.50/hour, pay at automated kiosks). Avoid the yellow lines—these spots are for locals only. From here it's about a five-minute walk to Porta Sant'Anna.

Parking is always free in Piazzale Don Franco, a five-minute walk north of the city walls. If you must park inside the city walls, try just inside Porta Santa Maria (€1/hour). Or consider parking outside the gates near the train station or on the boulevard surrounding the city (meter rates vary; also about €1/hour). Overnight parking (20:00-8:00) on city streets and in city lots is usually free. Check with your hotel to be sure.

Helpful Hints

Combo-Tickets: A €7 combo-ticket includes visits to the Ilaria del Carretto tomb in San Martino Cathedral (€3), Cathedral Museum (€4), and San Giovanni Church (€4). A €6 combo-ticket combines the Guinigi Tower (€4) and the Clock Tower (€4). Yet another combo-ticket covers Palazzo Mansi and Villa Guinigi for €6.50 and is valid for three days (€4 each if purchased separately).

Shops and Museums Alert: Shops close most of Sunday and Monday mornings. Many museums are closed on Monday as well.

Markets: Lucca's atmospheric markets are worth visiting. Every third weekend of the month (whenever the third Sun falls), one of the largest **antiques markets** in Italy unfurls in the blocks between Piazza Antelminelli and Piazza San Giovanni (8:00-19:00). The last weekend of the month, local artisans sell **arts and crafts** around town, mainly near the cathedral (also 8:00-19:00). At the **general market,** held Wednesdays and Saturdays, you'll find produce and household goods (8:30-13:00, from Porta Elisa to Porta San Jacopo on Via dei Bacchettoni).

Concerts: San Giovanni Church hosts one-hour concerts featuring a pianist and singers performing highlights from hometown composer Giacomo Puccini (€17 at the door, some hotels offer tickets for the same price or cheaper, daily April-Oct at 19:00, Nov-March check schedule and location at www .puccinielasualucca.com).

Festival: On September 13 and 14, the city celebrates Volto Santo ("Holy Face"), with a procession of the treasured local crucifix and a fair in Piazza Antelminelli.

Internet Access: You can get online at the main TI on Piazzale Giuseppe Verdi (€2/hour, two terminals, Wi-Fi same price) or at **Betty Blue,** a wine bar handy to the recommended launderette (€4.50/hour, two terminals and cables to plug in your laptop, Thu-Tue 11:00-24:00, closed Wed, Via del Gonfalone 18, tel. 0583-492-166).

Baggage Storage: For train travelers, the most convenient storage spot is the TI on **Piazza Curtatone** (2 bags for €4.50/5 hours, €7/day, daily 9:00-17:30, they need to photocopy your passport). The TI on **Piazzale Giuseppe Verdi** is more convenient to the buses and has longer hours (same prices and passport procedure as other TI, daily 9:00-18:30). In a pinch, you also may be able to store bags at the recommended Hotel

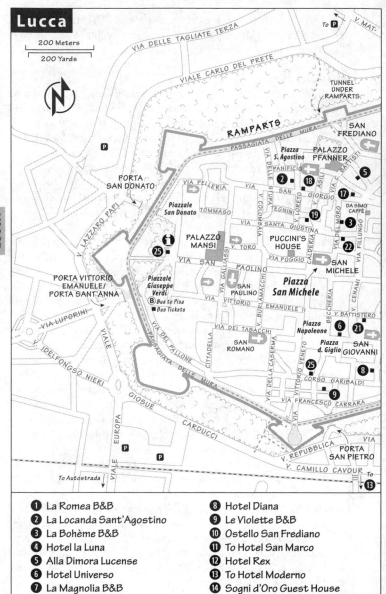

Lucca

LUCCA

Legend:

1. La Romea B&B
2. La Locanda Sant'Agostino
3. La Bohème B&B
4. Hotel la Luna
5. Alla Dimora Lucense
6. Hotel Universo
7. La Magnolia B&B
8. Hotel Diana
9. Le Violette B&B
10. Ostello San Frediano
11. To Hotel San Marco
12. Hotel Rex
13. To Hotel Moderno
14. Sogni d'Oro Guest House

LUCCA

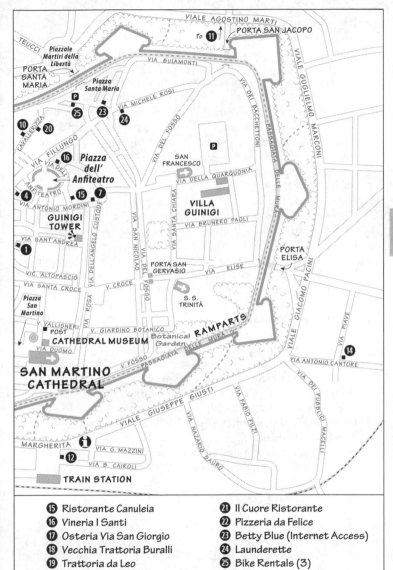

15 Ristorante Canuleia
16 Vineria I Santi
17 Osteria Via San Giorgio
18 Vecchia Trattoria Buralli
19 Trattoria da Leo
20 Bella 'Mbriana Pizzeria

21 Il Cuore Ristorante
22 Pizzeria da Felice
23 Betty Blue (Internet Access)
24 Launderette
25 Bike Rentals (3)

Rex (near the train station).

Laundry: Lavanderia Self-Service Niagara is just off Piazza Santa Maria at Via Rosi 26 (€9 wash and dry, daily 7:00-23:00).

Bike Rental: A one-hour rental gives you time for two leisurely loops around the ramparts. Several places with identical prices cluster around Piazza Santa Maria (€3/hour, €15/day, tandem bikes available, helmets available on request, daily about 9:00-19:00 or sunset). Try these easygoing shops: **Antonio Poli** (Piazza Santa Maria 42, tel. 0583-493-787, enthusiastic Cristiana) and, right next to it, **Cicli Bizzarri** (Piazza Santa Maria 32, tel. 0583-496-682, Australian Dely). At the west end of town, the **TI** on Piazzale Giuseppe Verdi rents bikes (€3/hour). At the south end, at Porta San Pietro, you'll find **Chrono** (same rates and hours as the competition, Corso Garibaldi 93, tel. 0583-490-591, www.chronobikes.com).

Local Magazine: For insights into American and British expat life and listings of concerts, markets, festivals, and other special events, pick up a copy of the *Grapevine* (€2), available at newsstands.

Cooking Class: Gianluca Pardini invites you to the hills above Lucca to learn to make Tuscan fare. You prepare and then eat a three-course meal. Depending on how many others attend, the price ranges from €50 (a steal) to a whopping €125 per person. This is great for groups of four or more (€14 cab ride from town, 3-hour lesson plus time to dine, includes wine, reserve at least 2 days in advance, Via di San Viticchio 414, tel. 0583-378-071, mobile 347-678-7447, www.italiancuisine.it, info@italiancuisine.it).

Updates to this Book: For news about changes to this book's coverage since it was published, see www.ricksteves.com/update.

Tours in Lucca

Walking Tours—The TI offers two-hour city walks with a local guide, departing from the office on Piazzale Giuseppe Verdi (€10, Mon-Sat at 14:30, Sun at 9:30, tel. 0583-583-150).

Local Guide—Gabriele Calabrese knows and shares his hometown well (€120/3 hours, by foot or bike, mobile 347-788-0667, www.turislucca.com, turislucca@turislucca.com).

Sights in Lucca

▲▲**Bike the Ramparts**—Lucca's most remarkable feature, its Renaissance wall, is also its most enjoyable attraction—especially when circled on a rental bike. Stretching for 2.5 miles, this is an

ideal place to come for an overview of the city by foot or bike.

Lucca has had a protective
wall for 2,000 years. You can
read three walls into today's map:
the first rectangular Roman wall,
the later medieval wall (nearly
the size of today's), and the 16th-
century Renaissance wall that
still survives.

With the advent of cannons,
thin medieval walls were suddenly vulnerable. A new design—
the same one that stands today—was state-of-the-art when it was
built (1550-1650). Much of the old medieval wall (look for the old
stones) was incorporated into the Renaissance wall (with uniform
bricks). The new wall was squat: a 100-foot-wide mound of dirt
faced with bricks, engineered to absorb a cannonball pummeling.
The townspeople cleared a wide no man's land around the town,
exposing any attackers from a distance. Eleven heart-shaped bas-
tions (now inviting picnic areas) were designed to minimize exposure to cannonballs and to maximize defense capabilities. The
ramparts were armed with 130 cannons.

The town invested a third of its income for more than a century to construct the wall, and—since it kept away the Florentines
and nasty Pisans—it was considered a fine investment. In fact,
nobody ever bothered to try to attack the wall. Locals say that the
only time it actually defended the city was during an 1812 flood of
the Serchio River, when the gates were sandbagged and its ramparts kept out the high water.

Today, the ramparts seem made-to-order for a leisurely bike
ride (20-minute pedal, wonderfully smooth). You can rent bikes
cheaply and easily from one of several bike-rental places in town
(listed earlier, under "Helpful Hints").

Piazza dell'Anfiteatro—Just off the main shopping street, the
architectural ghost of a Roman amphitheater can be felt in the
delightful Piazza dell'Anfiteatro. With the fall of Rome, the the-

ater (which seated 10,000) was gradually cannibalized for its stones and
inhabited by people living in a mishmash of huts. The huts were cleared
away at the end of the 19th century
to better appreciate the town's illus-
trious past. Today, the square is a
circle of touristy shops and mediocre restaurants that becomes a lively
bar-and-café scene after dark. The

The History of Lucca

Lucca began as a Roman settlement. In fact, the grid layout of the streets (and the shadow of an amphitheater) survives from Roman times. Trace the rectangular Roman wall—indicated by today's streets—on the map. As in typical Roman towns, two main roads quartered the fortified town, crossing at what was the forum (main market and religious/political center)—today's Piazza San Michele.

Christianity came here early; it's said that the first bishop of Lucca was a disciple of St. Peter. While churches were built here as early as the fourth century, the majority of Lucca's elegant Romanesque churches date from about the 12th century.

Feisty Lucca, though never a real power, enjoyed a long period of independence (maintained by clever diplomacy). Aside from 30 years of being ruled from Pisa in the 14th century, Lucca was basically an independent city-state until Napoleon came to town.

In the Middle Ages, wealthy Lucca's economy was built on the silk industry, dominated by the Guinigi (gwee-NEE-gee) family. Without silk, Lucca would have been just another sleepy Italian town. In 1500, the town had 3,000 silk looms employing 25,000 workers. Banking was also big. Many pilgrims stopped here on their way to the Holy Land, deposited their money for safety...and never returned to pick it up.

In its heyday, Lucca packed 160 towers—one on nearly every corner—and 70 churches within its walls. Each tower was the home of a wealthy merchant family. Towers were many stories tall, with single rooms stacked atop each other: ground-floor shop, upstairs living room, and top-floor fire-safe kitchen, all connected by exterior wooden staircases. The rooftop was generally a vegetable garden, with trees providing shade. Later, the wealthy city folk moved into the countryside, trading away life in their city palazzos to establish farm estates complete with fancy villas. (You can visit some of these villas today—the TI has a brochure—but they're convenient only for drivers and are generally not worth the cost of admission.)

In 1799, Napoleon stormed into Italy and took a liking to Lucca. He liked it so much that he gave it to his sister as a gift (who ruled 1805-14). After Napoleon was toppled, Europe's ruling powers gave Lucca to Maria Luisa, the daughter of the king of Spain. Duchess Maria Luisa (who ruled 1817-24) was partially responsible for turning the city's imposing (but no longer particularly useful) fortified wall into a fine city park that is much enjoyed today. Her statue stands on Piazza Napoleone, near Palazzo Ducale.

LUCCA

modern street level is nine feet above the original arena floor. The only bits of surviving Roman stonework are a few arches on the northern exterior (at Via Fillungo 42 and on Via dell'Anfiteatro).

Via Fillungo—This main pedestrian drag stretches southwest from Piazza dell'Anfiteatro. *The* street to stroll, Via Fillungo takes you from the amphitheater almost all the way to the cathedral. Along the way, you'll get a taste of Lucca's rich past, including several elegant, century-old storefronts. Many of the original storefront paintings, reliefs, and mosaics survive—even if today's shopkeeper sells something entirely different.

At #97 is a classic old **jewelry store** with a rare storefront that has kept its T-shaped arrangement (when closed, you see a wooden T, and during open hours it unfolds with a fine old-time display). This design dates from a time when the merchant sold his goods in front, did his work in the back, and lived upstairs.

Di Simo Caffè, at #58, has long been the hangout of Lucca's artistic and intellectual elite. Composer and hometown boy Giacomo Puccini tapped his foot while sipping coffee here. Pop in to check out the 1880s ambience (daily 9:00-24:00).

A surviving five-story **tower house** is at #67. There was a time when nearly every corner sported its own tower (see the sidebar). The stubby stones that still stick out once supported wooden staircases (there were no interior connections between floors). So many towers cast shadows over this part of town that the street just before it is called Via Buia (Dark Street). Look away from this tower and down Via San Andrea for a peek at the town's tallest tower, Guinigi, in the distance—with its characteristic oak trees sprouting from the top.

At #45 and #43, you'll see two more good examples of tower houses. Across the street, the **Clock Tower** (Torre delle Ore) has a hand-wound Swiss clock that has clanged four times an hour since 1754 (€4 to climb up and see the mechanism flip into action on the quarter-hour—if it's actually working, €6 combo-ticket includes

Guinigi Tower, daily April-Oct 9:30-18:30, Nov-March 9:30-16:30, last entry 20 minutes before closing, corner of Via Fillungo and Via del'Arancio).

The intersection of Via Fillungo and Via Roma/Via Santa Croce marks the center of town (where the two original Roman roads crossed). As you go right down Via Roma, you'll pass the fine Edison Bookstore on your left before reaching Piazza San Michele.

Piazza San Michele—This square has been the center of town since Roman times, when it was the forum. It's dominated by the Church of San Michele. Towering above the church's fancy Pisan Romanesque facade, the archangel Michael stands ready to flap his wings—which he was known to do on special occasions.

The square is surrounded by an architectural hodgepodge. The loggia, which dates from 1495, is the first Renaissance building in town. There's a late 19th-century interior in Buccellato Taddeucci, a 130-year old pastry shop (#34). The left section of the BNL bank (#5; in front of the church) sports an Art Nouveau facade that celebrates both Amerigo Vespucci and Cristoforo Colombo.

Perhaps you've noticed that the statues of big shots that decorate many an Italian piazza are mostly absent from Lucca's squares. That's because unlike Venice, Florence, and Milan—which were dominated by a few powerful dynasties—Lucca was traditionally run by an oligarchy of a hundred leading families, with no one central figure to commemorate in stone. But after Italian unification, when leaders were fond of saying, "We have created Italy... now we need to create Italians," stirring statues of national heroes popped up everywhere—even in Lucca. The statue on Piazza San Michele is a two-bit local guy, dredged up centuries after his death because he favored strong central government.

Look back at the church facade, which also has an element of patriotism—designed to give roots and legitimacy to Italian statehood. Perched above many of the columns are the faces of heroes in the Italian independence and unification movement: Victor Emmanuel II (above the short red column on the right), the Count of Cavour (next to Victor, above the column with black zigzags), and Giuseppe Mazzini.

▲**San Martino Cathedral**—This cathedral, begun in the 11th century, is an entertaining mix of architectural and artistic styles. It's also home to the exquisite 15th-century tomb of Ilaria del Carretto, who married into the wealthy Guinigi family.

Cost and Hours: Cathedral—free, Ilaria tomb—€3, €7 combo-ticket includes Cathedral Museum and San Giovanni Church; Mon-Fri 9:30-17:45, Sat 9:30-18:45; Sun open sporadically between Masses: 9:00-10:15 & 11:30-18:00; Piazza San Martino.

Visiting the Cathedral: The cathedral's elaborate Pisan Romanesque **facade** features Christian teaching scenes, animals, and candy-cane-striped columns.

The central figure is St. Martin, a Roman military officer from Hungary who, by offering his cloak to a beggar, more fully understood the beauty of Christian compassion. (The impressive original, a fine example of Romanesque sculpture, hides from pollution just inside, to the right of the main entrance.) Each of the columns on the facade is unique. Notice how the facade is asymmetrical: The 11th-century bell tower was already in place when the rest of the cathedral was built, so the builders cheated on the right side to make it fit the space. Over the right portal (as if leaning against the older tower), the architect Guideo from Como

holds a document declaring that he finished the facade in 1204. On the right (at eye level on the pilaster), a labyrinth is set into the wall. The maze relates the struggle and challenge our souls face in finding salvation. (French pilgrims on their way to Rome could relate to this, as it's the same pattern they knew from the floor of the church at Chartres.) The Latin plaque just left of the main door is where moneychangers and spice traders met to seal deals (on the doorstep of the church—to underscore the reliability of their promises). Notice the date: *An Dni MCXI* (A.D. 1111).

The interior features Gothic arches, Renaissance paintings, and stained glass from the 19th century. On the left side of the nave, a small, elaborate, birdcage-like temple contains the wooden crucifix—beloved by locals—called **Volto Santo.** It's said to have been sculpted by Nicodemus in Jerusalem and set afloat in an unmanned boat that landed on the coast of Tuscany, from where wild oxen miraculously carried it to Lucca in 782. The sculpture (which is actually 12th-century Byzantine-style) has quite a jewelry collection, which you can see in the Cathedral Museum (described next).

On the right side of the nave, the sacristy houses the enchantingly beautiful **memorial tomb of Ilaria del Carretto** by Jacopo della Quercia (1407). Pick up a handy English description to the right of the door as you enter the sacristy. This young bride of silk baron Paolo Guinigi is decked out in the latest, most expensive fashions, with the requisite little dog (symbolizing her loyalty) curled up at her feet in eternal sleep. She's so realistic that the statue was nicknamed "Sleeping Beauty." Her nose is partially worn off because of a long-standing tradition of lonely young ladies rubbing it for luck in finding a boyfriend.

Cathedral Museum (Museo della Cattedrale)—This beautifully presented museum houses original paintings, sculptures, and vestments from the cathedral and other Lucca churches. The first room displays jewelry made to dress up the Volto Santo crucifix (described above), including gigantic gilded silver shoes. Upstairs, notice the fine red brocaded silk—a reminder that this precious fabric is what brought riches and power to the city. The exhibits in this museum have very brief descriptions and are meaningful only with the slow-talking €1 audioguide—if you're not in the mood to listen, skip the place altogether.

Cost and Hours: €4, €7 combo-ticket includes Ilaria tomb and San Giovanni Church; April-Oct daily 10:00-18:00; Nov-March Mon-Fri 10:00-14:00, Sat-Sun 10:00-17:00; to the left of the cathedral as you're facing it, Piazza Antelminelli, tel. 0583-490-530, www.museocattedralelucca.it.

San Giovanni Church—This first cathedral of Lucca is interesting only for its archaeological finds. The entire floor of the 12th-century church has been excavated in recent decades, revealing layers of Roman houses, ancient hot tubs that date back to the time of Christ, early churches, and theological graffiti. Sporadic English translations help you understand what you're looking at. As you climb under the church's present-day floor and wander the lanes of Roman Lucca, remember that the entire city sits on similar ruins. If it's open, climb the *campanile* (bell tower) of the church for a panoramic view of the city.

Cost and Hours: €4, €7 combo-ticket includes Ilaria tomb and Cathedral Museum, audioguide-€1; mid-March-Oct daily 10:00-18:00; Nov-mid-March Sat-Sun 10:00-17:00, closed Mon-Fri; see concert info on page 433; kitty-corner from cathedral at Piazza San Giovanni.

Church of San Frediano—This impressive church was built in 1112 by the pope to counter Lucca's bishop and his spiffy cathedral. Lucca was the first Mediterranean stop on the pilgrim route from northern Europe, and the pope wanted to remind pilgrims that the action, the glory, and the papacy awaited them in Rome. Therefore, he had the church made "Roman-esque." The pure marble facade frames an early Christian Roman-style mosaic of Christ with his 12 apostles. Step inside and you're struck by the sight of 40 powerful (if recycled) ancient Roman columns. The message: Lucca may be impressive, but the finale of your pilgrimage—in Rome—is worth the hike.

Inside, there's a notable piece of art in each corner: At rear left is the 12th-century baptistery, with some interesting Church propaganda showing the story of Moses (the evil Egyptians are played by Holy Roman Empire troops). At rear right is St. Zita's actual body, put there in 1278. At front left is a particularly elegant Virgin Mary, depicted at the moment she gets the news that she'll bring the Messiah into the world (carved and painted by Lucchesi artist Matteo Civitali, c. 1460). And at front right is a painting on wood of the *Assumption of the Virgin* (c. 1510), with Doubting Thomas receiving Mary's red belt as she ascends so he'll doubt no more. The pinball-machine composition serves as a virtual catalog of the fine silk material produced in Lucca—a major industry in the 16th century.

Cost and Hours: Free, Mon-Sat 8:30-12:00 & 15:00-17:30, Sun 9:00-11:30 & 15:00-17:30, Piazza San Frediano, tel. 0583-493-627.

Palazzo Mansi—Minor paintings by Tintoretto, Pontormo, Veronese, and others vie for attention, but the palace itself—a sumptuously furnished and decorated 17th-century confection—steals the show. This is your chance to appreciate the wealth of Lucca's silk merchants. Since all visitors must be accompanied by a museum employee, during high season you may have to wait a bit for your chance to enter.

Cost and Hours: €4, €6.50 combo-ticket includes Villa Guinigi, hours prone to change but generally Tue-Sat 8:30-19:30, Sun 8:30-13:30, closed Mon, no photos, request English booklet at ticket desk, Via Galli Tassi 43, tel. 0583-55-570.

Guinigi Tower (Torre Guinigi)—Many Tuscan towns have towers, but none is quite like the Guinigi family's. Up 227 steps is a small garden with fragrant trees, surrounded by fantastic views.

Cost and Hours: €4, €6 combo-ticket includes Clock Tower, daily April-May 9:30-18:30, June-Sept 9:30-19:30, March and Oct 9:30-17:30, Nov-Feb 9:30-16:30, Via Sant'Andrea 41.

Puccini's House—Opera enthusiasts (but nobody else) will want to visit the home where Giacomo Puccini (1858-1924) grew up. The museum has the great composer's piano and a small collection of his personal belongings, as well as opera costumes and memorabilia.

Cost and Hours: €7; April-Oct Wed-Mon 10:00-18:00, Nov-March Wed-Mon 11:00-17:00, closed Tue year-round; Corte San Lorenzo 9, ring to be let in, tel. 0583-584-028, www.puccini museum.it.

Palazzo Pfanner—Garden enthusiasts (and anyone needing a break from churches) will enjoy this 18th-century palace built for a rich Swiss expat who came to Lucca to open a brewery. His sudsy legacy includes Baroque furniture, elaborate frescoes, a centuries-old kitchen, and a lavish garden.

Cost and Hours: Garden or residence-€4.50 apiece, €6 for both, April-Oct daily 10:00-18:00, closed Nov-March, Via degli Asili 33, tel. 0583-954-029, www.palazzopfanner.it.

Villa Guinigi—Built by Paolo Guinigi in 1418, the family villa is now a stark, abandoned-feeling museum displaying a hodge-podge of Etruscan artifacts, religious sculptures, paintings, inlaid woodwork, and ceramics. Monumental paintings by the multi-talented Giorgio Vasari are the best reason to visit.

Cost and Hours: €4, €6.50 combo-ticket includes Palazzo Mansi, Tue-Sat 8:30-19:30, Sun 8:30-13:30, closed Mon, may have to wait in high season for a museum employee to accompany you, Via della Quarquonia, tel. 0583-496-033.

Sleeping in Lucca

Fancy Little Boutique B&Bs Within the Walls

$$$ La Romea B&B, in an air-conditioned, restored, 14th-century palazzo near Guinigi Tower, feels like a royal splurge. Its four posh rooms and one suite are lavishly decorated in handsome colors and surround a big, plush lounge with stately Venetian-style floors (Db-€100-135 depending on season, big suite-€160, extra bed-€20-25; 10 percent discount when you book direct, show this book, and pay cash; Wi-Fi; from the train station, take Via Fillungo, turn right on Via Sant'Andrea, then take the second right to Vicolo delle Ventaglie 2; tel. 0583-464-175, www.laromea .com, info@laromea.com, Giulio and wife Gaia).

$$$ La Locanda Sant'Agostino has three romantic, bright, and palatial rooms. The vine-draped terrace, beautiful breakfast spread, and quaint views invite you to relax (Db-€160, extra bed-€25, air-con, Internet access and Wi-Fi, from Via Fillungo take Via San Giorgio to Piazza Sant'Agostino 3, best to reserve by email, tel. 0583-443-100, mobile 347-989-9069, www.locandasant agostino.it, info@locandasantagostino.it).

$$ La Bohème B&B has a cozy yet elegant ambience, offering six large, charming, chandeliered rooms, each painted with a different rich color scheme (Db-€125, less off-season, 10 percent discount with this book if you pay cash and book direct, air-con, free Wi-Fi, Via del Moro 2, tel. & fax 0583-462-404, www .boheme.it, info@boheme.it, Sara).

Sleeping More Forgettably Within the Walls

$$ Hotel la Luna, run by the Barbieri family, has 29 rooms in a great location, right in the heart of the city. Updated rooms are split between two adjacent buildings just off of the main shopping street. The annex may have an elevator, but I prefer the rooms in the main building, which are larger and classier (Sb-€90, Db-€125, suite-€190, these prices for Rick Steves readers who book direct, air-con, pay Internet access and Wi-Fi, parking-€15/day, Via Fillungo at Corte Compagni 12, tel. 0583-493-634, fax 0583-490-021, www.hotellaluna.com, info@hotellaluna.com, Sara).

$$ Alla Dimora Lucense's seven newer rooms are bright, modern, clean, and peaceful, with all the comforts. Enjoy their

Sleep Code

(€1 = about $1.40, country code: 39)
S = Single, **D** = Double/Twin, **T** = Triple, **Q** = Quad, **b** = bathroom,
s = shower only.

Unless otherwise noted, credit cards are accepted, English is spoken, and breakfast is included (but usually optional). Many towns in Italy levy a hotel tax of about €2 per person, per night, which is generally not included in the rates I've quoted.

To help you sort easily through these listings, I've divided the accommodations into three categories based on the price for a standard double room with bath:

$$$ Higher Priced—Most rooms €125 or more.
  $$ Moderately Priced—Most rooms between €80-125.
    $ Lower Priced—Most rooms €80 or less.

Prices can change without notice; verify the hotel's current rates online or by email.

relaxing, sunny interior courtyard (Db-€125, suite for 2-4 people-€150-200; 10 percent discount if you pay cash, book direct, and show this book; air-con, Wi-Fi, half a block from Via Fillungo at Via Fontana 19, tel. 0583-495-722, fax 0583-441-210, www.dimora lucense.it, info@dimoralucense.it).

$$ Hotel Universo, renting 55 rooms right on Piazza Napoleone and facing the theater and Palazzo Ducale, is a 19th-century town fixture. While it clearly was once elegant, now it's old and tired, with a big Old World lounge and soft prices ("comfort" Db-€100, "superior" Db with updated bath-€130, Wi-Fi, Piazza del Giglio 1, tel. 0583-493-678, www.universolucca.com, info@universolucca.com).

$$ La Magnolia B&B offers five basic rooms and one apartment with an intimate atmosphere and relaxing garden. It's buried in a ramshackle old palace in a central location (may have new owners in 2013, Sb-€65, Db-€85, Qb-€90, includes breakfast at nearby bar, 5 percent discount with this book if you pay cash and book direct, a block behind amphitheater at Via Mordini 63, tel. 0583-467-111, www.lamagnolia .com, info@lamagnolia.com).

$ Hotel Diana is a dreary little family-run hotel, with nine rooms in the main building and another six slightly nicer, soundproofed, and air-conditioned rooms in the annex just around the corner (D-€50, Db-€65, annex Db-€85, Wi-Fi, parking-€6/day, south of the cathedral at Via del Molinetto 11, tel. 0583-492-202, fax 0583-467-795, www.albergodiana.com, info@albergodiana.com).

$ At Le Violette B&B, friendly Anna (who's still learning English) will settle you into one of her six homey rooms near the train station inside Porta San Pietro (D-€60, Db-€75, extra bed-€15, Wi-Fi, communal kitchen, €5 to use washer and dryer, Via della Polveriera 6, tel. 0583-493-594, mobile 349-823-4645, fax 0583-429-305, www.leviolette.it, leviolette@virgilio.it).

$ Ostello San Frediano, in a central, sprawling ex-convent with a peaceful garden, is a cut above the average hostel, though it's still filled mainly with a young crowd. Its 29 rooms are bright and modern, and some have fun lofts (€20 beds in 6- to 8-person dorms, 140 beds, Db-€65, Tb-€80, Qb-€105, includes sheets, €3 extra/night for non-members, cash only, breakfast extra, no curfew, lockers, Internet access and Wi-Fi, cheap restaurant, free parking, Via della Cavallerizza 12, tel. 0583-469-957, fax 0583-461-007, www.ostellolucca.it, info@ostellolucca.it).

Outside the Walls

$$$ Hotel San Marco, a seven-minute walk outside the Porta Santa Maria, is a postmodern place decorated à la Stanley Kubrick. Its 42 rooms are sleek, with all the comforts (Sb-€87, Db-€136, extra bed-€10, includes nice breakfast spread, air-con, Wi-Fi, elevator, pool, bikes-€6/half-day, free parking, taxi from station-€6, Via San Marco 368, tel. 0583-495-010, fax 0583-490-513, www .hotelsanmarcolucca.com, info@hotelsanmarcolucca.com).

$$ Hotel Rex rents 25 rooms in a practical contemporary building on the train station square. While in the modern world, you're just 200 yards away from the old town and get more space for a better price (Db-€80-100; 10 percent discount with this book if you pay cash and book direct, does not apply to prepaid/nonrefundable rooms booked online; air-con, Wi-Fi, free bike rental, a few steps from the train station at Piazza Ricasoli 19, tel. 0583-955-443, www.hotelrexlucca.com, info@hotelrexlucca.com).

$$ Hotel Moderno is indeed modern, with 11 good-value rooms tastefully decorated in shades of white. Although it backs up to the train tracks, the rooms are quiet (Sb-€70, Db-€90, air-con, Wi-Fi, Via Vincenzo Civitali 38—turn left out of train station and go over bridge across tracks, tel. 0583-55-840, fax 0583-53-830, www.albergomodernolucca.com, info@albergomodernolucca.com).

$ Sogni d'Oro Guest House ("Dreams of Gold"), run by Davide, is a handy budget option for drivers, with five basic rooms and a cheery communal kitchen (grocery store next door). It's a 10-minute walk from the train station and a five-minute walk from the city walls (D-€50, Db-€65, Q-€70, 10 percent discount with cash; free ride to and from station with advance notice—then call when your train arrives in Lucca; from the station, head straight out to Viale Regina Margherita and turn right, follow the main boulevard as it turns into Viale Giuseppe Giusti, at the curve turn right onto Via Antonio Cantore to #169; tel. 0583-467-768, mobile 329-582-5062, fax 0583-957-612, www.bbsognidoro.com, info @bbsognidoro.com).

Eating in Lucca

Ristorante Canuleia makes everything fresh in their small kitchen. While the portions aren't huge, the food is tasty. You can eat in their dressy little dining room or outside on the garden courtyard (€10 pastas, €17 *secondi*, Mon-Sat 12:30-14:00 & 19:30-21:30, closed Sun, Via Canuleia 14, tel. 0583-467-470, reserve for dinner).

Vineria I Santi is pricey but good if you appreciate quality food and fine wine, and just want to lie back and be pampered. The sexy jazz ambience would work well in a bordello. Relax in the peaceful indoors among wine bottles, or on a quiet square outside (€11 pastas, €18 *secondi*, Thu-Tue 12:30-14:30 & 19:30-22:00, closed Wed, Via dell'Anfiteatro 29, tel. 0583-496-124).

Osteria Via San Giorgio, owned by Daniela and her brother Piero, is a cheery family eatery that satisfies both fish-lovers and meat-lovers. Sample the splittable *antipasto fantasia*—five small courses such as *ceviche* (seafood salad), scallops au gratin, squid sautéed with potatoes, or whatever else was caught that day in Viareggio; they also offer a meatier version. Dinner-size salads are bright and fresh, pasta is homemade, and Daniela's desserts tempt (daily 12:00-16:00 & 19:00-23:00, Via San Giorgio 26, tel. 0583-953-233).

Vecchia Trattoria Buralli, on quiet Piazza Sant'Agostino, is a good bet for traditional cooking and juicy steaks, with fine indoor and piazza seating (€7 pastas, €10 *secondi*, €12-30 fixed-price meals, Thu-Tue 12:00-14:45 & 19:00-22:30, closed Wed, Piazza Sant'Agostino 10, tel. 0583-950-611).

Trattoria da Leo packs in chatty locals for typical, cheap home-cooking in a hash-slingin' Mel's-diner atmosphere. This place is a high-energy winner...you know it's going to be good as soon as you step in. Arrive early or reserve in advance (€6 pastas, €10 *secondi*, Mon-Sat 12:00-14:30 & 19:30-22:30, sometimes open Sun, cash only, leave Piazza San Salvatore on Via Asili and take the first left to Via Tegrimi 1, tel. 0583-492-236).

Bella 'Mbriana Pizzeria focuses on doing one thing very well: turning out piping-hot, wood-fired pizzas to happy locals in a welcoming wood-paneled dining room. Order and pay at the counter, take a number, and they'll call you when your pizza's ready. Consider take-out to munch on the nearby walls (Wed-Mon 12:30-14:30 & 18:30-23:00, closed Tue, to the right as you

Specialties in Lucca

Lucca has some tasty specialties worth seeking out. *Ceci* (CHEH-chee), also called *cecina* (cheh-CHEE-nah), makes an ideal cheap snack any time of day. This garbanzo-bean crepe is sold in pizza shops and is best accompanied by a nip of red wine.

Farro, a grain (spelt) dating back to ancient Roman cuisine, shows up in restaurants in soups or as a creamy rice-like dish *(risotto di farro).*

Tordelli, the Lucchesi version of *tortelli,* is homemade ravioli. It's traditionally stuffed with meat and served with more meat sauce, but chefs creatively pair cheeses and vegetables, too.

Meat, not fish, is the star at most restaurants, especially steak, which is listed on menus as *filetto di manzo* (filet), *tagliata di manzo* (thin slices of grilled tenderloin), or the king of steaks, *bistecca alla fiorentina.* Order *al sangue* (rare), *medio* (medium rare), *cotto* (medium), or *ben cotto* (well). Anything more than *al sangue* is considered a travesty for steak connoisseurs.

Note that steaks (as well as fish) are often sold by weight, noted on menus as *s.q.* (according to quantity ordered) or *l'etto* (cost per 100 grams—250 grams is about an 8-ounce steak).

For something sweet, bakeries sell *buccellato*, bread dotted with raisins, lightly flavored with anise, and often shaped like a wreath. It's only sold in large sizes, but luckily it stays good for a few days (and it also pairs well with *vin santo*— fortified Tuscan dessert wine). An old proverb says, "Coming to Lucca without eating the *buccellato* is like not having come at all." *Buon appetito!*

face the Church of San Frediano, Via della Cavallerizza 29, tel. 0583-495-565).

Il Cuore Enogastronomia includes a delicatessen and restaurant. For a fancy picnic, drop in the deli for ready-to-eat lasagna, saucy meatballs, grilled and roasted vegetables, vegetable soufflés, Tuscan bean soup, fruit salads, and more, sold by weight and dished up in disposable trays to go. Ask them to heat your order *(riscaldare),* then picnic on nearby Piazza Napoleone. For curious traveling foodies on a budget who want to eat right there, they can assemble a €10 "degustation plate"—just point to what you want from among the array of tasty treats under the glass (Tue-Sun 9:30-19:30, closed Mon, Via del Battistero 2, tel. 0583-493-196, Cristina).

Il Cuore Ristorante, located across the way, is a trendy find for wine-tasting or a meal on a piazza. Try the €8 *aperitivo* (available

18:00-20:00), which includes a glass of wine and a plate of cheese, *salumi*, and snacks, or feast on fresh pastas and other high-quality dishes from their lunch and dinner menus (Wed-Sun 12:00-22:00 with limited menu 15:00-19:30, Tue 12:00-15:00, closed Mon, Via del Battistero, tel. 0583-493-196).

Pizzeria da Felice is a little mom-and-pop hole-in-the-wall serving *cecina* (garbanzo-bean crepes) and slices of freshly baked pizza to throngs of snackers. Grab an *etto* of *cecina* and a short glass of wine for €2.50 (Mon-Sat 10:00-20:30, closed Sun and 3 weeks in Aug, Via Buia 12, tel. 0583-494-986).

Lucca Connections

From Lucca by Train to: Florence (2/hour, 1.5 hours), **Pisa** (roughly 1-2/hour, 30 minutes, bus is better except on Sun), **Livorno** (about hourly, 1-1.25 hours, transfer at Pisa Centrale, €3.70), **Milan** (2/hour except Sun, 4-5 hours, transfer in Florence), **Rome** (1/hour except Sun, 3-4 hours, change in Florence).

From Lucca by Bus to Pisa: Direct buses from Lucca's Piazzale Giuseppe Verdi drop you right at the Leaning Tower, making Pisa an easy day trip (Mon-Sat hourly, fewer on Sun, 30 minutes, also stops at Pisa's airport, €3). Even with a car, I'd opt for this much faster and cheaper option. For more on Pisa, see those chapters.

TUSCAN HILL TOWNS

San Gimignano • Volterra •
Montepulciano • Pienza •
Montalcino • Cortona

Tuscany is rich in history, and proud locals will remind you that their ancestors, the Etruscans, were thriving long before anyone had heard of Julius Caesar. The region offers a delightful mix of scenic beauty and deep traditions...and a taste of the rustic Italian good life.

Many of the hill towns—so emblematic of Tuscany—trace their roots to Etruscan times (well before ancient Rome). Others date from the fall of Rome, when barbarian invasions chased lowland townsfolk to the hills, where they built fortified communities. The Middle Ages were formative times for many cities, when warring factions divided towns between those loyal to the pope (Guelphs) and to the Holy Roman Emperor (Ghibellines). Cities developed monumental defensive walls and built great towers. Then, the Black Death swept through Tuscany in 1348 and devastated the region. The plague, plus the increasing dominance of Florence, turned many bustling cities into docile backwaters. Ironically, what was bad news in the 14th century is good news today: The hill towns enjoy a tourist-fueled affluence and retain a unique, medieval charm.

Tuscan towns are best enjoyed by adapting to the pace of the countryside. So, slow...down...and savor the delights that this region offers. Spend the night if you can, as many hill towns are mobbed by day-trippers from Florence and Siena.

But how in Dante's name does a traveler choose from Italy's hundreds of hill towns? I've listed some of my favorites in this chapter. The one(s) you visit will depend on your interests, time, and mode of transportation.

Multitowered San Gimignano is a classic, but because it's such an easy hill town to visit (about 1.5 hours by bus from Florence), peak-season crowds can overwhelm its charms. For rustic vitality not completely trampled by tourist crowds, out-of-the-way Volterra is the clear winner. Wine aficionados head for Montalcino and Montepulciano—each a happy gauntlet of wine shops and art galleries (Montepulciano being my favorite). Fans of architecture and urban design appreciate Pienza's well-planned streets and squares. Those enamored by Frances Mayes' memoir *(Under the Tuscan Sun)* make the pilgrimage to Cortona.

One of the greatest Tuscan treats—the food—varies wildly depending on where you are. The areas around Florence and Siena are famed for serving hearty "farmer food," but as you move west, dishes become lighter, based more on seafood and grains. Each town proudly boasts local specialties—ask for the *specialità della città*. While Siena is the town that excels at sweets, you can find good local desserts anywhere (watch for the phrase "*fatta in casa*," which means it's homemade). Wine is good throughout Tuscany, with pleasing selections for both amateurs and connoisseurs. (See "Wine Labels and Lingo" on page 34 for a description of Tuscan wines.)

Getting Around Tuscany
Most hill towns are easier and more efficient to visit by car.

By Bus or Train
Traveling by public transportation is cheap and connects you with the locals. While trains link some of the towns, hill towns—being on hills—don't quite fit the railroad plan. Stations are likely to be in the valley a couple of miles from the town center, usually connected efficiently by a local bus.

Buses are often the only public-transportation choice to get between small hill towns. But, as with trains, they don't always drive up into the town itself. Fortunately, bus stations are sometimes connected to the town by escalator or elevator.

Buy bus tickets at newsstands or tobacco shops (with the big *T* signs). Confirm the departure point *("Dov'è la fermata?")*—some piazzas have more than one bus stop, so double-check that the posted schedule lists your destination and departure time. In most cases, orange buses are local city buses, and blue buses are for long distances.

Once the bus arrives, confirm the destination with the driver. You are expected to stow big backpacks underneath the bus (open the luggage compartment yourself if it's closed).

Sundays and holidays are problematic; even from cities such as Siena, schedules are sparse, departing buses are jam-packed, and ticket offices are often closed. Plan ahead and buy your ticket in advance. Most travel agencies book bus and train tickets with little or no commission.

Tuscan Hill Towns Public Transportation

- - - - - Rail
━━━━━ High Speed Rail
- - - - Bus

20 Kilometers
20 Miles

To Cinque Terre
Carrara
To Bologna, Ravenna, Milan & Venice
Monte-catini
Pistoia
Viareggio
Lucca
Prato
Vespucci ✈
Fiesole
Pisa
Empoli
Florence
Galileo ✈
Livorno
T U S C A N Y
San Gimignano
Poggibonsi
Arezzo
Volterra
"Corse Rapide" Direct Bus
Camucia
Cortona
Cecina
Saline di Volterra
Colle Val d'Elsa
Siena
To Assisi
Ligurian Sea
San Galgano
Buonconvento
Montepulciano Stazione
Teron-tola
Campiglia
Montalcino
Monte-pulciano
Chiusi
Piombino
Braccagni
Pienza
Elba Portoferraio
Grosseto
Orvieto
To Rome
To Rome

If you're pinched for time, it makes sense to narrow your focus to one or two hill towns, or rent a car to see more.

By Car

Exploring small-town Tuscany by car can be a great experience. But since a car is an expensive, worthless headache in Florence and

Siena, wait to pick up your car until the last big city you visit (or pick it up at the nearest airport to avoid big-city traffic). Then use the car for lacing together the hill towns and exploring the country-side. For more on car rentals and driving in Italy, see the appendix.

A big, detailed regional road map (buy one at a newsstand or gas station) and a semiskilled navigator are essential. Freeways (such as the toll autostrada and the non-toll *superstrada*) provide the fastest way to connect two points, but the smaller roads, including the super-scenic S-222, which runs through the heart of the Chianti region (connecting Florence and

Siena), are more rewarding. For more joyrides—from Siena to Montalcino, and from Montalcino to Montepulciano—see "The Crete Senese" on page 515.

Parking throughout this region can be challenging. Some towns don't allow visitors to park in the city center, so you'll need to leave your car outside the walls and walk into town. Signs reading *Zona Traffico Limitato (ZTL)*—often above a red circle—mark areas where no driving or parking is allowed. Parking lots, indicated by big blue *P* signs, are usually free and plentiful outside city walls (and in some cases, are linked to the town center by elevators or escalators). In some towns, you can park on the street; nearby kiosks sell "pay and display" tickets. In general, white lines indicate free parking, blue lines mean you have to pay, and yellow lines are spaces reserved for local residents. To reduce the threat of theft (no guarantees, though), choose a parking lot over street parking when possible. Your hotelier can also recommend safe parking options.

Sleeping in Tuscany
Hotels, Rooms, and Apartments

Smaller towns offer few hotels to choose from. Prices are lower than in Florence, but a nice double will still run about €80, including breakfast. Many towns have an abundance of *affitta camere,* or rental rooms. This can be anything from a set of keys and a basic bed to a cozy B&B with your own Tuscan grandmother. TIs book rooms and apartments and have lists of each. Private rooms are generally a good budget option, but since they vary in quality, shop around to find the best value. It's always OK to ask to see the room before you commit. Apartments usually offer a couple of bedrooms, a sitting area, and a teensy *cucinetta,* typically stocked with dishes and flatware—a great value for families traveling together who'd rather cook than eat out all the time.

Agriturismo

Agriturismo (agricultural tourism), or rural B&Bs, began in the 1980s as a way to allow small farmers in the countryside to survive in a modern economy where, like in the US, so many have been

run out of business by giant agricultural corporations. By renting rooms to travelers, farmers can remain on their land and continue to produce food. A peaceful home base for exploring the region, these rural Italian B&Bs are ideal for those traveling by car—especially families.

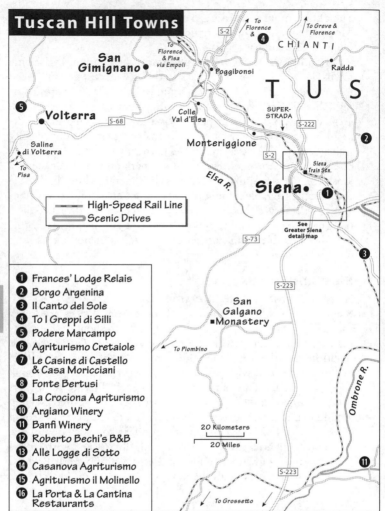

Tuscan Hill Towns

TUSCAN HILL TOWNS

San Gimignano •

5 • Volterra   S-68

Saline di Volterra •

To Pisa

San Gimignano •

To Florence & Pisa via Empoli

Poggibonsi

Colle Val d'Elsa

Monteriggione

S-2

To Florence &

4   C H I A N T I

To Greve & Florence

Radda

T U S

SUPER-STRADA   S-222

2

Elsa R.

Siena Train Stn.

Siena •   **1**

See Greater Siena detail map

S-73   **3**

S-223

San Galgano ■ Monastery

To Piombino

Ombrone R.

20 Kilometers

20 Miles

11

S-223

To Grosseto

━━━ High-Speed Rail Line
▱▱▱ Scenic Drives

1 Frances' Lodge Relais
2 Borgo Argenina
3 Il Canto del Sole
4 To I Greppi di Silli
5 Podere Marcampo
6 Agriturismo Cretaiole
7 Le Casine di Castello & Casa Moricciani
8 Fonte Bertusi
9 La Crociona Agriturismo
10 Argiano Winery
11 Banfi Winery
12 Roberto Bechi's B&B
13 Alle Logge di Sotto
14 Casanova Agriturismo
15 Agriturismo il Molinello
16 La Porta & La Cantina Restaurants

It's wise to book several months in advance for high season (May-Sept). Weeklong stays are preferred in July and August, but shorter stays are possible off-season. To sleep cheaper, avoid peak season. A farmhouse that rents for as much as $2,000 a week in July can go for as little as $700 in late September or October. In the winter, you might be charged extra for heat, so confirm the price ahead of time. Payment policies vary, but generally a 25 per-cent deposit is required (lost if you cancel), and the balance is due one month before arrival.

As the name implies, *agriturismi* are in the countryside, although some are located within a mile of town. Most are family-

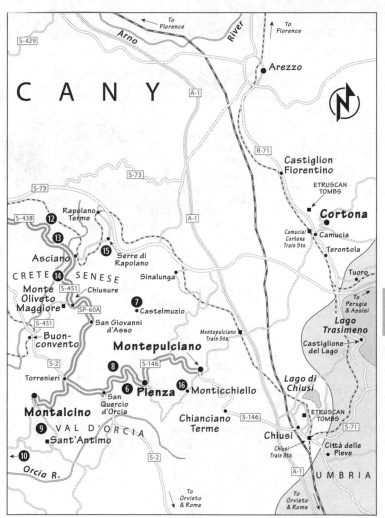

run. *Agriturismi* vary dramatically in quality—some properties are rustic, while others are downright luxurious, offering amenities such as swimming pools and riding stables. The rooms are usually clean and comfortable. Breakfast is often included, and *mezza pensione* (half-pension, which in this case means a home-cooked dinner) might be built into the price whether you want it or not. Most places serve tasty homegrown food; some are vegetarian or organic, others are gourmet. Kitchenettes are often available to cook up your own feast.

To qualify officially as an *agriturismo*, the farm must still generate more money from its farm activities, thereby insuring that

Tips for Enjoying an *Agriturismo* Farmhouse Stay

- To sleep cheap, avoid peak season. Rental prices follow the old rule of supply and demand. Prices that are sky-high in summer can drop dramatically in fall.
- Make sure your trip fits their requirements. Many properties rent on a traditional Saturday-to-Saturday time period. You might be unable to rent for a different or shorter time, especially during peak season.
- If you want amenities, be willing to pay more. A swimming pool can add substantially to the cost, but at the height of summer, could be worth every extra euro, particularly if you're bringing kids.
- Consider renting a rural apartment rather than an entire villa or farmhouse. Often the owners have renovated an original rambling farmhouse or medieval estate into a series of well-constructed apartments with private kitchens, bathrooms, living areas, and outdoor terraces. They usually share a common pool.
- You will need private transportation, such as a rental car, to fully enjoy—or even reach—your accommodations.
- To make the most of your time, ask an expert—the owner—for suggestions on restaurants, sights, and activities. Make sure you know how to operate the appliances.
- Slow down. One of the joys of staying for at least a week in one location is you can develop a true *dolce far niente* (sweetness of doing nothing) attitude. If it rains, grab a book from the in-house library and curl up on the sofa.
- While your time in the countryside may not be action-packed, staying put in one spot leaves you open to the unexpected pleasures that come when you just let the days unwind without a plan.

the land is worked and preserved. Some farmhouse B&Bs aren't working farms, but are still fine places to stay. Many people who think they want *agriturismi* are really looking for countryside B&Bs and villas that offer a bit more upscale comfort (while skipping the farm smells and sounds). If you want the real thing, make sure the owners call their place an *agriturismo*.

In this chapter, I've listed a broad range of options under the towns that they're nearest to, but there are many, many more. Local TIs can give you a list of places in their area, and many *agriturismi* now have their own websites. For a sampling, visit www.agriturismoitaly.it or search online for *agriturismo*. One booking agency among many is Farm Holidays in Tuscany (closed Sat-Sun, tel. 0564-417-418, www.byfarmholidays.com, info @byfarmholidays.com).

Between Florence and Siena

Two fine hill towns—one famous, the other underrated—sit in the middle of the triangle formed by three major destinations: Florence, Siena, and Pisa. If driving between those cities, it makes sense to detour either to picturesque but touristy San Gimignano, or charming and authentic-feeling Volterra. (Or you could use one of them as a home base for reaching the bigger towns.) While they're only about a 30-minute drive apart, they're poorly connected to each other by public transit (requiring an infrequent two-hour connection); if relying on buses, San Gimignano is easier to reach, but Volterra rewards the additional effort.

San Gimignano

The epitome of a Tuscan hill town, with 14 medieval towers still standing (out of an original 72), San Gimignano (sahn jee-meen-

YAH-noh) is a perfectly preserved tourist trap. There are no important interiors to sightsee, and the town is packed with crass commercialism. The locals seem spoiled by the easy money of tourism, and most of the rustic is faux. The fact that this small town supports two torture museums is a comment on the caliber of the masses who choose to visit. But San Gimignano is so easy to reach and visually so beautiful that it remains a good stop. It's enchanting at night, when it's yours alone. For this reason, San Gimignano is an ideal place to go against the touristic flow—arrive late in the day, enjoy it at twilight, then take off in the morning before the deluge begins.

In the 13th century—back in the days of Romeo and Juliet—feuding noble families ran the hill towns. They'd periodically battle things out from the protection of their respective family towers.

Pointy skylines, like San Gimignano's, were the norm in medieval Tuscany.

San Gimignano's cuisine is mostly what you might find in Siena—typical Tuscan home cooking. *Cinghiale* (cheeng-GAH-lay, boar) is served in almost every way: stews, soups, cutlets, and, my favorite, salami. Most shops will give you a sample before you commit to buying. The area is well known for producing some of the best saffron in Italy (collected from the purple flowers of *Crocus sativus*); you'll find the spice for sale in shops (it's fairly expensive) and as a flavoring in meals at finer restaurants. Although Tuscany is normally a red-wine region, the most famous Tuscan white wine comes from here: the inexpensive, light, and fruity Vernaccia di San Gimignano. Look for the green "DOCG" label around the neck for the best quality (see "Wines Labels and Lingo" on page 34).

Orientation to San Gimignano

While the basic ▲▲▲ sight here is the town of San Gimignano itself, there are a few worthwhile stops. From the town gate, head straight up the traffic-free town's cobbled main drag to Piazza della Cisterna (with its 13th-century well). The town sights cluster around the adjoining Piazza del Duomo.

Tourist Information

The helpful TI is in the old center on Piazza del Duomo (daily March-Oct 10:00-13:00 & 15:00-19:00, Nov-Feb 10:00-13:00 & 14:00-18:00, free maps, sells bus tickets, books rooms, handles VAT refunds, tel. 0577-940-008, www.sangimignano.com).

The town offers a two-hour **guided walk** in English and Italian several days a week (April-Oct Sat-Sun at 11:00, €20; includes admission either to the Duomo or to the Civic Museum and Tower; pay and meet at TI). They also offer a two-hour minibus tour to a countryside winery for the same price (April-Oct Tue and Thu at 17:00).

Arrival in San Gimignano

The **bus** stops at the main town gate, Porta San Giovanni. There's no baggage storage anywhere in town, so you're better off leaving your bags in Siena or Florence.

You can't **drive** within the walled town. There are three pay lots a short walk outside the walls: The handiest is Parcheggio Montemaggio, just outside the main gate, Porta San Giovanni (€2/hour, €20/day). The one below the roundabout and Co-op supermarket, called Parcheggio Giubileo, is least expensive (€1.50/hour, €6/day). And at the north end of town, by Porta San Jacopo,

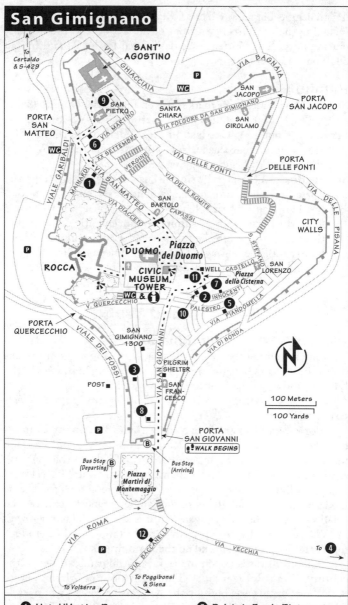

San Gimignano

TUSCAN HILL TOWNS

1. Hotel l'Antico Pozzo
2. Hotel la Cisterna
3. Palazzo al Torrione
4. To Ponte a Nappo Rooms
5. Le Vecchie Mura Camere & Ristorante
6. Locanda il Pino
7. Dulcis in Fundo Ristorante
8. Trattoria Chiribiri
9. Locanda di Sant'Agostino
10. diVinorum Wine Bar
11. Gelateria Pluripremiata "di Piazza"
12. Co-op Supermarket

is Parcheggio Bagnaia (€2/hour, €15/day). Note that some lots—including the one directly in front of the Co-op and the one just outside Porta San Matteo—are designated for locals and have a one-hour limit for tourists.

Helpful Hints

Market Day: Thursday is market day on Piazza del Duomo (8:00-13:00), but for local merchants, every day is a sales frenzy.

Services: A public **WC** is just off Piazza della Cisterna (€0.50); others are at the Rocca fortress, just outside Porta San Matteo, and at the Parcheggio Bagnaia parking lot.

Shuttle Bus: A little electric shuttle bus does its laps all day from Porta San Giovanni to Piazza della Cisterna to Porta San Matteo. Route #1 runs back and forth through town; route #2—which runs only in summer—conveniently connects the three parking lots to the town center. Each route runs about hourly (€0.75 one-way, €1.50 for all-day pass, buy ticket in advance from TI or tobacco shop, possible to buy on bus for extra charge).

Self-Guided Walk

Welcome to San Gimignano

This quick walking tour will take you across town, from the bus stop at Porta San Giovanni through the town's main squares to the Duomo, and on to the Sant'Agostino Church.

• *Start, as most tourists do, at the Porta San Giovanni gate at the bottom end of town.*

Porta San Giovanni: San Gimignano lies about 25 miles from both Siena and Florence, a good stop for pilgrims en route to those cities, and on a naturally fortified hilltop that encouraged settlement. The town's walls were built in the 13th century, and gates like this helped regulate who came and went. Today, modern posts keep out all but service and emergency vehicles. The small square just outside the gate features a memorial to the town's WWII dead. Follow the pilgrims' route (and flood of modern tourists) through the gate and up the main drag.

About 100 yards up, on the right, is a pilgrims' shelter (12th-century, Pisan Romanesque). The eight-pointed Maltese cross indicates that this was built by the Knights of Malta, whose early mission (before they became a military unit) was to provide hospitality for pilgrims. It was one of 11 such shelters in town. Today, only the wall of this shelter remains.

• *Carry on past all manner of touristy rip-off shops, up to the town's central Piazza della Cisterna. Sit on the steps of the well.*

Piazza della Cisterna: The piazza is named for the cistern that is served by the old well standing in the center of this square.

A clever system of pipes drained rainwater from the nearby rooftops into the underground cistern. This square has been the center of the town since the ninth century. Turn in a slow circle and observe the commotion of rustic-yet-proud facades crowding in a tight huddle around the well. Imagine this square in pilgrimage times, lined by inns and taverns for the town's guests. Now finger the grooves in the lip of the well and imagine generations of maids and children fetching water. Each Thursday, the square fills with a market—as it has for more than a thousand years.

• *Notice San Gimignano's famous towers.*

The Towers: Of the original 72 towers, only 14 survive. Before effective city walls were developed, rich people fortified their own homes with these towers: They provided a handy refuge when ruffians and rival city-states were sacking the town. If under attack, tower owners would set fire to the external wooden staircase, leaving the sole entrance unreachable a story up; inside, fleeing nobles pulled the ladders that connected each level up behind them, leaving invaders no way to reach the stronghold at the tower's top. These towers became a standard part of medi-

eval skylines. Even after town walls were built, the towers continued to rise—now to fortify noble families feuding within a town (Montague and Capulet-style).

In the 14th century, San Gimignano's good times turned very bad. In the year 1300, about 13,000 people lived within the walls. Then in 1348, a six-month plague decimated the population, leaving the once-mighty town with barely 4,000 survivors. Once fiercely independent, now crushed and demoralized, San Gimignano came under Florence's control and was forced to tear down its towers. (The Banca CR Firenze building occupies the remains of one such toppled tower.) And, to add insult to injury, Florence redirected the vital trade route away from San Gimignano. The town never recovered, and poverty left it in a 14th-century architectural time warp. That well-preserved cityscape, ironically, is responsible for the town's prosperity today.

• *From the well, walk 30 yards uphill to the adjoining square with the cathedral.*

Piazza del Duomo: The square faces the former cathedral. The twin towers to the right are 10th century, among the first in town. The stubby tower oppo-

site the church is typical of a merchant's tower: main door on ground floor, warehouse upstairs, holes to hold beams that once supported wooden balconies and exterior staircases, heavy stone on the first floor, cheaper and lighter brick for upper stories.

• *On the piazza are the Civic Museum and Tower, worth checking out (see "Sights in San Gimignano," later). You'll also see the...*

Duomo (or Collegiata): Inside San Gimignano's Romanesque cathedral, Sienese Gothic art (14th century) lines the nave with parallel themes—Old Testament on the left and New Testament on the right. (For example, from back to front: Creation facing the Annunciation, the birth of Adam facing the Nativity, and the suffering of Job opposite the suffering of Jesus.) This is a classic use of art to teach. Study the fine Creation series (top left). Many scenes are portrayed with a local 14th-century "slice of life" setting, to help lay townspeople relate to Jesus—in the same way that many white Christians are more comfortable thinking of Jesus as Caucasian (€3.50, €5.50 combo-ticket includes mediocre Religious Art Museum—skip it; April-Oct Mon-Fri 10:00-19:30, Sat 10:00-17:30, Sun 12:30-19:30; Nov-March Mon-Sat 10:00-17:00, Sun 12:30-17:00; last entry 20 minutes before closing, buy ticket and enter from the courtyard around the left side).

• *From the church, hike uphill (passing the church on your left) following signs to Rocca e Parco di Montestaffoli. Keep walking until you enter a peaceful hilltop park and olive grove within the shell of a 14th-century fortress.*

Hilltop Views at the Rocca: On the far side, 33 steps take you to the top of a little tower (free) for the best views of San Gimignano's skyline; the far end of town and the Sant'Agostino Church (where this walk ends); and a commanding 360-degree view of the Tuscan countryside. San Gimignano is surrounded by olives, grapes, cypress trees, and—in the Middle Ages—lots of wild dangers. Back then, farmers lived inside the walls and were thankful for the protection.

• *Return to the bottom of Piazza del Duomo, turn left, and continue your walk across town, cutting under the double arch (from the town's first wall). In around 1200, this defined the end of town. The **Church of San Bartolo** stood just outside the wall (on the right). The Maltese*

TUSCAN HILL TOWNS

cross over the door indicates that it likely served as a hostel for pilgrims. As you continue down Via San Matteo, notice that the crowds have dropped by at least half. Enjoy the breathing room as you pass a fascinating array of stone facades from the 13th and 14th centuries—now a happy cancan of wine shops and galleries. Reaching the gateway at the end of town, follow signs to the right to reach...

Sant'Agostino Church: This tranquil church, at the far end of town (built by the Augustinians who arrived in 1260), has fewer crowds and more soul. Behind the altar, a lovely fresco cycle by Benozzo Gozzoli (who painted the exquisite Chapel of the Magi in the Medici-Riccardi Palace in Florence) tells of the life of St. Augustine, a North African monk who preached simplicity. The kind, English-speaking friars (from Britain and the US) are happy to tell you about their church and way of life, and also have Mass in English on Sundays at 11:00. Pace the peaceful cloister before heading back into the tourist mobs (free, €0.50 lights the frescoes; April-Oct daily 7:00-12:00 & 15:00-19:00; Nov-March Tue-Sun 7:00-12:00 & 15:00-18:00, Mon 16:00-18:00). Their fine little shop, with books on the church and its art, is worth a look.

Sights in San Gimignano

▲ **Civic Museum and Tower (Museo Civico and Torre Grossa)**—This small, fun museum, consisting of just three unfurnished rooms and a tower, is inside City Hall (Palazzo Comunale). The main room (across from the ticket desk), called the **Sala di Consiglio** (a.k.a. Dante Hall), is covered in festive frescoes, including the *Maestà* by Lippo Memmi. This virtual copy of Simone Martini's *Maestà* in Siena proves that Memmi didn't have quite the same talent as his famous brother-in-law.

Upstairs, the **Pinacoteca** displays a classy little painting collection of mostly altarpieces. The highlight is a 1422 altarpiece by Taddeo di Bartolo honoring St. Gimignano (far end of last room). You can see the saint, with the town—bristling with towers—in his hands, surrounded by events from his life.

Before going back downstairs, be sure to stop by the **Mayor's Room** (Camera del Podestà, across the stairwell from the Pinacoteca). Frescoed in 1310 by Memmo di Filippuccio, it offers an intimate and candid peek into the 14th century. The theme: profane love. As you enter, look to the left corner where a young man is ready to experience the world. He hits his parents up for a bag of money and is free. On the opposite wall (above the window), you'll see a series of bad decisions: Almost immediately he's entrapped by two prostitutes, who lead him into a tent where he loses his money, is turned out, and is beaten. Above the door, from left to right, you see a parade of better choices: marriage, the cradle of love, the bride led to the groom's house, and newlyweds bathing together and retiring happily to their bed.

The highlight for most visitors is a chance to climb the **Tower** (Torre Grossa, entrance halfway down the stairs from the Pinacoteca). The city's tallest

tower, 200 feet and 218 steps up, rewards those who climb it with a commanding view. See if you can count the town's 14 towers (yes, that includes the stubby little one just below this tower). It's a sturdy, modern staircase most of the way, but the last stretch is a steep, ladder-like climb.

Coming back down to earth, you leave the complex via a delightful stony loggia and courtyard out back.

Cost and Hours: €5 includes museum and tower, daily April-Sept 9:30-19:00, Oct-March 11:00-17:30, Piazza del Duomo, tel. 0577-990-310.

San Gimignano 1300—This small but interesting attraction, located inside the Palazzo Ficarelli on a quiet street a block over from the main street, is a trip back in time. When possible, attendants like to lead visitors on individual tours around the small exhibit. The highlight is a painstakingly rendered 1:100 scale clay model of San Gimignano at the turn of the 14th century. You can see the 72 original "tower houses," and marvel at how unchanged the street plan remains today. You'll peek into cross-sections of buildings, view scenes of medieval life both within and outside the city walls, and watch videos about town history and the making of the model. After walking through a gallery of modern Italian sculpture, your visit ends in the ceramics workshop next door, where models like this one are created from wet lumps of clay. (Conveniently, the "workshop" is one corner of a ceramics shop.) While cynics might view this as little more than a gimmick to sell more little ceramic buildings, the detail of the model is truly enchanting.

Cost and Hours: €5; April-Oct daily 9:00-19:00; Nov-March Wed-Mon 10:00-17:00, Sat-Sun until 18:00, closed Tue; Via Berignano 23, tel. 0577-941-078, www.sangimignano1300.com.

Sleeping in San Gimignano

Although the town is a zoo during the daytime, locals outnumber tourists when evening comes, and San Gimignano becomes mellow and enjoyable. Drivers can unload near their hotels, then park

---

Sleep Code

(€1 = about $1.40, country code: 39)

S = Single, **D** = Double/Twin, **T** = Triple, **Q** = Quad, **b** = bathroom, **s** = shower only. Unless otherwise noted, credit cards are accepted and breakfast is included (but usually optional). English is generally spoken, but I've noted exceptions. Many towns in Italy levy a hotel tax of about €2 per person, per night, which is generally not included in the rates I've quoted.

To help you sort easily through these listings, I've divided the accommodations into three categories based on the price for a standard double room with bath:

  $$$ Higher Priced—Most rooms €100 or more.
   $$ Moderately Priced—Most rooms between €70-100.
    $ Lower Priced—Most rooms €70 or less.

Prices can change without notice; verify the hotel's current rates online or by email.

---

outside the walls in recommended lots. Hotel websites provide instructions.

$$$ Hotel l'Antico Pozzo is an elegantly restored, 15th-century townhouse with 18 tranquil, comfortable rooms, a peaceful interior courtyard terrace, and an elite air (Sb-€100, small Db-€120, standard Db-€140, big Db-€180, includes breakfast, air-con, elevator, free Wi-Fi, near Porta San Matteo at Via San Matteo 87, tel. 0577-942-014, fax 0577-942-117, www.anticopozzo.com, info@anticopozzo.com; Emanuele, Elisabetta, and Mariangela). If arriving by bus, save a cross-town walk by asking for the Porta San Matteo stop (rather than getting off at the main stop near Porta San Giovanni).

$$$ Hotel la Cisterna, right on Piazza della Cisterna, feels old and stately, with 49 predictable rooms, some with panoramic view terraces (Sb-€78, Db-€100, Db with view-€125, Db with view terrace-€140, 10 percent discount with this book when you book direct, includes buffet breakfast, air-con, elevator, cheap Wi-Fi, good restaurant with great view, closed Jan-Feb, Piazza della Cisterna 23, tel. 0577-940-328, fax 0577-942-080, www.hotelcisterna.it, info@hotelcisterna.it, Alessio).

$$$ Ponte a Nappo, run by enterprising Carla Rossi (who doesn't speak English) and her son Francesco (who does), has seven comfortable rooms and two apartments in a kid-friendly farmhouse. Located a long half-mile below town (best for drivers, but doable for hardy walkers), this place has killer views. A picnic dinner lounging on their comfy garden furniture as the sun sets is good Tuscan living (Db-€100-130, 2-6 person apartment-€130-250, price depends on season and length of stay, for best price book direct and mention Rick Steves, air-con mid-June-mid-Sept only, free Wi-Fi, free parking, pool, free loaner bikes, lunch and dinner available to guests, 15-minute walk or 5-minute drive from Porta San Giovanni, tel. 0577-907-282, mobile 349-882-1565, fax 0577-941-268, www.accommodation-sangimignano .com, info@rossicarla.it). About 100 yards below the monument square at Porta San Giovanni, find Via Vecchia (not left or right, but down a tiny road) and follow it down a dirt road for five minutes by car. They also rent a dozen or so rooms and apartments in town (including some in the Palazzo Tortoli, a stone tower right on the main square, for Db-€75-110; each one is described on their website).

$$ Palazzo al Torrione, on an untrampled side street just inside Porta San Giovanni, is quiet and handy, and generally better than most hotels (even though they don't have a full-time reception). Their 10 modern rooms are spacious and tastefully appointed (Db-€90, terrace Db-€110, Tb-€110, terrace Tb-€120, Qb-€120-130, 10 percent discount with this book when you book direct, breakfast-€7, communal kitchen, parking-€6/day, inside and left of gate at Via Berignano 76; operated from tobacco shop 2 blocks away, on the main drag at Via San Giovanni 59; tel. 0577-940-480, mobile 338-938-1656, fax 0577-955-605, www.palazzoal torrione.com, palazzoaltorrione@palazzoaltorrione.com, Vanna and Francesco).

$ Le Vecchie Mura Camere offers three good rooms above their restaurant in the old town (Db-€60, no breakfast, air-con, free Wi-Fi, Via Piandornella 15, tel. 0577-940-270, www.vecchie mura.it, info@vecchiemura.it, Bagnai family).

$ Locanda il Pino has just seven rooms and a big living room. It's dank but clean and quiet. Run by English-speaking Elena and her family, it sits above their elegant restaurant just inside Porta San Matteo (Db-€55, no breakfast, free Wi-Fi in lobby, easy parking just outside the gate, Via Cellolese 4, tel. 0577-940-415, locanda@ristoranteilpino.it). If you're arriving by bus, ask for the Porta San Matteo stop, rather than the main stop near Porta San Giovanni.

Eating in San Gimignano

My first two listings cling to quiet, rustic lanes overlooking the Tuscan hills (yet just a few steps off the main street); the rest are buried deep in the old center.

Dulcis in Fundo Ristorante, small and family-run, proudly serves modest portions of "revisited" Tuscan cuisine (with a modern twist and gourmet presentation) in a jazzy ambience. This enlightened place, whose menu identifies the sources of their ingredients, offers lots of vegetarian options and gladly caters to gluten-free diets—rare in Tuscany (€12 pastas, €13-16 *secondi*, meals served 12:30-14:30 & 19:15-21:30, closed Wed, Vicolo degli Innocenti 21, tel. 0577-941-919).

Le Vecchie Mura Ristorante has good and fast service, great prices, tasty if unexceptional home cooking, and the ultimate view. It's romantic indoors or out. They have a dressy, modern interior where you can dine with a view of the busy stainless-steel kitchen under rustic vaults, but the main reason to come is for the incredible cliffside garden terrace. Cliffside tables are worth reserving in advance by calling or dropping by: Ask for "front view" (€8-11 pastas, €12-15 *secondi*, open only for dinner from 18:00, last order at 22:00, closed Tue, Via Piandornella 15, tel. 0577-940-270, Bagnai family).

Trattoria Chiribiri, just inside Porta San Giovanni, serves homemade pastas and desserts at remarkably fair prices. While its petite size and tight seating make it hot in the summer, it's a good budget option—and as such, it's in all the guidebooks (€7 pastas, €9 *secondi*, daily 11:00-23:00, Piazza della Madonna 1, tel. 0577-941-948, Maria and Maurizio).

Locanda di Sant'Agostino spills out onto the peaceful square, facing Sant'Agostino Church. It's cheap and cheery, serving lunch and dinner daily—big portions of basic food in a restful setting. Dripping with wheat stalks and atmosphere on the inside, there's shady on-the-square seating outside (€8 pizzas, pastas, and *bruschette*; €9-14 *secondi*, daily 11:00-22:00, closed Tue off-season and Jan-Feb, Piazza Sant'Agostino 15, tel. 0577-943-141, Genziana and sons).

Enoteca: diVinorum, a cool wine bar with a small entrance right on Piazza Cisterna, has a contemporary cellar atmosphere and—best of all—a row of tables out back overlooking rolling Tuscan hills (just downhill and toward the main drag from Dulcis in Fundo, recommended above; at mealtimes, you'll have to order food to sit at the outdoor tables). They have local wines by the glass (€3-5) as well as snacks that can easily make a light meal (€10-15 *antipasti* plates, €7-8 *bruschette* and warm plates, daily 11:00-21:30, Nov-April until 20:00, Piazza Cisterna 30 or Via degli Innocenti 5, tel. 0577-907-192, Matteo).

Picnics: The big, modern **Co-op supermarket** sells all you need for a nice spread (Mon-Sat 8:30-20:00, Sun 8:30-12:30 except closed Sun Nov-March, at parking lot below Porta San Giovanni). Or browse the little shops guarded by boar heads within the town walls; they sell pricey boar meat *(cinghiale)*. Pick up 100 grams (about a quarter pound) of boar, cheese, bread, and wine and enjoy

TUSCAN HILL TOWNS

a picnic in the garden at the Rocca or the park outside Porta San Giovanni.

Gelato: To cap the evening and sweeten your late-night city stroll, stop by **Gelateria Pluripremiata "di Piazza"** on Piazza della Cisterna (at #4). Gelato-maker Sergio was a member of the Italian team that won the official Gelato World Cup—and his gelato really is a cut above (daily 8:00-24:00, tel. 0577-942-244, Dondoli family).

San Gimignano Connections

Bus tickets are sold at the bar just inside the town gate or at the TI. Many connections require a change at Poggibonsi (poh-jee-BOHN-see, with a soft "g"), which is also the nearest train station.

From San Gimignano by Bus to: Florence (hourly, less on Sun, 1.5-2 hours, change in Poggibonsi, €6.80), **Siena** (8/day direct, on Sun must change in Poggibonsi, 1.25 hours, €6), **Volterra** (4/day Mon-Sat; on Sun only 1/day—in the late afternoon and usually crowded—with no return to San Gimignano; 2 hours, change in Colle Val d'Elsa, €5.45). Note that the bus connection to Volterra is four times as long as the drive; if you're desperate to get there faster, you can pay about €70 for a taxi.

By Car: San Gimignano is an easy 45-minute drive from Florence (take the A-1 exit marked *Firenze Certosa,* then a right past tollbooth following *Siena per 4 corsie* sign; exit the freeway at Poggibonsi). From San Gimignano, it's a scenic and windy half-hour drive to Volterra.

TUSCAN HILL TOWNS

Volterra

Encircled by impressive walls and topped with a grand fortress, Volterra sits high above the rich farmland surrounding it. More than 2,000 years ago, Volterra was one of the most important Etruscan cities, one much larger than we see today. Greek-trained Etruscan artists worked here, leaving a significant stash of art, particularly funerary urns. Eventually Volterra was absorbed into the Roman Empire, and for centuries it was an independent city-state. Volterra fought bitterly against the

Florentines, but like many Tuscan towns, it lost in the end and was given a fortress atop the city to "protect" its citizens.

Unlike other famous towns in Tuscany, Volterra feels neither cutesy nor touristy...but real, vibrant, and almost oblivious to the allure of the tourist dollar. This probably stems from the Volterrans' feisty resistance to change. (At a recent town meeting about whether to run high-speed Internet cable to the town, a local grumbled, "The Etruscans didn't need it—why do we?") This stubbornness helps make Volterra a refreshing change of pace from its more commercial neighbors. It also boasts some particularly fine sights for a small town, from a remarkably intact ancient Roman theater, to a finely decorated Pisan Romanesque cathedral, to an excellent museum of Etruscan artifacts. All in all, Volterra is my favorite small town in Tuscany.

Orientation to Volterra

Compact and walkable, the city stretches out from the pleasant Piazza dei Priori to the old city gates.

Tourist Information
The helpful TI is on the main square, at Piazza dei Priori 19 (daily 10:00-13:00 & 14:00-18:00, tel. 0588-87257, www.volterratur.it). The TI's excellent €5 audioguide narrates 20 stops (2-for-1 discount on audioguides with this book).

Arrival in Volterra
By Public Transport: Buses stop at Piazza Martiri della Libertà in the town center. Train travelers can reach the town with a short bus ride (see "Volterra Connections," later.)

By Car: Drivers will find the town ringed with easy numbered parking lots (#5, #6, and #8 are free; #3 is for locals only). The most central lots are the pay lots at Porta Fiorentina and underground at Piazza Martiri della Libertà (€1.50/hour, €11/24 hours).

Helpful Hints
Market Day: The market is on Saturday morning near the Roman Theater (8:00-13:00, at parking lot #5; in winter, it's right on Piazza dei Priori). The TI hands out a list of other market days in the area.

Festivals: Volterra's Medieval Festival takes place the third and fourth Sundays of August. Fall is a popular time for food festivals—check with the TI for dates and events planned.

Internet Access: Web & Wine has a few terminals, fine wine by the glass, and organic vegetarian food (€3/hour, no minimum, summer daily 9:30-1:00 in the morning, closed

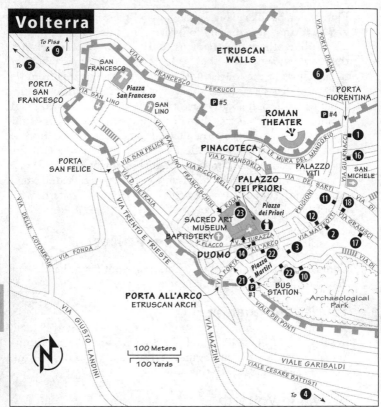

Thu in Sept-May, Via Porta all'Arco 11-15, tel. 0588-81531, www.webandwine.com, Lallo speaks English). **Enjoy Café Internet Point** has a couple of terminals in their basement (€3/hour, daily 6:30-1:00 in the morning, Piazza dei Martiri 3, tel. 0588-80530).

Laundry: The handy self-service **Lavanderia Azzurra** is just off the main square (€3 wash, €3-4 dry, daily 7:00-23:00, Via Roma 7, tel. 0588-80030).

Tours in Volterra

▲▲**Guided Volterra Walk**—Annie Adair (also listed individually, below) and her colleagues offer a great one-hour, English-only introductory walking tour of Volterra for €10. The walk touches on Volterra's Etruscan, Roman, and medieval history, as well as the contemporary cultural scene (April-July and Sept-Oct daily, rain or shine, at 18:00; meet in front of alabaster shop on Piazza Martiri della Libertà, no need to reserve—just show up, they need

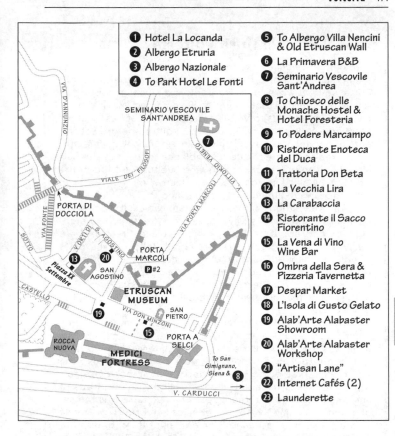

1. Hotel La Locanda
2. Albergo Etruria
3. Albergo Nazionale
4. To Park Hotel Le Fonti
5. To Albergo Villa Nencini & Old Etruscan Wall
6. La Primavera B&B
7. Seminario Vescovile Sant'Andrea
8. To Chiosco delle Monache Hostel & Hotel Foresteria
9. To Podere Marcampo
10. Ristorante Enoteca del Duca
11. Trattoria Don Beta
12. La Vecchia Lira
13. La Carabaccia
14. Ristorante il Sacco Fiorentino
15. La Vena di Vino Wine Bar
16. Ombra della Sera & Pizzeria Tavernetta
17. Despar Market
18. L'Isola di Gusto Gelato
19. Alab'Arte Alabaster Showroom
20. Alab'Arte Alabaster Workshop
21. "Artisan Lane"
22. Internet Cafés (2)
23. Launderette

TUSCAN HILL TOWNS

a minimum of 3 people—or €30—to make the tour go, www.volterrawalkingtour.com or www.tuscantour.com, info@volterrawalkingtour.com). There's no better way to spend €10 and one hour in this city.

Local Guide—American **Annie Adair** is an excellent city guide. She and her husband Francesco, a sommelier, organize private food and wine tours and even Tuscan weddings for Americans (€50/hour, minimum 2 hours, tel. 0588-086-201, mobile 347-143-5004, www.tuscantour.com, info@tuscantour.com). Francesco leads a crash one-hour "Wine Tasting 101" class in sampling Tuscan wines, held at a local wine bar (€50 per group plus cost of wine).

Sights in Volterra

I've arranged these sights as a handy little town walk, connected by directions on foot. Not all the sights will interest everyone, so skim the listings to decide which detours appeal to you.

• *Begin your visit of town at the Etruscan Arch. To find it, go all the*

Vampire Volterra?

Fans of the *Twilight* books and films may recognize Volterra as the home of the powerful clan of vampires called the Volturi. For a while, a wave of *Twilight* interest swept through the town—but most of that seems to have passed. Maybe that's because *Twilight* ties to Volterra were tenuous at best. Author Stephanie Meyer had never been to Volterra before setting part of her second novel, *New Moon,* in the town; she simply picked the name for its resemblance to the one she had already given to her characters, the "Volturi." Although the novel takes place in Volterra, most scenes in the *New Moon* film (2009) were filmed in Montepulciano.

And yet, although it was a random choice, it was serendipitous. Sitting on its stony main square at midnight, watching bats dart about as if they own the place, I realize there really is something supernatural about Volterra. The cliffs of Volterra inspired Dante's "cliffs of hell." In the winter, the town's vibrancy is smothered under a deadening cloak of clouds. The name Volterra means "land that floats"—referring to the clouds that often seem to cut it off from the rest of the world below.

The people of Volterra live in a cloud of mystery, too. Their favorite cookie, crunchy with almonds, is called Ossi di Morta ("bones of the dead"). Through the 1980s, Volterra was home to Italy's second-biggest psychiatric hospital. The town's first disco was named Catacombs. Volterra's top sight—the Etruscan Museum—is filled with hundreds of ancient caskets. And in the 1970s, when Volterra was the set of a wildly popular TV horror series called *Ritratto di Donna Velata (Portrait of a Veiled Woman),* all of Italy tuned in to Volterra every week for a good scare. Perhaps *Twilight* is just one more chapter in a long tale of a town that revels in being otherworldly.

way down to the bottom of Via Porta all'Arco (you'll find the top of this street between Piazza Martiri della Libertà, with the town bus stop, and the main square, Piazza dei Priori).

▲**Etruscan Arch (Porta all'Arco)**—Volterra's most famous sight is its Etruscan arch, built of massive, volcanic tuff stones in the fourth century B.C. (for more information on tuff, see the sidebar on page 474). Volterra's original wall was four miles around—twice the size of the wall that encircles it today. With 25,000 people, Volterra was a key trading center and one of 12 leading towns in the confederation of *Etruria Propria.* The three seriously eroded heads, dating from the first century B.C., show what happens when you leave something outside for 2,000 years. The newer stones are part of the 13th-century city wall, which incorporated parts of the

much older Etruscan wall.

A plaque just outside remembers June 30, 1944. That night, Nazi forces were planning to blow up the arch to slow the Allied advance. To save their treasured landmark, Volterrans ripped up the stones that pave Via Porta all'Arco and plugged the gate, managing to convince the Nazi commander that there was no need to blow up the arch. Today, all the stones are back in their places, and like silent heroes, they welcome you through the oldest standing Etruscan gate into Volterra. Locals claim this as the only surviving round arch of the Etruscan age; most experts believe this is where Romans got the idea for using a keystone in their arches.

• *Go through the arch and head up Via Porta all'Arco, which I like to call...*

"Artisan Lane" (Via Porta all'Arco)—This steep and atmospheric strip is lined with interesting shops featuring the work of artisans and producers. Because of its alabaster heritage, Volterra attracted craftsmen and artists, who brought with them a rich variety of handiwork (shops generally open Mon-Sat 10:00-13:00 & 16:00-19:00, closed Sun; the TI produces a free booklet called *Handicraft in Volterra*).

From the Etruscan Arch, browse your way up the hill, checking out these shops and items (listed from bottom to top): La Mia Fattoria—a co-op of producers of cheese, salami, and olive oil lets you buy direct at farm prices (just up Via Laberinti near #52); alabaster shops (#57, #50, and #45); book bindery and papery (#26); jewelry (#25); etchings (#23); Web & Wine (Internet access; #11-15); and bronze work (#6).

• *Reaching the top of Via Porta all'Arco, turn left and walk a few steps into Volterra's main square, Piazza dei Priori. It's dominated by the...*

Palazzo dei Priori—Volterra's City Hall (c. 1209) claims to be the oldest of any Tuscan city-state. It clearly inspired the more famous Palazzo Vecchio in Florence. Town halls like this are emblematic of an era when city-states were powerful. They were architectural exclamation points declaring that, around here, no pope or emperor called the shots. Towns such as Volterra were truly city-states—proudly independent and relatively democratic. They had their own armies, taxes, and even weights and measures. Notice the horizontal "cane" cut into the City Hall wall (right of the door). For a thousand years, this square hosted a market, and the "cane" was the local yardstick. When not in use for meetings or weddings, the city council chambers—lavishly painted and lit

Italy Is Made of Tuff Stuff

Tuff (*tufo* in Italian) is a light-colored volcanic rock that is common in Italy. A part of Tuscany is even called the "Tuff Area." The seven hills of Rome are made of tuff, and quarried blocks of this stone can be seen in the Colosseum, Pantheon, and Castel Sant'Angelo. Just outside of Rome, the catacombs were carved from tuff. Sorrento rises above the sea on a tuff outcrop. Orvieto, Civita di Bagnoregio (pictured), and many other hill towns perch on bluffs of tuff.

Italy's early inhabitants, including the Etruscans and Romans, carved caves, tunnels, burial niches, and even roads out of tuff. Blocks of this rock were quarried to make houses and walls. Tuff is soft and easy to carve when it's first exposed to air, but hardens later, which makes it a good building stone.

Italy's tuff-producing volcanoes resulted from a lot of tectonic-plate bumping and grinding. This violent geologic history is reflected in Italy's volcanoes, like Vesuvius and Etna, and earthquakes such as the 2009 quake in the L'Aquila area northeast of Rome.

Tuff is actually just a big hardened pile of old volcanic ash. When volcanoes hold magma that contains a lot of water, they erupt explosively (think heat + water = steam = POW!). The exploded rock material gets blasted out as hot volcanic ash, which settles on the surrounding landscape, piles up, and over time welds together into the rock called tuff.

So when you're visiting an area in Italy of ancient caves or catacombs built out of this material, you'll know that at least once (and maybe more) upon a time, it was a site of a lot of volcanic activity.

with fun dragon lamps, as they have been for centuries of town meetings—are open to visitors.

Cost and Hours: €1.50, mid-March-Oct daily 10:30-17:30, Nov-mid-March Sat-Sun only 10:00-17:00.

• *Facing the City Hall, notice the black-and-white-striped wall to the right (set back from the square). The door in that wall leads into Volterra's...*

Duomo—This church is not as elaborate as its cousin in Pisa, but the simple 13th-century facade and the interior (rebuilt in the late 16th century), with its central nave flanked by monolithic stone columns, are beautiful examples of the Pisan Romanesque style.

Cost and Hours: Free, daily 8:00-12:30 & 15:00-18:00, Nov-

March until 17:00.

Visiting the Church: Enter through the back door, and take a moment to let your eyes adjust to this dark, Romanesque space. (If you come through the main door around front, do this tour in reverse.) The interior was decorated mostly in the late 16th century, during Florentine rule under the Medici family. Their coat of arms, with its distinctive balls (called *palle*), is repeated multiple times throughout the building.

Head down into the nave to face the main altar. Up the stairs just to the right is a dreamy painted and gilded-wood *Deposition* (Jesus being taken down from the cross), restored to its original form. Carved in 1228, a generation before Giotto, it shows emotion and motion way ahead of its time (€1 buys some light).

The glowing **windows** in the transept and behind the altar are sheets of alabaster. These, along with the recorded Gregorian chants, add to the church's wonderful ambience.

The 12th-century marble **pulpit** is also beautifully carved. In the relief panel of the Last Supper, all the apostles are together except Judas, who's under the table with the evil dragon (his name is the only one not carved into the relief).

Just past the pulpit on the right (at the Rosary Chapel), check out the *Annunciation* by Fra Bartolomeo (who was a student of Fra Angelico and painted this in 1497). Bartolomeo delicately gives worshippers a way to see Mary "conceived by the Holy Spirit." Note the vibrant colors, exaggerated perspective, and Mary's *contrapposto* pose—all attributes of the Renaissance.

At the end of the nave, the **chapel** to the right of the doors has painted terra-cotta statue groups of the Nativity and the Adoration of the Magi, thought to be the work of master ceramists Luca and Andrea della Robbia. Luca is credited with inventing the glazing formula that makes his inventive sculptures shine even in poorly lit interiors.

Step outside the main door to see a classically Pisan space. A common arrangement in the Middle Ages was for the church to face the baptistery (you couldn't enter the church until you were baptized)...and for the hospital to face the cemetery (now the site of the local ambulance corps). These buildings all overlooked the same square. That's how it is in Pisa, and that's how it is here.

• *Exiting the cathedral out the front door, it's a short detour (to the right and around the corner) to the skippable Sacred Art Museum; otherwise, head back to the main square (either returning through the church to the back door, or looping around the block).*

Sacred Art Museum (Museo d'Arte Sacra)—This humble four-room museum collects sacred art and vestments from deconsecrated churches and small, unguarded churches from nearby villages. The museum may close in 2013, but if it does, you're not missing much.

Cost and Hours: Only possible with a €10 combo-ticket that includes the Etruscan Museum and Pinacoteca—no individual ticket, daily 9:00-13:00 & 15:00-18:00, morning only Nov-mid-March, well-explained in English, next to the Duomo at Via Roma 13, tel. 0588-86290.

• *Head back to the main square. Facing the City Hall, go down the street to the left; after one short block, you're standing at the head (on the left) of...*

▲**Via Matteotti**—The town's main drag, named after the popular Socialist leader Giacomo Matteotti (killed by the Fascists in 1924), provides a good cultural scavenger hunt.

At #1 is a typical Italian bank security door. (Step in and say, "Beam me up, Scotty.") Back outside, stand at the corner, and look up and all around. Find the medieval griffin torch holder—symbol of Volterra—and imagine it holding a lit torch. The pharmacy sports the symbol of its medieval guild. Across the street from the bank, #2 is the base of what was a San Gimignano-style fortified Tuscan tower. Look up and imagine heavy beams cantilevered out, supporting extra wooden rooms and balconies crowding out over the street. Throughout Tuscany, today's stark and stony old building fronts once supported a tangle of wooden extensions.

As you head down Via Matteotti, notice how the doors show centuries of refitting work. Doors that once led to these extra rooms are now partially bricked up to make windows. Contemplate urban density in the 14th century, before the plague thinned out the population. Be careful: There's a wild boar (a local delicacy) at #10.

At #12, notice the line of doorbells: This typical palace, once the home of a single rich family, is now occupied by many middle-class families. After the social revolution in the 18th century and the rise of the middle class, former palaces were condominium-ized. Even so, like in *Dr. Zhivago,* the original family still lives here. Apartment #1 is the home of Count Guidi.

At #16, pop in to an alabaster showroom. Alabaster, mined nearby, has long been a big industry here. Volterra alabaster—softer and more porous than marble—was sliced thin to serve as windows for Italy's medieval churches.

At #19, the recommended La Vecchia Lira is a lively cafeteria. The Bar L'Incontro across the street is a favorite for pastries; in the summer, they sell homemade gelato, while in the winter they make chocolates.

Across the way, up Vicolo delle Prigioni, is a fun bakery *(panificio).* They're happy to sell small quantities if you want to try the local *cantuccini* (almond biscotti) or another treat (closed 14:00-17:30, Sat after 14:00, and all day Sun).

Continue to the end of the block. At #51, a bit of Etruscan wall is artfully used to display more alabaster art. And #56A is the alabaster art gallery of Paolo Sabatini.

Locals gather early each evening at Osteria dei Poeti (at #57) for some of the best cocktails in town—served with free munchies. The cinema is across the street. Movies in Italy are rarely in *versione originale;* Italians are used to getting their movies dubbed into Italian. To bring some culture to this little town, they also show live transmissions of operas and concerts (advertised in the window).

At #66, another Tuscan tower marks the end of the street. This noble house has a ground floor with no interior access to the safe upper floors. Rope ladders were used to get upstairs. The tiny door was wide enough to let in your skinny friends...but definitely not anyone wearing armor and carrying big weapons.

Across the street stands the ancient Church of St. Michael. After long years of barbarian chaos, the Lombards moved in from the north and asserted law and order in places like Volterra. That generally included building a Christian church on the old Roman forum to symbolically claim and tame the center of town. (Locals still call this San Michele in Foro—"in the forum.") The church standing here today is Romanesque, dating from the 12th century. Around the right side, find the crude little guy and the smiling octopus under its eaves—they've been making faces at the passing crowds for 800 years.

• *Two more sights—Palazzo Viti (fancy old palace) and the Pinacoteca (gallery of gilded altarpieces)—are a short stroll down Via dei Sarti: From the end of Via Matteotti, turn left. If you want to skip straight down to the Roman Theater, just head straight from the end of Via Matteotti onto Via Guarnacci, then turn left when you get to the Porta Fiorentina gate. To head directly to Volterra's top sight, the Etruscan Museum, just turn around, walk a block back up Via Matteotti, turn left on Via Gramsci, and follow it all the way through Piazza XX Settembre up Via Don Minzoni to the museum.*

Palazzo Viti—Go behind the rustic, heavy stone walls of the city and see how the nobility lived (in this case, rich from 19th-century alabaster wealth). One of the finest private residential buildings in Italy, with 12 rooms open to the public, Palazzo Viti feels remarkably lived in—because it is. You'll also find Signora Viti herself selling admission tickets. It's no wonder this time warp is so popular with Italian movie directors. Remember, you're helping keep a noble family in leotards.

Cost and Hours: €5, pick up the loaner English description, April-Oct daily 10:00-13:00 & 14:30-18:30, closed Nov-March, Via dei Sarti 41, tel. 0588-84047, www.palazzoviti.it.

• *A block past Palazzo Viti, also on Via dei Sarti, is the...*

Pinacoteca—This museum fills a 15th-century palace with fine paintings that feel more Florentine than Sienese—a reminder of whose domain this town was in. You'll see roomfuls of gilded altarpieces and saintly statues. Head upstairs to the first floor. If you go left, you'll circle all the way around and save the best for last—but to cut to the chase, turn right at the landing and go directly into the best room, with Luca Signorelli's beautifully lit *Annunciation* (1491), an example of classic High Renaissance (from the town cathedral), and (to the right) *Deposition from the Cross* (1521), the groundbreaking Mannerist work by Rosso Fiorentino (note the elongated bodies and harsh emotional lighting and colors). In the adjacent room, see Ghirlandaio's *Christ in Glory* (1492). The two devout-looking kneeling women are actually pagan, pre-Christian Etruscan demigoddesses, Attinea and Greciniana, but the church identified them as obscure saints to make the painting acceptable. Rather than attempt to get locals to stop venerating them (as their images were all over town), the church simply sainted them. Upstairs, the second floor has three more rooms of similar art. Before leaving, duck into the fine, tranquil, cloister-like courtyard.

Cost and Hours: €6, €10 combo-ticket includes Etruscan and (if it's open) Sacred Art museums, daily 9:00-18:45, Nov-mid-March until 13:45, Via dei Sarti 1, tel. 0588-87580.

• *Exiting the Pinacoteca, turn right, then right again down the Passo del Gualduccio passage into the parking-lot square; at the end of this square, turn right and walk along the wall, with fine views of the...*

Roman Theater—Built in about 40 B.C., this well-preserved theater has good acoustics. Because a fine aerial view is available from the city wall promenade, you may find it unnecessary to pay admission to enter. Belly up to the 13th-century wall and look down. The wall that you're standing on divided the theater from the town center...so, naturally, the theater became the town dump. Over time, the theater was forgotten—covered in the garbage of Volterra. Luckily, it was rediscovered in the 1950s, by an administrator (and armchair historian) at the local mental hospital. Since they couldn't secure government funding for the dig, the theater was first excavated by mental patients who found the activity therapeutic.

The stage wall was standard Roman design—with three levels from which actors would appear: one level for mortals, one for heroes, and the top one for gods. Parts of two levels still stand. Gods leaped out onto the third level for the last time around the third century A.D., which is when the town began to use the theater stones to build fancy baths instead. You can see the remains of the baths behind the theater, including the round sauna with brick supports that raise the heated floor.

From the vantage point on the city wall promenade, you can trace Volterra's vast Etruscan wall. Find the church in the distance, on the left, and notice the stones just below. They are from the Etruscan wall that followed the ridge into the valley and defined Volterra in the fourth century B.C.

Cost and Hours: €3.50, but you can view the theater free from Via Lungo le Mure; the entrance is near the little parking lot just outside Porta Fiorentina—you can see the entry to the right as you survey the theater from above; mid-March-Oct daily 10:30-17:30, Nov-mid-March Sat-Sun only 10:00-16:00.

• *From the Roman Theater, make your way back to Via Matteotti (follow Via Guarnacci straight up from Porta Fiorentina). A block down Via Matteotti, you can't miss the wide, pedestrianized shopping street called Via Gramsci. Follow this up to Piazza XX Settembre, walk through that leafy square, and continue uphill on Via Don Minzoni. Watch on your left for the...*

▲▲**Etruscan Museum (Museo Etrusco Guarnacci)**—Filled top to bottom with rare Etruscan artifacts, this museum—even with few English explanations and its dusty, almost neglectful, old-school style—makes it easy to appreciate how advanced this pre-Roman culture was.

Cost and Hours: €8, €10 combo-ticket includes the Pinacoteca and (if it's open) Sacred Art Museum; daily mid-March-Oct 9:00-19:00, Nov-mid-March 8:30-13:45; ask at the ticket window for mildly interesting English pamphlet, audioguide-€3, Via Don Minzoni 15, tel. 0588-86347, www.comune.volterra.pi.it/english.

Visiting the Museum: The museum's three floors feel dusty and disorganized. As there are scarcely any English explanations, consider the serious but interesting audioguide-€3; the information below hits the highlights.

Ground Floor: The collection starts with a small gathering of pre-Etruscan Villanovian artifacts (c. 1500 B.C., to the left as you enter), but its highlight is straight ahead, sprawling through several rooms: a seemingly endless collection of Etruscan **funerary urns** (dating from the seventh to the first century B.C.). Designed to contain the ashes of cremated loved ones, each urn is tenderly carved with a unique scene, offering a peek into the still-mysterious Etruscan society. Etruscan urns have two parts: The casket on the bottom contained the remains (with elaborately carved panels), while the lid was decorated with a sculpture of the departed.

First pay attention to the people on top. While contemporaries of the Greeks, the Etruscans were more libertine. Their religion was less demanding, and their women were a respected part of both the social and public spheres. Women and men alike are depicted lounging on Etruscan urns. While they seem to be just

Under the Etruscan Sun
(c. 900 B.C.-A.D. 1)

Around 550 B.C.—just before the Golden Age of Greece—the Etruscan people of central Italy had their own Golden Age. Though their origins are mysterious, their mix of Greek-style art with Roman-style customs helped lay a civilized foundation for the rise of the Roman empire. As you travel through Italy—particularly in Tuscany (from "Etruscan")—you'll find traces of this long-lost people.

Etruscan tombs and artifacts are still being discovered, often by farmers in the countryside. Museums in Volterra and Cortona house fine collections of urns, pottery, and devotional figures. You can visit several domed tombs outside Cortona.

The Etruscans first appeared in the ninth century B.C., when a number of cities sprouted up in sparsely populated Tuscany and Umbria, including today's hill towns of Cortona, Chiusi, and Volterra. Possibly immigrants from Turkey, but more likely local farmers who moved to the city, they became traders and craftsmen, and welcomed new ideas from Greece.

More technologically advanced than their neighbors, the Etruscans mined metal, exporting it around the Mediterranean, both as crude ingots and as some of the finest-crafted jewelry in the known world. They drained and irrigated large tracts of land, creating the fertile farmland of central Italy's breadbasket. With their disciplined army, warships, merchant vessels, and (from the Greek perspective) pirate galleys, they ruled central Italy and the major ports along the Tyrrhenian Sea. For nearly two centuries (c. 700-500 B.C.), much of Italy lived a Golden Age of peace and prosperity under the Etruscan sun.

Judging from the frescoes and many luxury items that have survived, the Etruscans enjoyed the good life: They look healthy and vibrant as they play flutes, dance with birds, or play party games. Etruscan artists celebrated individual people, showing their wrinkles, crooked noses, silly smiles, and funny haircuts.

Thousands of surviving ceramic plates and cups attest to the importance of food. Men and women ate together, propped on their elbows on dining couches, surrounded by colorful decor. According to contemporary accounts, the Etruscans, even their slaves, were Europe's best-dressed people. The banqueters were entertained with music and dancing, and served by elegant and well-treated slaves.

Scholars today have deciphered the Etruscans' Greek-style alphabet and some individual words, but they have yet to fully crack the code. Much of what we know of the Etruscans comes from their tombs. The tomb was a home in the hereafter, complete with all of the deceased's belongings. The sarcophagus might have a statue on the lid of the deceased at a banquet—

The Etruscan Empire

Bologna

Ravenna

Adriatic Sea

Appenine Mountains

La Spezia

Florence ▪Fiesole

Arno R.

▪Pisa

Ligurian Sea

** E T R U S C A N**

Volterra (M)

Siena ●

Cortona ▪ (M)

Chiusi (M)

Lake Trasimeno

▪Perugia

▪Populonia

E M P I R E

▪Vetulonia

Elba

▪Roselle

Orvieto (M)

▪Bolsena

Lake Bolsena

Tiber R.

Tyrrhenian Sea

▪Vulci

Tarquinia ▪

Veio ▪

Cerveteri ▪

● Rome (M)

30 Kilometers

30 Miles

▪	Etruscan Cities
●	Modern Cities
(M)	Etruscan Museum
— --	Border of Tuscany

TUSCAN HILL TOWNS

lying across a dining couch, spooning with his wife, smiles on their faces, living the good life for all eternity.

Seven decades of wars with the Greeks (545-474 B.C.) disrupted their trade routes and drained the Etruscan League, just as a new Mediterranean power was emerging: Rome. In 509 B.C., the Romans overthrew their Etruscan king, and Rome expanded, capturing Etruscan cities one by one (the last in 264 B.C.). Etruscan resisters were killed, the survivors intermarried with Romans, and their kids grew up speaking Latin. By Julius Caesar's time, the only remnants of Etruscan culture were its priests, who became Rome's professional soothsayers. Interestingly, the Etruscan prophets had foreseen their own demise, having predicted that Etruscan civilization would last 10 centuries.

But Etruscan culture lived on in Roman religion (pantheon of gods, household gods, and divination rituals), art (realism), lifestyle (the banquet), and in a taste for Greek styles—the mix that became our "Western civilization."

hanging out, the lounging dead were actually offering the gods a banquet—in order to gain their favor in the transition to the next life. The banquet—where Etruscans really did lounge like this in front of a table—was the epitome of their social structure. But the outcome of this particular banquet had eternal consequences. The dearly departed are often depicted holding scrolls, blank wax tablets (symbolizing blank new lives in the next world), and containers that would generally be used at banquets, including libation cups for offering wine to the gods. The women in particular are finely dressed, sometimes holding a pomegranate (symbolizing fertility) or a mirror. Look at the faces, and imagine the lives they lived and the loved ones they left behind.

Now tune into the reliefs carved into the fronts of the caskets. The motifs vary widely, from floral patterns to mystical animals (such as a Starbucks-like mermaid) to parades of magistrates. Most show journeys on horseback—appropriate for someone leaving this world and entering the next. The most evocative scenes show the fabled horseback-and-carriage ride to the underworld, where the dead are greeted by Charon, an underworld demon, with his hammer and pointy ears.

While the finer urns are carved of alabaster, most are made of limestone. Originally they were colorfully painted. Many lids are mismatched—casualties of reckless 18th- and 19th-century archaeological digs.

First Floor: You'll enter a room with a circular mosaic in the floor (a Roman original, found in Volterra and transplanted here). Turn left into a series of green rooms—the best presented (and most important) of the museum.

The first room, Sala XIV, collects scenes of Ulysses carved into the fronts of caskets. Turn left and head into Sala XV, with the museum's prize piece. Fans of Alberto Giacometti will be amazed at how the tall, skinny figure called *The Evening Shadow* (*L'Ombra della Sera*, third century B.C.) looks just like the modern Swiss sculptor's work—but is 2,500 years older. This is an exceptional example of the *ex-voto* bronze statues that the Etruscans created to thank the gods. With his supremely lanky frame, distinctive wavy hairdo, and inscrutable Mona Lisa smirk, this Etruscan lad captures the illusion of a shadow stretching long late in the day. Admire the sheer artistry of the statue; with its right foot shifted slightly forward, it even hints at the *contrapposto* pose that would become common in this same region during the Renaissance, two millennia later.

Continue circling clockwise, through Sala XVI (alabaster urns with more Greek myths), Sala XVII (ex-voto water-bearer statues, kraters—vases with handles, and bronze hand mirrors), and Sala XVIII (golden jewelry). Sala XIX shows off the museum's other top piece, the *Urn of the Spouses* (*Urna degli Sposi,* first century B.C.). It's unique for various reasons, including its material (it's in terra-cotta—a relatively rare material for these funerary urns) and its depiction of two people rather than one. Looking at this elderly couple,

it's easy to imagine the long life they spent together and their desire to pass eternity lounging with each other at a banquet for the gods.

The rest of this floor has black glazed pottery; thousands of Etruscan, Greek, and Roman coins; and many more bronze ex-votos and jewelry.

Top Floor: From the top of the stairs, turn right, then immediately right again to find a re-created grave site, with several neatly aligned urns and artifacts that would have been buried with the deceased. Some of these were funeral dowries (called *corredo*) that the dead would pack along. You'll see artifacts such as mirrors, coins, hardware for vases, votive statues, pots, pans, and jewelry. On the landing are fragments from Volterra's acropolis—a site now occupied by the Medici Fortress.

• *After your visit, duck across the street to the alabaster showroom and the wine bar (both described next).*

▲**Alabaster Workshop**—Alab'Arte offers a fun peek into the

art of alabaster. Their showroom is across from the Etruscan Museum, but to find their powdery workshop, go a block downhill, in front of Porta Marcoli, where you can watch Roberto Chiti and Giorgio Finazzo at work. They are delighted to share their art with visitors.

(Everything—including Roberto and Giorgio—is covered in a fine white dust.) Lighting shows off the translucent quality of the stone and the expertise of these artists. This is not a touristy guided visit, but something far more special: the chance to see busy artisans practicing their craft. For more such artisans in action, visit "Artisan Lane" (Via Porta all'Arco) described earlier, or ask the TI for their list of the town's many workshops open to the public.

Cost and Hours: Free, showroom—daily 10:30-13:00 & 15:30-19:00, Via Don Minzoni 18; workshop—March-Oct Mon-Sat 9:30-13:00 & 15:00-19:00, closed Sun, usually closed Nov-Feb—call ahead, Via Orti Sant'Agostino 28; tel. 0588-87968, www.alabarte.com.

▲La Vena di Vino (Wine-Tasting with Bruno and Lucio)—
La Vena di Vino, also just across from the Etruscan Museum, is

a fun *enoteca* where two guys who have devoted themselves to the wonders of wine share it with a fun-loving passion. Each day Bruno and Lucio open six or eight bottles, serve your choice by the glass, pair it with characteristic munchies, and offer fine music (guitars available for patrons) and an unusual decor (the place is strewn with bras). Hang out here with the local characters. This is your chance to try the Super Tuscan wine—a creative mix of international grapes grown in Tuscany. According to Bruno, the Brunello (€7/glass) is just right with wild boar, and the Super Tuscan (€6) is perfect for meditation. Food is served all day, including some microwaved hot dishes or a plate of meats and cheeses. Although Volterra is famously quiet late at night, this place is full of action. Downstairs is a rustic cellar that doubles on weekend nights as a sort of disco.

Cost and Hours: Pay per glass, open Wed-Mon 11:30-1:00 in the morning, closed Tue, 3- to 5-glass wine tastings, shipping options available, Via Don Minzoni 30, tel. 0588-81491, www .lavenadivino.com.

• *Volterra's final sight is perched atop the hill just above the wine bar. Climb up one of the lanes nearby, then walk (to the right) along the formidable wall to find the park.*

Medici Fortress and Archaeological Park—The Parco Archeologico marks what was the acropolis of Volterra from 1500 B.C. until A.D. 1472, when Florence conquered the pesky city and burned its political and historic center, turning it into a grassy commons and building the adjacent Medici Fortezza. The old fortress—a symbol of Florentine dominance—now keeps people in rather than out. It's a maximum-security prison housing only about 100 special prisoners. (When you're driving from San Gimignano to Volterra, you pass another big, modern prison—almost surreal in the midst of all the Tuscan wonder.) Authorities prefer to keep organized crime figures locked up far away from their family ties in Sicily.

The park sprawling next to the fortress (toward the town center) is a rare, grassy meadow at the top of a rustic hill town—a favorite place for locals to relax and picnic on a sunny day. Nearby is an archaeological dig, which costs €3 to enter, but can be viewed through a fence for free.

Cost and Hours: Park—free to enter, closes at 20:00 in summer, 17:00 in winter.

Countryside Strolls—All the sights listed above are in a tight little zone of the old town, about a 10-minute walk from each other. But if you have time for a stroll, Volterra—perched on a ridge overlooking pristine Tuscan hills—has countryside galore to explore. Get some advice from the TI.

One popular walk is to head to the west end of town, out Porta San Francesco, into a workaday area (dubbed "Borgi," literally "neighborhoods") that sees few tourists. Continuing downhill (past the Church of San Giusto), you'll come to a cliff with a stretch of the original fourth-century B.C. Etruscan wall. Peering over the cliff from here, you can see that Volterra sits upon orange sandy topsoil packed onto clay cliffs, called Le Balze. At various points in its history, the town has been threatened by landslides, and parts of its hilltop have simply disappeared. The big church you see in the distance was abandoned in the late 1800s for fear that it would be swallowed up by the land. The distinctive cliffs surrounding Volterra are called *calanchi* (similar to the French *calanques* that slash the Mediterranean coast).

Sleeping in Volterra

(€1 = about $1.40, country code: 39)
Predictably for a small town, Volterra's accommodations are limited, and all have their quirks—but there are plenty of places offering a good night's sleep at a fair price. While it's convenient to stay inside the old town, the lodgings that are a short walk away are generally a bit cheaper (and much easier for drivers).

Inside Volterra's Old Town
$$$ Hotel La Locanda feels stately and old-fashioned. This well-located place (just inside Porta Fiorentina) rents 18 decent rooms with flowery decor and modern comforts (Db-€104, less off-season, 10 percent Rick Steves discount, includes breakfast, air-con, free Wi-Fi, Via Guarnacci 24/28, tel. 0588-81547, www .hotel-lalocanda.com, staff@hotel-lalocanda.com, Giulia, Stefania, and Irina).

$$ Albergo Etruria, on Volterra's main drag, rents 21 fresh, modern, and spacious rooms within an ancient stone structure. They have a welcoming TV lounge and a peaceful rooftop garden (Sb-€75, Db-€95, Tb-€115, 10 percent discount with cash and this book when you book direct, includes breakfast, fans, free but spotty Wi-Fi, Via Matteotti 32, tel. 0588-87377, fax 0588-92784, www .albergoetruria.it, info@albergoetruria.it, Lisa and Giuseppina are fine hosts).

$$ Albergo Nazionale, with 38 big rooms, is simple, a little musty, short on smiles, popular with school groups, and steps from the bus stop. While the place feels dated, it's an exceptionally handy location (Sb-€60-70, Db-€80-90, Tb-€105, 10 percent discount with cash and this book if you book direct, reception closes at midnight, includes breakfast, free Wi-Fi, Via dei Marchesi 11, tel. 0588-86284, fax 0588-84097, www.hotelnazionale-volterra.it, info@hotelnazionale-volterra.it).

Just Outside the Old Town

These accommodations are within a 5- to 15-minute walk of the city walls.

$$$ Park Hotel Le Fonti, a dull 10-minute walk downhill from Porta all'Arco, can't decide whether it's a business hotel or a resort. The spacious, imposing building feels old and stately, and has 67 rooms, many with views. While generally overpriced (the management knows it's the only hotel of its kind in Volterra), it can be a good value if you manage to snag a deal. In addition to the swimming pool, guests can use a small spa with sauna, hot tub, and an intriguing "emotional shower" (Db-€89-165, average is about Db-€129 but prices vary wildly depending on season, "superior" room is identical to others but has a view for €20 extra, "deluxe" room with terrace costs €30 extra, includes breakfast, elevator, pay Wi-Fi in lobby, on-site restaurant, wine bar, free parking, Via di Fontecorrenti 5, tel. 0588-85219, fax 0588-92728, www.park hotellefonti.com, info@parkhotellefonti.com).

$$ Albergo Villa Nencini, just outside of town, is big, professional, and older-feeling, with 36 cheaply furnished rooms. A few rooms have terraces and many have views. Guests also enjoy the large pool and free parking (Sb-€67, Db-€88, Tb-€115, 10 percent discount with cash and this book, includes breakfast, pay Wi-Fi, Borgo Santo Stefano 55, a 15-minute uphill walk to main square, tel. 0588-86386, fax 0588-80601, www.villanencini.it, info@villa nencini.it, Nencini family).

$ La Primavera B&B is a great value just a few minutes' walk outside Porta Fiorentina (near the Roman Theater). Silvia rents five charming, tidy rooms that share a cutesy-country, heavily perfumed lounge. The house is along a fairly busy road, but set back along a pleasant courtyard (Db-€70, Tb-€90, includes breakfast, free Wi-Fi, free parking, Via Porta Diana 15, tel. 0588-87295, mobile 328-865-0390, www.affittacamere-laprimavera.com, info @affittacamere-laprimavera.com).

$ Seminario Vescovile Sant'Andrea has been training priests for more than 500 years. Today, the remaining eight priests still train students, but when classes are over, their 16 rooms—separated by vast and holy halls in an echoing old mansion—are rented very cheaply. Look for the 15th-century Ascension ceramic by Andrea della Robbia, tucked away in a corner upstairs (S-€17, Sb-€22,

D-€32, Db-€40, T-€48, Tb-€60, no breakfast, closed Oct-March, elevator, closes at 24:00, groups welcome, free parking, 10-minute walk from Etruscan Museum, Viale Vittorio Veneto 2, tel. 0588-86028, semvescovile@diocesivolterra.it; Alberto, Angela, and Sergio).

$ **Chiosco delle Monache,** Volterra's youth hostel, fills a wing of the restored Convent of San Girolamo with 68 beds in 23 rooms. It's modern, spacious, and very institutional, with lots of services and a tranquil cloister to wander. However, it's about a 20-minute hike out of town, in a boring area near deserted hospital buildings (bed in 6-bed dorm-€18, breakfast-€6 extra, lockers; Db-€69, includes breakfast; reception closed 13:00-15:00 and after 22:00, elevator, pay Wi-Fi, free parking, Via dell Teatro 4, look for hospital sign from main Volterra-San Gimignano road, tel. 0588-86613, www.ostellovolterra.it, info@ostellovolterra.it). Nearby and run by the same organization, $ **Hotel Foresteria** has 35 big, utilitarian, new-feeling rooms with great prices but the same location woes as the hostel; it's worth considering for budget travelers, families, and drivers (Sb-€44, Db-€62, Tb-€83, Qb-€102, 5b-€122, includes breakfast, air-con, elevator, pay Wi-Fi, restaurant, free parking, Borgo San Lazzaro, tel. 0588-80050, www.foresteriavolterra.it, info@foresteriavolterra.it).

Near Volterra

$$ **Podere Marcampo** is a newer *agriturismo* about 2.5 miles outside Volterra on the road to Pisa. Run by Genuino (owner of the recommended Ristorante Enoteca del Duca), his wife Ivana, and their English-speaking daughter Claudia, this peaceful spot has three well-appointed rooms and three apartments, plus a swimming pool with panoramic views. Genuino produces his award-winning Merlot on site and offers €20 wine-tastings with cheese and homemade salami. Cooking classes at their restaurant in town are also available (Db-€94, apartment-€118-145, more expensive mid-July-Aug, includes breakfast with this book, air-con, free Wi-Fi, free parking, tel. 0588-85393, Claudia's mobile 328-174-4605, www.agriturismo-marcampo.com, info@agriturismo-marcampo.com).

Eating in Volterra

Menus feature a Volterran take on regional dishes. *Zuppa alla Volterrana* is a fresh vegetable-and-bread soup, similar to *ribollita* (except that it isn't made from leftovers). *Torta di ceci,* also known as *cecina,* is a savory-pancake-like dish made with garbanzo beans. Those with more adventurous palates dive into *trippa* (tripe; comes in a bowl like stew), the traditional breakfast of the alabaster carvers. *Fegatelli* are meatballs made with liver.

Ristorante Enoteca del Duca, with a locally respected chef named Genuino, serves well-presented and creative Tuscan cuisine. You can dine under a medieval arch with walls lined with wine bottles, in a sedate, high-ceilinged dining room (with an Etruscan statuette at each table), on a nice little patio out back, or in their little *enoteca* (wine cellar). It's a good place for truffles, and has a friendly staff and a fine wine list (which includes Genuino's own merlot, plus several much pricier options—choose carefully). The spacious seating, dressy clientele, and calm atmosphere make this a good choice for a romantic splurge (€42 food-sampler fixed-price meal, €10-15 pastas, €15-22 *secondi*, Wed-Mon 12:30-15:00 & 19:30-22:00, closed Tue, near City Hall at Via di Castello 2, tel. 0588-81510).

Don Beta is a family-run trattoria on the main drag, popular with travelers for its stylish home cooking. Mirko supervises the lively young team as they whisk out steaming plates of pasta and homemade desserts (€6-10 pastas, €12-18 *secondi*, daily 12:00-14:30 & 19:00-22:00, lighter menu available until 24:00, reservations smart, Via Matteotti 39, tel. 0588-86730).

La Vecchia Lira, bright and cheery, is a classy self-serve eatery that's a hit with locals as a quick and cheap lunch spot by day (with €5-10 meals), and a fancier restaurant at night (€9-10 pastas, €11-18 *secondi*; Fri-Wed 12:00-14:30 & 19:00-22:30, closed Thu, Via Matteotti 19, tel. 0588-86180, Lamberto and Massimo).

La Carabaccia feels like an old-school Italian eatery, with a 1950s turquoise color scheme, a deli up front, and a country-rustic dining room in back. They serve only two pastas and two *secondi* on any given night, so check the menu by the door to be sure you like the choices. Committed to tradition, on Fridays they serve only fish. They whip up €3-4 take-away sandwiches at the deli up front (€7-9 pastas and *secondi*, Tue-Sun 12:30-14:30 & 19:30-22:00, closed Mon, Piazza XX Settembre 4/5, tel. 0588-86239).

Ristorante il Sacco Fiorentino is a local favorite for traditional cuisine and seasonal seafood specials (€8-10 pastas, €10-15 *secondi*, Thu-Tue 12:00-15:00 & 19:00-22:00, closed Wed, Via Giusto Turazza 13, tel. 0588-88537).

La Vena di Vino is an *enoteca* serving up simple and traditional dishes and the best of Tuscan wine in a fun atmosphere. As their hot dishes are microwaved (there's no real kitchen), come here more for the wine and ambience than for the food (€8-12 meals, closed Tue, Via Don Minzoni 30, tel. 0588-81491). For more details, read the description on page 484.

Pizzerias: Ombra della Sera dishes out what local kids consider the best pizza in town. At €6-8 a pop, their pizzas make for a cheap date (Tue-Sun 12:00-15:00 & 19:00-22:00, closed Mon, Via Guarnacci 16, don't confuse this with their second, pricier location on Via Gramsci; tel. 0588-85274). **Pizzeria Tavernetta,** next door, is more romantic, with delightful indoor and on-the-street seating. Its romantically frescoed dining room upstairs is the classiest I've seen in a pizzeria. Marco, who looks like a younger Billy Joel, serves €5-8 pizzas (Thu-Tue 12:00-16:00 & 18:30-22:00, closed Wed, Via Guarnacci 14, tel. 0588-87630).

Picnic: You can assemble a picnic at the few *alimentari* around town (try Despar Market at Via Gramsci 12, Mon-Sat 7:30-13:00 & 16:00-20:00, Sun 8:00-13:00) and eat in the breezy Archaeological Park.

Gelato: Of the many ice-cream stands in the center, I've found **L'Isola di Gusto** to be reliably high quality (Tue-Sun 11:00-late, closed Mon, Via Gramsci 3).

Volterra Connections

In Volterra, buses come and go from Piazza Martiri della Libertà (buy tickets at the tobacco shop on the main square, two short blocks away). Most connections—except to Pisa—are with the C.P.T. bus company through Colle Val d'Elsa ("koh-leh" for short), a workaday town in the valley (4/day Mon-Sat, 1/day Sun, 50 minutes, €2.75). Once in Colle, you must buy another ticket (from another bus company) at the newsstand near the bus stop, or from the blue automated machine at the bus stop (press "F" to toggle to English, then punch in the number for your destination). I've listed total journey fares below. The nearest train station is in Saline di Volterra, a 15-minute bus ride away (7/day, 4/day Sun); however, trains from Saline run only to the coast, not to the major bus destinations listed next.

From Volterra by Bus to: Florence (4/day Mon-Sat, 1/day Sun, 2 hours, change in Colle Val d'Elsa, €8.35), **Siena** (4/day Mon-Sat, no buses on Sun, 2 hours, change in Colle Val d'Elsa, €5.75), **San Gimignano** (4/day Mon-Sat, 1/day Sun, 2 hours, change in Colle Val d'Elsa, €5.45), **Pisa** (9/day, 2 hours, change in Pontedera, €5.50).

South of Siena

Just an hour south of Siena (or two hours south of Florence), you'll find a trio of inviting hill towns, with an emphasis on good wine and scenic country drives: The biggest and most interesting, Montepulciano, has an engaging medieval cityscape draped in a Renaissance coat, wine cellars that plunge deep down into the cliffs it sits upon, and a classic town square. Pienza is a tidily planned Renaissance town that once gave the world a pope. And mellow Montalcino is (even more than most towns around here) all about its wine: Brunello di Montalcino. All three are within about a half-hour drive of each other, making any one of them a good home base for the entire region. Just to the north are the rippling hills of the Crete Senese. Dressed in vibrant green in spring and parched brown in fall, this area is blessed with quintessential Tuscan scenery and dotted with worthwhile countryside accommodations. While my favorite home base for the region is the most interesting town, Montepulciano, you can't go wrong staying in the countryside or in Montalcino.

Montepulciano

Curving its way along a ridge, Montepulciano (mohn-teh-pull-chee-AH-noh) delights visitors with *vino* and views. Alternately under Sienese and Florentine rule, the city still retains its medieval *contrade* (districts), each with a mascot and flag. The neighborhoods compete the last Sunday of August in the Bravio delle Botti, where teams of men push large wine casks uphill from Piazza Marzocco to Piazza Grande, all

hoping to win a banner and bragging rights. The entire last week of August is a festival: Each *contrada* arranges musical entertainment and serves food at outdoor eateries along with generous tastings of the local *vino*.

The city is a collage of architectural styles, but the elegant San Biagio Church, at the base of the hill, is its best Renaissance building. Most visitors ignore the architecture and focus more on the city's other creative accomplishment, the tasty Vino Nobile di Montepulciano red wine.

Orientation to Montepulciano

The commercial action in Montepulciano centers in the lower town, mostly along Via di Gracciano nel Corso (nicknamed "Corso"). This stretch begins at the town gate called Porta al Prato (near the TI, bus station, and some parking) and winds slowly up, up, up through town—narrated by my self-guided walk, later. Strolling here, you'll find eateries, gift shops, and tourist traps. The back streets are worth exploring. The main square, at the top of town (up a steep switchback lane from Corso), is Piazza Grande. Standing proudly above all the touristy sales energy, it has a noble, Florentine feel.

Tourist Information

The TI is just outside the Porta al Prato city gate, directly underneath the small tree-lined parking lot. It offers a paltry town map for €0.50, books hotels and rooms for no fee, sells train tickets (€1 fee), has an Internet terminal (€3.50/hour), and can book one of the town's few taxis (Mon-Sat 9:30-12:30 & 15:00-18:00, Sun 9:30-12:30, daily until 20:00 in July-Aug, Piazza Don Minzoni, tel. 0578-757-341, www.prolocomontepulciano.it).

Note that on the main square there is an office that looks like a TI, but this is actually a privately run "Strada del Vino" (Wine Road) agency. They don't have city info, but they do provide wine-road maps, organize **wine tours** in the city, and lead minibus winery tours farther afield. They also offer other tours (olive oil, cheese, and slow food), cooking classes, and more, depending on season and demand (Mon-Fri 10:00-13:00 & 15:00-18:00, closed Sat-Sun but likely open Sat in summer, Piazza Grande 7, tel. 0578-717-484, www.stradavinonobile.it).

Arrival in Montepulciano

Buses leave passengers at the station on Piazza Nenni, steeply downhill from the Porta al Prato gate. From the station, cross the street and head inside the modern orange-brick structure burrowed into the hillside, where there's an elevator. Ride to level 1, walk straight ahead down the corridor (following signs for *centro storico*), and ride another elevator to level 1. You'll pop out at the Poggiofanti Gardens; walk to the end of this park and hook left to find the gate. From here, it's a 15-minute walk uphill along the Corso, the bustling main drag, to the main square, Piazza Grande (following my self-guided walk, described later). Alternatively, you can wait for the orange shuttle bus that takes you all the way up to Piazza Grande (2/hour, €1.10); it's a good strategy to take the bus up and walk back down.

Drivers arriving by car should park outside the walls. The city center is a "ZTL" zone—marked with a red circle—where you'll be fined if you drive; even if you were allowed, you wouldn't want to tackle the tiny roads inside the city. (If you're sleeping in town, your hotelier will give you a permit to park within the walls; be sure to get very specific instructions.) Well-signed pay-and-display parking lots ring the city center. To get the full Montepulciano experience of walking the full length of the town up the Corso, park just outside the Porta al Prato gate (#1 is handiest, but may be full; #2, #3, and #4 are nearby; #5 is near the bus station—you can ride up to the gate on the elevator described above). For a quick surgical strike, make a beeline to the lots up at the top end of town. Follow signs for *centro storico, duomo,* and *Piazza Grande,* and use the *Fortezza* or *San Donato* lots (flanking the fortress at the top of town). Drivers, be aware that Montepulciano is a very vertical town, and it's easy to get turned around. Mercifully, it's also a small town, so backtracking isn't too time-consuming. Just avoid the ZTL areas.

Helpful Hints

Market Day: It's on Thursday morning (8:00-13:00), near the bus station.

Services: There's no official **baggage storage** in town, but the TI might let you leave bags with them if they have space and you ask nicely. Public **WCs** are located at the TI, to the right of Palazzo Comunale, and at the Sant'Agostino Church.

Laundry: A self-service launderette is at Via del Paolino 2 (€4 wash, €4 dry, daily 8:00-22:00, tel. 0578-717-544).

Taxis: For a taxi, call any one of four local drivers direct: 335-617-7126, 330-173-2723, 348-286-8790, or 348-702-4124.

Self-Guided Walk

Welcome to Montepulciano

This two-part walk traces the spine of the town, from its main entrance up to its hilltop seat of power. Part 1 begins at Porta al Prato (where you'll enter if arriving at the bus station, parking at certain lots, or visiting the TI). Note that this part of the walk is uphill; if you'd rather skip straight to the more level part of town, ride the twice-hourly shuttle bus up, or park at one of the lots near the Fortezza. In that case, you can still do Part 1, backwards, on the way down.

Part 1: Up the Corso

This guided stroll takes you up through Montepulciano's commercial (and touristic) gamut, which curls ever so gradually from the

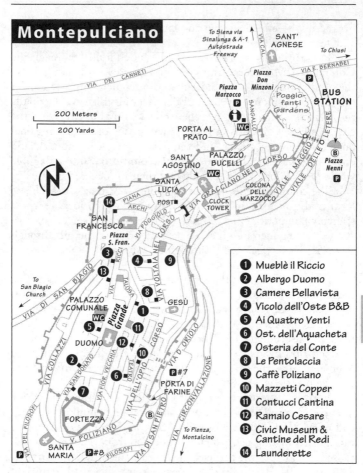

Montepulciano

To Siena via Sinalunga & A-1 Autostrada Freeway
SANT' AGNESE
To Chiusi
VIA E. BERNABEI
VIA DEI CANNETI
VIA CAL...
Piazza Don Minzoni
Piazza Marzocco
P
Poggio- fanti Gardens
BUS STATION
SANGALLO
PORTA AL PRATO
i
WC
Piazza Nenni
P
VIALE DELLE LETERE
VIALE 1 MAGGIO
CORSO
B
200 Meters
200 Yards
N
SANT' AGOSTINO
SANTA LUCIA
PALAZZO BUCELLI
WC
VIA GRACCIANO NEL CORSO
COLONA DELL MARZOCCO
POST
PIANA ARCHI
CLOCK TOWER
14
SAN FRANCESCO
Piazza S. Fran.
VIA POGGIOLO
VIA VOLTAIA NEL CORSO
3
RICCI
4
9
13
VIA TALOSA
8
GESÙ
To San Biagio Church
VIA DI SAN BIAGIO
PALAZZO COMUNALE
WC
5
Piazza Grande
DUOMO
1
11
12
10
CORSO
VIA DELL OPIO
VIA DI ORIOLO
2
VIA COLLAZZI
VIA SAN DONATO
6
P #7
VIA FIOR. VECCHIA
7
PORTA DI FARINE
TEATRO
B
VIA CIRCONVALLAZIONE
FORTEZZA
V. POLIZIANO
VIA DI SAN PIETRO
To Pienza, Montalcino
P
SANTA MARIA
P #8
VIA DEL FILOSOFI
FILOSOFI
VIA DI ...

1 Mueblè il Riccio
2 Albergo Duomo
3 Camere Bellavista
4 Vicolo dell'Oste B&B
5 Ai Quattro Venti
6 Ost. dell'Aquacheta
7 Osteria del Conte
8 Le Pentolaccia
9 Caffè Poliziano
10 Mazzetti Copper
11 Contucci Cantina
12 Ramaio Cesare
13 Civic Museum & Cantine del Redi
14 Launderette

TUSCAN HILL TOWNS

bottom of town to the top. While the street is lined mostly with gift shops, you'll pass a few relics of an earlier, less commercial age.

Begin in front of the imposing Porta al Prato, one of the many stout city gates that once fortified this highly strategic town. Facing the gate, find the sign for the Porta di Bacco *"passagio secreto"* on the left. While Montepulciano did have secret passages tunneled through the rock beneath it for coming and going in case of siege, this particular passage—right next to the city's front door—was probably no *secreto*...though it works great for selling salami.

Walk directly below the entrance to the **Porta al Prato,** and look up to see the slot where the portcullis (heavily fortified gate) could slide down to seal things off. Notice that there are two gates, enabling defenders to trap would-be invaders in a no-man's land where they could be doused with hot tar (sticky and painful). Besides having a drop-down portcullis, each gate also had a hinged door—effectively putting four barriers between the town and its enemies.

Pass through the gate and head a block uphill to reach the **Colona dell' Marzocco.** This column, topped with a lion holding the Medici shield, is a reminder that Montepulciano existed under the auspices of Florence—but only for part of its history. Originally the column was crowned by a she-wolf suckling human twins, the civic symbol of Siena. At a strategic crossroads of mighty regional powers (Florence, Siena, and the papal states), Montepulciano often switched allegiances—and this column became a flagpole where the overlords du jour could tout their influence.

The column is also the starting point for Siena's masochistic local tradition, **Bravio delle Botti,** in which each local *contrada* (fiercely competitive neighborhood, like Siena's) selects its two stoutest young men to roll a 180-pound barrel up the hill through town. If the vertical climb through town wears you out, be glad you're only toting a camera.

A few steps up, on the right (at #91), is one of the many fine noble palaces that front Montepulciano's main strip. The town is fortunate to be graced with so many bold and noble palazzos— Florentine nobility favored Montepulciano as a breezy and relaxed place for a secondary residence. Grand as this palace is, with its stylized lion heads, it's small potatoes—the higher you go in Montepulciano, the closer you are to the town center...and the fancier the mansions.

Farther up on the right, at #75 (Palazzo Bucelli), take a moment to examine the **Etruscan and Roman fragments** embedded in the wall (left here by a 19th-century antiques dealer). You can quickly distinguish which pieces came from the Romans and those belonging to the earlier Etruscans by the differences in their alphabets: The "backwards" Etruscan letters (they read from right to left) look closer to Greek than the more modern Roman letters. Many of the fragments show a circle flanked by a pair of inward-facing semicircular designs. The circle represents the libation cup used for drinking at an Etruscan banquet. Banquets were at the center of Etruscan social life, and burial urns depict lounging nobles presenting a feast for the gods.

At the top of the block on the right, pass by the Baroque-style Church of Sant'Agostino. Huff up a few more steps (imagine pushing a barrel now), then take a breather to look back and see the **clock tower** in the middle of the street. The bell ringer at the top takes the form of the character Pulcinella, one of the wild and carefree revelers familiar from Italy's comedy theater *(commedia dell'arte).*

Keep on going, bearing right (uphill) at the fork. At the *ali-mentari* on the right (at #23), notice the classic old sign advertising milk, butter, margarine, and olive and canola oil. Soon after, you'll pass under another sturdy **gateway**—indicating that this city grew in concentric circles. Passing through the gate and facing the loggia (with the Florentine Medici seal—a shield with balls), turn left and keep on going.

As you huff and puff, notice (on your right, and later on both sides) the steep, narrow, often covered lanes called *vicolo* ("little street"). You're getting a peek at the higgledy-piggledy medieval Montepulciano. Only when the rationality of Renaissance aesthetics took hold was the main street realigned, becoming symmetrical and pretty. Beneath its fancy suit, though, Montepulciano remains a rugged Gothic city.

On the left, watch for the hulking former palace (I told you they'd get bigger) that's now home to Banca Etruria. "Etruria"—a name you'll see everywhere around here—is a term for the Etruscan territory of today's Tuscany.

Just after is a fine spot for a coffee break (on the left, at #27): **Caffè Poliziano,** the town's most venerable watering hole (from 1868). Step inside to soak in the genteel atmosphere, with a busy espresso machine, newspapers on long sticks, and a little terrace with spectacular views (open long hours daily). It's named for a famous Montepulciano-born 15th-century poet who was a protégé of Lorenzo the Magnificent de Medici and tutored his two sons. So important is he to civic pride that townspeople are nicknamed *poliziani*.

A bit farther up and on the right, notice the precipitous Vicolo dello Sdrucciolo—literally "slippery lane." Any *vicolo* on the right can be used as a steep shortcut to the upper part of town, while those on the left generally lead to fine views. Many of these side lanes are spanned by brick arches, allowing the centuries-old buildings to lean on each other for support rather than toppling over—a fitting metaphor for the tight-knit communities that vitalize Italian small towns.

Soon the street levels out. Near the end, on the right (at #64), look for the **Mazzetti** copper shop, crammed full of both decorative and practical items. Because of copper's unmatched heat conductivity, it's a favored material in premium kitchens. The production of hand-hammered copper vessels like these is a dying art; in this shop, you can meet gregarious Cesare, who makes them in his workshop just up the street.

To get there, go up the covered lane just after the copper shop (Vicolo Benci, on the right). You'll emerge partway up the steep street just below the main square. Cesare's workshop and museum are across the street and a bit to the left (look for *Ramaio*; for details on him, see page 498). Steeply uphill, on the right just before reaching the square, Cesare's buddy Adamo loves to introduce travelers to Montepulciano's fine wines at the Contucci Cantina (described on page 498). Visit Cesare and Adamo now, or head up to the square for Part 2 of this walk before coming back down.

Either way, Montepulciano's main square is just ahead. You made it!

Part 2: Piazza Grande and Nearby

This pleasant, lively piazza is surrounded by a grab bag of architectural sights. If the medieval **Palazzo Comunale**, or town hall, reminds you of Palazzo Vecchio in Florence, it's because Florence dominated Montepulciano in the 15th and 16th centuries. The crenellations along the roof were never intended to hide soldiers—they're just meant to symbolize power. But the big, square central tower makes it clear that the city is keeping an eye out in all directions.

Take a moment to survey the square, where the town's four great powers stare each other down. Face the Palazzo Comunale, and keep turning to the right to see: the one-time building of the courts (Palazzo del Capitano); the noble Palazzo Tarugi, a Renaissance-arcaded confection; and the aristocratic Palazzo Contucci, with its 16th-century Renaissance facade. (The Contucci family still lives in their palace, producing and selling their own wine.) Continuing your spin, you see the unfinished Duomo looking glumly on, wishing the city hadn't run out of money for its facade. (Its interior, described later under "Sights and Experiences in Montepulciano," looks much better.)

A cistern system fed by rainwater draining from the roofs of surrounding palaces supplied the fine **well** in the corner. Check out its 19th-century pulleys, the grills to keep animals from contaminating the water supply, and the Medici coat of arms (with lions symbolizing the political power of Florence).

Climbing the town hall's **tower** rewards you with a windy but commanding view from the terrace below the clock. Go into the Palazzo Comunale, head up the stairs to your left, and pay on the second floor (€3, daily 10:00-18:00, closed in winter).

The street to the left as you face the tower leads to the **Fortezza**, or fortress. While you might expect the town to be huddled protectively around its fortress, in Montepulciano's case, it's built on a distant ledge at the very edge of town. That's because this fort wasn't meant to protect the townspeople—but to safeguard its rulers by keeping an eye on those townspeople.

Detour to the Church of San Francesco and Views: From the main square, it's a short, mostly level walk to a fine viewpoint. You could head down the wide street to the right as you face the tower. But for a more interesting look at Montepulciano behind its pretty Renaissance facades, go instead up the narrow lane between the two Renaissance palaces in the corner of the square. Within just a few steps, you'll be surrounded not by tidy columns and triangles, but by a mishmash of brick and stone. Pause at the Mueblè il Riccio B&B (with a fine courtyard—peek inside) and look high up across the street to see how centuries of structures have been stitched together, sometimes gracelessly.

Follow along this lane as it bends left, and eventually you'll pop out just below the main square, facing the recommended Cantine del Redi wine cellar (described later). Turn right and head down toward the church. At #21 (on the left), look for a red-and-gold shield, over a door, with the name *Talosa*. This marks the home of one of Montepulciano's *contrade*, or neighborhoods; birth and death announcements for the *contrada* are posted on the board next to the door.

Soon you'll come to a viewpoint (on the right) that illustrates Montepulciano's highly strategic position. The ancient town sitting on this high ridge was surrounded by powerful forces—everything you see in this direction was part of the Papal States, ruled from Rome. In the distance is Lake Trasimeno, once a notorious swampland that made it even harder to invade this town.

Continue a few steps farther to the big parking lot in front of the church. Head out to the terrace for a totally different view: the rolling hills that belonged to Siena. And keep in mind that Montepulciano itself belonged to Florence. For the first half of the 16th century, those three formidable powers—Florence, Siena, and Rome (the papacy)—vied to control this small area. Take in the view of Montepulciano's most impressive church, San Biagio—well worth a visit for drivers or hikers (described later).

From here, you can head back up to the main square, or drop into Cantine del Redi to spelunk its wine cellars.

Sights and Experiences in Montepulciano

These are listed in the order you'll reach them on the self-guided walk, above. For me, Montepulciano's best "experiences" are personal: dropping in on either Adamo, the winemaker at Contucci Cantina, or Cesare, the coppersmith at Ramaio Cesare. Either one will greet you with a torrent of cheerful Italian; just smile and nod, pick up what you can from gestures, and appreciate this rare opportunity to meet a true local character.

▲▲**Contucci Cantina**—Montepulciano's most popular attraction isn't made of stone...it's the famous wine, Vino Nobile. This robust red can be tasted in any of the cantinas lining Via Ricci and Via di Gracciano nel Corso, but the cantina in the basement of Palazzo Contucci is both historic and fun. Skip the palace's formal wine-tasting showroom facing the square, and instead head down the lane on the right to the actual cellars, where you'll meet lively

Adamo (ah-DAH-moh), who has been making wine since 1953 and welcomes tourists into his cellar. While at the palace, you may meet Andrea Contucci, whose family has lived here since the 11th century. He loves to share his family's products with the public. Adamo and Signor Contucci usually have a dozen bottles open.

After sipping a little wine with Adamo, explore the palace basement, with its 13th-century vaults. Originally part of the town's wall, these chambers have been filled since the 1500s with huge barrels of wine. Dozens of barrels of Croatian, Italian, and French oak (1,000-2,500 liters each) cradle the wine through a two-year in-the-barrel aging process, while the wine picks up the personality of the wood. After about 35 years, an exhausted barrel has nothing left to offer its wine, so it's retired. Adamo explains that the French oak gives the wine "pure elegance," the Croatian is more masculine, and the Italian oak is a marriage of the two. Each barrel is labeled with the size in liters, the year the wine was barreled, and the percentage of alcohol (determined by how much sun shone in that year). "Nobile"-grade wine needs a minimum of 13 percent alcohol.

Cost and Hours: Free drop-in tasting, daily 8:30-12:30 & 14:30-18:30, Sat-Sun from 9:30, Piazza Grande 13, tel. 0578-757-006, www.contucci.it.

▲**Ramaio Cesare**—Cesare (CHEH-zah-ray) the coppersmith is an institution in Montepulciano, carrying on his father's and grandfather's trade by hammering into existence an immense selection of copper objects in his cavernous workshop. Though his English is limited, he's happy to show you photos of his work—including the copper top of the Duomo in Siena and the piece he designed and personally delivered to Pope Benedict. Next door, he has assembled a fine museum with items he and his relatives have made, as well as pieces from his personal collection. Cesare is evangelical about copper, and if he's not too busy, he'll create personalized mementoes for visitors—he loves meeting people from around the world who appreciate his handiwork (as his brimming photo album demonstrates). Cesare's justifiable pride in his vocation evokes the hardworking, highly skilled craft guilds that once dominated small-town Italy's commercial and civic life.

Cost and Hours: Demonstration and museum are free; Cesare is generally in his workshop Mon-Sat 8:00-12:30 & 14:30-18:30, Piazzetta del Teatro, tel. 0578-758-753, www.rameria.com. Cesare's shop *(negozio)* is on the main drag, just downhill at Corso #64—look for Rameria Mazzetti, open long hours daily.

Duomo—This church's unfinished facade—rough stonework left waiting for the final marble veneer—is not that unusual. Many Tuscan churches were built just to the point where they had a functional interior, and then, for various practical reasons, the facades were left unfinished. But step inside and you'll be rewarded with some fine art. A beautiful Andrea della Robbia blue-and-white, glazed-terra-cotta *Altar of the Lilies* is behind the baptismal font (on the left as you enter). The high altar, with a top like a pine forest, features a luminous, early-Renaissance Assumption triptych by the Sienese artist Taddeo di Bartolo. Showing Mary in her dreamy eternal sleep as she ascends to be crowned by Jesus, it illustrates how Siena clung to the Gothic aesthetic—elaborate gold leaf and lacy pointed arches—to show heavenly grandeur at the expense of realism.

Cost and Hours: Free, daily 9:00-13:00 & 15:00-18:30.

▲**Cantine del Redi**—The most impressive wine cellars in Montepulciano sit below the Palazzo Ricci, just a few steps off the main square (toward the Church of San Francesco). Enter through the unassuming door and find your way down a spiral staircase—with rounded steps designed to go easy on fragile noble feet, and lined with rings held in place by finely crafted tiny wrought-iron goat heads. You'll wind up in the dramatic cellars, with gigantic barrels under even more gigantic vaults—several stories high. As you go deeper and deeper into the cellars, high up, natural stone seems to take over the brick. At the deepest point, the atmospheric cave, surrounding a filled-in well, a warren of corridors holds fine wine aging in bottles. Finally you wind up in the shop, where you're welcome to taste two or three Redi wines for free—or, if you show them this book, they'll offer you the free wines along with some light food in their spacious tasting room.

Cost and Hours: Free tasting, €7-20 bottles, affordable shipping, daily 10:30-19:00, next to Palazzo Ricci, tel. 0578-757-166, www.dericci.com.

Civic Museum (Museo Civico)—Eclectic and surprisingly modern, but small and ultimately forgettable, this museum collects bits and pieces of local history with virtually no English explanation. The ground floor and cellar hold ancient artifacts and vases, including some Etruscan items. The next two floors are the pinacoteca

TUSCAN HILL TOWNS

(art gallery), of which the highlight is the first-floor room filled with colorful Andrea della Robbia ceramic altarpieces. You'll find a similar della Robbia altarpiece in situ, in the Duomo, for free.

Cost and Hours: €5, Tue-Sun 10:00-13:00 & 15:00-18:00, closed Mon, Via Ricci 10, tel. 0578-717-300.

Just Outside Montepulciano

San Biagio Church—At the base of Montepulciano's hill, down a picturesque driveway lined with cypresses, this church—designed by Antonio da Sangallo and built of locally quarried travertine—is Renaissance perfection. The proportions of the Greek cross floor plan give the building a pleasing rhythmic quality. Bramante, who designed St. Peter's at the Vatican in 1516, was inspired by this dome. The lone tower was supposed to have a twin, but it was never built. The soaring interior, with a high dome and lantern, creates a fine Renaissance space. Walk around the building to study the freestanding towers, and consider a picnic or snooze on the grass in back. The street called Via di San Biagio, leading from the church up into town, makes for an enjoyable, if challenging, walk.

Cost and Hours: Free, normally open daily 8:30-18:30.

Sleeping in Montepulciano

(€1 = about $1.40, country code: 39)

$$$ Mueblè il Riccio ("Hedgehog") is medieval-elegant, with 10 modern and spotless rooms, an awesome roof terrace, and friendly owners. Five are new "superior" rooms with grand views across the Tuscan valleys (Sb-€80, Db-€100, view Db-€110, superior Db-€150, superior Db with balcony-€160, Tb-€116, superior Tb-€180, superior Qb-€200, breakfast-€8, air-con, Internet access and Wi-Fi, limited free parking—request when you reserve, a block below the main square at Via Talosa 21, tel. & fax 0578-757-713, www.ilriccio.net, info@ilriccio.net, Gió and Ivana speak English). Gió and his son Iacopo give tours of the countryside (€50/hour) in one of their classic Italian cars; for details, see their website. Ivana makes wonderful breakfast tarts.

$$ Albergo Duomo is big, modern, and nondescript, with 13 rooms (with small bathrooms) and a comfortable lounge downstairs (small Db-€75, standard Db-€95, Tb-€115, family deals, elevator, air-con in some rooms for €5 extra, free Wi-Fi, free parking nearby, Via di San Donato 14, tel. 0578-757-473, www.albergo duomo.it, albergoduomo@libero.it, Elisa and Saverio).

$$ Camere Bellavista has 10 charming, tidy rooms. True to its name, each room has a fine view—though some are better than others. Room 6 has a view terrace worth reserving (Db-€75, terrace Db-€100, cash only, optional €3-10 breakfast at a bar in the piazza, lots of stairs with no elevator, free Wi-Fi, Via Ricci 25, no reception—call before arriving or ring bell, mobile 347-823-2314, fax 0578-716-341, www.camerebellavista.it, bellavista@bccmp .com, Gabriella speaks only a smidgen of English).

$$ Vicolo dell'Oste B&B, just off the main drag halfway up through town, has five modern rooms with fully outfitted kitchenettes (Db-€95-100, Tb-€130, Qb-€140, includes breakfast at nearby café, free Wi-Fi, Via dell'Oste 1, tel. 0578-758-393, www .vicolodelloste.it, info@vicolodelloste.it, Luisa and Giuseppe).

Countryside Options near Montepulciano: If you'd rather be in the country than in town, don't miss the nearby options listed under "Sleeping near Pienza," later—about a 15-minute drive from Montepulciano.

Eating in Montepulciano

Ai Quattro Venti is fresh, flavorful, fun, and right on Piazza Grande, with a simple dining room and outdoor tables right on the square. It distinguishes itself by offering reasonable portions of tasty, unfussy Tuscan food in an unpretentious setting. Try their very own organic olive oil and wine (€8-9 pastas and *secondi*, Fri-Wed 12:30-14:30 & 19:30-22:30, closed Thu, next to City Hall on Piazza Grande, tel. 0578-717-231, Chiara).

Osteria dell'Aquacheta is a carnivore's dream come true, famous among locals for its excellent beef steaks. Its long, narrow room is jammed with shared tables and tight seating, with an open fire in back and a big hunk of red beef lying on the counter like a corpse on a gurney. Giulio, with a pen tucked into his ponytail, whacks off slabs with a cleaver, confirms the weight and price with the diner, and tosses the meat on the grill—seven minutes per side. Steaks are sold by weight (€3/100 grams, or *etto,* one kilo is about the smallest they serve, two can split it for €30). They also serve hearty €6 pastas and salads and a fine house wine. In

the tradition of old trattorias, they serve one glass, which you use alternately for wine and water (Wed-Mon 12:30-15:00 & 19:30-22:30, closed Tue, Via del Teatro 22, tel. 0578-758-443).

Osteria del Conte, an attractive but humble family-run bistro, offers a €30 *menù del Conte*—a four-course dinner of local specialties including wine—as well as à la carte options and cooking like mom's. While the interior is very simple, they also have outdoor tables on a stony street at the edge of the historic center (€7-8 pastas, €9-14 *secondi*, Thu-Tue 12:30-14:30 & 19:30-21:30, closed Wed, Via San Donato 19, tel. 0578-756-062).

Le Pentolaccia is a small, family-run restaurant at the upper, relatively untouristy end of the main drag. With both indoor and outdoor seating, they serve traditional Tuscan dishes as well as daily fish specials (€8-10 pastas, €8-15 *secondi*, Fri-Wed 12:00-15:00 & 19:30-22:30, closed Thu, Corso 86, tel. 0578-757-582).

Near Montepulciano, in Monticchiello

If you'd enjoy getting out of town for dinner—but not too far—consider the 15-minute drive to the smaller, picturesque hill town of Monticchiello. Just inside the town's gate is the highly regarded **La Porta** restaurant, where Daria pleases diners either indoors or out with well-executed traditional Tuscan dishes (€9 pastas, €12-15 *secondi*, reservations smart; seatings at 12:30, 14:00, 19:30, and 21:30; closed Thu, Via del Piano 1, tel. 0578-755-163). If La Porta is closed or you want a bit more contemporary preparation in a modern atmosphere, continue 50 yards up into town and turn right to find **La Cantina,** run by daughter Deborah (similar prices, Tue-Thu 12:30-15:00 & 19:30-22:00, closed Wed, Via San Luigi 3, tel. 0578-755-280).

Getting There: It's a straight shot to Monticchiello, but finding the road is the hard part. At the base of Montepulciano, head toward Pienza. Shortly after passing the road to San Biagio Church (on the right), watch on the left for the Albergo San Biagio. Turn off and take the road that runs up past the left side of this big hotel, and follow it all the way to Monticchiello. This is a rough (gravel at times), middle-of-nowhere drive. As a bonus, right near Monticchiello is a twisty serpentine lined with stoic cypress trees—one of those classic Tuscan images you'll see on calendars and postcards. It's also possible to reach Monticchiello more directly from Pienza (ask locals for directions).

Montepulciano Connections

Schedule information and bus tickets are available at the TI. All buses leave from Piazza Pietro Nenni. The bus station seems to double as the town hangout, with a lively bar and locals chatting inside. In fact, there's no real ticket window—you'll buy your tickets at the bar. Check www.sienamobilita.it for schedules.

From Montepulciano by Bus to: Florence (2/day with a change in Bettole, 2 hours, €8.70), **Siena** (8/day, none on Sun, 1.25 hours, €5.45), **Pienza** (8/day, 30 minutes, €2.05), **Montalcino** (4/day Mon-Fri, 3/day Sat, none Sun, change in Torrenieri, 1-1.25 hours total, €3.85). There are hourly bus connections to **Chiusi,** a town on the main Florence-Rome rail line (40 minutes, €2.70);

Chiusi is a much better bet than the distant Montepulciano station (5 miles away), which is served only by milk-run trains. Buses connect Montepulciano's bus station and its train station (8/day, none on Sun).

To Montalcino: This connection is problematic by public transportation—consider asking at the TI for a **taxi.** Although expensive (about €60), a taxi could make sense for two or more people. Otherwise you can take a bus to Buonconvento, then change to get to Montalcino (2 hours). **Drivers** find route S-146 to Montalcino particularly scenic (see "The Crete Senese" on page 515).

Pienza

Set on a crest and surrounded by green, rolling hills, the small town of Pienza packs a lot of Renaissance punch. In the 1400s,

locally born Pope Pius II of the Piccolomini family decided to remodel his birthplace in the style that was all the rage: Renaissance. Propelled by papal clout, the town of Corsignano was transformed—in only five years' time—into a jewel of Renaissance architecture. It was

renamed Pienza, after Pope Pius. The plan was to remodel the entire town, but work ended in 1464 when both the pope and his architect, Bernardo Rossellino, died. Their vision—what you see today—was completed a century later. The architectural focal point is the square, Piazza Pio II, surrounded by the Duomo and the pope's family residence, Palazzo Piccolomini. While Piazza Pio II is Pienza's pride and joy, the entire town—a mix of old stonework, potted plants, and grand views—is fun to explore, especially with a camera or sketchpad in hand. You can walk every lane in the tiny town in a few minutes.

Cute as the town is, it's far from undiscovered; tourists can flood Pienza in peak season, and boutiques selling gifty packages of pecorino cheese and local wine greatly outnumber local shops. While it offers fine views of the surrounding countryside, Pienza is situated on a relatively flat plateau rather than the steep pinnacle of more dramatic towns like Montepulciano and Montalcino. For these reasons, it's made to order as a stretch-your-legs break to enjoy the setting, and perhaps tour the palace, but it's not ideal for lingering overnight.

Nearly every shop sells the town's specialty: Pecorino cheese.

This pungent sheep's cheese is available fresh *(fresco)* or aged *(secco)*, and sometimes contains other ingredients, such as truffles or peppers. Look on menus for warm Pecorino *(al forno* or *alla griglia)*, often topped with honey or pears and served with bread. Along with a glass of local wine, this just might lead you to a new understanding of *la dolce vita.*

Orientation to Pienza

Tourist Information: The TI is 10 yards up the street from Piazza Pio II, inside the Diocesan Museum (Wed-Mon 10:00-13:00 & 15:00-18:00, closed Tue, Sat-Sun only in Nov-March, Corso il Rossellino 30, tel. 0578-749-905). Ignore the kiosk just outside the gate, labeled *Informaturista,* which is a private travel agency.

Arrival in Pienza: Buses drop you just a couple of blocks directly in front of the town's main entrance. If **driving,** read signs carefully—some parking spots are reserved for locals, others require the use of a cardboard clock, and others are pay-and-display. Parking is tight, so if you don't see anything quickly, head for the large lot at Piazza del Mercato near Largo Roma outside the old town: As you approach town and reach the "ZTL" cul-de-sac (marked with a red circle) surrounding the park right in front of the town gate, head up the left side of town and look for the turnoff on the left for parking (€1.50/hour, closed Fri morning during market).

Helpful Hints: Market day is Friday morning at Piazza del Mercato, just outside the town walls. A public **WC,** marked *gabinetti pubblici,* is on the right as you face the town gate from outside, on Piazza Dante Alighieri (down the lane next to the faux TI).

Sights in Pienza

▲**Piazza Pio II**—One of Italy's classic piazzas, this square is

famous for its elegance and artistic unity. The square and the surrounding buildings were all designed by Rossellino to form an "outdoor room." Spinning around clockwise, you'll see City Hall (13th-century bell tower with a Renaissance facade and a fine loggia), the Bishop's Palace (now the Diocesan Museum), the Duomo, and the Piccolomini family palace. Just to the left of the church, a lane leads to the best viewpoint in town (described later).

Duomo—Its classic, symmetrical Renaissance facade—dated 1462 with the Piccolomini family coat of arms immodestly front and center—dominates Piazza Pio II. The interior is charming, with several Gothic altarpieces and painted arches. Windows feature the crest of Pius II, with five half-moons advertising the number of crusades that his family funded. The interior art is Sienese Gothic, on the cusp of the Renaissance. As the local clay and *tufo* stone did not make an ideal building foundation, the church is slouching. The church's cliff-hanging position bathes the interior in light, but also makes it feel as if the building could break in half if you jumped up and down. See the cracks in the apse walls, and get seasick behind the main altar.

Cost and Hours: Free, generally open daily 7:00-13:00 & 14:30-19:00.

▲**Palazzo Piccolomini**—The home of Pius II (see page 367) and the Piccolomini family (until 1962) can only be visited on an escorted audioguide tour (about 30 minutes total). You'll see six rooms (dining room, armory, bedroom, library, and so on), three galleries (art-strewn hallways), and the panoramic loggia before being allowed to linger in the beautiful hanging gardens. The drab interiors, faded paintings, coffered ceilings, and scuffed furniture have a mothballed elegance that makes historians wish they'd seen it in its heyday. The audioguide very dryly identifies each item in each room but (sadly) does little to muster enthusiasm for this small-town palace that once hosted a big-name player in European politics. While it's not quite the fascinating slice of 15th-century aristocratic life that it could be (I'd like to know more about the pope's toilet), this is still the best small-town palace experience I've found in Tuscany (it famously starred as the Capulets' home in Franco Zeffirelli's 1968 Academy Award-winning *Romeo and Juliet*). You can peek inside the door for free to check out the well-preserved, painted courtyard. In Renaissance times, most buildings were covered with elaborate paintings like these.

Cost and Hours: €7, Tue-Sun 10:00-13:00 & 14:00-18:30, first tour departs at 10:30, last tour at 18:00, closed Mon, Piazza Pio II 2, tel. 0578-748-392, www.palazzopiccolominipienza.it.

Diocesan Museum (Museo Diocesano)—This measly collection of religious paintings, ecclesiastical gear, altarpieces, and old giant hymnals from local churches fills one room of the cardinal's Renaissance palace. The art is provincial Sienese, displayed in chronological order from the 12th through 17th centuries (but with no English information).

Cost and Hours: €4.10, same hours as TI—which is where you'll buy the ticket, Corso il Rossellino 30.

View Terrace—As you face the church, the upper lane leading left brings you to the panoramic promenade. Views from the terrace include the Tuscan countryside and, in the distance, Monte Amiata, the largest mountain in southern Tuscany.

Sleeping near Pienza

While I wouldn't hang my hat in sleepy Pienza itself, some fine countryside options sit just outside town—including one of my favorite Italian *agriturismo* experiences, La Cretaiole. Location-wise, this is an ideal home base: midway between Montepulciano and Montalcino, and immersed in Tuscan splendor. Three or four of *the* iconic Tuscan landscape vistas are within 10 or 15 minutes' drive of Pienza; you'll make your sightseeing commute along extremely scenic roads with plenty of strategically located pullouts.

$$$ **Agriturismo Cretaiole,** in pristine farmland just out-side Pienza, is a terrific value if you want to call Tuscany home for a long stay. It's warmly run by reformed city-slicker Isabella, her country-boy husband Carlo, and their family. This family-friendly farm, deeply rooted in the culture, welcomes visi-tors for weeklong stays (gener-ally Sat-Sat) in six comfortable apartments. Eager to share

their local traditions, they create a community of about 20 travel-ers who are looking for a rich cultural education. Carlo is a pro-fessional olive-oil taster. Carlo's father, Luciano, is in charge of the grappa and tends the vegetable garden (take your pick of the free veggies). And Isabella is a tireless Jill-of-all-trades, who prides herself on personally assisting each of her guests to find exactly the Tuscan experience they're dreaming of. Included in your stay are a pasta-making class hosted by Isabella followed by a Tuscan din-ner, a visit to their family farm (with samples), a tour of their very own Etruscan-era hermitage, and an olive oil tasting lesson. You may also have the chance to go on a truffle hunt and/or help with grape and olive harvesting. While there's no swimming pool—for philosophical reasons—many thoughtful touches and extras, such as Wi-Fi, mountain bikes, and loaner mobile phones, are provided. Isabella also organizes fairly priced optional activities, such as tours to the studios of local artisans, side-trips to Siena, watercolor classes, dinner at a local monastery, and more (Db-€825/week, small Db apartment-€990/week, large Db apartment-€1,290/week, same apartment for four-€1,595/week, these prices promised with this book in 2013, fewer activities and lower prices mid-Nov-mid-March, tel. & fax 0578-748-083, Isabella's mobile 338-740-9245, www.cretaiole.it, info@cretaiole.it). It's on the Montalcino-Pienza

TUSCAN HILL TOWNS

road (S-146), about 11 miles out of Montalcino, and about 2.5 miles from Pienza. While they prefer weeklong stays, when things are slow they may accept guests for as few as three nights (for this you must book less than a month in advance, Db-€110, 3-night minimum). The same family runs two other properties, with the same activities and personal attention as the main *agriturismo*: **Le Casine di Castello** is a townhouse with two units and the same prices as La Cretaiole, but guests have more independence. The more upscale **Casa Moricciani** is a swanky villa featuring dreamy views, plush interiors, loads of extras, and pure Tuscan luxury (€2,900/week upstairs or €3,900/week downstairs, each with 2 bedrooms and 2 bathrooms). Both properties are in the untouristy medieval village of Castelmuzio, five miles north of Pienza; for details, see www.buongiornotoscana.it.

$$$ Fonte Bertusi, nearly across the road from La Cretaiole, is well-run by young couple Manuela and Andrea, Andrea's father Eduardo, and their attention-starved cats. This imaginative family has scattered vivid, whimsical bits and pieces of artwork around the grounds and in the rooms. The eight apartments are simple—mixing rustic decor with avant-garde creations—and a bit pricey, but the setting is sublime (nightly rate: 1-bedroom apartment-€130, 2-bedroom apartment-€260, includes breakfast; weekly rate: €710-1,010, €40 extra per person for breakfast all week; free Wi-Fi, laundry service, swimming pool, communal BBQ and outdoor kitchen, just outside Pienza toward San Quirico d'Orcia on the right—don't confuse it with the turnoff for "Il Fonte" just before, tel. 0578-748-077, www.fontebertusi.it, info@fontebertusi.it).

Pienza Connections

Bus tickets are sold at the bar/café (marked *Il Caffè*) just outside Pienza's town gate (or pay a little extra and buy tickets from the driver). Buses leave from a few blocks up the street, directly in front of the town entrance. Montepulciano is the nearest transportation hub to other points.

From Pienza by Bus to: Siena (6/day, none on Sun, 1.5 hours, €4.40), **Montepulciano** (8/day, 30 minutes, €2.05), **Montalcino** (4/day Mon-Fri, 3/day Sat, none sun, change in Torrenieri, 45-60 minutes total, €2.70).

Montalcino

On a hill overlooking vineyards and valleys, Montalcino—famous for its delicious and pricey Brunello di Montalcino red wines—is

a must for wine lovers. It's a pleasant, low-impact town with a fine ambience but little sightseeing. Everyone touring this area seems to be relaxed and in an easy groove... as if enjoying a little wine buzz.

In the Middle Ages, Montalcino (mohn-tahl-CHEE-noh) was considered Siena's biggest ally. Originally aligned with Florence, the town switched sides after the Sienese beat up Florence in the Battle of Montaperti in 1260. The Sienese persuaded the Montalcini to join their side by forcing them to sleep one night in the bloody Florentine-strewn battlefield.

Montalcino prospered under Siena, but like its ally, it waned after the Medici family took control of the region. The village became a humble place. Then, in the late 19th century, the Biondi Santi family created a fine, dark red wine, calling it "the brunette" (Brunello). Today's affluence is due to the town's much-sought-after wine.

If you're not a wine lover, you may find Montalcino a bit too focused on *vino,* but one sip of Brunello makes even wine skeptics believe that Bacchus was onto something. Note that Rosso di Montalcino (a younger version of Brunello) is also very good, at half the price. Those with a sweet tooth will enjoy crunching the Ossi di Morta ("bones of the dead") cookies popular in Tuscany.

Orientation to Montalcino

Sitting atop a hill amidst a sea of vineyards, Montalcino is surrounded by walls and dominated by the Fortezza (a.k.a. "La Rocca"). From here, roads lead down into the two main squares: Piazza Garibaldi and Piazza del Popolo.

Tourist Information: The helpful TI, just off Piazza Garibaldi in City Hall, can find you a room for no fee. They sell bus tickets; can call ahead to book a visit at a countryside winery (€1-per-person service fee); and have information on taxi service to nearby towns, abbeys, and monasteries (daily 10:00-13:00 & 14:00-17:30, closed Mon Nov-March, tel. & fax 0577-849-331, www.proloco montalcino.com).

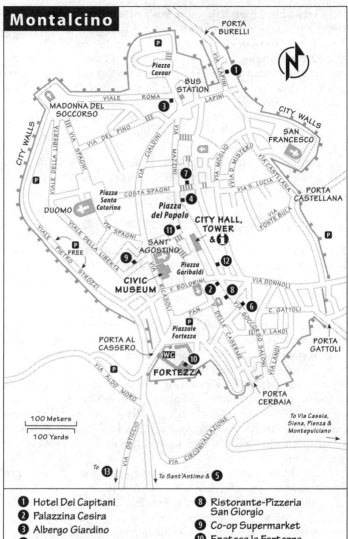

Montalcino

PORTA BURELLI

VIA LAPINI

Piazza Cavour

P

BUS STATION

VIALE ROMA

VIA LAPINI

MADONNA DEL SOCCORSO

CITY WALLS

CITY WALLS

SAN FRANCESCO

VIA DEL PINO

VIA DELLA LIBERTA

VIALE SPAGNI

VIA CIALDINI

VIA MAZZINI

VIA MOGLIO

VIA D. MISTERO

VIA CASTELLANA

PORTA CASTELLANA

VIA S. LUCIA

COSTA SPAGNI

Piazza Santa Catarina

Piazza del Popolo

VIA FONTE BULA

P

DUOMO

VIA SPAGNI

VIALE DELLA LIBERTA

CITY HALL, TOWER &

SANT' AGOSTINO

Piazza Garibaldi

VIALE PIETRO STROZZI

P FREE

CIVIC MUSEUM

VIA RICASOLI

VIA V. BOLDRINI

VIA DONNOLI

P

PAN

V. DELLE CASERME

C. GATTOLI

V. LANDI

Piazzale Fortezza

VIA SOCCORSO SALONI

VIA LANDI

PORTA GATTOLI

PORTA AL CASSERO

WC

FORTEZZA

PORTA CERBAIA

VIA ALDO MORO

P

VIA OSTICCIO

VIA CIRCONVALLAZIONE

To Via Cassia, Siena, Pienza & Montepulciano

100 Meters

100 Yards

To

To Sant'Antimo &

TUSCAN HILL TOWNS

① Hotel Dei Capitani
② Palazzina Cesira
③ Albergo Giardino
④ Affittacamere Mariuccia
⑤ To La Crociona Agriturismo
⑥ Re di Macchia
⑦ Taverna il Grappolo Blu
⑧ Ristorante-Pizzeria San Giorgio
⑨ Co-op Supermarket
⑩ Enoteca la Fortezza di Montalcino
⑪ Caffè Fiaschetteria Italiana
⑫ Enoteca di Piazza
⑬ To Banfi & Argiano Wineries

Arrival in Montalcino: The **bus** station is on Piazza Cavour, about 300 yards from the town center. From here, simply follow Via Mazzini straight into town.

Drivers coming in for a short visit should drive right through the old gate under the fortress (follow signs to *Fortezza;* it looks almost forbidden) and grab a spot in the pay lot at the fortress (€1.50/hour, free 20:00-8:00). If you miss this lot—or if it's full—follow the town's western wall toward the Madonna del Socorrso church and a long pay lot with the same prices. Otherwise, park for free a short walk away.

Helpful Hints: Market day is Friday (7:00-13:00) on Viale della Libertà (near the Fortezza). Day-trippers be warned: Montalcino has **no baggage storage.**

Sights in Montalcino

Fortezza—This 14th-century fort, built under the rule of Siena, is now little more than an empty shell. People visit for its wine bar (see page 513). You can climb the ramparts to enjoy a panoramic view of the Asso and Orcia valleys, or enjoy a picnic in the park surrounding the fort.

Cost and Hours: €4 for rampart walk—buy ticket and enter in the wine bar, €6 combo-ticket includes Civic Museum (sold only at museum), daily 9:00-20:00, until 18:00 Nov-March, last entry 30 minutes before closing.

Piazza del Popolo—All roads in tiny Montalcino seem to lead to the main square, Piazza del Popolo ("People's Square").

Since 1888, the recommended **Caffè Fiaschetteria Italiana** has been *the* elegant place to enjoy a drink. Its founder, inspired by Caffè Florian in Venice, brought fine coffee to this humble town of woodcutters.

City Hall was the fortified seat of government. It's decorated by the coats of arms of judges who, in the interest of fairness, were from outside of town. Like Siena, Montalcino was a republic in the Middle Ages. When Florentines took Siena in 1555, Siena's ruling class retreated here and held out for four more years. The Medici coat of arms (with the six pills), which supersedes all the others, is a reminder that in 1559 Florence finally took Montalcino.

The one-handed **clock** was the norm until 200 years ago. For five centuries the arcaded **loggia** hosted the town market. And, of course, it's fun to simply observe the *passeggiata*—these days mostly a parade of tourists here for the wine.

Montalcino Museums (Musei di Montalcino)—While it's technically three museums in one (archaeology, medieval art, and modern art), and it's surprisingly big and modern for this little town, Montalcino's lone museum ranks only as a decent bad-weather activity. The archaeology collection, filling the cellar, includes interesting artifacts from the area dating back as far as—gulp—200,000 B.C. With good English explanations, this section also displays a mannequin dressed as an Etruscan soldier and a model of the city walls in early Roman times. The ground, first, and second floors hold the medieval and modern art collections, with an emphasis on Gothic sacred art (with works from Montalcino's heyday, the 13th to 16th centuries). Most of the art was created by local artists. The ground floor is best, with a large collection of crucifixes and the museum's highlights, a glazed terra-cotta altarpiece and statue of St. Sebastian, both by Andrea della Robbia.

Cost and Hours: €4.50, €6 combo-ticket includes rampart walk at Fortezza, Tue-Sun 10:00-13:00 & 14:00-17:50, closed Mon, Via Ricasoli 31, to the right of Sant'Agostino Church, tel. 0577-846-014.

Sleeping in Montalcino

(€1 = about $1.40, country code: 39)

$$$ Hotel Dei Capitani, at the end of town near the bus station, has plush public spaces, an inviting pool, and a cliffside terrace offering plenty of reasons for lounging. About half of the 29 rooms come with vast Tuscan views for the same price (request a view room when you reserve), the nonview rooms are bigger, and everyone has access to the terrace (Db-€138 with this book in 2013, extra bed-€40, air-con, elevator, free Internet access and Wi-Fi, limited free parking—first come, first served, Via Lapini 6, tel. 0577-847-227, www.deicapitani.it, info@deicapitani.it).

$$ Palazzina Cesira, right in the heart of the old town, is a gem renting five spacious and tastefully decorated rooms in a fine 13th-century residence with a palatial lounge and a pleasant garden. You'll enjoy a refined and tranquil ambience, a nice breakfast (with eggs), and the chance to get to know Lucilla and her American husband Roberto, who are generous with local advice (Db-€95, suites-€115, cash only, 2-night minimum, 3-night minimum on holiday weekends, air-con, free Internet access and Wi-Fi, free off-street parking, Via Soccorso Saloni 2, tel. & fax 0577-846-055, www.montalcinoitaly.com, p.cesira@tin.it).

$ Affittacamere Mariuccia has three small, colorful, good-value, Ikea-chic rooms on the main drag over a heaven-scented bakery (Sb-€35, Db-€50, no breakfast, check-in across the street at Enoteca Pierangioli before 20:00 or let them know arrival time, Piazza del Popolo 16, rooms at #28, tel. 0577-849-113, mobile 348-392-4780, www.affittacameremariuccia.it, enotecapierangioli @hotmail.com, Alessandro and Stefania speak English).

$ Albergo Giardino, old and basic, has nine big simple rooms, no public spaces, and a convenient location near the bus station (Db-€55-60, 10 percent discount with this book outside May and Sept, no breakfast, Piazza Cavour 4, tel. & fax 0577-848-257, mobile 338-684-3163, albergoilgiardino@virgilio.it; Roberto speaks English; dad Mario doesn't).

Near Montalcino

$$ La Crociona, an *agriturismo* farm and working vineyard, rents seven fully equipped apartments. Fiorella Vannoni and Roberto and Barbara Nannetti offer cooking classes and tastes of the Brunello wine grown and bottled on the premises (Db-€95, or €65 in Oct-mid-May; Qb-€130, or €95 in Oct-mid-May; lower weekly rates, metered gas heating, laundry-€8/load, pool, fitness room, La Croce 15, tel. 0577-847-133, fax 0577-846-994, www.la crociona.com, info@lacrociona.com). The farm is two miles south of Montalcino on the road to the Sant'Antimo Monastery; don't turn off at the first entrance to the village of La Croce—wait for the second one, following directions to Tenuta Crocedimezzo e Crociona). A good restaurant is next door.

Eating in Montalcino

Restaurants

Re di Macchia is an invitingly intimate restaurant where Antonio serves up the Tuscan fare Roberta cooks. Look for their seasonal menu and Montalcino-only wine list. Try the €25 fixed-price meal, and for €17 more, have it paired with local wines carefully selected to accompany each dish (€9-10 pastas, €16 *secondi*, Fri-Wed 12:00-14:00 & 19:00-21:00, closed Thu, reservations strongly recommended, Via Soccorso Saloni 21, tel. 0577-846-116).

Taverna il Grappolo Blu is unpretentious, friendly, and serious about its wine, serving local specialties and vegetarian options to an enthusiastic crowd (€8-9 pastas, €9-14 *secondi*, daily 12:00-15:00 & 19:00-22:00, reservations smart, near the main square, a few steps off Via Mazzini at Scale di Via Moglio 1, tel. 0577-847-150, Luciano).

Ristorante-Pizzeria San Giorgio is a homey trattoria/pizzeria with kitschy decor and reasonable prices. It's a reliable choice for a simple meal (€4-7 pizzas, €8 pastas, €8-12 *secondi*, daily 12:00-15:00 & 19:00-22:30, Via Soccorso Saloni 10-14, tel. 0577-848-507, Mara).

Picnic: Gather ingredients at the **Co-op supermarket** on Via Sant'Agostino (Mon-Sat 8:30-13:00 & 16:00-20:00, closed Sun, just off Via Ricasoli in front of Sant'Agostino Church), then enjoy your feast up at the Madonna del Soccorso Church, with vast territorial views.

Wine Bars: Note that two of the places listed under "Wine Bars *(Enoteche)* in Town," later, also serve light food.

Wine Tasting and Wineries

There are two basic approaches for sampling Montalcino's wines: at an *enoteca* in town, or at a countryside winery. Serious wine connoisseurs will enjoy a day of winery-hopping, sipping the wines right where they were created. But if you don't have the time, or want to try more than one producer's wines, you might prefer to simply visit a wine bar in town, where you can comfortably taste a variety of vintages before safely stumbling back to your hotel.

Wine Bars *(Enoteche)* in Town

Enoteca la Fortezza di Montalcino offers a chance to taste top-end wines by the glass, each with an English explanation. While wine snobs turn up their noses, the medieval setting inside Montalcino's fort is a hit for most visitors. Spoil yourself with Brunello in the cozy *enoteca* or at an outdoor table (€13 for 3 tastings, or €22 for 3 "top-end" tastings; €10-18 two-person sampler plates of cheeses, *salumi,* honeys, and olive oil; daily 9:00-20:00, closes at 18:00 Nov-March, inside the Fortezza, tel. 0577-849-211, www.enotecalafortezza.com).

Caffè Fiaschetteria Italiana, a classic, venerable café/wine bar, was founded by Ferruccio Biondi Santi, the creator of the famous Brunello wine. The wine library in the back of the café boasts many local choices. A meeting place since 1888, this grand café also serves light lunches and espresso to tourists and locals alike (€6-12 Brunellos by the glass, €3-5 light snacks, €8-12 plates; same prices inside, outside, or in back room; daily 7:30-23:00, closed Thu Nov-Easter, free Wi-Fi, Piazza del Popolo 6, tel. 0577-849-043). And if it's coffee you need, this place—with its classic 1961 espresso machine—is considered the best in town.

Enoteca di Piazza is one of a chain of wine shops with a system of mechanical dispensers. A "drink card" (like a debit card) keeps track of the samples you take, for which you'll pay from €1 to €9 for each 50-milliliter taste of the 100 different wines, including some whites—rare in this town. The only nibbles are saltine-type crackers. They hope you'll buy a bottle of the samples you like, and are happy to educate you in English. (Rule of thumb: A bottle costs about 10 times the cost of the sample. If you buy a bottle, the sample of that wine is free.) While the place feels a little formulaic, it can be fun—the wine is great, and the staff is casual and helpful (daily 9:00-20:00, near Piazza del Popolo at Via Matteotti 43, tel.

0577-848-104, www.enotecadipiazza.com). Confusingly, there are three similarly named places in this same area—this tasting room is a block below the main square.

Wineries in the Countryside

The surrounding countryside is littered with wineries, some of which offer tastings. A few require an appointment, but many are happy to serve a glass to potential buyers and show them around. The Montalcino TI can give you a list of more than 150 regional wineries and will call ahead for you (€1 fee per person). Or check with the vintners' consortium (tel. 0577-848-246, www.consorzio brunellodimontalcino.it, info@consorziobrunellodimontalcino.it). These two places listed below are big and capable of handling a steady flow of international visitors; they don't offer an "authentic" Tuscan or cozy experience, but they are convenient and user-friendly.

Argiano claims to be one of the oldest working wineries in the region, dating back to 1580. About a 10-minute drive south of Montalcino at Sant'Angelo in Colle, their one-hour tour in English includes the vineyards, the exterior of a historic villa, and ancient moldy cellars full of wine casks. They also rent on-site apartments—handy for those who have oversampled (€20 tour includes six wine samples, reserve in advance, tel. 0577-844-037, www.argiano.net, coming by car the last two miles are along a rough-but-drivable track through vineyards).

Banfi, run by the Italian-American Mariani brothers, is huge and touristy. While it's not an intimate family winery, the grounds are impressive and they're well set up to introduce the passing hordes to their wines (€13 for 3 tastings, €3.50-25 per glass, daily 10:00-18:00, free tours Mon-Fri at 16:00—reserve in advance, 10-minute drive south of Montalcino in Sant'Angelo Scalo, tel. 0577-877-500, www.castellobanfi.com, reservations@banfi.it).

Bus Tour: If you lack a car (or don't want to drive), you can take a tour on the **Brunello Wine Bus,** which laces together a variety of wineries (€25, mid-June-Oct Tue, Thu, and Sat, departs at 9:00, returns at 20:00, tel. 0577-846-021, www.lecameredibacco .com, info@lecameredibacco.com).

Montalcino Connections

Montalcino is poorly connected to just about everywhere except Siena, but connections are generally workable. Montalcino's bus station is on Piazza Cavour, within the town walls. Bus tickets are sold at the bar on Piazza Cavour, at the TI, and at some tobacco shops, but not on board (except for the bus to Sant'Antimo). Check schedules at the TI, at the bus station, or at www.sienamobilita

.it. The nearest train station is a 20-minute bus ride away, in Buonconvento (bus runs nearly hourly, €2.05).

From Montalcino by Bus: The handiest direct bus is to **Siena** (6/day Mon-Sat, 4/day Sun, 1.5 hours, €3.85). To reach **Pienza** or **Montepulciano,** ride the bus to Torrenieri (5/day Mon-Sat, none on Sun, 20 minutes), where you'll switch to line #114 for the rest of the way (from Torrenieri: 25 minutes and €2.70 total to Pienza; 45 minutes and €3.85 total to Montepulciano). A local bus runs to **Sant'Antimo** (3/day Mon-Fri, 2/day Sat, none on Sun, 15 minutes, €1.50, buy tickets on board). Anyone going to **Florence** by bus changes in Siena; since the bus arrives at Siena's train station, it's handier to go the rest of the way to Florence by train. Alternatively, you could take the bus to Buonconvento (described earlier), and catch the train there to Florence.

The Crete Senese

Between Siena and the trio of towns described above (Montepulciano, Pienza, Montalcino), the hilly area known as the "Sienese Clay Hills" is full of colorful fields and curvy, scenic roads. The Crete Senese (KRAY-teh seh-NAY-zeh) begins at Siena's doorstep and tumbles south through some of the most eye-pleasing scenery in Italy. You'll see an endless parade of classic Tuscan scenes, rolling hills topped with medieval towns, olive groves, rustic stone farmhouses, and a skyline punctuated with cypress trees. You won't find many wineries here, since the clay soil is better for wheat and sunflowers, but you will find the pristine, panoramic Tuscan countryside featured on countless calendars and postcards.

During the spring, the fields are painted in yellow and green with fava beans and broom, dotted by red poppies on the fringes. Sunflowers decorate the area during June and July, and expanses of windblown grass fill the landscape for much of the early spring and summer.

Most roads to the southeast of Siena will give you a taste of this area, but one of the most scenic stretches is the Lauretana road (Siena-Asciano-San Giovanni d'Asso, S-438, S-451, and SP-60a on road maps; the numbering changes as you drive, but it feels like the same road). To find the Lauretana road from Siena, follow signs for the A-1 expressway; you'll turn off onto S-438 (look for the sign for *Asciano*) well before you reach the expressway. You'll come across plenty of turnouts for panoramic photo opportunities on this road, as well as a few roadside picnic areas and several good accommodations (see "Sleeping in the Crete Senese," later).

For a break from the winding road, about 15 miles from Siena,

The Beauty of Tuscany's Geology (and Vice Versa)

While North Americans have romanticized notions of the "Tuscan" landscape, there's a surprisingly wide variety of land forms in the region. Never having been crushed by a glacier, Tuscany is anything but flat. The hills and mountains scattered around the area are made up of different substances, each of which is ideal for very different types of cultivation.

The Chianti region (between Florence and Siena) is rough and rocky, with an inhospitable soil that challenges grape vines to survive while coaxing them to produce excellent wine grapes.

Farther south, the soil switches from rock to clay, silt, and sand. The region called the Crete Senese is literally translated as the "Sienese Clay Hills"—a perfect description of the landscape. Seen from a breezy viewpoint, it's easy to imagine that these clay hills were once at the bottom of the sea floor. The soil here is the yin to Chianti's yang: not ideal for wine, but perfect for truffles and for vast fields of cereal crops such as wheat, fava beans, and sun-yellow rapeseed (for canola oil). In the spring and summer, the Crete Senese is blanketed with brightly colorful crops and flowers. But by the fall, after the harvest, it's a brown and dusty desolate wasteland punctuated with pointy cypress trees—still picturesque, but in a surface-of-the-moon way. Within the Crete Senese, you can distinguish two types of hills shaped by erosion: smooth, rounded *biancane* and pointy, jagged *calanchi*.

The area around Montepulciano and Montalcino is more varied, with rocky protuberances breaking up the undulating clay hills (and providing a suitable home for wine grapes). Even farther south is the Val d'Orcia, the valley of the Orcia River, with its own beauty that mixes clay hills and jutting rock.

You'll see many hot springs in this part of Tuscany, as well as town names with the word Terme (for "spa" or "hot spring"). These generally occur where clay meets rock: water moving through the clay encounters a barrier and gets trapped. Aside from hot water, another byproduct of this change in landscapes is travertine, explaining the quarries you may see in or near spa towns.

you'll find the quaint and non-touristy village of **Asciano.** With a medieval town center and several interesting churches and museums, this town offers a rare look at everyday Tuscan living—and it's a great place for lunch (TI open Tue-Sun 10:30-13:00 & 15:00-18:00, Mon 10:00-13:00, at Corso Matteotti 18, tel. 0577-718-811). If you're in town on Saturday, gather a picnic at the outdoor market (Via Amendola, 8:00-13:00).

A bit farther along, in **Chiusure** (about 6 miles south of Asciano, on S-451), follow signs up a steep driveway to the *casa di reposo* (nursing home) for a fine viewpoint over the Crete Senese, including classic views of jagged *calanchi* cliffs. From that hilltop, you can also see the **Abbey of Monte Oliveto Maggiore.** Located 1.5 miles west of Chiusure, the abbey houses a famous fresco cycle of the life of St. Benedict, painted by Renaissance masters Il Sodoma and Luca Signorelli (free, daily 9:15-12:00 & 15:15-18:00, Nov-March until 17:00, Gregorian chanting Sun at 11:00 and Mon-Sat at 18:15, call to confirm, tel. 0577-707-611, www.monte olivetomaggiore.it).

Once you reach the town of **San Giovanni d'Asso**—in the heart of the truffle region—it's a short drive southwest to Montalcino, or southeast to Pienza (each about 12 miles away).

Another scenic drive is the lovely stretch between Montalcino and Montepulciano. This route (S-146 on road maps) alternates between the grassy hills of the Crete Senese and sunbathed vineyards of the Orcia River valley. Stop by Pienza en route.

Sleeping in the Crete Senese

If pastoral landscapes and easy access to varied towns are your goals, you can't do much better than sleeping in the Crete Senese. These countryside options sit between Siena, Montepulciano, Pienza, and Montalcino (a 15- to 45-minute drive from any of them). These options line up on (or just off) the scenic roads (S-438 and S-451) south of Siena; I've listed them from north to south.

$$$ Recommended local guide **Roberto Bechi** (see page 345) has built a new house from scratch that's immersed in gorgeous Crete Sense scenery (about 15 minutes south of Siena). He plans to begin renting five spacious rooms there in late 2012; contact him to see if they're ready yet. The house (which Roberto designed and built himself) is entirely "green," with a zero carbon footprint (likely Db-€100, mobile 328-425-5648, www.toursby roberto.com, toursbyroberto@gmail.com). It's just off road S-438; take the turn off for Fontanelle.

$$$ Alle Logge di Sotto, right along route S-438 (with some road noise), is a pleasant country home with dramatic Crete Senese views, an immaculate garden, a swimming pool, and five tidy, nicely appointed rooms (Db-€110, includes breakfast, €700/ week includes one dinner, cheaper in winter, €35/person for full dinner, Lauretana 14, Pievnia/Asciano, tel. 0577-717-199, mobile 338-969-6073, www.alleloggedisotto.it, contact@alleloggedisotto .it, Alessandro and Alessandra). They also offer cooking classes for their guests (€100/2 hours).

$ **Casanova Agriturismo** is for people who *really* want to stay on an authentic, working farm. This rustic place comes with tractors, plenty of farm smells and noises, and a barn full of priceless Chianina cows. If the five simple rooms and one apartment take a back seat to the farm workings, the lodgings are accordingly inexpensive, and you'll appreciate the results of their hard work when you dig into one of their fine farm-fresh dinners (€20/person). German Wiebke (who speaks great English and runs the accommodations), her Tuscan husband Bartolo (who works the fields), his mama Paola (who cooks), and the rest of the Conte clan make this a true *agriturismo* experience (Db-€60, apartment-€70 for 2 and €10 per additional person up to 4, breakfast-€5, free Wi-Fi in some areas, swimming pool, just outside Asciano on road S-451 toward Chiusure, tel. 0577-718-324, mobile 346-792-0859, www .agriturismo-casanova.it, info@agriturismo-casanova.it).

$$ **Agriturismo il Molinello** ("Little Mill") rents five apartments, two built over a medieval mill, on the grounds of a working farm with organic produce, olives, and a truffle ground. Hardworking Alessandro and Elisa share their organic produce and offer weekly wine tastings for a minimum of four people; they also lead cooking classes on request. From May through October, they give free guided tours of Siena on Tuesday afternoons. More rustic than romantic, and lacking the dramatic views of some places, this is a nice mix of farm and style. With children, friendly dogs, toys, and a swimming pool, it's ideal for families (Db-€50-80, Qb-€70-100, apartment for up to 8-€80-200 depending on season and number of people, optional organic breakfast-€9.50, one-week stay required in July-Aug, discounts and no minimum stay off-season, free Internet access, free Wi-Fi in public areas, mountain-bike rentals, biking maps and guided bike tours, between Asciano and the village of Serre di Rapolano—on the road toward Rapolano, 30 minutes southeast of Siena, tel. 0577-704-791, mobile 335-692-5720, fax 0577-705-605, www.molinello .com, info@molinello.com).

Cortona

Cortona blankets a 1,700-foot hill surrounded by dramatic Tuscan and Umbrian views. Frances Mayes' book *Under the Tuscan Sun* placed this town in the touristic limelight, just as Peter Mayle's books popularized the Luberon region in France. But long before Mayes ever published a book, Cortona was popular with Romantics and considered one of the classic Tuscan hill towns. Although it's unquestionably touristy, unlike San Gimignano, Cortona main-

tains a rustic and gritty personality—even with its long history of foreigners who, enamored with its Tuscan charm, made it their adopted home.

The city began as one of the largest Etruscan settlements, the remains of which can be seen at the base of the city walls, as well as in the nearby tombs. It grew to its present size in the 13th to 16th centuries, when it was a colorful and crowded city, eventually allied with Florence. The farmland that fills almost every view from the city was marshy and uninhabitable until about 200 years ago, when it was drained and turned into some of Tuscany's most fertile land.

Art lovers know Cortona as the home of Renaissance painter Luca Signorelli, Baroque master Pietro da Cortona (Berretini), and the 20th-century Futurist artist Gino Severini. The city's museums and churches reveal many of the works of these native sons.

Orientation to Cortona

Most of the main sights, shops, and restaurants cluster around the level streets on the Piazza Garibaldi-Piazza del Duomo axis, but Cortona will have you huffing and puffing up some steep hills. From Piazza Garibaldi, it's a level five-minute walk down bustling shop-lined Via Nazionale to Piazza della Repubblica, the heart of the town, which is dominated by City Hall (Palazzo del Comune). From this square, a two-minute stroll leads you past the TI, the interesting Etruscan Museum, and the theater to Piazza del Duomo, where you'll find the recommended Diocesan Museum. These sights are along the more-or-less level spine that runs through the bottom of town; from here, Cortona sprawls upward. Steep streets, many of them stepped, go from Piazza della Repubblica up to the San Niccolò and Santa Margherita churches and the Medici Fortress (a 30-minute climb from Piazza della Repubblica). In this residential area, you'll see fewer tourists and get a better sense of the "real" Cortona.

In the flat valley below Cortona sprawls the modern, workaday town of Camucia (kah-moo-CHEE-ah), with the train station and other services (such as launderettes) that you won't find in the hill town itself.

Tourist Information

To reach the helpful TI, head to Piazza Signorelli, then walk through the courtyard of the Etruscan Museum and up a short

TUSCAN HILL TOWNS

flight of steps, at the back (Mon-Fri 9:00-13:00 & 15:00-18:00, Sat 9:00-13:00, closed Sun, possibly longer hours May-Sept, tel. 0575-637-223 or 0575-637-276, www.turismo.provincia.arezzo.it).

Arrival in Cortona

Cortona is challenging but doable by public transportation. There are few intercity buses, so your best bet for reaching the town is by train or by car.

By Train: Trains arrive at the unstaffed Camucia station, in the valley four miles below Cortona. Sporadic local buses connect the train station and Piazza Garibaldi in Cortona in about 10 minutes. (If you choose to walk, it's a long steep climb, and there are no sidewalks.) From the station, walk out the front door and look left to find the bus shelter (with schedules posted). Unfortunately, buses depart only about once per hour—and only twice daily on Sundays—and the schedule is not well-coordinated with train times (purchase €1.60 from driver; you want a bus marked for Cortona rather than the opposite direction, Terontola). On the schedule, departures marked with S do not run during school vacations; those marked with N run only during school vacations. If you'd rather not wait, consider taking a taxi into town (€10, call for Dejan and his seven-seater cab, mobile 348-402-3501—Dejan also arranges day trips, see "Local Guides," later; or you can ask your hotel to arrange a taxi).

By Car: You'll find several lots ringing the walls; some are free (white lines), others require payment (blue lines), and still others are for local residents only (yellow lines), so check signs carefully. Your best bet is the large, free lot on Viale Cesare Battisti, just after the big Santo Spirito Church. From here, a series of stairs and escalators take you steeply up to Piazza Garibaldi. Piazza Garibaldi itself may have a handful of pay spots available (marked by blue lines, pay & display, free 20:00-8:00). The small town is actually very long, and it can be smart to drive to the top for sightseeing up there (free parking at Santa Margherita Basilica).

Helpful Hints

Market Day: The market is on Saturday on Piazza Signorelli (from early morning until 14:00).

Services: The town has **no baggage storage,** so try asking nicely at a hotel to leave your bag there. The best public **WC** is located in Piazza del Duomo, under Santa Margherita's statue.

Tuscan Cooking Classes: Husband-and-wife team **Romano and Agostina** hold morning hands-on cooking and cheesemaking classes, as well as wine-, cheese-, and oil-tasting courses three mornings a week in the kitchen of their recommended Ristorante La Bucaccia. In the five-hour class, you'll prepare two *antipasti*, two types of pasta, an entrée, and a dessert, which you then get to eat (roughly €90/person, price includes wine, 5 percent discount if you show this book, classes start at 9:30). A three-hour version starts at 11:00 (€70/person; try to book a few weeks in advance, evening and personalized classes available, Via Ghibellina 17, tel. 0575-606-039, www .labucaccia.it, info@labucaccia.it).

Local Guides: Giovanni Adreani exudes energy and a love of his city and Tuscan high culture. He is great at bringing the fine points of the city to life and can take visitors around in his car for no extra charge. As this region is speckled with underap-preciated charms, having Giovanni for a day as your driver/guide promises to be a fascinating experience (€110/half-day, €200/day, tel. 0575-630-665, mobile 347-176-2830, www .adreanigiovanni.com, adreanigiovanni@libero.it). Reliable, English-speaking taxi driver **Dejan** (DAY-zhan) **Prvulovic** can also take you on full-day tours to Pienza, Montalcino, Siena, Assisi, and Chianti—email him and devise your own itinerary (€220-250/day depending on number of passengers, mobile 348-402-3501, dejanprvi70@yahoo.it).

Self-Guided Walk

Welcome to Cortona

This introductory walking tour will take you from Piazza Garibaldi and up the main strip to the town center, its piazzas, and the Duomo.

• *Start at the bus stop in...*

Piazza Garibaldi: Many visits start and finish in this square, thanks to its bus stop. While the piazza, bulging out from the town fortifications like a big turret, looks like part of an old rampart, it's really a souvenir of those early French and English Romantics—the ones who first created the notion of a dreamy, idyllic Tuscany. During the Napoleonic Age, the French built this balcony (and the scenic little park behind the adjacent San Domenico Church) simply to enjoy a commanding view of the Tuscan countryside.

With Umbria about a mile away, Cortona marks the end of Tuscany. This is a major cultural divide, as Cortona was the last town in Charlemagne's empire and the last under Medici rule. Umbria, just to the south, was papal territory for centuries. These deep-seated cultural disparities were a great challenge for the visionaries who unified the fractured region to create the modern nation of Italy during the 1860s. An obelisk in the center of this square honors one of the heroes of the struggle for Italian unifica-tion—the brilliant revolutionary general Giuseppe Garibaldi.

Enjoy the commanding view from here. Assisi is just over

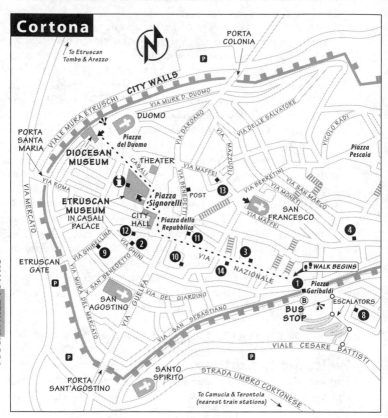

TUSCAN HILL TOWNS

the ridge on the left. Lake Trasimeno peeks from behind the hill, looking quite normal today. But, according to legend, it was blood-red after Hannibal defeated the Romans here in 217 B.C., when 15,000 died in the battle. The only sizable town you can see, on the right, is Montepulciano. Cortona is still defined by its Etruscan walls—remnants of these walls, with stones laid 2,500 years ago, stretch from here in both directions.

Frances Mayes put Cortona on the map for many Americans with her book (and later movie) *Under the Tuscan Sun*. The book describes her real-life experience buying, fixing up, and living in a run-down villa in Cortona with her husband, Ed. The movie romanticized the story, turning Frances into a single, recently divorced writer who restores the villa and her peace of mind. Mayes' villa isn't "under the Tuscan sun" very often; it's

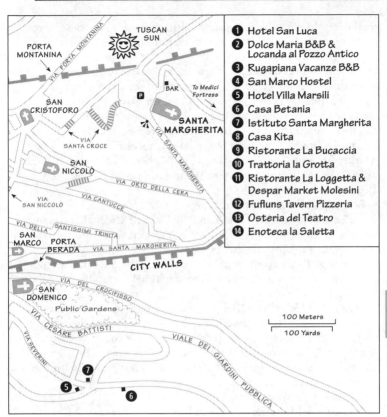

TUSCAN SUN

PORTA
MONTANINA

BAR   To Medici
Fortress

SAN
CRISTOFORO

SANTA
MARGHERITA

VIA SANTA CROCE

SAN
NICCOLÒ

VIA ORTO DELLA CERA

VIA
SAN NICCOLÒ

VIA CANTUCCE

VIA DELLA SANTISSIMI TRINITA

SAN
MARCO   PORTA
BERADA   VIA SANTA MARGHERITA

CITY WALLS

SAN
DOMENICO
Public Gardens

VIA DEL CROCIFISSO

VIA CESARE BATTISTI

VIALE DEL GIARDINI PUBBLICA

VIA SEVERINI

100 Meters
100 Yards

❶ Hotel San Luca
❷ Dolce Maria B&B &
   Locanda al Pozzo Antico
❸ Rugapiana Vacanze B&B
❹ San Marco Hostel
❺ Hotel Villa Marsili
❻ Casa Betania
❼ Istituto Santa Margherita
❽ Casa Kita
❾ Ristorante La Bucaccia
❿ Trattoria la Grotta
⓫ Ristorante La Loggetta &
   Despar Market Molesini
⓬ Fufluns Tavern Pizzeria
⓭ Osteria del Teatro
⓮ Enoteca la Saletta

TUSCAN HILL TOWNS

named "Bramasole"—literally, "craving sun." On the wrong side of the hill, it's in the shade after 15:00. She and her husband still live there part of each year and are respected members of their adopted community (outside the walls, behind the hill on the left—a 20-minute walk away; ask at the TI for directions if you'd like to see it up close).

• *From this square, head into town along...*

Via Nazionale: The only level road in town, locals have nicknamed Via Nazionale the *ruga piana* (flat wrinkle). This is the main commercial street in this town of 2,500, and it's been that way for a long time. Every shop seems to have a medieval cellar or an Etruscan well. Notice the crumbling sandstone door frames. The entire town is constructed from this grainy, eroding rock.

• *Via Nazionale leads to...*

Piazza della Repubblica: City Hall faces Cortona's main square. Note how City Hall is a clever hodgepodge of twin medieval towers, with a bell tower added to connect them, and a grand staircase to lend some gravitas. Notice also the fine wood balconies on the left. In the Middle Ages, wooden extensions like these were common features on the region's stone buildings. These balconies (not original, but rebuilt in the 19th century) would have fit right into the medieval cityscape. These days, you usually see only the holes that once supported the long-gone wooden beams.

This spot has been the town center since Etruscan times. Four centuries before Christ, an important street led from here up to the hill-capping temple. Later, the square became the Roman forum. Opposite City Hall is the handy, recommended Despar Market Molesini, good for cheap sandwiches. Above that is the loggia—once a fish market, now the recommended Ristorante La Loggetta.

• *The second half of the square, to the right of City Hall, is...*

Piazza Signorelli: Dominated by Casali Palace, this square was the headquarters of the Florentine captains who used to control the city. Peek into the palace entrance (under the MAEC sign) for a look at the coats of arms. Every six months, Florence would send a new captain to Cortona, who would help establish his rule by inserting his family coat of arms into the palace's wall. These date from the 15th to the 17th century, and were once painted with bright colors. Cortona's fine Etruscan Museum (described later, under "Sights in Cortona") is in the Casali Palace courtyard, which is lined with many more of these family coats of arms. The inviting Caffè del Teatro fills the loggia of the theater that is named for the town's most famous artist, Luca Signorelli.

• *Head down the street just to the right of the museum to...*

Piazza del Duomo: Here you'll find the Diocesan Museum (listed later, under "Sights in Cortona"), cathedral, and (closer to the top of the square) a statue of Santa Margherita. The cathedral's facade, though recently renovated, still seems a little underwhelming and tucked away. Cortona so loves its hometown saint, Margherita, that it put the energy it would otherwise have invested in its cathedral into the Santa Margherita Basilica, at the top of the hill (at the other end of town—not visible from here). Margherita was a 13th-century rich girl who took good care of the poor and was an early follower of St. Francis and St. Clare. Many locals believe that Margherita protected Cortona from WWII bombs.

The Piazza del Duomo terrace comes with a commanding view of the Tuscan countryside. Notice the town cemetery in the foreground. If you were standing here before the time of Napoleon, you'd be surrounded by tombstones. But Cortona's graveyards—like other urban graveyards throughout Napoleon's realm—were cleaned out in the early 1800s to reclaim land and improve hygiene.

• *Next, enter the...*

Duomo: The Cortona cathedral is not—strictly speaking—a

cathedral, because it no longer has a bishop. The white-and-gray Florentine Renaissance-style interior is mucked up with lots of Baroque chapels filling once-spacious side niches. In the rear (on the right) is an altar cluttered with relics. Technically, any Catholic altar, in order to be consecrated, needs a relic embedded in it. Gently lift up the tablecloth (go ahead—the priest here doesn't mind), and you'll see a little marble patch that holds a bit of a saint (daily in summer 7:30-13:00 & 15:00-18:30, daily in winter 8:00-12:30 & 15:00-17:30, closed during Mass).

• *From here, you can visit the nearby Diocesan Museum, or head back toward Piazza della Repubblica to visit the Etruscan Museum in Piazza Signorelli (both listed next) or to get a bite to eat (see "Eating in Cortona," later).*

Sights in Cortona

▲**Etruscan Museum (Museo dell'Accademia Etrusca e della Città di Cortona)**—Located in the 13th-century Casali Palace and called MAEC for short, this fine gallery (established in 1727) is one of the first dedicated to artifacts from the Etruscan civilization. (In the logo, notice the E is backwards—in homage to the Etruscan alphabet.) This sprawling collection is nicely installed on four big floors with plenty of English information. The bottom two floors (underground) are officially the "Museum of the Etruscan and Roman City of Cortona." You'll see an exhibit on the Roman settlement and take a virtual tour of the Etruscan "Il Sodo" tombs (in the nearby countryside). The Cortona Tablet (*Tabula Cortonensis,* second century B.C.), a 200-word contract inscribed in bronze, contains dozens of Etruscan words archaeologists had never seen before its discovery in 1992. Along with lots of gold and jewelry, you'll find a seventh-century B.C. grater (for some *very* aged Parmesan cheese). The top two floors, called the "Accademia," display an even more eclectic collection, including more Etruscania, Egyptian artifacts, fine Roman mosaics, and a room dedicated to 20th-century abstract works by Severini, all lovingly described in English. A highlight is the magnificent fourth-century B.C. bronze oil lamp chandelier with 16 spouts. On the top floor, peek into the classic old library of the Etruscan Academy, founded in 1727 to promote an understanding of the city through the study of archaeology.

Cost and Hours: €10, €13 combo-ticket includes Diocesan Museum; April-Oct daily 10:00-19:00; Nov-March Tue-Sun 10:00-17:00, closed Mon; Casali Palace on Piazza Signorelli, tel. 0575-637-235, www.cortonamaec.org.

▲**Diocesan Museum (Museo Diocesano)**—This small collection contains some very choice artworks from the town's many churches, including works by Fra Angelico and Pietro Lorenzetti, and masterpieces by hometown hero and Renaissance master Luca Signorelli.

Cost and Hours: €5, €13 combo-ticket includes Etruscan Museum, helpful audioguide-€3; April-Oct daily 10:00-19:00; Nov-March Tue-Sun 10:00-17:00, closed Mon; Piazza del Duomo 1, tel. 0575-62-830.

Visiting the Museum: From the entrance, head straight into the Signorelli Room (Sala 4). Signorelli was a generation ahead of Michelangelo and, with his passion for painting ideas, was an inspiration for the younger artist (for more on Signorelli, visit the San Niccolò Church, described later). Take a slow stroll past his very colorful canvases, mostly relocated here from local churches. Among the most striking is *Lamentation over the Dead Christ (Compianto sul Cristo Morto, 1502)*. Everything in Signorelli's painting has a meaning: The skull of Adam sits under the sacrifice of Jesus; the hammer represents the Passion (the Crucifixion leading to the Resurrection); the lake is blood; and so on. I don't understand all the medieval symbolism, but it is intense.

Then cut across the top of the stairwell into Sala 3, which was once the nave of the Gesù Church (look up at the beautiful wood-carved ceiling). In Fra Angelico's sumptuous *Annunciation* (c. 1430), Mary says "Yes," consenting to bear God's son. The angel's words are top and bottom, while Mary's answer is upside down (logically, since it's directed to God, who would be reading while looking down from heaven). Notice how the house sits on a pillow of flowers...the new Eden. The old Eden, featuring the expulsion of Adam and Eve from Paradise, is in the upper left. The bottom edge of the painting comes with comic strip-like narration of scenes from Mary's life. On the wall to the right, the crucifix (by Pietro Lorenzetti, c. 1325) is striking in its severity. Notice the gripping realism—even the tendons in Jesus' arms are pulled tight.

Now head back to the stairwell, which is lined with colorful Stations of the Cross scenes by another local but much later artist, the 20th-century's Gino Severini. These are actually "cartoons," models used to create permanent pieces for the approach up to the Santa Margherita Basilica. Downstairs, the lower refectory (Sala 6) has a vault with beautiful frescoes (1545) designed by Giorgio Vasari. Back up near the entrance, another staircase leads down to an important but dull collection of vestments and ecclesiastical gear.

San Francesco Church—Established by St. Francis' best friend, Brother Elias, this church dates from the 13th century. The wooden beams of the ceiling are original. While the place was redecorated in the Baroque age, some of the original frescoes that once wall-papered the church peek through the whitewash in the second chapel on the left. Francis fans visit for its precious Franciscan relics. To the left of the altar, you'll find one of Francis' tunics, his pillow (inside a fancy cover), and his gospel book. Notice how the entire high altar seems designed to frame its precious relic—a piece of the cross Elias brought back from his visit to the patriarch in Constantinople. You're welcome to climb the altar for a close-up look. In the humble choir area behind the main altar is Elias' very simple tomb (just a stone slab in the middle of the floor—on a nearby slab, see the *Frate Elia da Cortona* plaque).

Cost and Hours: Free, daily 9:00-17:30; Mass Mon-Sat at 17:00, Sun at 10:00.

San Niccolò Church—Signorelli enthusiasts will want to make the pilgrimage up to this tiny church, a steep 10-minute walk above the San Francesco Church. While it's not worth going out of the way for (the picturesque neighborhood surrounding it is, for many, more interesting), it's an easy detour if you're hiking up to Santa Margherita. The highlight of this humble church is an altar-piece painted on both sides by Signorelli, which is usually pulled halfway open so you can see both sides.

Cost and Hours: €1 donation, April-Oct Sat-Sun 11:00-13:00 & 15:00-18:00, likely daily in June-Sept, generally closed Nov-March, verify hours with TI before making the trip.

Santa Margherita Basilica—From San Niccolò Church, another steep path leads uphill 10 minutes to this basilica, which houses the remains of Margherita, the town's favorite saint. The red-and-white-striped interior boasts some colorfully painted vaults. Santa Margherita, an unwed mother from Montepulciano, found her calling with the Franciscans in Cortona, tending to the sick and poor. The well-preserved and remarkably emotional 13th-century crucifix on the right is the cross that, according to legend, talked to Margherita.

Cost and Hours: Free, daily 9:00-12:00 & 15:00-19:00 except closed Mon morning, tel. 0575-603-116.

Nearby: Still need more altitude? Head uphill five more minutes to the recently renovated **Medici Fortezza Girifalco** (€3, usually open daily late April-Sept 9:00-13:00 & 15:00-18:00, likely later in July-Aug, closed Oct-late April, sometimes closed for rehearsals by Italian rock legend Jovanotti, who lives in a villa beyond San Niccolò Church—check with TI). The views are stunning, stretching all the way to distant Lago Trasimeno.

Etruscan Tombs near Cortona—Guided tours to the tombs (called *melone* for their melon-like shape), in the locality of Sodo, are complicated to arrange. But the excavation site and bits of the ruins are easy to visit and can be seen from outside the fence in the morning. It's just a couple of miles northwest of Cortona on the Arezzo road (R-71), at the foot of the Cortona hill; ask anyone for "Il Sodo."

Sleeping in Cortona

(€1 = about $1.40, country code: 39)

Inside the Old Town

$$$ Hotel San Luca, perched on the side of a cliff, has 54 impersonal business-class rooms, half with stunning views of Lago Trasimeno. While the hotel feels tired and the rooms have seen better days, it's friendly and conveniently located, right at the bus stop on Piazza Garibaldi at the entrance to the Old Town (Sb-€70, Db-€100, Tb-€130, request a view room when you reserve for no extra charge, popular with Americans and groups, air-con, elevator, pay Wi-Fi, Piazza Garibaldi 2, tel. 0575-630-460, fax 0575-630-105, www.sanlucacortona.com, info@sanlucacortona.com). If driving, you might find a spot at the small public parking lot at the hotel; otherwise you can park at the big lot down below and ride the escalator up.

$$ Dolce Maria B&B is located in a 16th-century building with high-beamed ceilings. Though the breakfast area is small, the six rooms themselves are good-value, luminous, and spacious, with tasteful period furnishings and modern bathrooms. The B&B is run by warm and efficient Paola, who also runs the Antico Pozzo restaurant next door—the two businesses share a patio (Db-€80-100, air-con, free Wi-Fi, Via Ghini 12, tel. 0575-601-577, fax 057-560-4627, www.cortonastorica.com, info@cortonastorica.com).

$ San Marco Hostel, at the top of town, is housed in a remodeled 13th-century palace (bunk in 4- to 6-bed dorm-€17, in 2-bed room-€22, includes breakfast, lunch or dinner-€10.50, lockout 10:00-13:00; from Piazza Garibaldi head up steep Via Santa Margherita, then turn left to find Via Maffei 57; tel. & fax 0575-601-392, www.cortonahostel.com, ostellocortona@libero.it).

Outside the Old Town

These accommodations line up along the road that angles downhill from Piazza Garibaldi, within a 10-minute (uphill) walk to the entrance to the Old Town. Drivers may find these handier than the places in town.

$$$ Hotel Villa Marsili is a comfortable splurge just below town. It was originally a 15th-century church, then an elegant 18th-century home. Its 26 rooms and public areas have been recently redecorated and restored, and come with lots of thoughtful little touches. Guests can enjoy an evening aperitif with free snacks on the panoramic terrace. In general, the higher up the room, the fancier the decor and the higher the price. Diane Lane slept in one of the suites while filming *Under the Tuscan Sun* (Sb-€90, small standard Db-€150, superior Db-€180, deluxe Db-€230, Db suite-

€350, extra bed-€25/child or €50/adult, Jacuzzi in deluxe room and suites, air-con, elevator, free Internet access and Wi-Fi, free street parking nearby—first come, first served, Viale Cesare Battisti 13, tel. 0575-605-252, fax 0575-605-618, www.villamarsili.net, info @villamarsili.net, Marina).

$ Casa Betania, a big, wistful convent with an inviting view terrace, rents 30 fine rooms (mostly twin beds) for the best price in town. While it's primarily for "thoughtful travelers," anyone looking for a peaceful place to call home will feel welcome in this pilgrims' resort. Marco, a big-city lawyer escaping from the rat race, has taken over this place and is turning it into an impressive retreat facility, with conference rooms, a chapel, wine cellar, cooking classes, and more (S-€32, D-€44, Db-€48, Tb-€66, extra bed-€20, breakfast-€4, free Wi-Fi, free parking, about a third of a mile out of town, a few minutes' walk below Piazza Garibaldi and through iron gates on the right at Via Gino Severini 50, tel. & fax 0575-630-423, www.casaperferiebetania.com, info@casaperferie betania.com).

$ Istituto Santa Margherita, run by the Serve di Maria Riparatrici sisters, rents 22 nicely renovated rooms in a smaller and more traditional-feeling convent just up the street from Casa Betania (Sb-€42, Db-€58, Tb-€75, Qb-€86, breakfast-€5, elevator, pay Wi-Fi, free parking, Viale Cesare Battisti 17, tel. 0575-178-7203 or 0575-630-336, fax 0575-630-549, www.santamargherita .smr.it, comunitacortona@smr.it).

$ Casa Kita, renting four slightly quirky rooms, is a homey place just below Piazza Garibaldi with fine views from its terrace. You'll really feel like you're staying in someone's home, but the prices are good (Db-€65, free Wi-Fi, 100 yards below Piazza Garibaldi at Vicolo degli Orti 7, tel. 389-557-9893, www.casakita .com, info@casakita.com, Lorenzini family).

Eating in Cortona

Ristorante La Bucaccia is a family-run eatery set in a rustic medieval wine cellar. It's dressy and romantic. Taking an evangelical pride in their Chianina beef dishes and homemade pastas, Romano hosts and his wife Agostina cooks. Reservations are required for dinner—and worth making (€8-9 pastas, €12-15 *secondi,* daily 12:00-15:30 & 19:00-24:00, show this book for a 5 percent discount and a small free appetizer, Via Ghibellina 17, tel. 0575-606-039).

Trattoria la Grotta, just off Piazza della Repubblica, is a traditional place serving daily specials to an enthusiastic clientele under grotto-like vaults (€7-9 pastas, €7-16 *secondi*, good wine by the glass, Wed-Mon 12:00-14:30 & 19:00-22:00, closed Tue, Piazza Baldelli 3, tel. 0575-630-271).

Locanda al Pozzo Antico offers an affordable menu of Tuscan fare, with a focus on fresh, quality produce, and using their own homemade olive oil. Eat in a classy, minimalist dining room or tucked away in a tranquil secret courtyard. Paola is a charming hostess (€6-9 pastas, €10-16 *secondi*, Fri-Wed 12:30-14:30 & 19:30-22:00, closed Thu, Via Ghini 12, tel. 0575-62091 or 0575-601-577; Paola, husband Franco, and son Gianni).

Ristorante La Loggetta serves up big portions of well-presented Tuscan cuisine on the loggia overlooking Piazza della Repubblica. While they have fine indoor seating under stone vaults, I'd eat here for the chance to gaze at the square over a meal (€8-10 pastas, €8-15 *secondi*, Thu-Tue 12:30-15:00 & 19:30-23:00, closed Wed, Piazza Pescheria 3, tel. 0575-630-575).

Fufluns Tavern Pizzeria (that's the Etruscan name for Dionysus) is easy-going, friendly, and remarkably unpretentious for its location in the town center. It's popular with locals for its good, inexpensive Tuscan cooking, friendly staff, and stone-and-beam-cozy interior (€5-7 pizza and €6-10 pastas plus big salads, good house wine, Wed-Mon 12:15-14:30 & 19:15-22:30, closed Tue, a block below Piazza della Repubblica at Via Ghibellina 3, tel. 0575-604-140).

Osteria del Teatro tries very hard to create a romantic Old World atmosphere, and does it well. Chef and owner Emiliano serves nicely presented and tasty Italian and local cuisine (taking creative liberties with traditions). There's good outdoor seating, too. It feels upscale and a bit self-important (€8-9 pastas, €11-16 *secondi,* Thu-Tue 12:30-14:30 & 19:30-22:00, closed Wed, 2 blocks uphill from the main square at Via Maffei 2—look for the gnomes on the steps, tel. 0575-630-556).

Enoteca la Saletta, dark and classy with a nice mellow vibe, is good for fine wine and a light meal. You can sit inside surrounded by wine bottles or outside to people-watch on the town's main drag (€3-5 sandwiches and pizzas, €7-12 pastas and *secondi,* daily 7:30-24:00, meals served 12:00-24:00, closed Wed in winter, free Wi-Fi, Via Nazionale 26, tel. 0575-603-366).

Picnic: On the main square, the chic little **Despar Market Molesini** makes tasty sandwiches, served with a smile (see list on counter and order by number, or invent your own), and sells whatever else you might want for a picnic (Mon-Sat 7:00-13:30 & 16:00-20:00, Sun 9:00-13:00, Piazza della Repubblica 23). Munch your picnic across the square on the steps of City Hall, or just past Piazza Garibaldi in the public gardens behind San Domenico Church.

TUSCAN HILL TOWNS

Cortona Connections

Cortona has good train connections with the rest of Italy through its Camucia-Cortona station. Arrive with small bills and coins, as the station is usually unstaffed, and its very basic ticket machine takes only cash—and for change gives only vouchers (which you can use to pay for a future journey). The machine will ask the following: *stazione di partenza* (departure station—select Camucia), *stazione di arrivo* (arrival station—key in the number of your destination from the posted list), *tipo di bilgietto* (select *solo andata*, one-way), *classe* (I go for *seconde*—second class), type of ticket (select *adulti*), and *quantità biglietti da emettare* (how many tickets you want). Then *premiere OK* (press OK) and insert the cash. After buying your ticket, immediately validate it in the yellow box next to the machine. It's possible to buy tickets on board the train for €5 extra—but you have to find the conductor before he finds you, or you'll pay a €40 fine.

To get to the train station at the foot of the hill, take a €10 taxi or hop the €1.20 bus (see "Arrival in Cortona," earlier; runs only about once hourly; buy tickets at newsstand, TI, or tobacco shop, or buy from driver for €0.40 more). Some buses from Piazza Garibaldi only take you as far as the newsstand that's 200 yards in front of the station.

From Camucia-Cortona by Train to: Rome (9/day, 2.5 hours, 4 direct, others with change), **Florence** (hourly, 1.5 hours), **Assisi** (every 2 hours, 70 minutes, change in Terontola), **Montepulciano** (9/day, 1.5-2 hours, change in Chiusi; because few buses serve Montepulciano's town center from its distant train station, it's better to go by train to Chiusi, then by hourly 40-minute bus to Montepulciano), **Chiusi** (9/day, 40 minutes).

Most trains stop at the Camucia-Cortona train station, but each day, two or three high-speed trains to/from Rome, Florence, and Assisi stop at **Terontola**, 10 miles away (buses go about hourly to Terontola, leaves from Piazza Garibaldi, 25-30 minutes, €2, check the schedule at the bus stop by the tree in the square or pick up printed bus schedule from the TI). Note that these trains require reservations, which you can't make on the spot; if taking one, reserve online in advance.

TUSCAN HILL TOWNS

More Tuscan Sights

▲Florence American Cemetery and Memorial

The compelling sight of endless rows of white marble crosses and Stars of David recalls the heroism of the young Americans who fought so valiantly to free Italy (and ultimately Europe) from the grip of fascism. This particular cemetery is the final resting place of more than 4,000 Americans who died in the liberation of Italy during World War II. Climb the hill past the perfectly manicured lawn lined with grave markers, to the memorial, where maps and a history of the Italian campaign detail the Allied advance.

Cost and Hours: Free, daily 9:00-17:00; 7.5 miles south of Florence, off Via Cassia, which parallels the *superstrada* between Florence and Siena, 2 miles south of Florence Certosa exit on A-1 autostrada; buses from Florence stop just outside the cemetery; tel. 055-202-0020, www.abmc.gov.

▲San Galgano Monastery

Of southern Tuscany's several evocative monasteries, San Galgano is the best. Set in a forested area called the Montagnolo ("Medium-Size Mountains"), the isolated abbey and chapel are postcard-perfect, though you'll need a car to get here. Other, more accessible Tuscan monasteries worth visiting include Sant'Antimo (6 miles south of Montalcino) and Monte Oliveto Maggiore (15 miles south of Siena, mentioned in "The Crete Senese," earlier).

Cost and Hours: €2, June-Aug daily 9:00-20:00, shoulder season until 19:00, Nov-Feb daily 10:00-17:00, tel. 0577-756-738, www.prolocochiusdino.it; concerts sometimes held here in summer—info tel. 055-597-8309, www.festivalopera.it. For a quick snack, a small, touristy bar at the end of the driveway is your only option.

Getting There: Although a bus reportedly comes here from Siena, this sight is realistically accessible only for drivers. It's just outside Monticiano (not Montalcino), about an hour south of Siena. A warning to the queasy: These roads are curvy.

Visiting the Monastery: St. Galgano was a 12th-century saint who renounced his past as a knight to become a hermit. Lacking a cross to display, he created his own by miraculously burying his sword up to its hilt in a stone, à la King Arthur, but in reverse. After his death, a large Cistercian monastery complex grew. Today, all you'll see is the roofless, ruined abbey and, on a nearby hill, the Chapel of San Galgano with its fascinating dome and sword in the stone.

This picturesque Cistercian **abbey** was once a powerful institution in Tuscany. Known for their skill as builders, the Cistercians oversaw the construction of Siena's cathedral. But after losing most of its population in the plague of 1348, the abbey never really recovered and was eventually deconsecrated.

The Cistercian order was centered in France, and the architecture of the abbey shows a heavy French influence. Notice the

large, high windows and the pointy, delicate arches. This is pure French Gothic, a style that never fully caught on in Italy (compare it with the chunky, elaborately decorated cathedral in Siena, built about the same time).

As you enter the church, look to the left to see a small section of the cloister wall. This used to surround the garden and was the only place where the monks were allowed to talk, for one hour each day. From inside the church, the empty windows frame the view of the chapel up on the hill.

In 2013, the upper floor of the actual monks' quarters (to the side of the abbey) may open to the public.

A path from the abbey leads up the hill to the **Chapel of San Galgano.** The unique, beehive-like interior houses St. Galgano's sword and stone, recently confirmed to date back to the 12th century. Don't try and pull the sword from the stone—the small chapel to the left displays the severed arms of the last guy who tried. The chapel also contains some deteriorated frescoes and more interesting *sinopie* (fresco sketches). The adjacent gift shop sells a little bit of everything, from wine to postcards to herbs, some of it monk-made.

▲Chiusi

This small hill town (rated ▲▲ for Etruscan fans) was once one of the most important Etruscan cities. Today, it's a key train junction and a pleasant, workaday Italian village with an enjoyable historic center and few tourists. The hill upon which Chiusi sits is honeycombed with Etruscan tunnels, which you can see in a variety of ways.

Tourist Information: The well-organized TI faces the main square (daily April-Aug 9:00-13:00 & 15:00-18:00, Sept 10:00-13:00 & 15:00-18:00, Oct 9:00-13:00, Nov-March 9:30-12:30, Via Porsenna 79, tel. 0578-227-667, www.prolocochiusi.it).

Arrival in Chiusi: The region's **trains** (to Florence, Siena, and Rome—each of these is about an hour away) go through or change at this hub, making Chiusi an easy day trip. There's no luggage storage at the station, but the TI may be willing to take your bags for a short time. Buses link the train station with the town center two miles away (every 40 minutes, buy tickets at tobacco shop, bus doesn't run during a gap in the afternoon, taxi costs €10). All buses from the station drop off at a stop just below the center of town (follow well-marked pedestrian signs up to the TI and museums); about half continue on to a stop near the town theater, right downtown. **Drivers** follow signs for *centro storico*, then the TI. Easy and free parking lots are a five-minute walk from the center; pay spaces (marked with blue lines) are right downtown, next to the TI and museums. Hertz has a rental-car office near the train station (Via M. Buonarroti 21, tel. 057-822-3000).

Sights in Chiusi: All the town's sights are within a five-minute walk of each other and the TI.

The **Archaeological Museum** (Museo Archeologico Nazionale, a.k.a. the Etruscan Museum) thoughtfully presents a high-quality collection with plenty of explanations in English. The collection of funerary urns, some in painted terra-cotta and some in *pietra fetida* ("stinky stone"), are remarkably intact. You'll also see exhibits on two tombs in the nearby countryside: a model of the Tomba della Pellegrina, and small-scale reproductions of the frescoes from the Tomba della Scimmia—both mentioned below (€4, daily 9:00-20:00, in the stately Neoclassical-looking building just off the main square at Via Porsenna 93, tel. 0578-20177, www.archeotoscana.beniculturali.it).

The museum also arranges tours to visit the actual Pellegrina and Scimmia **tombs;** to take part, you'll need to have your own car and to join a guide (meet at the museum 15 minutes before the tour time). For the Tomba della Pellegrina (Tomb of the Pilgrim), from the Hellenistic period (4th century B.C.), tours depart daily at 11:00 and 16:00 (or 14:30 in winter). This is included in museum admission, and no reservations are necessary—just ask when you arrive. The other, the Tomba della Scimmia (Tomb of the Monkey), is a century earlier and has some well-preserved frescoes (€2; Mon, Tue, and Sat only; March-Oct at 11:00 and 16:00, Nov-Feb at 11:00 and 14:30; this tomb requires an advance reservation).

Troglodyte alert! The **Cathedral Museum** on the main square has a dark, underground labyrinth of Etruscan tunnels. The mandatory guided tour of the tunnels ends in a large Roman cistern, from which you can climb the church bell tower for an expansive view of the countryside (museum-€2, labyrinth-€3, combo-ticket-€4, daily June-mid-Oct 9:45-12:45 & 16:00-18:30, mid-Oct-May 9:45-12:45 only, 30-minute tunnel tours run every

40 minutes during museum hours, Piazza Duomo 1, tel. 0578-226-490).

Craving more underground fun? The **Museo Civico** provides hourly tours of the Etruscan water system, which includes an underground lake (€4; May-Oct Tue-Sun at 10:15, 11:30, 12:45, 15:15, 16:30, and 17:45; closed Mon, fewer tours and closed Mon-Wed off-season, call to confirm times, Via II Ciminia 1, tel. 0578-20530, mobile 334-626-6851).

FLORENTINE HISTORY

Two Millennia of Eras

59 B.C.-A.D. 1200: Roman, Early Christian, Medieval

It's the usual Rome story—military outpost, thriving provincial capital, conversion to Christianity, over-run by barbarians—except Florence really didn't fall. Proud medieval Florentines traced their roots back to civilized Rome, and the city remained a Tuscan commercial center during the Dark Ages.

Sights
- Piazza della Repubblica (the old Forum)
- Find the ancient Roman military camp on today's street map. You can still see the rectangular grid plan—aligned by compass points, rather than the river.
- Baptistery (built c. 1050), likely on site of Roman temple
- Roman and Etruscan fragments (Duomo Museum)

1200s: Urban Growth

Woolen cloth manufacture, trade, and banking made urban merchants—organized into guilds—more powerful than rural, feudal nobles. Florence, now a largely independent city-state, allied with nearby cities.

Sights
- Bargello (it was built as the City Hall)

- Santa Croce and Santa Maria Novella churches
- Baptistery interior mosaics

1300s: Prosperity, Plague, Recovery

As part of a budding democracy with civic pride, Florence's guilds and merchants financed major construction projects (some begun in the late 1200s). But the population of 90,000 suddenly was cut nearly in half by the Black Death (bubonic plague) of 1348. Recovery was slowed by more plagues, bank failures, and political rivalries.

Sights

- Duomo and Campanile (original decorations in Duomo Museum)
- Palazzo Vecchio
- Orsanmichele Church
- Santa Croce, Santa Maria Novella, and Giotto's bell-tower design (Campanile) and his paintings in Uffizi

1400s: Renaissance and the Medici Dynasty

While 1500 marks Europe's Renaissance, in Florence—where the whole revival of classical culture got its start—the Renaissance

began and ended in the 1400s (the Quattrocento). The Medici, a rich textile-and-banking family whose wealth gave them political leverage around Europe, ruled the most prosperous city in Italy, appeasing the masses with philanthropy and public art.

Sights

- Brunelleschi's Duomo dome and Pazzi Chapel
- Donatello's statues in Bargello, Duomo Museum, and on Orsanmichele exterior
- Ghiberti's two bronze doors on Baptistery (originals in Duomo Museum)
- Botticelli's paintings in Uffizi
- The Uffizi, tracing painting's history from medieval to Michelangelo
- The Bargello, tracing sculpture's history
- Masaccio's frescoes in Santa Maria Novella and Brancacci Chapel

FLORENTINE HISTORY

Church Architecture

History comes to life when you visit a centuries-old church. Even if you wouldn't know your apse from a hole in the ground, learning a few simple terms will enrich your experience. Note that not every church has every feature, and that a "cathedral" isn't a type of church architecture, but rather a designation for a church that's a governing center for a local bishop.

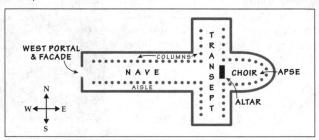

FLORENTINE HISTORY

Aisles: The long, generally low-ceilinged arcades that flank the nave.

Altar: The raised area with a ceremonial table (often adorned with candles or a crucifix), where the priest prepares and serves the bread and wine for Communion.

Apse: The space beyond the altar, generally bordered with small chapels.

Barrel Vault: A continuous round-arched ceiling that resembles an extended upside-down U.

Choir: A cozy area, often screened off, located within the church nave and near the high altar, where services are sung in a more intimate setting.

Cloister: A square-shaped series of hallways surrounding an open-air courtyard, traditionally where monks and nuns got fresh air.

Facade: The outer wall of the church's main (west) entrance, generally highly decorated.

Groin Vault: An arched ceiling formed where two equal barrel vaults meet at right angles. Less common usage: term for a medieval jock strap.

Narthex: The area (portico or foyer) between the main entry and the nave.

Nave: The long, central section of the church (running west to east, from the entrance to the altar) where, in medieval times, the congregation stood through the service.

Transept: The north-south part of the church, which crosses (perpendicularly) the east-west nave. In a traditional Latin cross-shaped floor plan, the transept forms the "arms" of the cross.

West Portal: The main entry to the church (on the west end, opposite the main altar).

- Fra Angelico paintings (and Savonarola history) in San Marco Museum

1500-1800: Decline, Medici Dukes, Renaissance Goes South

Bankrupt, the antidemocratic Medici were exiled to Rome, where they married into royalty and returned—backed by foreign powers—as even less democratic nobles. The "Renaissance spirit" moved elsewhere, taking Michelangelo, Leonardo, and Raphael with it. In succeeding centuries, the Medici dukes ruled an economically and politically declining city, but still financed art.

Sights
- Michelangelo's Florentine works—*David*, Medici Chapels, and Laurentian Library
- Pitti Palace and Boboli Gardens (the later Medici palace)
- Later paintings (Uffizi) and statues (Bargello)
- Destruction of the original Duomo facade (Duomo Museum)
- Medici Chapels—pompous tombs of (mostly) later Medici
- Ponte Vecchio cleaned up for jewelry shops
- Baroque interiors of many older churches
- Galileo's fingers, telescopes, and experiments in the Galileo Science Museum

1800s: Italian Unification

After years of rule by Austrian nobles, Florence peacefully booted out the *Ausländer*s and joined the Italian unification movement. It even served briefly as modern Italy's capital (1865-1870). Artistic revival of both medieval (Neo-Gothic) and Renaissance (Neoclassical) styles.

Sights
- Duomo's current Neo-Gothic facade
- Piazza della Repubblica (commemorating unification), with its fine 19th-century cafés

1900s to Today: Uncontrolled Urbanization, Urban Renewal

Population growth, rapid indus-
trialization, WWII destruction, and the 20-foot-high flood
of 1966 made Florence a chaotic,
noisy, dirty, traffic-choked city.
In the last 30 years, however, the
tourist zone has been cleaned
and cleared, museums revamped,
hours extended, and the people
have become accustomed to welcoming foreign visitors. Now if
they could just do something about those Vespas....

Florence Timeline

500 B.C.-A.D. 1000: Etruscans, Romans, and "Barbarians"

c. 550 B.C.	Etruscans settle in Fiesole, near Florence.
59 B.C.	Julius Caesar establishes the Roman town of Florentia (meaning "flowering" or "flourishing") at a convenient crossing point on the Arno River.
c. A.D. 200	Thriving Roman city, pop. 10,000.
c. 350	In the wake of Constantine's legalization of Christianity, Bishop (and Saint) Zenobius builds a church where the Duomo stands today.
450	Rome falls. Ostrogoths from the east, Byzantines from modern-day Turkey, and Germanic barbarians sweep through in waves. But Florence survives as a small trading town.
800	Charlemagne's Franks sweep through; he becomes the first Holy Roman Emperor. Florence is part of the Empire for the next 300 years, and is the regional capital (rather than Fiesole).

1000-1400: Medieval Rise and Political Squabbles

c. 1050	Baptistery built, likely on site of ancient Roman temple.
1100	Matilda, Countess of Tuscany, allies with the pope and rises against the German-based Holy Roman Empire, gaining independence for Florence.
1200	Florence is the leading city in Tuscany, thriving on wool textile manufacture, trade, banking, and money lending.

Guelphs vs. Ghibellines

In medieval times, Italy was divided between two competing political factions, characterized by these differences:

	Guelphs	**Ghibellines**
Leader	Pope	Emperor
Constituency	Middle-class merchants and craftsmen	Aristocrats of feudal order
Economics	Urban (new economy)	Rural (traditional economy)
Politics	Independence of city-states under local Italian leaders	Unification of small states under traditional dukes and kings

Their conflict had more to do with power than ideology. (It wasn't what you believed, but with whom you were allied.) The names could mean something different depending on the particular place and time.

1215 Power struggles erupt among nobles (Ghibellines), rich merchants and craftsmen (Guelphs), and laborers. The different factions seek support from outsiders—Guelphs ally with pope, Ghibellines with emperor. In general, Ghibellines dominate in first half of 1200s.

1222-1235 Florentine armies defeat Pisa, Siena, and Pistoia. Florence is the dominant city-state in Tuscany, heading a rich, commercial marketplace.

1252 Gold florin minted, one of Europe's strongest currencies.

1266 Merchants and craftsmen (Guelphs) organize into guilds, oust nobles and establish the *primo popolo,* the first "rule by the people."

1293 Guelphs solidify rule by the rich middle class, establishing a constitution that forbids nobles and laborers from holding office. The Ghibellines are gone, but bitter political infighting continues, with Florence divided between Black and White Guelphs.

1296 Construction begins on the Duomo. Santa Croce and Santa Maria Novella are also being built.

1302 The poet Dante, a prominent White Guelph, is exiled. Traveling around Europe and Italy, he writes his epic poem, *The Divine Comedy.*

1347 Florence's population is 90,000, making it one of Europe's biggest cities.

1348 Population nearly halved after the horrific Black Death (bubonic plague). Bank failures and ongoing political squabbles make recovery more difficult.

1378 The Ciompi revolt, led by wool-factory workers, is suppressed by rich merchant families. The guilds (craftsmen unions) lose power as a few wealthy families rise—the Strozzi, Ricci, Alberti, and...Medici.

1400s, The Quattrocento: A Prosperous Renaissance City Under Medici Princes

1401 Baptistery door competition energizes an already civic-minded city.

1406 Florence, by conquering Pisa, gains a port and becomes a sea-trading power.

1421 Giovanni de' Medici, a shrewd businessman, expands the Medici family business from textiles into banking.

1434 Cosimo the Elder (Giovanni's son) returns triumphant from exile to rule Florence. Outwardly, he honors the Florentine constitution, but, in fact, he uses his great wealth to rule as a tyrant, buying popularity with lavish patronage of public art.

1436 Dedication of the Duomo, topped by Brunelleschi's dome.

1440 Battle of Anghiari—Florence defeats Milan.

c. 1440 Donatello's *David*.

1458 Cosimo the Elder creates a rubber-stamp Council of the Hundred.

1464 Cosimo the Elder's son, Piero the Gouty, rules stiffly but ably.

1469 Lorenzo the Magnificent, Cosimo the Elder's grandson, rules over the most powerful city in Italy. He is a popular politician but a so-so businessman.

1492 Lorenzo dies. Many Medici banks go bankrupt. Lorenzo's son, Piero the Unfortunate, faces an invasion force from France and appears to side with the foreigners.

1494 Reviled for being morally, financially, and politically bankrupt, the Medici family is exiled. In the political vacuum, the monk Girolamo

Savonarola appears as a voice of moral authority. He reestablishes the Florentine constitution.

1498 Savonarola is hanged and burned on Piazza della Signoria by political enemies and a citizenry tired of his morally strict rule. The constitution-driven republic continues.

1500-1800: The "Later" Medici Oversee Florence's Decline

1501 Michelangelo begins sculpting *David*.

1512 The Medici family, having established a power base in Rome, returns to take political power as tyrants, backed by the pope and the Spanish army of Holy Roman Emperor Charles V.

1513 Lorenzo the Magnificent's son, Giovanni, becomes Pope Leo X.

1523 Lorenzo's nephew, Giulio de' Medici, becomes Pope Clement VII.

1527 Renegade, unpaid, mercenary troops loot Rome. In the political chaos that follows, Florentines drive the Medici from Florence, re-establishing a republic.

1530 After a yearlong siege, Pope Clement VII and Charles V retake Florence, abolishing the republic and reinstalling Medici rulers.

1533 The Medici marry off Catherine de' Medici to the future King Henry II of France.

1537 Cosimo I, a Medici descended from Cosimo the Elder's brother, is made Duke of Florence. He and his wife, Eleonora of Toledo, rule as tyrannical nobles but beautify the city with the Uffizi, a renovated Palazzo Vecchio, and a rebuilt Pitti Palace.

1574 Francesco I becomes duke, soon to be followed by various Ferdinandos and Cosimos. Florence is now a minor player in world affairs, a small dukedom with a stagnant economy.

1587 The medieval facade of the Duomo is torn down. It remains bare brick for the next 200 years while different proposals are debated.

1600 Maria de' Medici marries Henry IV to become queen of France.

1610-1633 Galileo, backed by the Medici family, works in Florence.

1737 Gian Gastone, the last of the Medici line, dies. Florence is ruled by Austrian Habsburg nobles.

1800-Present: Florence Enters the Modern World

1799   Napoleon "liberates" the city, briefly establishing a pseudo-democracy with his sister as duchess.

1814   Napoleon falls, and the city returns to Austrian rule, under a distant descendant of the Medici family.

1848   Florentine citizens join an uprising all over Italy against foreign rule. The Risorgimento (unification movement) is on.

1860   Florence joins the kingdom of Victor Emmanuel II, forming the nucleus of united, democratic, modern Italy.

1865   Florence is made Italy's capital.

1870   Rome is liberated from papal forces and becomes the de facto capital of a unified Italy (officially in 1871).

1944   Under Nazi occupation as the Allies close in, all the Arno bridges except Ponte Vecchio are blown up.

1966   A disastrous flood, up to nearly 20 feet high, covers the city's buildings and art treasures in mud. The city is a cultural, economic, and touristic mess. An international effort of volunteer "mud angels" slowly brings these treasures back into view.

1993   The Mafia tries to strike terror with a bomb that destroys a section of the Uffizi, but the museum and the city recover. With a thriving university, plentiful cafés, and sparkling clean museums, Florence is a model cultural destination.

2009   The area around the Duomo is declared traffic-free. As in Renaissance times, Florence proves itself to be a trendsetter for other cities.

2013   You visit Florence, the art capital of Europe.

Renaissance Florence: Cradle of the Modern World

There was something dynamic about the Florentines. Pope Boniface VIII said there were five elements: earth, air, fire, water... and Florentines. For 200 years, starting in the early 1300s, their city was a cultural hub.

Florence's contributions to Western culture are immense: the revival of the arts, humanism, and science after centuries of medieval superstition and oppression; the seeds of democracy; the modern Italian language (which grew out of the popular Florentine dialect); the art of Botticelli, Leonardo, and Michelangelo; the writings of Machiavelli, Boccaccio, and Dante; and the explorations of Amerigo Vespucci, who gave his name to a newly discovered continent. Florentines considered themselves descendants of the highly cultured people of the Roman Empire. But Florence, even in its Golden Age, was always a mixture of lustiness and refinement. The streets were filled with tough-talking, hardened, illiterate merchants who strode about singing verses from Dante's *Divine Comedy*.

Florentine culture came from money, and that money came from the wool trade, silk factories, and banking. The city had a large middle class and strong guilds (trade associations for skilled craftsmen). Success was a matter of civic pride, and Florentines showed that pride in the mountains of money they spent to rebuild and beautify the city.

Technically, Florence was a republic, ruled by elected citizens rather than nobility. While there was some opportunity for upward mobility among the middle class, most power was in the hands of a few wealthy banking families. The most powerful was the Medici family. The Medici bank had branches in 10 European cities, including London, Geneva, Bruges (Belgium), and Lyon (France). The pope kept his checking account in the Rome branch. The Florentine florin was the monetary standard of the continent.

Florence dominated Italy economically and culturally, but not militarily. The independent Italian city-states squabbled and remained scattered until the nationalist movement four centuries later. (When someone suggested to the Renaissance Florentine Niccolò Machiavelli that the Italian city-states might unite against their common enemy, France, he wrote back, "Don't make me laugh.")

Lorenzo de' Medici (1449-1492), inheritor of the family's wealth and power, and his grandfather Cosimo's love of art, was a central figure of the Golden Age. He was young (20 when he took power), athletic, and intelligent, in addition to being a poet, horseman, musician, and leader. He wrote love songs and humorous ditties to be performed loudly and badly at carnival time. His marathon drinking bouts and illicit love affairs were legendary. He learned Greek and Latin and read the classics, yet his great passion was hunting. He was the Renaissance Man—a man of knowledge and action, a patron of the arts, and a scholar and man of the world. He was Lorenzo the Magnificent.

Lorenzo epitomized the Florentine spirit of optimism. Born on New Year's Day and raised in the lap of luxury (Donatello's *David* stood in the family courtyard) by loving parents, he grew up feeling that there was nothing he couldn't do. Florentines saw themselves as part of a "new age," a great undertaking of discovery and progress in man's history. They boasted that within the city walls, there were more "nobly gifted souls than the world has seen in the entire thousand years before." These people invented the term "Dark Ages" for the era that preceded theirs.

Lorenzo surrounded himself with Florence's best and brightest. They created an informal "Platonic Academy," based on that of ancient Greece, to meet over a glass of wine under the stars at the Medici villa and discuss literature, art, music, and politics—witty conversation was considered an art in itself.

Their neo-Platonic philosophy stressed the goodness of man and the created world; they believed in a common truth behind all religion. The Academy was more than just an excuse to go out with the guys: The members were convinced that their discussions were changing the world and improving their souls.

Sandro Botticelli (1445-1510) was a member of the Platonic Academy. He painted scenes from the classical myths that the group read, weaving contemporary figures and events into the ancient subjects. He gloried in the nude body, which he considered God's greatest creation.

Artists such as Botticelli thrived on the patronage of wealthy individuals, government, the Church, and guilds. Botticelli commanded as much as 100 florins for one work, enough to live on for a year in high style, which he did for many years. In Botticelli's art we see the lightness, gaiety, and optimism of Lorenzo's court.

Another of Lorenzo's protégés was the young **Michelangelo Buonarroti** (1475-1564). Impressed with his work, Lorenzo took the poor, unlearned 13-year-old boy into the Medici household and treated him like a son.

Michelangelo's playmates were the Medici children, later to become Popes Leo X and Clement VII, who would give him important commissions. For all the encouragement, education, and contacts Michelangelo received, his most important gift from Lorenzo was simply a place at the dinner table, where he could absorb the words of the great men of the time and their love of art for art's sake.

Even with all the art and philosophy of the Renaissance, violence, disease, and warfare were still present in medieval proportions. For the lower classes, life was as harsh as it had always been. Many artists and scholars wore swords and daggers as part of everyday dress. This was the time of the ruthless tactics of the Borgias (known for murdering their political enemies) and of other families battling for power. Lorenzo himself barely escaped assassination in the cathedral during Easter Mass; his brother died in the attack.

The center of the Renaissance gradually shifted to Rome, but its artists were mostly Florentine. In the 15th century, the Holy City of Rome was a dirty, decaying, crime-infested place. Then a series of popes, including Lorenzo's son and nephew, launched a building and beautification campaign. They used fat commissions (and outright orders) to lure Michelangelo, Raphael, and others to Rome. The Florentine Renaissance headed south.

APPENDIX

Contents

Tourist Information

The Italian national tourist offices **in the US** are a wealth of information. Before your trip, scan their website (www.italia .it) or contact the nearest branch to briefly describe your trip and request information. They'll mail you a general brochure and you can download many other brochures free of charge. If you have a specific problem, they're a good source of sympathy.

In New York: Tel. 212/245-5618, fax 212/586-9249, newyork @enit.it; 630 Fifth Ave. #1965, New York, NY 10111.

In Chicago: Tel. 312/644-0996, fax 312/644-3019, chicago @enit.it; 500 N. Michigan Ave. #506, Chicago, IL 60611.

In Los Angeles: Tel. 310/820-1898, fax 310/820-6357, los angeles@enit.it; 12400 Wilshire Blvd. #550, Los Angeles, CA 90025.

In Italy, your best first stop in every town is generally the tourist information office (abbreviated **TI** in this book); for TIs in Florence, see page 46 (www.firenzeturismo.it). TIs are good places to get a city map and information on public transit (including bus and train schedules), walking tours, special events, and nightlife. While Italian TIs are about half as helpful as those in other countries, their information is twice as important. Prepare a list of questions and a proposed plan to double-check. Many TIs have information on the entire country or at least the region, so try to pick up maps for destinations you'll be visiting later in your trip. If you're arriving in a town after the TI closes, call ahead or pick up a map in a neighboring town.

Be wary of the travel agencies or special information services that masquerade as TIs but serve fancy hotels and tour companies. They're in the business of selling things you don't need.

While TIs are eager to book you a room, use their room-finding service only as a last resort. They are unable to give hard opinions on the relative value of one place over another. The accommodations stakes are too high to go potluck through the TI. Even if there's no "fee," you'll save yourself and your host money by going direct with the listings in this book.

Communicating

Hurdling the Language Barrier

Many Italians—especially those in the tourist trade and in big cities such as Florence—speak English. Still, you'll get better treatment if you learn and use Italian pleasantries. In smaller, non-touristy towns, Italian is the norm. Italians have an endearing habit of talking to you even if they know you don't speak their language—and yet, thanks to gestures and thoughtfully simplified words, it somehow works. Don't stop them to tell them you don't understand every word—just go along for the ride. For a list of survival phrases, see page 589.

Note that Italian is pronounced much like English, with a few exceptions, such as: *c* followed by *e* or *i* is pronounced ch (to ask, *"Per centro?"*—To the center?—you say, pehr CHEHN-troh). In Italian, *ch* is pronounced like the hard c in Chianti (*chiesa*—church—is pronounced kee-AY-zah). Give it your best shot. Italians appreciate your efforts.

Telephones

Smart travelers use the telephone to reserve or reconfirm rooms, get tourist information, reserve restaurants, confirm tour times, or phone home. This section covers dialing instructions, phone cards, and types of phones (for more information, see www.ricksteves.com/phoning).

How to Dial

Calling from the US to Italy, or vice versa, is simple—once you break the code. The European calling chart later in this chapter will walk you through it.

Dialing Domestically Within Italy

Italy has a direct-dial phone system (no area codes). To call anywhere within Italy, just dial the number. For example, the number of one of my recommended Florence hotels is 055-289-592. That's the number you dial whether you're calling it from Florence's train station or from Rome.

These instructions apply to dialing from a landline (such as a pay phone or your hotel-room phone) or an Italian mobile phone.

If you're making calls within Italy using your US mobile phone, you may need to dial as if it's a domestic call, or you may need to dial as if you're calling from the US (see "Dialing Internationally," next). Try it one way, and if it doesn't work, try it the other way.

Italy's land lines start with 0 and mobile lines start with 3. The country's toll-free lines begin with 80. These 80 numbers—called *freephone* or *numero verde* (green number)—can be dialed free from any phone without using a phone card. Note that you can't call Italy's toll-free numbers from the US, nor can you count on reaching American toll-free numbers from Italy. Any Italian phone number that starts with 8 but isn't followed by a 0 is a toll call, generally costing €0.10-0.50 per minute.

Italian phone numbers vary in length; a hotel can have, say, an eight-digit phone number and a nine-digit fax number.

Dialing Internationally to or from Italy

If you want to make an international call, follow these steps:

• Dial the international access code (00 if you're calling from Europe, 011 from the US or Canada). If you're dialing from a mobile phone, you can replace the international access code with +, which works regardless of where you're calling from. (On many mobile phones, you can insert a + by pressing and holding the 0 key.)

• Dial the country code of the country you're calling (39 for Italy, or 1 for the US or Canada).

• Dial the local number. Note that in most European countries, you have to drop the zero at the beginning of the local number—but in Italy, you dial it. (The European calling chart lists specifics per country.)

Calling from the US to Italy: To call from the US to my recommended Florence hotel, dial 011 (the US international access code), 39 (Italy's country code), then 055-289-592.

European Calling Chart

Just smile and dial, using this key:
AC = Area Code, LN = Local Number.

European Country	Calling long distance within ...	Calling from the US or Canada to ...	Calling from a European country to ...
Austria	AC + LN	011 + 43 + AC (without the initial zero) + LN	00 + 43 + AC (without the initial zero) + LN
Belgium	LN	011 + 32 + LN (without initial zero)	00 + 32 + LN (without initial zero)
Bosnia-Herzegovina	AC + LN	011 + 387 + AC (without initial zero) + LN	00 + 387 + AC (without initial zero) + LN
Britain	AC + LN	011 + 44 + AC (without initial zero) + LN	00 + 44 + AC (without initial zero) + LN
Croatia	AC + LN	011 + 385 + AC (without initial zero) + LN	00 + 385 + AC (without initial zero) + LN
Czech Republic	LN	011 + 420 + LN	00 + 420 + LN
Denmark	LN	011 + 45 + LN	00 + 45 + LN
Estonia	LN	011 + 372 + LN	00 + 372 + LN
Finland	AC + LN	011 + 358 + AC (without initial zero) + LN	999 (or other 900 number) + 358 + AC (without initial zero) + LN
France	LN	011 + 33 + LN (without initial zero)	00 + 33 + LN (without initial zero)
Germany	AC + LN	011 + 49 + AC (without initial zero) + LN	00 + 49 + AC (without initial zero) + LN
Gibraltar	LN	011 + 350 + LN	00 + 350 + LN
Greece	LN	011 + 30 + LN	00 + 30 + LN
Hungary	06 + AC + LN	011 + 36 + AC + LN	00 + 36 + AC + LN
Ireland	AC + LN	011 + 353 + AC (without initial zero) + LN	00 + 353 + AC (without initial zero) + LN

European Country	Calling long distance within ...	Calling from the US or Canada to ...	Calling from a European country to ...
Italy	LN	011 + 39 + LN	00 + 39 + LN
Montenegro	AC + LN	011 + 382 + AC (without initial zero) + LN	00 + 382 + AC (without initial zero) + LN
Morocco	LN	011 + 212 + LN (without initial zero)	00 + 212 + LN (without initial zero)
Netherlands	AC + LN	011 + 31 + AC (without initial zero) + LN	00 + 31 + AC (without initial zero) + LN
Norway	LN	011 + 47 + LN	00 + 47 + LN
Poland	LN	011 + 48 + LN	00 + 48 + LN
Portugal	LN	011 + 351 + LN	00 + 351 + LN
Slovakia	AC + LN	011 + 421 + AC (without initial zero) + LN	00 + 421 + AC (without initial zero) + LN
Slovenia	AC + LN	011 + 386 + AC (without initial zero) + LN	00 + 386 + AC (without initial zero) + LN
Spain	LN	011 + 34 + LN	00 + 34 + LN
Sweden	AC + LN	011 + 46 + AC (without initial zero) + LN	00 + 46 + AC (without initial zero) + LN
Switzerland	LN	011 + 41 + LN (without initial zero)	00 + 41 + LN (without initial zero)
Turkey	AC (if there's no initial zero, add one) + LN	011 + 90 + AC (without initial zero) + LN	00 + 90 + AC (without initial zero) + LN

- The instructions above apply whether you're calling a land line or mobile phone.

- The international access code (the first numbers you dial when making an international call) is 011 if you're calling from the US or Canada. It's 00 if you're calling from virtually anywhere in Europe (except Finland, where it's 999 or another 900 number, depending on the phone service you're using).

- To call the US or Canada from Europe, dial 00, then 1 (the country code for the US and Canada), then the area code and number. In short, 00 + 1 + AC + LN = Hi, Mom!

Calling from any European country to the US: To call my office in Edmonds, Washington, from anywhere in Europe, I dial 00 (Europe's international access code), 1 (the US country code), 425 (Edmonds' area code), and 771-8303.

Mobile Phones

Traveling with a mobile phone is handy and practical. Whether you're using a smartphone or a conventional cell phone, the basics for how to make calls and send texts is the same. For specifics on using your smartphone to get online, see the sidebar.

Roaming with Your Mobile Phone: Your US mobile phone works in Europe if it's GSM-enabled, tri-band or quad-band, and on a calling plan that includes international calls. Phones from AT&T and T-Mobile, which use the same GSM technology that Europe does, are more likely to work overseas than Verizon or Sprint phones (if you're not sure, ask your service provider). Most US providers will charge you $1.29-1.99 per minute to make or receive calls while roaming internationally, and 20-50 cents to send or receive text messages. If you bother to sign up for an international calling plan with your provider, you'll save a few dimes per minute. Though pricey, roaming on your own phone is easy and can be a cost-effective way to keep in touch—especially on a short trip or if you won't be making many calls.

Buying and Using SIM Cards in Europe: You'll pay much cheaper rates if you put a European SIM card in your mobile phone; to do this, your phone must be electronically "unlocked" (ask your provider about this, buy an unlocked phone before you leave, or get one in Europe—see "Other Mobile-Phone Options," next). Then, in Europe, you can buy a fingernail-size **SIM card,** which gives you a European phone number. SIM cards are sold at mobile-phone stores, post offices, and some newsstand kiosks for $5-10, and often include at least that much prepaid domestic calling time (making the card itself virtually free). When you buy a SIM card, you may need to show ID, such as your passport.

Insert the SIM card in your phone (usually in a slot behind the battery or on the side), and it'll work like a European mobile phone. Before purchasing a SIM card, always ask about fees for domestic and international calls, roaming charges, and how to check your credit balance and buy more time. This can be tricky to accomplish if you don't speak some Italian, but the major mobile phone companies usually have English-speaking staff at their stores. (Also, be aware that prompts for voice mail or topping up the card are in Italian.) When you're in the SIM card's home country, domestic calls average 10 to 20 cents per minute, and incoming calls are free. Rates are higher if you're roaming in another country, and you may pay more to call a toll number than you'd pay to

Smartphones and Data Roaming

I take my smartphone to Europe, using it to make phone calls (sparingly) and send texts, but also to check email, listen to audiotours, and browse the Internet. If you're clever, you can do all this without incurring huge data-roaming fees. Here's how.

Many smartphones, such as the iPhone, Android, and BlackBerry, work in Europe (though some older Verizon iPhones don't). For voice calls and text messaging, smartphones work like any mobile phone (as described under "Using Your Mobile Phone," earlier)—unless you're connected to free Wi-Fi, in which case you can use Skype, Google Talk, or FaceTime to call for free (or at least very cheaply; see "Calling over the Internet," next page).

The (potentially) really expensive aspect of using smartphones in Europe is not voice calls or text messages, but sky-high rates for using data: checking email, browsing the Internet, streaming videos, using certain apps, and so on. If you don't proactively adjust your settings, these charges can mount up even if you're not actually using your phone—because the phone is constantly "roaming" to update your email and such. (One tip is to switch your email settings from "push" to "fetch," so you can choose when to download your emails rather than having them automatically "pushed" over the Internet to your device.)

The best solution: Disable data roaming entirely, and use your device to access the Internet only when you find free Wi-Fi (at your hotel, for example). Then you can surf the net to your heart's content, or make free (or extremely cheap) phone calls via Skype. You can manually turn off data roaming on your phone's menu (check under the "Network" settings). For added security, you can call and ask your service provider to temporarily suspend your data account entirely for the length of your trip.

Some travelers enjoy the flexibility of getting online even when they're not on free Wi-Fi. But be careful. If you simply switch on data roaming, you'll pay exorbitant rates of about $20 per megabyte (figure around 40 cents per email downloaded, or about $3 to view a typical web page)—much more expensive than it is back home. If you know you'll be doing some data roaming, it's far more affordable to sign up for a limited international data-roaming plan through your carrier (but be very clear on your megabyte limit to avoid inflated overage charges). In general, ask your provider in advance how to avoid unwittingly roaming your way to a huge bill.

APPENDIX

dial it from a fixed line.

Other Mobile-Phone Options: Many travelers like to carry two phones: both their own US mobile phone (allowing them to stay reachable on their own phone number) and a second, unlocked European phone (which lets them do all their local calling at far cheaper rates). You could either bring two phones from home, or get one in Europe. If you have an old mobile phone sitting around, ask your provider for the "unlock code" so it can be used with European SIM cards. Or buy a cheap, basic phone before you go (search your favorite online shopping site for "unlocked quad-band GSM phone"). In Europe, basic phones are sold at hole-in-the-wall vendors at many airports and train stations, and at phone desks within larger department stores. Phones that are "locked" to work with a single provider start around $40; "unlocked" phones (which work with any SIM card) start around $60. Regardless of how you get your phone, remember that you'll need a SIM card to make it work.

Car-rental companies and mobile-phone companies offer the option to rent a mobile phone with a European number. While this seems convenient, hidden fees (such as high per-minute charges or expensive shipping costs) can really add up—which usually makes it a bad value. One exception is Verizon's Global Travel Program, available only to Verizon customers.

Calling over the Internet

Some things that seem too good to be true...actually are true. If you're traveling with a laptop, tablet, or smartphone, you can make free calls over the Internet to another wireless device, anywhere in the world, for free. (Or you can pay a few cents to call a telephone from your device). The major providers are Skype (www.skype.com, also available as a smartphone app), Google Talk (www.google.com/talk), and FaceTime (this app is preloaded on most Apple devices). You can get online at a Wi-Fi hotspot and use these apps to make calls without ringing up expensive roaming charges (though call quality can be spotty on slow connections). You can make Internet calls even if you're traveling without your own mobile device: Many European Internet cafés have Skype, as well as microphones and webcams, on their terminals—just log on and chat away.

Landline Telephones

As in the US, these days most Italians do most of their phoning on mobile phones. But for those sticking with landlines, here are the different places from which to make landline calls:

Hotel-Room Phones: Calling from your hotel room can be great for local calls and for calls using cheap international phone cards (described later). Otherwise, hotel-room phones can be an almost criminal rip-off for long-distance or international calls. Many hotels charge a fee for local and sometimes even "toll-free" numbers—always ask for the rates before you dial. Incoming calls are free, making this a cheap way for friends and family to stay in touch (provided they have a long-distance plan with good international rates—and a list of your hotels' phone numbers).

Public Pay Phones: Coin-op phones are virtually extinct. Most pay phones require an insertable phone card, described below.

Metered Phones: In Italy, some call shops have phones with meters. You can talk all you want, then pay the bill when you leave—but be sure you know the rates before you have a lengthy conversation. Note that charges can be "per unit" rather than per minute; find out the length of a unit.

Types of Telephone Cards

There are two types of phone cards: insertable (for pay phones) and international (cheap for overseas calls and usable from any type of phone). If you purchase either type of card in Italy, it'll work only in Italy. If you have a live card at the end of your trip, give it to another traveler to use.

Insertable Phone Cards: This type of card, which works only at pay phones, is sold by Italy's largest phone company, Telecom Italia. They give you the best deal for calls within Italy and are reasonable for international calls. You can buy Telecom cards (in €5 or €10 denominations) at tobacco shops, post offices, and machines near phone booths (many phone booths have signs indicating where the nearest phone-card sales outlet is located).

Rip off the perforated corner to "activate" the card, and then physically insert it into a slot in the pay phone. It displays how much money you have remaining on the card. Then just dial away. The price of the call is automatically deducted while you talk.

International Phone Cards: With these cards, phone calls from Italy to the US can cost less than a nickel a minute. They can also be used to make local calls, and work from any type of phone, including your hotel-room phone or a mobile phone with a European SIM card. To use the card, you'll dial a toll-free access number, then enter your scratch-to-reveal PIN code. If you're calling from a hotel, be sure to dial the *freephone* number (starts with "80") provided on the card rather than the "local access" number (which would incur a charge).

You can buy the cards at small newsstand kiosks, tobacco shops, Internet cafés, hostels, and hole-in-the-wall long-distance phone shops. Because there are so many brand names, ask for an international phone card (*carta telefonica prepagata internazionale*,

KAR-tah teh-leh-FOHN-ee-kah pray-pah-GAH-tah in-ter-naht-zee-oh-NAH-lay). Tell the vendor where you'll be making most calls (*"per Stati Uniti"*—to America), and he'll select the brand with the best deal.

Buy a lower denomination in case the card is a dud. I've had good luck with the Europa card, which offers up to 350 minutes from Italy to the US for €5. Some shops also sell cardless codes, printed right on the receipt. Since you don't need the actual card or receipt to use the account, you can write down the access number and code and share it with friends.

US Calling Cards: These cards, such as the ones offered by AT&T, Verizon, or Sprint, are a rotten value and are being phased out. Try any of the options outlined earlier.

Useful Phone Numbers
Emergency Needs
English-Speaking Police Help: 113
Ambulance: 118
Road Service: 116

Embassies and Consulates
US Embassy: 24-hour emergency line—tel. 06-46741, non-emergency—tel. 06-4674-2406 (access only by appointment, Via Vittorio Veneto 121, Rome, www.usembassy.it)
US Consulate: Tel. 055-266-951 (Mon-Fri 8:30-12:30, closed Sat-Sun and US and Italian holidays, Lungarno Vespucci 38, Florence, http://florence.usconsulate.gov)
Canadian Embassy: Tel. 06-854-441 (Mon-Fri 9:00-12:00, closed Sat- Sun, Via Zara 30, Rome, www.italy.gc.ca)

Travel Advisories
US Department of State: Tel. 202/647-5225, www.travel.state.gov
Canadian Department of Foreign Affairs: Canadian tel. 800-267-6788, www.international.gc.ca
US Centers for Disease Control and Prevention: Tel. 800-CDC-INFO (800-232-4636), www.cdc.gov/travel

Directory Assistance
Telephone Help (in English; free directory assistance): 170
Directory Assistance (for €0.50, an Italian-speaking robot gives the number twice, very clearly): 12

Airports
Florence: Amerigo Vespucci Airport (airport code: FLR)—tel. 055-306-1300 (for flight info, tel. 055-306-1700), www.aeroporto.firenze.it

Pisa: Galileo Galilei Airport (airport code: PSA)—tel. 050-849-300, www.pisa-airport.com

Internet Access

It's useful to get online periodically as you travel—to confirm trip plans, check train or bus schedules, get weather forecasts, catch up on email, blog or post photos from your trip, or call folks back home (explained earlier, under "Calling over the Internet").

Your Mobile Device: The majority of accommodations in Italy offer Wi-Fi (sometimes called "WLAN"), as do many cafés, making it easy for you to get online with your laptop, tablet, or smartphone. Access is often free, but sometimes there's a fee.

Some hotel rooms and Internet cafés have high-speed Internet jacks that you can plug into with an Ethernet cable. A cellular modem—which lets your device access the Internet over a mobile phone network—provides more extensive coverage, but is much more expensive than Wi-Fi (in Italy, www.wind.it and www.tim.it offer pay-as-you-go mobile broadband).

Public Internet Terminals: Many accommodations offer a computer in the lobby with Internet access for guests. If you ask politely, smaller places may sometimes let you sit at their desk for a few minutes just to check your email. If your hotelier doesn't have access, ask to be directed to the nearest place to get online.

Security: Whether you're accessing the Internet with your own device or at a public terminal, using a shared network or computer comes with the potential for increased security risks. Be careful about storing personal information online, such as passport and credit-card numbers. If you're not convinced a connection is secure, avoid accessing any sites that could be vulnerable to fraud (e.g., online banking).

Mail

You can mail one package per day to yourself worth up to $200 duty-free from Europe to the US (mark it "personal purchases"). If you're sending a gift to someone, mark it "unsolicited gift." For details, visit www.cbp.gov and search for "Know Before You Go."

Mail service in Italy has improved over the last few years, but even so, mail nothing precious from an Italian post office. For quick transatlantic delivery (in either direction), consider services such as DHL (www.dhl.com).

Transportation

To Drive or Not to Drive?

The answer is a resounding "yes" if you want to get off the beaten path, free yourself from bus and train schedules, and stop on a

APPENDIX

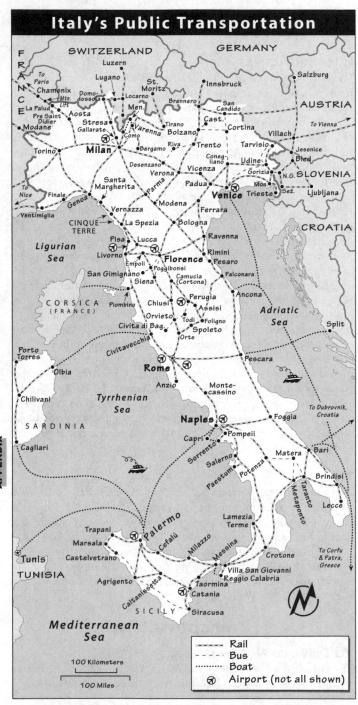

Italy's Public Transportation

Rail

Bus

Boat

Airport (not all shown)

100 Kilometers

100 Miles

whim for that perfect photo of undulating, cypress-lined hills. But don't rent a car if you find driving stressful or if your destinations are easily accessible by public transportation. If your itinerary includes only Florence, Siena, Pisa, and Lucca, a rental car is an unnecessary cost and hassle. However, if you want to stay in an out-of-the-way *agriturismo* and focus on isolated hill towns and Etruscan tombs, having your own wheels will save you time and headaches. (I've noted which areas are best by train or by car, and offered route and arrival instructions, throughout this book.)

Public Transportation
Trains

To travel by train cheaply in Italy, you can simply buy tickets as you go. Ticket machines in stations work well and are easy to use (see "Buying Tickets," later), so you can usually avoid long lines at ticket windows. Pay all ticket costs in the station before you board or pay a penalty on the train.

Types of Trains: Most trains in Italy are operated by the state-run Trenitalia company (a.k.a. Ferrovie dello Stato Italiane or FS). Since ticket prices depend on the speed of the train, it helps to know the different types of trains: pokey R *(regionali)*, medium-speed RV *(regionali espresso)*, and E *(espresso)*; fast IC (InterCity) and EC (EuroCity); and super-fast ES (Eurostar Italia, including Alta Velocità and Frecciarossa). If you're traveling with a railpass, note that reservations are optional for IC trains, but required for EC and international trains (€5) and ES trains (€10). You can't make reservations for regional trains, such as most Florence-Pisa-Cinque Terre connections.

Beginning in mid-2012, a brand-new, private train company called Italo began running fast trains on major routes in Italy, attempting to challenge Trenitalia's monopoly. Italo is focusing on the high-speed Venice-Milan-Bologna-Florence-Rome-Naples corridor, running trains at more or less the same speed as Trenitalia's high-speed trains, but often at lower fares. Italo does not currently accept railpasses. As this is a new venture, it's difficult to know how effective Italo will be—or if it'll even be around by the time you read this.

Schedules: At the train station, the easiest way to check schedules is at a handy automated ticket machine (described later, under "Buying Tickets"). Enter the desired date, time, and destination to see all your options. Printed schedules are also posted at the station (departure posters are always yellow).

Newsstands sell up-to-date regional and all-Italy timetables (€5, ask for the *orario ferroviario*). On the Web, check www.trenitalia.it and www.italotreno.it (domestic journeys only); for international trips, use www.bahn.de (Germany's excellent all-Europe

Train Costs in Italy

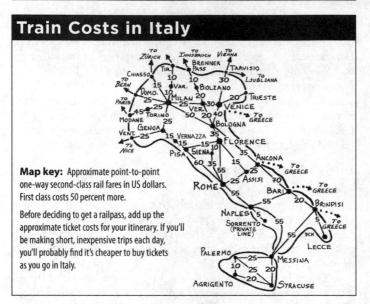

Map key: Approximate point-to-point one-way second-class rail fares in US dollars. First class costs 50 percent more.

Before deciding to get a railpass, add up the approximate ticket costs for your itinerary. If you'll be making short, inexpensive trips each day, you'll probably find it's cheaper to buy tickets as you go in Italy.

schedule website). Trenitalia offers a single all-Italy telephone number for train information (24 hours daily, tel. 892-021, in Italian only, consider having your hotelier call for you). For Italo trains, call 06-0708.

Be aware that Trenitalia and Italo don't cooperate at all, so if you ask for information from one company, they will most likely ignore the other's options.

Point-to-Point Tickets

Train tickets are a good value in Italy. Fares are shown on the map above, though fares can vary for the same journey, mainly depending on the time of day, the speed of the train, and more. **First-class** tickets cost 50 percent more than **second-class.** While second-class cars go as fast as their first-class neighbors, Italy is one country where I would consider the splurge of first class. The easiest way to "upgrade" a second-class ticket once on board a crowded train is to nurse a drink in the snack car.

Speed vs. Savings: For point-to-point tickets on mainline routes, fast trains save time, but charge a premium. For example, super-fast Florence-Rome trains run hourly, cost €45 in second class, and make the trip in 1.5 hours, while less-frequent InterCity options cost €30 and take 3 hours.

Discounts: Families with young children can get price breaks—kids ages 4 and under travel free; ages 4-11 at half-price. Sometimes the parents get a 20 percent price break. Ask for the "Offerta Familia" deal when buying tickets at a counter (or, at a ticket machine, choose "Yes" at the "Do you want ticket issue?" prompt, then choose "Familia"). With the discount, families of three to five people with at least one kid (age 12 or under) get 50 percent off the child fare, and 20 percent off the adult fare. The deal doesn't apply to all trains at all times, but it's worth checking out.

Discounts for youths and seniors require purchase of a separate card (Carta Verde for ages 12-26 costs €40; Carta Argento for ages 60 and over is €30), but the discount on tickets is so minor (10-15 percent respectively for domestic travel), it's not worth it for most.

Buying Tickets: Avoid train station ticket lines whenever possible by using the automated ticket machines found in station halls. You'll be able to easily purchase tickets for travel within Italy (not international trains), make seat reservations, and even book a *cuccetta* (koo-CHEHT-tah; overnight berth).

Trenitalia's automated ticket machines (usually green-and-white, marked *Biglietto Veloce/Fast Ticket*) are user-friendly and found in all but the tiniest stations in Italy. You can pay by cash (they give change) or by debit or credit card (even for small amounts). Select English, then your destination. If you don't immediately see the city you're traveling to, keep keying in the spelling until it's listed. You can choose from first- and second-class seats, request tickets for more than one traveler, and (on the high-speed Eurostar Italia trains) choose an aisle or window seat. If the machine prompts you—"Fidelity Card?"—choose no. Don't select a discount rate without being sure that you meet the criteria (for example, Americans are not eligible for certain EU or resident discounts). Railpass-holders can use the machines to make seat reservations. If you need to validate your ticket, you can do it in the same machine if you're boarding your train right away.

For nearby destinations only, you can also buy tickets from the older, gray-and-blue machines marked *Rete regionale* (cash only, push button for English).

It's possible, but generally unnecessary, to buy Trenitalia tickets in advance online at www.trenitalia.it. Because most Italian trains run frequently and there's no deadline to buy tickets, you can keep your travel plans flexible by buying tickets as you go, or buy several tickets at one station when you are ready to reserve.

To buy tickets for high-speed **Italo** trains, look for a dedicated service counter (in most major rail stations), or a red automated ticket machine labeled *Italo*. You can also book Italo tickets by phone (tel. 06-0708) or online (www.italotreno.it).

Note that if you buy a ticket for one train line, you must travel with only that company—your ticket is not valid on the competitor's train line. Survey your options carefully before you choose.

APPENDIX

Open or Non-Reserved Ticket—Need to Validate

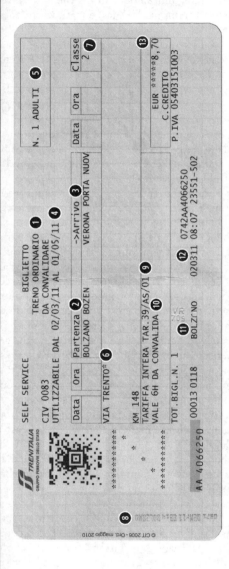

1 Open ticket for non-express trains, must be validated
2 Point of departure
3 Destination
4 Validity of ticket (use once within 2 months of purchase)
5 Number of passengers
6 Route
7 Class of travel (1 = 1st, 2 = 2nd)
8 Validation stamp
9 Full fare for non-express train
10 Once stamped, ticket is good for 1 trip within 6 hours
11 Location of ticket sale
12 Date ticket was purchased
13 Ticket cost

Reserved Ticket (Fast Train)—Need Not Validate

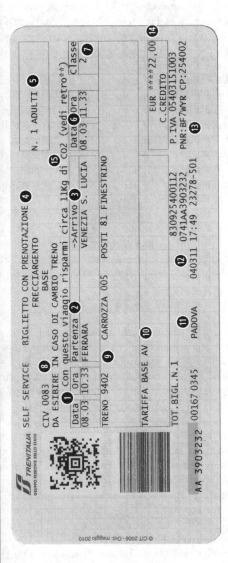

1. Departure date & time
2. Point of departure
3. Destination
4. "Ticket with reservation"
5. Number of passengers
6. Arrival date & time
7. Class of travel (1 = 1st, 2 = 2nd)
8. "Present to official if changing trains"
9. Train #, train car # & seat # (finestrino = window seat)
10. Fast-train fare (other types of trains can be cheaper and don't require reservations)
11. Location of ticket sale
12. Date ticket was purchased
13. Booking ID
14. Ticket cost
15. Amount of CO_2 usage reduced by this train trip

Be aware that you can't buy international tickets from machines; for this and anything else that requires a real person, try a local travel agency, a good alternative to the ticket windows at the station. They also sell domestic tickets and make reservations. The cost is only a little more (agencies charge a small fee); it can be more convenient (if you find yourself near a travel agency while you're sightseeing); there are no crowds; and the language barrier can be smaller than at the station's ticket windows.

Validating Tickets: If your ticket includes a seat reservation on a specific train, you're all set and can just get on board. However, many tickets (especially for slower trains) are flexible—not tied to a particular train or specific reserved seat—and so must be validated before you board. You always need to validate the small, paper-slip tickets that you buy from newsstands or older ticket machines. Tickets from the newer machines must also be validated if they say *"Da convalidare"* near the top. To validate your ticket, stamp it in the yellow box near the platform. Once you validate a ticket, you must complete your trip within the timeframe shown on the ticket (within 6 hours for medium-distance trips; within 1.25 hours for short rides under 6 miles). If you forget to validate your ticket, go right away to the train conductor—before he comes to you—or you'll pay a fine. Note that you don't need to validate a railpass or e-ticket.

Railpasses

The **Italy Pass** for Italian State Railways may save you money if you're taking three long train rides or prefer first-class travel, but don't count on it for hop-on convenience on every train. Use the price map on page 562 to add up your ticket costs (ticket prices on the map are for the fastest trains on a given route, many of which have reservation costs built in). Remember that railpasses are not valid on high-speed Italo trains.

Railpass travelers must make separate seat reservations for the fastest trains between major Italian cities (€10-15 each). Railpass travelers can just hop on InterCity trains (optional €5 reservation) and regional trains (no reservations possible). Making a reservation at a train station or travel agency is the same as the process to buy a ticket, so you may need to stand in line either way. Reservations for berths on overnight trains cost extra, aren't covered by railpasses, and aren't reflected on the ticket cost map.

A 23-country **Eurail Global Pass** can work well for an all-Europe trip, but is a bad value for travel exclusively in Italy. A cheaper version, the **Eurail Select Pass,** allows you to tailor a pass to your trip, provided you're traveling in three, four, or five adjacent countries directly connected by rail or ferry. For instance, with a three-country pass allowing 10 days of train travel within

APPENDIX

Railpasses

Prices listed are for 2013 and are subject to change. For the latest prices, details, and train schedules (and easy online ordering), see my comprehensive *Guide to Eurail Passes* at www.ricksteves.com/rail.

"Saver" prices are per person for two or more people traveling together. "Youth" means under age 26. The fare for children 4–11 is half the adult individual fare or Saver fare. Kids under age 4 travel free.

ITALY PASS

	Individual 1st Class	Individual 2nd Class	Saver 1st Class	Saver 2nd Class	Youth 2nd Class
3 days in 2 months	$298	$244	$254	$208	$198
Extra rail days (max 7)	32-39	26-30	28-32	32-36	22-25

ITALY RAIL & DRIVE PASS
Any 3 rail days and 2 car days in 2 months.

Car Category	1st Class	2nd Class	Extra Car Day
Economy 2-Door	$367	$311	$64
Economy 4-Door	375	320	72
Compact	394	339	92
Intermediate	420	365	118
Economy Automatic	403	347	100
Premium	520	464	217
Extra rail days (max 2)	32	26	

Prices are per person, two traveling together. Solo travelers pay about 20 percent more. To order a Rail & Drive pass, call your travel agent or Rail Europe at 800-438-7245. *This pass is not sold by Europe Through the Back Door.*

FRANCE–ITALY PASS

	Individual 1st Class	Individual 2nd Class	Saver 1st Class	Saver 2nd Class	Youth 2nd Class
4 days in 2 months	$417	$355	$355	$303	$273
Extra rail days (max 6)	45-51	38-44	38-44	33-37	29-33

Be aware of your route. Direct Paris–Italy trains (day and overnight) and trains via Switzerland aren't covered by this pass.

GREECE–ITALY PASS

	Individual 1st Class	Individual 2nd Class	Saver 1st Class	Saver 2nd Class	Youth 2nd Class
4 days in 2 months	$387	$310	$329	$265	$253
Extra rail days (max 6)	38-40	31-32	33-34	26-27	25-26

Covers deck passage on overnight Superfast Ferries between Patras, Greece and Bari or Ancona, Italy (starts use of one travel day). Does not cover travel to or on Greek islands, except a 30% discount on Blue Star Ferries. Very few trains run in Greece.

SELECTPASS
This pass covers travel in three adjacent countries, not including France. Please visit **www.ricksteves.com/rail** for four- and five-country options.

	Individual 1st Class	Saver 1st Class	Youth 2nd Class
5 days in 2 months	$492	$419	$322
6 days in 2 months	544	463	355
8 days in 2 months	643	547	419
10 days in 2 months	745	634	486

APPENDIX

Deciphering Italian Train Schedules

At the station, look for the big yellow posters labeled *Partenze*—Departures (ignore the white posters, which show arrivals).

Schedules are listed chronologically, hour by hour, showing the trains leaving the station throughout the day. Each schedule has columns:

- The first column *(Ora)* lists the time of departure.
- The next column *(Treno)* shows the type of train.
- The third column *(Classi Servizi)* lists the services available (first- and second-class cars, dining car, *cuccetta* berths, etc.) and, more importantly, whether you need reservations (usually denoted by an R in a box). Note that all Eurostar Italia (ES) and Alta Velocità (AV) trains, many InterCity (IC) and EuroCity (EC) trains, and most international trains require reservations.
- The next column lists the destination of the train *(Principali Fermate Destinazioni)*, often showing intermediate stops, followed by the final destination, with arrival times listed throughout in parentheses. Note that your final destination may be listed in fine print as an intermediate destination. For example, if you're going from Florence to Cortona, scan the schedule and you'll notice that many trains that terminate in Rome stop in Cortona en route (and fast trains stop in Terontola, near Cortona). Travelers who read the fine print end up with a far greater choice of trains.
- The next column *(Servizi Diretti e Annotazioni)* has pertinent notes about the train, such as "also stops in..." *(ferma anche a...)*, "doesn't stop in..." *(non ferma a...)*, "stops in every station" *(ferma in tutte le stazioni)*, "delayed..." *(ritardo...)*, and so on.
- The last column lists the track *(Binario)* the train departs from. Confirm the *binario* with an additional source: a ticket seller, the electronic board that lists immediate departures, TV monitors on the platform, or the railway officials who are usually standing by the train unless you really need them.

For any odd symbols on the poster, look at the key at the end. Some of the phrasing can be deciphered easily, such as *servizio periodico* (periodic service—doesn't always run). For the trickier ones, ask a local or railway official, try your *Rick Steves' Italian Phrase Book & Dictionary*, or simply take a different train.

You can also check schedules—for trains anywhere in Italy, not just from the station you're currently in—at the handy ticket machines. Enter the date and time of your departure (to or from any Italian station), and you can view all your options.

a two-month period (about $730 for a single adult in 2012), you could choose France-Italy-Greece or Germany-Austria-Italy. A **France and Italy Pass** combines just those two countries. (If your route includes a connection in Switzerland, you'll pay extra—so the Select Pass is a better choice if you want to see the Alps). Note that none of these passes cover direct day or night trains between Italy and Paris, which require a separate ticket. Before you buy a Select Pass or France and Italy Pass, consider how many travel days you'll really need. Use the pass only for travel days that involve long hauls or several trips. Pay out of pocket for tickets on days you're taking only short, cheap rides.

For a summary of railpass deals and the latest prices, check my Guide to Eurail Passes at www.ricksteves.com/rail. If you decide to get a railpass, this guide will help you know you're getting the right one for your trip.

Train Tips

This section contains information on making seat reservations, storing baggage, avoiding theft, and dealing with strikes.

Seat Reservations: Trains can fill up, even in first class. If you're on a tight schedule, you'll want to reserve a few days ahead for fast trains (see "Types of Trains," earlier). Purchasing tickets or passholder reservations onboard a train comes with a nasty penalty. Buying them at the station can be a time-waster unless you use the automatic ticket machines.

If you don't need a reservation, and if your train originates at your departure point (e.g., you're catching the Florence-Rome train in Florence), arriving at least 15 minutes before the departure time will help you snare a seat.

Some major stations have train composition posters on the platforms showing where first- and second-class cars are located when the trains arrive (letters on the poster are supposed to correspond to letters posted over the platform—but they don't always). Since most trains now allow you to make reservations up to the time of departure, conductors are no longer marking reserved seats with a card—instead, they simply post a list of the reservable and non-reservable seat rows (sometimes in English) in each train car's vestibule. This means that if you board a crowded train and get one of the last seats, you may be ousted when the reservation holder comes along.

Baggage Storage: Many stations have *deposito bagagli* where you can safely leave your bag for about €8 per 12-hour period (payable when you pick up the bag, double-check closing hours). Due to security concerns, no Italian stations have lockers.

Theft Concerns: Italian trains are famous for their thieves. Never leave a bag unattended. Police do ride the trains, cutting down on theft. Still, for an overnight trip, I'd feel safe only in a *cuccetta* (a bunk in a special sleeping car with an attendant who keeps track of who comes and goes while you sleep—approximately €21 in a six-bed compartment, €26 in a less-cramped four-bed compartment, €50 in a more private, double compartment).

Strikes: Strikes, which are common, generally last a day. Train employees will simply explain, *"Sciopero"* (strike). But in actuality, sporadic trains, following no particular schedule, lumber down the tracks during most strikes. When a strike is pending, travel agencies (and Web-savvy hoteliers) can check the Internet for you to see when the strike goes into effect and which trains will continue to run. Revised schedules may be posted in Italian at stations, and station personnel still working can often tell you what trains are expected to run. If I need to get somewhere and know a strike is imminent, I leave early (before the strike, which often begins at 9:00), or I just go to the station with extra patience in tow and hop on anything rolling in the direction I want to go.

Renting a Car

If you're renting a car in Italy, bring your driver's license. You're also technically required to have an International Driving Permit—an official translation of your driver's license (sold at your local AAA office for $15 plus the cost of two passport-type photos; see www .aaa.com). While that's the letter of the law, I've often rented cars in Italy without having—or being asked to show—this permit.

Rental companies require you to be at least 21 years old and have held your license for one year. Drivers under the age of 25 may incur a young-driver surcharge, and some rental companies do not rent to anyone 75 and over. If you're considered too young or old, look into leasing (described later), which has less-stringent age restrictions.

Research car rentals before you go. It's cheaper to arrange most car rentals from the US. Call several companies and look online to compare rates, or arrange a rental through your home-town travel agent.

Most of the major US rental agencies (including National, Avis, Budget, Hertz, and Thrifty) have offices throughout Europe. Also consider the two major Europe-based agencies, Europcar and Sixt. It can be cheaper to use a consolidator, such as Auto Europe or Europe by Car, which compares rates at several companies to get you the best deal. However, my readers have reported problems with consolidators, ranging from misinformation to unexpected fees; because you're going through a middleman, it can be more challenging to resolve disputes that arise with the rental agency.

Regardless of the car-rental company you choose, always read the contract carefully. The fine print can conceal a host of common add-on charges—such as one-way drop-off fees, airport surcharges, or mandatory insurance policies—that aren't included in the "total price," but can be tacked on when you pick up your car. You may need to query rental agents pointedly to find out your actual cost.

For the best rental deal, rent by the week with unlimited mileage. To save money on gas, ask for a diesel car. I normally rent the smallest, least-expensive model—with a stick shift (it's cheaper than an automatic). An automatic transmission adds about 50 percent to the car-rental cost. Almost all rentals are manual by default, so if you need an automatic, you must request one in advance; beware that these cars are usually larger models (not as maneuverable on narrow, winding roads). Roads and parking spaces are narrow in Tuscany, so you'll do yourself a favor by renting the smallest car that meets your needs.

For a three-week rental, allow $900 per person (based on two people sharing a car), including insurance, tolls, gas, and parking. For trips of this length, look into leasing (see next page); you'll save money on insurance and taxes.

You can sometimes get a GPS unit with your rental car or leased vehicle for an additional fee (around $15/day; be sure it's set to English and has all the maps you need before you drive off). Or, if you have a portable GPS device at home, consider taking it with you to Europe (buy and upload European maps before your trip). GPS apps are also available for smartphones, but downloading maps on one of these apps in Europe could lead to an exorbitant data-roaming bill.

Big companies have offices in most cities; ask whether they can pick you up at your hotel. Small local rental companies can be cheaper but aren't as flexible. Compare pickup costs (downtown can be less expensive than the airport) and explore drop-off options. When choosing where to pick up or drop off your car, don't trust the agency's description of "downtown" or "city center." In some cases, a "downtown" branch can be on the outskirts of the city—a long, costly taxi ride from the center. Before choosing, plug the address into a mapping website to compare locations. You may find that the "train station" location is handier. Returning a car at a big-city train station or downtown agency can be tricky; get precise details on the car drop-off location and hours. Note that rental offices usually close from midday Saturday until Monday.

When you pick up the rental car, check it thoroughly and make sure any damage is noted on your rental agreement. Find out how your car's lights, turn signals, wipers, and fuel cap function, and know what kind of gas the car takes. When you return the car, make sure the agent verifies its condition with you.

If you want a car for only a couple of days, a rail-and-drive pass (such as a EurailDrive, Select Pass Drive, or Italy Rail and Drive) can be put to thoughtful use. The basic Italy Rail and Drive Pass, which includes theft insurance and CDW (described next), comes with two days of car rental and three days of rail in two months. While rail-and-drive passes are convenient, they're also pricey, particularly for solo travelers.

Car Insurance Options

Accidents can happen anywhere, but when you're on vacation, the last thing you need is stress over car insurance. When you rent a car, you're liable for a very high deductible, sometimes equal to the entire value of the car. Limit your financial risk in case of an accident by choosing one of these two options: Buy Collision Damage Waiver (CDW) coverage from the car-rental company (figure roughly 30 percent extra), or get coverage through your credit card (free, but more complicated).

In Italy, most car-rental companies' rates automatically include CDW coverage. Even if you try to decline CDW when you reserve your Italian car, you may find when you show up at the counter that you must buy it after all.

While each rental company has its own variation, the basic **CDW** costs $15-35 a day and reduces your liability, but does not eliminate it. When you pick up the car, you'll be offered the chance to "buy down" the deductible to zero (for an additional $10-30/day; this is sometimes called "super CDW").

If you opt for **credit-card coverage,** there's a catch. You'll technically have to decline all coverage offered by the car-rental company, which means they can place a hold on your card (which can be up to the full value of the car). In case of damage, it can be time-consuming to resolve the charges with your credit-card company. Before you decide on this option, quiz your credit-card company about how it works.

For more on car-rental insurance, see www.ricksteves.com/cdw.

Theft Insurance: Note that theft insurance (separate from CDW insurance) is mandatory in Italy. The insurance usually costs about $15-20 a day, payable when you pick up the car.

Leasing

For trips of three weeks or more, consider leasing (which automatically includes zero-deductible collision and theft insurance). By technically buying and then selling back the car, you save lots of money on tax and insurance. Leasing provides you a new car with unlimited mileage and a 24-hour emergency assistance program. You can lease for as little as 21 days to as long as six months. Car

Driving in Tuscany: Distance & Time

m = miles h = hours
Note: Your times may vary based on traffic, construction, and road conditions.

leases must be arranged from the US. One of many companies offering affordable lease packages is Europe by Car (US tel. 800-223-1516, www.ebctravel.com).

Driving

Driving in Italy can be scary—a video game for keeps, and you only get one quarter. Italian drivers can be aggressive. They drive fast and tailgate as if it were required. They pass where Americans are taught not to—on blind corners and just before tunnels. Roads have narrow shoulders or none at all. Driving in the countryside is less stressful than driving through urban areas, but stay alert. On one-lane roads, larger vehicles have the right-of-way. If you're on a truckers' route, stifle your Good Samaritan impulse when you see provocatively dressed women standing by camper-vans at the side of the road; they're not having car trouble. (For more on driving in Tuscany, see page 452.)

Road Rules: Stay out of restricted traffic zones or you'll risk

APPENDIX

huge fines. Car traffic is restricted in many city centers, including Florence, Lucca, Siena, San Gimignano, Volterra, Montepulciano, Pienza, and Cortona. Don't drive or park anywhere with signs reading *Zona Traffico Limitato* (*ZTL,* often shown above a red circle; see image). If you do, your license plate will likely be photographed and a hefty (€100-plus) ticket mailed to your home without you ever having met a cop. Bumbling in and out of these zones can net you multiple fines. If your hotel is within a restricted area, it's best to ask your hotelier to direct you to parking outside the zone. (Although your hotelier can register your car as an authorized vehicle permitted to enter the zone, this usually isn't worth the hassle.)

As for other road rules, seatbelts are mandatory, and you should keep headlights on at all times outside of urban areas. It's illegal to use your mobile phone without a hands-free headset while driving. In Europe, you're not allowed to turn right on a red light, unless there is a sign or signal specifically authorizing it. Ask your car-rental company about these rules, or check the US State Department website (www.travel.state.gov, click on "International Travel," then specify your country of choice and click "Traffic Safety and Road Conditions").

Tolls: Italy's freeway system, the *autostrada,* is as good as our interstate system, but you'll pay about a dollar for every 10 minutes of use. While I favor the freeways because I feel they're safer, cheaper (saving time and gas), and less nerve-racking than smaller roads, savvy local drivers know which toll-free *superstradas* are actually faster and more direct than the *autostrada* (e.g., Florence to Pisa). For more information, visit www.autostrade.it.

Fuel: Gas is expensive—often about $8.50 per gallon. Diesel cars are more common in Europe than back home, so be sure you know what type of gas your car takes before you fill up. Gas pumps are color-coded for unleaded *(senza piombo)* or diesel. *Autostrada* rest stops are self-service stations open daily without a siesta break. Many 24-hour-a-day stations are entirely automated. Small-town stations are usually cheaper and offer full service but shorter hours.

Maps and Signage: A good map is essential. Learn the universal road signs (explained in charts in most road atlases and at service stations). Although roads are numbered on maps, actual road signs don't list route numbers. Instead, roads are indicated by blue signs with a city name on them (for example, if you want to take the road heading west out of Montepulciano—marked route S-146 on your map—you'd follow signs to Pienza, the next town

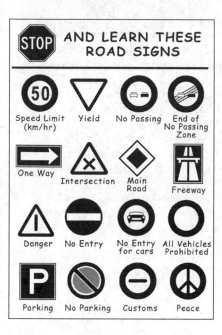

AND LEARN THESE ROAD SIGNS

Speed Limit (km/hr) — Yield — No Passing — End of No Passing Zone

One Way — Intersection — Main Road — Freeway

Danger — No Entry — No Entry for cars — All Vehicles Prohibited

Parking — No Parking — Customs — Peace

along this road). But the signs are inconsistent: They may direct you to the nearest big city or simply the next town along the route.

Theft: Cars are routinely vandalized and stolen. Thieves easily recognize rental cars and assume they are filled with a tourist's gear. Try to make your car look locally owned by hiding the "tourist-owned" rental-company decals and putting an Italian newspaper in your back window. Be sure all of your valuables are out of sight and locked in the trunk, or even better, with you or in your room.

Parking: White lines generally mean parking is free. Yellow lines mean that parking is reserved for residents only (who have permits). Blue lines mean you'll have to pay—usually around €1.50 per hour (use machine, leave time-stamped receipt on dashboard). If there's no meter, there's probably a roving attendant who will take your money. Study the signs. Often the free zones have a 30- or 60-minute time limit. Signs showing a street cleaner and a day of the week indicate which day the street is cleaned; there's a €100 tow-fee incentive to learn the days of the week in Italian.

Zona disco has nothing to do with dancing. Italian cars come equipped with a time disk (a cardboard clock), which you set at your arrival time and lay on the dashboard so the attendant knows how long you've been parked. This is a fine system that all drivers should take advantage of. (If your rental car doesn't come with a *zona disco*, pick one up at a tobacco shop or just write your arrival time on a piece of paper and place it on the dashboard.)

Garages are safe, save time, and help you avoid the stress of parking tickets. Take the parking voucher with you to pay the cashier before you leave.

Cheap Flights

If you're considering a train ride that's more than five hours long, a flight may save you both time and money. When comparing your options, factor in the time it takes to get to the airport and how early you'll need to arrive to check in.

APPENDIX

The best comparison search engine for both international and intra-European flights is www.kayak.com. For inexpensive flights within Europe, try www.skyscanner.com or www.hipmunk.com. If you're not sure who flies to your destination, check its airport's website for a list of carriers.

Budget airlines out of Florence (airport code: FLR) include Belle Air (www.belleair.it), Flybaboo (www.flybaboo.com), and Vueling (www. vueling.com). Cheaper airlines use Pisa (airport code: PSA), including well-known carriers easyJet and Ryanair (see www.pisa-airport.com for full list) and the Italian-based discount airline Air One (www.flyairone.com). Airport websites may list small airlines that serve your destination.

Remember that Florence is well-connected by train to plenty of airports—giving you more options—including Parma, Perugia, Bologna, and Rimini (which all have budget flights available). Rome, Milan, and Venice are only a two-hour train ride away.

Be aware of the potential drawbacks of flying on the cheap: nonrefundable and nonchangeable tickets, minimal or nonexistent customer service, treks to airports far outside of town, and stingy baggage allowances with steep overage fees. If traveling with lots of luggage, a cheap flight can quickly become a bad deal. To avoid unpleasant surprises, read the small print before you book.

Resources

Resources from Rick Steves

Books: *Rick Steves' Florence & Tuscany 2013* is one of many books in my series on European travel, which includes country guidebooks, city guidebooks (Venice, Rome, Paris, London, etc.), Snapshot Guides (excerpted chapters from my country guides), Pocket Guides (full-color little books on big cities), and my budget-travel skills handbook, *Rick Steves' Europe Through the Back Door*. Most of my titles are available as ebooks. My phrase books—for Italian, French, German, Spanish, and Portuguese—are practical and budget-oriented. My other books include *Europe 101* (a crash course on art and history), *Mediterranean Cruise Ports* (how to make the most of your time in port), and *Travel as a Political Act* (a travelogue sprinkled with tips for bringing home a global perspective). A more complete list of my titles appears near the end of this book.

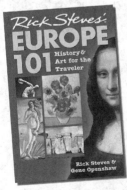

Video: My public television series, *Rick Steves' Europe*, covers European destinations in 100 shows, with 17 episodes on Italy,

Begin Your Trip at www.ricksteves.com

At ricksteves.com, you'll find a wealth of free information on European destinations, including fresh monthly news and helpful tips from thousands of fellow travelers. You'll find my latest guidebook updates (www.ricksteves.com/update), a monthly travel e-newsletter (easy and free to sign up), my personal travel blog, and my free Rick Steves Audio Europe smartphone app (if you don't have a smartphone, you can access the same content via podcasts). You can even follow me on Facebook and Twitter.

Our **online Travel Store** offers travel bags and accessories that I've designed specifically to help you travel smarter and lighter. These include my popular carry-on bags (roll-aboard and backpack versions), money belts, totes, toiletries kits, adapters, other accessories, and a wide selection of guidebooks, planning maps, and DVDs.

Choosing the right **railpass** for your trip—amid hundreds of options—can drive you nutty. We'll help you choose the best pass for your needs and ship it to you for free.

Want to travel with greater efficiency and less stress? We organize **tours** with more than three dozen itineraries and more than 500 departures reaching the best destinations in this book...and beyond. Our Italy tours include "the best of" in 17 days, Village Italy in 14 days, South Italy in 13 days, Sicily in 10 days, Venice-Florence-Rome in 10 days, the Heart of Italy in nine days, My Way: Italy "unguided" tour in 13 days, and a week-long Rome tour. You'll enjoy great guides, a fun bunch of travel partners (with small groups of generally around 24-28), and plenty of room to spread out in a big, comfy bus. You'll find European adventures to fit every vacation length. For all the details, and to get our Tour Catalog and a free Rick Steves Tour Experience DVD (filmed on location during an actual tour), visit www.ricksteves.com or call us at 425/608-4217.

APPENDIX

including four on Florence and Tuscany. To watch episodes online, visit www.hulu.com; for scripts and local airtimes, see www.rick steves.com/tv.

Audio: My weekly public radio show, *Travel with Rick Steves*, features interviews with travel experts from around the world. I've also produced several free, self-guided **audio tours** of the top sights and neighborhoods in Florence: the Renaissance Walk, Accademia, and Uffizi Gallery. All of this audio content is available for free at Rick Steves Audio Europe, an extensive online library organized by destination. Choose whatever interests you, and download it for free via the Rick Steves Audio Europe smartphone app, www .ricksteves.com/audioeurope, iTunes, or Google Play.

Maps

The black-and-white maps in this book are concise and simple, designed to help you locate recommended places and get to local TIs, where you can pick up more in-depth maps of cities or regions (usually free). Better maps are sold at newsstands and bookstores. Before you buy a map, look at it to be sure it has the level of detail you want. Drivers will want to pick up a good, detailed map in Europe (I'd recommend a 1:200,000- or 1:300,000-scale map).

Other Guidebooks

If you're like most travelers, this book is all you need. But if you're heading beyond my recommended destinations, $40 for extra maps and books can be money well-spent. For several people traveling by car, the extra weight and expense of a small trip library are negligible. If you'll be traveling elsewhere in Italy, consider *Rick Steves' Italy*, *Rick Steves' Venice*, or *Rick Steves' Rome*.

The following books are worthwhile, though most are not updated annually; check the publication date before you buy. The Access guide (which combines Florence and Venice) is well-researched, organized by neighborhood, and color-coded for sights, hotels, and restaurants. Focusing mainly on sights, the colorful Eyewitness guides on Florence and Tuscany are fun for their great graphics and photos, but they're relatively skimpy on written content and weigh a ton. You can buy the guides in Florence (no more expensive than in the US) or simply borrow one for a minute from other travelers at certain sights to make sure that you're aware of that place's highlights. *Let's Go Rome, Venice & Florence: The Student Travel Guide* is youth-oriented, with good coverage of hostels and nightlife.

Recommended Books and Movies

To learn more about Florence and Tuscany past and present, check out a few of these books or films.

Nonfiction

Among the classics of Italian literature with particular relevance to Florence are Niccolò Machiavelli's *The Prince* and *Florentine Histories*.

For a historical overview of the whole city, try *The City of Florence* (R. W. B. Lewis), which has a biographer's perspective. In *Florence: A Portrait*, Michael Levey writes with a curator's expertise. *The Stones of Florence* bubbles with Mary McCarthy's wit. *Dark Water* (Robert Clark) vividly recounts the determination of the Florentines in the face of the city's destructive floods.

Architecture fans should consider reading the novel-like *Brunelleschi's Dome* (Ross King) or *The Architecture of the Italian Renaissance* (Peter Murray), which presents a (not too dry) textbook overview. *The Lives of the Artists* offers anecdote-filled biographies from Giorgio Vasari, a 16th-century author/painter/architect who was the contemporary of many of his subjects. For a more academic take on Italian art history, try *Italian Renaissance Art* (Laurie Schneider Adams).

Christopher Hibbert tells of the intrigues of Florence's first family in *The House of Medici* (his *Florence* is also recommended). *Fortune Is a River* (Roger D. Masters) describes a scheme between Machiavelli and da Vinci to re-route the Arno (which, thankfully, never happened).

If you'll be traveling to the area outside of Florence, consider the sensuous travel memoir, *The Hills of Tuscany* (Ferenc Máté). Also worthwhile is *A Tuscan Childhood* (Kinta Beevor), about growing up in a sun-drenched villa. *Under the Tuscan Sun* was a bestseller for Frances Mayes (and is better than the movie of the same name). Another memoir on the adventure of renovating a Tuscan farmhouse is *A Small Place in Italy* (Eric Newby).

Fiction

Florence was a favorite destination for European aristocrats and artists in the 19th and early 20th centuries. The Italian influence lives on in classics written during that time, including George Eliot's *Romola* and E. M. Forster's *A Room with a View*.

For a modern read, consider *The Passion of Artemisia*, by Susan Vreeland (who also wrote the bestselling *Girl in Hyacinth Blue*) and *The Sixteen Pleasures* (Robert Hellenga), set during the great floods that wracked the city in 1966. *Birth of Venus*, by Sarah Dunant, is set during Savonarola's reign, and *Galileo's Daughter* (Dava

APPENDIX

Sobel) is based on the real-life letters between the scientist and his daughter.

Page-turning mysteries set in Florence include *A Rich Full Death* (Michael Dibdin), *Death of an Englishman* (Magdalen Nabb), *The Dante Game* (Jane Langton), and *Bella Donna* (Barbara Cherne). For a fun Michelangelo potboiler, try *The Agony and the Ecstasy* (Irving Stone).

The Light in the Piazza (Elizabeth Spencer), the story of a mother and daughter visiting in the 1950s, was a movie (from 1962) and later became an award-winning Broadway musical.

And for the lover of classical tales, Giovanni Boccaccio's *Decameron*, written in the mid-1300s, is set in plague-ridden medieval Florence.

Films

For a well-done Shakespeare flick that was filmed in Tuscany, try *Much Ado About Nothing* (1993), which is actually set in Sicily. *A Room with a View* (1986) captures the charm of the book of the same name (described earlier). *Under the Tuscan Sun*—filled with eye-candy views—falls flat in comparison. The Oscar-winning Holocaust tragicomedy *Life Is Beautiful* (1997) has sections set in a Tuscan town. The warm-hearted Italian epic *Best of Youth* (2003) takes place in several Italian locations, including Florence and rural Tuscany.

For an excellent PBS docudrama about Florence's first family, look for *Medici: Godfathers of the Renaissance* (2005); its fine website is at www.pbs.org/empires/medici.

If Siena is on your itinerary, try *Palio* (1932), *Stealing Beauty* (1996), and *Up at the Villa* (2000), which also has scenes set in Florence. *The English Patient* (1996) was partially shot in Montepulciano, as was the vampire romance, *New Moon* (2009, part of the *Twilight* series). Filmed in Lucca, *The Triumph of Love* (2001) has a Baroque feel, while *The Portrait of a Lady* (1996) stays true to Henry James' bleak novel.

If bound for San Gimignano, consider watching films set in that locale: *Prince of Foxes* (1949), *Where Angels Fear to Tread* (1991), and two of Franco Zeffirelli's films, *Brother Sun, Sister Moon* (1972) and *Tea with Mussolini* (1999).

Although it's not a film, the video game *Assassin's Creed II* takes place in Renaissance Florence, San Gimignano, and other real Tuscan locations. The action is violent (hence the title), but you spend the game exploring astonishingly detailed, fully interactive

3-D models of the towns at their Renaissance peak. Leonardo da Vinci, Machiavelli, and other real-life Florentines are characters in the game, and when you approach a famous landmark, historical information about the place pops up on the screen.

Holidays and Festivals

In Italy, holidays seem to strike without warning. For instance, every town has a festival honoring its patron saint.

This list includes selected festivals in Florence in 2013, plus national holidays observed throughout Italy. Many sights and banks close on national holidays—keep this in mind when planning your itinerary. Before planning a trip around a festival, verify its dates by checking the festival's website or TI sites (www.italia.it and www.firenzeturismo .it); www.whatsonwhen.com also lists many festival dates.

In Florence, hotels get booked up on Easter weekend (from Good Friday through Monday), April 25 (Liberation Day), May 1 (Labor Day), May 9 (Feast of the Ascension Day), June 24 (St. John the Baptist), November 1 (All Saints' Day), and on Fridays and Saturdays year-round. Some hotels require you to book the full three-day weekend around a holiday.

For sports events, see www.sportsevents365.com for schedules and ticket information.

Jan	Florence fashion convention
Jan 1	New Year's Day
Jan 6	Epiphany
Early Feb	Carnival Celebrations/Mardi Gras in Florence (costumed parades, street water fights, jousting competitions)
March 31	Easter Sunday. Explosion of the Cart (Scoppio del Carro) in Florence (fireworks, bonfire in wooden cart)
April	Italy's Cultural Heritage Week (check www.beniculturali.it for dates)
April 1	Easter Monday
April 25	Italian Liberation Day
May 1	Labor Day
May 9	Ascension Day

APPENDIX

2013

JANUARY
S	M	T	W	T	F	S
		1	2	3	4	5
6	7	8	9	10	11	12
13	14	15	16	17	18	19
20	21	22	23	24	25	26
27	28	29	30	31		

FEBRUARY
S	M	T	W	T	F	S
					1	2
3	4	5	6	7	8	9
10	11	12	13	14	15	16
17	18	19	20	21	22	23
24	25	26	27	28		

MARCH
S	M	T	W	T	F	S
					1	2
3	4	5	6	7	8	9
10	11	12	13	14	15	16
17	18	19	20	21	22	23
24/31	25	26	27	28	29	30

APRIL
S	M	T	W	T	F	S
	1	2	3	4	5	6
7	8	9	10	11	12	13
14	15	16	17	18	19	20
21	22	23	24	25	26	27
28	29	30				

MAY
S	M	T	W	T	F	S
			1	2	3	4
5	6	7	8	9	10	11
12	13	14	15	16	17	18
19	20	21	22	23	24	25
26	27	28	29	30	31	

JUNE
S	M	T	W	T	F	S
						1
2	3	4	5	6	7	8
9	10	11	12	13	14	15
16	17	18	19	20	21	22
23/30	24	25	26	27	28	29

JULY
S	M	T	W	T	F	S
	1	2	3	4	5	6
7	8	9	10	11	12	13
14	15	16	17	18	19	20
21	22	23	24	25	26	27
28	29	30	31			

AUGUST
S	M	T	W	T	F	S
				1	2	3
4	5	6	7	8	9	10
11	12	13	14	15	16	17
18	19	20	21	22	23	24
25	26	27	28	29	30	31

SEPTEMBER
S	M	T	W	T	F	S
1	2	3	4	5	6	7
8	9	10	11	12	13	14
15	16	17	18	19	20	21
22	23	24	25	26	27	28
29	30					

OCTOBER
S	M	T	W	T	F	S
		1	2	3	4	5
6	7	8	9	10	11	12
13	14	15	16	17	18	19
20	21	22	23	24	25	26
27	28	29	30	31		

NOVEMBER
S	M	T	W	T	F	S
					1	2
3	4	5	6	7	8	9
10	11	12	13	14	15	16
17	18	19	20	21	22	23
24	25	26	27	28	29	30

DECEMBER
S	M	T	W	T	F	S
1	2	3	4	5	6	7
8	9	10	11	12	13	14
15	16	17	18	19	20	21
22	23	24	25	26	27	28
29	30	31				

APPENDIX

Mid-May	Cricket Festival in Florence (music, entertainment, food, crickets sold in cages)
Late May	Gelato Festival, Florence
Late May	Florence fashion convention
June 1-30	Annual Flower Display in Florence (carpet of flowers on the main square, Piazza della Signoria)
June 2	Anniversary of the Republic
June 16-17	Festival of St. Ranieri in Pisa
June 24	Festival of St. John the Baptist in Florence (parades, dances, boat races). Also Calcio Fiorentino (costumed soccer game on Florence's Piazza Santa Croce)
Late June-early Sept	Florence's annual outdoor cinema season (contemporary films)

June-July	Florence Dance Festival (www.florence dance.org)
July 2	Palio horse race in Siena
Aug 15	Assumption of Mary (Ferragosto)
Aug 16	Palio horse race in Siena
Early Sept	Festa della Rificolona in Florence (children's procession with lanterns, street performances, parade)
Sept 13-14	Volto Santo in Lucca (procession and fair)
Oct	Musica dei Popoli Festival in Florence (ethnic and folk music and dances)
Nov 1	All Saints' Day
Dec 8	Feast of the Immaculate Conception
Dec 25	Christmas
Dec 26	St. Stephen's Day

Conversions and Climate

Numbers and Stumblers

- Europeans write a few of their numbers differently than we do. 1 = 1, 4 = 4, 7 = 7.
- In Europe, dates appear as day/month/year, so Christmas is 25/12/13.
- Commas are decimal points, and decimal points are commas. A dollar and a half is 1,50, one thousand is 1.000, and there are 5.280 feet in a mile.
- When pointing, use your whole hand, palm down.
- When counting with fingers, start with your thumb. If you hold up your first finger to request one item, you'll probably get two.
- What Americans call the second floor of a building is the first floor in Europe.
- On escalators and moving sidewalks, Europeans keep the left "lane" open for passing. Keep to the right.

Roman Numerals

In the US, you'll see Roman numerals—which originated in ancient Rome—used for copyright dates, clocks, and the Super Bowl. In Italy, you're likely to observe these numbers chiseled on statues and buildings. If you want to do some numeric detective work, here's how: In Roman numerals, as in ours, the highest numbers (thousands, hundreds) come first, followed by smaller numbers. Many numbers are made by combining numerals into sets: V = 5, so VIII = 8 (5 plus 3). Roman numerals follow a subtraction principle for multiples of four (4, 40, 400, etc.) and nine

APPENDIX

(9, 90, 900, etc.); the number four, for example, is written as IV (1 subtracted from 5), rather than IIII. The number nine is IX (1 subtracted from 10).

Rick Steves' Florence & Tuscany 2013—written in Roman numerals—would translate as Rick Steves' Florence & Tuscany MMXIII. Big numbers such as dates can look daunting at first. The easiest way to handle them is to read the numbers in discrete chunks. For example, Michelangelo was born in MCDLXXV. Break it down: M (1,000) + CD (100 subtracted from 500, or 400) + LXX (50 + 10 + 10, or 70) + V (5) = 1475. It was a very good year.

M = 1000	XL = 40
CM = 900	X = 10
D = 500	IX = 9
CD = 400	V = 5
C = 100	IV = 4
XC = 90	I = duh
L = 50	

Metric Conversions (approximate)

A kilogram is 2.2 pounds, and 1 liter is about a quart, or almost four to a gallon. A kilometer is six-tenths of a mile. I figure kilometers to miles by cutting them in half and adding back 10 percent of the original (120 km: 60 + 12 = 72 miles, 300 km: 150 + 30 = 180 miles).

1 foot = 0.3 meter	1 square yard = 0.8 square meter
1 yard = 0.9 meter	1 square mile = 2.6 square kilometers
1 mile = 1.6 kilometers	1 ounce = 28 grams
1 centimeter = 0.4 inch	1 quart = 0.95 liter
1 meter = 39.4 inches	1 kilogram = 2.2 pounds
1 kilometer = 0.62 mile	32°F = 0°C

Clothing Sizes

When shopping for clothing, use these US-to-European comparisons as general guidelines (but note that no conversion is perfect).

- Women's dresses and blouses: Add 30
  (US size 10 = European size 40)
- Men's suits and jackets: Add 10
  (US size 40 regular = European size 50)
- Men's shirts: Multiply by 2 and add about 8
  (US size 15 collar = European size 38)
- Women's shoes: Add about 30
  (US size 8 = European size 38-39)
- Men's shoes: Add 32-34
  (US size 9 = European size 41; US size 11 = European size 45)

Florence's Climate

First line, average daily high; second line, average daily low; third line, average days without rain. For more detailed statistics for destinations in this book (as well as the rest of the world), check www .worldclimate.com.

J	F	M	A	M	J	J	A	S	O	N	D
40°	46°	56°	65°	74°	80°	84°	82°	75°	63°	51°	43°
32°	35°	43°	49°	57°	63°	67°	66°	61°	52°	43°	35°
25	21	24	22	23	21	25	24	25	23	20	24

Temperature Conversion: Fahrenheit and Celsius

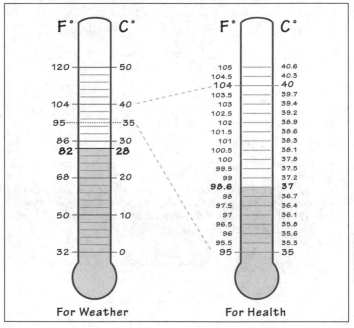

For Weather   For Health

Europe takes its temperature using the Celsius scale, while we opt for Fahrenheit. For a rough conversion from Celsius to Fahrenheit, double the number and add 30. For weather, remember that 28°C is 82°F—perfect. For health, 37°C is just right.

Hotel Reservation

To: _____   _____
              hotel   *email or fax*

From: _____   _____
              name   *email or fax*

Today's date: _____ / _____ / _____
                    day   *month*   *year*

Dear Hotel _____ ,

Please make this reservation for me:

Name: _____

Total # of people: _____   # of rooms: _____   # of nights: _____

Arriving: _____ / _____ / _____   My time of arrival (24-hr clock): _____
               day   *month*   *year*   (I will telephone if I will be late)

Departing: _____ / _____ / _____
                 day   *month*   *year*

Room(s): Single ___   Double ___   Twin ___   Triple ___   Quad ___

With: Toilet _____   Shower _____   Bath _____   Sink only _____

Special needs: View ___   Quiet ___   Cheapest ___   Ground Floor ___

Please email or fax confirmation of my reservation, along with the type of room reserved and the price. Please also inform me of your cancellation policy. After I hear from you, I will quickly send my credit-card information as a deposit to hold the room. Thank you.

_____
Name

_____
Address

_____
City   *State*   *Zip Code*   *Country*

Before hoteliers can make your reservation, they want to know the information listed above. You can use this form as the basis for your email, or you can photocopy this page, fill in the information, and send it as a fax (also available online at www.ricksteves.com/reservation).

Packing Checklist

Whether you're traveling for five days or five weeks, here's what you'll need to bring. Pack light to enjoy the sweet freedom of true mobility. Happy travels!

- ❑ 5 shirts: long- and short-sleeve
- ❑ 1 sweater or lightweight fleece
- ❑ 2 pairs pants
- ❑ 1 pair shorts
- ❑ 1 swimsuit
- ❑ 5 pairs underwear and socks
- ❑ 1 pair shoes
- ❑ 1 rainproof jacket with hood
- ❑ Tie or scarf
- ❑ Money belt
- ❑ Money—your mix of:
  - ❑ Debit card (for ATM withdrawals)
  - ❑ Credit card
  - ❑ Hard cash (in easy-to-exchange $20 bills)
- ❑ Documents plus photo-copies:
  - ❑ Passport
  - ❑ Printout of airline eticket
  - ❑ Driver's license
  - ❑ Student ID and hostel card
  - ❑ Railpass/car rental voucher
  - ❑ Insurance details
- ❑ Daypack
- ❑ Electronics—your choice of:
  - ❑ Camera (and related gear)
  - ❑ Computer/mobile devices (phone, MP3 player, ereader, etc.)
  - ❑ Chargers for each of the above
  - ❑ Plug adapter
- ❑ Empty water bottle

- ❑ Wristwatch and alarm clock
- ❑ Earplugs
- ❑ Toiletries kit
  - ❑ Toiletries
  - ❑ Medicines and vitamins
  - ❑ First-aid kit
  - ❑ Glasses/contacts/sunglasses (with prescriptions)
- ❑ Sealable plastic baggies
- ❑ Laundry soap
- ❑ Clothesline
- ❑ Small towel
- ❑ Sewing kit
- ❑ Travel information (guide-books and maps)
- ❑ Address list (for sending postcards)
- ❑ Postcards and photos from home
- ❑ Notepad and pen
- ❑ Journal

If you plan to carry on your luggage, note that all liquids must be in 3.4-ounce or smaller containers and fit within a single quart-size sealable baggie. For details, see www.tsa.gov/travelers.

Italian Survival Phrases

Good day.	Buon giorno.	bwohn JOR-noh
Do you speak English?	Parla inglese?	PAR-lah een-GLAY-zay
Yes. / No.	Sì. / No.	see / noh
I (don't) understand.	(Non) capisco.	(nohn) kah-PEES-koh
Please.	Per favore.	pehr fah-VOH-ray
Thank you.	Grazie.	GRAHT-seeay
You're welcome.	Prego.	PRAY-go
I'm sorry.	Mi dispiace.	mee dee-speeAH-chay
Excuse me.	Mi scusi.	mee SKOO-zee
(No) problem.	(Non) c'è un problema.	(nohn) cheh oon proh-BLAY-mah
Good.	Va bene.	vah BEHN-ay
Goodbye.	Arrivederci.	ah-ree-vay-DEHR-chee
one / two	uno / due	OO-noh / DOO-ay
three / four	tre / quattro	tray / KWAH-troh
five / six	cinque / sei	CHEENG-kway / SEHee
seven / eight	sette / otto	SEHT-tay / OT-toh
nine / ten	nove / dieci	NOV-ay / deeAY-chee
How much is it?	Quanto costa?	KWAHN-toh KOS-tah
Write it?	Me lo scrive?	may loh SKREE-vay
Is it free?	È gratis?	eh GRAH-tees
Is it included?	È incluso?	eh een-KLOO-zoh
Where can I buy / find...?	Dove posso comprare / trovare...?	DOH-vay POS-soh kohm-PRAH-ray / troh-VAH-ray
I'd like / We'd like...	Vorrei / Vorremmo...	vor-REHee / vor-RAY-moh
...a room.	...una camera.	OO-nah KAH-meh-rah
...a ticket to ___.	...un biglietto per ___.	oon beel-YEHT-toh pehr
Is it possible?	È possibile?	eh poh-SEE-bee-lay
Where is...?	Dov'è...?	DOH-veh
...the train station	...la stazione	lah staht-seeOH-nay
...the bus station	...la stazione degli autobus	lah staht-seeOH-nay DAYL-yee OW-toh-boos
...tourist information	...informazioni per turisti	een-for-maht-seeOH-nee pehr too-REE-stee
...the toilet	...la toilette	lah twah-LEHT-tay
men	uomini, signori	WOH-mee-nee, seen-YOH-ree
women	donne, signore	DON-nay, seen-YOH-ray
left / right	sinistra / destra	see-NEE-strah / DEHS-trah
straight	sempre diritto	SEHM-pray dee-REE-toh
When do you open / close?	A che ora aprite / chiudete?	ah kay OH-rah ah-PREE-tay / keeoo-DAY-tay
At what time?	A che ora?	ah kay OH-rah
Just a moment.	Un momento.	oon moh-MAYN-toh
now / soon / later	adesso / presto / tardi	ah-DEHS-soh / PREHS-toh / TAR-dee
today / tomorrow	oggi / domani	OH-jee / doh-MAH-nee

In an Italian-speaking Restaurant

I'd like...	Vorrei...	vor-REHee
We'd like...	Vorremmo...	vor-RAY-moh
...to reserve...	...prenotare...	pray-noh-TAH-ray
...a table for one / two.	...un tavolo per uno / due.	oon TAH-voh-loh pehr OO-noh / DOO-ay
Non-smoking.	Non fumare.	nohn foo-MAH-ray
Is this seat free?	È libero questo posto?	eh LEE-bay-roh KWEHS-toh POH-stoh
The menu (in English), please.	Il menù (in inglese), per favore.	eel may-NOO (een een-GLAY-zay) pehr fah-VOH-ray
service (not) included	servizio (non) incluso	sehr-VEET-seeoh (nohn) een-KLOO-zoh
cover charge	pane e coperto	PAH-nay ay koh-PEHR-toh
to go	da portar via	dah POR-tar VEE-ah
with / without	con / senza	kohn / SEHN-sah
and / or	e / o	ay / oh
menu (of the day)	menù (del giorno)	may-NOO (dayl JOR-noh)
specialty of the house	specialità della casa	spay-chah-lee-TAH DEHL-lah KAH-zah
first course (pasta, soup)	primo piatto	PREE-moh peeAH-toh
main course (meat, fish)	secondo piatto	say-KOHN-doh peeAH-toh
side dishes	contorni	kohn-TOR-nee
bread	pane	PAH-nay
cheese	formaggio	for-MAH-joh
sandwich	panino	pah-NEE-noh
soup	minestra, zuppa	mee-NEHS-trah, TSOO-pah
salad	insalata	een-sah-LAH-tah
meat	carne	KAR-nay
chicken	pollo	POH-loh
fish	pesce	PEH-shay
seafood	frutti di mare	FROO-tee dee MAH-ray
fruit / vegetables	frutta / legumi	FROO-tah / lay-GOO-mee
dessert	dolci	DOHL-chee
tap water	acqua del rubinetto	AH-kwah dayl roo-bee-NAY-toh
mineral water	acqua minerale	AH-kwah mee-nay-RAH-lay
milk	latte	LAH-tay
(orange) juice	succo (d'arancia)	SOO-koh (dah-RAHN-chah)
coffee / tea	caffè / tè	kah-FEH / teh
wine	vino	VEE-noh
red / white	rosso / bianco	ROH-soh / beeAHN-koh
glass / bottle	bicchiere / bottiglia	bee-keeAY-ray / boh-TEEL-yah
beer	birra	BEE-rah
Cheers!	Cin cin!	cheen cheen
More. / Another.	Ancora un po.' / Un altro.	ahn-KOH-rah oon poh / oon AHL-troh
The same.	Lo stesso.	loh STEHS-soh
The bill, please.	Il conto, per favore.	eel KOHN-toh pehr fah-VOH-ray
tip	mancia	MAHN-chah
Delicious!	Delizioso!	day-leet-seeOH-zoh

For more user-friendly Italian phrases, check out *Rick Steves' Italian Phrase Book & Dictionary* or *Rick Steves' French, Italian, and German Phrase Book*.

INDEX

INDEX

MAP INDEX

Audio Europe

NOW AVAILABLE:
eBOOKS, DVD & BLU-RAY

TRAVEL CULTURE

Europe 101
European Christmas
Postcards from Europe
Travel as a Political Act

eBOOKS

*Nearly all Rick Steves guides
are available as eBooks. Check
with your favorite bookseller.*

RICK STEVES' EUROPE DVDs

10 New Shows 2011–2012
Austria & the Alps
Eastern Europe
England & Wales
European Christmas
European Travel Skills & Specials
France
Germany, BeNeLux & More
Greece & Turkey
Iran
Ireland & Scotland
Italy's Cities
Italy's Countryside
Scandinavia
Spain
Travel Extras

BLU-RAY

Celtic Charms
Eastern Europe Favorites
European Christmas
Italy Through the Back Door
Mediterranean Mosaic
Surprising Cities of Europe

PHRASE BOOKS & DICTIONARIES

French
French, Italian & German
German
Italian
Portuguese
Spanish

JOURNALS

Rick Steves' Pocket Travel Journal
Rick Steves' Travel Journal

PLANNING MAPS

Britain, Ireland & London
Europe
France & Paris
Germany, Austria & Switzerland
Ireland
Italy
Spain & Portugal

Rick Steves books and DVDs are available at bookstores
and through online booksellers.

Rick Steves®

www.ricksteves.com

EUROPE GUIDES

Best of Europe
Eastern Europe
Europe Through the Back Door
Mediterranean Cruise Ports

COUNTRY GUIDES

Croatia & Slovenia
England
France
Germany
Great Britain
Ireland
Italy
Portugal
Scandinavia
Spain
Switzerland

CITY & REGIONAL GUIDES

Amsterdam, Bruges & Brussels
Athens & the Peloponnese
Barcelona
Budapest
Florence & Tuscany
Istanbul
London
Paris
Prague & the Czech Republic
Provence & the French Riviera
Rome
Venice
Vienna, Salzburg & Tirol

SNAPSHOT GUIDES

Berlin
Bruges & Brussels
Copenhagen & the Best of
    Denmark
Dublin
Dubrovnik
Hill Towns of Central Italy
Italy's Cinque Terre
Krakow, Warsaw & Gdansk
Lisbon
Madrid & Toledo
Munich, Bavaria & Salzburg
Naples & the Amalfi Coast
Northern Ireland
Norway
Scotland
Sevilla, Granada & Southern Spain
Stockholm

POCKET GUIDES

Athens
Barcelona
Florence
London
Paris
Rome
Venice

Rick Steves guidebooks are published by Avalon Travel,
a member of the Perseus Books Group.

Researchers

To help update this book, Rick a[...] [...] relied on...

Cameron Hewitt

Cameron writes an[...]
Rick Steves, specializes guidebooks for
For this book, he beat t[...] Eastern Europe.
Campanile, plied the Tus[...]es to climb the
search of *agriturismi*, and sa[...] countryside in
than he could count. When h[...] more frescoes
ing, Cameron lives in Seattle[...] not travel-
Shawna. [...]th his wife

Sarah Murdoch

Sarah has spent most of her adult li[...] split
between the US and Italy, ever since studying architecture in Rome during college.
She is passionate about history, art, and
pistachio gelato. When she isn't research-
ing guidebooks or leading tours, she lives in
Seattle with her patient husband Patrick and
sons Lucca and Nicola.